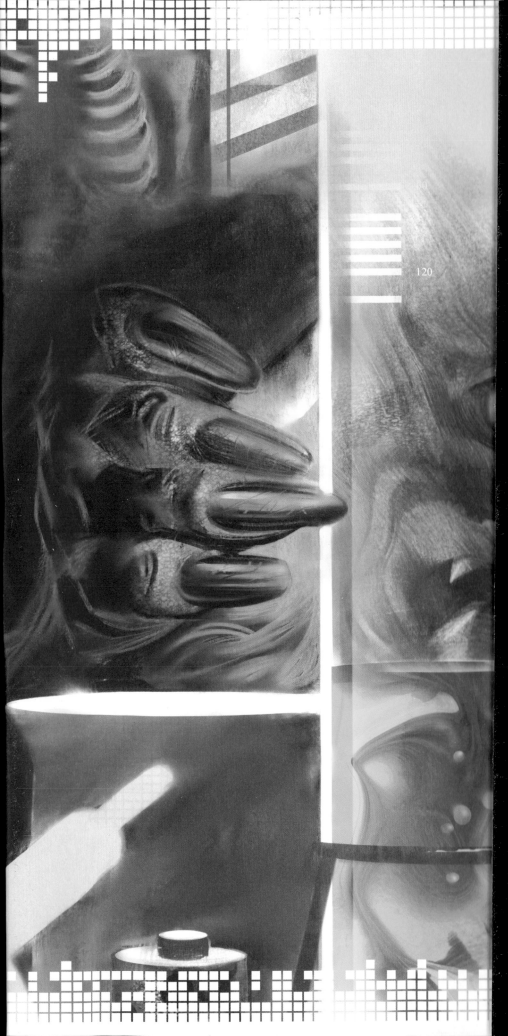

120

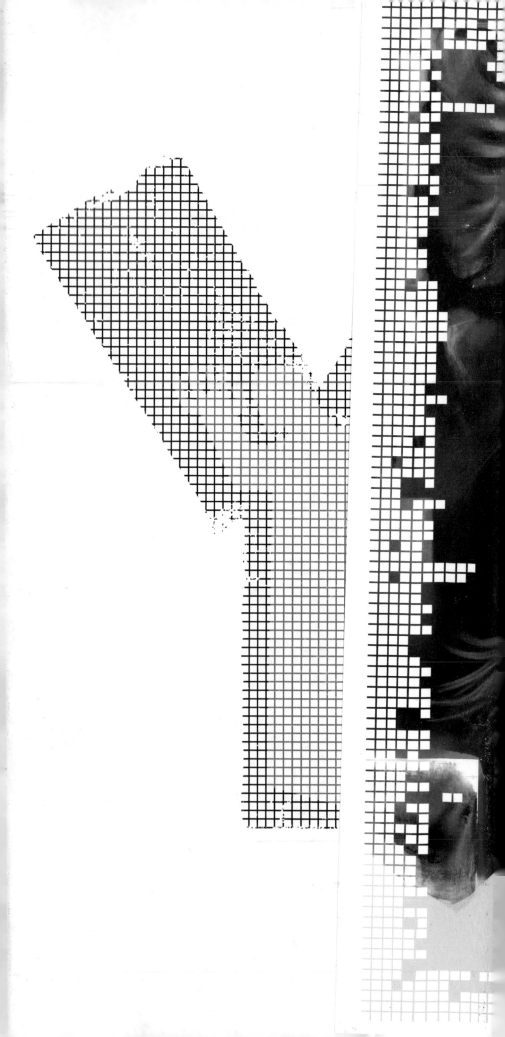

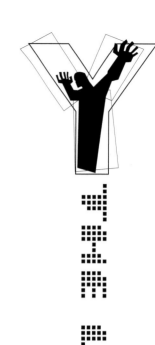

# Y: THE LAST MAN

The Deluxe Edition

Book Three

Brian K. Vaughan Writer

Pia Guerra, Goran Sudžuka Pencillers

José Marzán, Jr. Inker

Zylonol Colorist

Clem Robins Letterer

Massimo Carnevale Original Series Covers

Y: THE LAST MAN created by Brian K. Vaughan and Pia Guerra

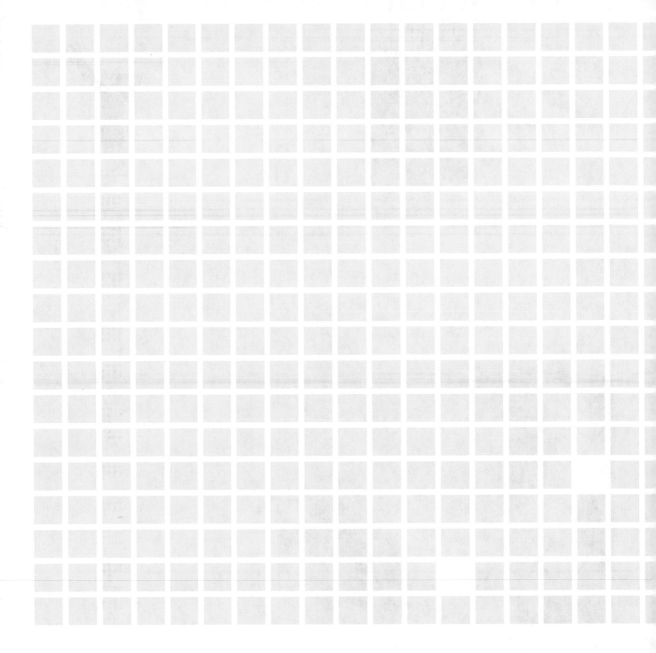

Will Dennis Editor – Original Series
Casey Seijas Assistant Editor – Original Series
Scott Nybakken Editor
Robbin Brosterman Design Director – Books
Louis Prandi Publication Design

Karen Berger Senior VP – Executive Editor, Vertigo
Bob Harras VP – Editor-in-Chief

Diane Nelson President
Dan DiDio and Jim Lee Co-Publishers
Geoff Johns Chief Creative Officer
John Rood Executive VP – Sales, Marketing and Business Development
Nairi Gardiner Senior VP – Finance
Jeff Boison VP – Publishing Operations
Mark Chiarello VP – Art Direction and Design
John Cunningham VP – Marketing
Terri Cunningham VP – Talent Relations and Services
Alison Gill Senior VP – Manufacturing and Operations
Hank Kanalz Senior VP – Digital
Jay Kogan VP – Business and Legal Affairs, Publishing
Jack Mahan VP – Business Affairs, Talent
Nick Napolitano VP – Manufacturing Administration
Sue Pohja VP – Book Sales
Courtney Simmons Senior VP – Publicity
Bob Wayne Senior VP – Sales

Cover illustration by
Massimo Carnevale.

Logo design by
Terry Marks.

Y: THE LAST MAN —
THE DELUXE EDITION
BOOK THREE

Published by DC Comics.
Cover and compilation
Copyright © 2010
DC Comics. All Rights
Reserved. Script Copyright
© 2005 Brian K. Vaughan
and Pia Guerra.
All Rights Reserved.

Originally published in
single magazine form as
Y: THE LAST MAN 24-36.
Copyright © 2004, 2005
Brian K. Vaughan and
Pia Guerra. All Rights
Reserved. All characters,
their distinctive likenesses
and related elements
featured in this publication
are trademarks of Brian K.
Vaughan and Pia Guerra.
VERTIGO is a trademark
of DC Comics. The stories,
characters and incidents
featured in this publication
are entirely fictional.
DC Comics does not read
or accept unsolicited
submissions of ideas,
stories or artwork.

DC Comics
1700 Broadway
New York, NY 10019
A Warner Bros.
Entertainment Company.
Printed and bound in
the USA. Third Printing.
ISBN: 978-1-4012-2578-0

Library of Congress
Cataloging-in-Publication
Data

Vaughan, Brian K.
Y, the last man. The
deluxe edition, Book three
/ Brian K. Vaughan, Pia
Guerra, José Marzán, Jr.,
Goran Sudzuka.
p. cm.
ISBN 978-1-4012-2578-0 (alk.
paper)
1. Graphic novels. I.
Guerra, Pia. II. Marzán,
José. III. Sudzuka, Goran.
IV. Title.
PN6728.Y2V46 2012
741.5'973—dc23

2012024703

SUSTAINABLE
FORESTRY
INITIATIVE

Certified Chain of Custody
At Least 25% Certified Forest Content

www.sfiprogram.org
SFI-01042
APPLIES TO TEXT STOCK ONLY

# Y: THE LAST MAN — Contents

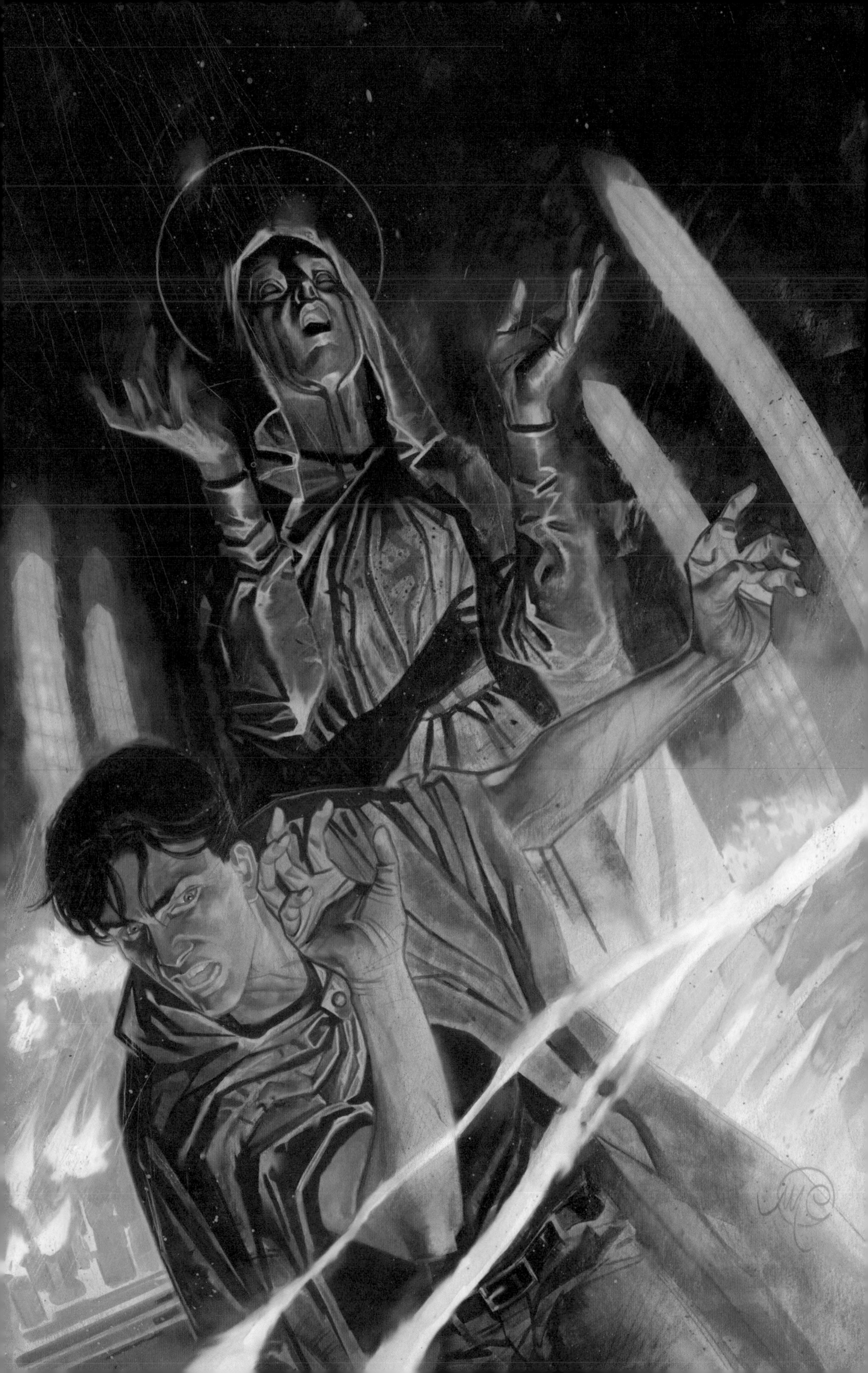

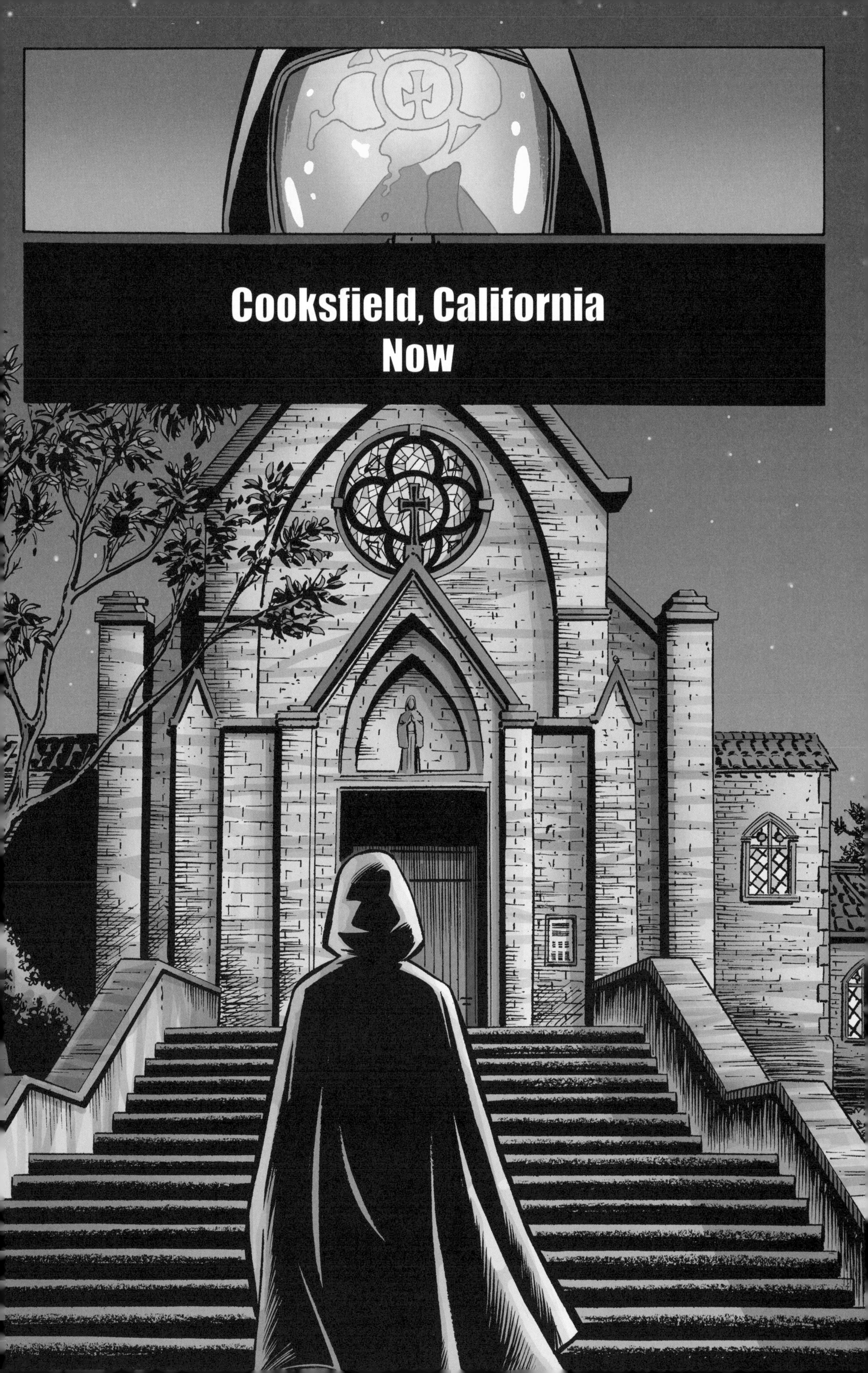
Cooksfield, California
Now

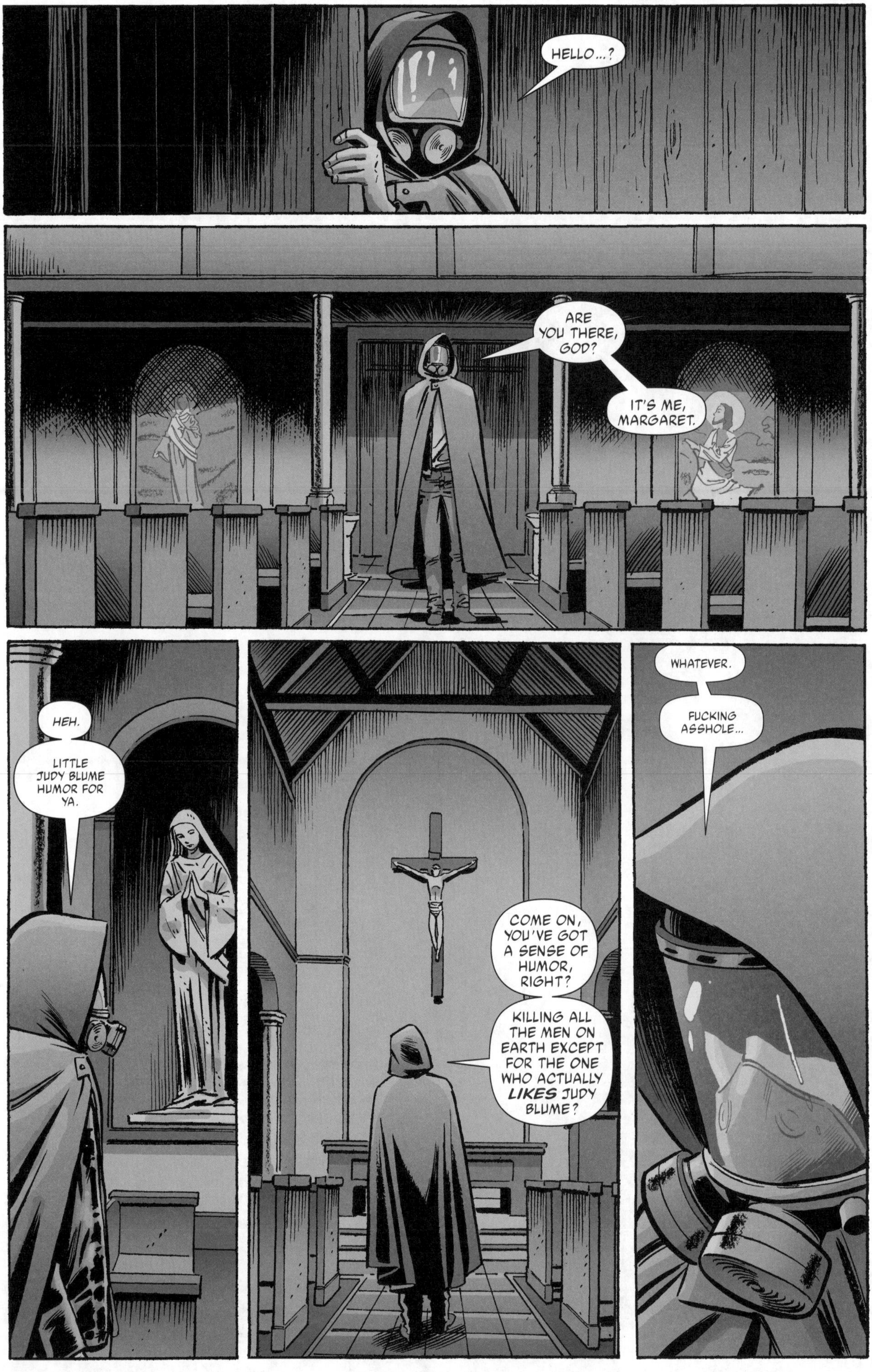
HELLO...?
ARE YOU THERE, GOD?
IT'S ME, MARGARET.
HEH.
LITTLE JUDY BLUME HUMOR FOR YA.
COME ON, YOU'VE GOT A SENSE OF HUMOR, RIGHT?
KILLING ALL THE MEN ON EARTH EXCEPT FOR THE ONE WHO ACTUALLY *LIKES* JUDY BLUME?
WHATEVER.
FUCKING ASSHOLE...

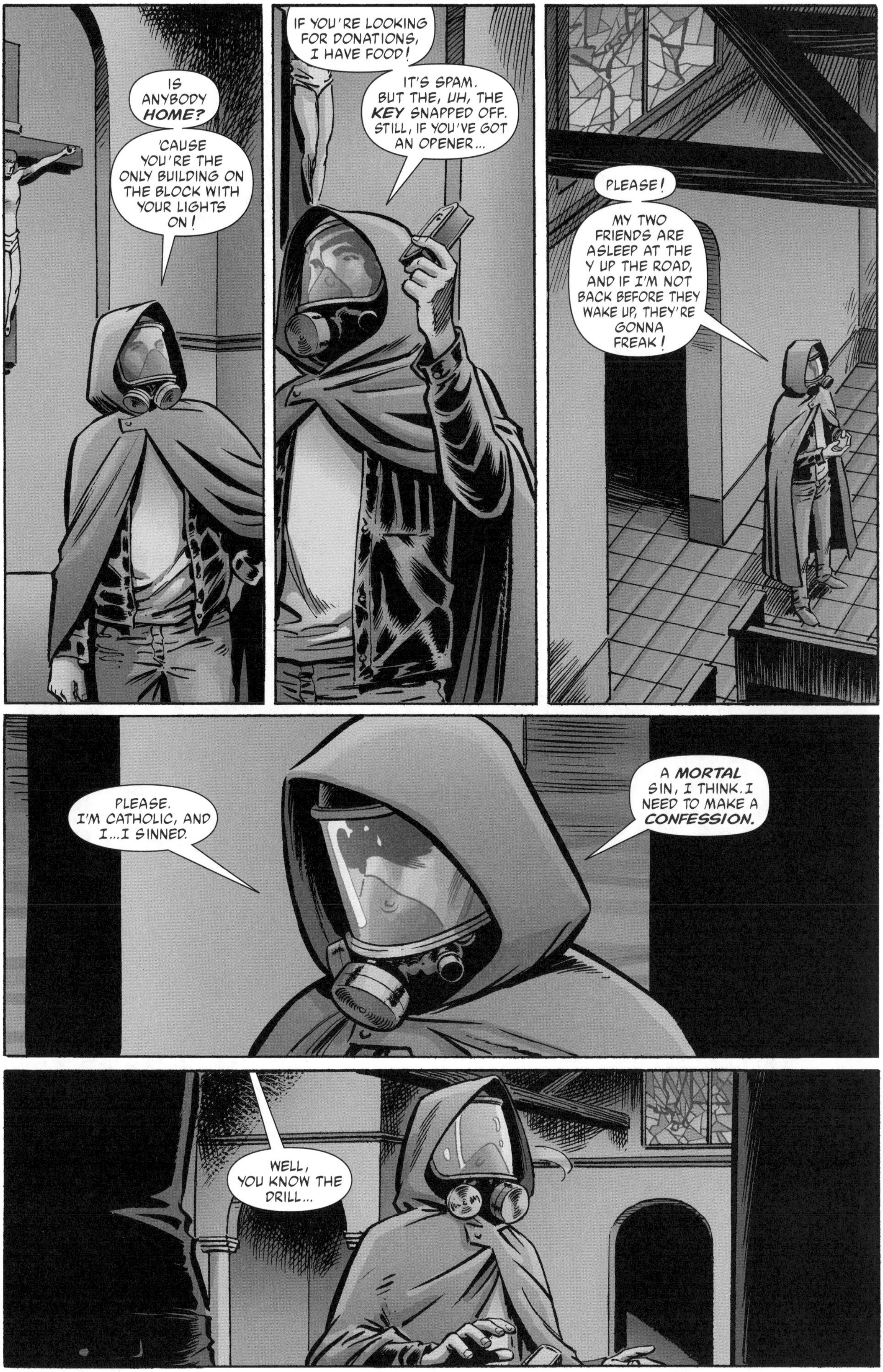
IS ANYBODY HOME?
'CAUSE YOU'RE THE ONLY BUILDING ON THE BLOCK WITH YOUR LIGHTS ON!
IF YOU'RE LOOKING FOR DONATIONS, I HAVE FOOD!
IT'S SPAM. BUT THE, UH, THE KEY SNAPPED OFF. STILL, IF YOU'VE GOT AN OPENER...
PLEASE!
MY TWO FRIENDS ARE ASLEEP AT THE Y UP THE ROAD, AND IF I'M NOT BACK BEFORE THEY WAKE UP, THEY'RE GONNA FREAK!
PLEASE. I'M CATHOLIC, AND I...I SINNED.
A MORTAL SIN, I THINK. I NEED TO MAKE A CONFESSION.
WELL, YOU KNOW THE DRILL...

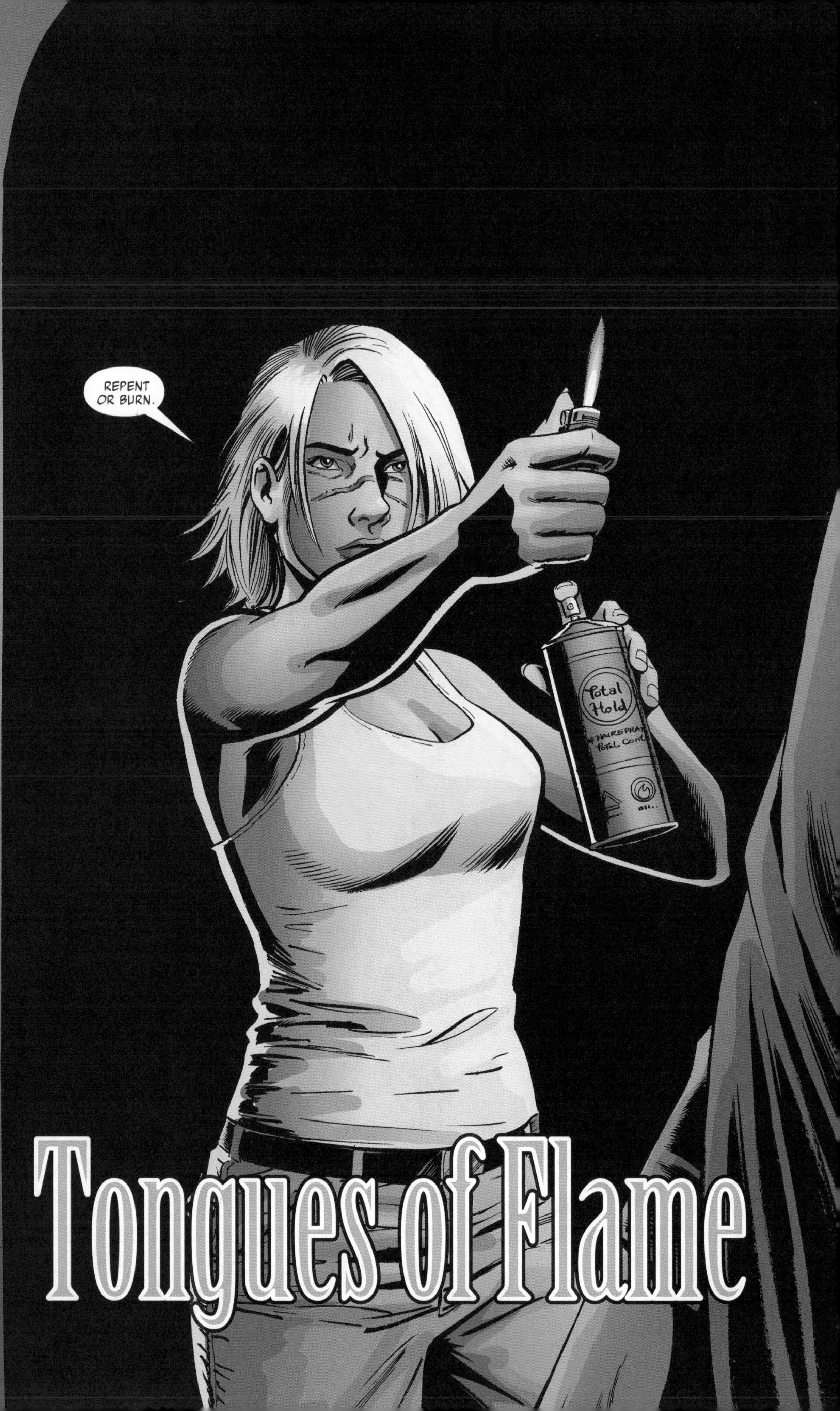
REPENT OR BURN.
Total Hold
Tongues of Flame

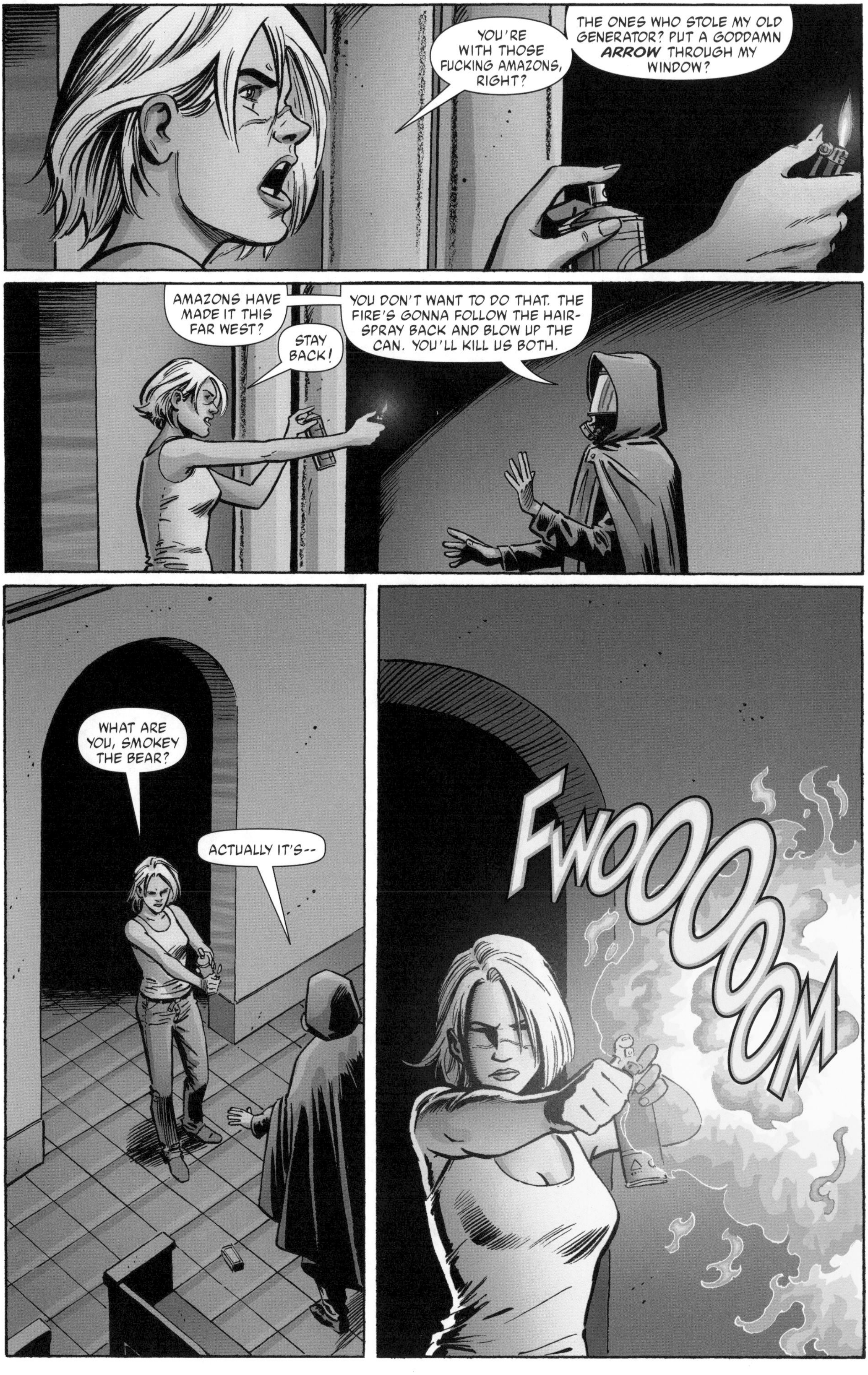
YOU'RE WITH THOSE FUCKING AMAZONS, RIGHT?
THE ONES WHO STOLE MY OLD GENERATOR? PUT A GODDAMN ARROW THROUGH MY WINDOW?
AMAZONS HAVE MADE IT THIS FAR WEST?
STAY BACK!
YOU DON'T WANT TO DO THAT. THE FIRE'S GONNA FOLLOW THE HAIR-SPRAY BACK AND BLOW UP THE CAN. YOU'LL KILL US BOTH.
WHAT ARE YOU, SMOKEY THE BEAR?
ACTUALLY IT'S--
FWOOOOOOM

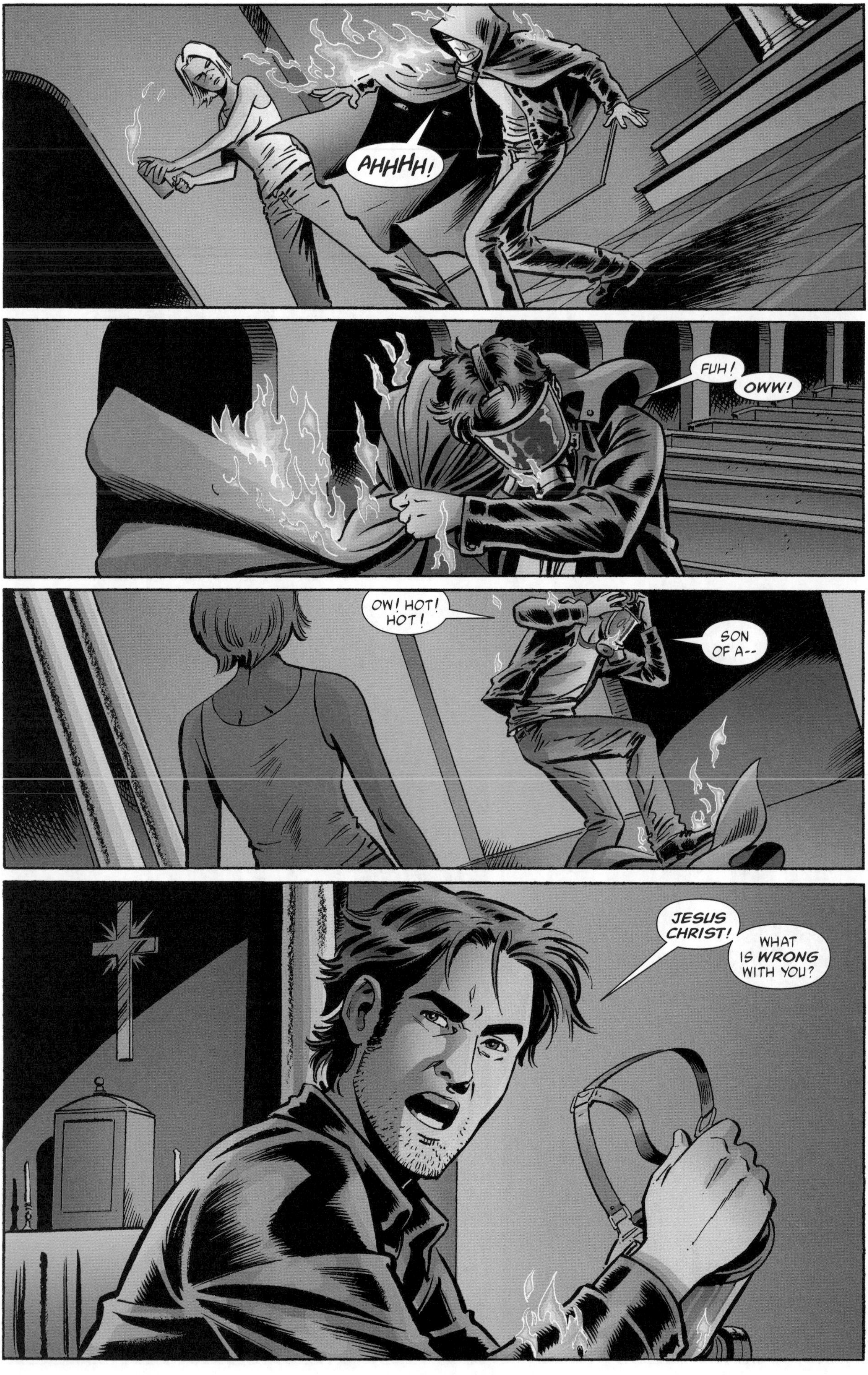
AHHHH!
FUH!
OWW!
OW! HOT! HOT!
SON OF A--
JESUS CHRIST!
WHAT IS WRONG WITH YOU?

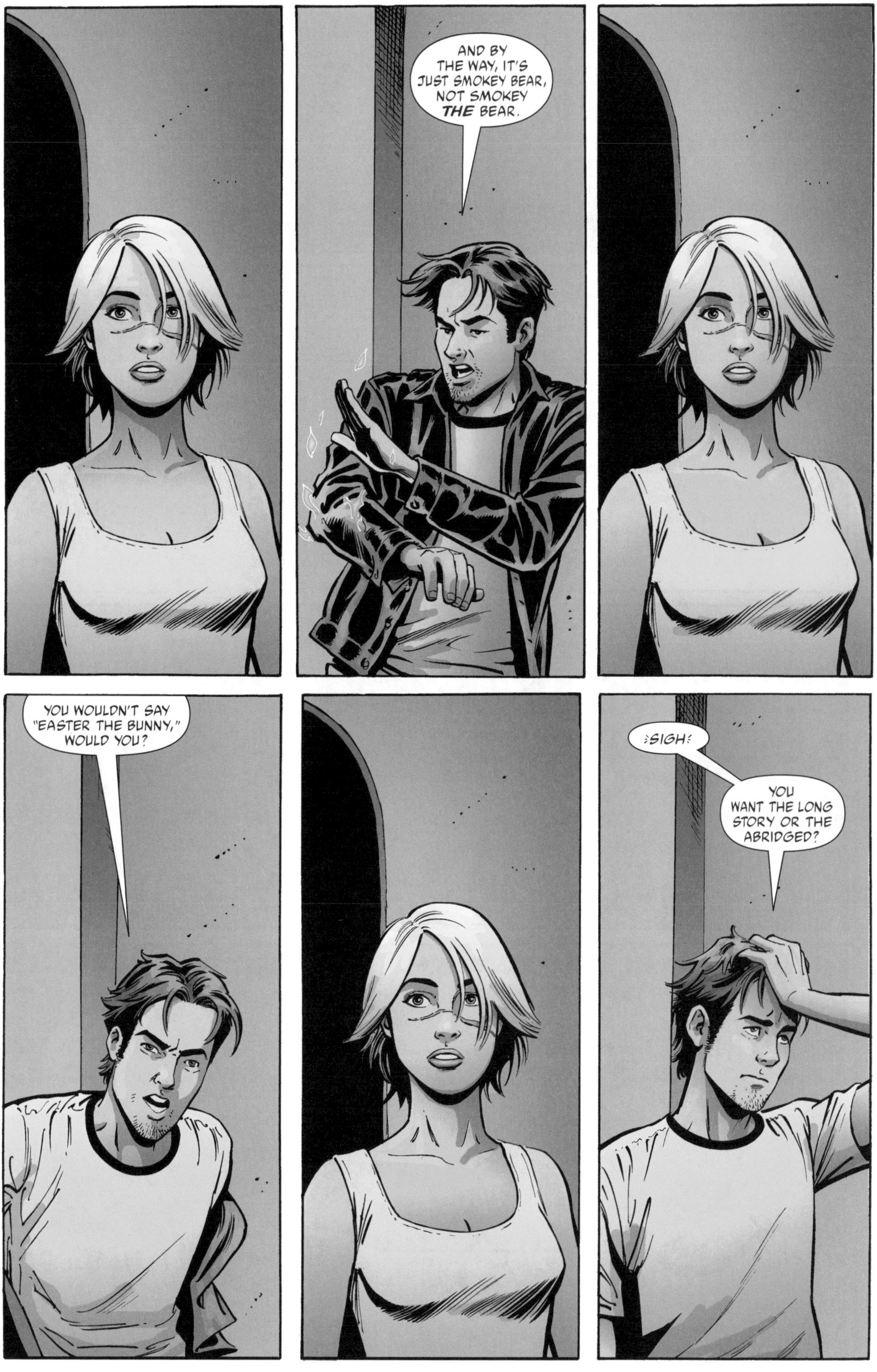
AND BY THE WAY, IT'S JUST SMOKEY BEAR, NOT SMOKEY THE BEAR.
YOU WOULDN'T SAY "EASTER THE BUNNY," WOULD YOU?
SIGH
YOU WANT THE LONG STORY OR THE ABRIDGED?

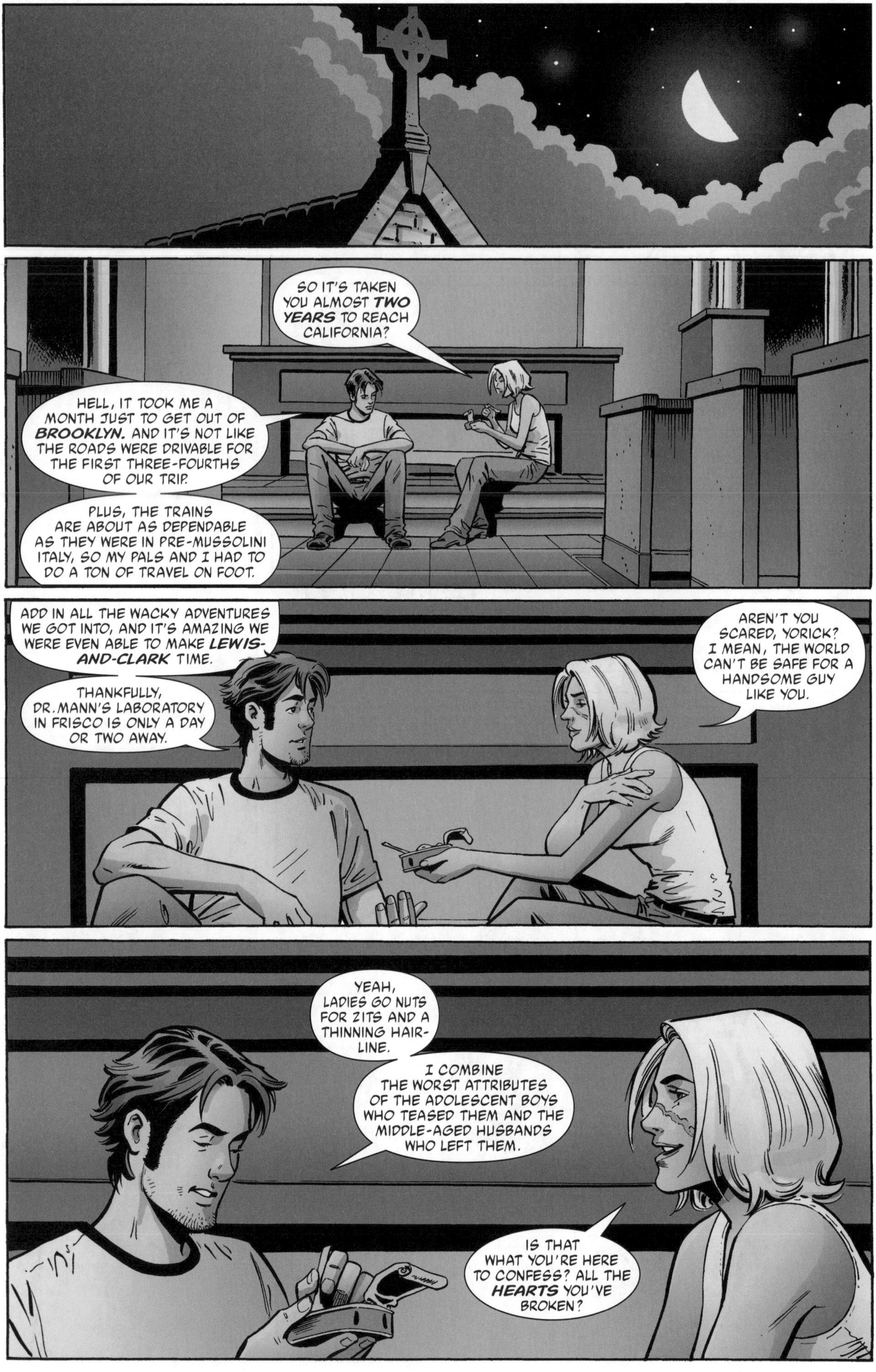
SO IT'S TAKEN YOU ALMOST **TWO YEARS** TO REACH CALIFORNIA?
HELL, IT TOOK ME A MONTH JUST TO GET OUT OF **BROOKLYN.** AND IT'S NOT LIKE THE ROADS WERE DRIVABLE FOR THE FIRST THREE-FOURTHS OF OUR TRIP.
PLUS, THE TRAINS ARE ABOUT AS DEPENDABLE AS THEY WERE IN PRE-MUSSOLINI ITALY, SO MY PALS AND I HAD TO DO A TON OF TRAVEL ON FOOT.
ADD IN ALL THE WACKY ADVENTURES WE GOT INTO, AND IT'S AMAZING WE WERE EVEN ABLE TO MAKE **LEWIS-AND-CLARK** TIME.
THANKFULLY, DR. MANN'S LABORATORY IN FRISCO IS ONLY A DAY OR TWO AWAY.
AREN'T YOU SCARED, YORICK? I MEAN, THE WORLD CAN'T BE SAFE FOR A HANDSOME GUY LIKE YOU.
YEAH, LADIES GO NUTS FOR ZITS AND A THINNING HAIR-LINE.
I COMBINE THE WORST ATTRIBUTES OF THE ADOLESCENT BOYS WHO TEASED THEM AND THE MIDDLE-AGED HUSBANDS WHO LEFT THEM.
IS THAT WHAT YOU'RE HERE TO CONFESS? ALL THE **HEARTS** YOU'VE BROKEN?

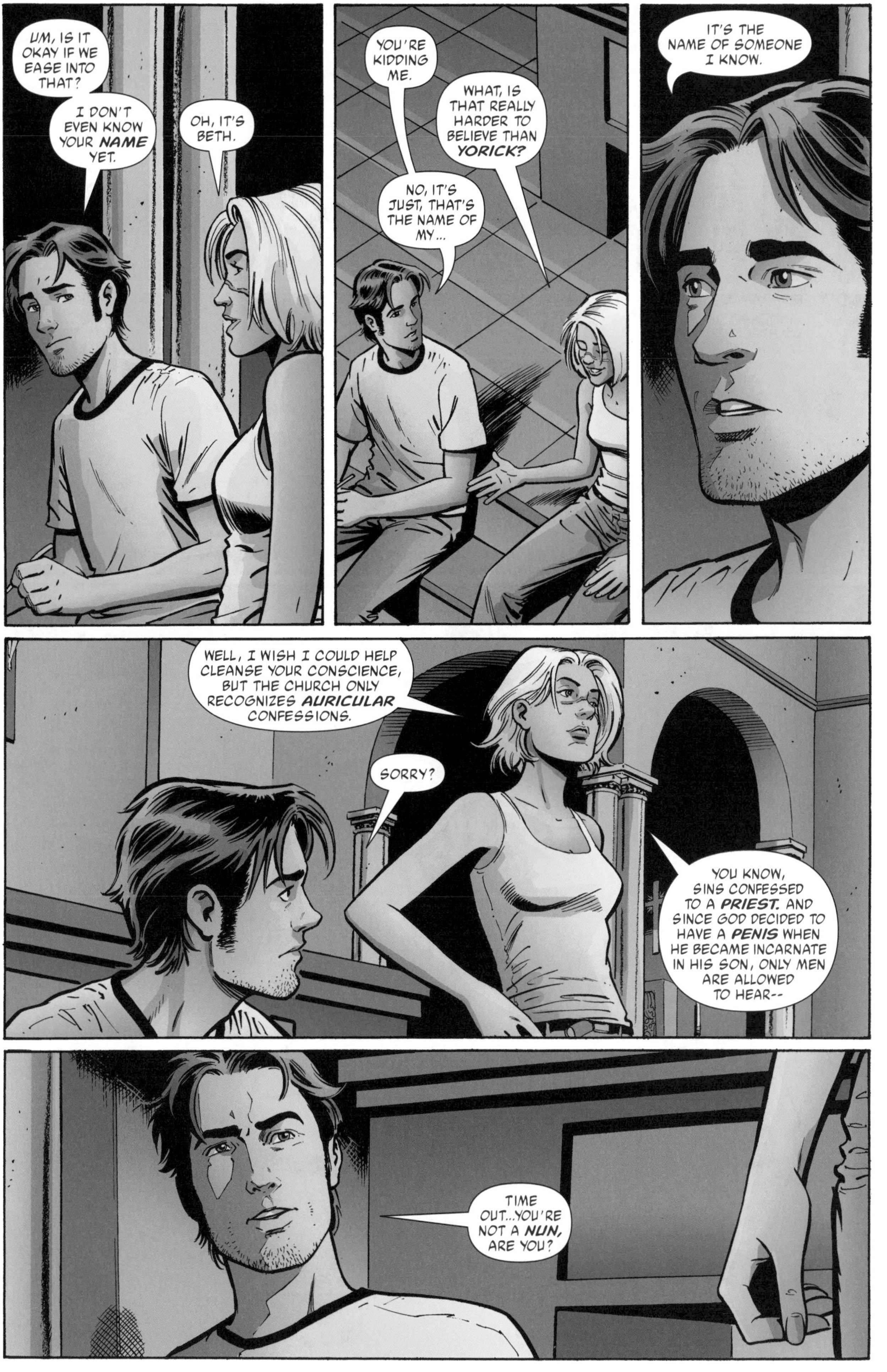
UM, IS IT OKAY IF WE EASE INTO THAT?
I DON'T EVEN KNOW YOUR NAME YET.
OH, IT'S BETH.
YOU'RE KIDDING ME.
NO, IT'S JUST, THAT'S THE NAME OF MY...
WHAT, IS THAT REALLY HARDER TO BELIEVE THAN YORICK?
IT'S THE NAME OF SOMEONE I KNOW.
WELL, I WISH I COULD HELP CLEANSE YOUR CONSCIENCE, BUT THE CHURCH ONLY RECOGNIZES AURICULAR CONFESSIONS.
SORRY?
YOU KNOW, SINS CONFESSED TO A PRIEST. AND SINCE GOD DECIDED TO HAVE A PENIS WHEN HE BECAME INCARNATE IN HIS SON, ONLY MEN ARE ALLOWED TO HEAR--
TIME OUT...YOU'RE NOT A NUN, ARE YOU?

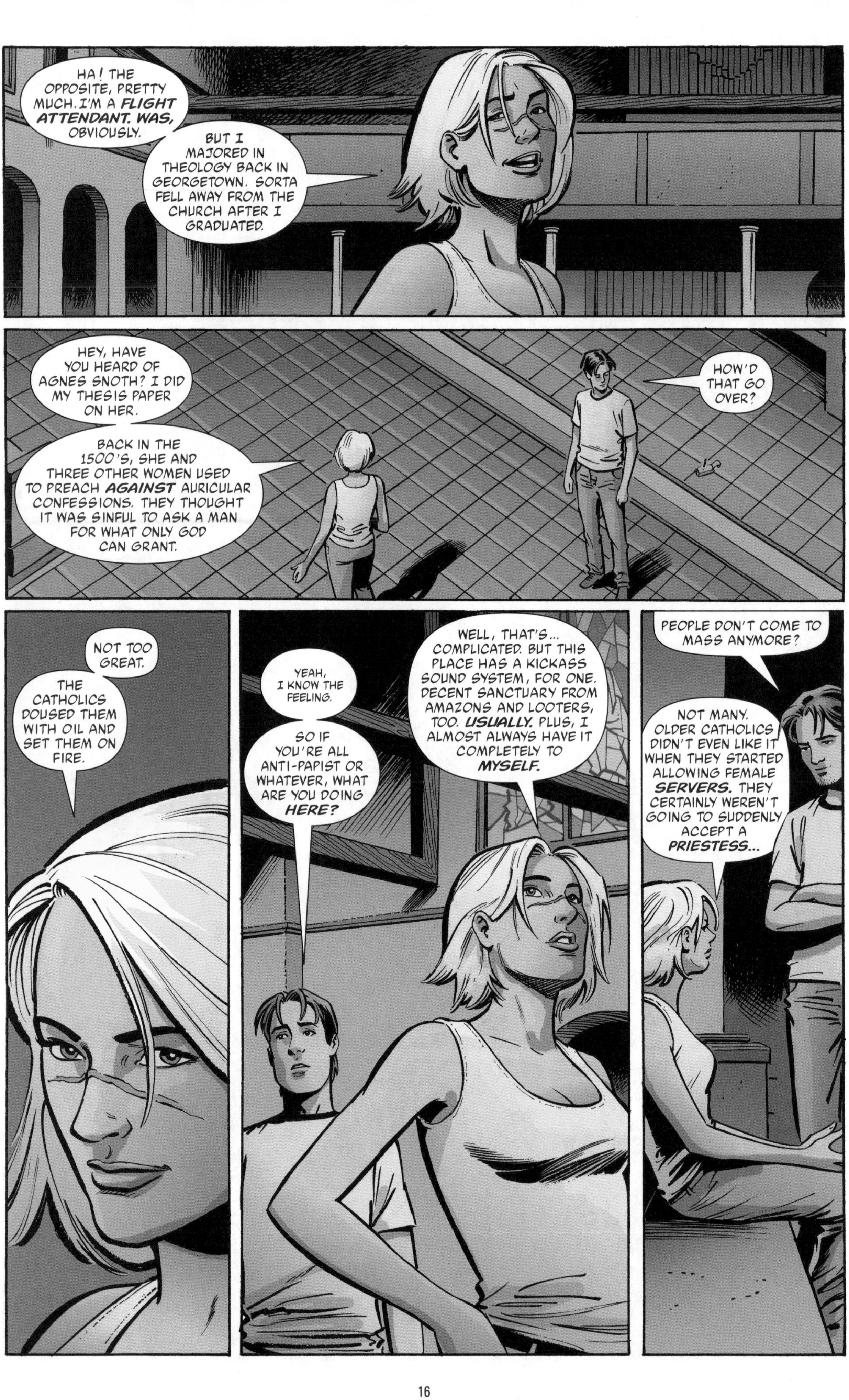
HA! THE OPPOSITE, PRETTY MUCH. I'M A FLIGHT ATTENDANT. WAS, OBVIOUSLY.
BUT I MAJORED IN THEOLOGY BACK IN GEORGETOWN. SORTA FELL AWAY FROM THE CHURCH AFTER I GRADUATED.
HEY, HAVE YOU HEARD OF AGNES SNOTH? I DID MY THESIS PAPER ON HER.
BACK IN THE 1500'S, SHE AND THREE OTHER WOMEN USED TO PREACH AGAINST AURICULAR CONFESSIONS. THEY THOUGHT IT WAS SINFUL TO ASK A MAN FOR WHAT ONLY GOD CAN GRANT.
HOW'D THAT GO OVER?
NOT TOO GREAT.
THE CATHOLICS DOUSED THEM WITH OIL AND SET THEM ON FIRE.
YEAH, I KNOW THE FEELING.
SO IF YOU'RE ALL ANTI-PAPIST OR WHATEVER, WHAT ARE YOU DOING HERE?
WELL, THAT'S... COMPLICATED. BUT THIS PLACE HAS A KICKASS SOUND SYSTEM, FOR ONE. DECENT SANCTUARY FROM AMAZONS AND LOOTERS, TOO. USUALLY. PLUS, I ALMOST ALWAYS HAVE IT COMPLETELY TO MYSELF.
PEOPLE DON'T COME TO MASS ANYMORE?
NOT MANY. OLDER CATHOLICS DIDN'T EVEN LIKE IT WHEN THEY STARTED ALLOWING FEMALE SERVERS. THEY CERTAINLY WEREN'T GOING TO SUDDENLY ACCEPT A PRIESTESS...

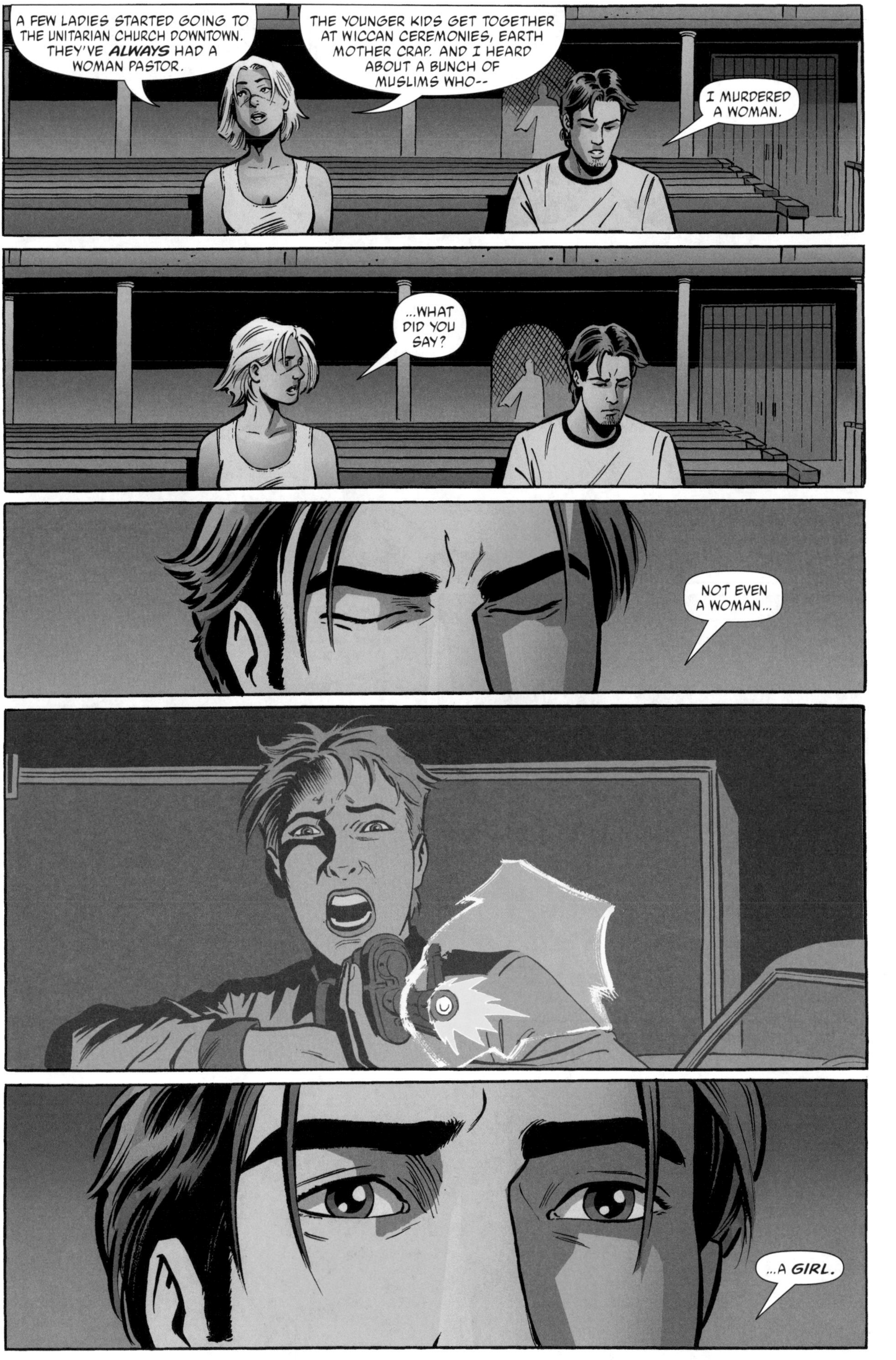
A FEW LADIES STARTED GOING TO THE UNITARIAN CHURCH DOWNTOWN. THEY'VE ***ALWAYS*** HAD A WOMAN PASTOR.
THE YOUNGER KIDS GET TOGETHER AT WICCAN CEREMONIES, EARTH MOTHER CRAP. AND I HEARD ABOUT A BUNCH OF MUSLIMS WHO--
I MURDERED A WOMAN.
...WHAT DID YOU SAY?
NOT EVEN A WOMAN...
...A ***GIRL.***

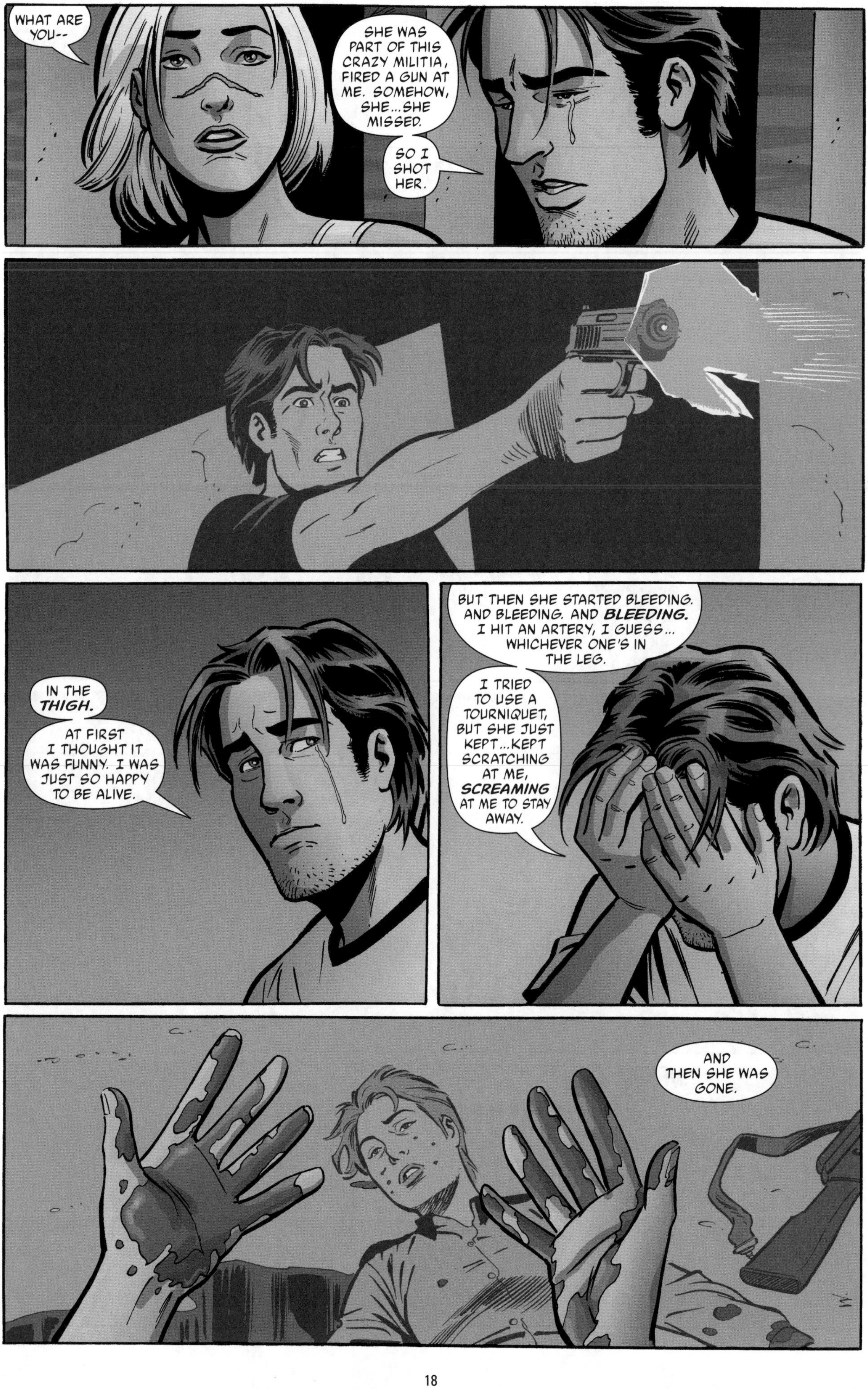
WHAT ARE YOU--
SHE WAS PART OF THIS CRAZY MILITIA, FIRED A GUN AT ME. SOMEHOW, SHE...SHE MISSED.
SO I SHOT HER.
IN THE *THIGH.*
AT FIRST I THOUGHT IT WAS FUNNY. I WAS JUST SO HAPPY TO BE ALIVE.
BUT THEN SHE STARTED BLEEDING. AND BLEEDING. AND *BLEEDING.* I HIT AN ARTERY, I GUESS... WHICHEVER ONE'S IN THE LEG.
I TRIED TO USE A TOURNIQUET, BUT SHE JUST KEPT...KEPT SCRATCHING AT ME, *SCREAMING* AT ME TO STAY AWAY.
AND THEN SHE WAS GONE.

FROM A BULLET TO THE *LEG?*

I DIDN'T EVEN KNOW THAT WAS *POSSIBLE.* I...I TRIED CPR, BUT--

YORICK, THAT'S NOT *MURDER.* YOU KILLED SOMEONE, BUT IN SELF-DEFENSE. IT'S NOT EVEN A SIN.

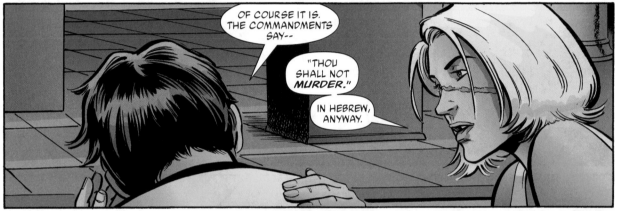

OF COURSE IT IS. THE COMMANDMENTS SAY--

"THOU SHALL NOT *MURDER.*"

IN HEBREW, ANYWAY.

BESIDES, IF THERE'S NO DIFFERENCE BETWEEN KILLING AND MURDER, I'D BE WORSE THAN *LIZZIE BORDEN.*

I'D MAKE AILEEN WUORNOS LOOK LIKE... LIKE...

I WAS WORKING THE LOGAN-L.A.X. RUN WHEN IT HAPPENED.

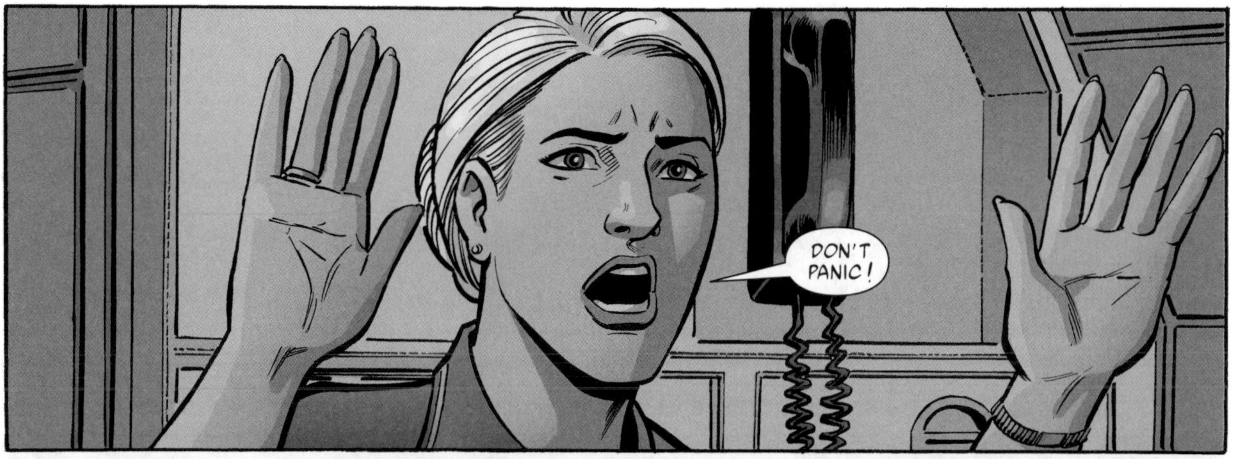
DON'T PANIC!

15,000 Feet Above Cooksfield
July 17, 2002

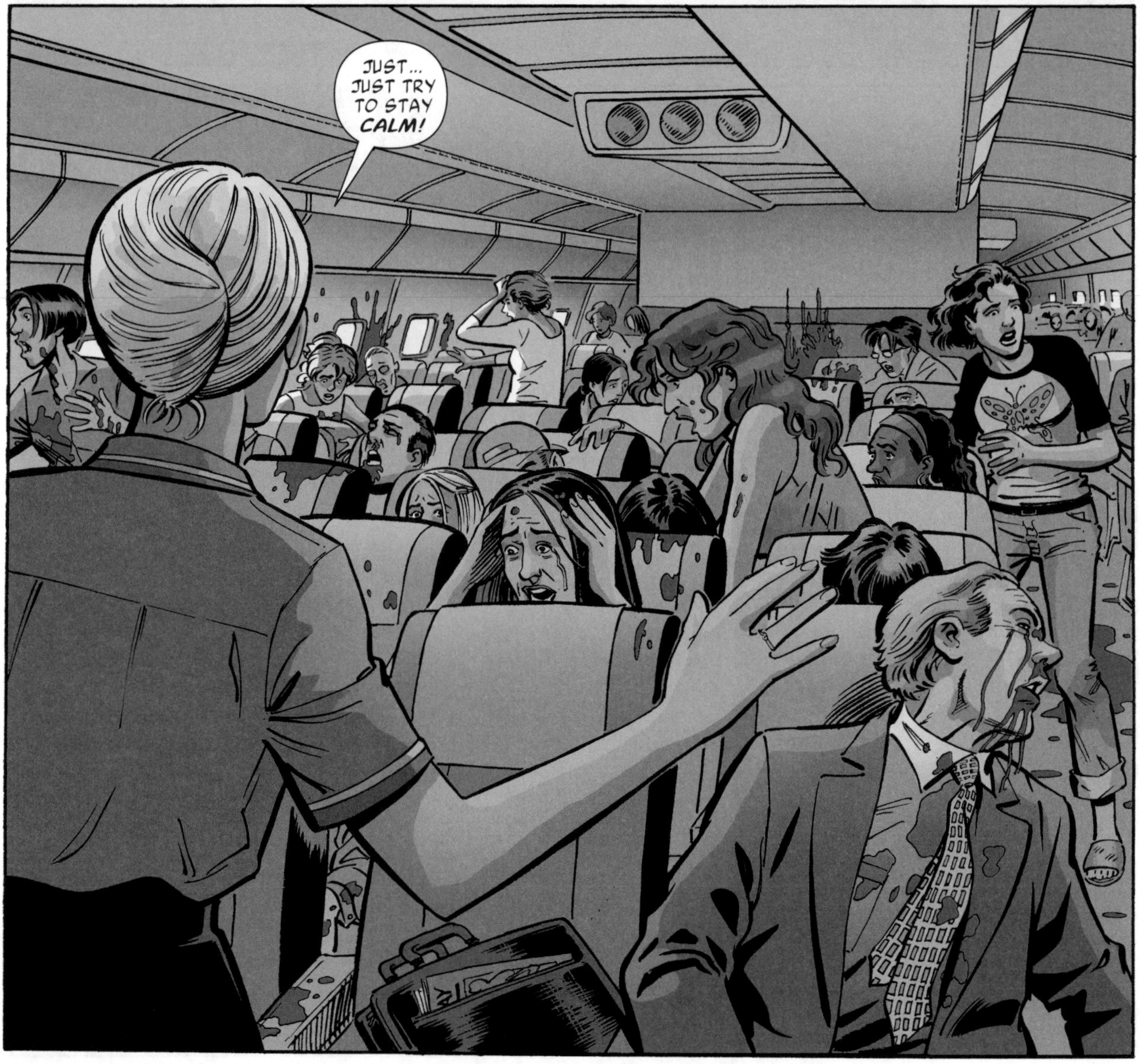
JUST... JUST TRY TO STAY CALM!

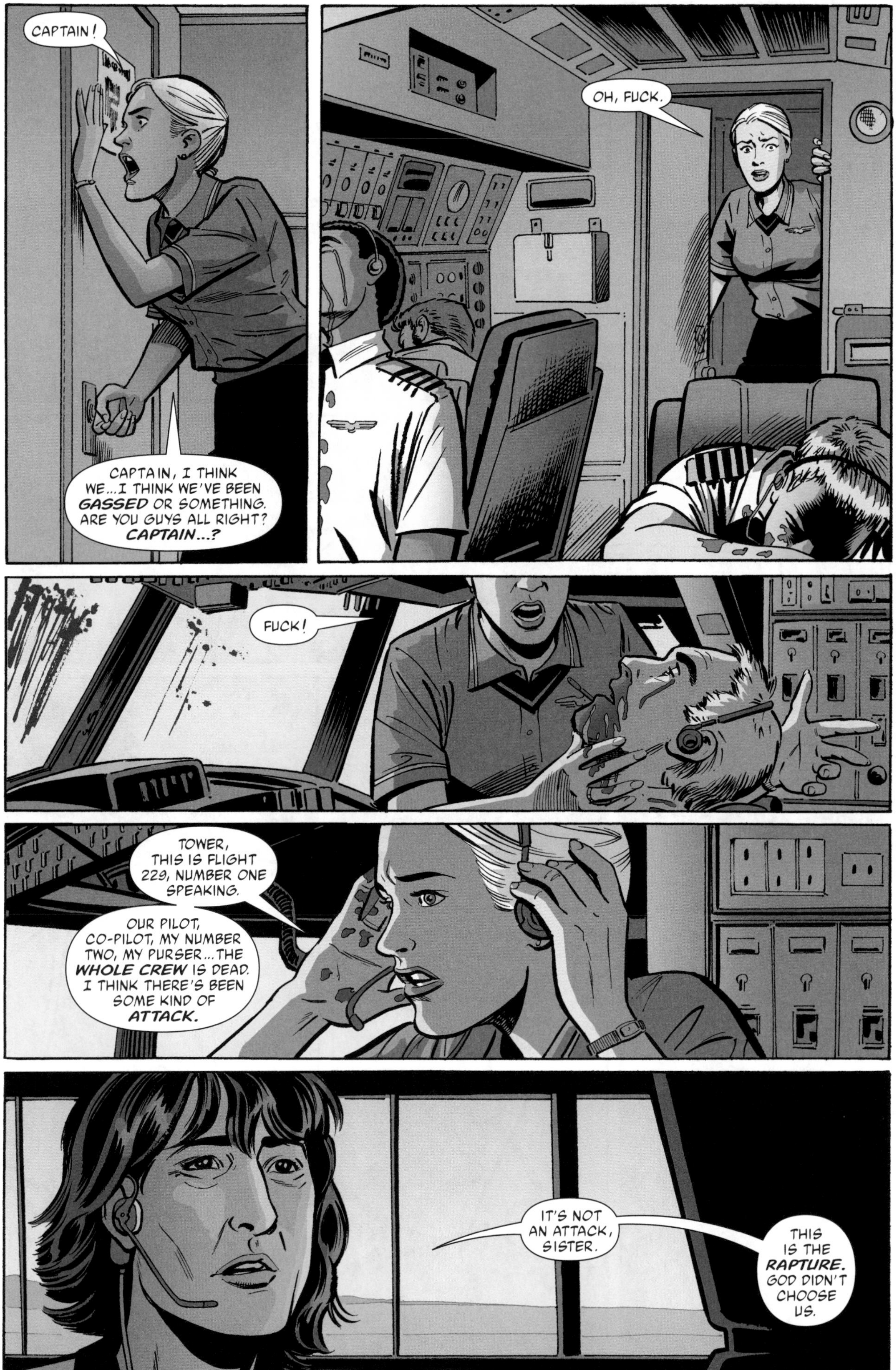
CAPTAIN!
CAPTAIN, I THINK WE...I THINK WE'VE BEEN GASSED OR SOMETHING. ARE YOU GUYS ALL RIGHT? CAPTAIN...?
OH, FUCK.
FUCK!
TOWER, THIS IS FLIGHT 229, NUMBER ONE SPEAKING.
OUR PILOT, CO-PILOT, MY NUMBER TWO, MY PURSER...THE WHOLE CREW IS DEAD. I THINK THERE'S BEEN SOME KIND OF ATTACK.
IT'S NOT AN ATTACK, SISTER.
THIS IS THE RAPTURE. GOD DIDN'T CHOOSE US.

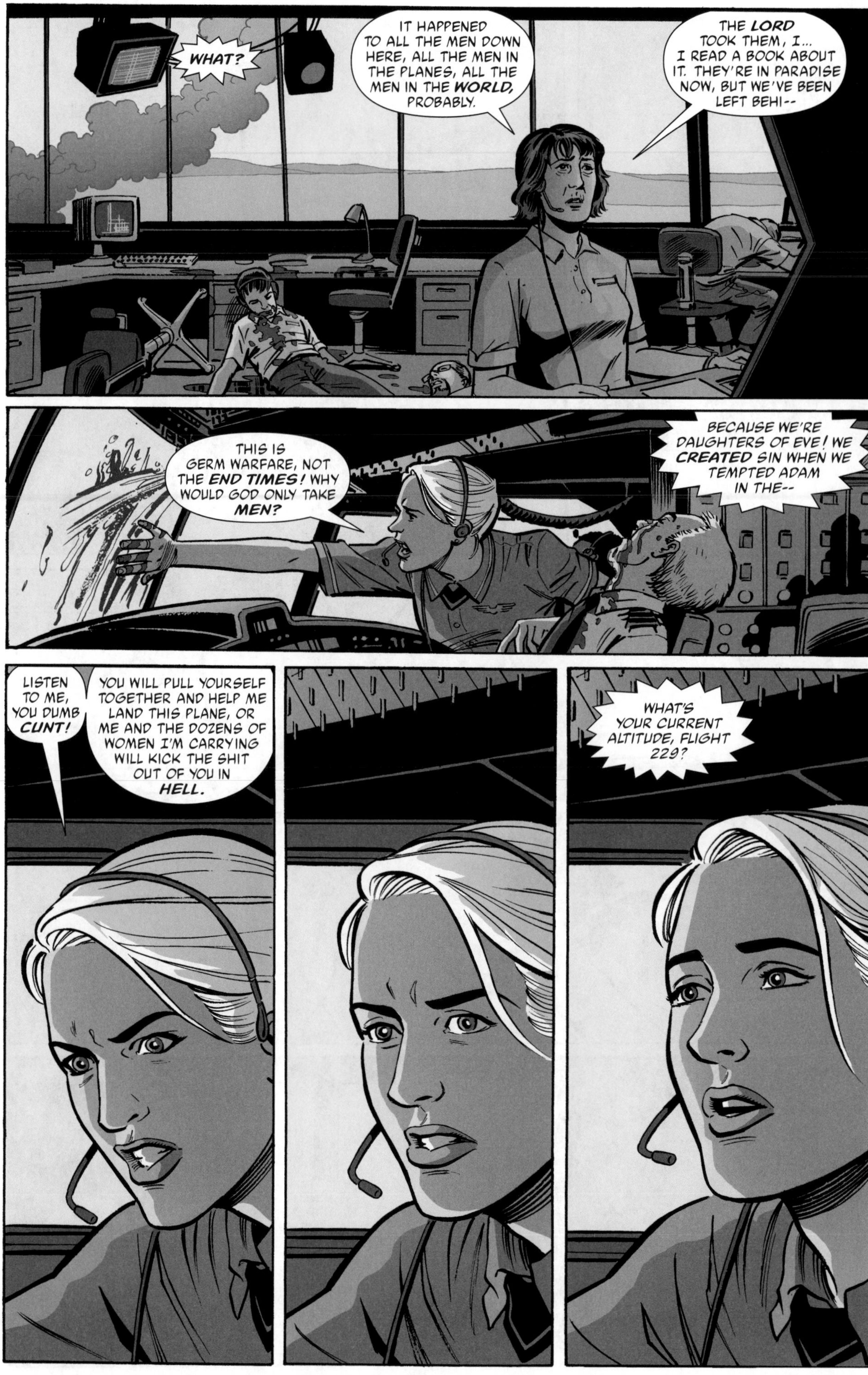
WHAT?
IT HAPPENED TO ALL THE MEN DOWN HERE, ALL THE MEN IN THE PLANES, ALL THE MEN IN THE WORLD, PROBABLY.
THE LORD TOOK THEM, I... I READ A BOOK ABOUT IT. THEY'RE IN PARADISE NOW, BUT WE'VE BEEN LEFT BEHI--
THIS IS GERM WARFARE, NOT THE END TIMES! WHY WOULD GOD ONLY TAKE MEN?
BECAUSE WE'RE DAUGHTERS OF EVE! WE CREATED SIN WHEN WE TEMPTED ADAM IN THE--
LISTEN TO ME, YOU DUMB CUNT!
YOU WILL PULL YOURSELF TOGETHER AND HELP ME LAND THIS PLANE, OR ME AND THE DOZENS OF WOMEN I'M CARRYING WILL KICK THE SHIT OUT OF YOU IN HELL.
WHAT'S YOUR CURRENT ALTITUDE, FLIGHT 229?

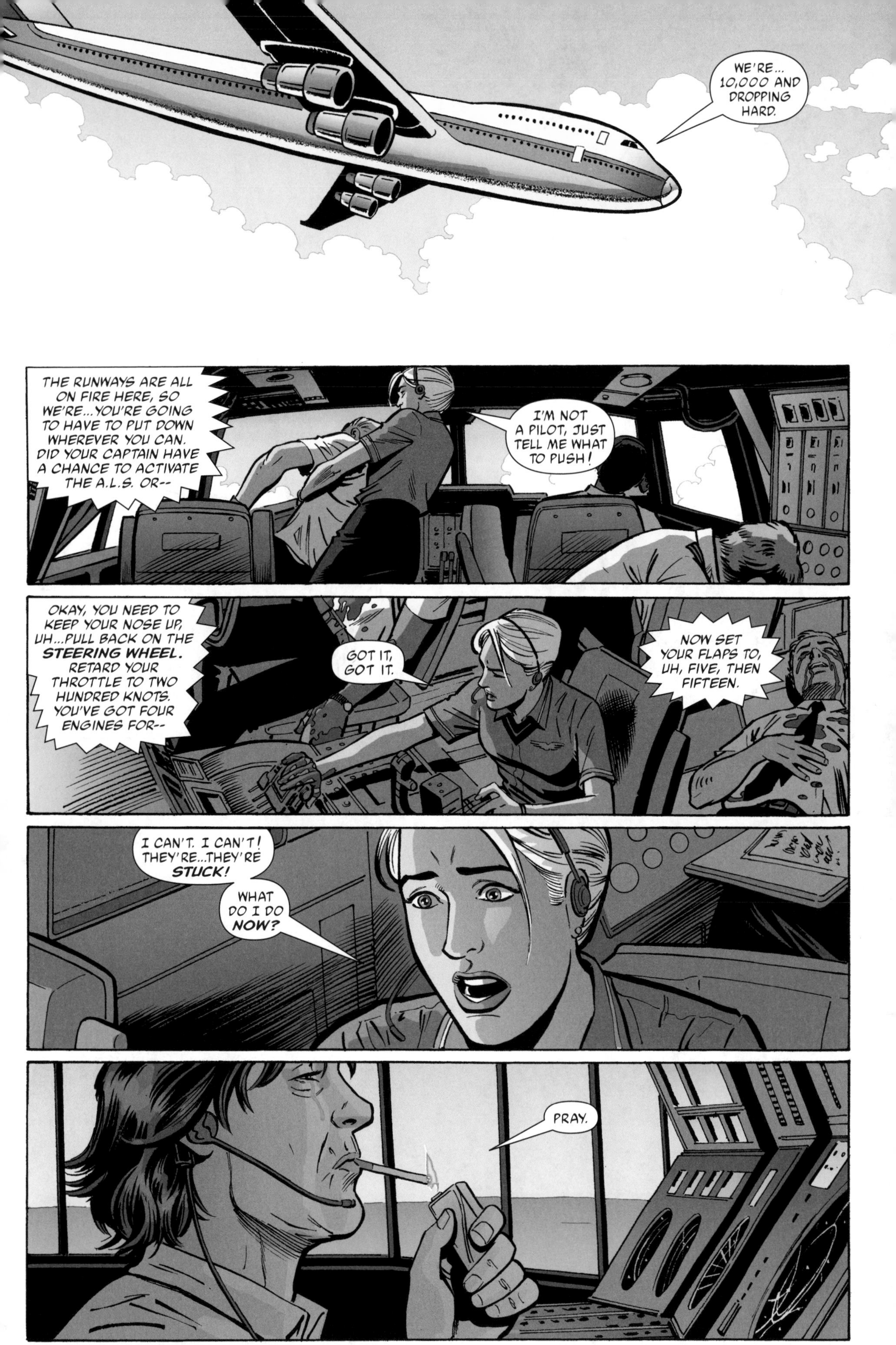
WE'RE... 10,000 AND DROPPING HARD.
THE RUNWAYS ARE ALL ON FIRE HERE, SO WE'RE... YOU'RE GOING TO HAVE TO PUT DOWN WHEREVER YOU CAN. DID YOUR CAPTAIN HAVE A CHANCE TO ACTIVATE THE A.L.S. OR--
I'M NOT A PILOT, JUST TELL ME WHAT TO PUSH!
OKAY, YOU NEED TO KEEP YOUR NOSE UP, UH...PULL BACK ON THE **STEERING WHEEL.** RETARD YOUR THROTTLE TO TWO HUNDRED KNOTS. YOU'VE GOT FOUR ENGINES FOR--
GOT IT, GOT IT.
NOW SET YOUR FLAPS TO, UH, FIVE, THEN FIFTEEN.
I CAN'T. I CAN'T! THEY'RE...THEY'RE **STUCK!**
WHAT DO I DO **NOW?**
PRAY.

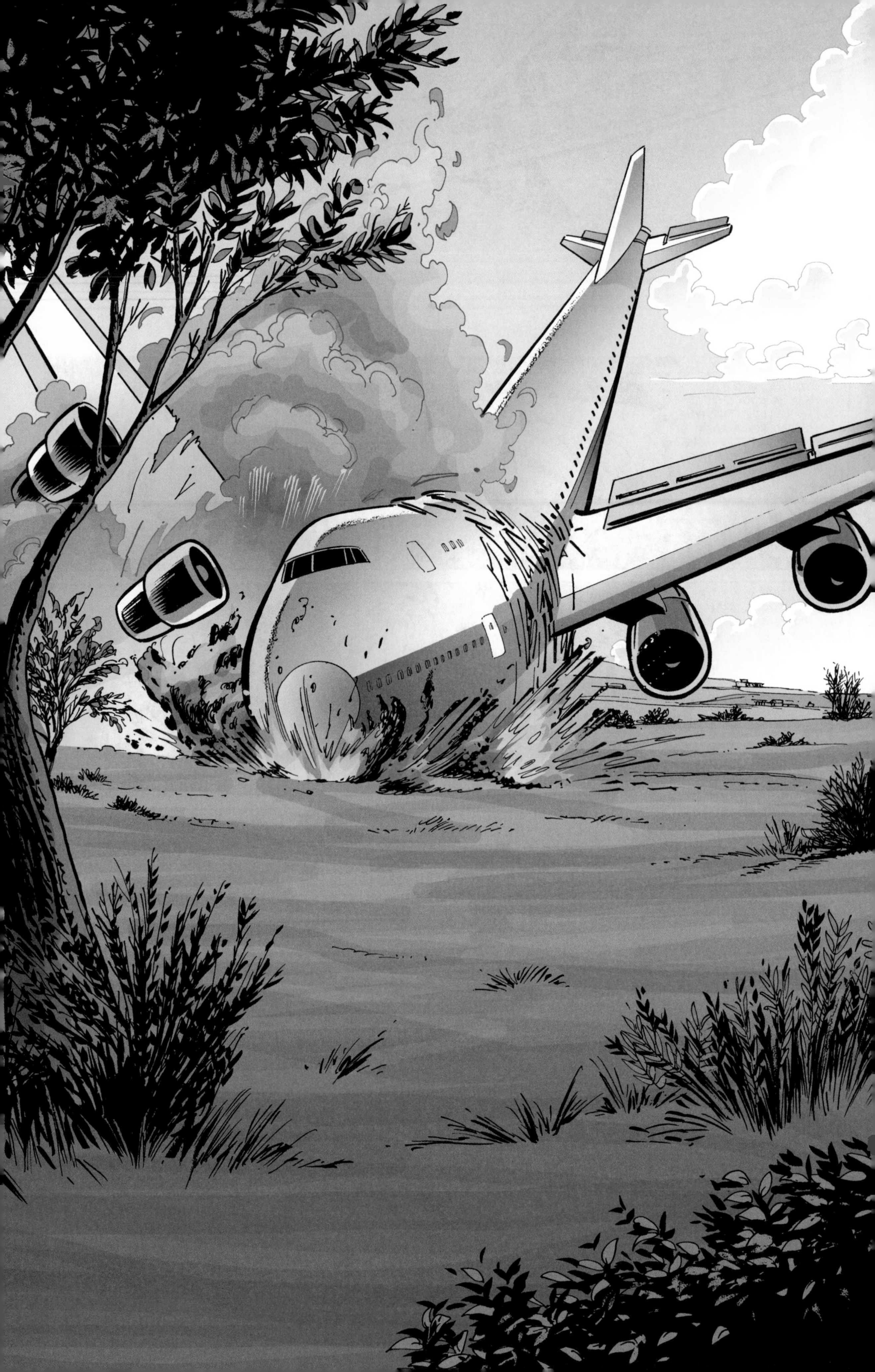

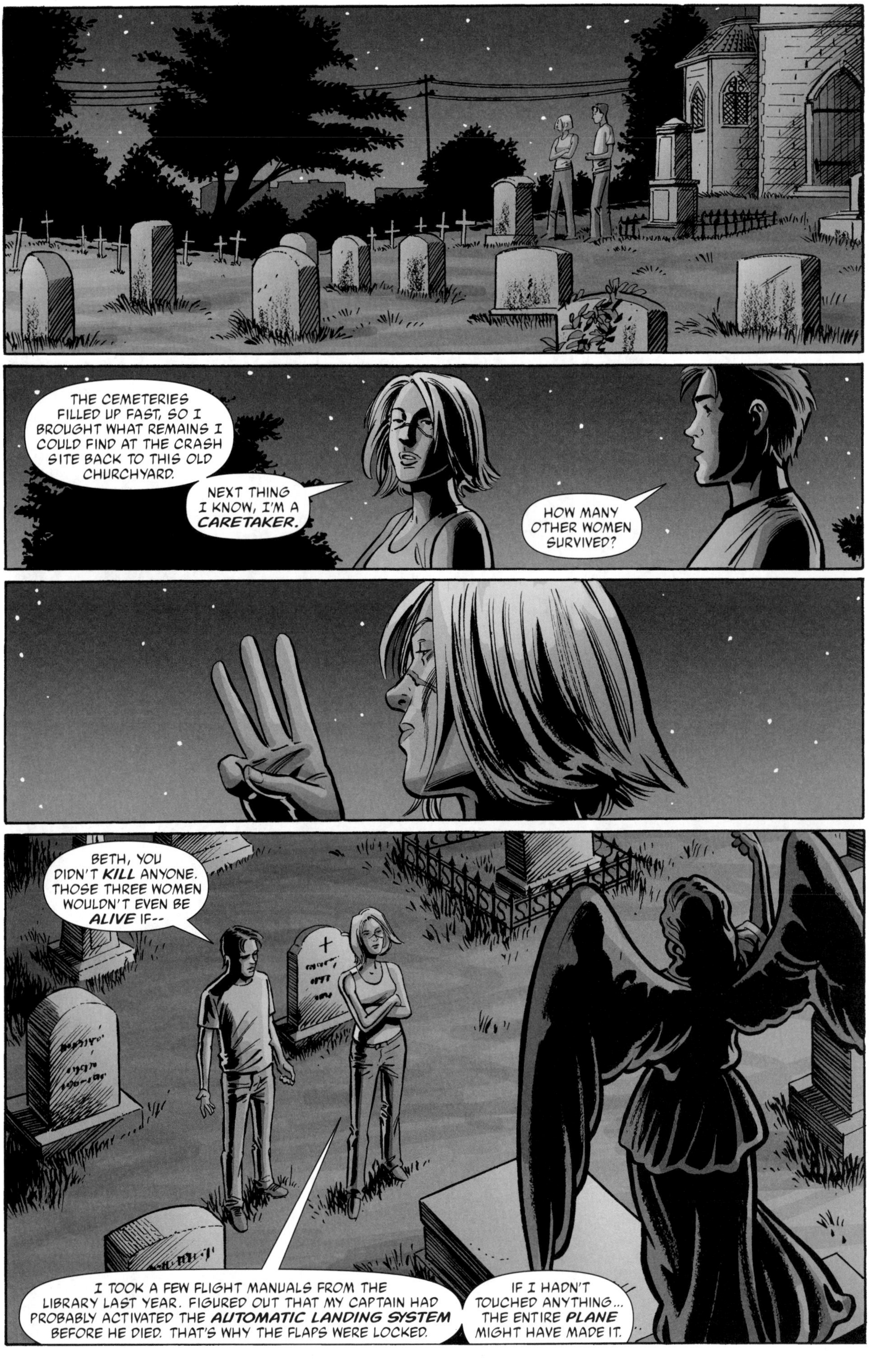
THE CEMETERIES FILLED UP FAST, SO I BROUGHT WHAT REMAINS I COULD FIND AT THE CRASH SITE BACK TO THIS OLD CHURCHYARD.
NEXT THING I KNOW, I'M A CARETAKER.
HOW MANY OTHER WOMEN SURVIVED?
BETH, YOU DIDN'T KILL ANYONE. THOSE THREE WOMEN WOULDN'T EVEN BE ALIVE IF--
I TOOK A FEW FLIGHT MANUALS FROM THE LIBRARY LAST YEAR. FIGURED OUT THAT MY CAPTAIN HAD PROBABLY ACTIVATED THE AUTOMATIC LANDING SYSTEM BEFORE HE DIED. THAT'S WHY THE FLAPS WERE LOCKED.
IF I HADN'T TOUCHED ANYTHING... THE ENTIRE PLANE MIGHT HAVE MADE IT.

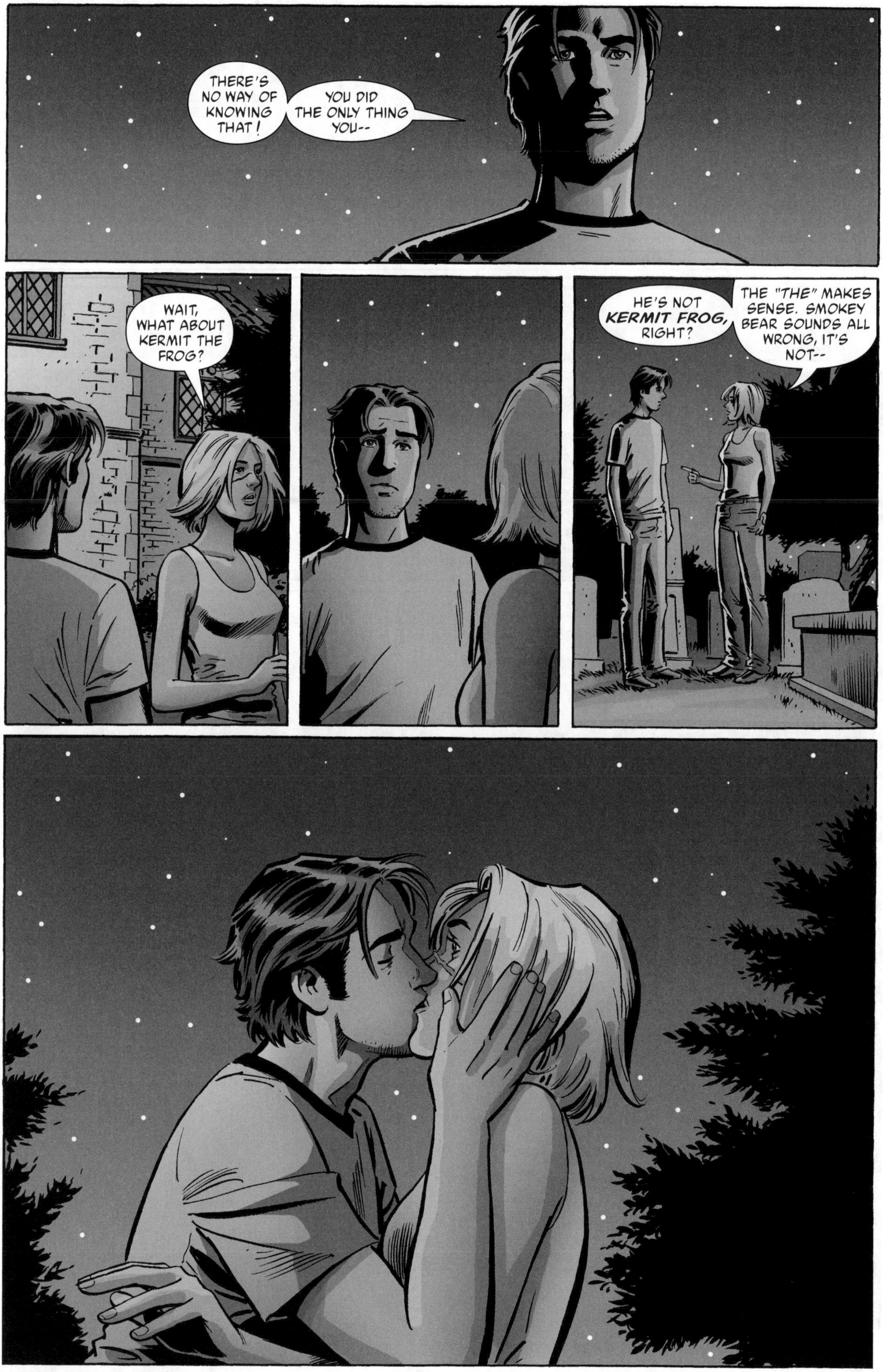
THERE'S NO WAY OF KNOWING THAT!
YOU DID THE ONLY THING YOU--
WAIT, WHAT ABOUT KERMIT THE FROG?
HE'S NOT KERMIT FROG, RIGHT?
THE "THE" MAKES SENSE. SMOKEY BEAR SOUNDS ALL WRONG, IT'S NOT--

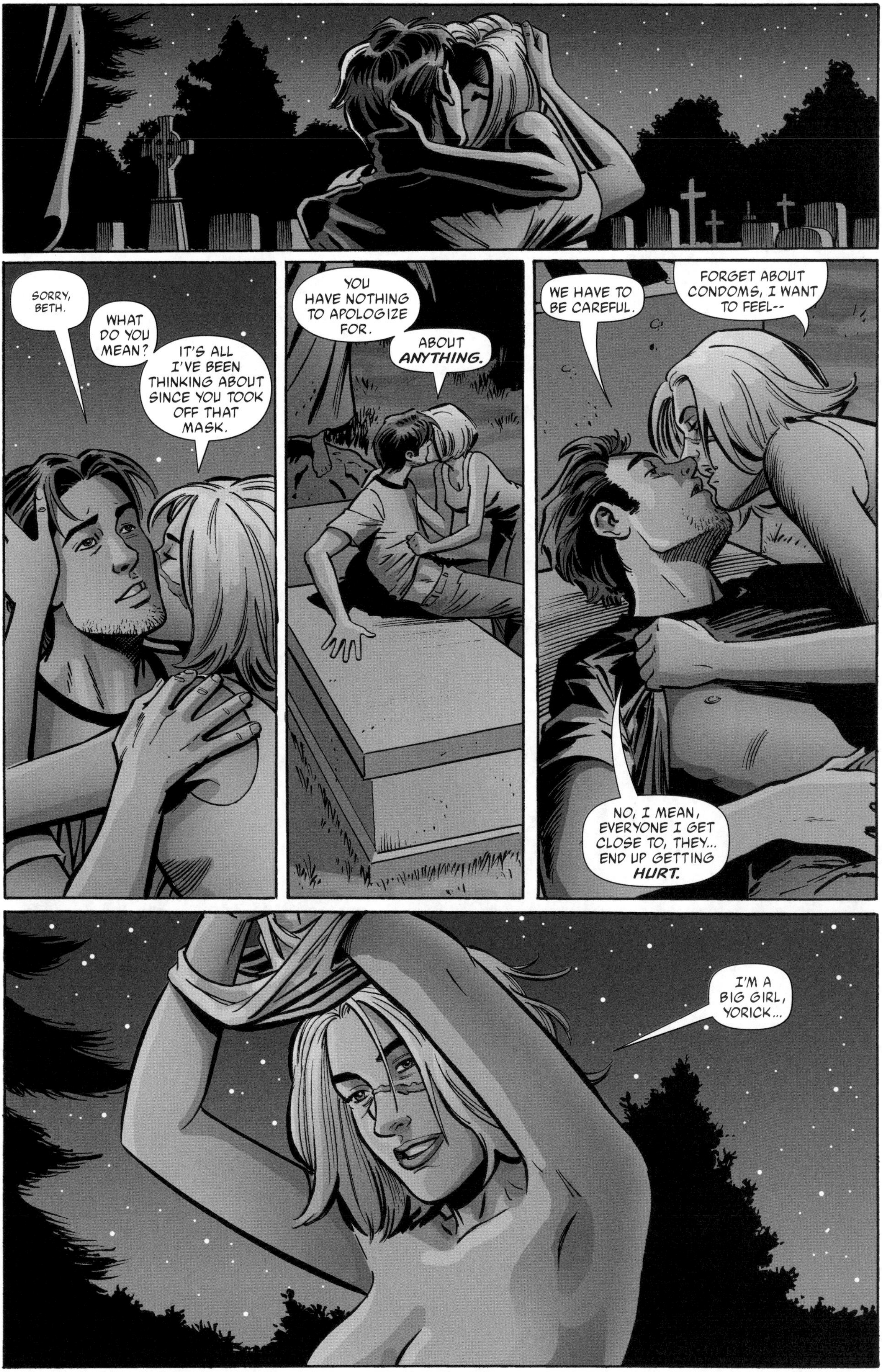
SORRY, BETH.
WHAT DO YOU MEAN?
IT'S ALL I'VE BEEN THINKING ABOUT SINCE YOU TOOK OFF THAT MASK.
YOU HAVE NOTHING TO APOLOGIZE FOR.
ABOUT ***ANYTHING.***
WE HAVE TO BE CAREFUL.
FORGET ABOUT CONDOMS, I WANT TO FEEL--
NO, I MEAN, EVERYONE I GET CLOSE TO, THEY... END UP GETTING ***HURT.***
I'M A BIG GIRL, YORICK...

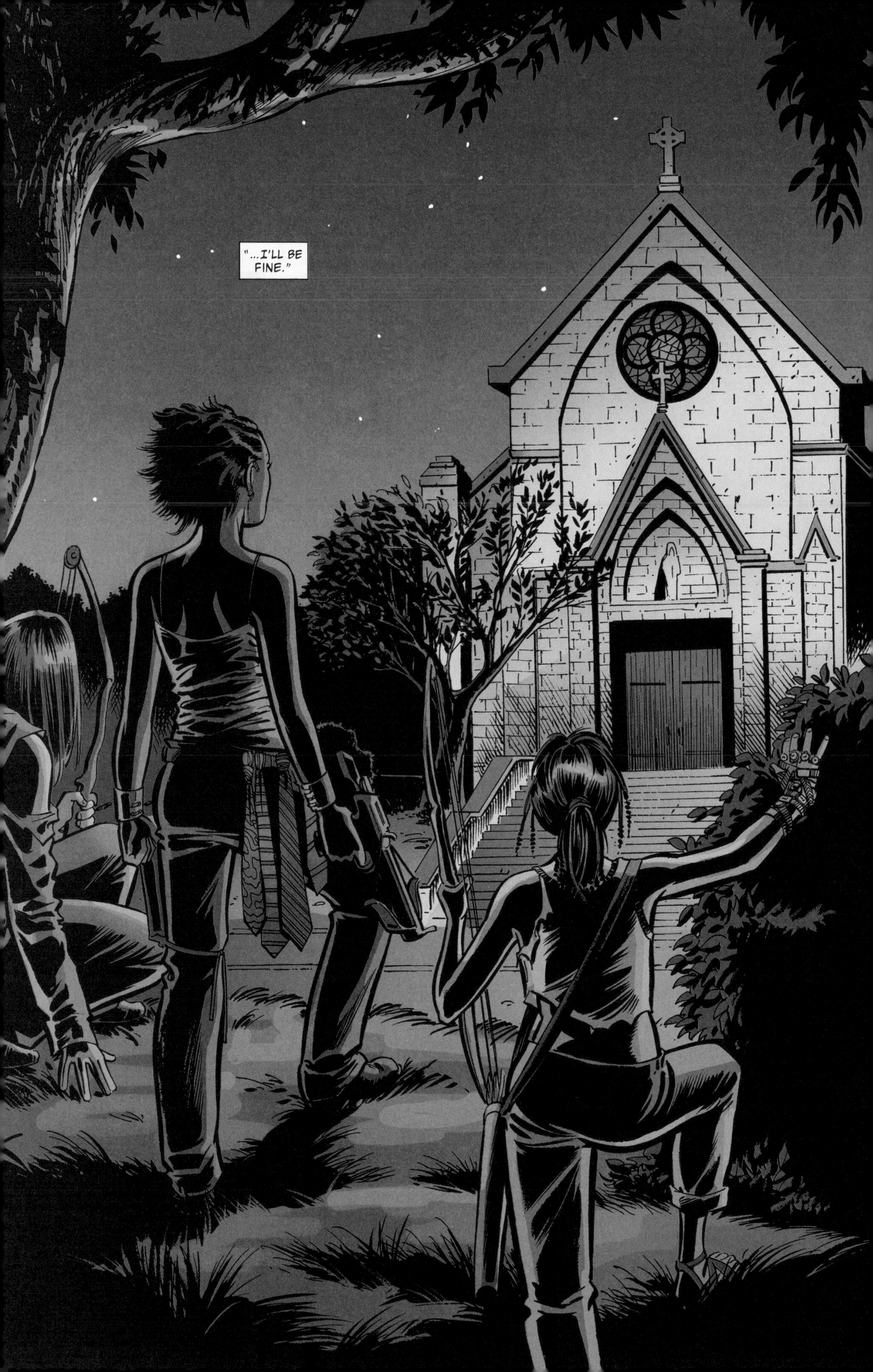
"...I'LL BE FINE."

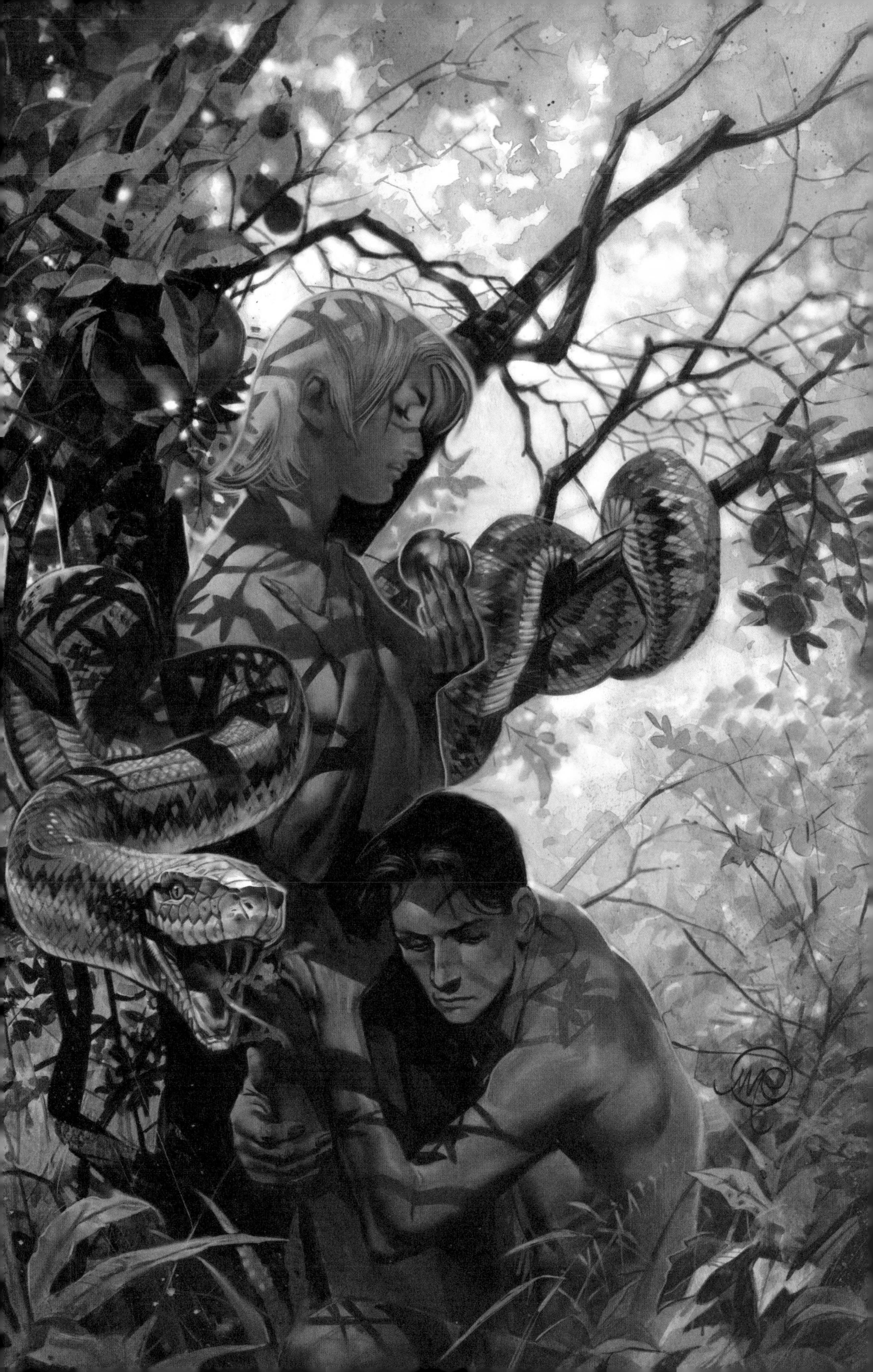

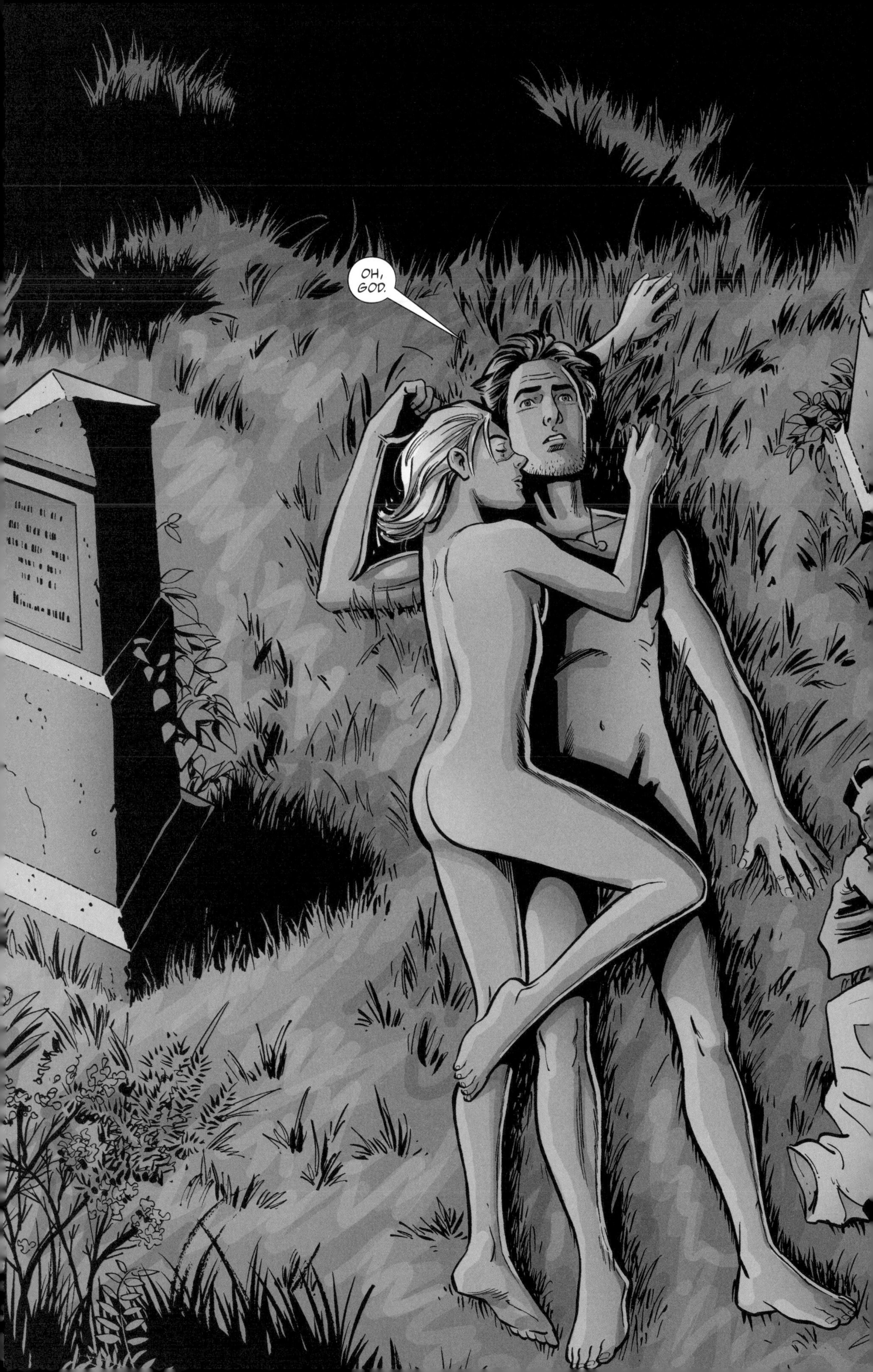
OH, GOD.

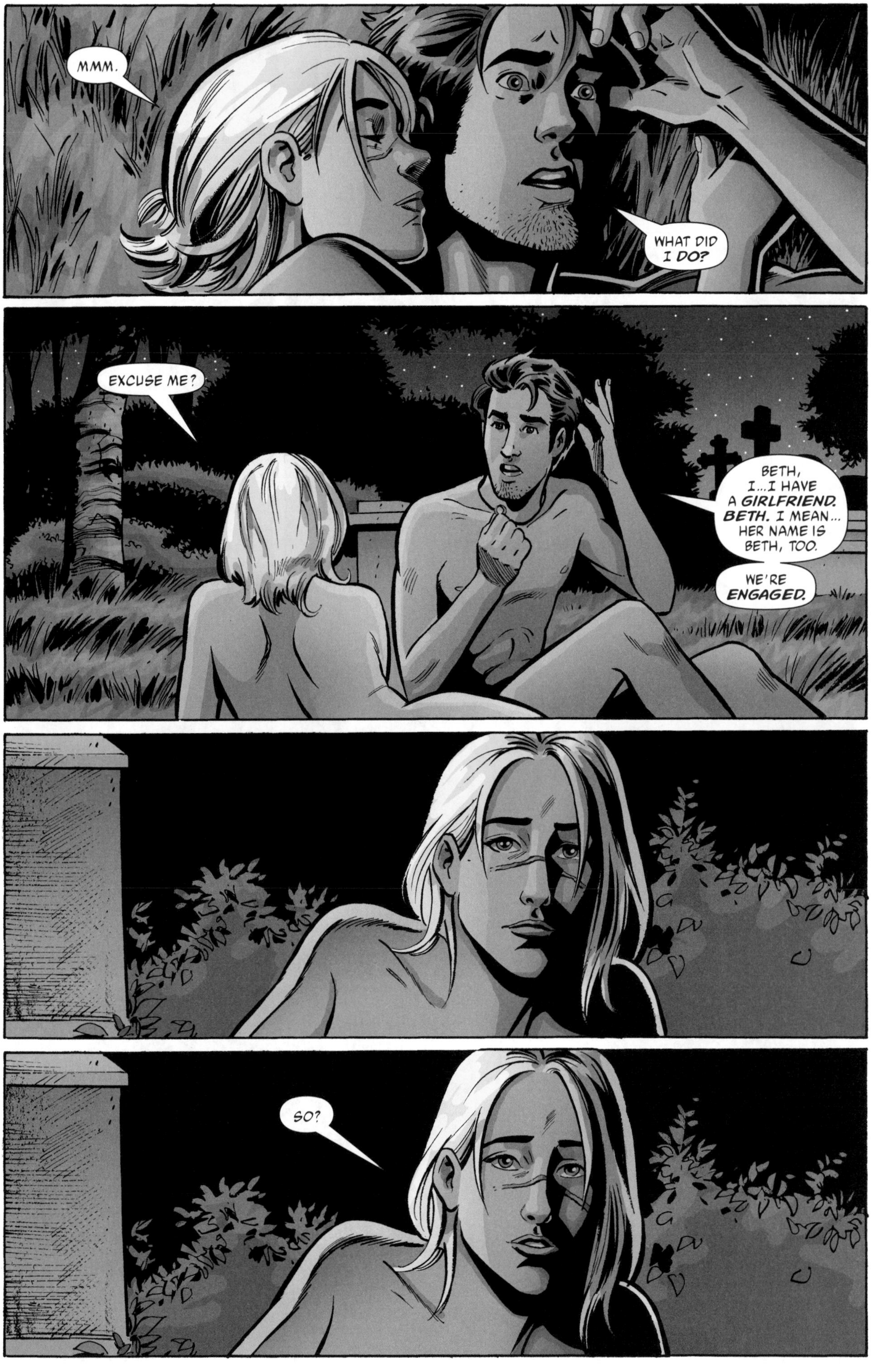
MMM.
WHAT DID I DO?
EXCUSE ME?
BETH, I...I HAVE A GIRLFRIEND. BETH. I MEAN... HER NAME IS BETH, TOO.
WE'RE ENGAGED.
SO?

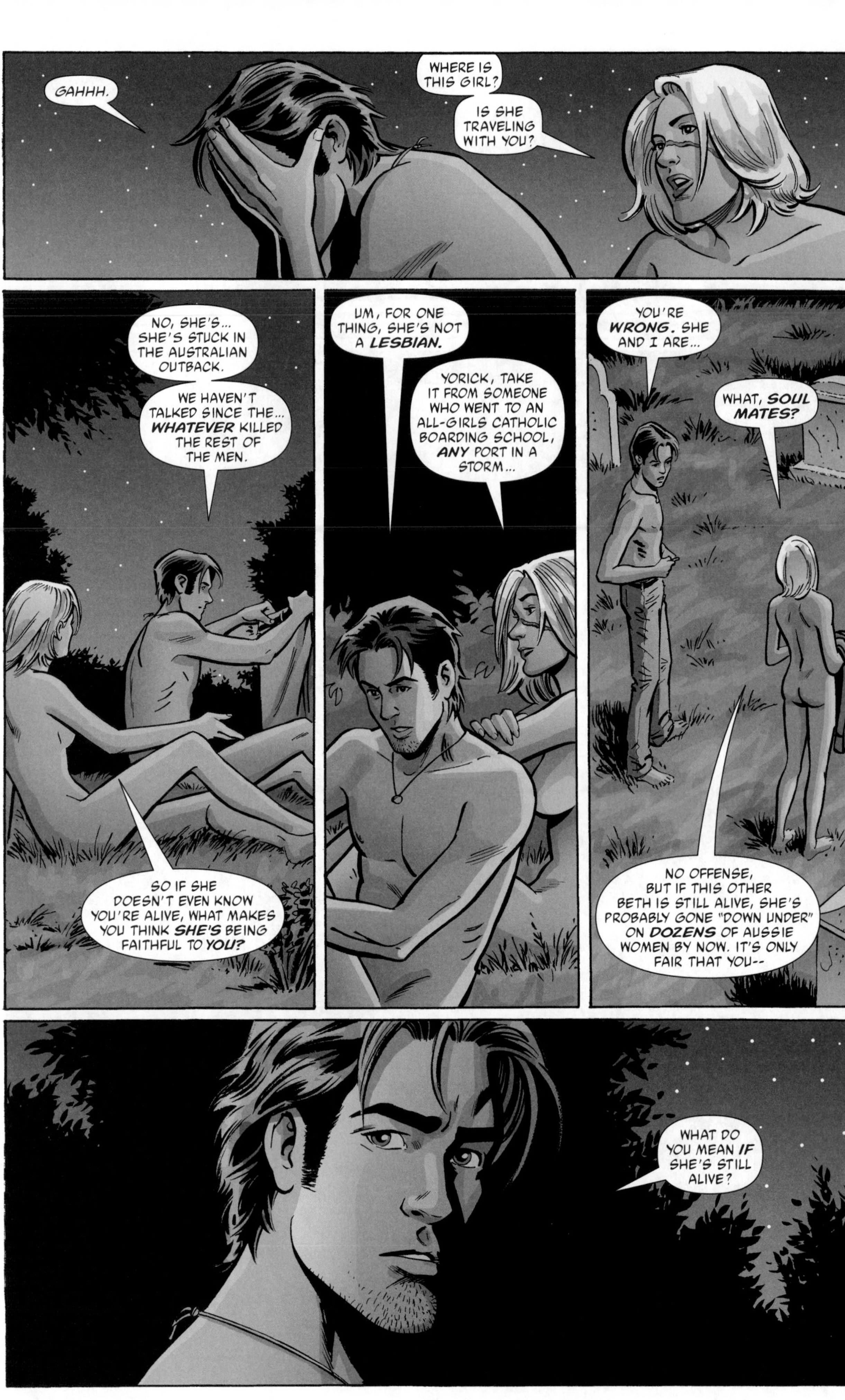
GAHHH.
WHERE IS THIS GIRL?
IS SHE TRAVELING WITH YOU?
NO, SHE'S... SHE'S STUCK IN THE AUSTRALIAN OUTBACK.
WE HAVEN'T TALKED SINCE THE... WHATEVER KILLED THE REST OF THE MEN.
SO IF SHE DOESN'T EVEN KNOW YOU'RE ALIVE, WHAT MAKES YOU THINK SHE'S BEING FAITHFUL TO YOU?
UM, FOR ONE THING, SHE'S NOT A LESBIAN.
YORICK, TAKE IT FROM SOMEONE WHO WENT TO AN ALL-GIRLS CATHOLIC BOARDING SCHOOL, ANY PORT IN A STORM...
YOU'RE WRONG. SHE AND I ARE...
WHAT, SOUL MATES?
NO OFFENSE, BUT IF THIS OTHER BETH IS STILL ALIVE, SHE'S PROBABLY GONE "DOWN UNDER" ON DOZENS OF AUSSIE WOMEN BY NOW. IT'S ONLY FAIR THAT YOU--
WHAT DO YOU MEAN IF SHE'S STILL ALIVE?

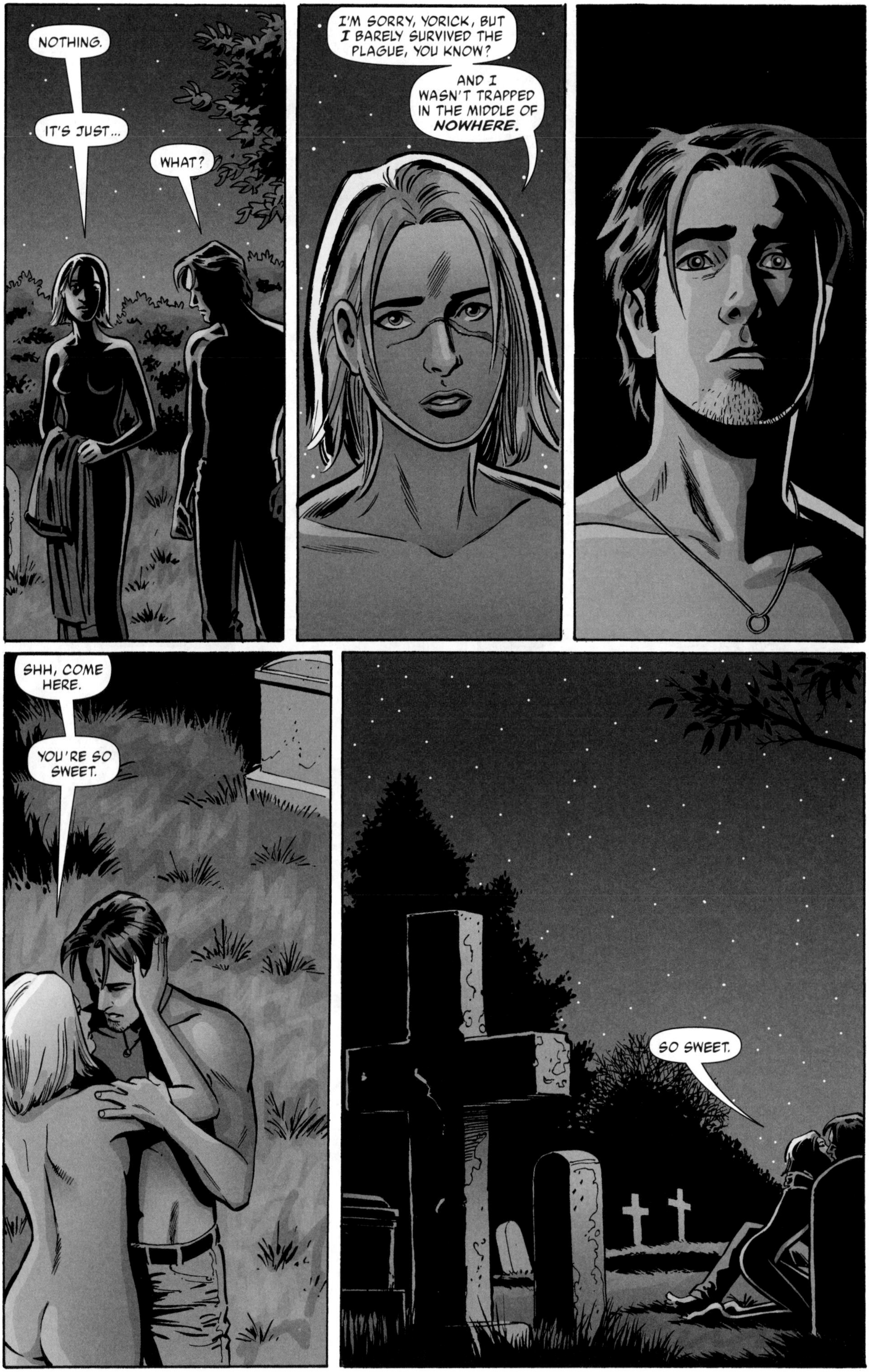
NOTHING.
IT'S JUST...
WHAT?
I'M SORRY, YORICK, BUT I BARELY SURVIVED THE PLAGUE, YOU KNOW?
AND I WASN'T TRAPPED IN THE MIDDLE OF NOWHERE.
SHH, COME HERE.
YOU'RE SO SWEET.
SO SWEET.

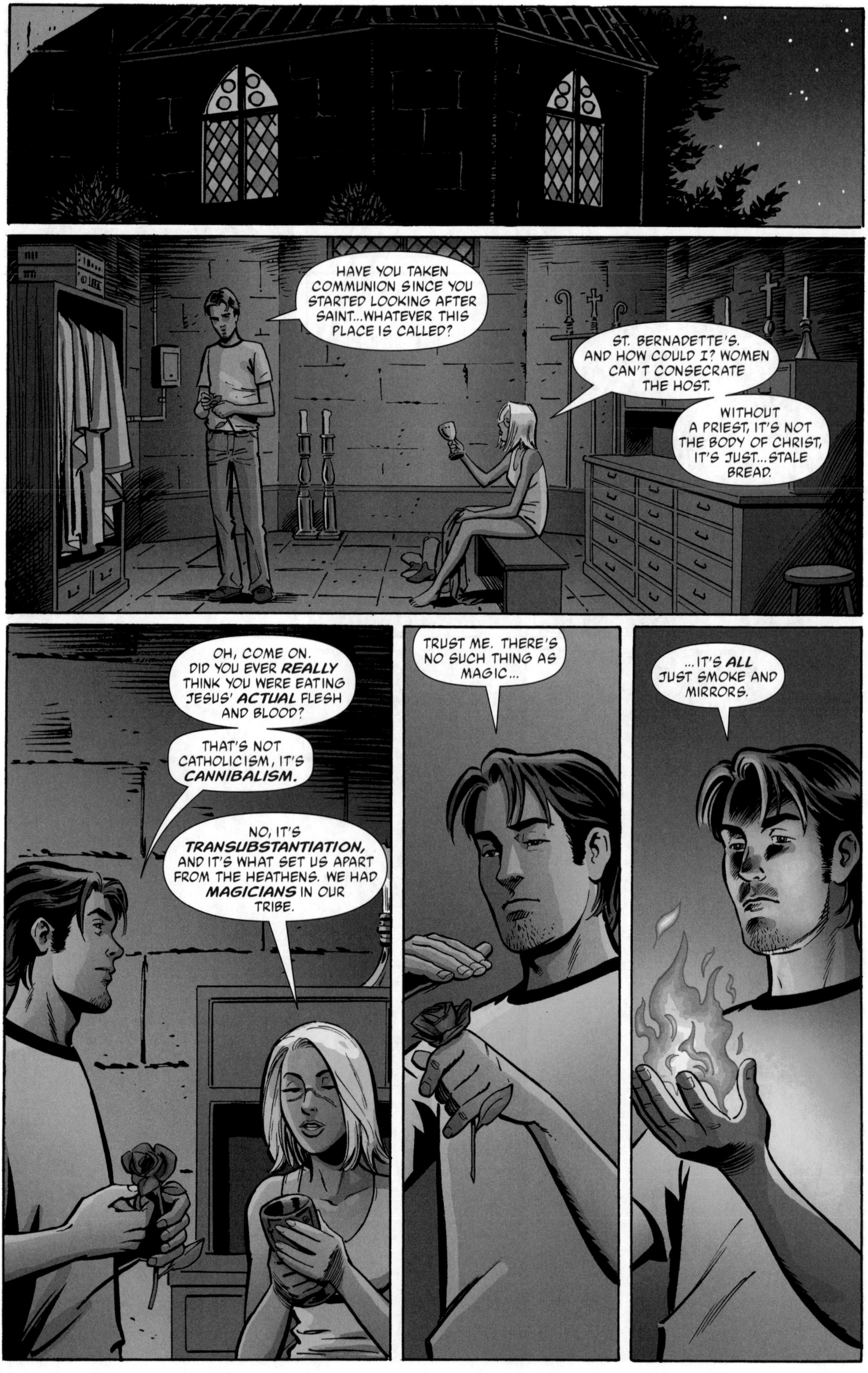
HAVE YOU TAKEN COMMUNION SINCE YOU STARTED LOOKING AFTER SAINT...WHATEVER THIS PLACE IS CALLED?
ST. BERNADETTE'S. AND HOW COULD I? WOMEN CAN'T CONSECRATE THE HOST.
WITHOUT A PRIEST, IT'S NOT THE BODY OF CHRIST, IT'S JUST...STALE BREAD.
OH, COME ON. DID YOU EVER REALLY THINK YOU WERE EATING JESUS' ACTUAL FLESH AND BLOOD?
THAT'S NOT CATHOLICISM, IT'S CANNIBALISM.
NO, IT'S TRANSUBSTANTIATION, AND IT'S WHAT SET US APART FROM THE HEATHENS. WE HAD MAGICIANS IN OUR TRIBE.
TRUST ME. THERE'S NO SUCH THING AS MAGIC...
...IT'S ALL JUST SMOKE AND MIRRORS.

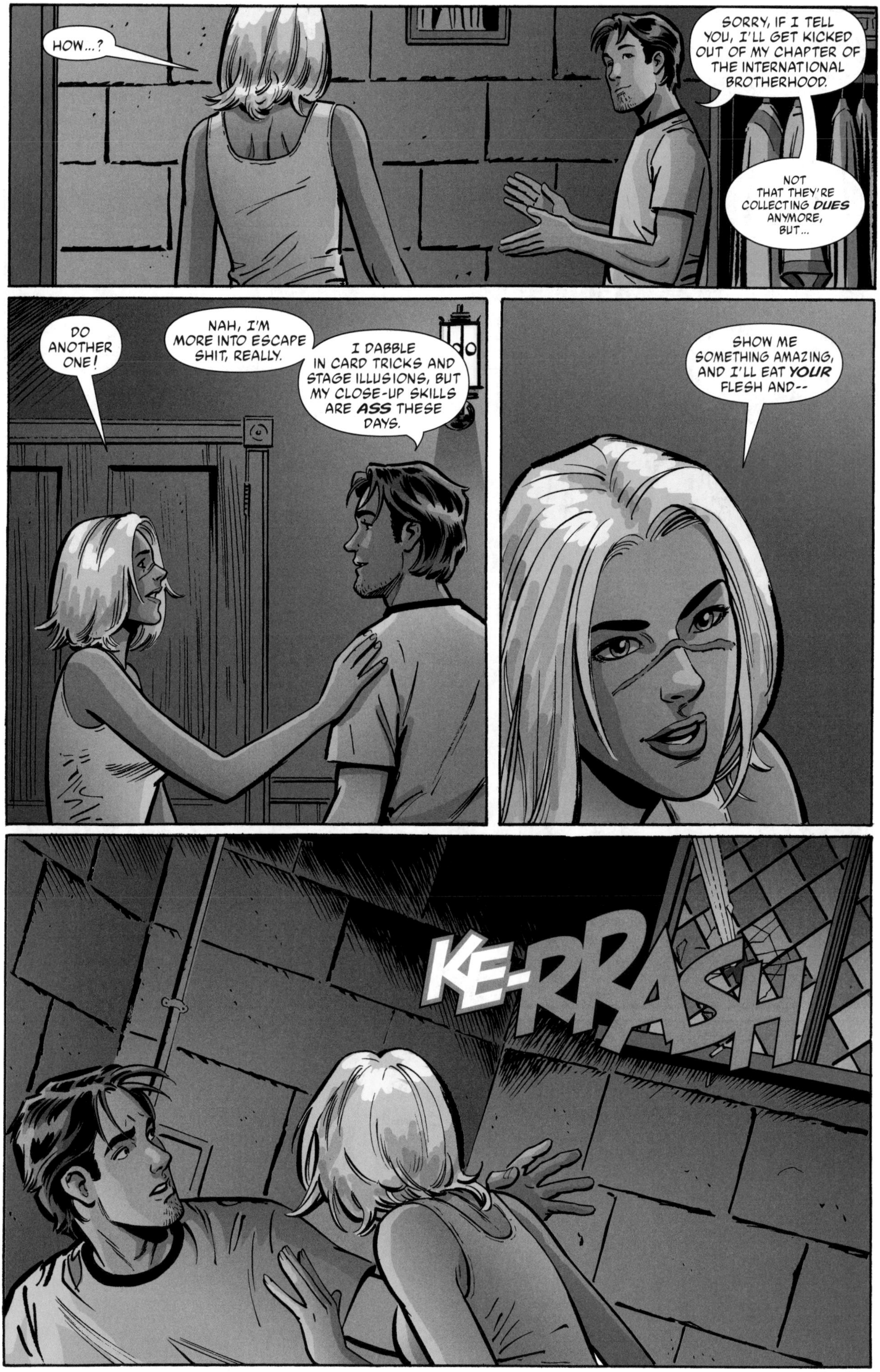
HOW...?
SORRY, IF I TELL YOU, I'LL GET KICKED OUT OF MY CHAPTER OF THE INTERNATIONAL BROTHERHOOD.
NOT THAT THEY'RE COLLECTING DUES ANYMORE, BUT...
DO ANOTHER ONE!
NAH, I'M MORE INTO ESCAPE SHIT, REALLY.
I DABBLE IN CARD TRICKS AND STAGE ILLUSIONS, BUT MY CLOSE-UP SKILLS ARE ASS THESE DAYS.
SHOW ME SOMETHING AMAZING, AND I'LL EAT YOUR FLESH AND--
KE-RRASH

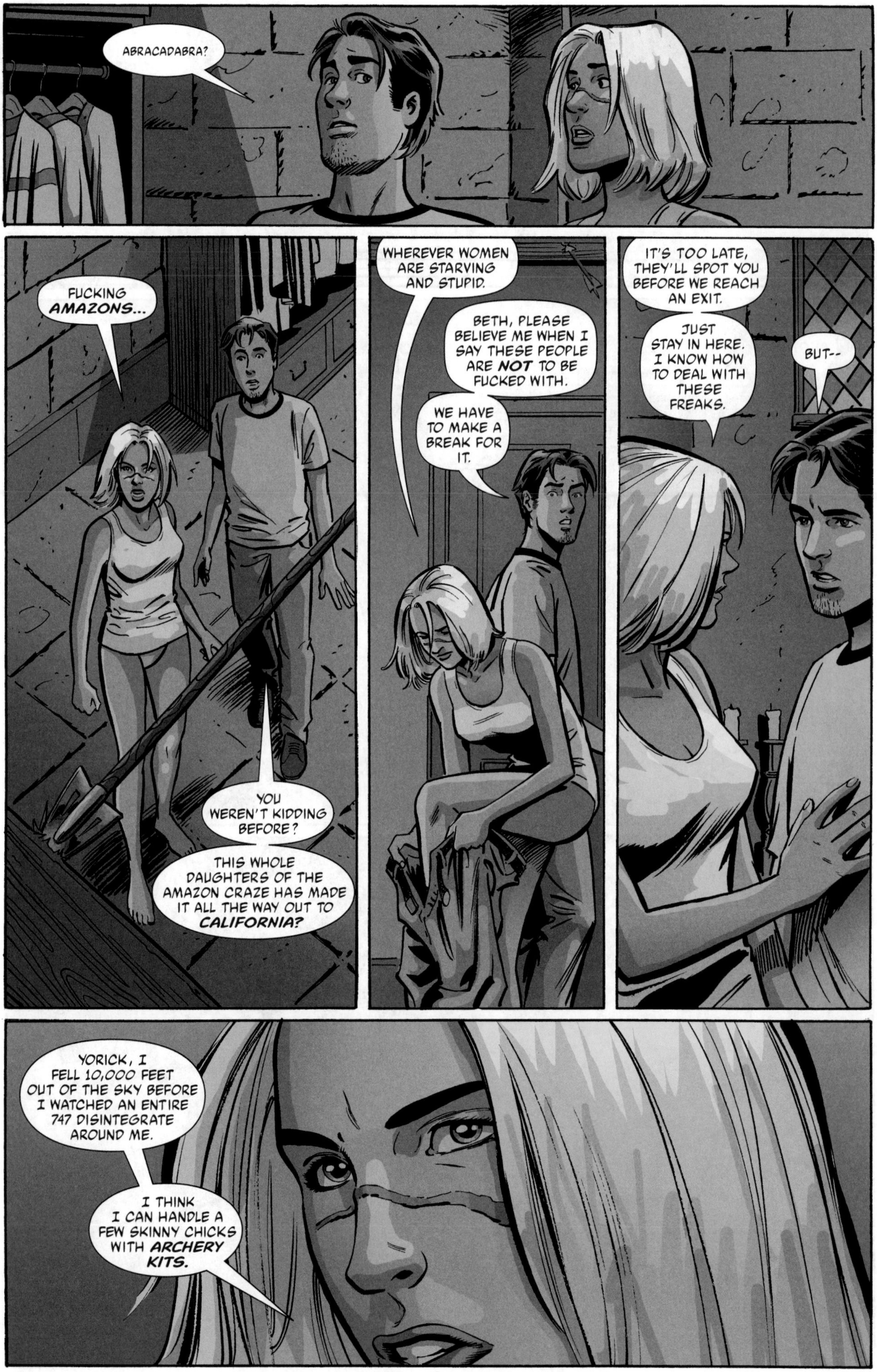
ABRACADABRA?
FUCKING AMAZONS...
YOU WEREN'T KIDDING BEFORE?
THIS WHOLE DAUGHTERS OF THE AMAZON CRAZE HAS MADE IT ALL THE WAY OUT TO CALIFORNIA?
WHEREVER WOMEN ARE STARVING AND STUPID.
BETH, PLEASE BELIEVE ME WHEN I SAY THESE PEOPLE ARE NOT TO BE FUCKED WITH.
WE HAVE TO MAKE A BREAK FOR IT.
IT'S TOO LATE, THEY'LL SPOT YOU BEFORE WE REACH AN EXIT.
JUST STAY IN HERE. I KNOW HOW TO DEAL WITH THESE FREAKS.
BUT--
YORICK, I FELL 10,000 FEET OUT OF THE SKY BEFORE I WATCHED AN ENTIRE 747 DISINTEGRATE AROUND ME.
I THINK I CAN HANDLE A FEW SKINNY CHICKS WITH ARCHERY KITS.

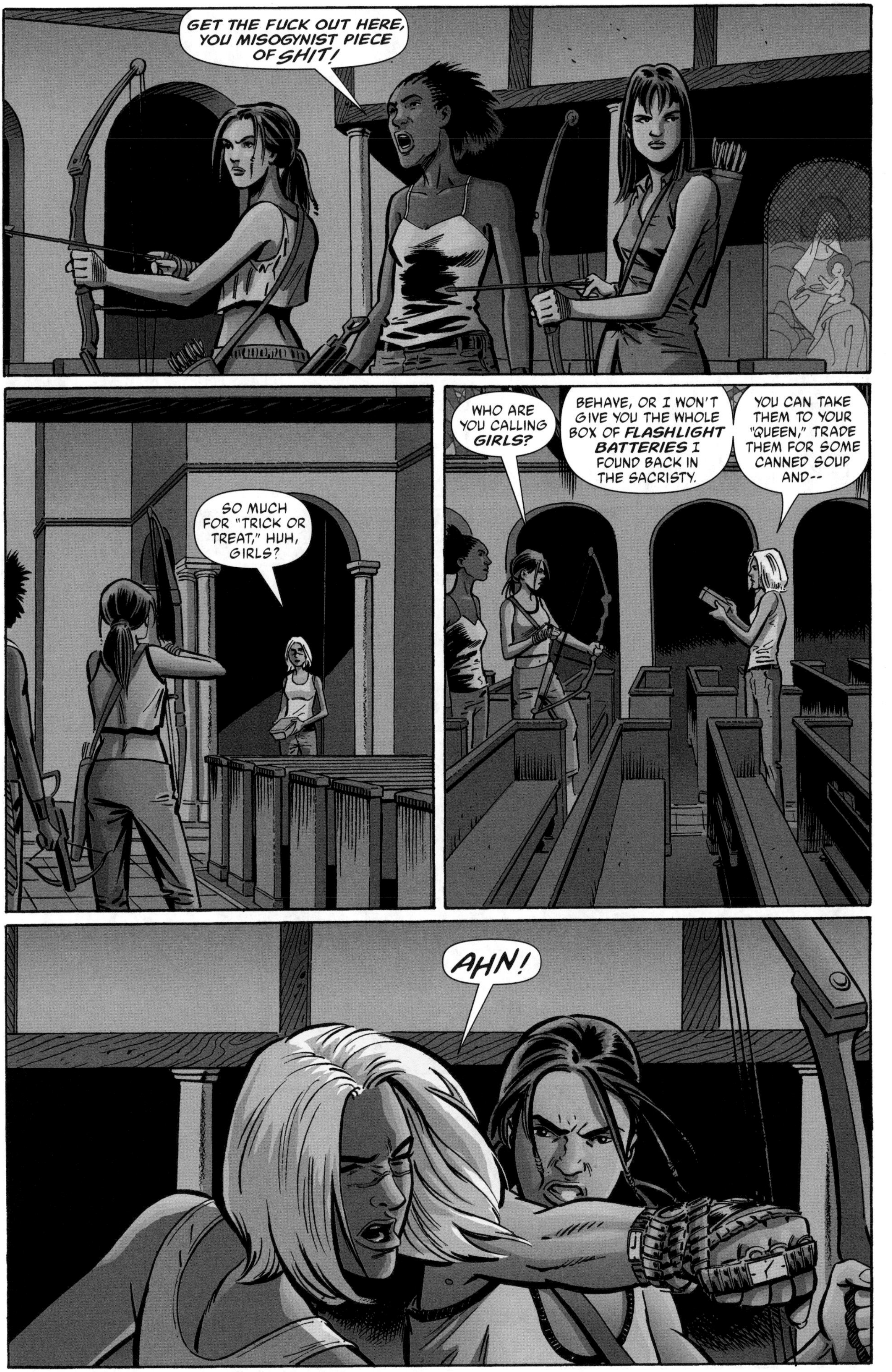
GET THE FUCK OUT HERE, YOU MISOGYNIST PIECE OF SHIT!
SO MUCH FOR "TRICK OR TREAT," HUH, GIRLS?
WHO ARE YOU CALLING GIRLS?
BEHAVE, OR I WON'T GIVE YOU THE WHOLE BOX OF FLASHLIGHT BATTERIES I FOUND BACK IN THE SACRISTY.
YOU CAN TAKE THEM TO YOUR "QUEEN," TRADE THEM FOR SOME CANNED SOUP AND--
AHN!

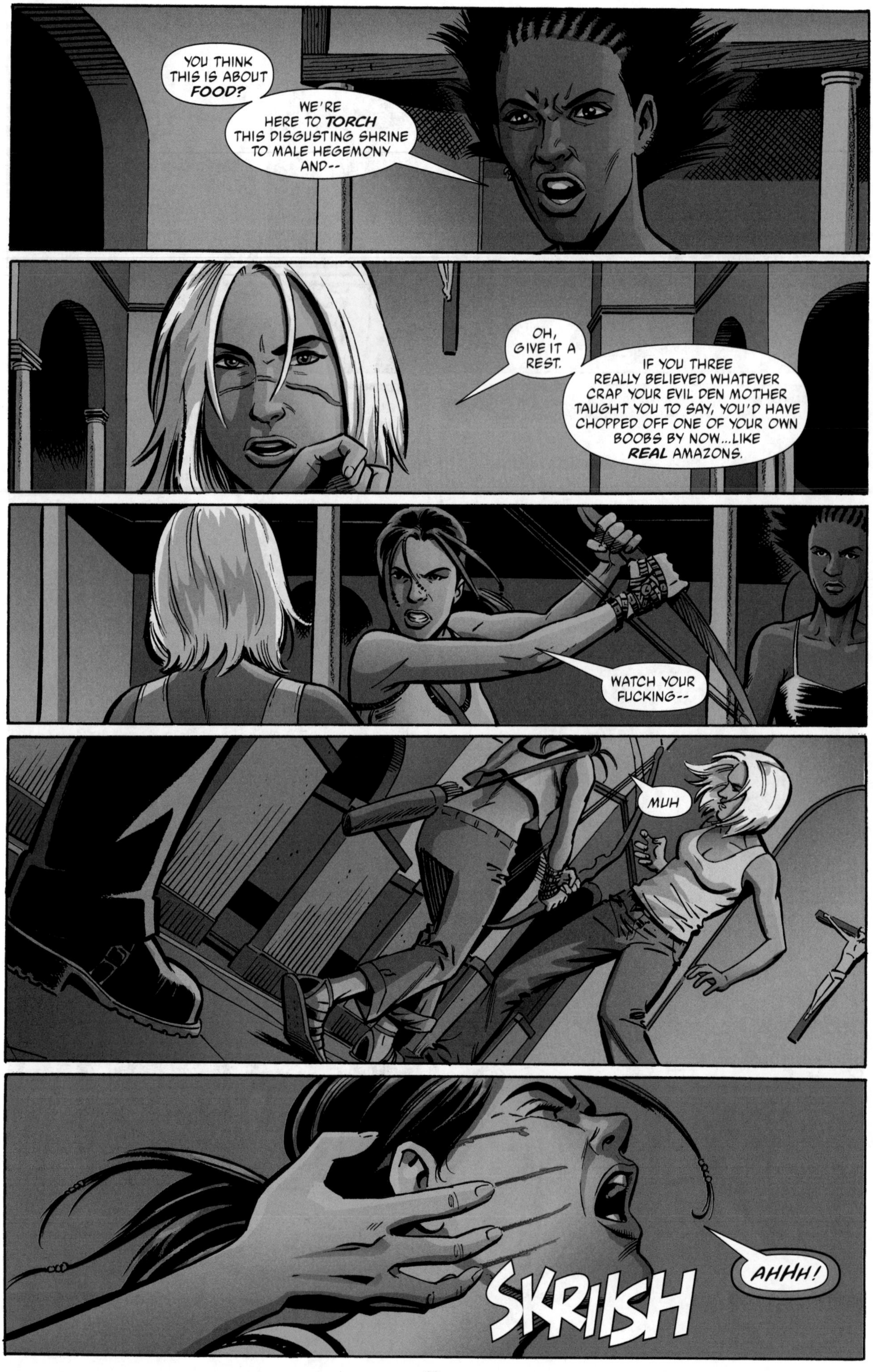
YOU THINK THIS IS ABOUT FOOD?
WE'RE HERE TO TORCH THIS DISGUSTING SHRINE TO MALE HEGEMONY AND--
OH, GIVE IT A REST.
IF YOU THREE REALLY BELIEVED WHATEVER CRAP YOUR EVIL DEN MOTHER TAUGHT YOU TO SAY, YOU'D HAVE CHOPPED OFF ONE OF YOUR OWN BOOBS BY NOW...LIKE REAL AMAZONS.
WATCH YOUR FUCKING--
MUH
SKRIISH
AHHH!

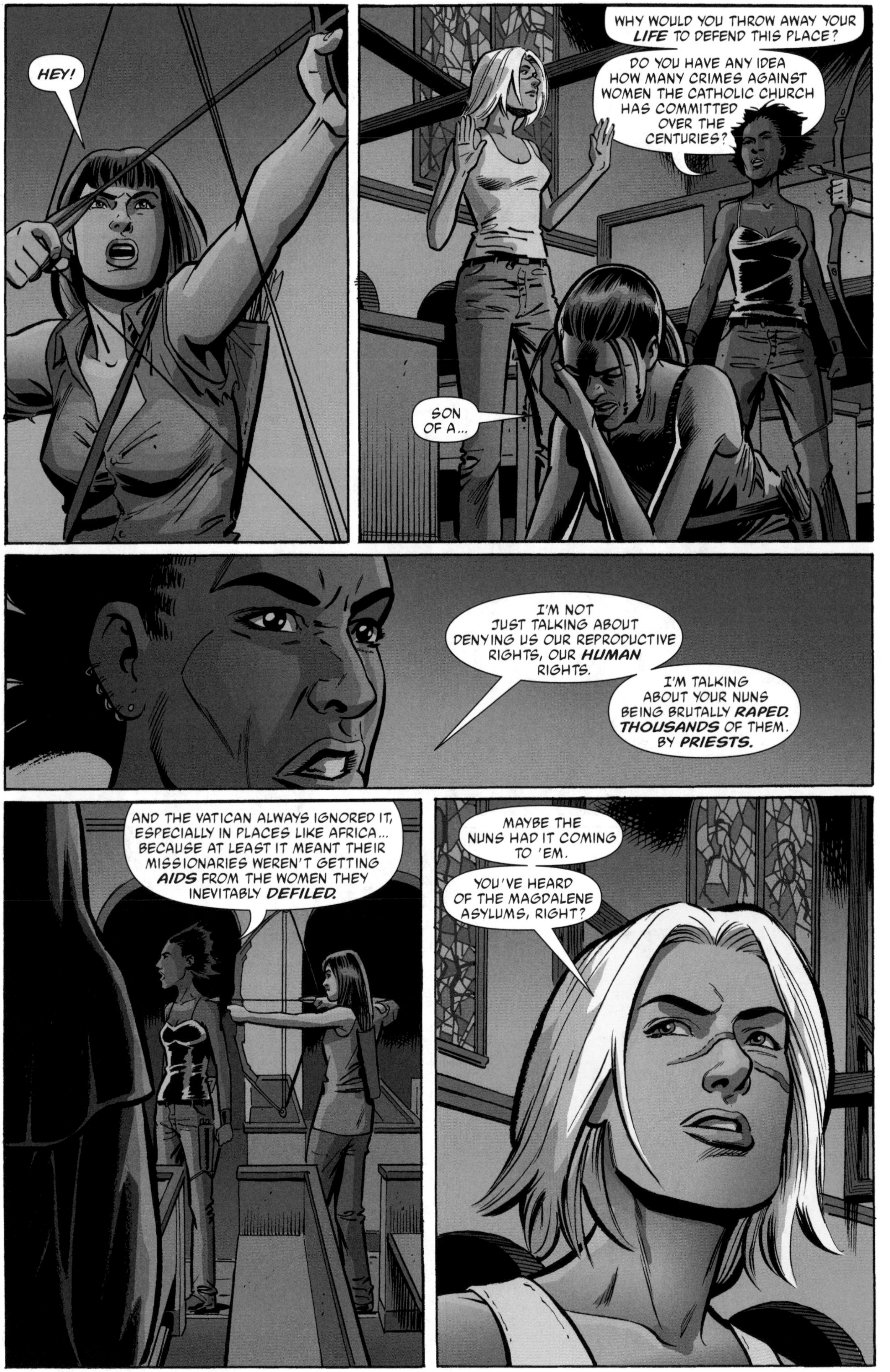
HEY!
WHY WOULD YOU THROW AWAY YOUR LIFE TO DEFEND THIS PLACE?
DO YOU HAVE ANY IDEA HOW MANY CRIMES AGAINST WOMEN THE CATHOLIC CHURCH HAS COMMITTED OVER THE CENTURIES?
SON OF A...
I'M NOT JUST TALKING ABOUT DENYING US OUR REPRODUCTIVE RIGHTS, OUR HUMAN RIGHTS.
I'M TALKING ABOUT YOUR NUNS BEING BRUTALLY RAPED. THOUSANDS OF THEM. BY PRIESTS.
AND THE VATICAN ALWAYS IGNORED IT, ESPECIALLY IN PLACES LIKE AFRICA... BECAUSE AT LEAST IT MEANT THEIR MISSIONARIES WEREN'T GETTING AIDS FROM THE WOMEN THEY INEVITABLY DEFILED.
MAYBE THE NUNS HAD IT COMING TO 'EM.
YOU'VE HEARD OF THE MAGDALENE ASYLUMS, RIGHT?

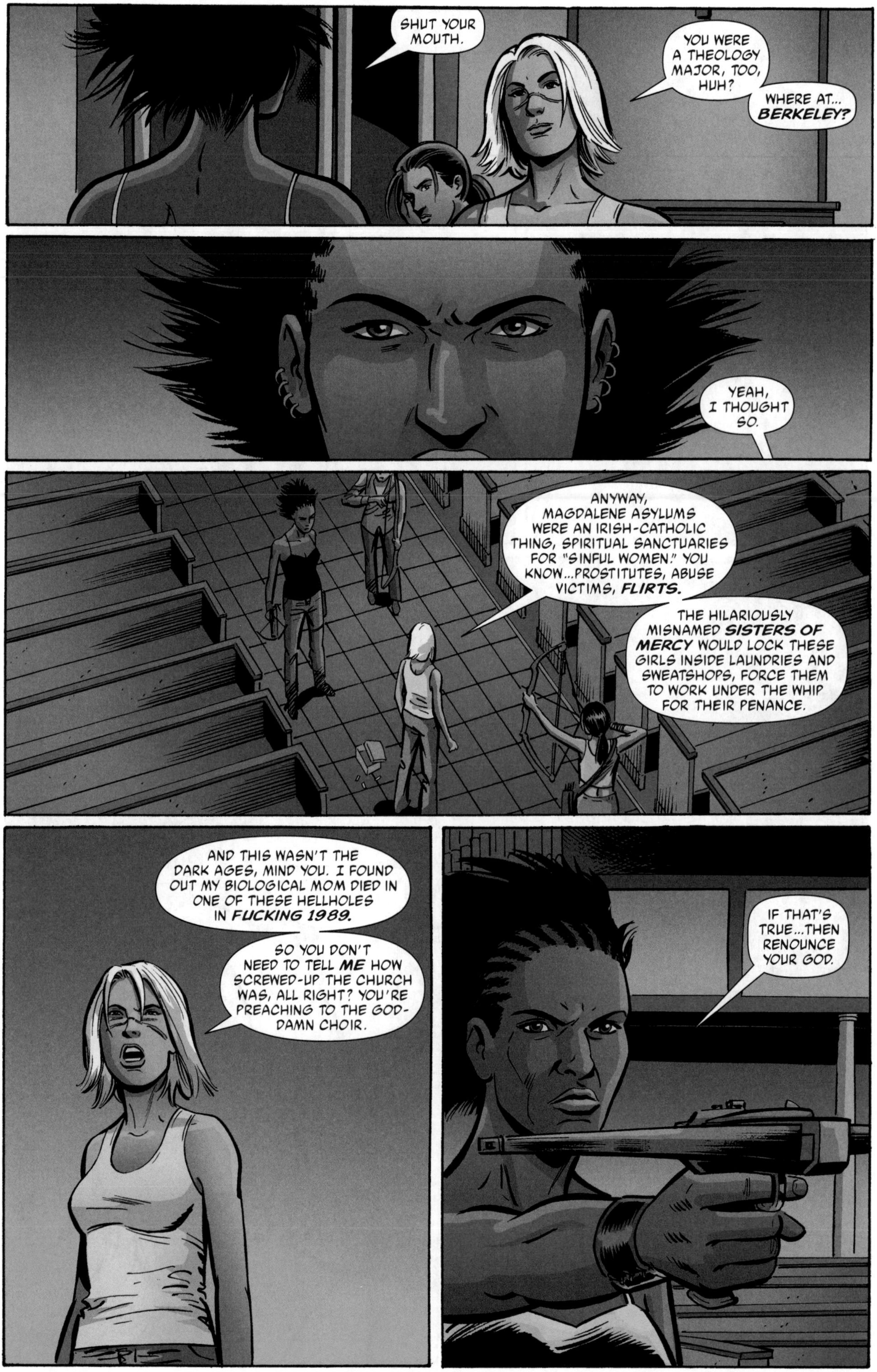
SHUT YOUR MOUTH.
YOU WERE A THEOLOGY MAJOR, TOO, HUH?
WHERE AT... **BERKELEY?**
YEAH, I THOUGHT SO.
ANYWAY, MAGDALENE ASYLUMS WERE AN IRISH-CATHOLIC THING, SPIRITUAL SANCTUARIES FOR "SINFUL WOMEN." YOU KNOW...PROSTITUTES, ABUSE VICTIMS, **FLIRTS.**
THE HILARIOUSLY MISNAMED **SISTERS OF MERCY** WOULD LOCK THESE GIRLS INSIDE LAUNDRIES AND SWEATSHOPS, FORCE THEM TO WORK UNDER THE WHIP FOR THEIR PENANCE.
AND THIS WASN'T THE DARK AGES, MIND YOU. I FOUND OUT MY BIOLOGICAL MOM DIED IN ONE OF THESE HELLHOLES IN **FUCKING 1989.**
SO YOU DON'T NEED TO TELL **ME** HOW SCREWED-UP THE CHURCH WAS, ALL RIGHT? YOU'RE PREACHING TO THE GOD-DAMN CHOIR.
IF THAT'S TRUE...THEN RENOUNCE YOUR GOD.

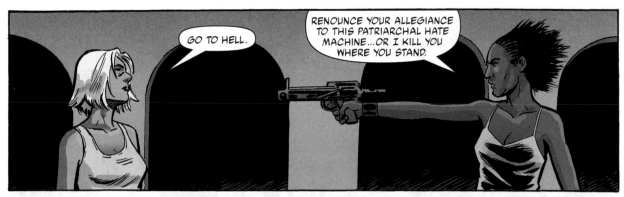

GO TO HELL.

RENOUNCE YOUR ALLEGIANCE TO THIS PATRIARCHAL HATE MACHINE...OR I KILL YOU WHERE YOU STAND.

PATRIARCHAL? DID YOU HEAR *ANYTHING* I JUST SAID?

THE CHURCH WASN'T FUCKED-UP BECAUSE IT WAS RUN BY *MEN*, IT WAS FUCKED-UP BECAUSE IT WAS RUN BY *HUMANS*.

IF YOUR PEOPLE START BURNING DOWN CATHEDRALS, WE WON'T HAVE ANYTHING LEFT TO REMIND US WHAT WE--

YOUR CALL, BITCH.

GET READY TO MEET YOUR--

--MAKER?

SILENCE!

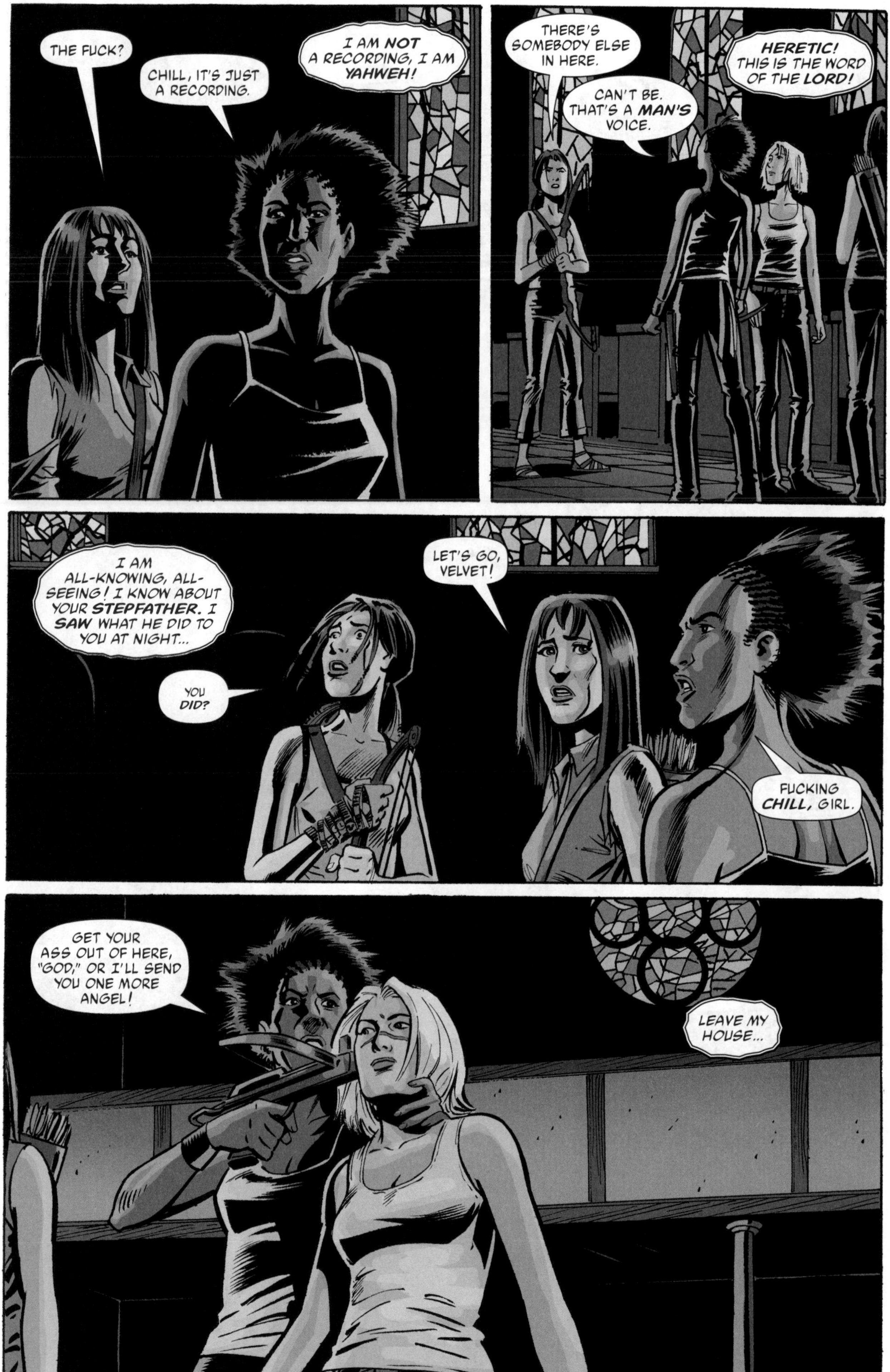
THE FUCK?
CHILL, IT'S JUST A RECORDING.
I AM NOT A RECORDING, I AM YAHWEH!
THERE'S SOMEBODY ELSE IN HERE.
CAN'T BE. THAT'S A MAN'S VOICE.
HERETIC! THIS IS THE WORD OF THE LORD!
I AM ALL-KNOWING, ALL-SEEING! I KNOW ABOUT YOUR STEPFATHER. I SAW WHAT HE DID TO YOU AT NIGHT...
YOU DID?
LET'S GO, VELVET!
FUCKING CHILL, GIRL.
GET YOUR ASS OUT OF HERE, "GOD," OR I'LL SEND YOU ONE MORE ANGEL!
LEAVE MY HOUSE...

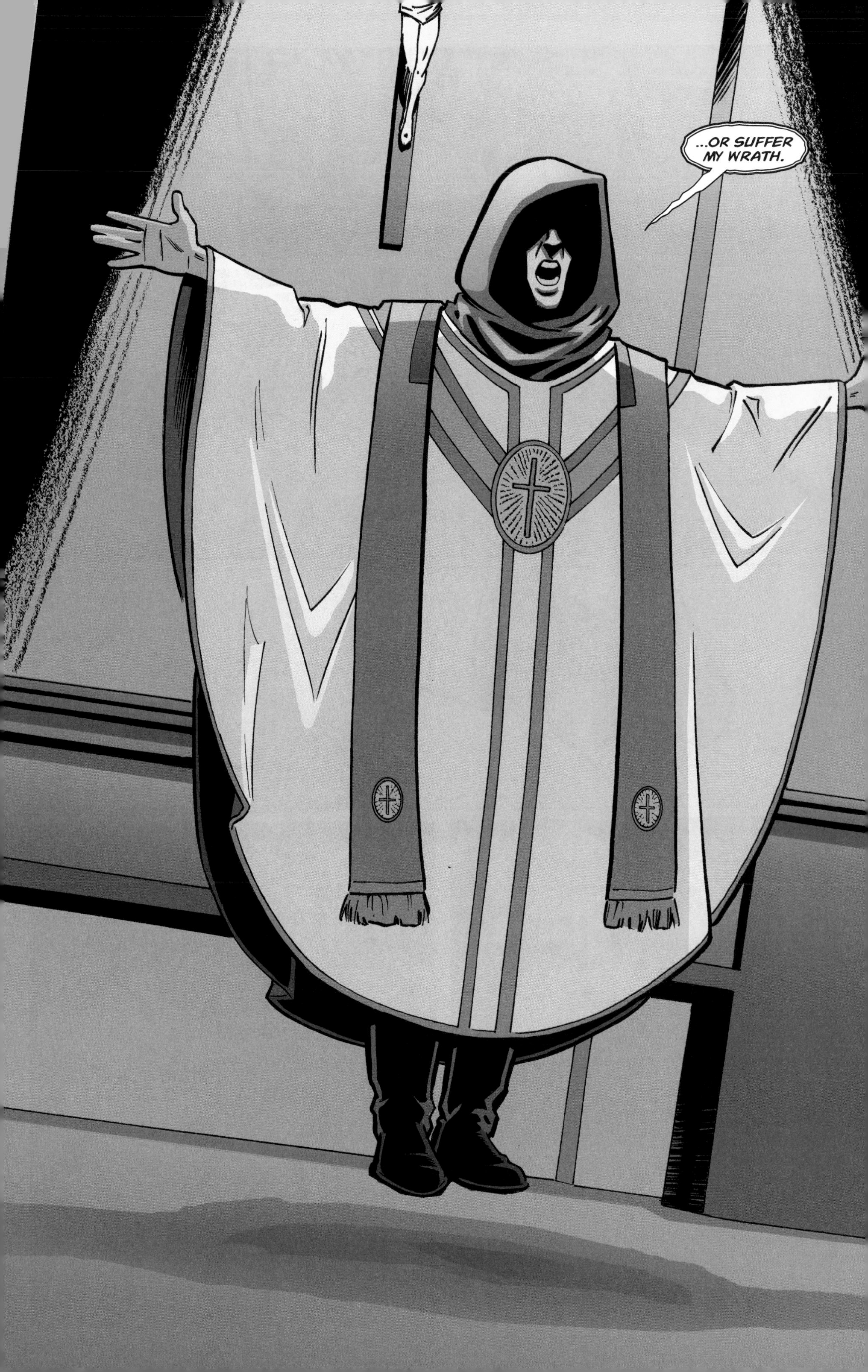
...OR SUFFER MY WRATH.

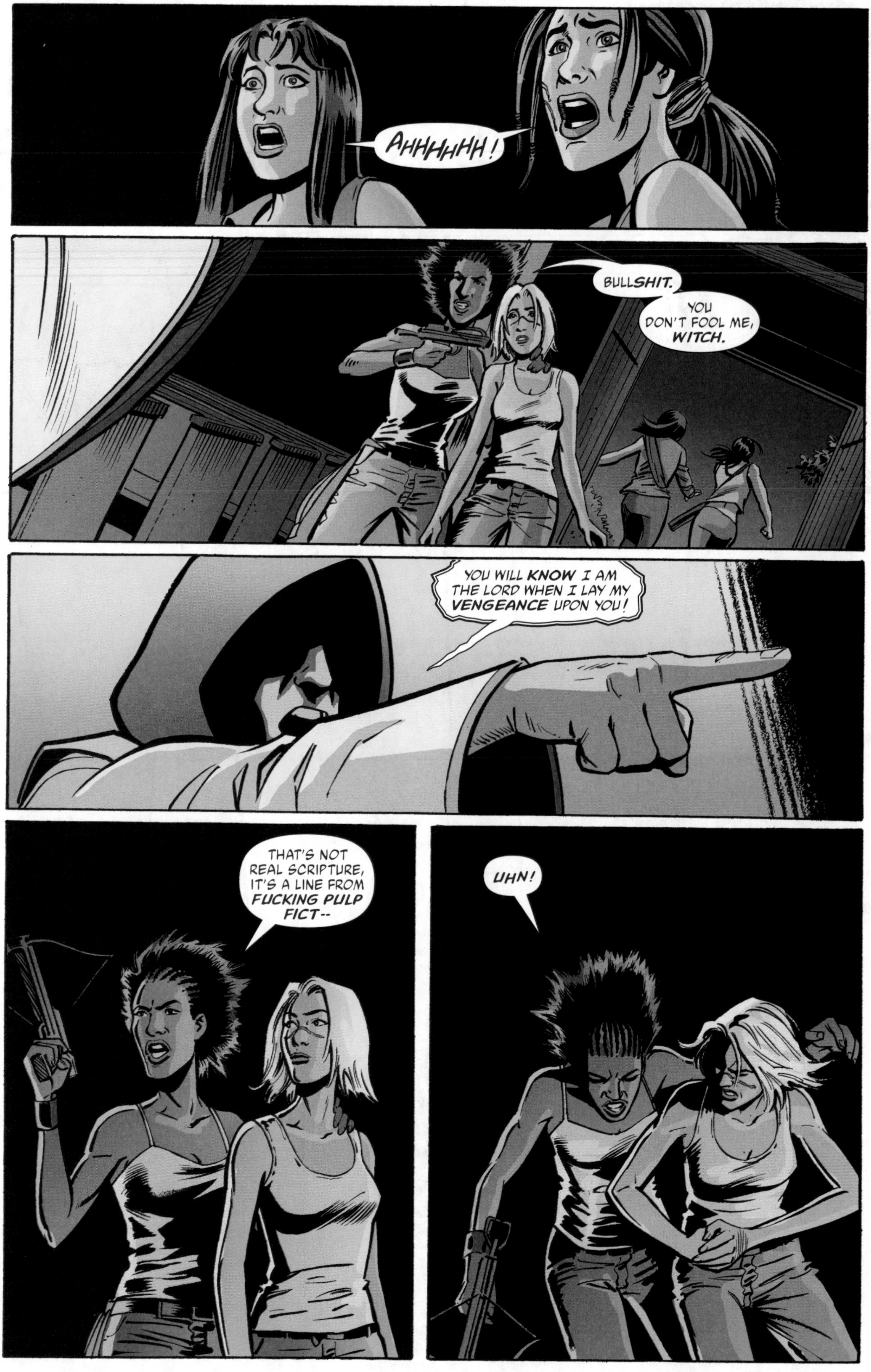
AHHHHHH!
BULLSHIT.
YOU DON'T FOOL ME, WITCH.
YOU WILL KNOW I AM THE LORD WHEN I LAY MY VENGEANCE UPON YOU!
THAT'S NOT REAL SCRIPTURE, IT'S A LINE FROM FUCKING PULP FICT--
UHN!

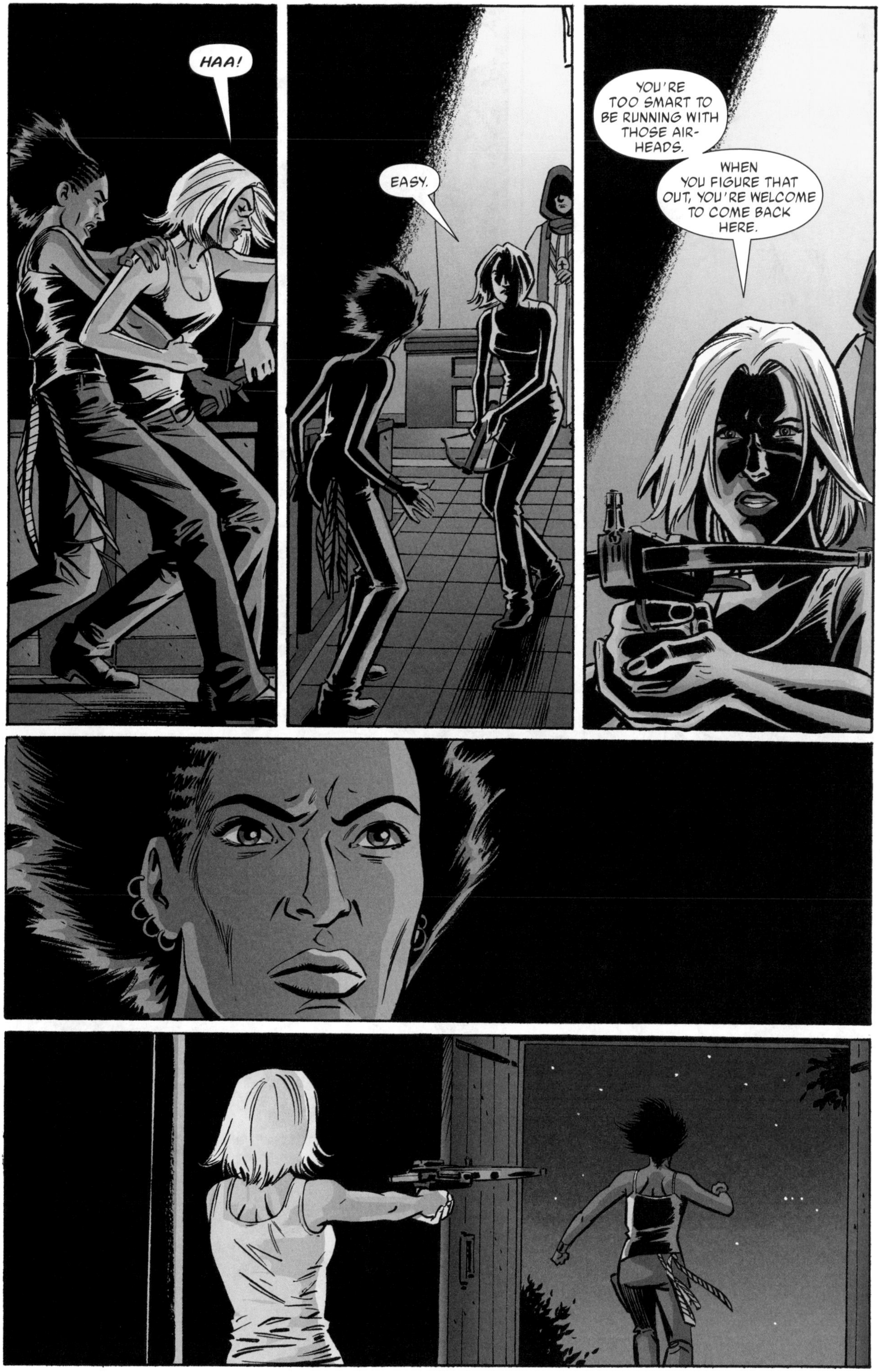
HAA!
EASY.
YOU'RE TOO SMART TO BE RUNNING WITH THOSE AIR-HEADS.
WHEN YOU FIGURE THAT OUT, YOU'RE WELCOME TO COME BACK HERE.

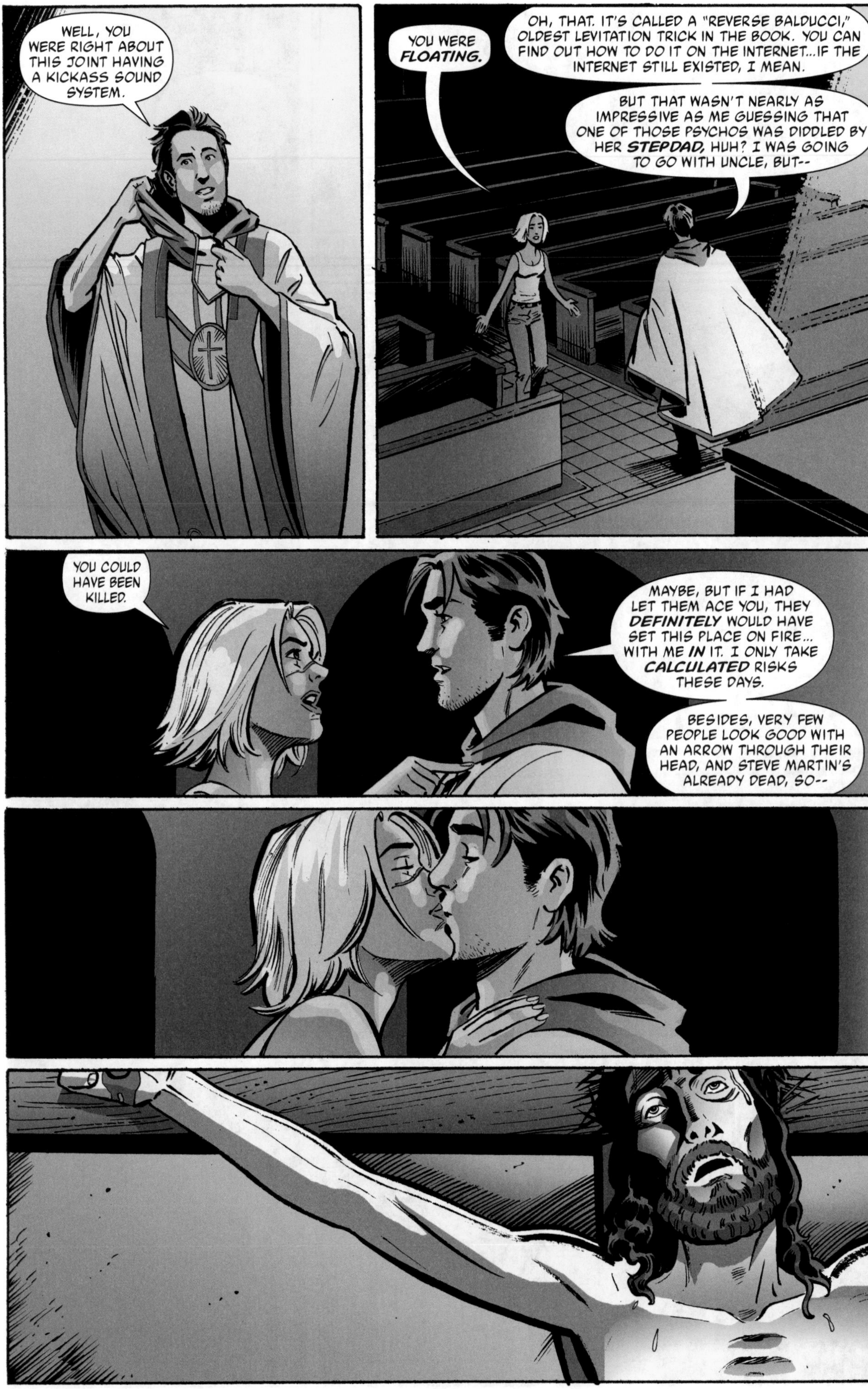
WELL, YOU WERE RIGHT ABOUT THIS JOINT HAVING A KICKASS SOUND SYSTEM.
YOU WERE FLOATING.
OH, THAT. IT'S CALLED A "REVERSE BALDUCCI," OLDEST LEVITATION TRICK IN THE BOOK. YOU CAN FIND OUT HOW TO DO IT ON THE INTERNET...IF THE INTERNET STILL EXISTED, I MEAN.
BUT THAT WASN'T NEARLY AS IMPRESSIVE AS ME GUESSING THAT ONE OF THOSE PSYCHOS WAS DIDDLED BY HER STEPDAD, HUH? I WAS GOING TO GO WITH UNCLE, BUT--
YOU COULD HAVE BEEN KILLED.
MAYBE, BUT IF I HAD LET THEM ACE YOU, THEY DEFINITELY WOULD HAVE SET THIS PLACE ON FIRE... WITH ME IN IT. I ONLY TAKE CALCULATED RISKS THESE DAYS.
BESIDES, VERY FEW PEOPLE LOOK GOOD WITH AN ARROW THROUGH THEIR HEAD, AND STEVE MARTIN'S ALREADY DEAD, SO--

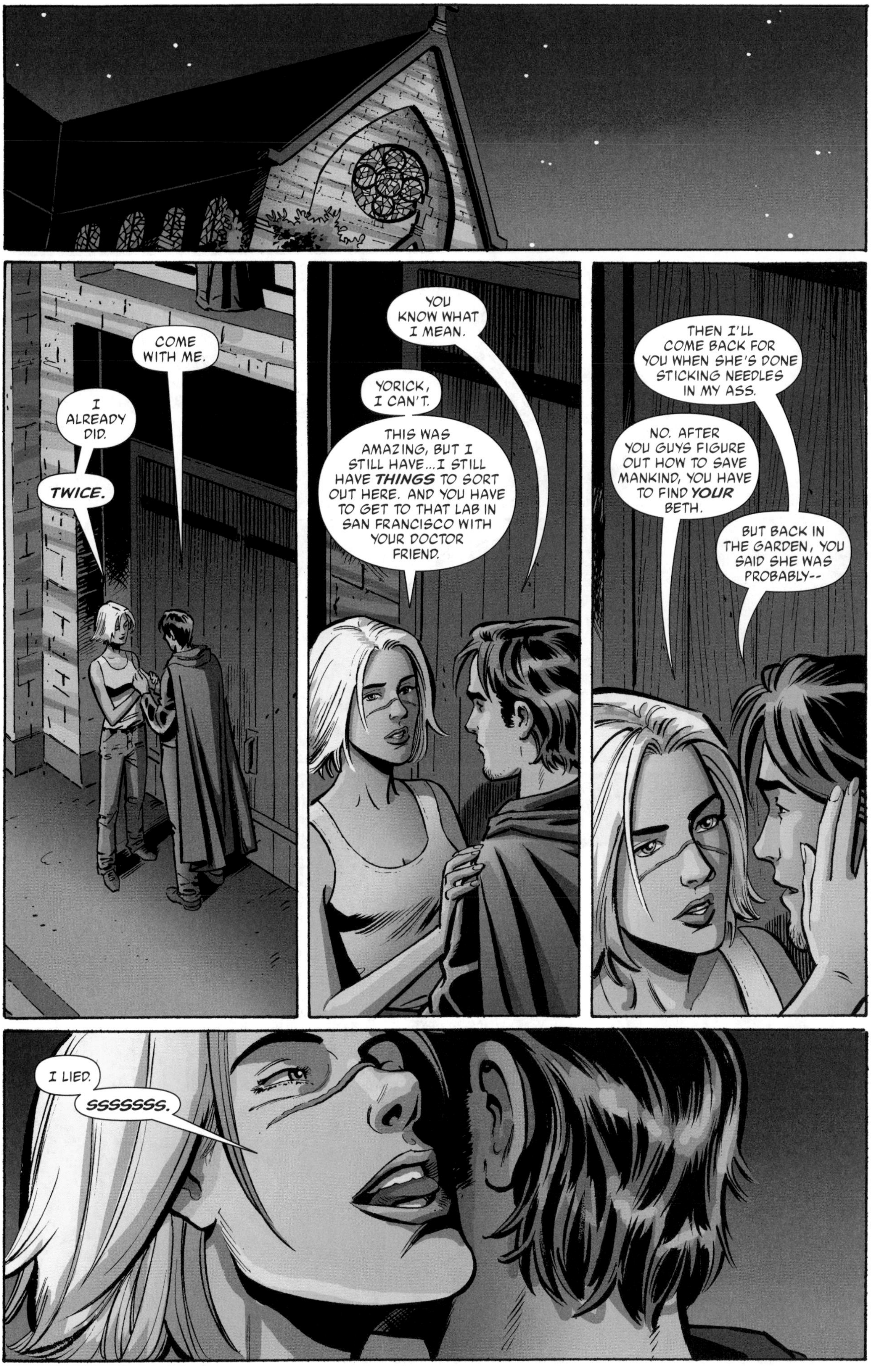
COME WITH ME.
I ALREADY DID.
TWICE.
YOU KNOW WHAT I MEAN.
YORICK, I CAN'T.
THIS WAS AMAZING, BUT I STILL HAVE...I STILL HAVE THINGS TO SORT OUT HERE. AND YOU HAVE TO GET TO THAT LAB IN SAN FRANCISCO WITH YOUR DOCTOR FRIEND.
THEN I'LL COME BACK FOR YOU WHEN SHE'S DONE STICKING NEEDLES IN MY ASS.
NO. AFTER YOU GUYS FIGURE OUT HOW TO SAVE MANKIND, YOU HAVE TO FIND YOUR BETH.
BUT BACK IN THE GARDEN, YOU SAID SHE WAS PROBABLY--
I LIED.
SSSSSSS.

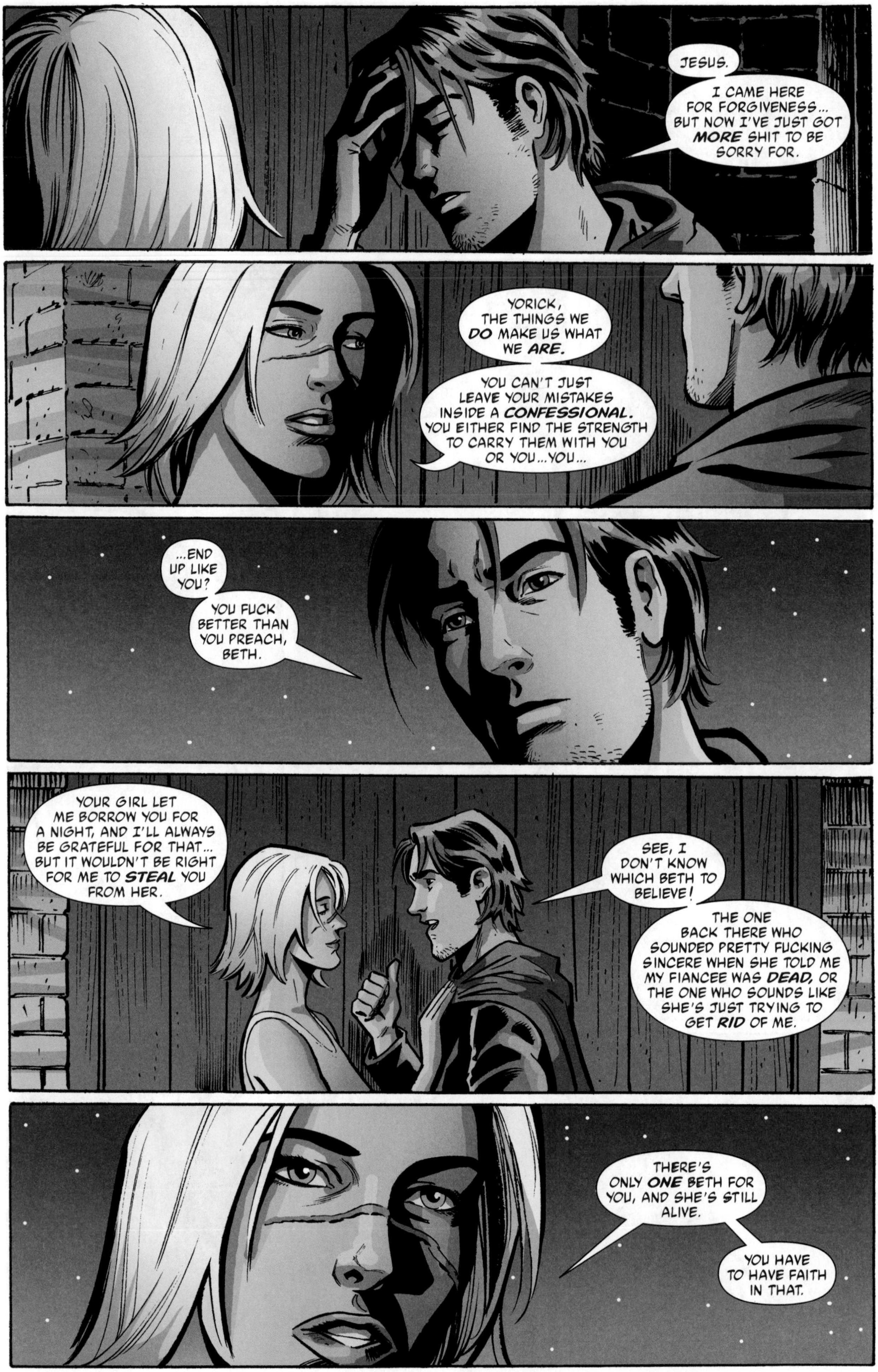
JESUS.
I CAME HERE FOR FORGIVENESS... BUT NOW I'VE JUST GOT MORE SHIT TO BE SORRY FOR.
YORICK, THE THINGS WE DO MAKE US WHAT WE ARE.
YOU CAN'T JUST LEAVE YOUR MISTAKES INSIDE A CONFESSIONAL. YOU EITHER FIND THE STRENGTH TO CARRY THEM WITH YOU OR YOU...YOU...
...END UP LIKE YOU?
YOU FUCK BETTER THAN YOU PREACH, BETH.
YOUR GIRL LET ME BORROW YOU FOR A NIGHT, AND I'LL ALWAYS BE GRATEFUL FOR THAT... BUT IT WOULDN'T BE RIGHT FOR ME TO STEAL YOU FROM HER.
SEE, I DON'T KNOW WHICH BETH TO BELIEVE!
THE ONE BACK THERE WHO SOUNDED PRETTY FUCKING SINCERE WHEN SHE TOLD ME MY FIANCEE WAS DEAD, OR THE ONE WHO SOUNDS LIKE SHE'S JUST TRYING TO GET RID OF ME.
THERE'S ONLY ONE BETH FOR YOU, AND SHE'S STILL ALIVE.
YOU HAVE TO HAVE FAITH IN THAT.

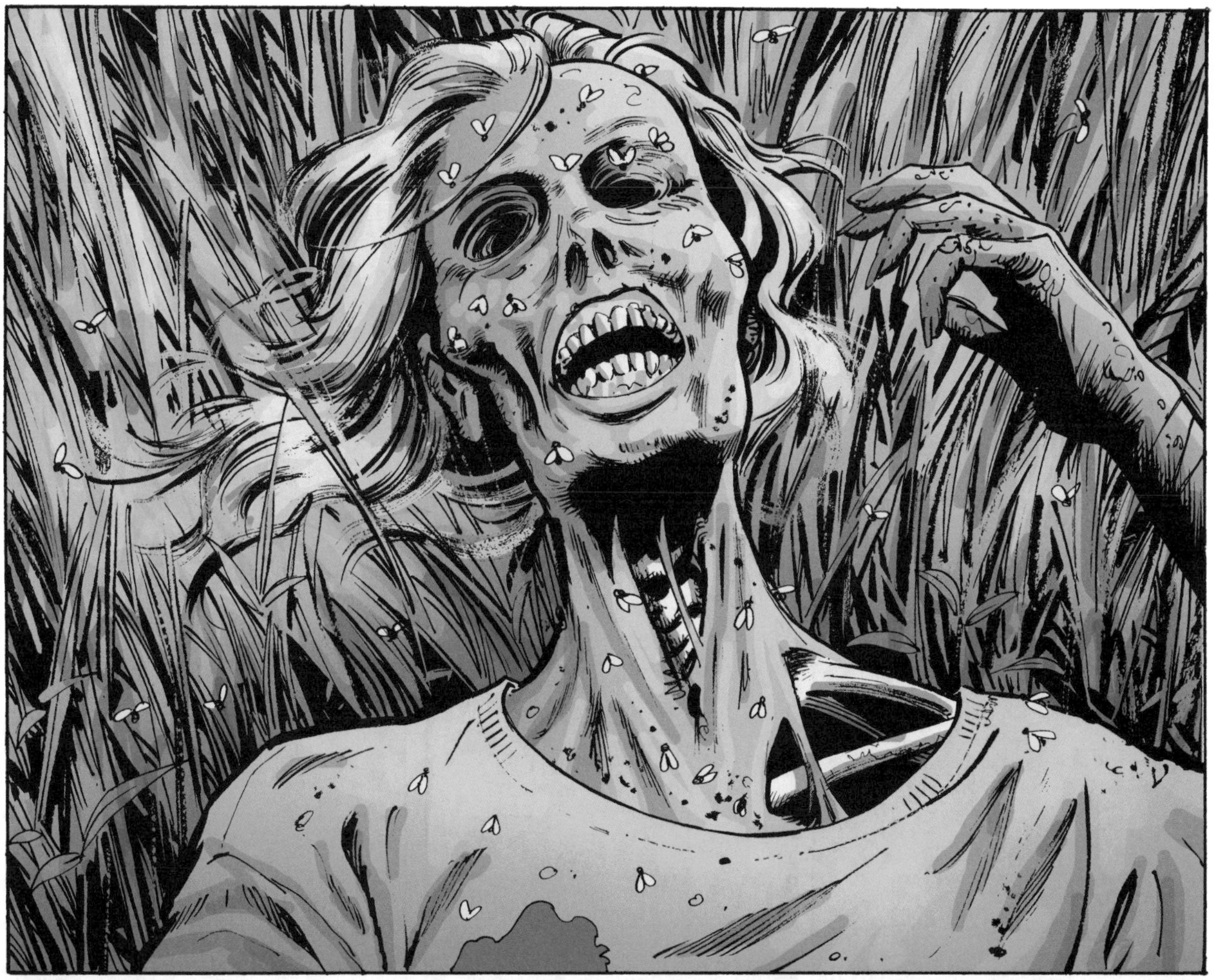

Somewhere in the Australian Outback
Now

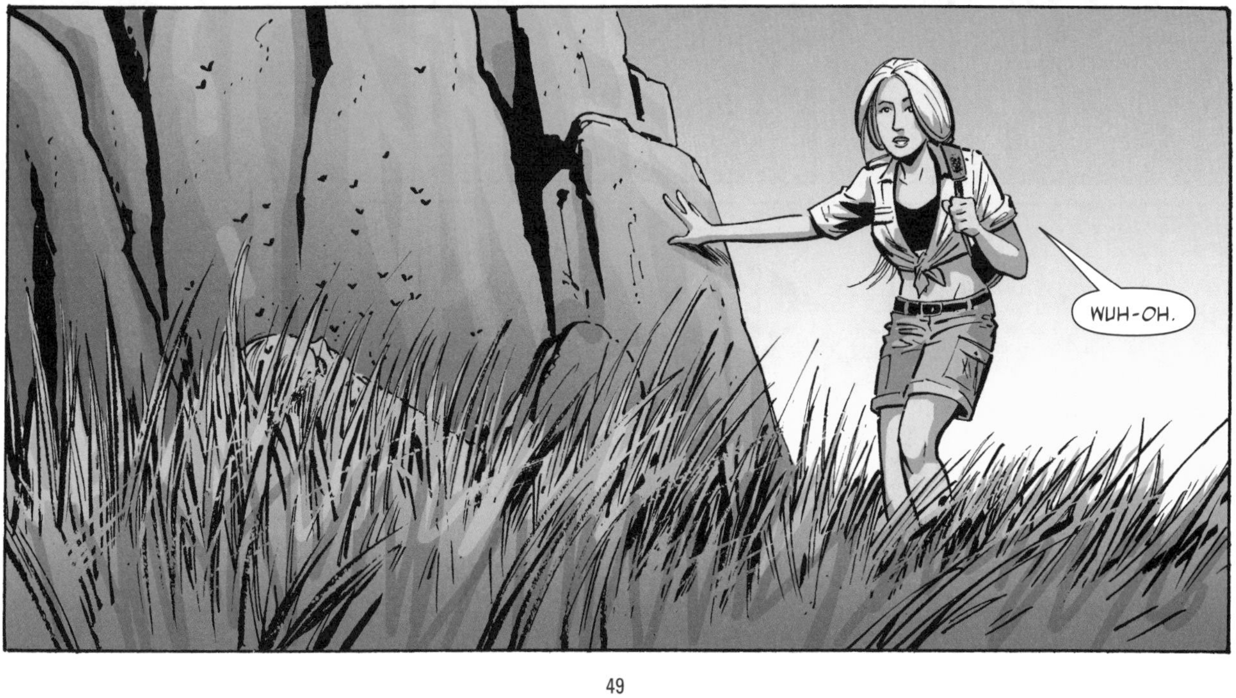
WUH-OH.

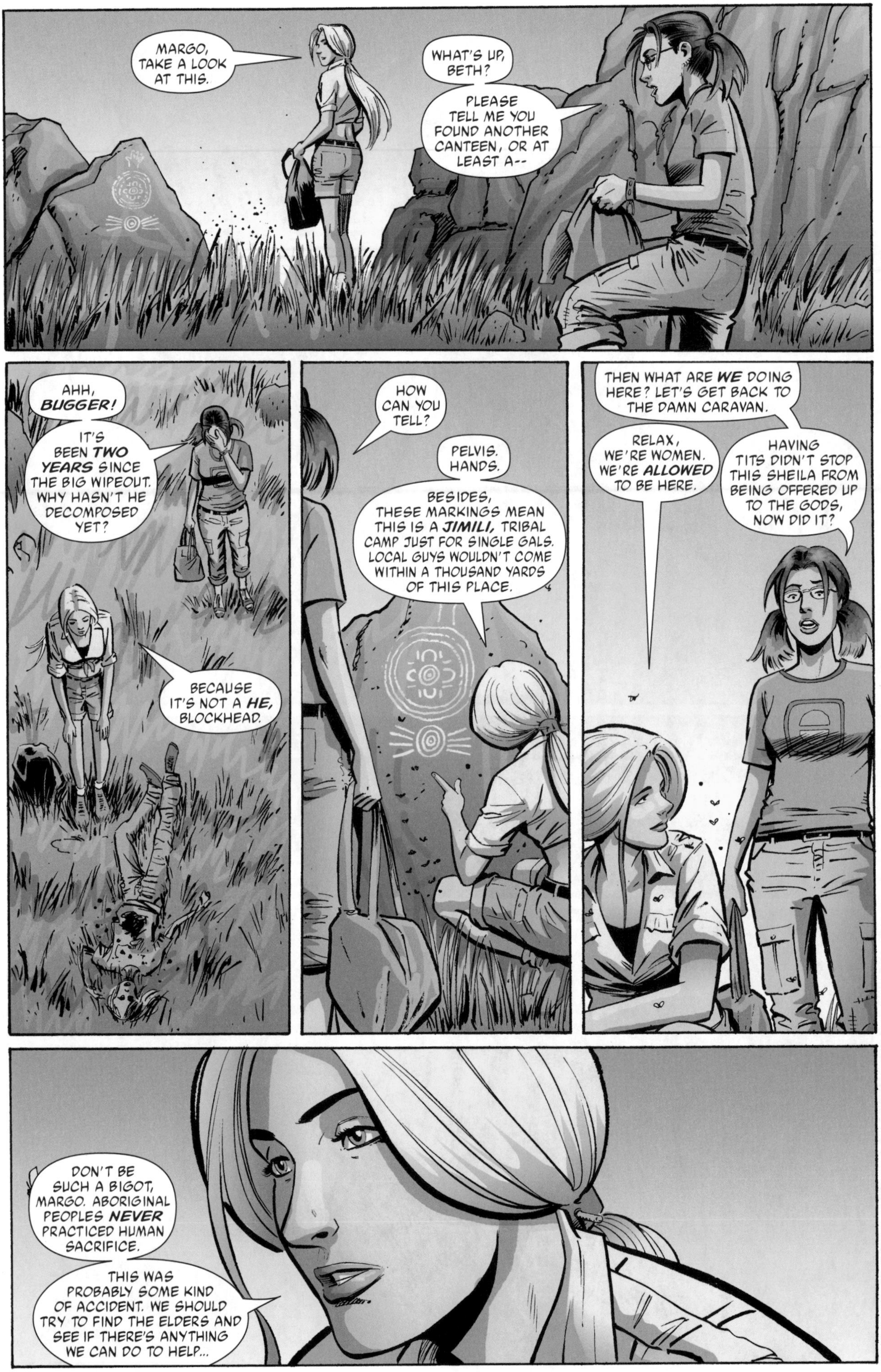
MARGO, TAKE A LOOK AT THIS.
WHAT'S UP, BETH?
PLEASE TELL ME YOU FOUND ANOTHER CANTEEN, OR AT LEAST A--
AHH, BUGGER!
IT'S BEEN TWO YEARS SINCE THE BIG WIPEOUT. WHY HASN'T HE DECOMPOSED YET?
BECAUSE IT'S NOT A HE, BLOCKHEAD.
HOW CAN YOU TELL?
PELVIS. HANDS.
BESIDES, THESE MARKINGS MEAN THIS IS A JIMILI, TRIBAL CAMP JUST FOR SINGLE GALS. LOCAL GUYS WOULDN'T COME WITHIN A THOUSAND YARDS OF THIS PLACE.
THEN WHAT ARE WE DOING HERE? LET'S GET BACK TO THE DAMN CARAVAN.
RELAX, WE'RE WOMEN. WE'RE ALLOWED TO BE HERE.
HAVING TITS DIDN'T STOP THIS SHEILA FROM BEING OFFERED UP TO THE GODS, NOW DID IT?
DON'T BE SUCH A BIGOT, MARGO. ABORIGINAL PEOPLES NEVER PRACTICED HUMAN SACRIFICE.
THIS WAS PROBABLY SOME KIND OF ACCIDENT. WE SHOULD TRY TO FIND THE ELDERS AND SEE IF THERE'S ANYTHING WE CAN DO TO HELP...

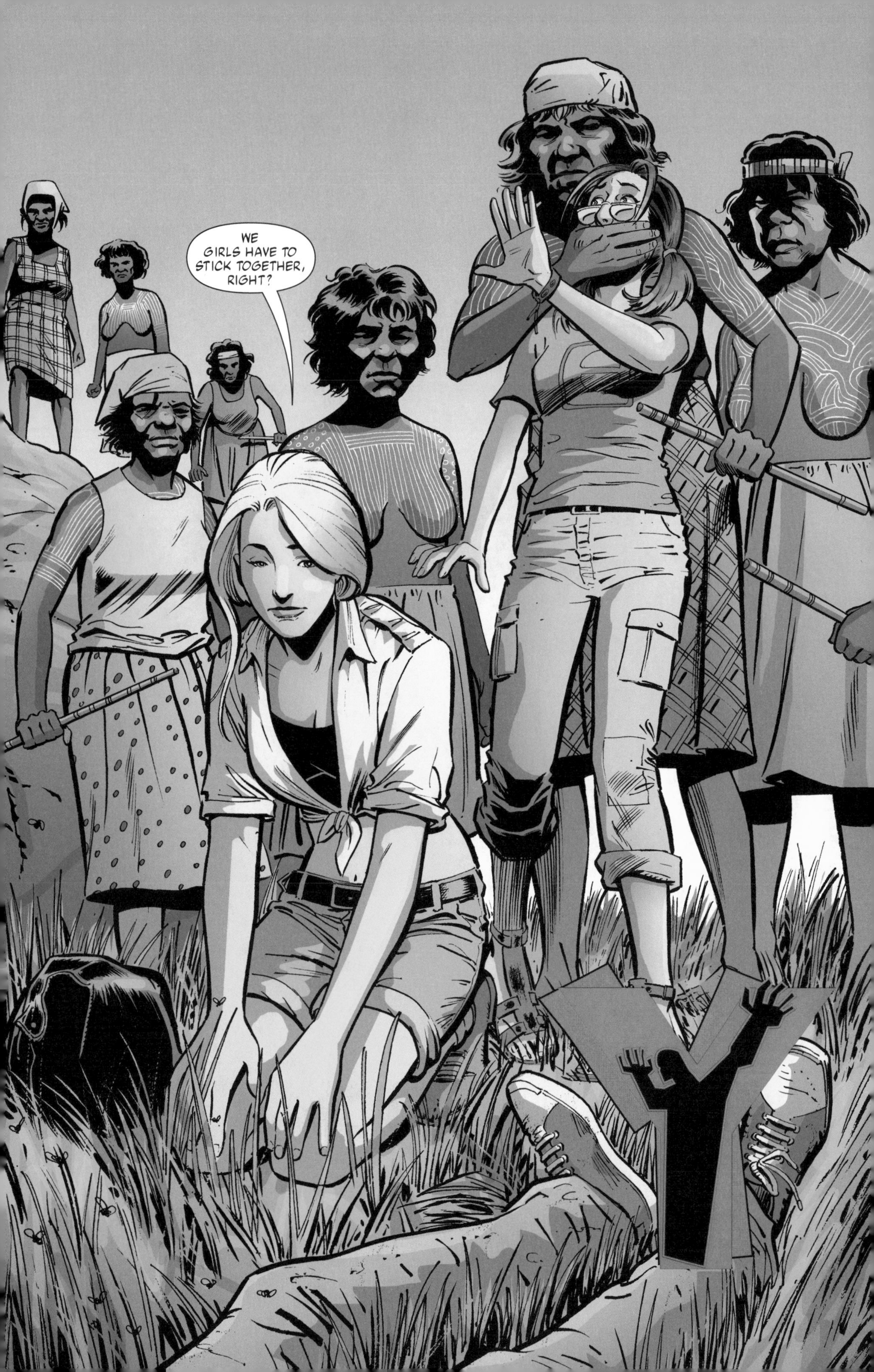
WE GIRLS HAVE TO STICK TOGETHER, RIGHT?

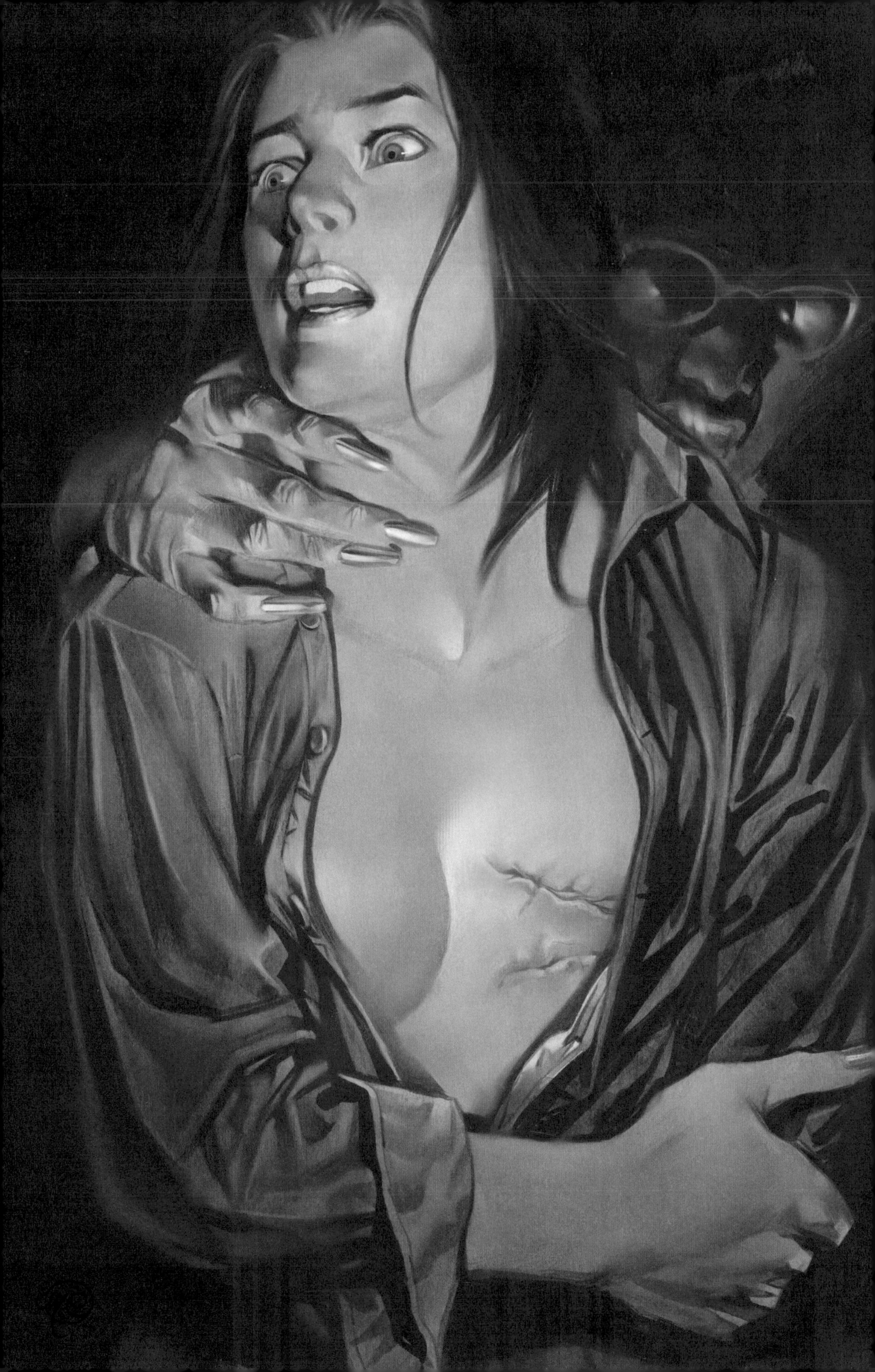

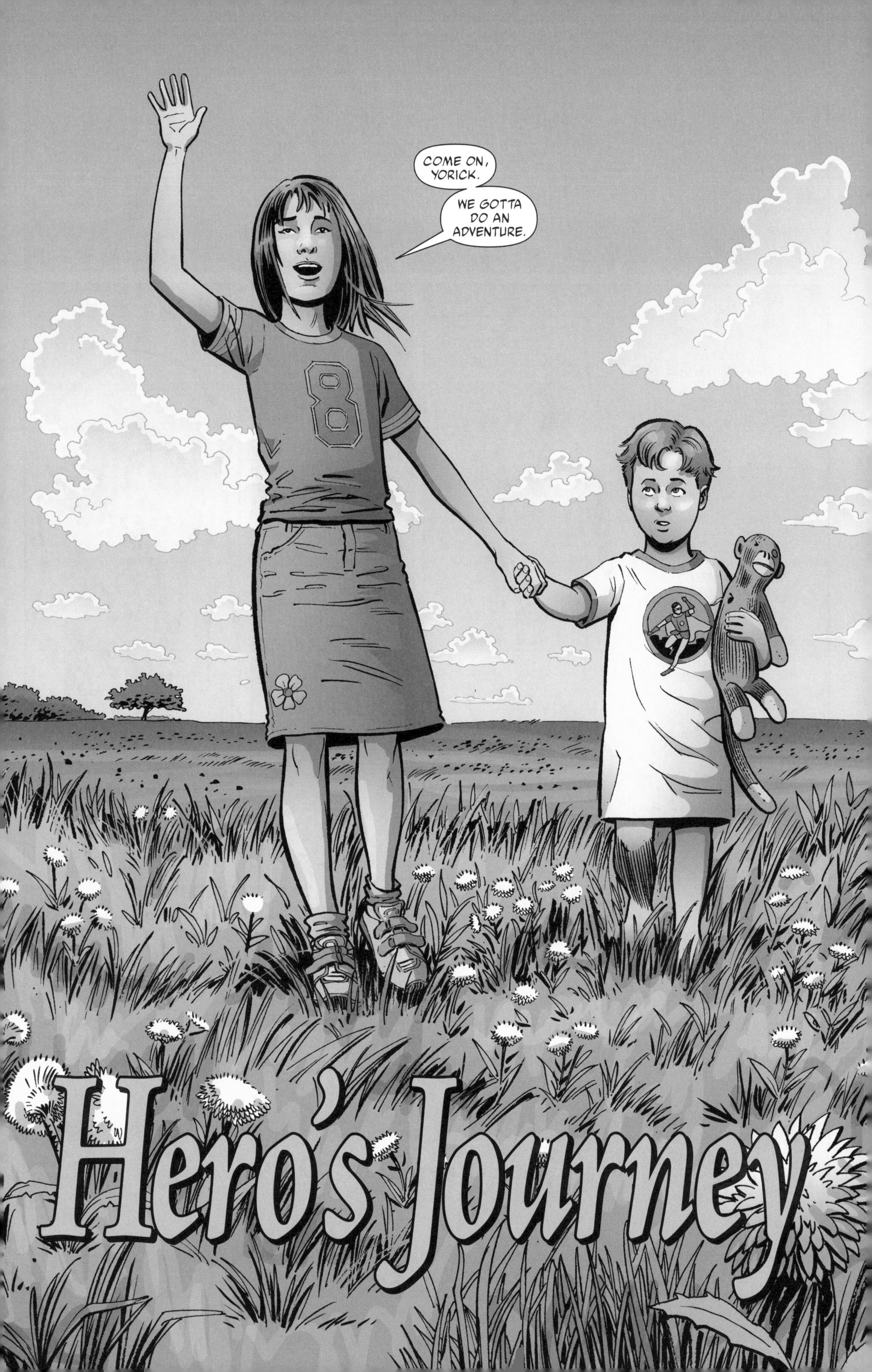
COME ON, YORICK.
WE GOTTA DO AN ADVENTURE.
Hero's Journey

WHY, HE-WO?

'CAUSE YOU HAVE TO MEET MY FRIEND. HER NAME IS QUEEN VICTORIA.

HELLO, QUEEN VICTORIA.

HELLO, HERO! WHO'S THIS?

HE'S MY LITTLE BROTHER. HIS NAME IS YORICK. HE'S GONNA JOIN OUR DANDELION LEAGUE.

HELLO, YORICK! NICE TO MEET YOU!

HI.

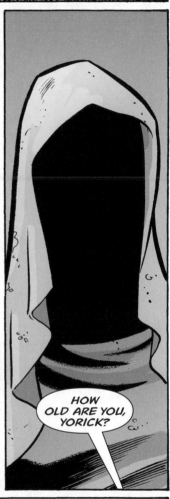

HOW OLD ARE YOU, YORICK?

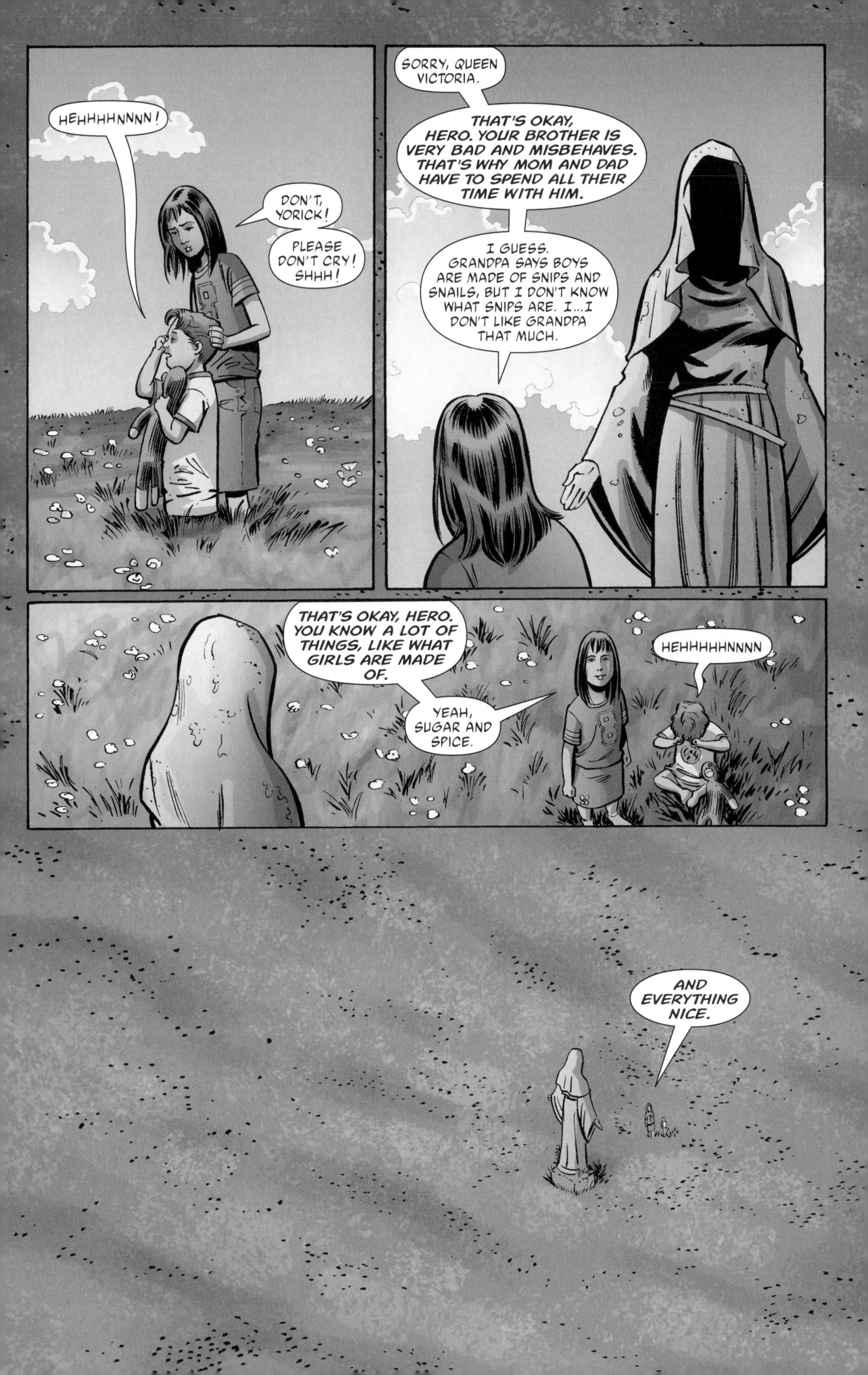
HEHHHHNNNN!
DON'T, YORICK!
PLEASE DON'T CRY! SHHH!
SORRY, QUEEN VICTORIA.
THAT'S OKAY, HERO. YOUR BROTHER IS VERY BAD AND MISBEHAVES. THAT'S WHY MOM AND DAD HAVE TO SPEND ALL THEIR TIME WITH HIM.
I GUESS. GRANDPA SAYS BOYS ARE MADE OF SNIPS AND SNAILS, BUT I DON'T KNOW WHAT SNIPS ARE. I...I DON'T LIKE GRANDPA THAT MUCH.
THAT'S OKAY, HERO. YOU KNOW A LOT OF THINGS, LIKE WHAT GIRLS ARE MADE OF.
YEAH, SUGAR AND SPICE.
HEHHHHHNNNN
AND EVERYTHING NICE.

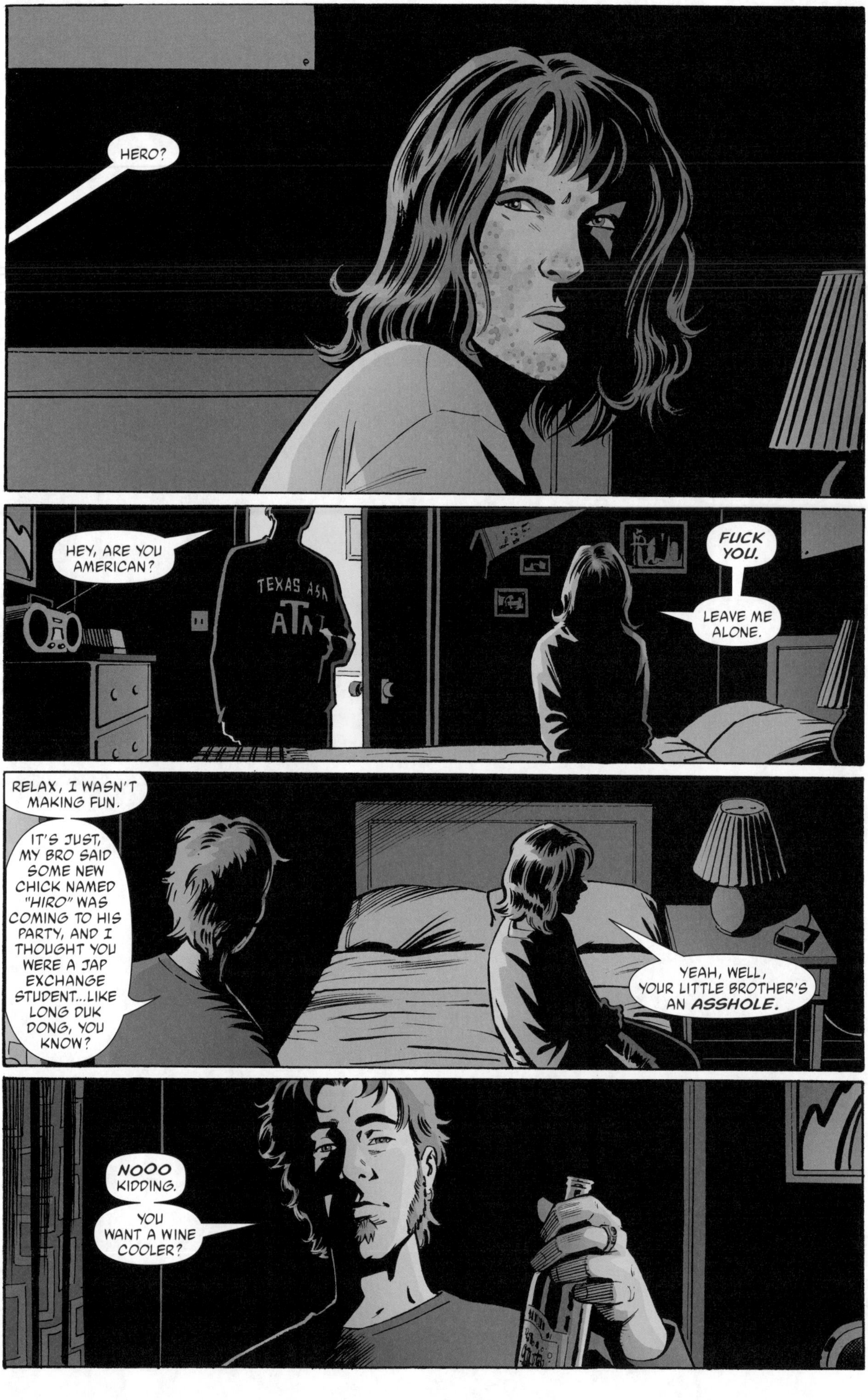
HERO?
HEY, ARE YOU AMERICAN?
TEXAS A&M
FUCK YOU.
LEAVE ME ALONE.
RELAX, I WASN'T MAKING FUN.
IT'S JUST, MY BRO SAID SOME NEW CHICK NAMED "HIRO" WAS COMING TO HIS PARTY, AND I THOUGHT YOU WERE A JAP EXCHANGE STUDENT...LIKE LONG DUK DONG, YOU KNOW?
YEAH, WELL, YOUR LITTLE BROTHER'S AN ASSHOLE.
NOOO KIDDING.
YOU WANT A WINE COOLER?

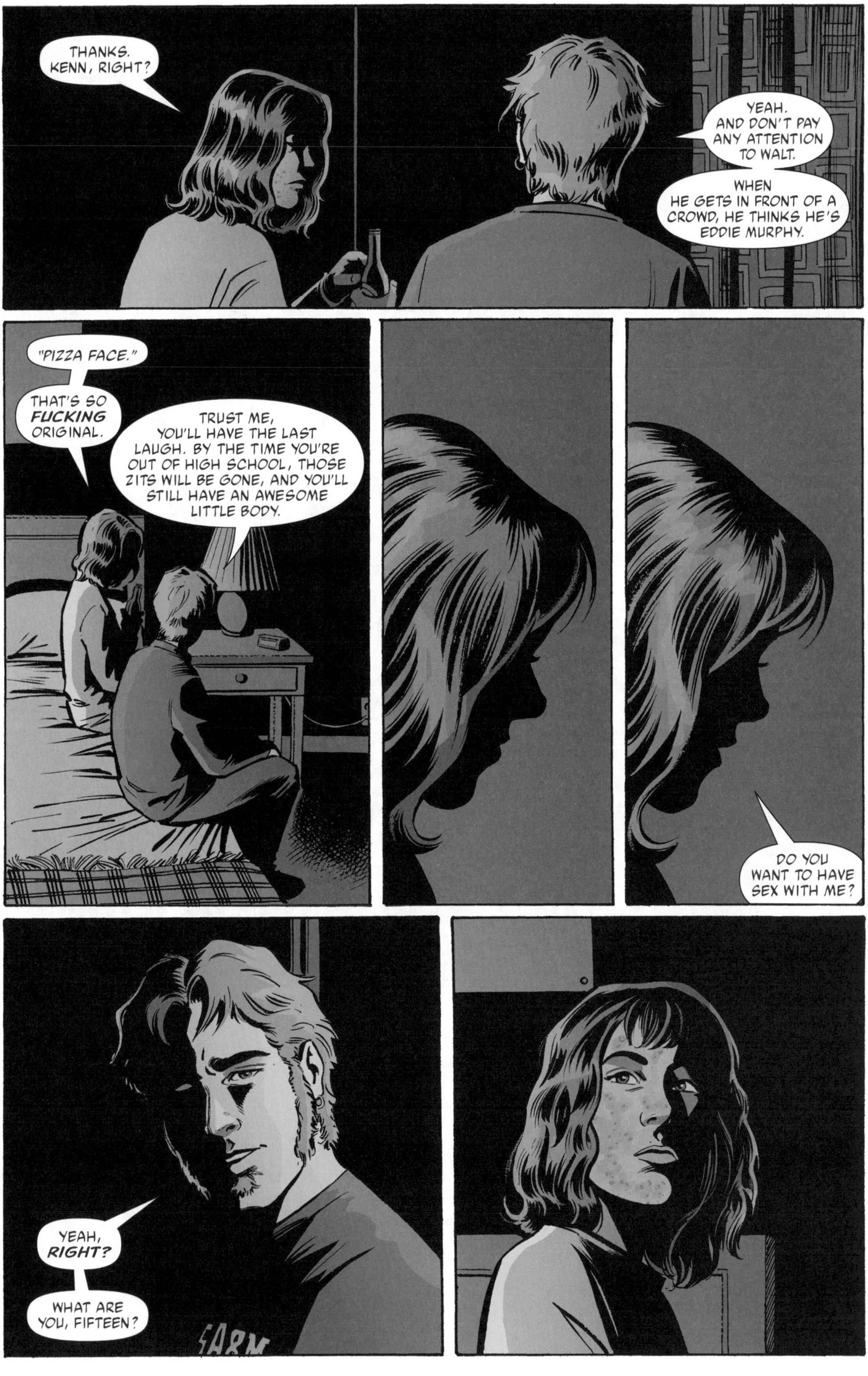
THANKS. KENN, RIGHT?
YEAH. AND DON'T PAY ANY ATTENTION TO WALT.
WHEN HE GETS IN FRONT OF A CROWD, HE THINKS HE'S EDDIE MURPHY.
"PIZZA FACE."
THAT'S SO **FUCKING** ORIGINAL.
TRUST ME, YOU'LL HAVE THE LAST LAUGH. BY THE TIME YOU'RE OUT OF HIGH SCHOOL, THOSE ZITS WILL BE GONE, AND YOU'LL STILL HAVE AN AWESOME LITTLE BODY.
DO YOU WANT TO HAVE SEX WITH ME?
YEAH, **RIGHT?**
WHAT ARE YOU, FIFTEEN?

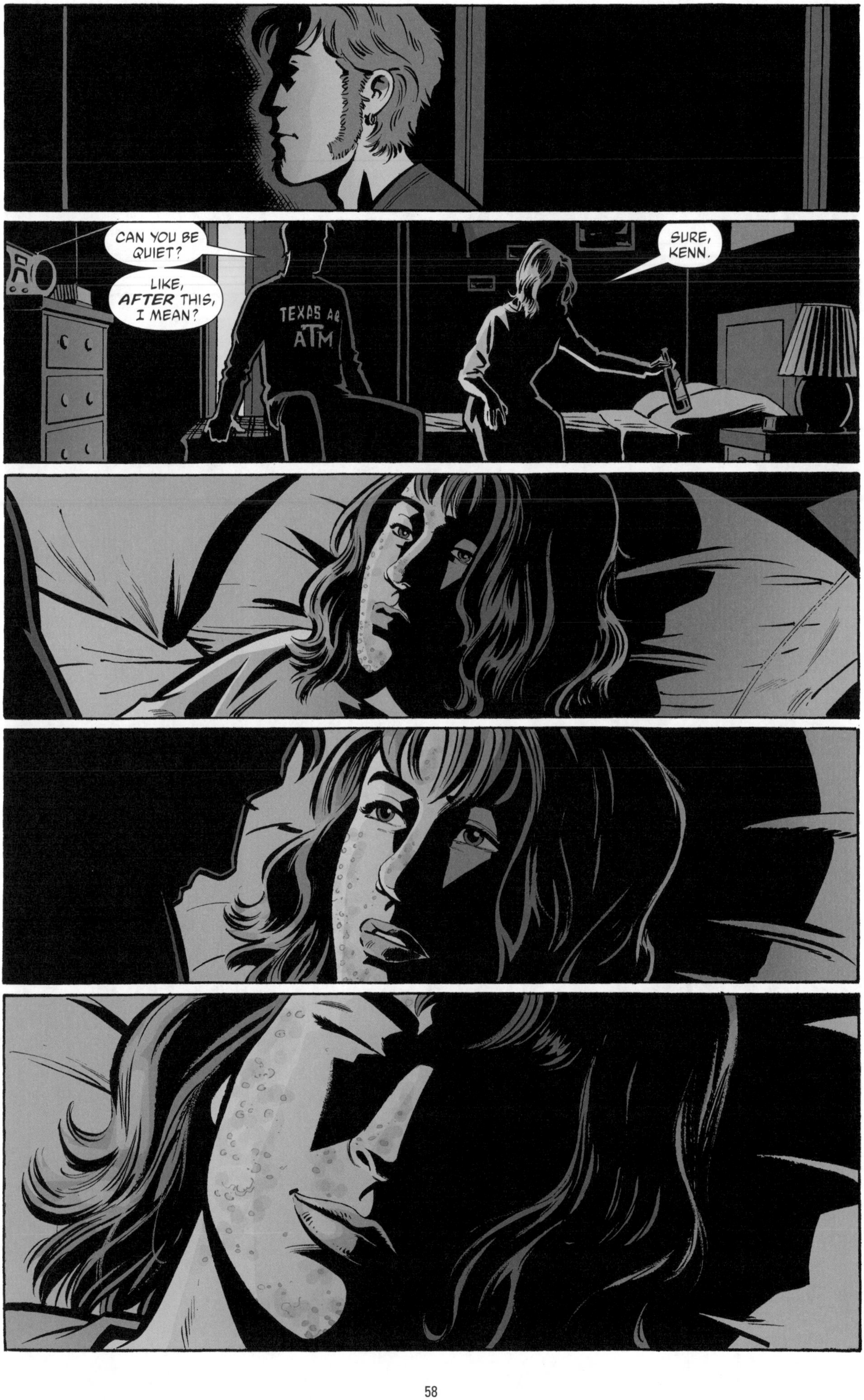
CAN YOU BE QUIET?
LIKE, AFTER THIS, I MEAN?
SURE, KENN.
TEXAS A&
ATM

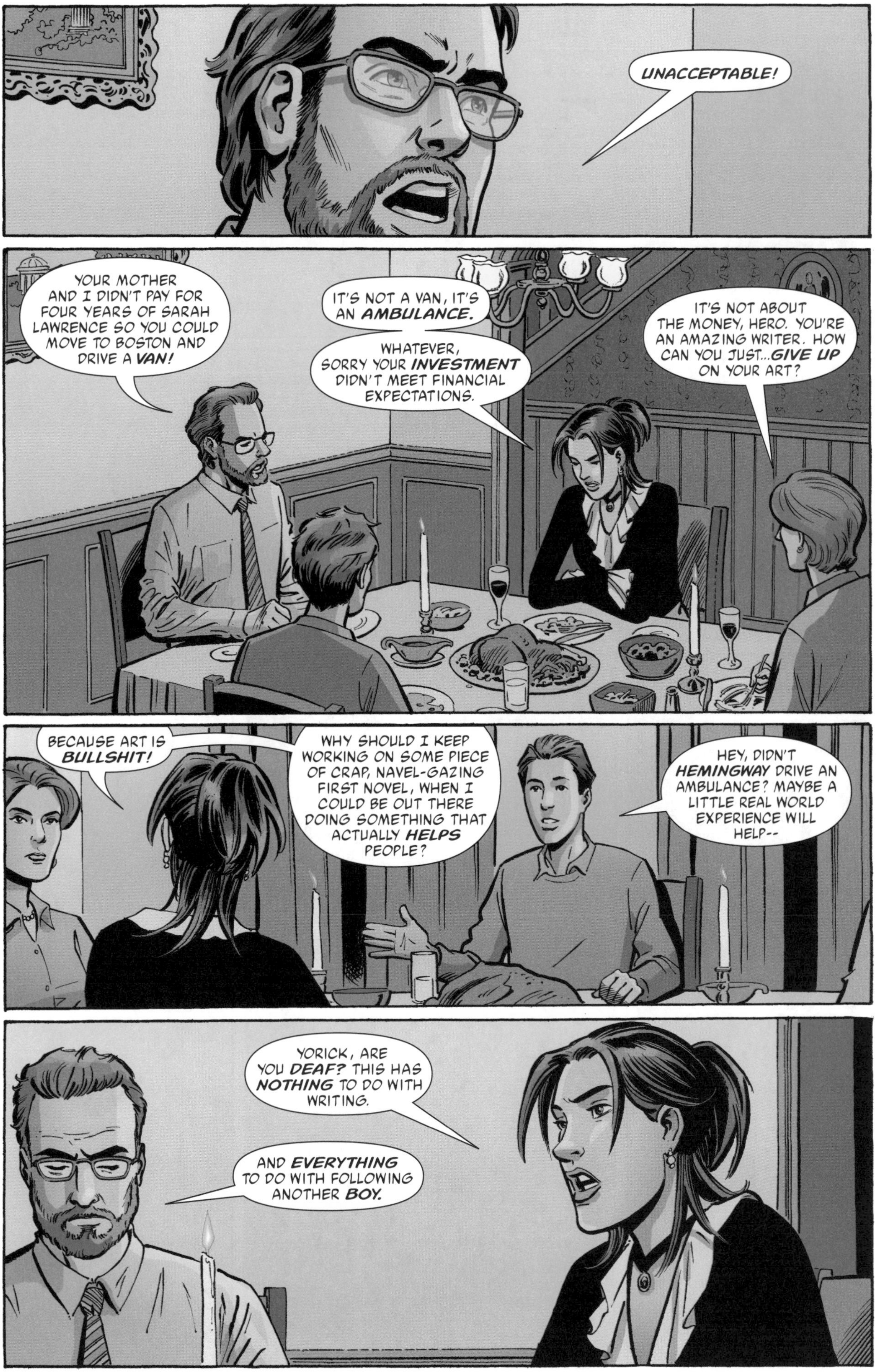
UNACCEPTABLE!
YOUR MOTHER AND I DIDN'T PAY FOR FOUR YEARS OF SARAH LAWRENCE SO YOU COULD MOVE TO BOSTON AND DRIVE A VAN!
IT'S NOT A VAN, IT'S AN AMBULANCE.
WHATEVER, SORRY YOUR INVESTMENT DIDN'T MEET FINANCIAL EXPECTATIONS.
IT'S NOT ABOUT THE MONEY, HERO. YOU'RE AN AMAZING WRITER. HOW CAN YOU JUST...GIVE UP ON YOUR ART?
BECAUSE ART IS BULLSHIT!
WHY SHOULD I KEEP WORKING ON SOME PIECE OF CRAP, NAVEL-GAZING FIRST NOVEL, WHEN I COULD BE OUT THERE DOING SOMETHING THAT ACTUALLY HELPS PEOPLE?
HEY, DIDN'T HEMINGWAY DRIVE AN AMBULANCE? MAYBE A LITTLE REAL WORLD EXPERIENCE WILL HELP--
YORICK, ARE YOU DEAF? THIS HAS NOTHING TO DO WITH WRITING.
AND EVERYTHING TO DO WITH FOLLOWING ANOTHER BOY.

JOE ISN'T "ANOTHER BOY," DAD.

HE RESPECTS ME FOR WHO I AM, WHICH IS MORE THAN I CAN SAY FOR ANY OF THE *OTHER* MEN IN MY LIFE.

DIAL IT DOWN, KIDDO. IT'S NOT LIKE WE'RE *MY* TOTALITARIAN PARENTS, TRYING TO FORCE YOU INTO THE FAMILY BUSINESS. YOUR FATHER JUST DOESN'T WANT YOU THROWING AWAY YOUR DREAMS OVER SOME *GUY* WHO DOESN'T EVEN--

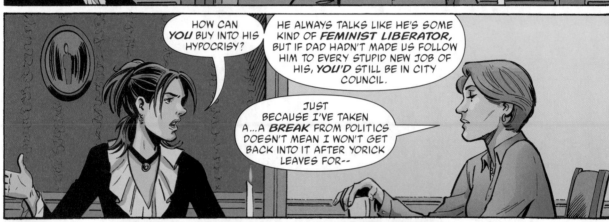

HOW CAN *YOU* BUY INTO HIS HYPOCRISY?

HE ALWAYS TALKS LIKE HE'S SOME KIND OF *FEMINIST LIBERATOR,* BUT IF DAD HADN'T MADE US FOLLOW HIM TO EVERY STUPID NEW JOB OF HIS, *YOU'D* STILL BE IN CITY COUNCIL.

JUST BECAUSE I'VE TAKEN A...A *BREAK* FROM POLITICS DOESN'T MEAN I WON'T GET BACK INTO IT AFTER YORICK LEAVES FOR--

FORGET IT!

I'M SO SICK OF THIS FAMILY'S *FICTION!*

IS IT JUST ME...OR IS CRANBERRY SAUCE *WAY* TOO AWESOME TO EAT JUST ONCE A YEAR?

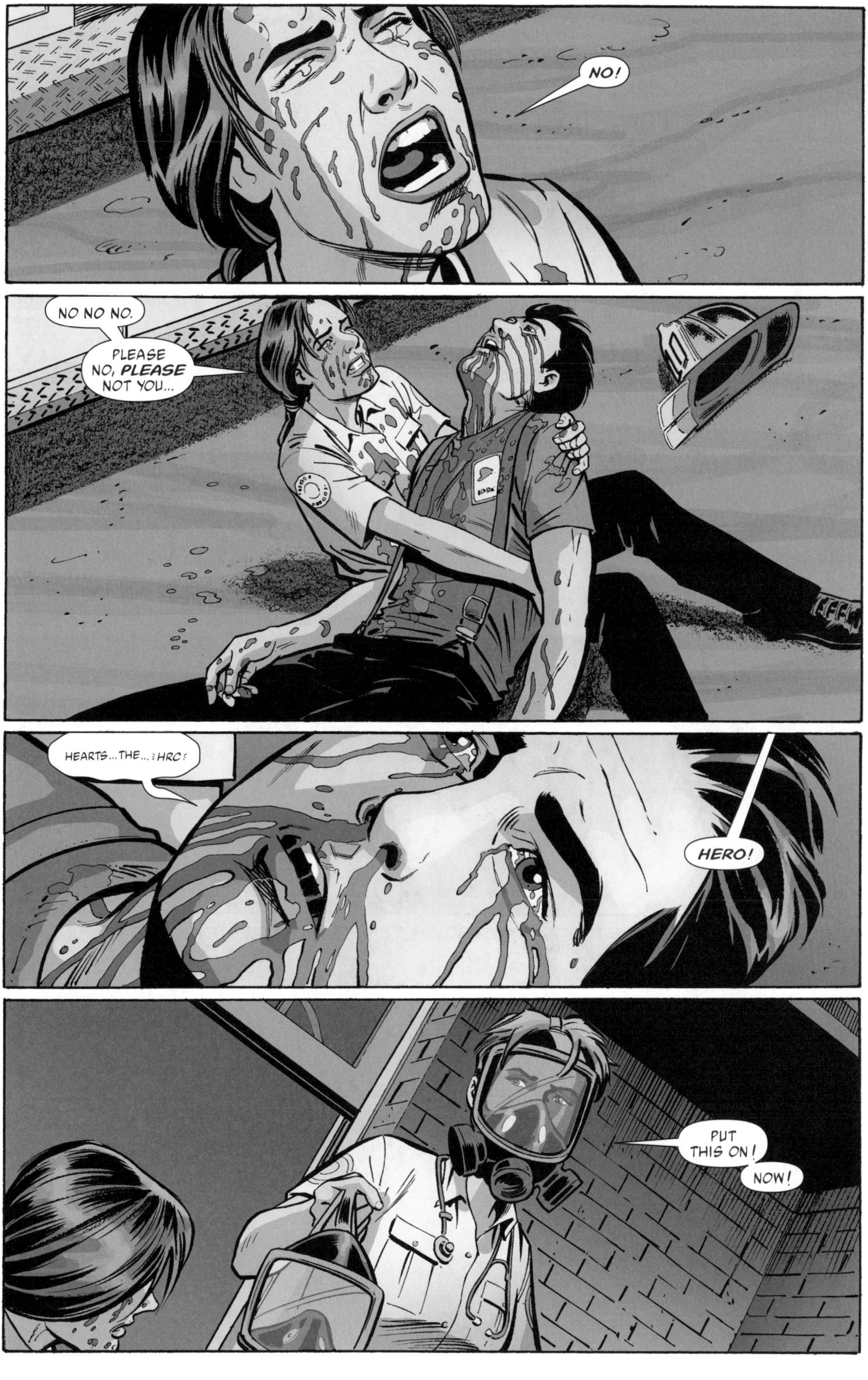
NO!
NO NO NO.
PLEASE NO, PLEASE NOT YOU...
HEARTS...THE...HRC
HERO!
PUT THIS ON!
NOW!

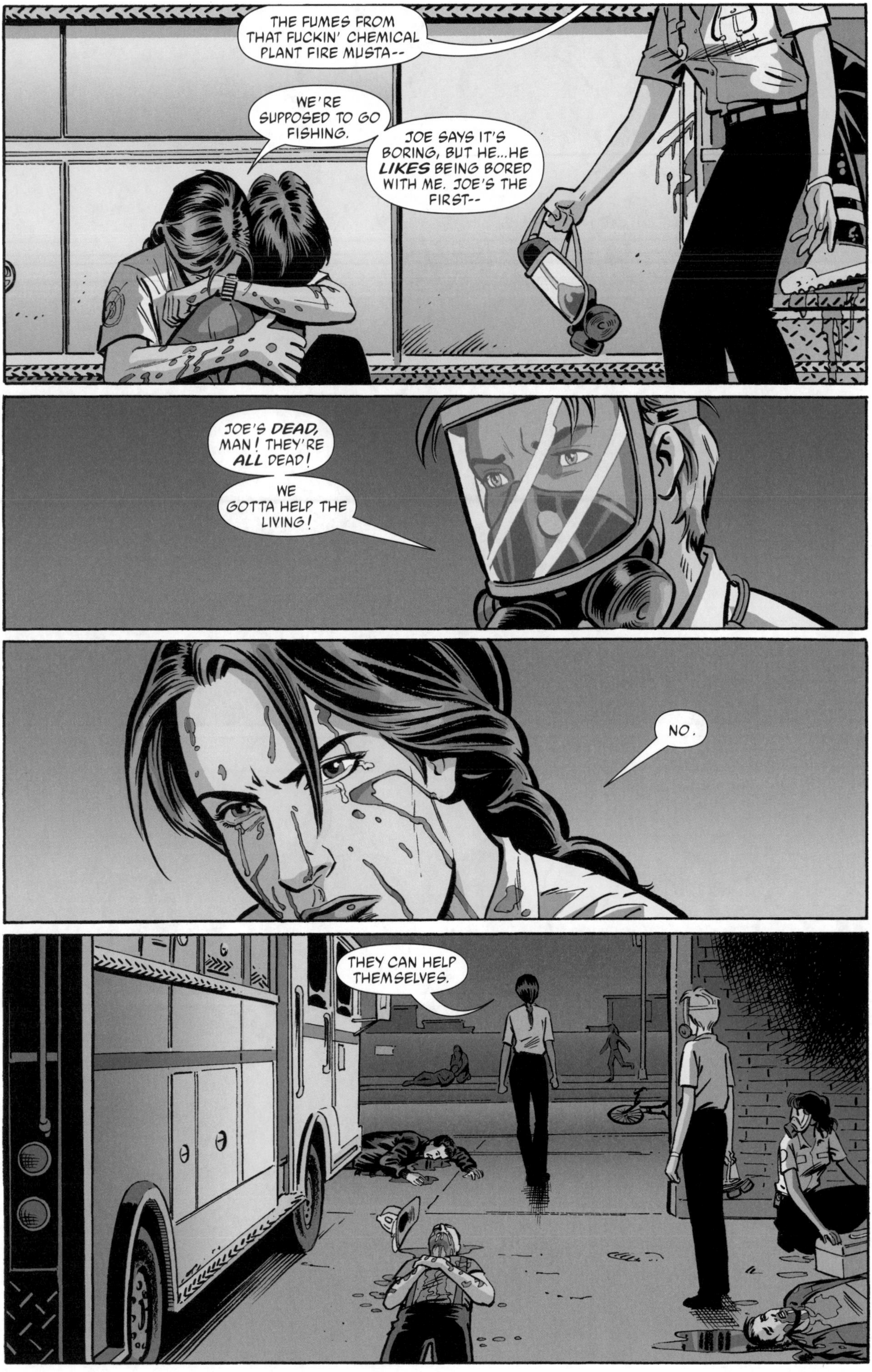
THE FUMES FROM THAT FUCKIN' CHEMICAL PLANT FIRE MUSTA--
WE'RE SUPPOSED TO GO FISHING.
JOE SAYS IT'S BORING, BUT HE...HE LIKES BEING BORED WITH ME. JOE'S THE FIRST--
JOE'S DEAD, MAN! THEY'RE ALL DEAD!
WE GOTTA HELP THE LIVING!
NO.
THEY CAN HELP THEMSELVES.

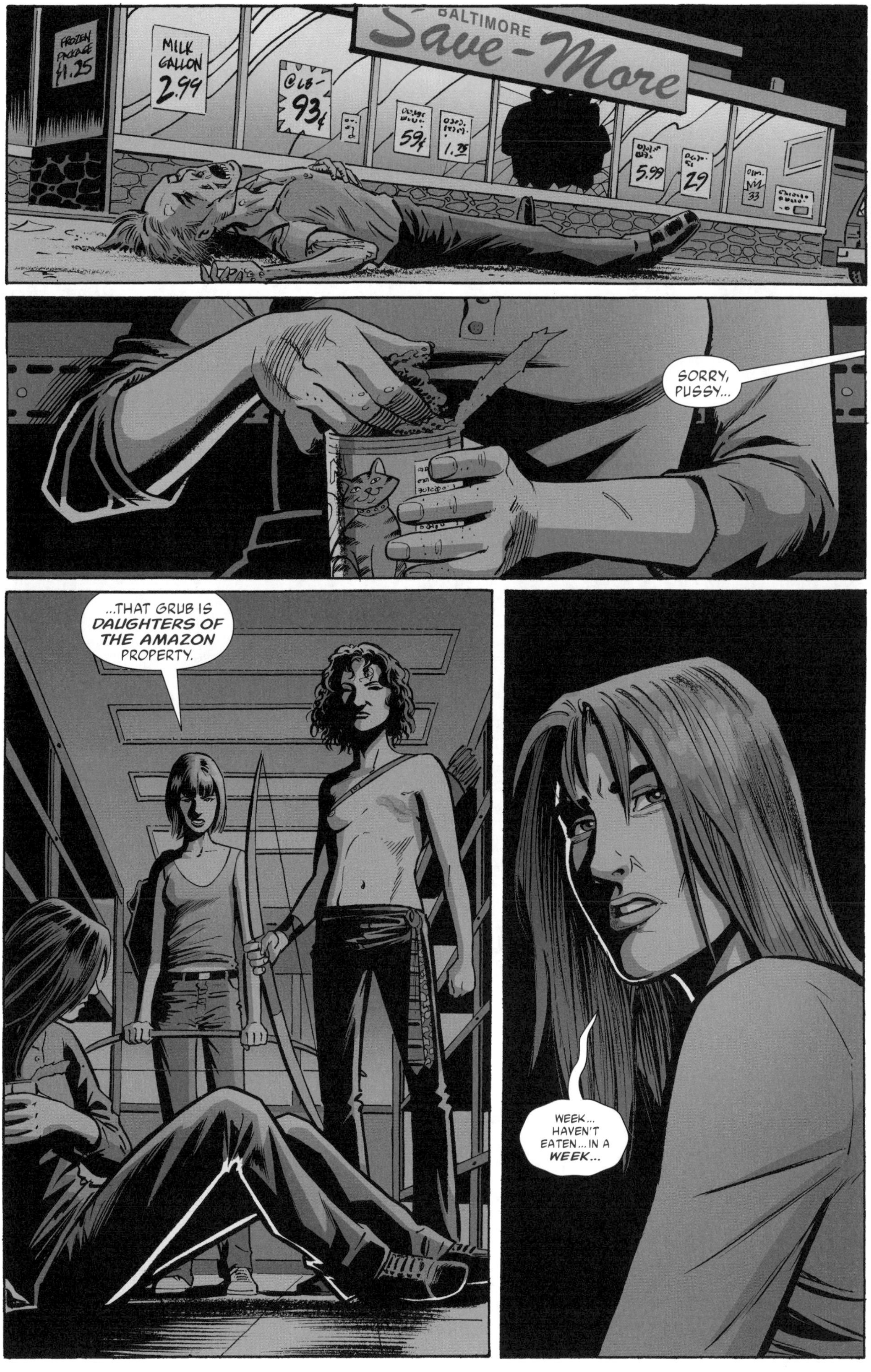
BALTIMORE
Save-More
FROZEN PACKAGE $1.25
MILK GALLON 2.99
@LB- 93¢
59¢
1.75
5.99
29
SORRY, PUSSY...
...THAT GRUB IS *DAUGHTERS OF THE AMAZON* PROPERTY.
WEEK... HAVEN'T EATEN...IN A *WEEK...*

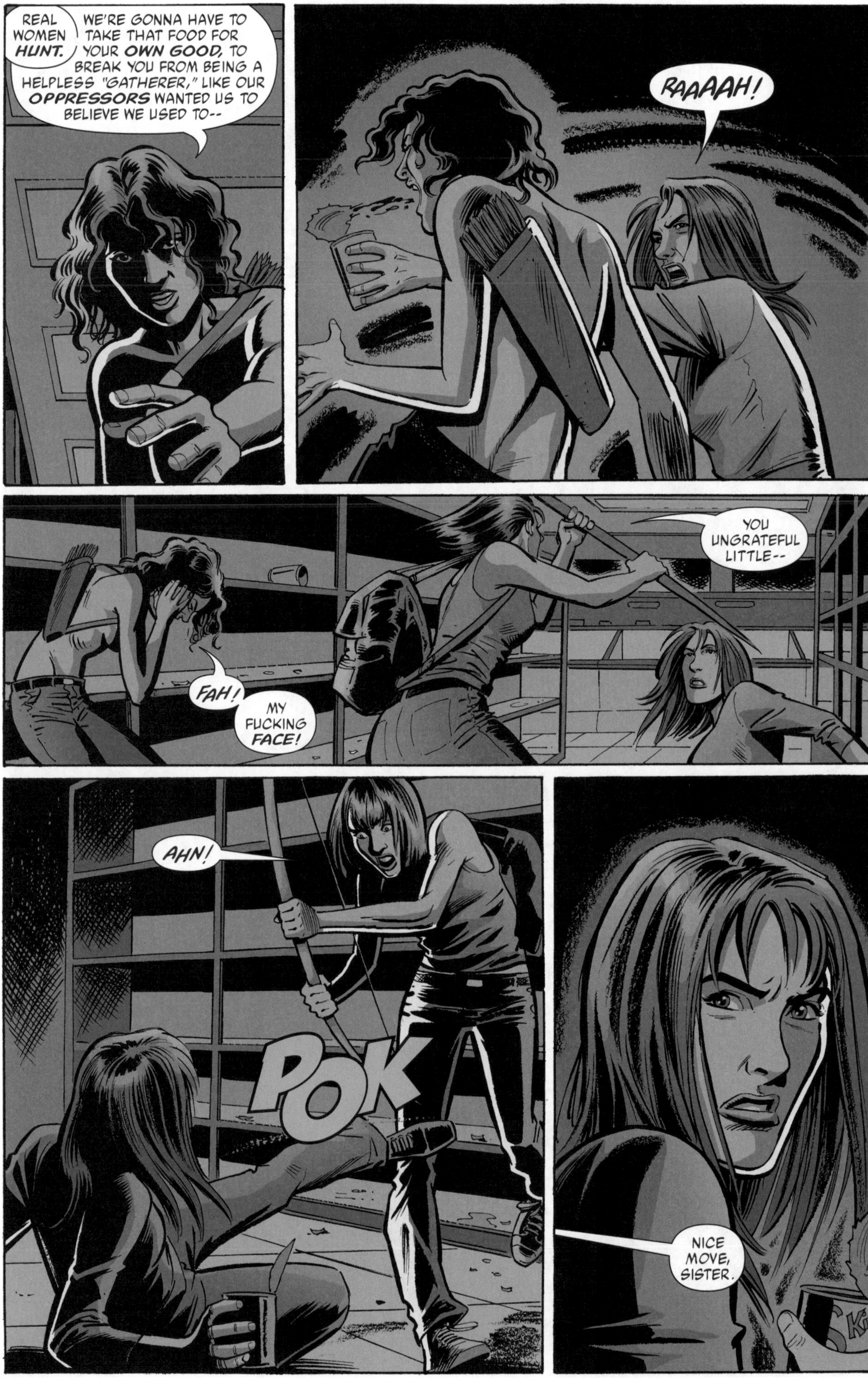
REAL WOMEN HUNT.
WE'RE GONNA HAVE TO TAKE THAT FOOD FOR YOUR OWN GOOD, TO BREAK YOU FROM BEING A HELPLESS "GATHERER," LIKE OUR OPPRESSORS WANTED US TO BELIEVE WE USED TO--
RAAAAH!
YOU UNGRATEFUL LITTLE--
FAH!
MY FUCKING FACE!
AHN!
POK
NICE MOVE, SISTER.

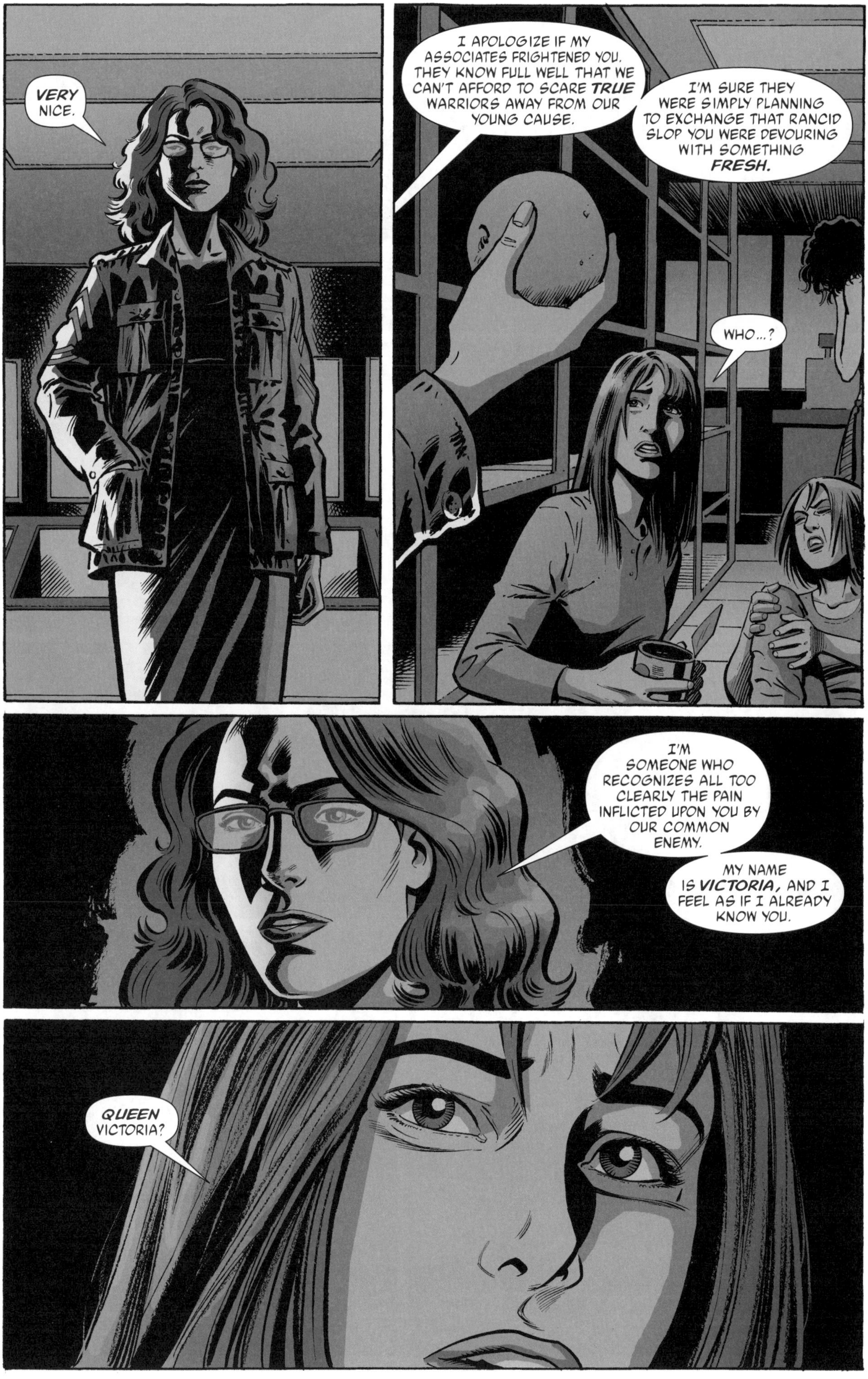
VERY NICE.
I APOLOGIZE IF MY ASSOCIATES FRIGHTENED YOU. THEY KNOW FULL WELL THAT WE CAN'T AFFORD TO SCARE TRUE WARRIORS AWAY FROM OUR YOUNG CAUSE.
I'M SURE THEY WERE SIMPLY PLANNING TO EXCHANGE THAT RANCID SLOP YOU WERE DEVOURING WITH SOMETHING FRESH.
WHO...?
I'M SOMEONE WHO RECOGNIZES ALL TOO CLEARLY THE PAIN INFLICTED UPON YOU BY OUR COMMON ENEMY.
MY NAME IS VICTORIA, AND I FEEL AS IF I ALREADY KNOW YOU.
QUEEN VICTORIA?

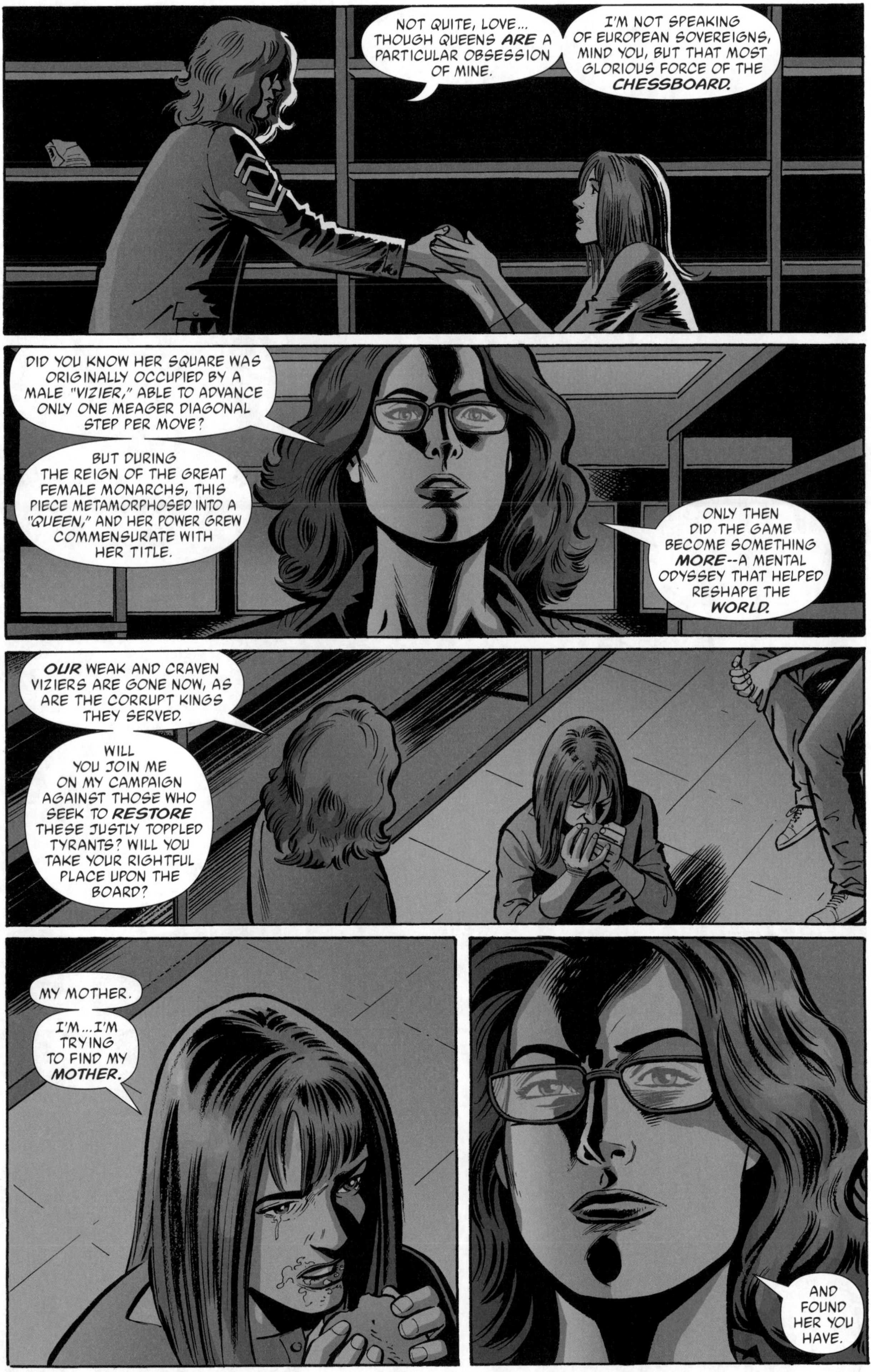
NOT QUITE, LOVE... THOUGH QUEENS ARE A PARTICULAR OBSESSION OF MINE.
I'M NOT SPEAKING OF EUROPEAN SOVEREIGNS, MIND YOU, BUT THAT MOST GLORIOUS FORCE OF THE CHESSBOARD.
DID YOU KNOW HER SQUARE WAS ORIGINALLY OCCUPIED BY A MALE "VIZIER," ABLE TO ADVANCE ONLY ONE MEAGER DIAGONAL STEP PER MOVE?
BUT DURING THE REIGN OF THE GREAT FEMALE MONARCHS, THIS PIECE METAMORPHOSED INTO A "QUEEN," AND HER POWER GREW COMMENSURATE WITH HER TITLE.
ONLY THEN DID THE GAME BECOME SOMETHING MORE--A MENTAL ODYSSEY THAT HELPED RESHAPE THE WORLD.
OUR WEAK AND CRAVEN VIZIERS ARE GONE NOW, AS ARE THE CORRUPT KINGS THEY SERVED.
WILL YOU JOIN ME ON MY CAMPAIGN AGAINST THOSE WHO SEEK TO RESTORE THESE JUSTLY TOPPLED TYRANTS? WILL YOU TAKE YOUR RIGHTFUL PLACE UPON THE BOARD?
MY MOTHER.
I'M...I'M TRYING TO FIND MY MOTHER.
AND FOUND HER YOU HAVE.

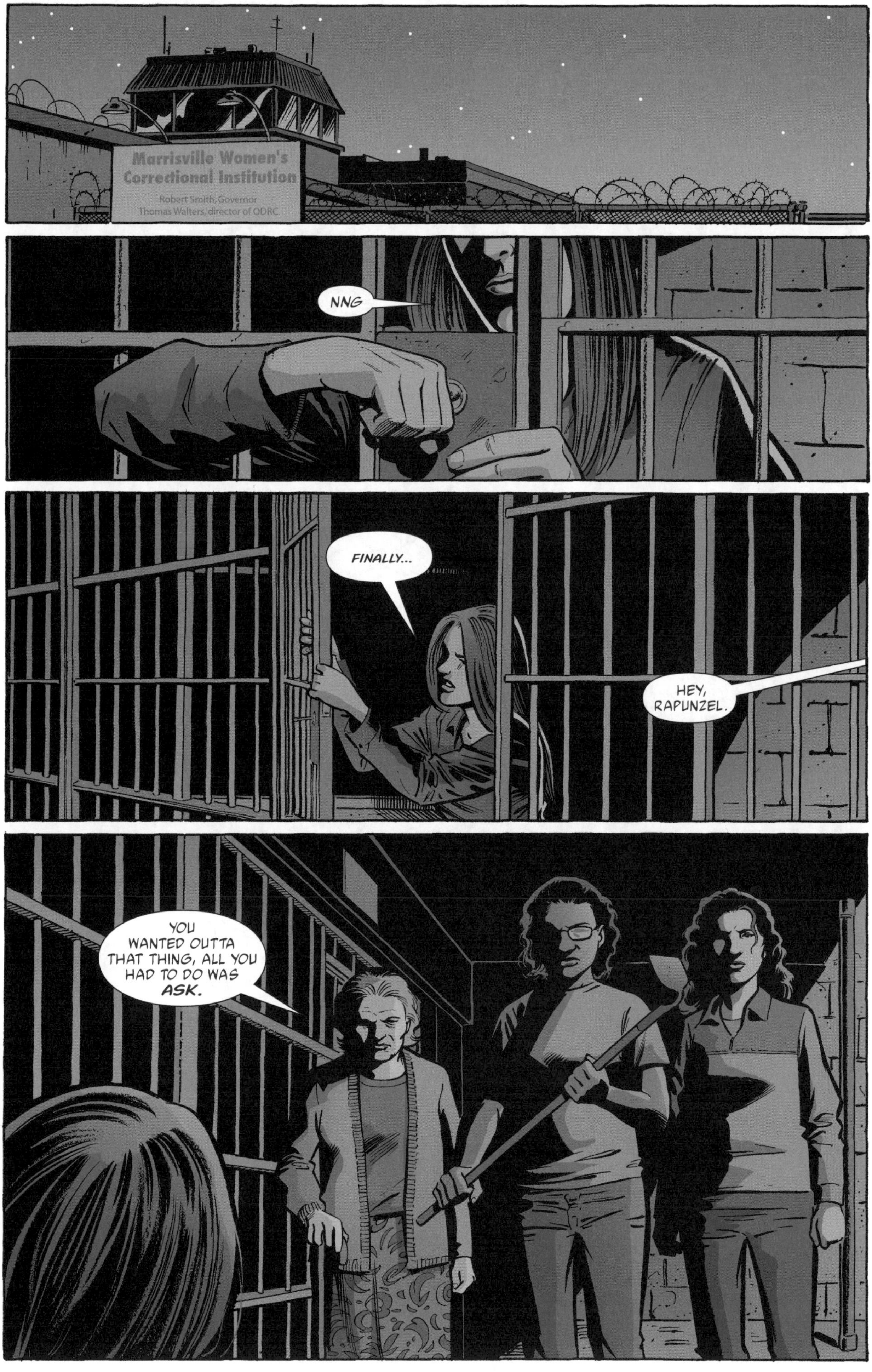
Marrisville Women's Correctional Institution
Robert Smith, Governor
Thomas Walters, director of ODRC
NNG
FINALLY...
HEY, RAPUNZEL.
YOU WANTED OUTTA THAT THING, ALL YOU HAD TO DO WAS ASK.

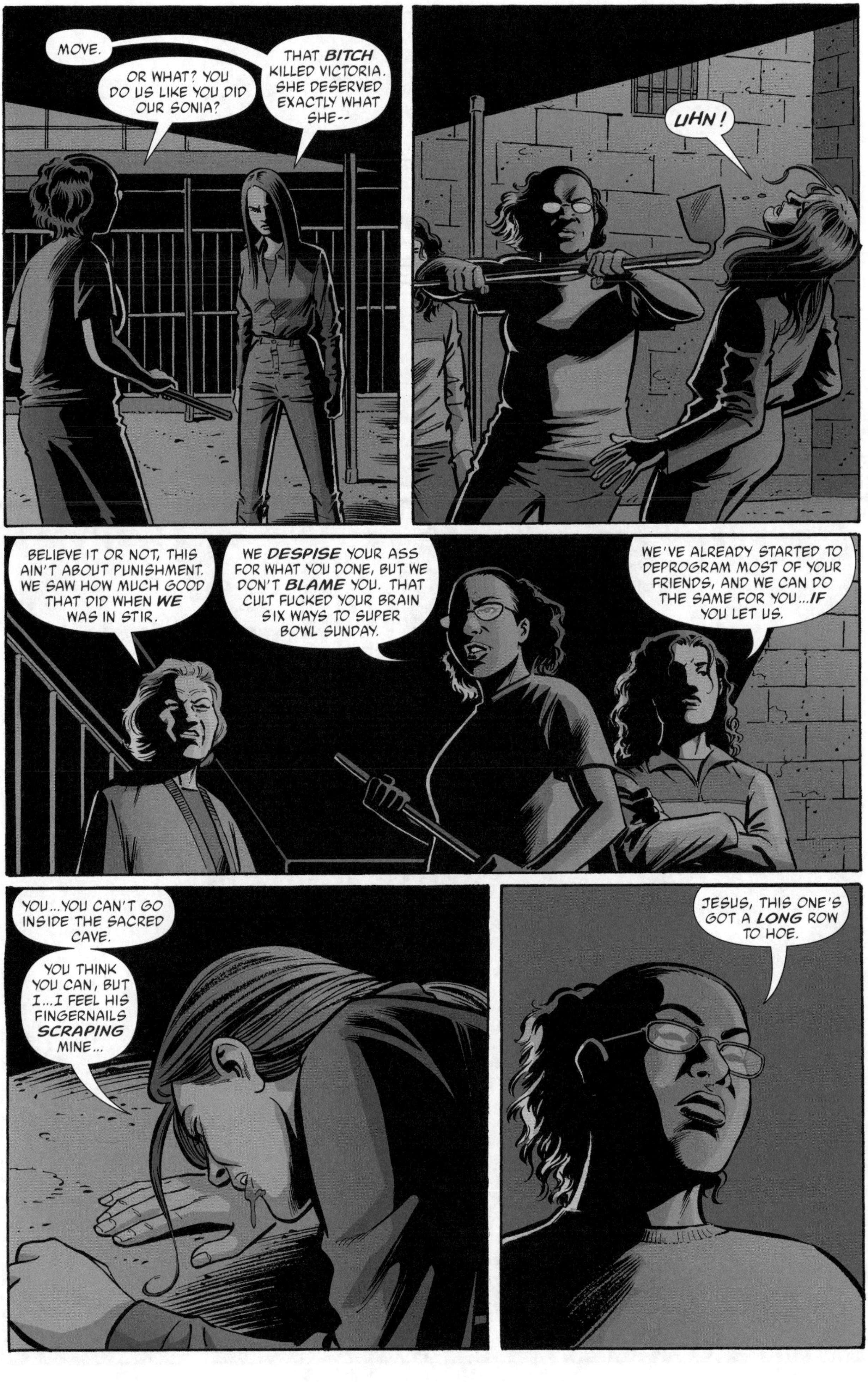
MOVE.
OR WHAT? YOU DO US LIKE YOU DID OUR SONIA?
THAT BITCH KILLED VICTORIA. SHE DESERVED EXACTLY WHAT SHE--
UHN!
BELIEVE IT OR NOT, THIS AIN'T ABOUT PUNISHMENT. WE SAW HOW MUCH GOOD THAT DID WHEN WE WAS IN STIR.
WE DESPISE YOUR ASS FOR WHAT YOU DONE, BUT WE DON'T BLAME YOU. THAT CULT FUCKED YOUR BRAIN SIX WAYS TO SUPER BOWL SUNDAY.
WE'VE ALREADY STARTED TO DEPROGRAM MOST OF YOUR FRIENDS, AND WE CAN DO THE SAME FOR YOU...IF YOU LET US.
YOU...YOU CAN'T GO INSIDE THE SACRED CAVE.
YOU THINK YOU CAN, BUT I...I FEEL HIS FINGERNAILS SCRAPING MINE...
JESUS, THIS ONE'S GOT A LONG ROW TO HOE.

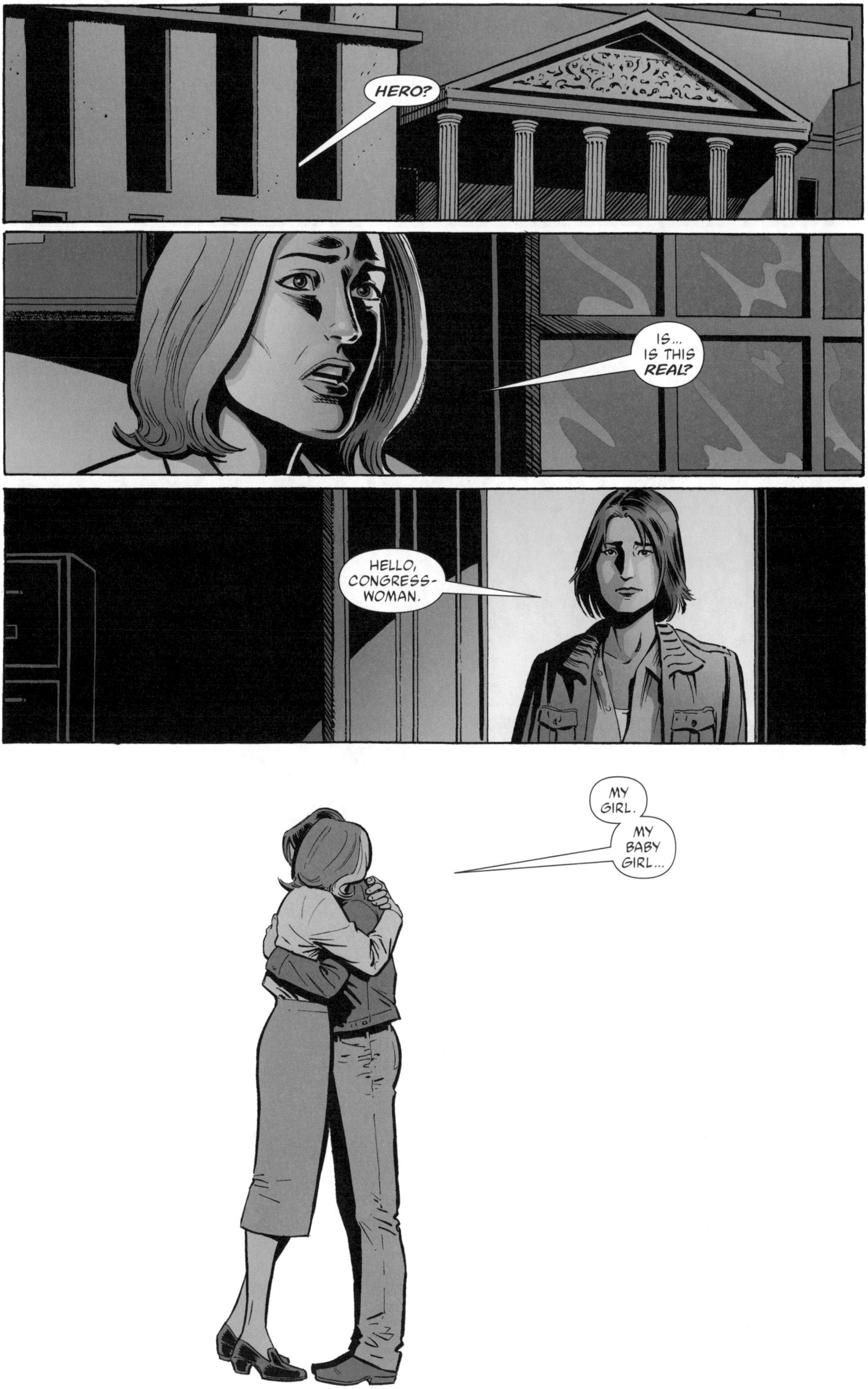
HERO?
IS... IS THIS REAL?
HELLO, CONGRESS-WOMAN.
MY GIRL.
MY BABY GIRL...

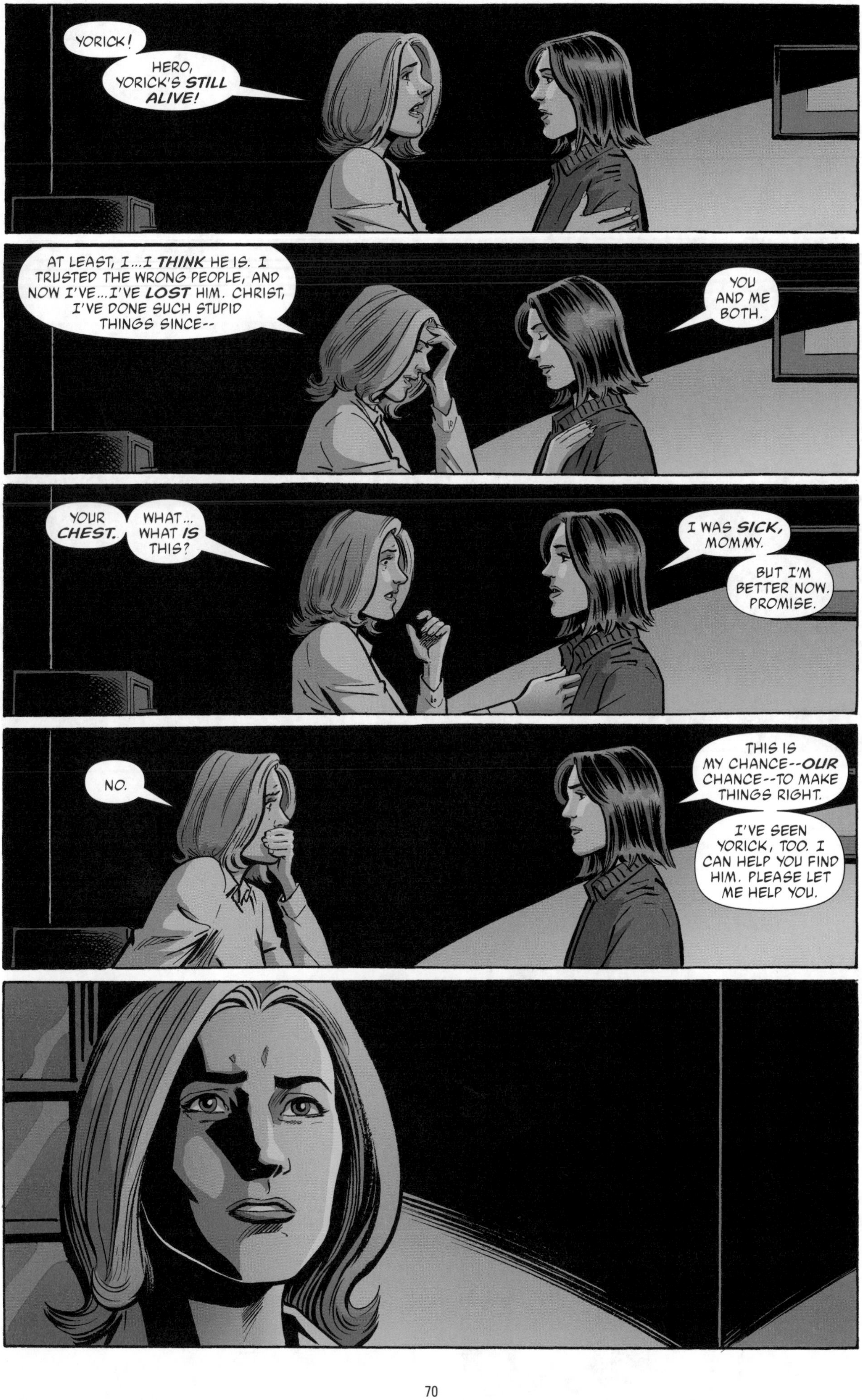
YORICK!
HERO, YORICK'S STILL ALIVE!
AT LEAST, I...I THINK HE IS. I TRUSTED THE WRONG PEOPLE, AND NOW I'VE...I'VE LOST HIM. CHRIST, I'VE DONE SUCH STUPID THINGS SINCE--
YOU AND ME BOTH.
YOUR CHEST.
WHAT... WHAT IS THIS?
I WAS SICK, MOMMY.
BUT I'M BETTER NOW. PROMISE.
NO.
THIS IS MY CHANCE--OUR CHANCE--TO MAKE THINGS RIGHT.
I'VE SEEN YORICK, TOO. I CAN HELP YOU FIND HIM. PLEASE LET ME HELP YOU.

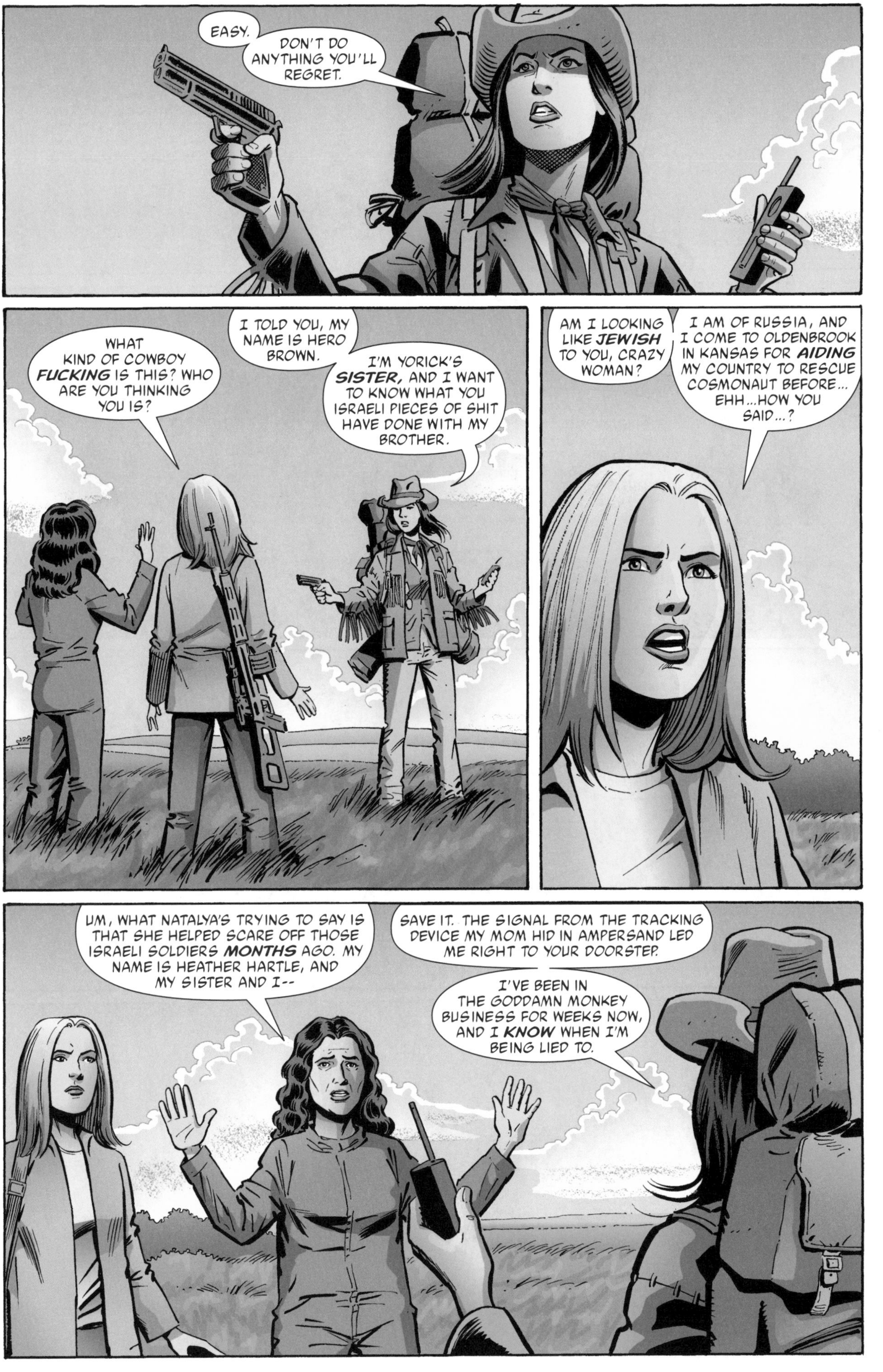
EASY.
DON'T DO ANYTHING YOU'LL REGRET.
WHAT KIND OF COWBOY FUCKING IS THIS? WHO ARE YOU THINKING YOU IS?
I TOLD YOU, MY NAME IS HERO BROWN.
I'M YORICK'S SISTER, AND I WANT TO KNOW WHAT YOU ISRAELI PIECES OF SHIT HAVE DONE WITH MY BROTHER.
AM I LOOKING LIKE JEWISH TO YOU, CRAZY WOMAN?
I AM OF RUSSIA, AND I COME TO OLDENBROOK IN KANSAS FOR AIDING MY COUNTRY TO RESCUE COSMONAUT BEFORE... EHH...HOW YOU SAID...?
UM, WHAT NATALYA'S TRYING TO SAY IS THAT SHE HELPED SCARE OFF THOSE ISRAELI SOLDIERS MONTHS AGO. MY NAME IS HEATHER HARTLE, AND MY SISTER AND I--
SAVE IT. THE SIGNAL FROM THE TRACKING DEVICE MY MOM HID IN AMPERSAND LED ME RIGHT TO YOUR DOORSTEP.
I'VE BEEN IN THE GODDAMN MONKEY BUSINESS FOR WEEKS NOW, AND I KNOW WHEN I'M BEING LIED TO.

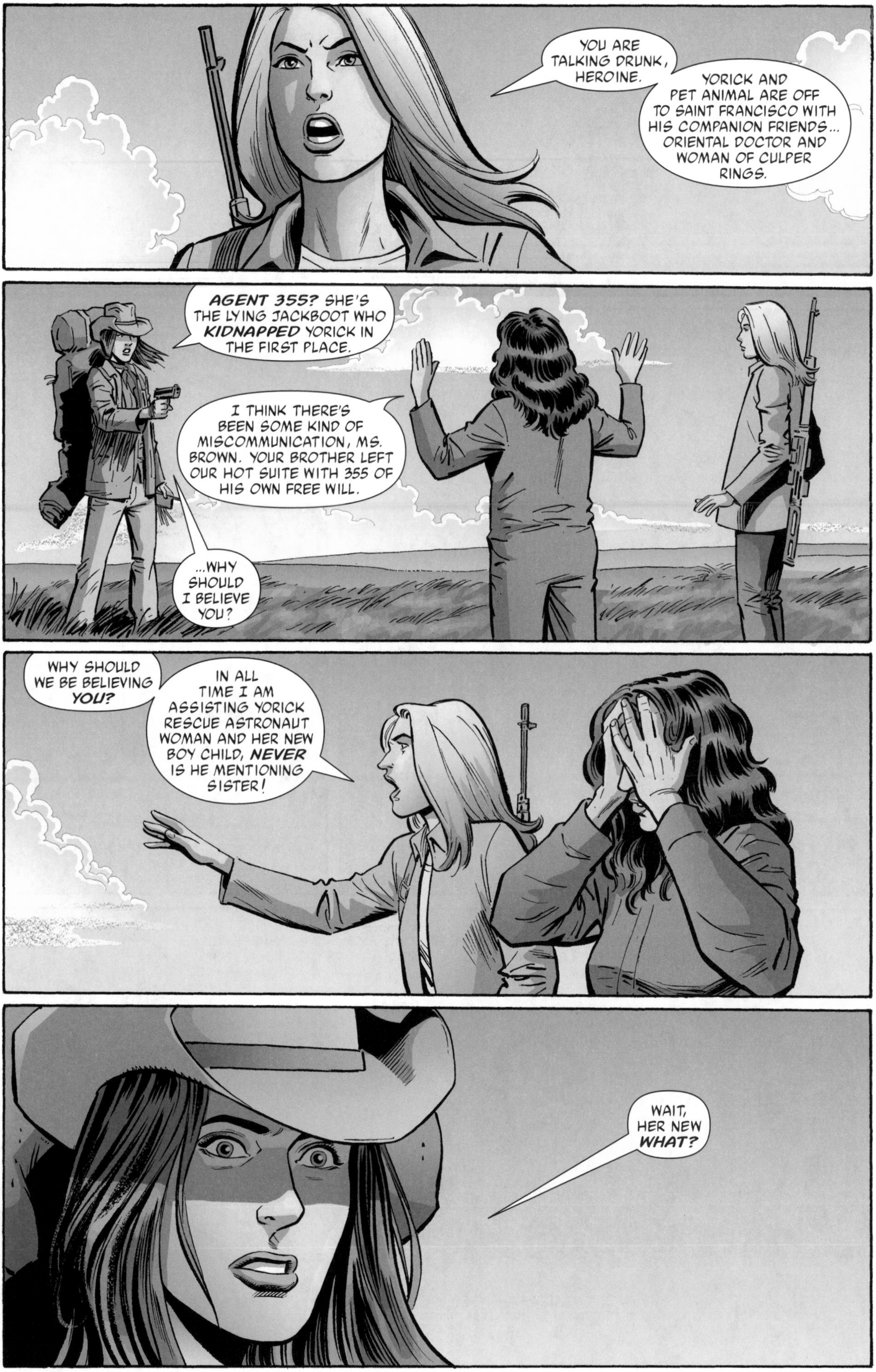
YOU ARE TALKING DRUNK, HEROINE.
YORICK AND PET ANIMAL ARE OFF TO SAINT FRANCISCO WITH HIS COMPANION FRIENDS... ORIENTAL DOCTOR AND WOMAN OF CULPER RINGS.
AGENT 355? SHE'S THE LYING JACKBOOT WHO KIDNAPPED YORICK IN THE FIRST PLACE.
I THINK THERE'S BEEN SOME KIND OF MISCOMMUNICATION, MS. BROWN. YOUR BROTHER LEFT OUR HOT SUITE WITH 355 OF HIS OWN FREE WILL.
...WHY SHOULD I BELIEVE YOU?
WHY SHOULD WE BE BELIEVING YOU?
IN ALL TIME I AM ASSISTING YORICK RESCUE ASTRONAUT WOMAN AND HER NEW BOY CHILD, NEVER IS HE MENTIONING SISTER!
WAIT, HER NEW WHAT?

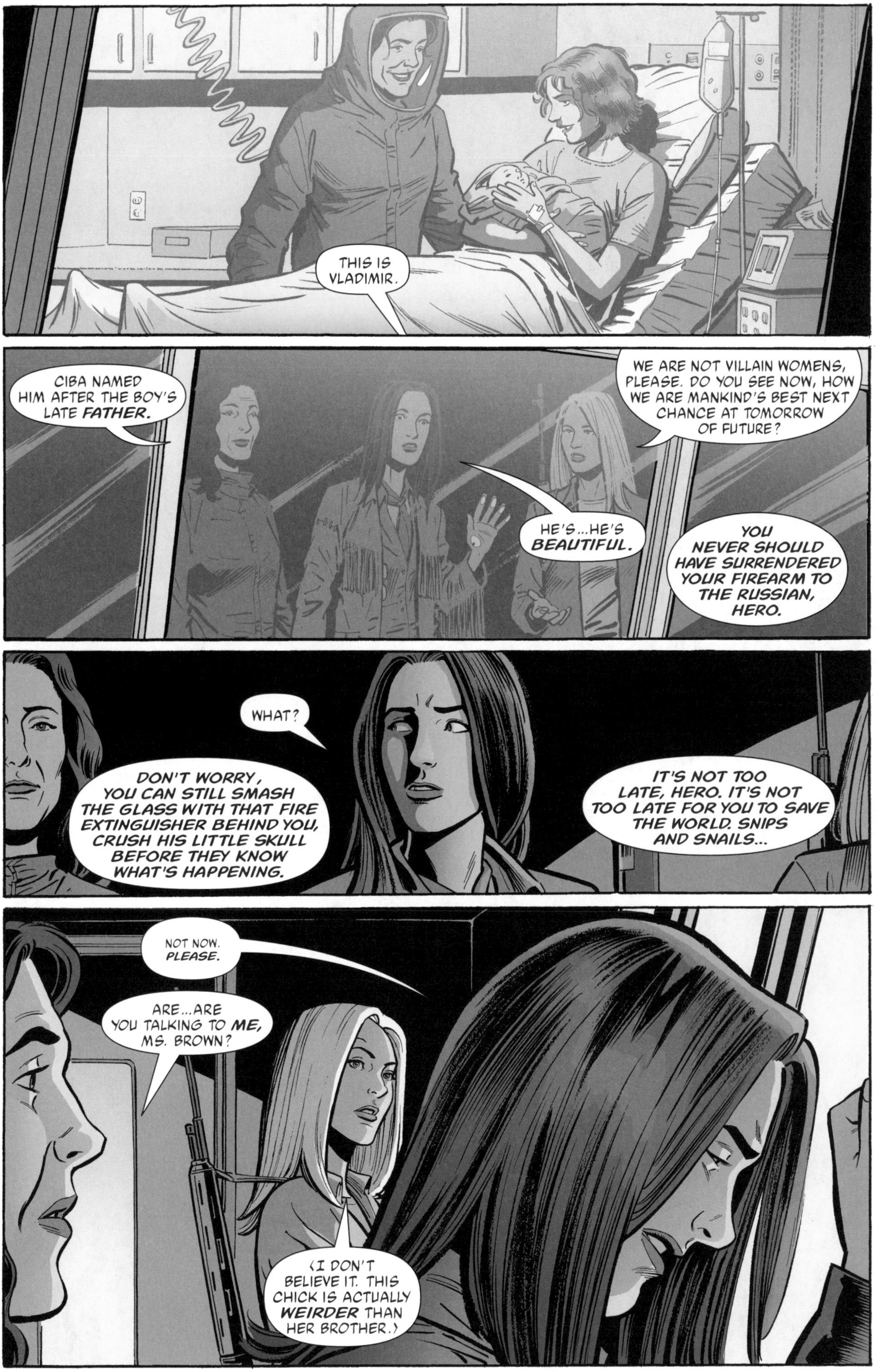
THIS IS VLADIMIR.
CIBA NAMED HIM AFTER THE BOY'S LATE FATHER.
WE ARE NOT VILLAIN WOMENS, PLEASE. DO YOU SEE NOW, HOW WE ARE MANKIND'S BEST NEXT CHANCE AT TOMORROW OF FUTURE?
HE'S...HE'S BEAUTIFUL.
YOU NEVER SHOULD HAVE SURRENDERED YOUR FIREARM TO THE RUSSIAN, HERO.
WHAT?
DON'T WORRY, YOU CAN STILL SMASH THE GLASS WITH THAT FIRE EXTINGUISHER BEHIND YOU, CRUSH HIS LITTLE SKULL BEFORE THEY KNOW WHAT'S HAPPENING.
IT'S NOT TOO LATE, HERO. IT'S NOT TOO LATE FOR YOU TO SAVE THE WORLD. SNIPS AND SNAILS...
NOT NOW. PLEASE.
ARE...ARE YOU TALKING TO ME, MS. BROWN?
‹I DON'T BELIEVE IT. THIS CHICK IS ACTUALLY WEIRDER THAN HER BROTHER.›

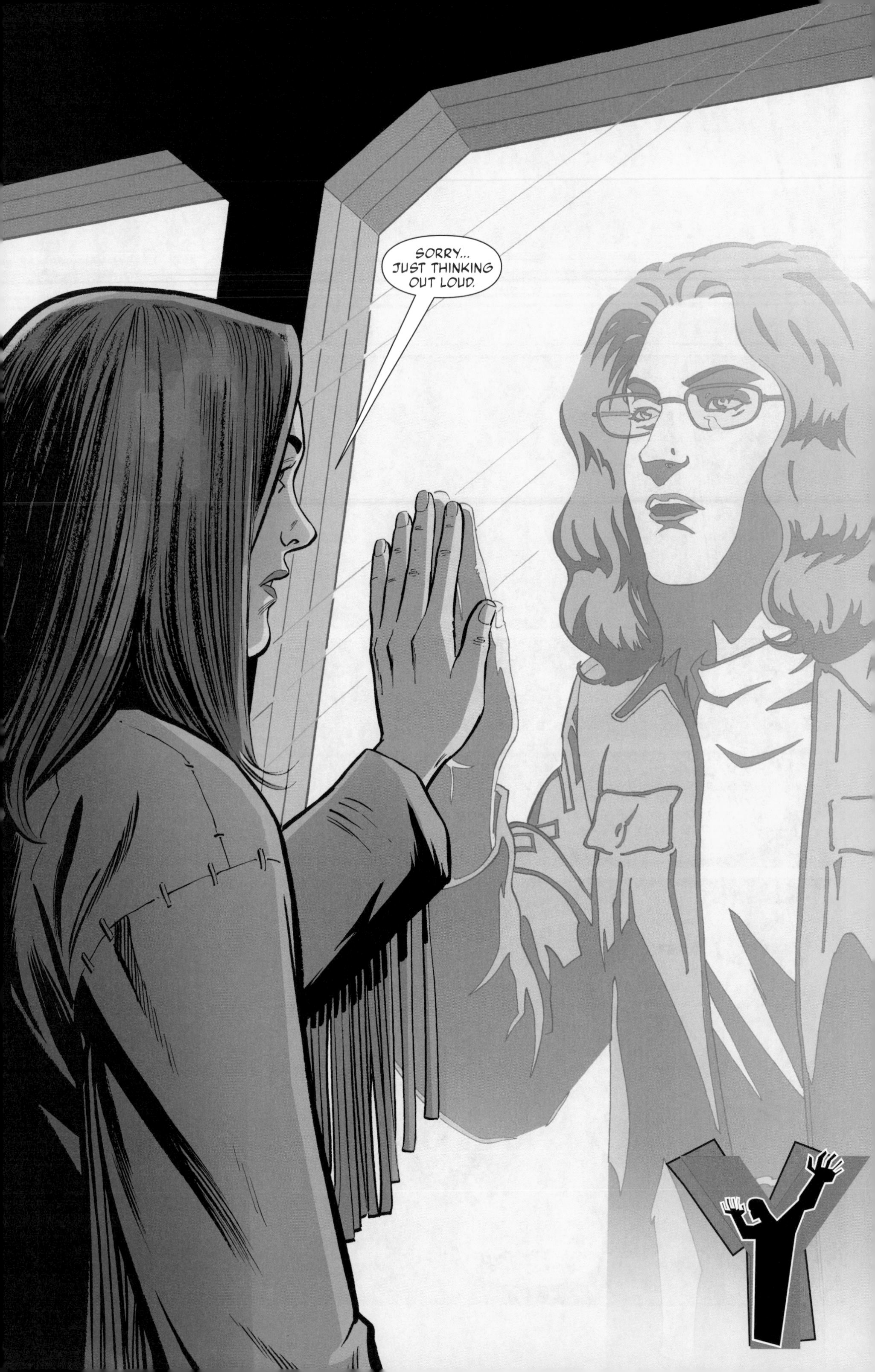
SORRY... JUST THINKING OUT LOUD.

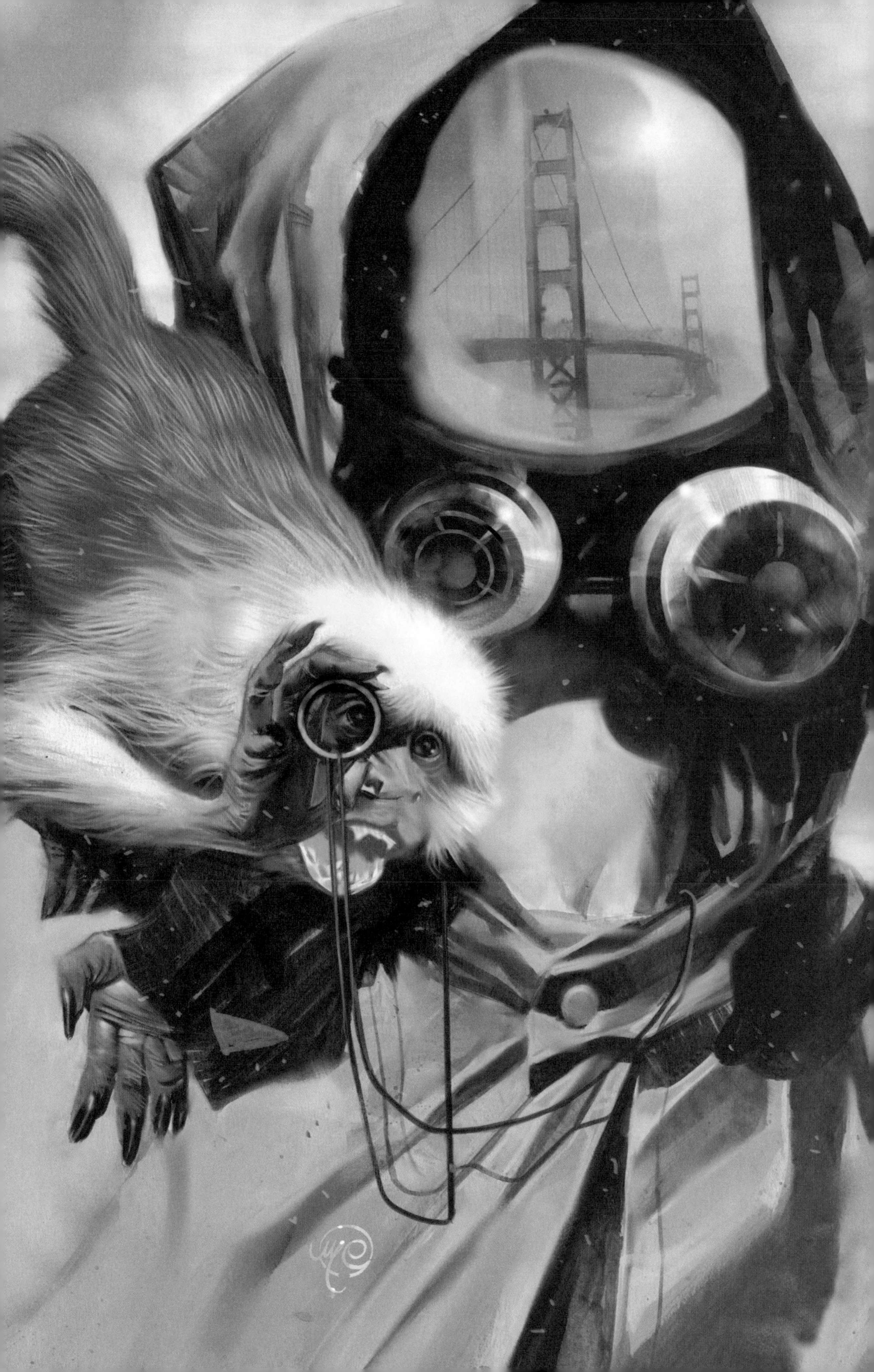

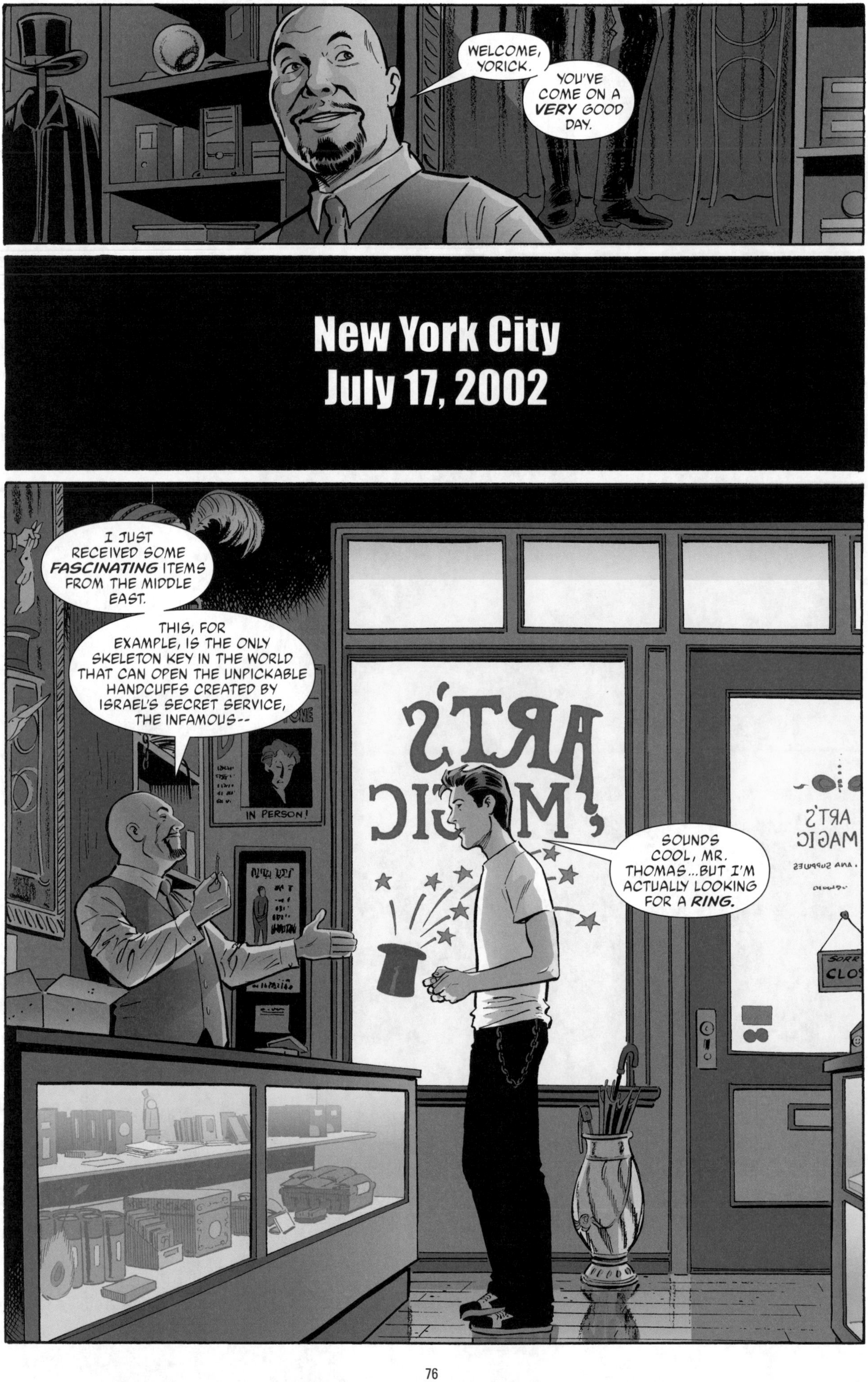
WELCOME, YORICK.
YOU'VE COME ON A VERY GOOD DAY.
New York City
July 17, 2002
I JUST RECEIVED SOME FASCINATING ITEMS FROM THE MIDDLE EAST.
THIS, FOR EXAMPLE, IS THE ONLY SKELETON KEY IN THE WORLD THAT CAN OPEN THE UNPICKABLE HANDCUFFS CREATED BY ISRAEL'S SECRET SERVICE, THE INFAMOUS--
IN PERSON!
SOUNDS COOL, MR. THOMAS...BUT I'M ACTUALLY LOOKING FOR A RING.

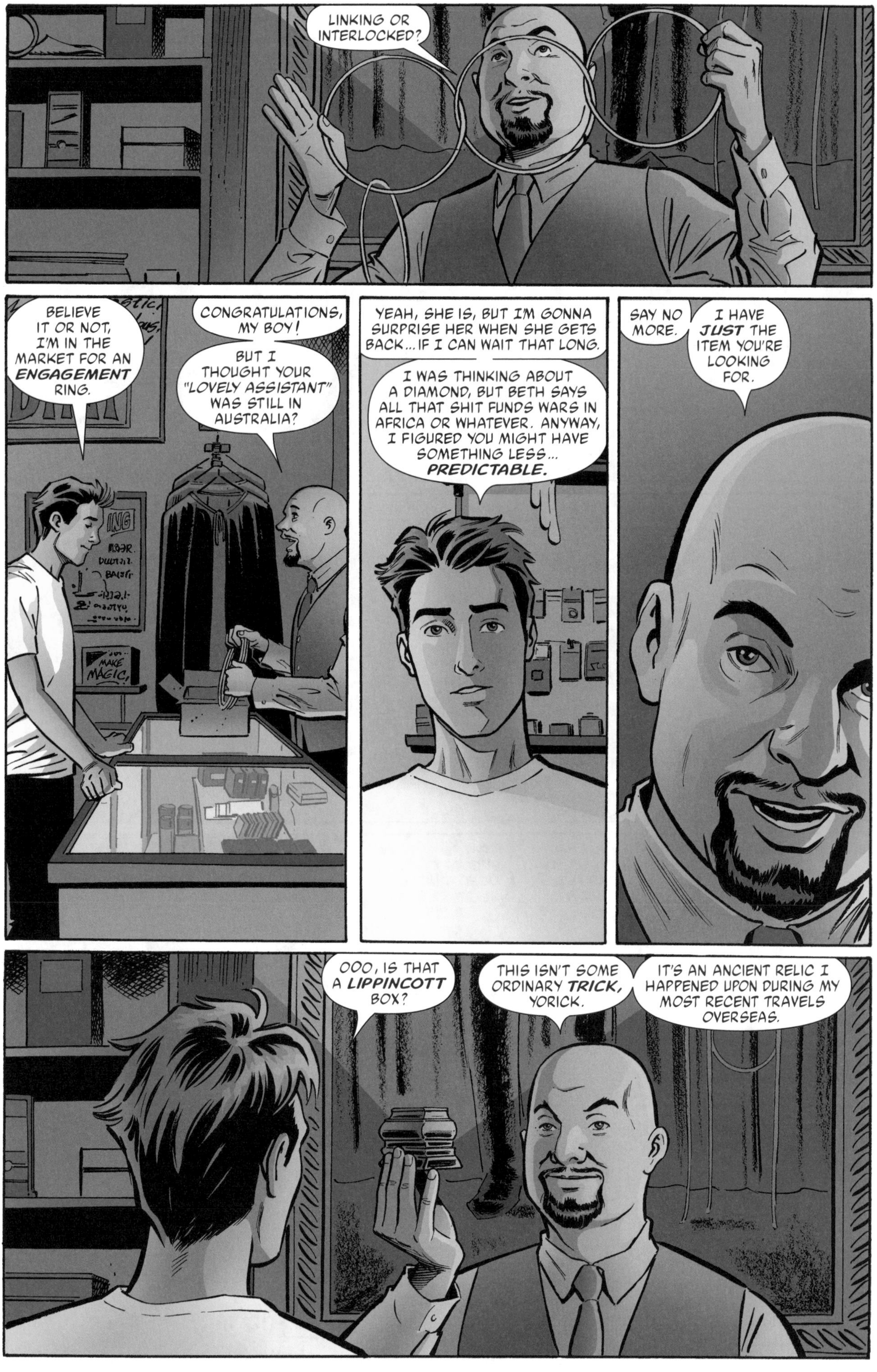
LINKING OR INTERLOCKED?
BELIEVE IT OR NOT, I'M IN THE MARKET FOR AN ENGAGEMENT RING.
CONGRATULATIONS, MY BOY!
BUT I THOUGHT YOUR "LOVELY ASSISTANT" WAS STILL IN AUSTRALIA?
MAKE MAGIC.
YEAH, SHE IS, BUT I'M GONNA SURPRISE HER WHEN SHE GETS BACK... IF I CAN WAIT THAT LONG.
I WAS THINKING ABOUT A DIAMOND, BUT BETH SAYS ALL THAT SHIT FUNDS WARS IN AFRICA OR WHATEVER. ANYWAY, I FIGURED YOU MIGHT HAVE SOMETHING LESS... PREDICTABLE.
SAY NO MORE.
I HAVE JUST THE ITEM YOU'RE LOOKING FOR.
OOO, IS THAT A LIPPINCOTT BOX?
THIS ISN'T SOME ORDINARY TRICK, YORICK.
IT'S AN ANCIENT RELIC I HAPPENED UPON DURING MY MOST RECENT TRAVELS OVERSEAS.

OH, SAVE THE OLD MAN FROM GREMLINS ROUTINE, MR. T.

IT'S TRUE!

DO YOU SEE HOW THE RING GLISTENS LIKE GOLD IN ONE LIGHT...

...AND SILVER IN THE NEXT? THIS REPRESENTS THE MALE AND FEMALE SIDES WHICH ALL OF US POSSESS.

MANY CULTURES BELIEVE THAT MEN AND WOMEN ARE *REVERSED* AT THE MOMENT OF PROPOSAL. THE YOUNG LADY'S FINGER IS TRANSFORMED INTO A SYMBOLIC *PHALLUS*, WHILE THE GENTLEMAN PRESENTING THE RING--

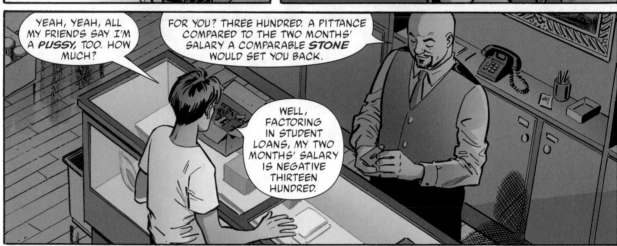

YEAH, YEAH, ALL MY FRIENDS SAY I'M A *PUSSY*, TOO. HOW MUCH?

FOR YOU? THREE HUNDRED. A PITTANCE COMPARED TO THE TWO MONTHS' SALARY A COMPARABLE *STONE* WOULD SET YOU BACK.

WELL, FACTORING IN STUDENT LOANS, MY TWO MONTHS' SALARY IS NEGATIVE THIRTEEN HUNDRED.

OF COURSE, IF YOU'D LIKE SOMETHING LESS *DISTINCTIVE* FOR YOUR BRIDE...

ARTS MAGIC

CLOSED

NO! NO, THAT ONE...THAT ONE FEELS *RIGHT*.

THROW IN FIFTY SHEETS OF FLASH PAPER, AND YOU'VE GOT YOURSELF A DEAL.

YOU, YOUNG MAN, ARE WISE BEYOND YOUR YEARS.

ABSOLUTELY NO REFUNDS

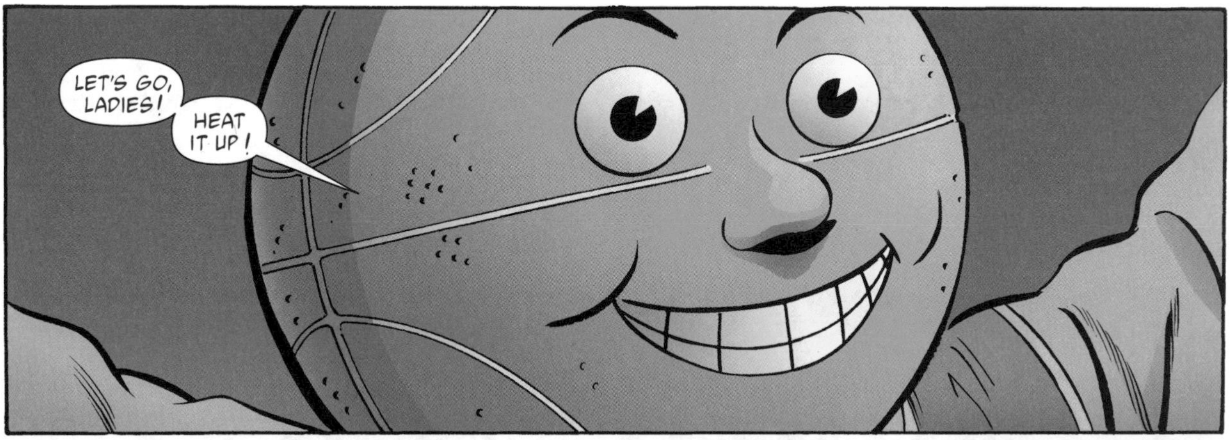
LET'S GO, LADIES!
HEAT IT UP!

**San Francisco, California**
**Now**

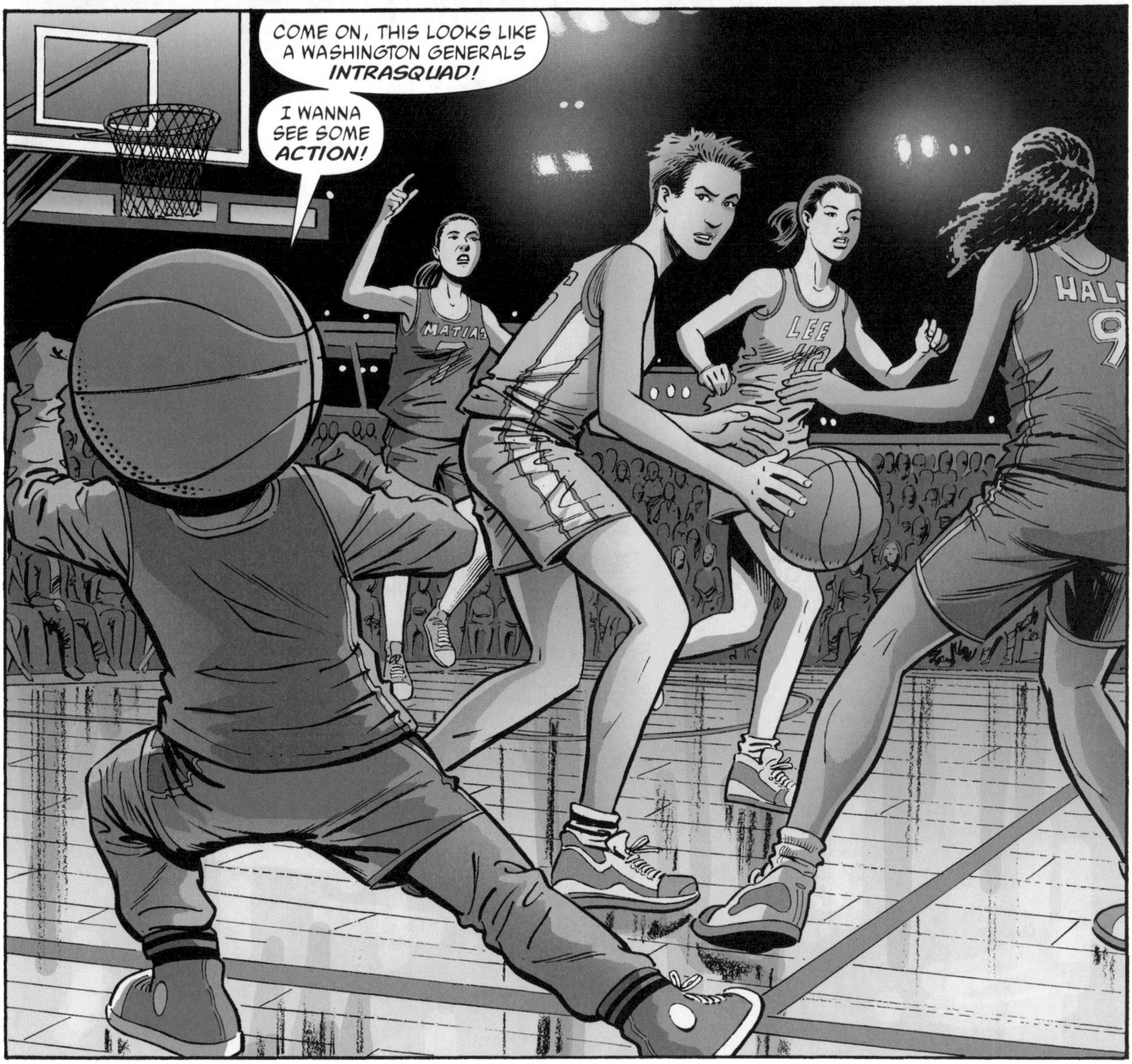
COME ON, THIS LOOKS LIKE A WASHINGTON GENERALS *INTRASQUAD!*
I WANNA SEE SOME *ACTION!*
MATIAS
LEE

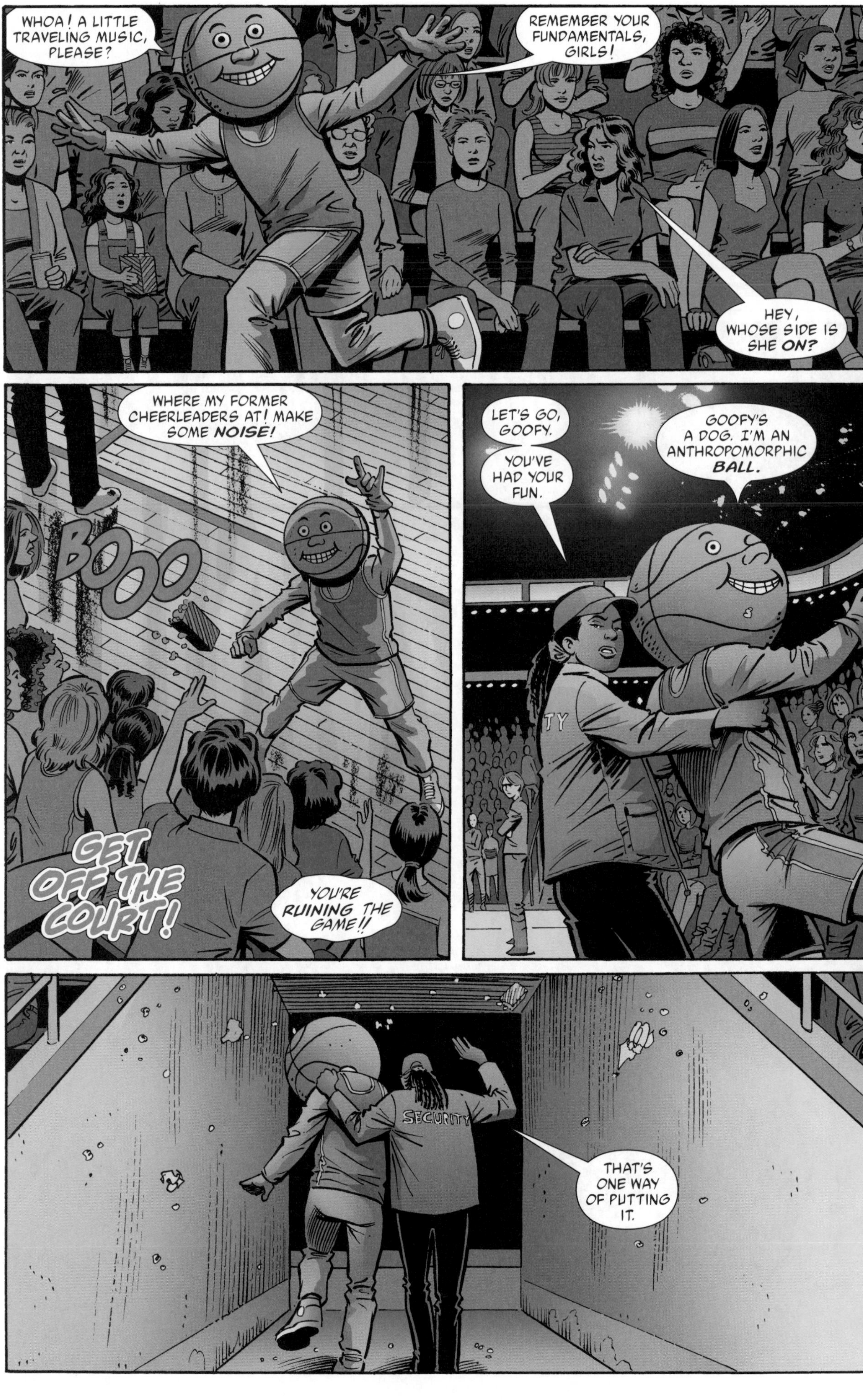
WHOA! A LITTLE TRAVELING MUSIC, PLEASE?
REMEMBER YOUR FUNDAMENTALS, GIRLS!
HEY, WHOSE SIDE IS SHE ON?
WHERE MY FORMER CHEERLEADERS AT! MAKE SOME NOISE!
BOOO
GET OFF THE COURT!
YOU'RE RUINING THE GAME!!
LET'S GO, GOOFY.
YOU'VE HAD YOUR FUN.
GOOFY'S A DOG. I'M AN ANTHROPOMORPHIC BALL.
SECURITY
THAT'S ONE WAY OF PUTTING IT.

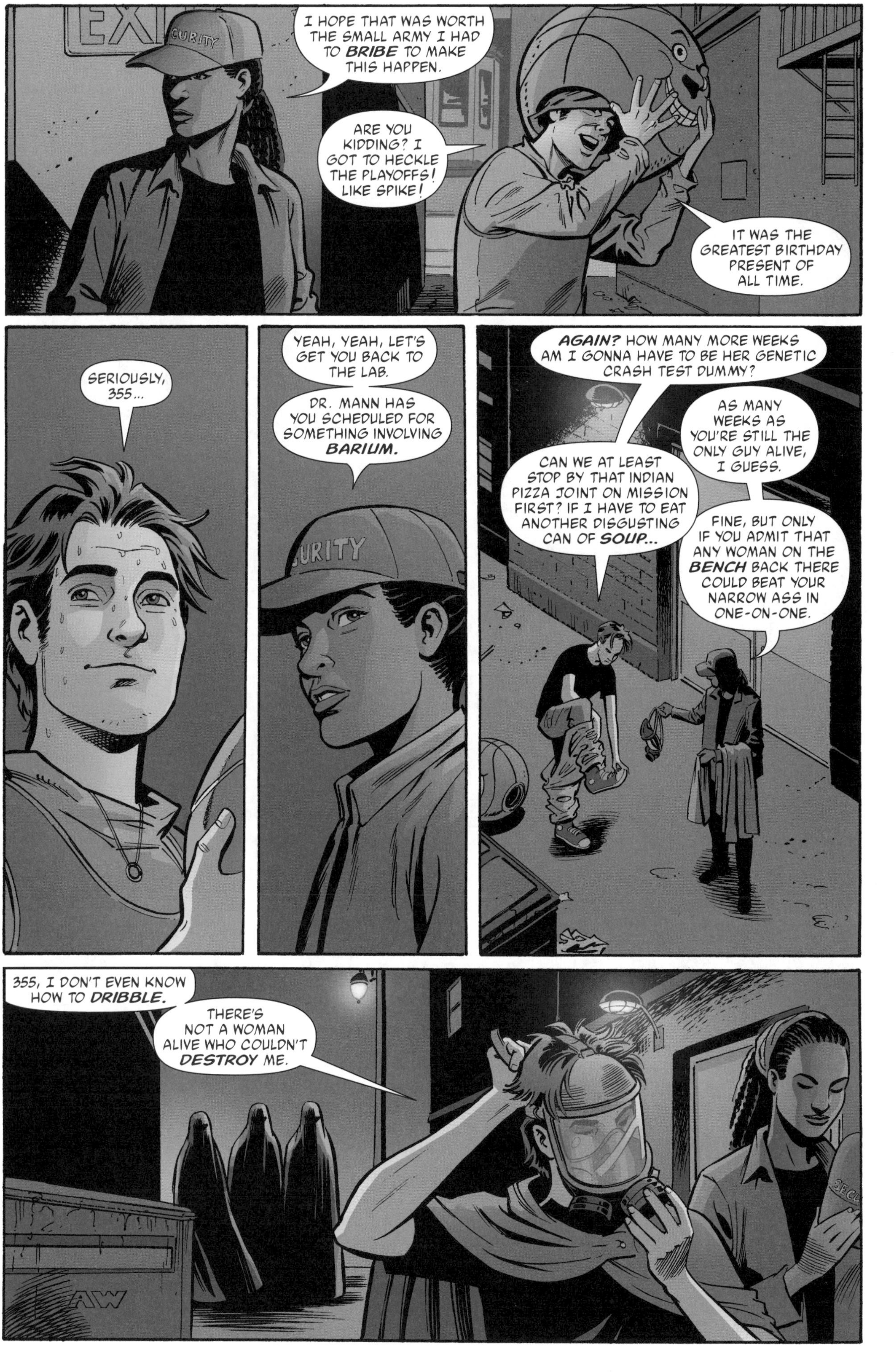
I HOPE THAT WAS WORTH THE SMALL ARMY I HAD TO **BRIBE** TO MAKE THIS HAPPEN.
ARE YOU KIDDING? I GOT TO HECKLE THE PLAYOFFS! LIKE SPIKE!
IT WAS THE GREATEST BIRTHDAY PRESENT OF ALL TIME.
SERIOUSLY, 355...
YEAH, YEAH, LET'S GET YOU BACK TO THE LAB.
DR. MANN HAS YOU SCHEDULED FOR SOMETHING INVOLVING **BARIUM.**
**AGAIN?** HOW MANY MORE WEEKS AM I GONNA HAVE TO BE HER GENETIC CRASH TEST DUMMY?
AS MANY WEEKS AS YOU'RE STILL THE ONLY GUY ALIVE, I GUESS.
CAN WE AT LEAST STOP BY THAT INDIAN PIZZA JOINT ON MISSION FIRST? IF I HAVE TO EAT ANOTHER DISGUSTING CAN OF **SOUP...**
FINE, BUT ONLY IF YOU ADMIT THAT ANY WOMAN ON THE **BENCH** BACK THERE COULD BEAT YOUR NARROW ASS IN ONE-ON-ONE.
355, I DON'T EVEN KNOW HOW TO **DRIBBLE.**
THERE'S NOT A WOMAN ALIVE WHO COULDN'T **DESTROY** ME.

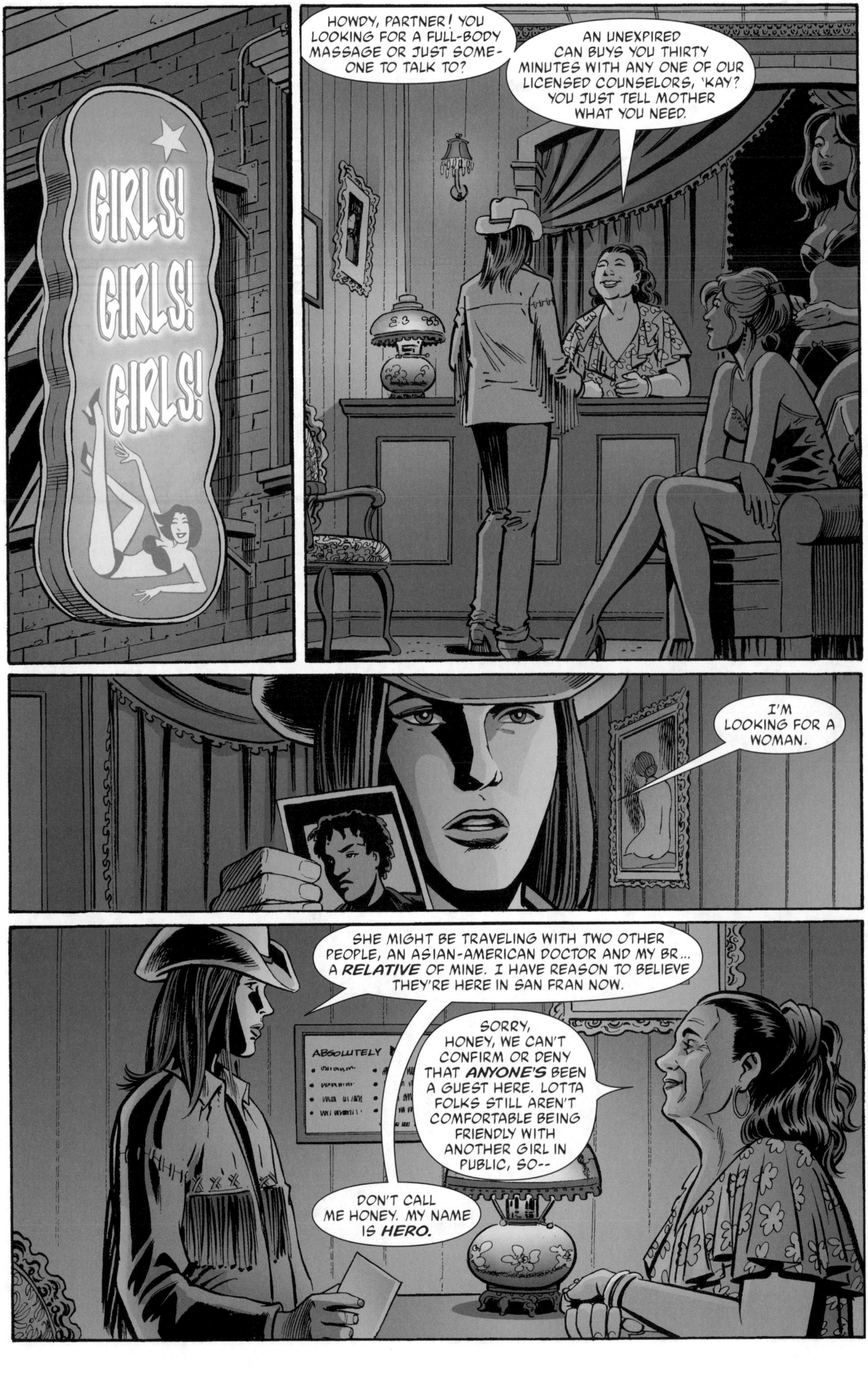
GIRLS! GIRLS! GIRLS!
HOWDY, PARTNER! YOU LOOKING FOR A FULL-BODY MASSAGE OR JUST SOME-ONE TO TALK TO?
AN UNEXPIRED CAN BUYS YOU THIRTY MINUTES WITH ANY ONE OF OUR LICENSED COUNSELORS, 'KAY? YOU JUST TELL MOTHER WHAT YOU NEED.
I'M LOOKING FOR A WOMAN.
SHE MIGHT BE TRAVELING WITH TWO OTHER PEOPLE, AN ASIAN-AMERICAN DOCTOR AND MY BR... A **RELATIVE** OF MINE. I HAVE REASON TO BELIEVE THEY'RE HERE IN SAN FRAN NOW.
SORRY, HONEY, WE CAN'T CONFIRM OR DENY THAT **ANYONE'S** BEEN A GUEST HERE. LOTTA FOLKS STILL AREN'T COMFORTABLE BEING FRIENDLY WITH ANOTHER GIRL IN PUBLIC, SO--
DON'T CALL ME HONEY. MY NAME IS ***HERO.***

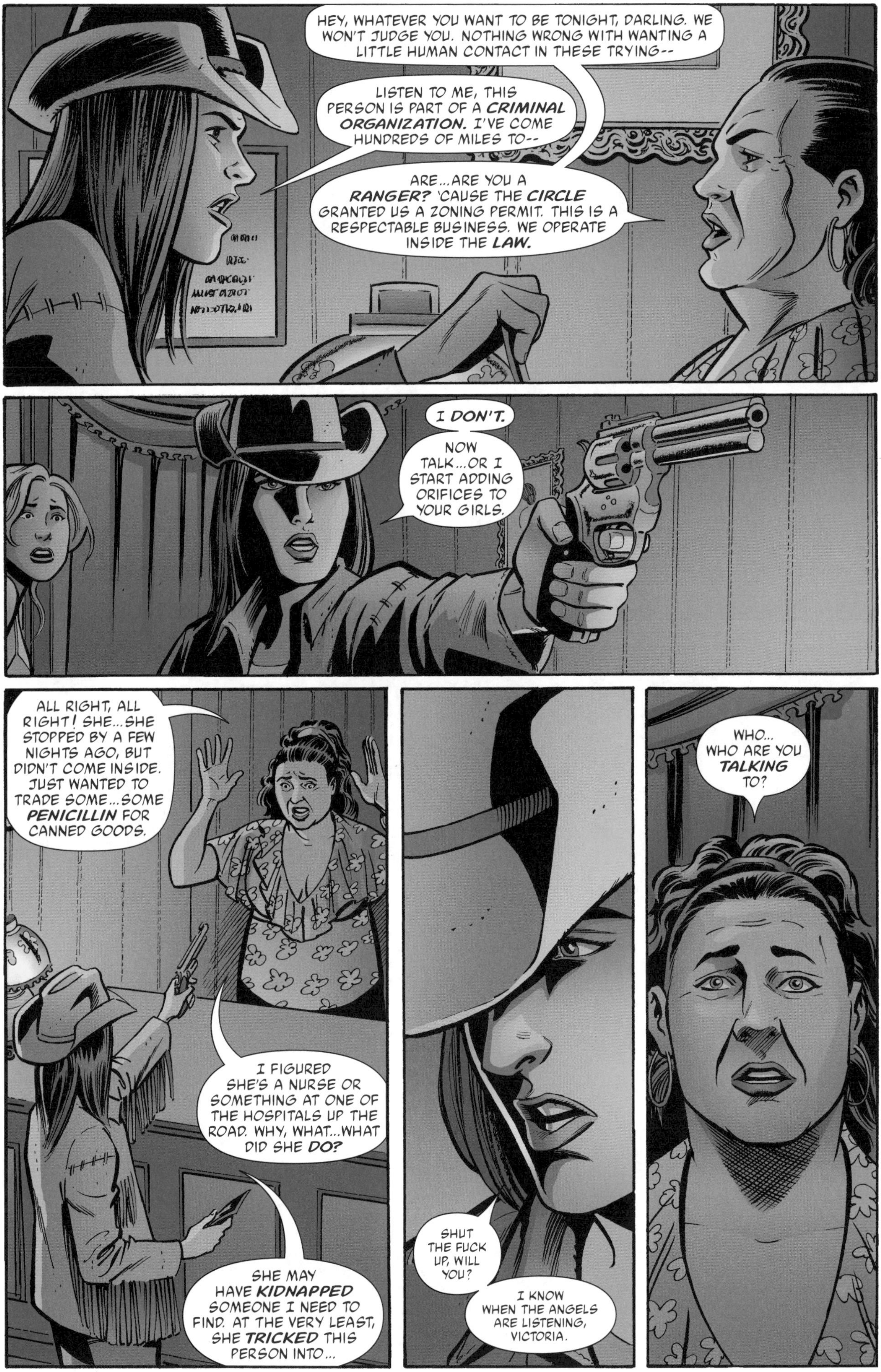
HEY, WHATEVER YOU WANT TO BE TONIGHT, DARLING. WE WON'T JUDGE YOU. NOTHING WRONG WITH WANTING A LITTLE HUMAN CONTACT IN THESE TRYING--
LISTEN TO ME, THIS PERSON IS PART OF A CRIMINAL ORGANIZATION. I'VE COME HUNDREDS OF MILES TO--
ARE...ARE YOU A RANGER? 'CAUSE THE CIRCLE GRANTED US A ZONING PERMIT. THIS IS A RESPECTABLE BUSINESS. WE OPERATE INSIDE THE LAW.
I DON'T.
NOW TALK...OR I START ADDING ORIFICES TO YOUR GIRLS.
ALL RIGHT, ALL RIGHT! SHE...SHE STOPPED BY A FEW NIGHTS AGO, BUT DIDN'T COME INSIDE. JUST WANTED TO TRADE SOME...SOME PENICILLIN FOR CANNED GOODS.
I FIGURED SHE'S A NURSE OR SOMETHING AT ONE OF THE HOSPITALS UP THE ROAD. WHY, WHAT...WHAT DID SHE DO?
SHE MAY HAVE KIDNAPPED SOMEONE I NEED TO FIND. AT THE VERY LEAST, SHE TRICKED THIS PERSON INTO...
SHUT THE FUCK UP, WILL YOU?
I KNOW WHEN THE ANGELS ARE LISTENING, VICTORIA.
WHO... WHO ARE YOU TALKING TO?

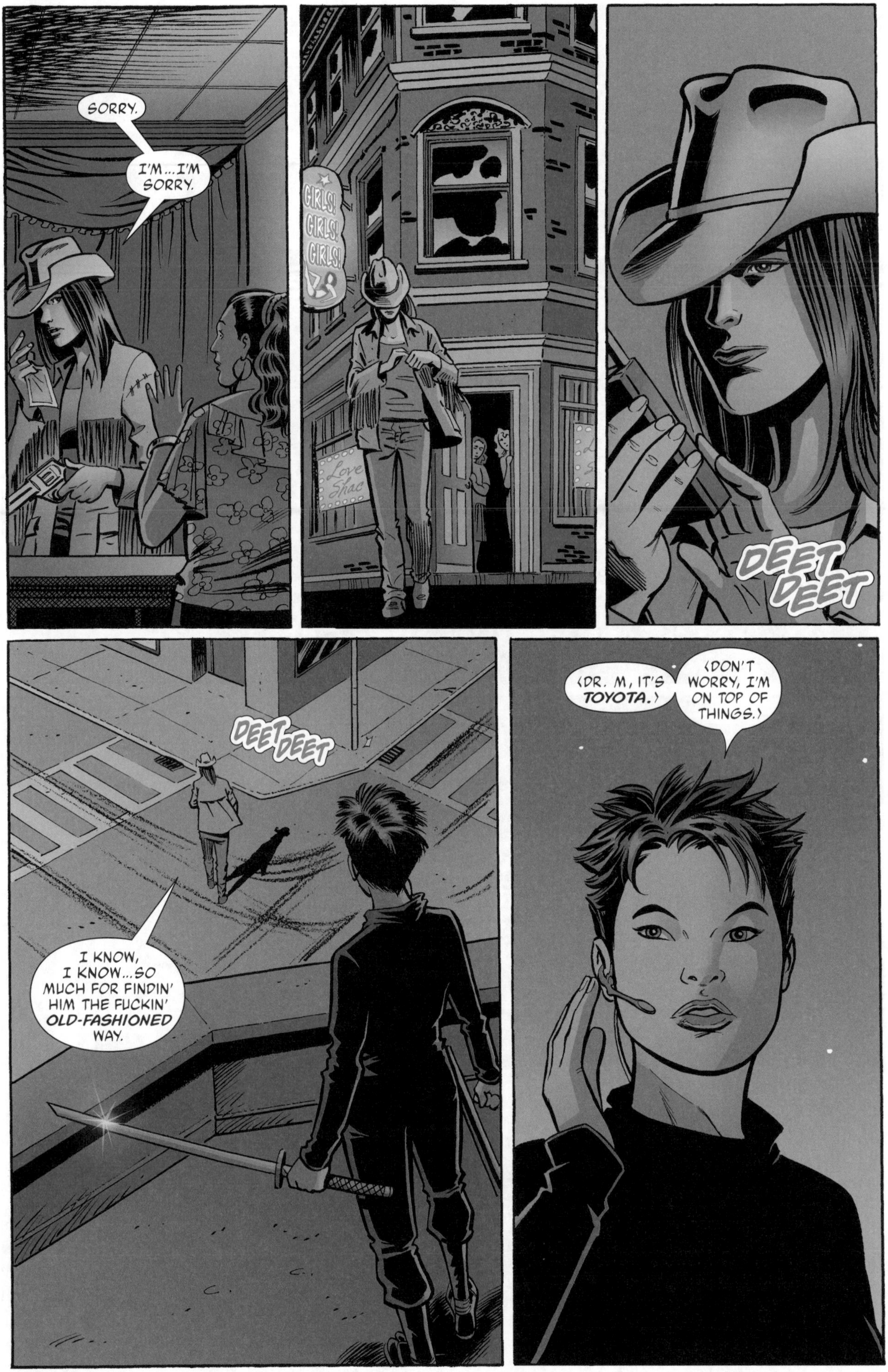
SORRY.
I'M...I'M SORRY.
GIRLS! GIRLS! GIRLS!
Love Shac
DEET DEET
DEET DEET
I KNOW, I KNOW...SO MUCH FOR FINDIN' HIM THE FUCKIN' OLD-FASHIONED WAY.
‹DR. M, IT'S TOYOTA.›
‹DON'T WORRY, I'M ON TOP OF THINGS.›

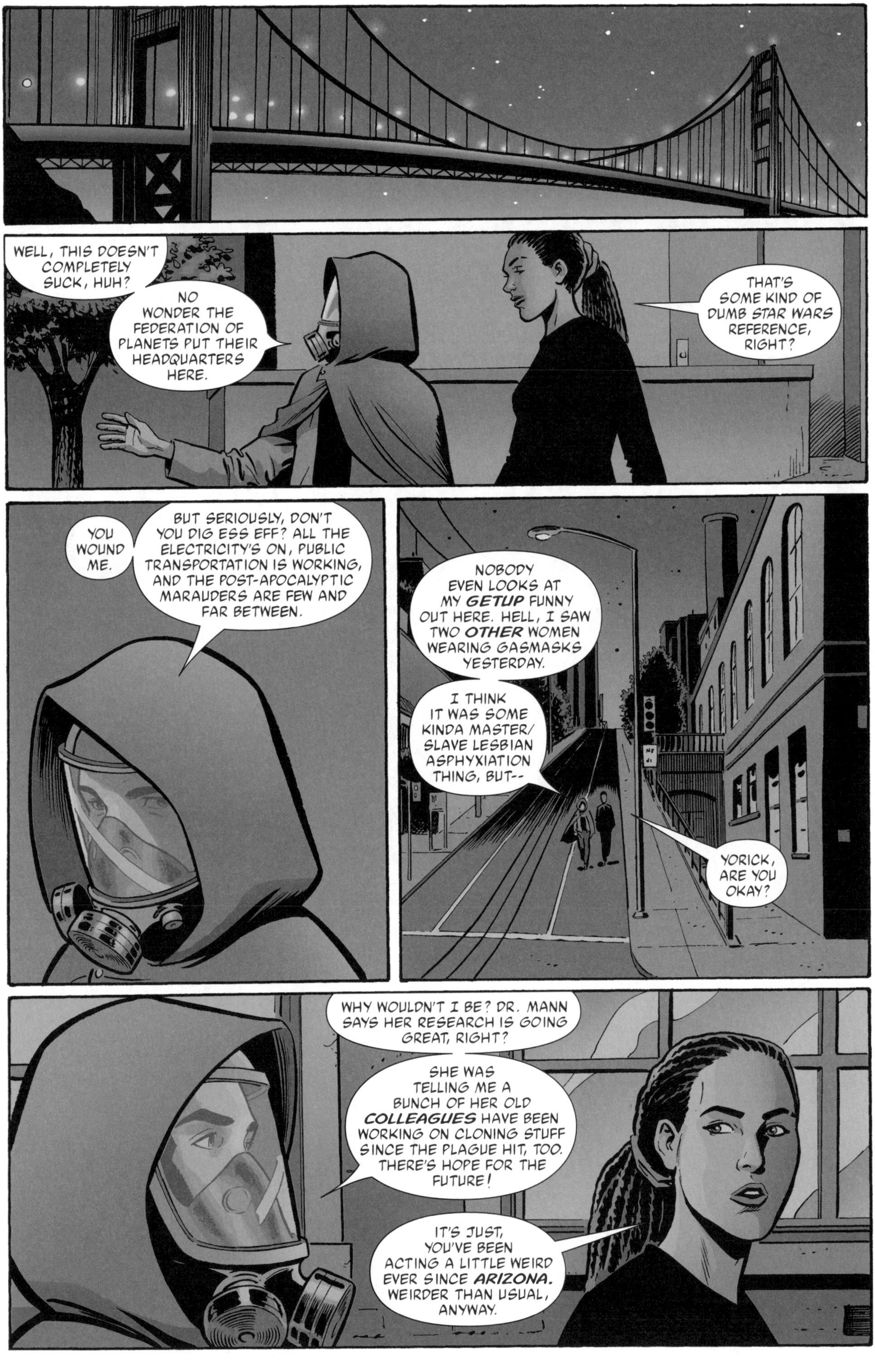
WELL, THIS DOESN'T COMPLETELY SUCK, HUH?
NO WONDER THE FEDERATION OF PLANETS PUT THEIR HEADQUARTERS HERE.
THAT'S SOME KIND OF DUMB STAR WARS REFERENCE, RIGHT?
YOU WOUND ME.
BUT SERIOUSLY, DON'T YOU DIG ESS EFF? ALL THE ELECTRICITY'S ON, PUBLIC TRANSPORTATION IS WORKING, AND THE POST-APOCALYPTIC MARAUDERS ARE FEW AND FAR BETWEEN.
NOBODY EVEN LOOKS AT MY GETUP FUNNY OUT HERE. HELL, I SAW TWO OTHER WOMEN WEARING GASMASKS YESTERDAY.
I THINK IT WAS SOME KINDA MASTER/SLAVE LESBIAN ASPHYXIATION THING, BUT--
YORICK, ARE YOU OKAY?
WHY WOULDN'T I BE? DR. MANN SAYS HER RESEARCH IS GOING GREAT, RIGHT?
SHE WAS TELLING ME A BUNCH OF HER OLD COLLEAGUES HAVE BEEN WORKING ON CLONING STUFF SINCE THE PLAGUE HIT, TOO. THERE'S HOPE FOR THE FUTURE!
IT'S JUST, YOU'VE BEEN ACTING A LITTLE WEIRD EVER SINCE ARIZONA. WEIRDER THAN USUAL, ANYWAY.

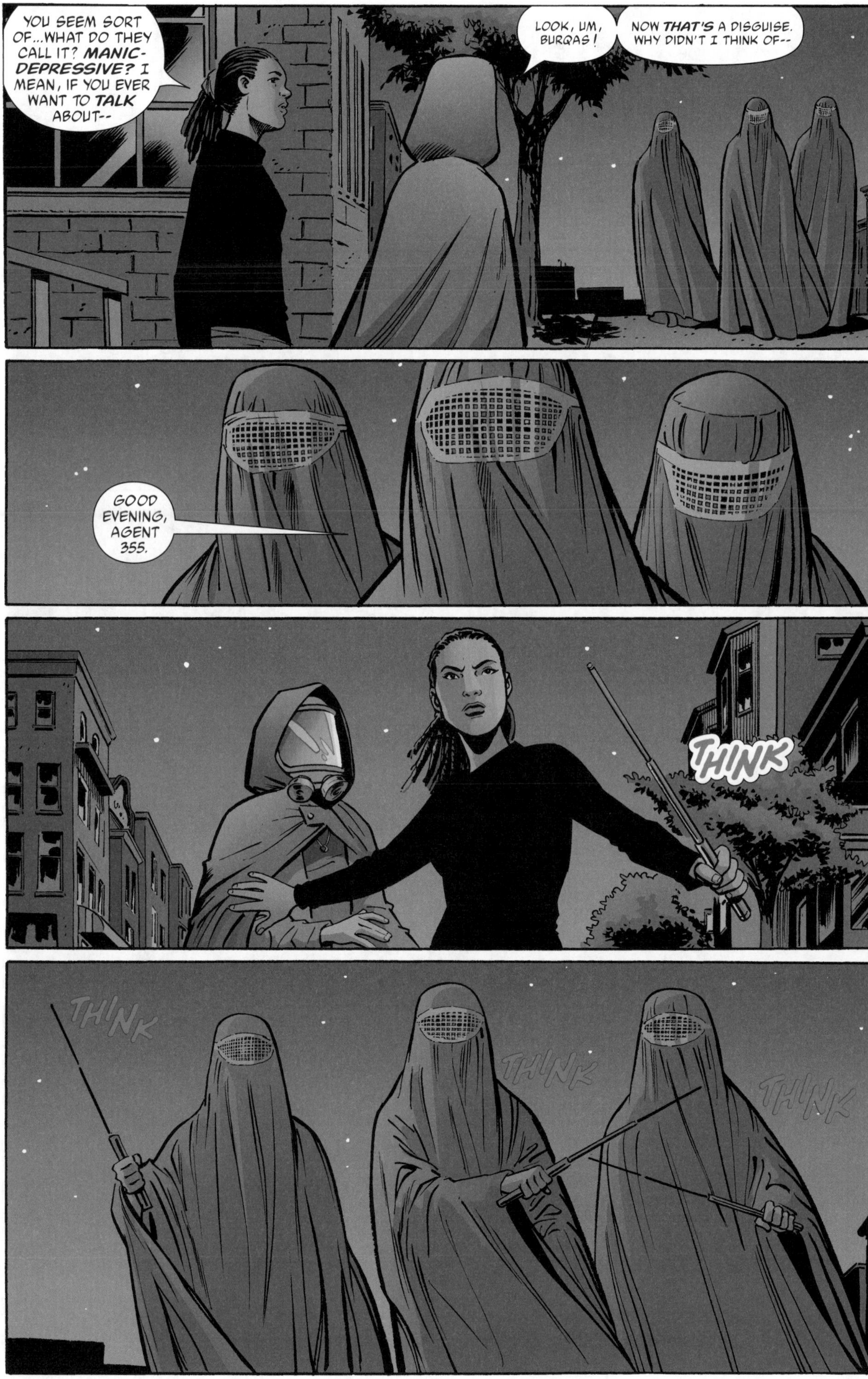
YOU SEEM SORT OF...WHAT DO THEY CALL IT? MANIC-DEPRESSIVE? I MEAN, IF YOU EVER WANT TO TALK ABOUT--
LOOK, UM, BURQAS!
NOW THAT'S A DISGUISE. WHY DIDN'T I THINK OF--
GOOD EVENING, AGENT 355.
THINK
THINK
THINK
THINK

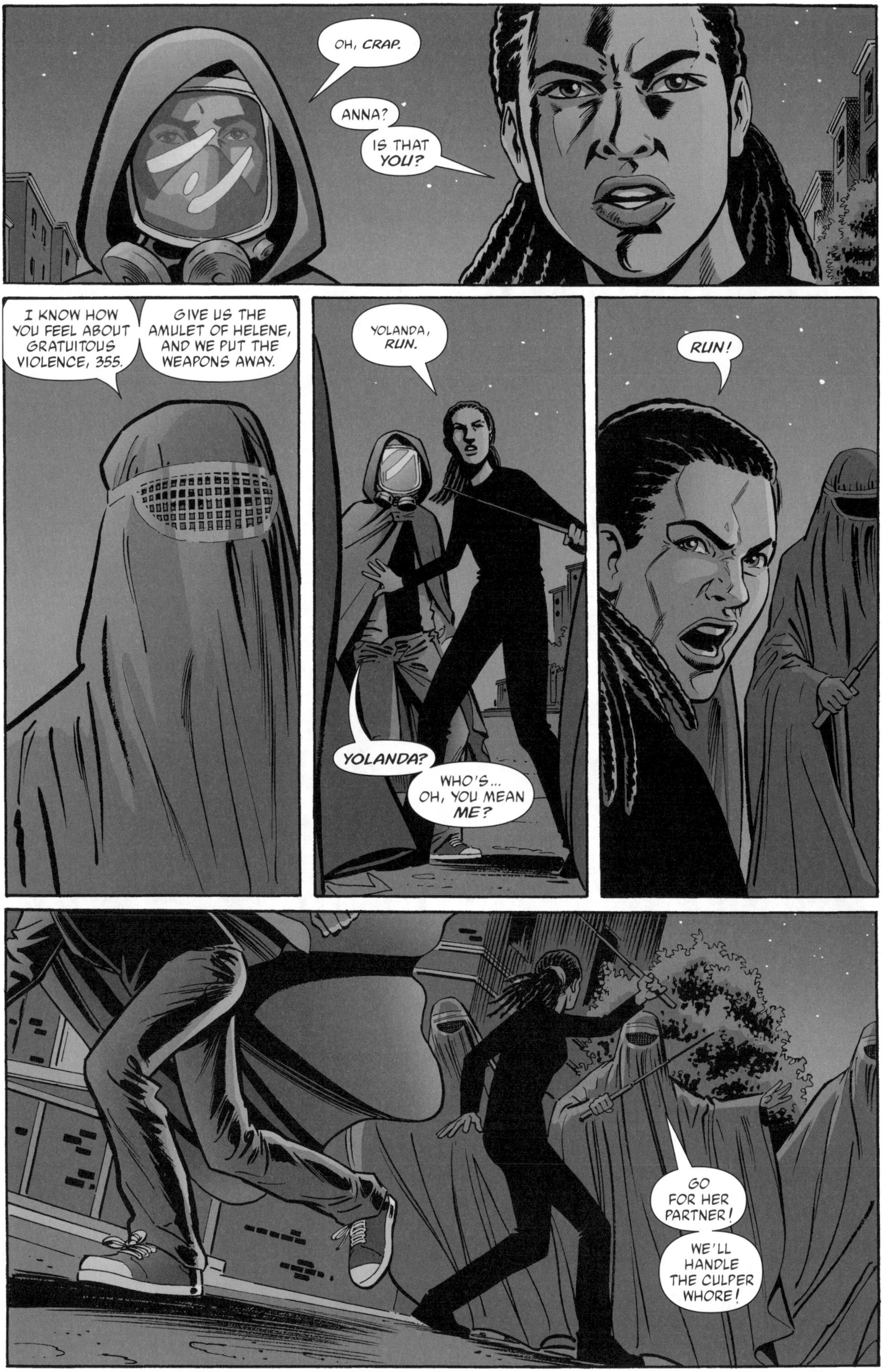
OH, CRAP.
ANNA?
IS THAT YOU?
I KNOW HOW YOU FEEL ABOUT GRATUITOUS VIOLENCE, 355.
GIVE US THE AMULET OF HELENE, AND WE PUT THE WEAPONS AWAY.
YOLANDA, RUN.
YOLANDA?
WHO'S... OH, YOU MEAN ME?
RUN!
GO FOR HER PARTNER!
WE'LL HANDLE THE CULPER WHORE!

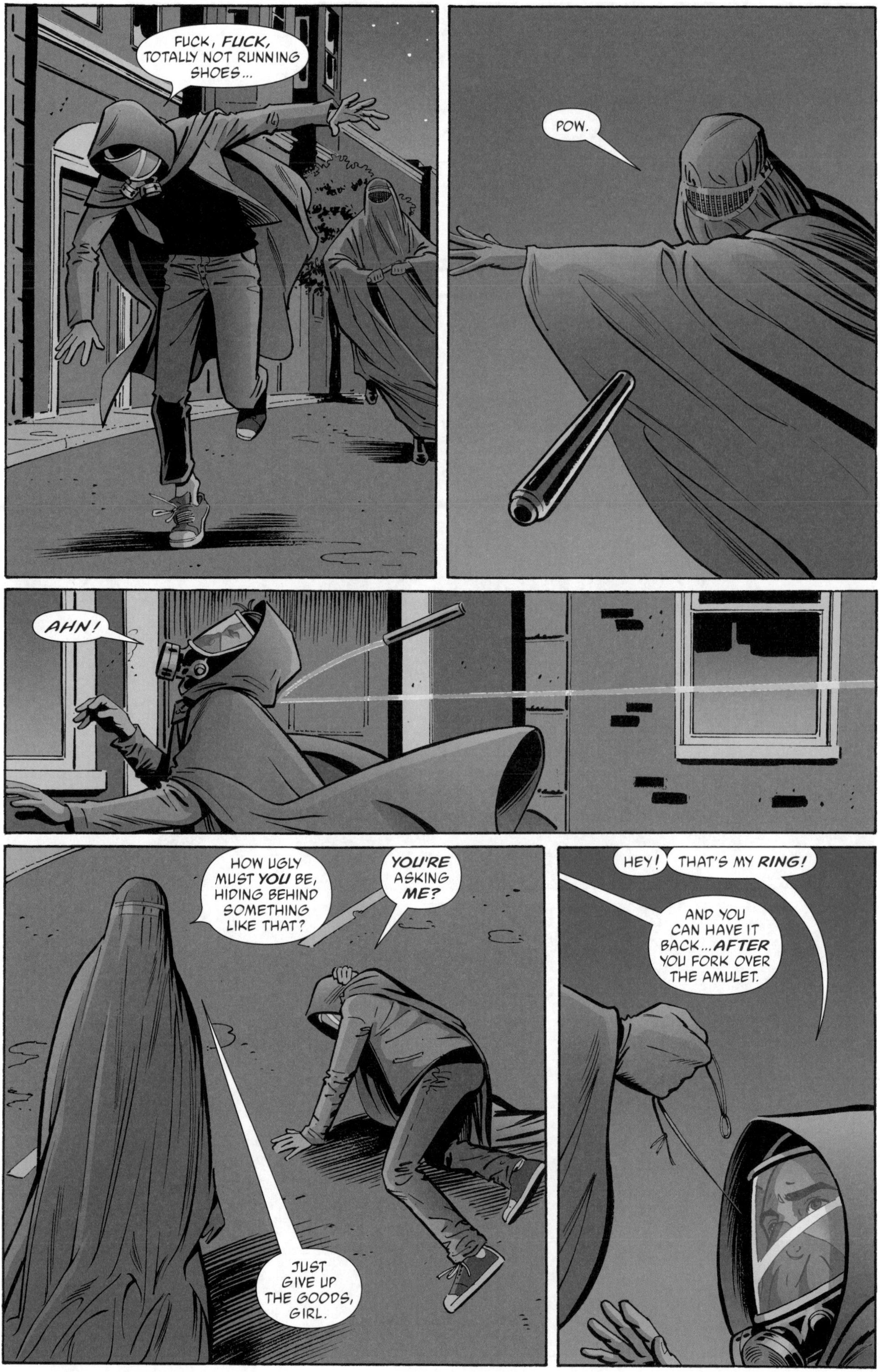
FUCK, FUCK, TOTALLY NOT RUNNING SHOES...
POW.
AHN!
HOW UGLY MUST YOU BE, HIDING BEHIND SOMETHING LIKE THAT?
YOU'RE ASKING ME?
JUST GIVE UP THE GOODS, GIRL.
HEY!
THAT'S MY RING!
AND YOU CAN HAVE IT BACK...AFTER YOU FORK OVER THE AMULET.

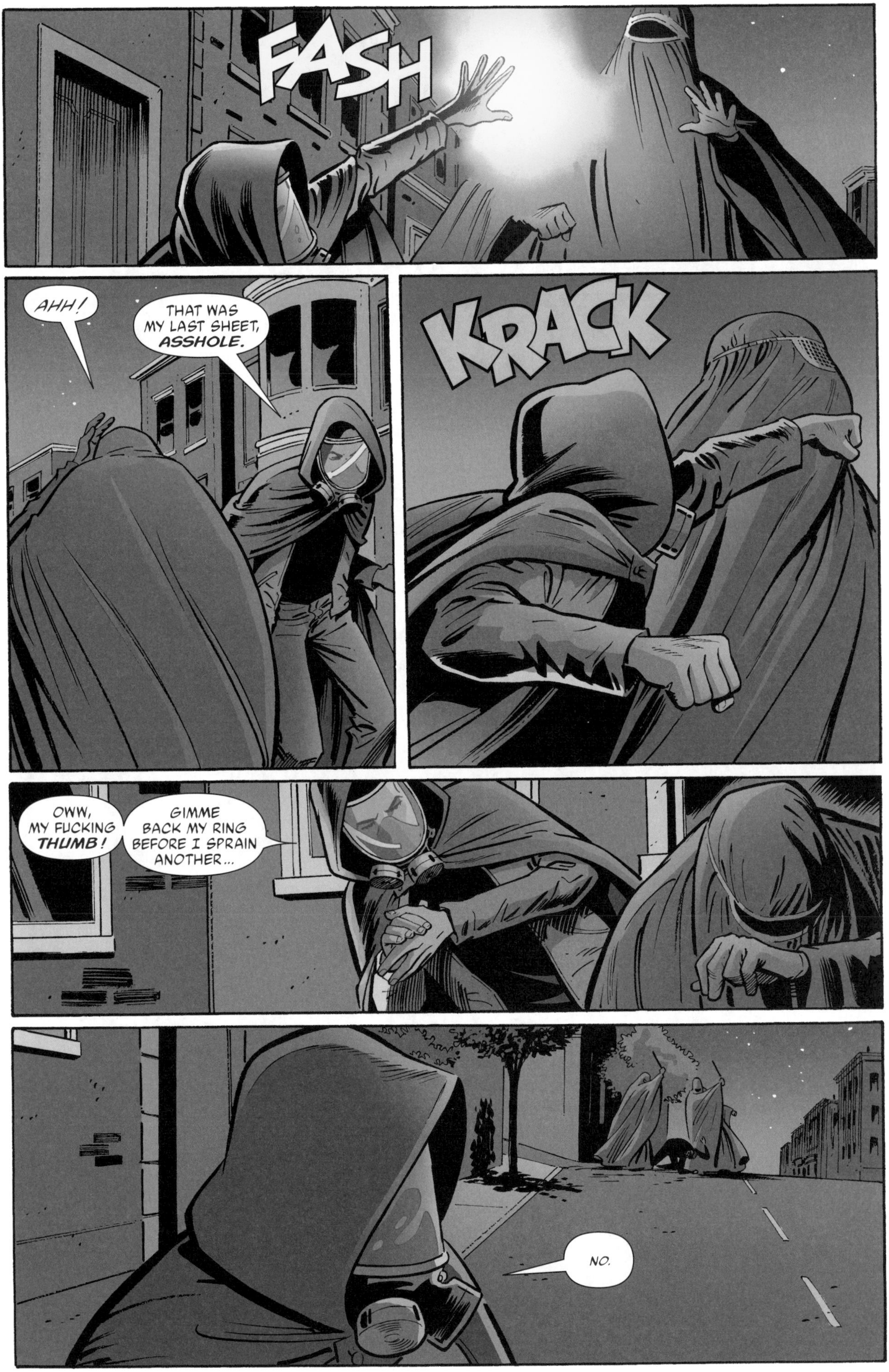
FASH
AHH!
THAT WAS MY LAST SHEET, ASSHOLE.
KRACK
OWW, MY FUCKING THUMB!
GIMME BACK MY RING BEFORE I SPRAIN ANOTHER...
NO.

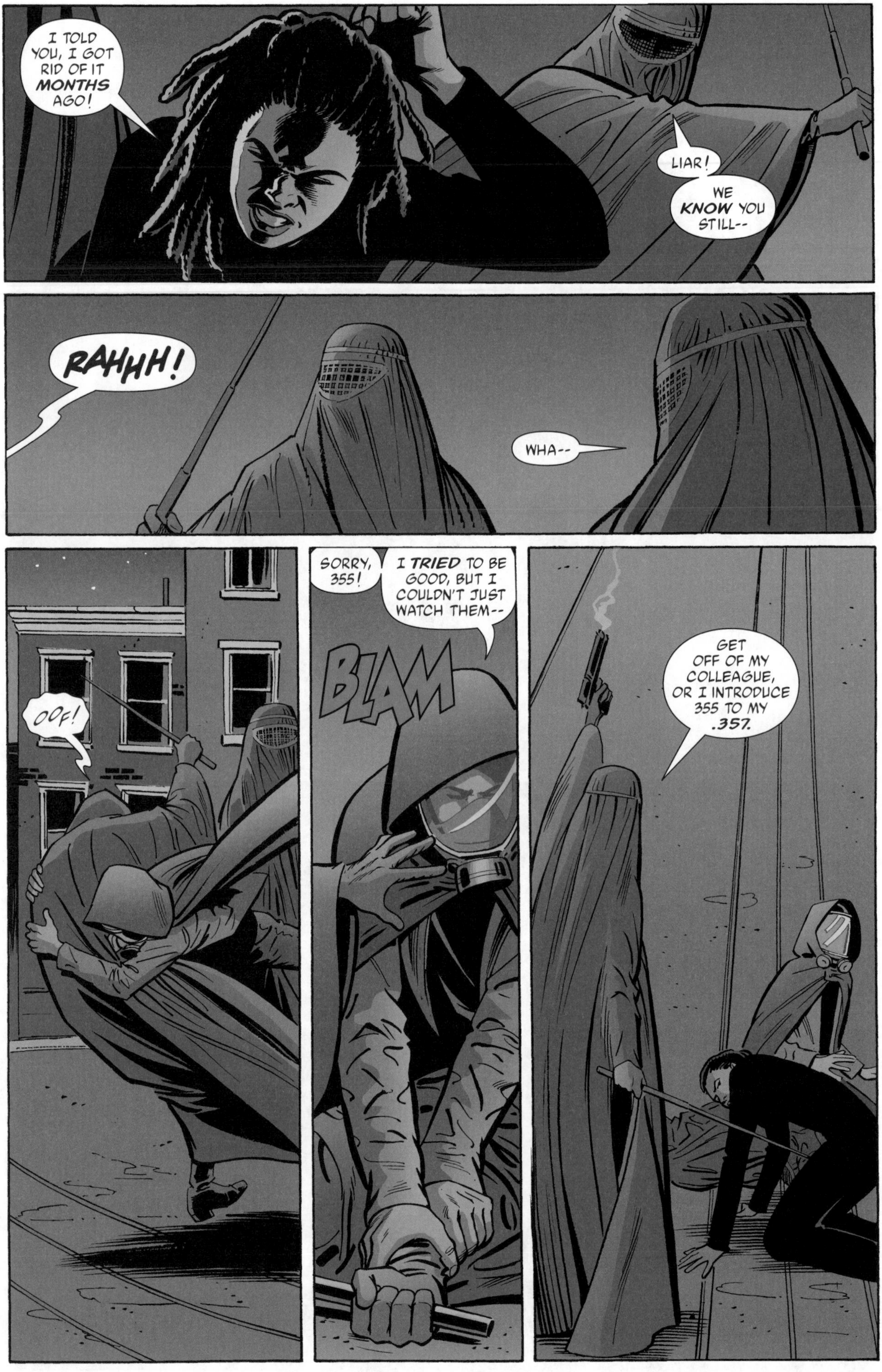
I TOLD YOU, I GOT RID OF IT MONTHS AGO!
LIAR!
WE KNOW YOU STILL--
RAHHH!
WHA--
OOF!
SORRY, 355!
I TRIED TO BE GOOD, BUT I COULDN'T JUST WATCH THEM--
BLAM
GET OFF OF MY COLLEAGUE, OR I INTRODUCE 355 TO MY .357.

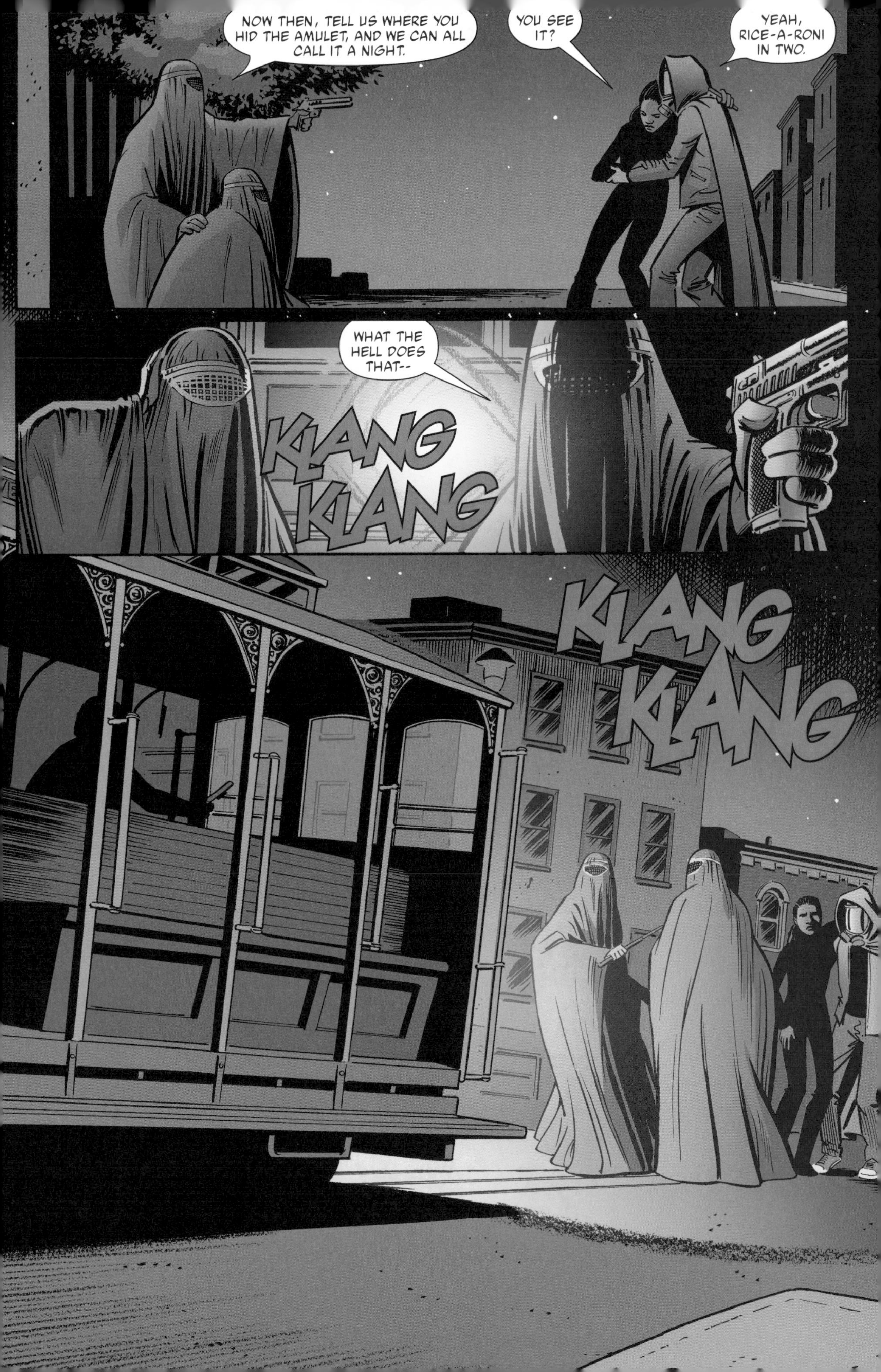
NOW THEN, TELL US WHERE YOU HID THE AMULET, AND WE CAN ALL CALL IT A NIGHT.
YOU SEE IT?
YEAH, RICE-A-RONI IN TWO.
WHAT THE HELL DOES THAT--
KLANG KLANG
KLANG KLANG

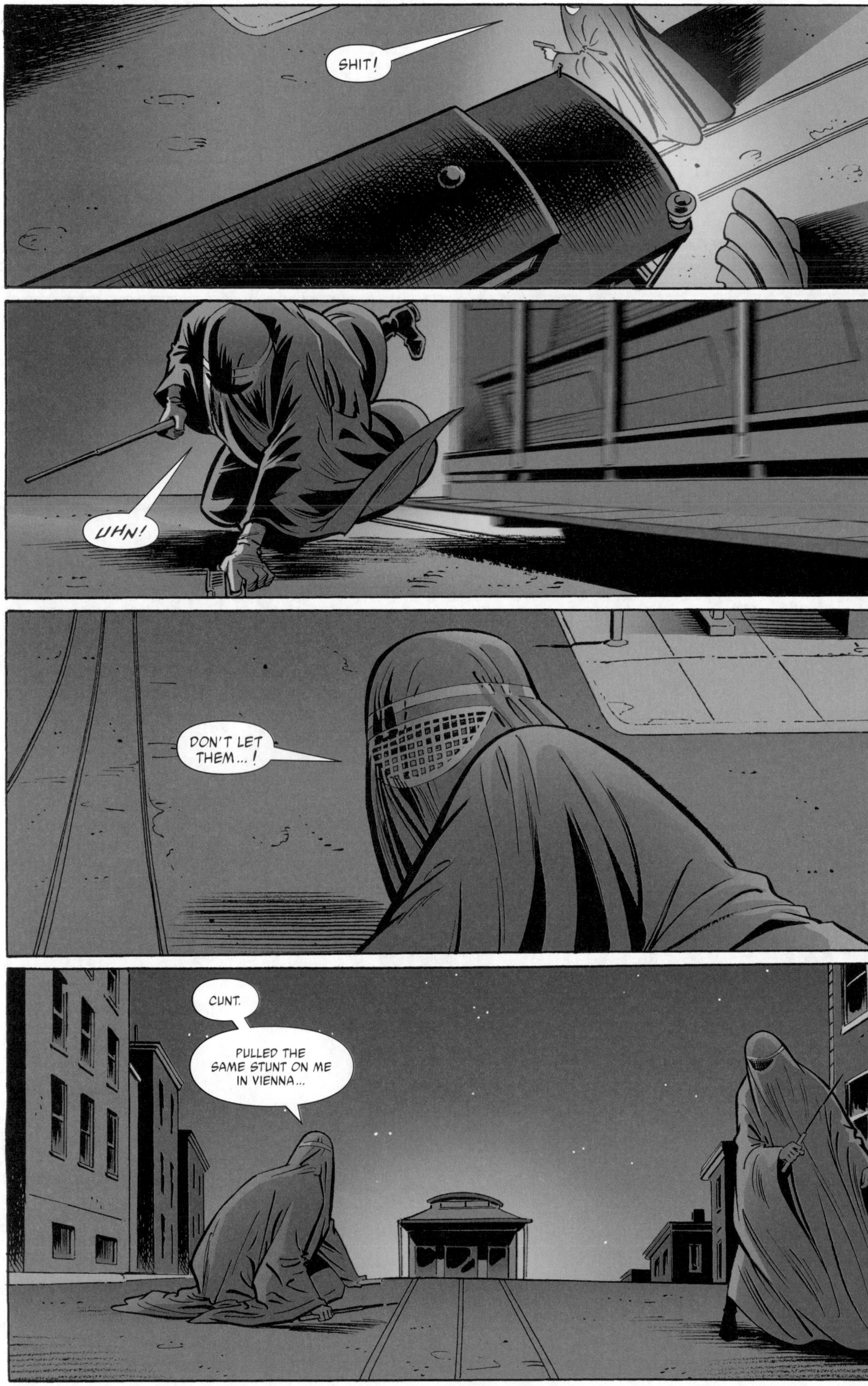
SHIT!
UHN!
DON'T LET THEM...!
CUNT.
PULLED THE SAME STUNT ON ME IN VIENNA...

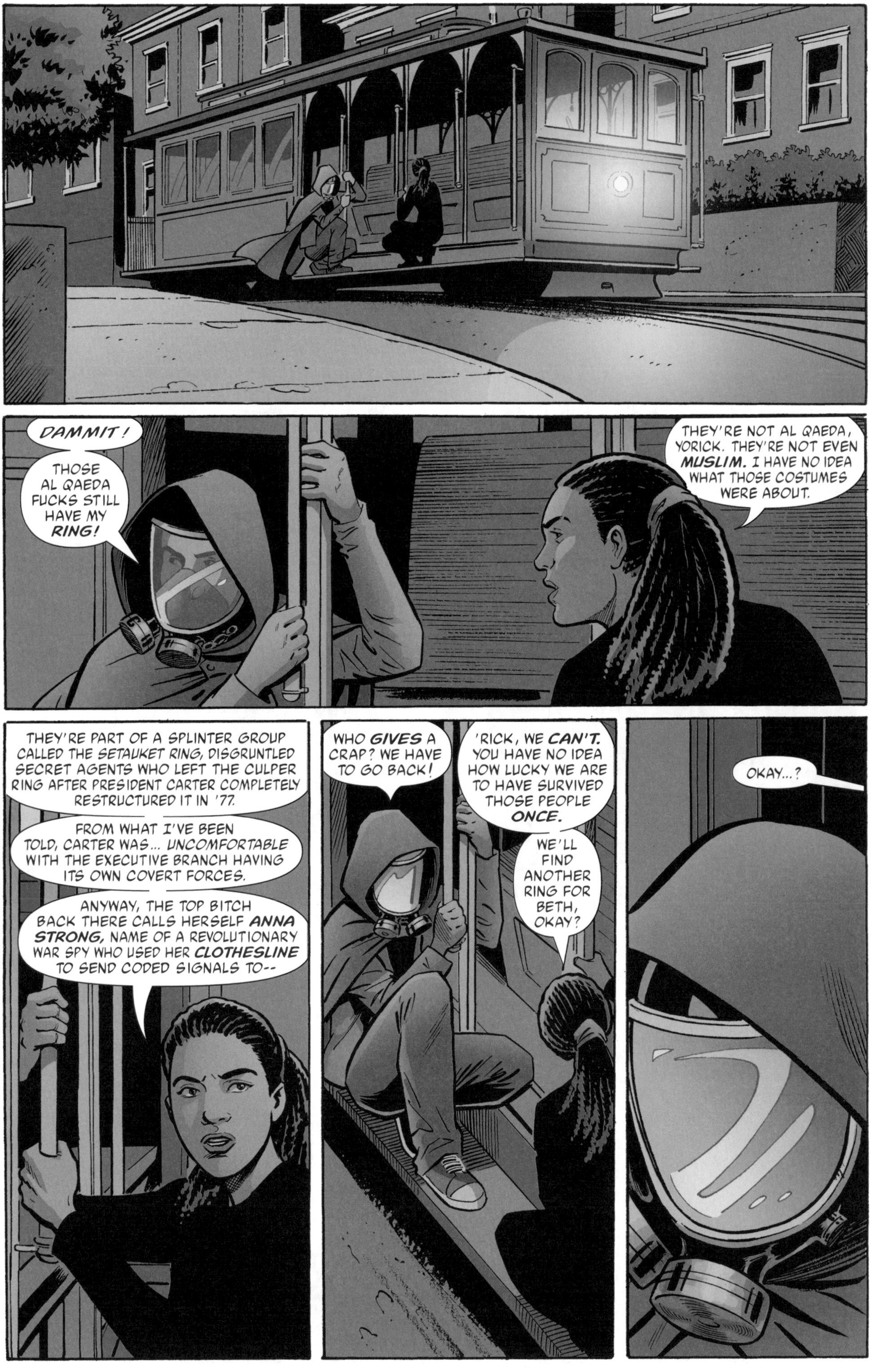
DAMMIT!
THOSE AL QAEDA FUCKS STILL HAVE MY RING!
THEY'RE NOT AL QAEDA, YORICK. THEY'RE NOT EVEN MUSLIM. I HAVE NO IDEA WHAT THOSE COSTUMES WERE ABOUT.
THEY'RE PART OF A SPLINTER GROUP CALLED THE SETAUKET RING, DISGRUNTLED SECRET AGENTS WHO LEFT THE CULPER RING AFTER PRESIDENT CARTER COMPLETELY RESTRUCTURED IT IN '77.
FROM WHAT I'VE BEEN TOLD, CARTER WAS... UNCOMFORTABLE WITH THE EXECUTIVE BRANCH HAVING ITS OWN COVERT FORCES.
ANYWAY, THE TOP BITCH BACK THERE CALLS HERSELF ANNA STRONG, NAME OF A REVOLUTIONARY WAR SPY WHO USED HER CLOTHESLINE TO SEND CODED SIGNALS TO--
WHO GIVES A CRAP? WE HAVE TO GO BACK!
'RICK, WE CAN'T. YOU HAVE NO IDEA HOW LUCKY WE ARE TO HAVE SURVIVED THOSE PEOPLE ONCE.
WE'LL FIND ANOTHER RING FOR BETH, OKAY?
OKAY...?

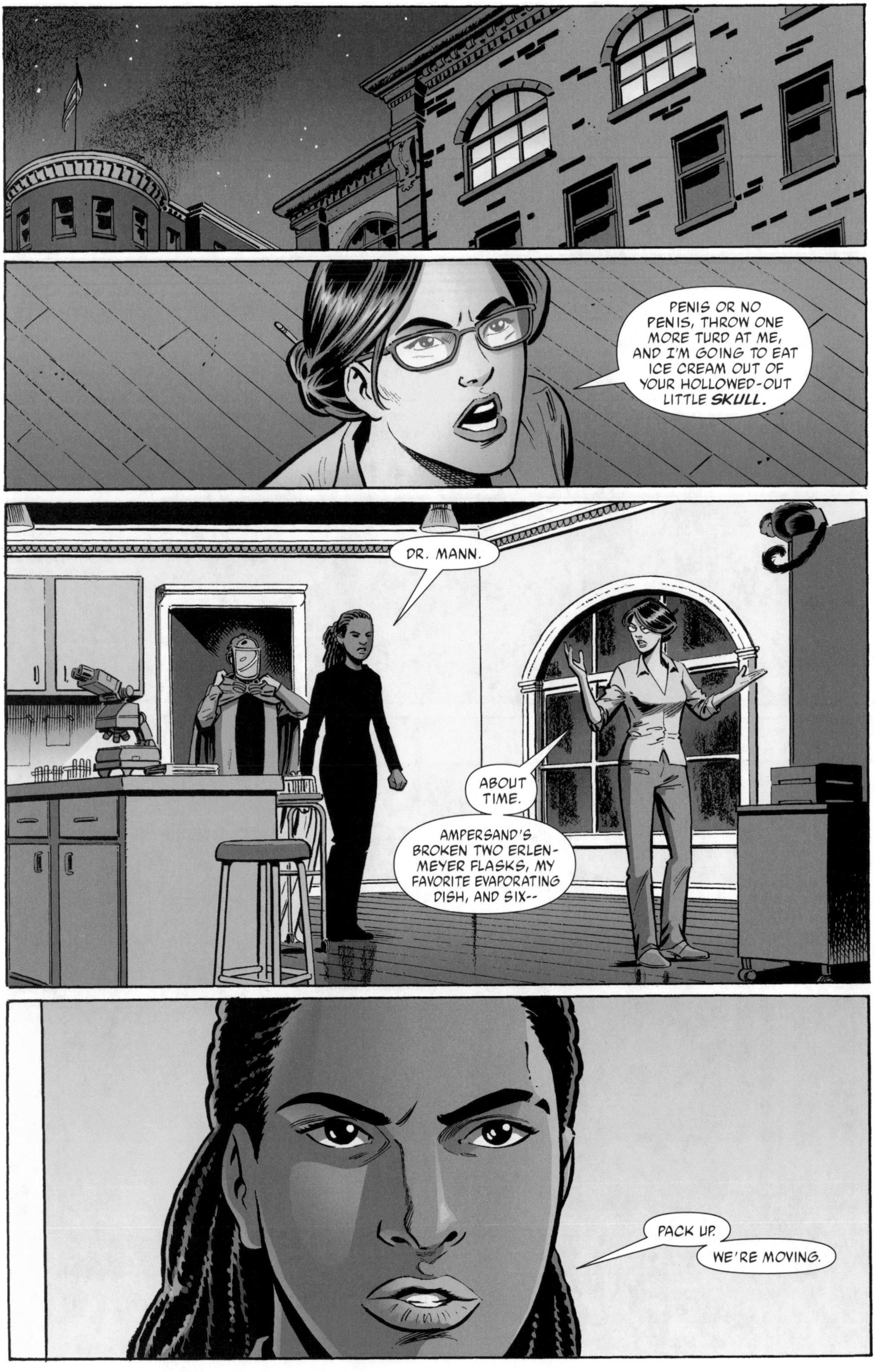
PENIS OR NO PENIS, THROW ONE MORE TURD AT ME, AND I'M GOING TO EAT ICE CREAM OUT OF YOUR HOLLOWED-OUT LITTLE **SKULL.**
DR. MANN.
ABOUT TIME.
AMPERSAND'S BROKEN TWO ERLEN-MEYER FLASKS, MY FAVORITE EVAPORATING DISH, AND SIX--
PACK UP.
WE'RE MOVING.

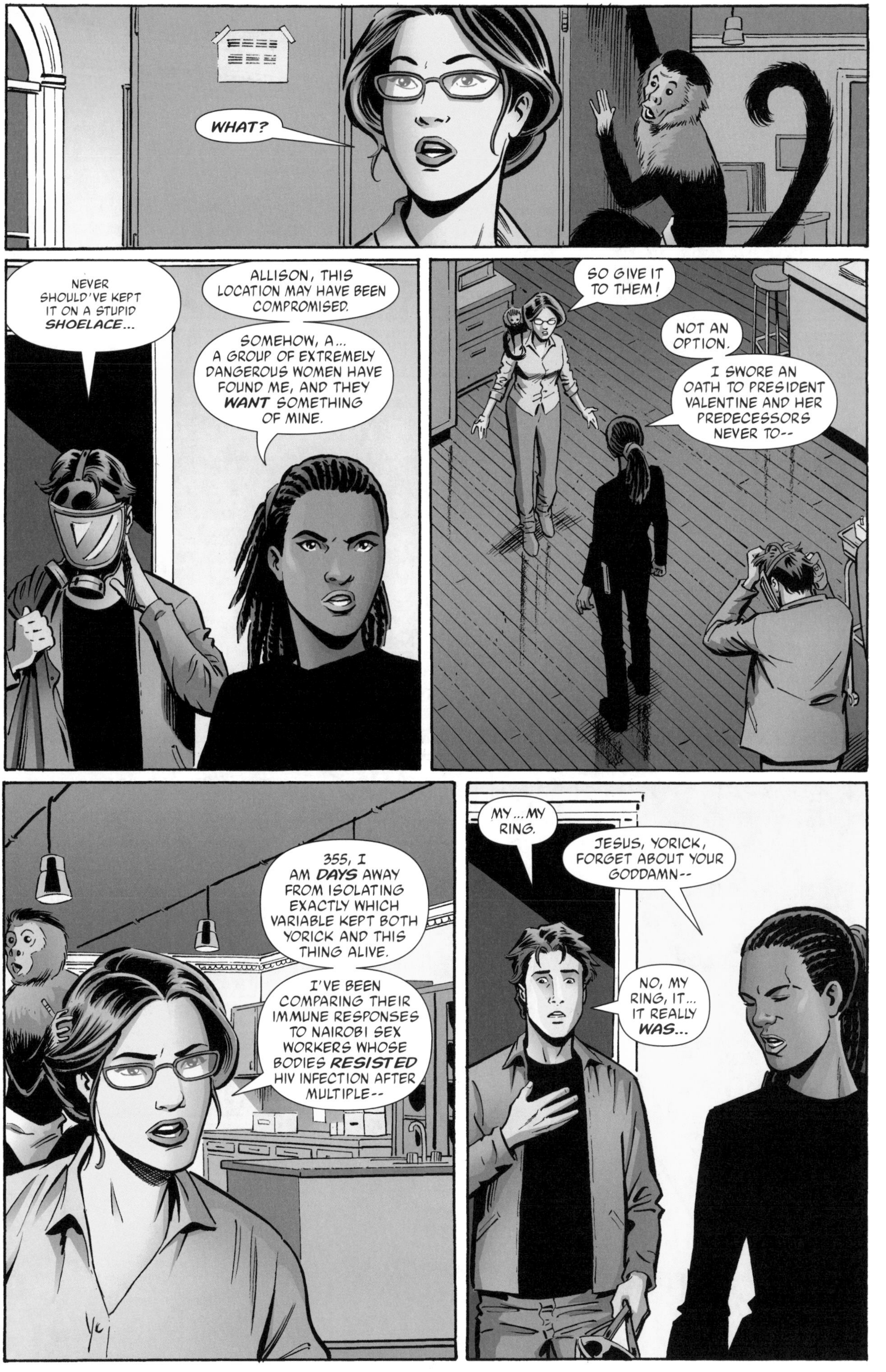

WHAT?
NEVER SHOULD'VE KEPT IT ON A STUPID SHOELACE...
ALLISON, THIS LOCATION MAY HAVE BEEN COMPROMISED.
SOMEHOW, A... A GROUP OF EXTREMELY DANGEROUS WOMEN HAVE FOUND ME, AND THEY WANT SOMETHING OF MINE.
SO GIVE IT TO THEM!
NOT AN OPTION.
I SWORE AN OATH TO PRESIDENT VALENTINE AND HER PREDECESSORS NEVER TO--
355, I AM DAYS AWAY FROM ISOLATING EXACTLY WHICH VARIABLE KEPT BOTH YORICK AND THIS THING ALIVE.
I'VE BEEN COMPARING THEIR IMMUNE RESPONSES TO NAIROBI SEX WORKERS WHOSE BODIES RESISTED HIV INFECTION AFTER MULTIPLE--
MY...MY RING.
JESUS, YORICK, FORGET ABOUT YOUR GODDAMN--
NO, MY RING, IT... IT REALLY WAS...

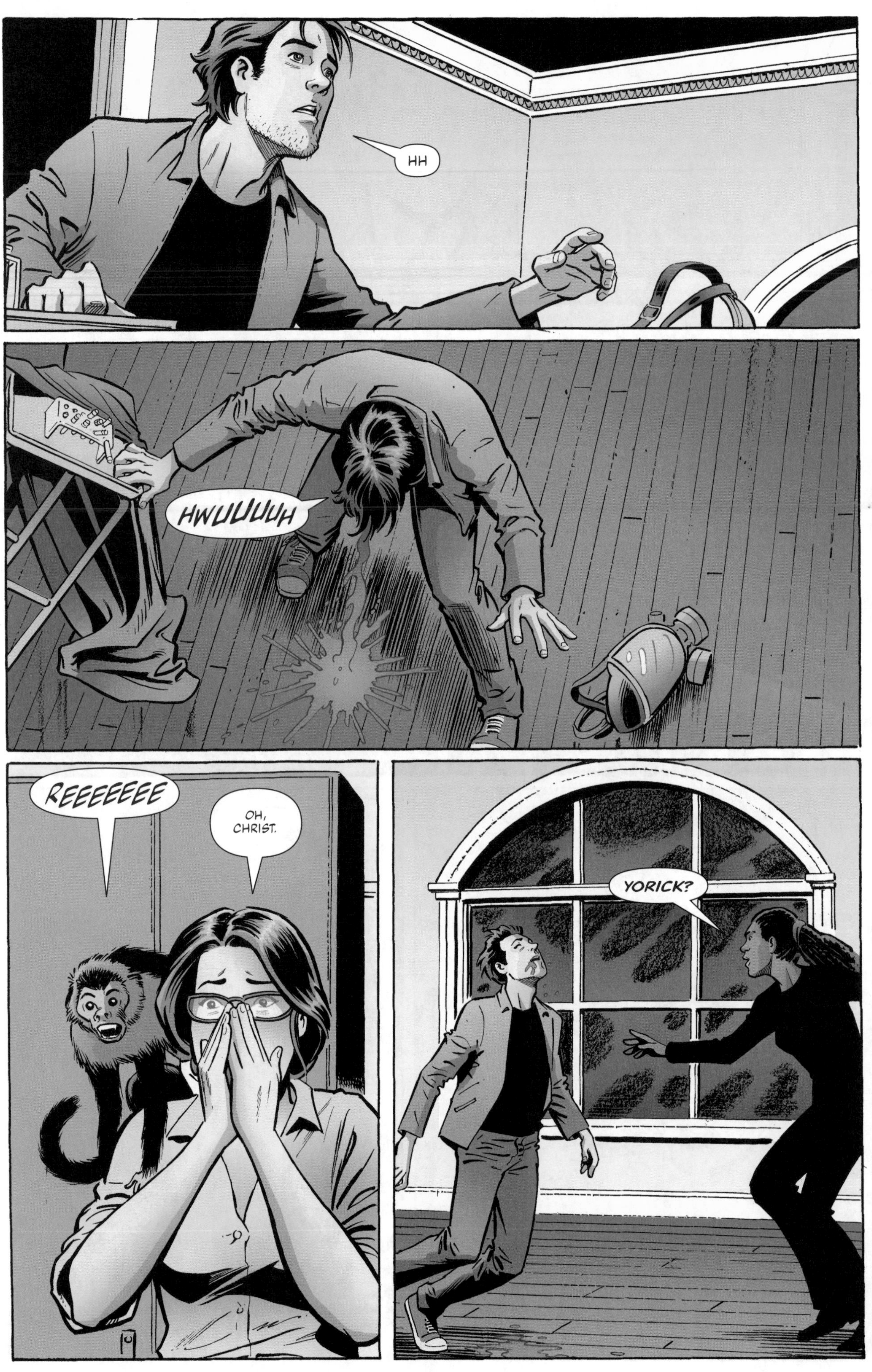
HH
HWUUUUH
REEEEEEE
OH, CHRIST.
YORICK?

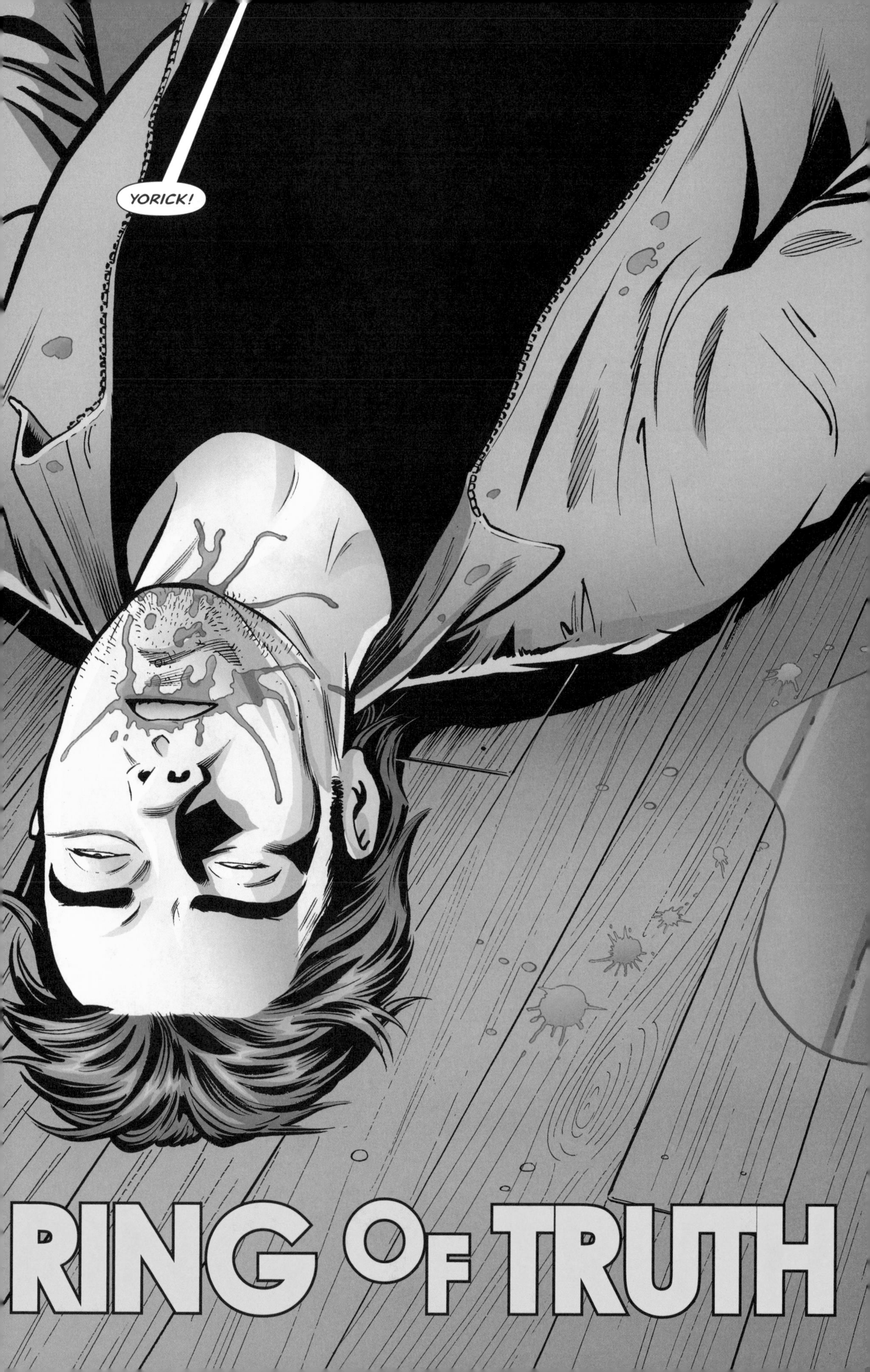
YORICK!
RING OF TRUTH

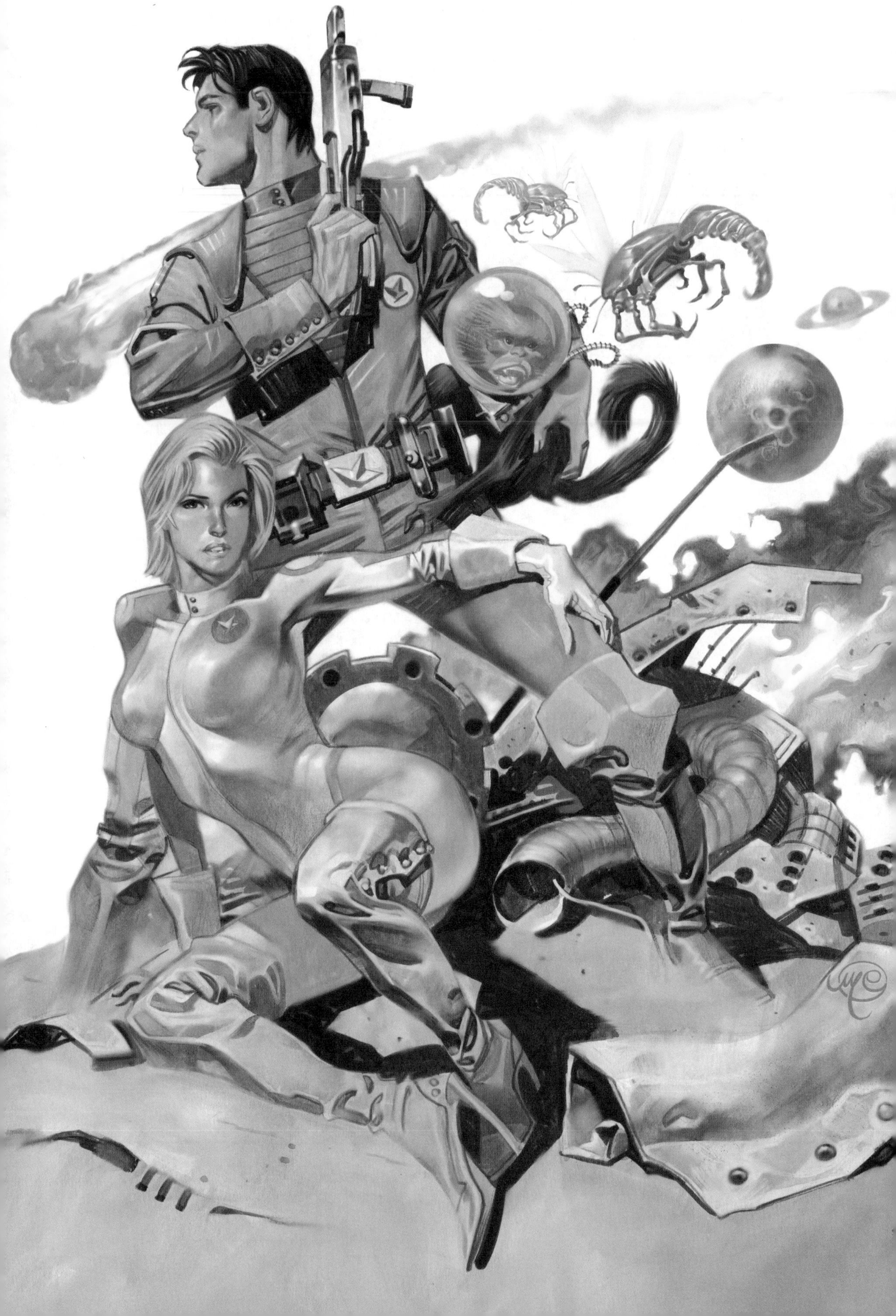

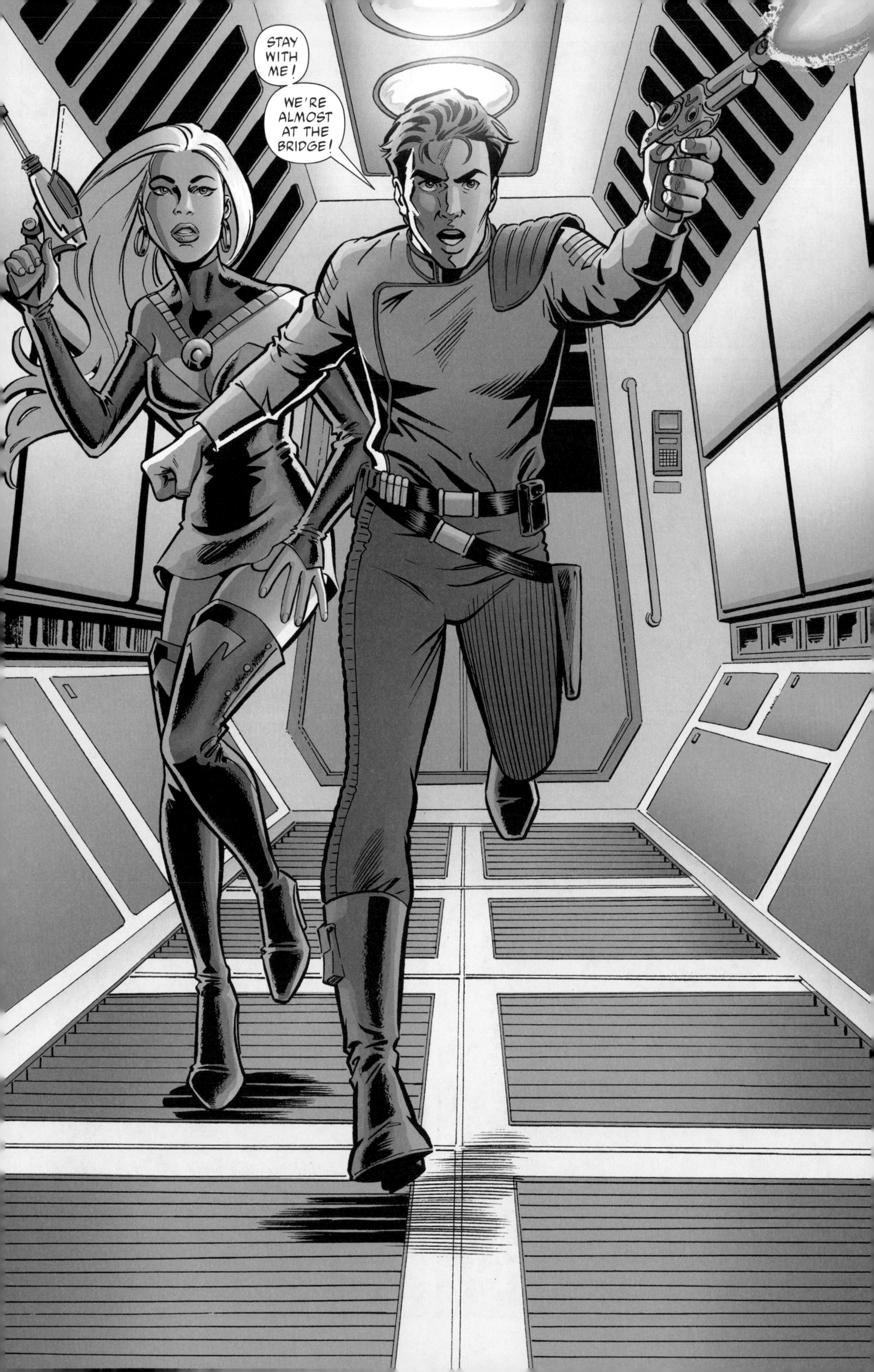
STAY WITH ME!
WE'RE ALMOST AT THE BRIDGE!

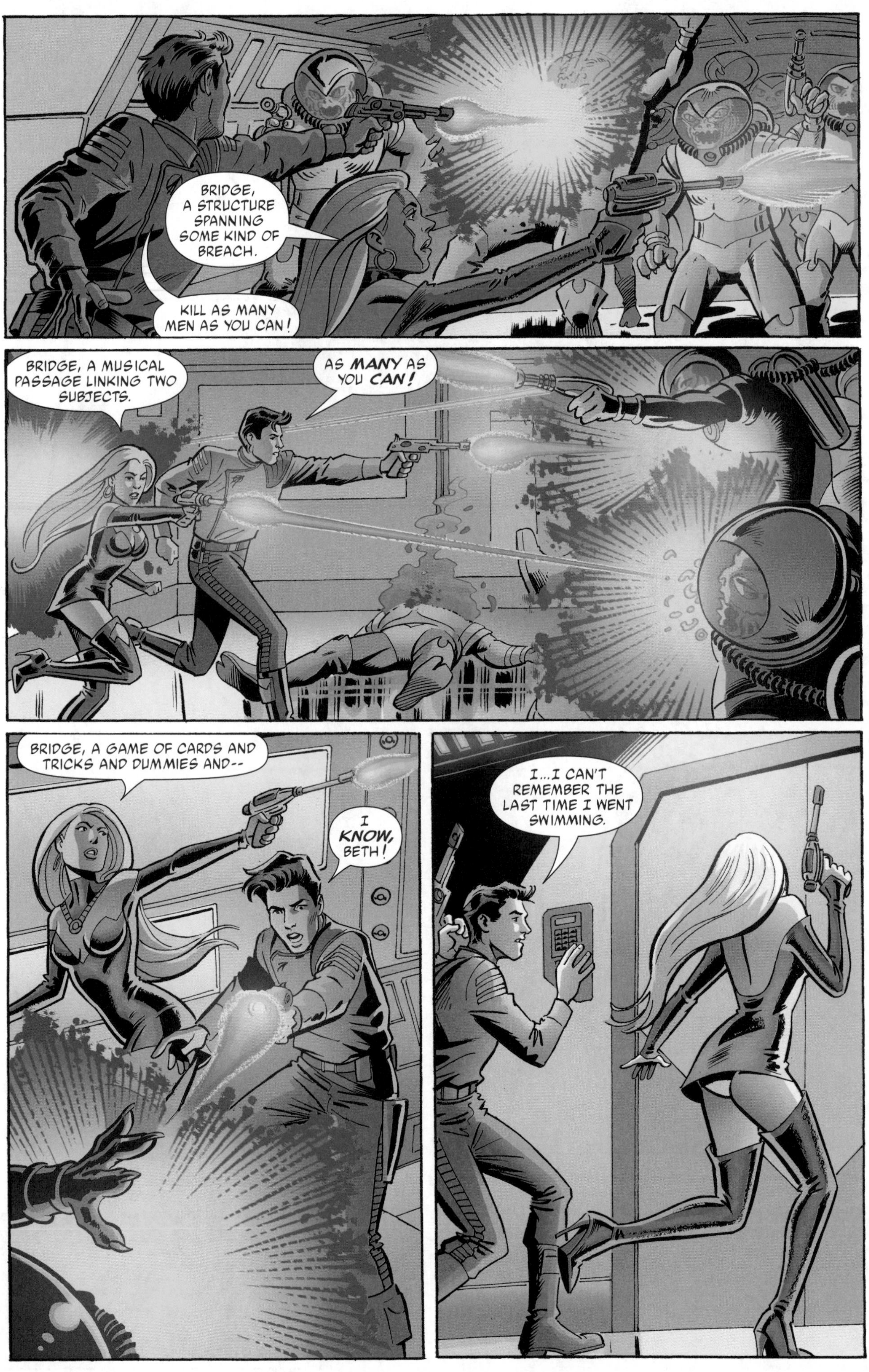
BRIDGE, A STRUCTURE SPANNING SOME KIND OF BREACH.
KILL AS MANY MEN AS YOU CAN!
BRIDGE, A MUSICAL PASSAGE LINKING TWO SUBJECTS.
AS MANY AS YOU CAN!
BRIDGE, A GAME OF CARDS AND TRICKS AND DUMMIES AND--
I KNOW, BETH!
I...I CAN'T REMEMBER THE LAST TIME I WENT SWIMMING.

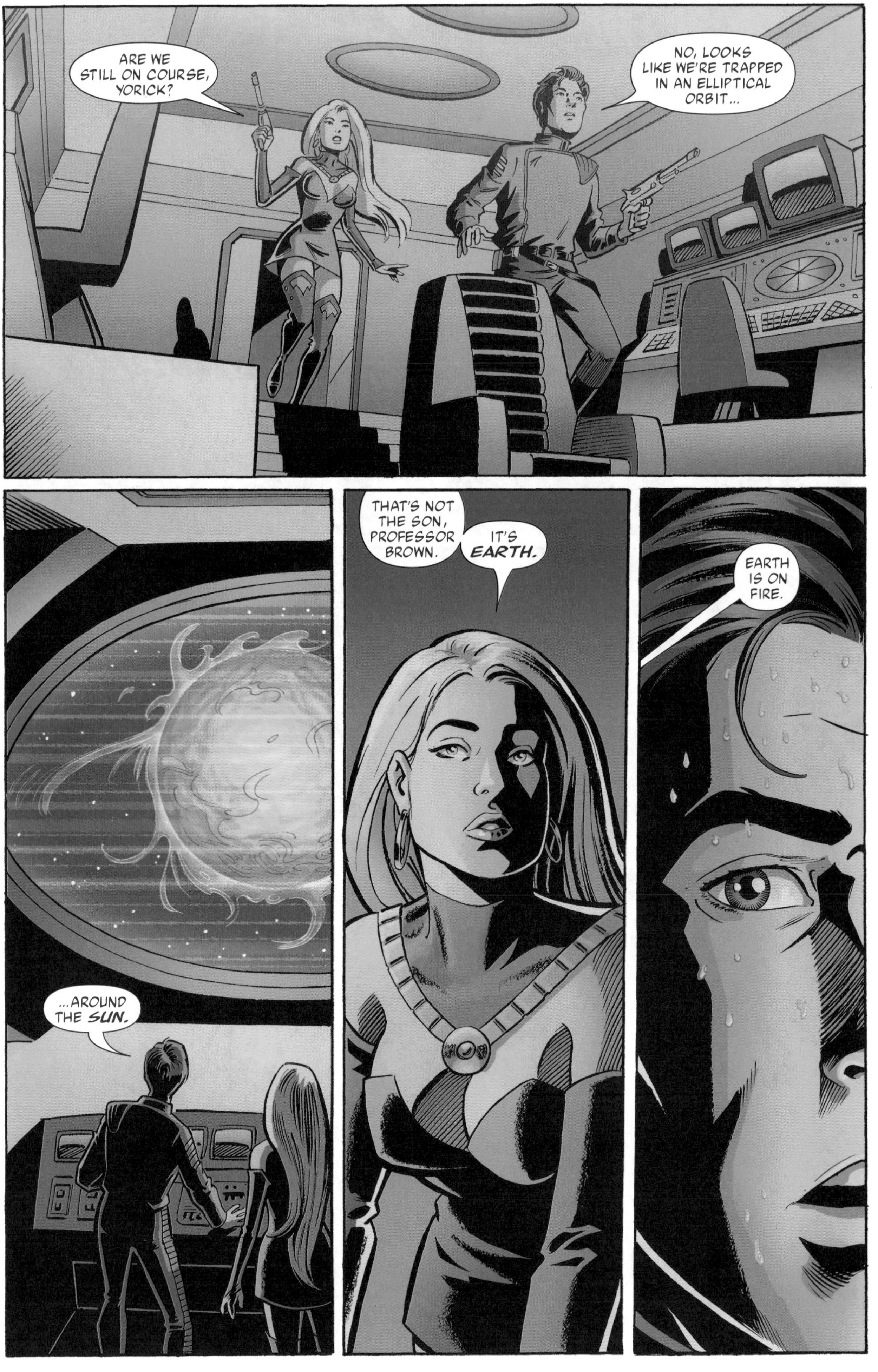
ARE WE STILL ON COURSE, YORICK?
NO, LOOKS LIKE WE'RE TRAPPED IN AN ELLIPTICAL ORBIT...
...AROUND THE SUN.
THAT'S NOT THE SON, PROFESSOR BROWN.
IT'S EARTH.
EARTH IS ON FIRE.

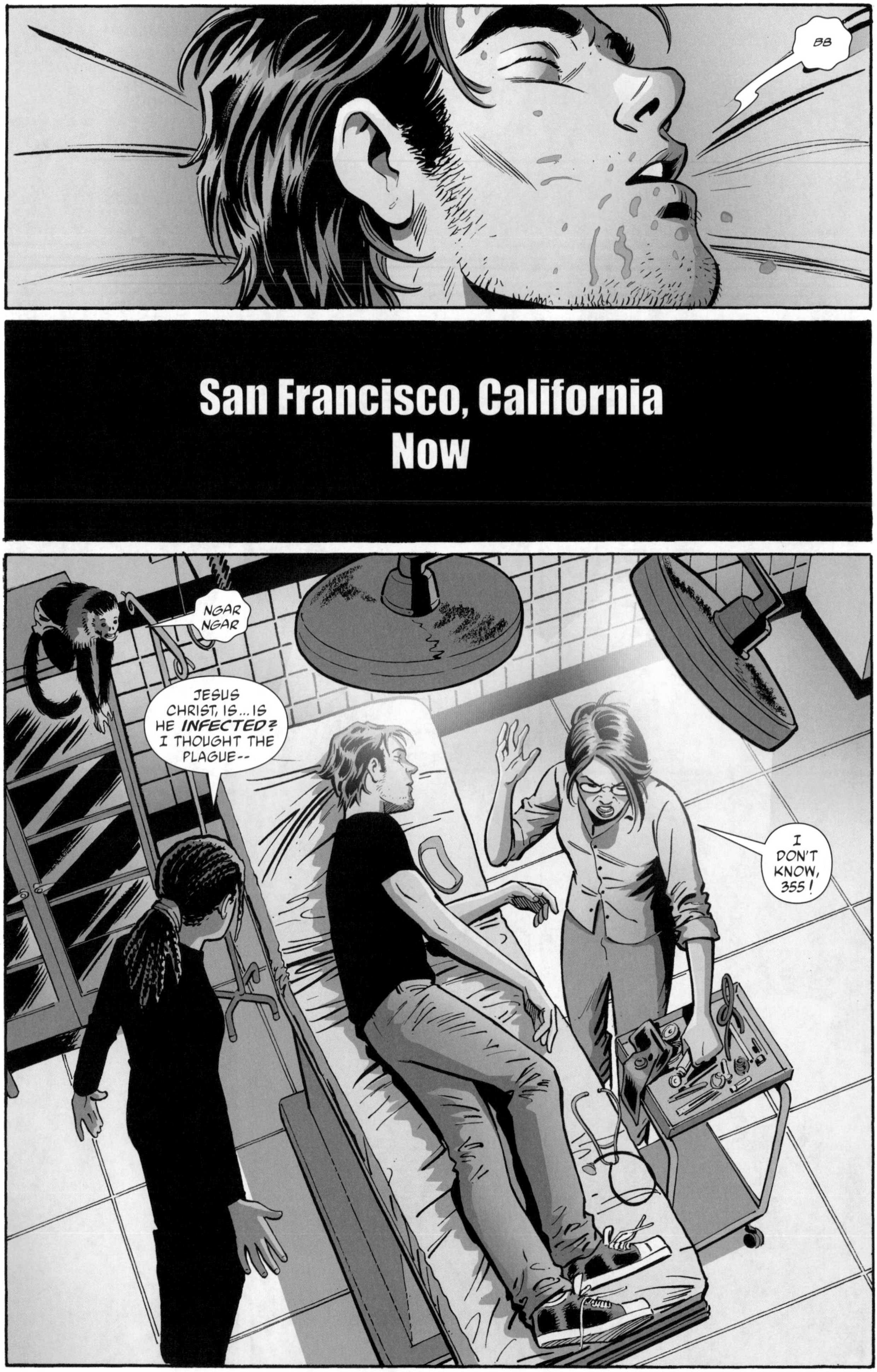
BB
San Francisco, California
Now
NGAR NGAR
JESUS CHRIST, IS...IS HE INFECTED? I THOUGHT THE PLAGUE--
I DON'T KNOW, 355!

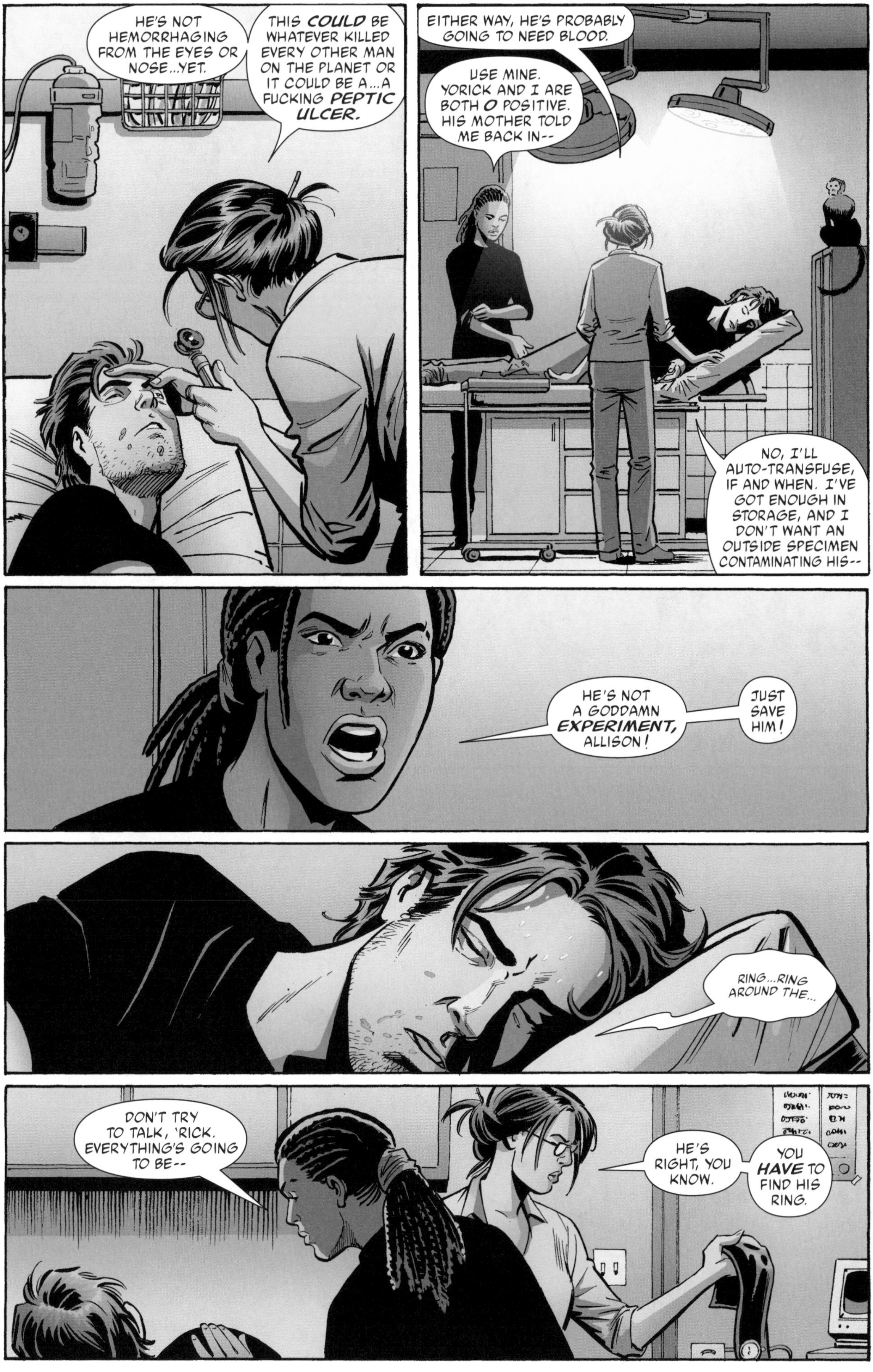
HE'S NOT HEMORRHAGING FROM THE EYES OR NOSE...YET.
THIS COULD BE WHATEVER KILLED EVERY OTHER MAN ON THE PLANET OR IT COULD BE A...A FUCKING PEPTIC ULCER.
EITHER WAY, HE'S PROBABLY GOING TO NEED BLOOD.
USE MINE. YORICK AND I ARE BOTH O POSITIVE. HIS MOTHER TOLD ME BACK IN--
NO, I'LL AUTO-TRANSFUSE, IF AND WHEN. I'VE GOT ENOUGH IN STORAGE, AND I DON'T WANT AN OUTSIDE SPECIMEN CONTAMINATING HIS--
HE'S NOT A GODDAMN EXPERIMENT, ALLISON!
JUST SAVE HIM!
RING...RING AROUND THE...
DON'T TRY TO TALK, 'RICK. EVERYTHING'S GOING TO BE--
HE'S RIGHT, YOU KNOW.
YOU HAVE TO FIND HIS RING.

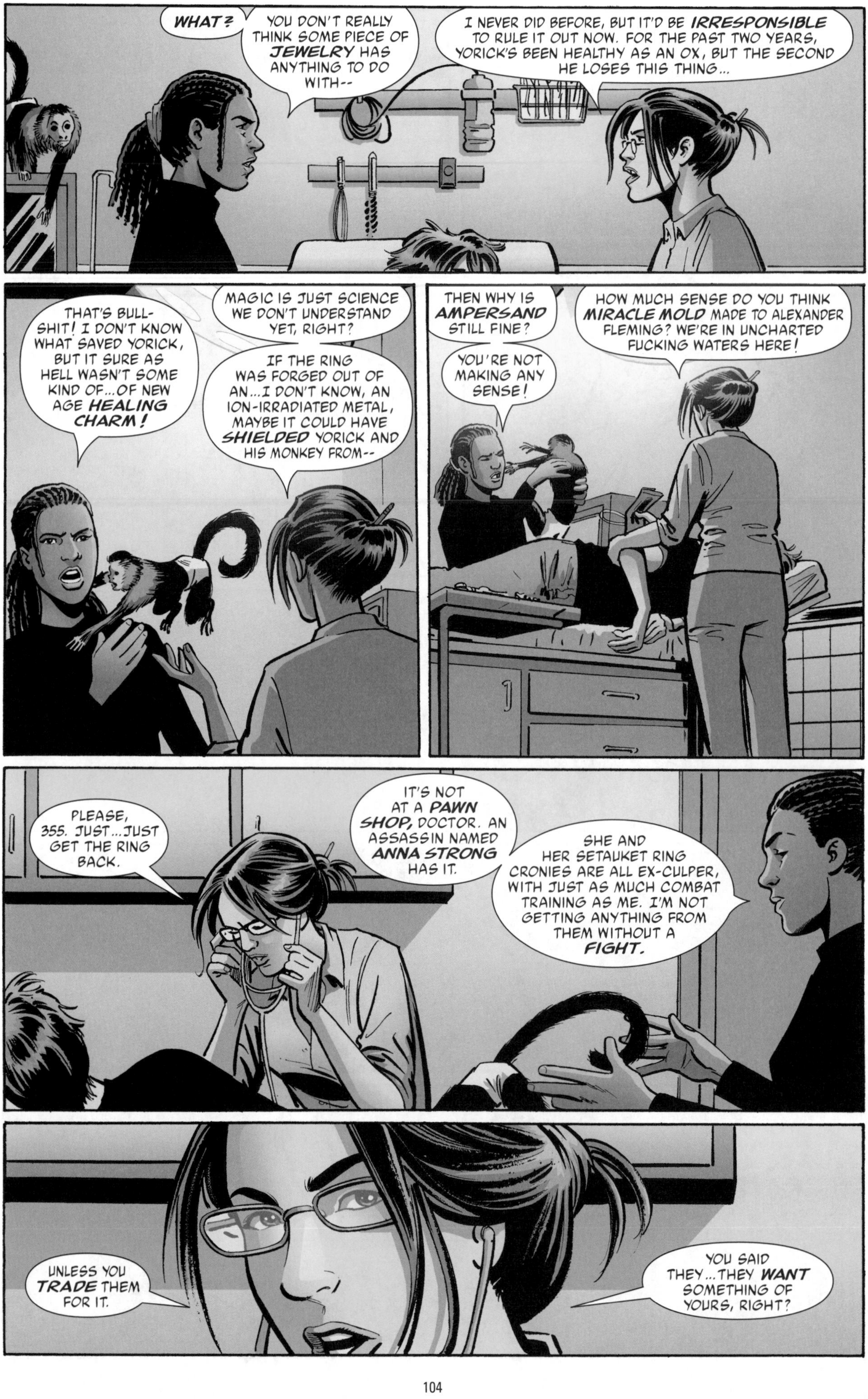

WHAT?
YOU DON'T REALLY THINK SOME PIECE OF JEWELRY HAS ANYTHING TO DO WITH--
I NEVER DID BEFORE, BUT IT'D BE IRRESPONSIBLE TO RULE IT OUT NOW. FOR THE PAST TWO YEARS, YORICK'S BEEN HEALTHY AS AN OX, BUT THE SECOND HE LOSES THIS THING...
THAT'S BULL-SHIT! I DON'T KNOW WHAT SAVED YORICK, BUT IT SURE AS HELL WASN'T SOME KIND OF...OF NEW AGE HEALING CHARM!
MAGIC IS JUST SCIENCE WE DON'T UNDERSTAND YET, RIGHT?
IF THE RING WAS FORGED OUT OF AN...I DON'T KNOW, AN ION-IRRADIATED METAL, MAYBE IT COULD HAVE SHIELDED YORICK AND HIS MONKEY FROM--
THEN WHY IS AMPERSAND STILL FINE?
YOU'RE NOT MAKING ANY SENSE!
HOW MUCH SENSE DO YOU THINK MIRACLE MOLD MADE TO ALEXANDER FLEMING? WE'RE IN UNCHARTED FUCKING WATERS HERE!
PLEASE, 355. JUST...JUST GET THE RING BACK.
IT'S NOT AT A PAWN SHOP, DOCTOR. AN ASSASSIN NAMED ANNA STRONG HAS IT.
SHE AND HER SETAUKET RING CRONIES ARE ALL EX-CULPER, WITH JUST AS MUCH COMBAT TRAINING AS ME. I'M NOT GETTING ANYTHING FROM THEM WITHOUT A FIGHT.
UNLESS YOU TRADE THEM FOR IT.
YOU SAID THEY...THEY WANT SOMETHING OF YOURS, RIGHT?

THAT'S WHAT THIS IS ABOUT, ISN'T IT?

YOU DON'T GIVE A DAMN ABOUT THE RING. YOU JUST WANT ME TO UNLOAD THE **AMULET OF HELENE.**

THESE SETAUKET PEOPLE ARE LOOKING FOR IT, AREN'T THEY? WELL, HOW LONG BEFORE THEY FIND **US?**

WE CAN'T MOVE YORICK WITH-OUT **KILLING** HIM, AND I'M NOT GOING TO BE ABLE TO TREAT HIM IF I'VE GOT YOUR OLD PLAYMATES SHOOTING UP THE JOINT.

EVEN IF THE RING HAS **NOTHING** TO DO WITH YORICK'S SURVIVAL, **BARTERING** WITH THESE SCUMBAGS COULD BUY ME ENOUGH TIME TO AT LEAST **STABILIZE** HIM.

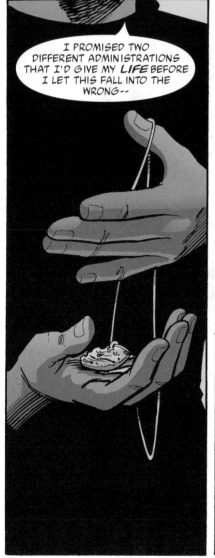

I PROMISED TWO DIFFERENT ADMINISTRATIONS THAT I'D GIVE MY **LIFE** BEFORE I LET THIS FALL INTO THE WRONG--

IT'S YOUR CALL, 355.

BUT I DON'T KNOW HOW LONG WE'VE GOT.

...RING AROUND...THE ROSIE...THE RIVETER...

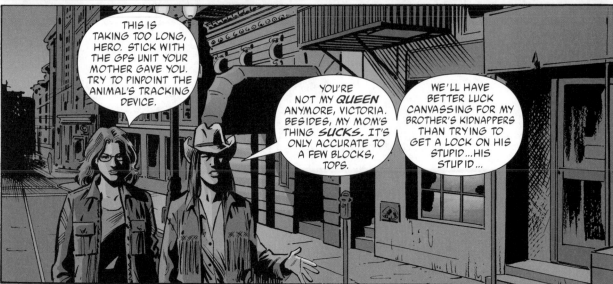

THIS IS TAKING TOO LONG, HERO. STICK WITH THE GPS UNIT YOUR MOTHER GAVE YOU. TRY TO PINPOINT THE ANIMAL'S TRACKING DEVICE.

YOU'RE NOT MY *QUEEN* ANYMORE, VICTORIA. BESIDES, MY MOM'S THING *SUCKS*. IT'S ONLY ACCURATE TO A FEW BLOCKS, TOPS.

WE'LL HAVE BETTER LUCK CANVASSING FOR MY BROTHER'S KIDNAPPERS THAN TRYING TO GET A LOCK ON HIS STUPID...HIS STUPID...

DAMMIT.

FUCKING *FOCUS*, GIRL.

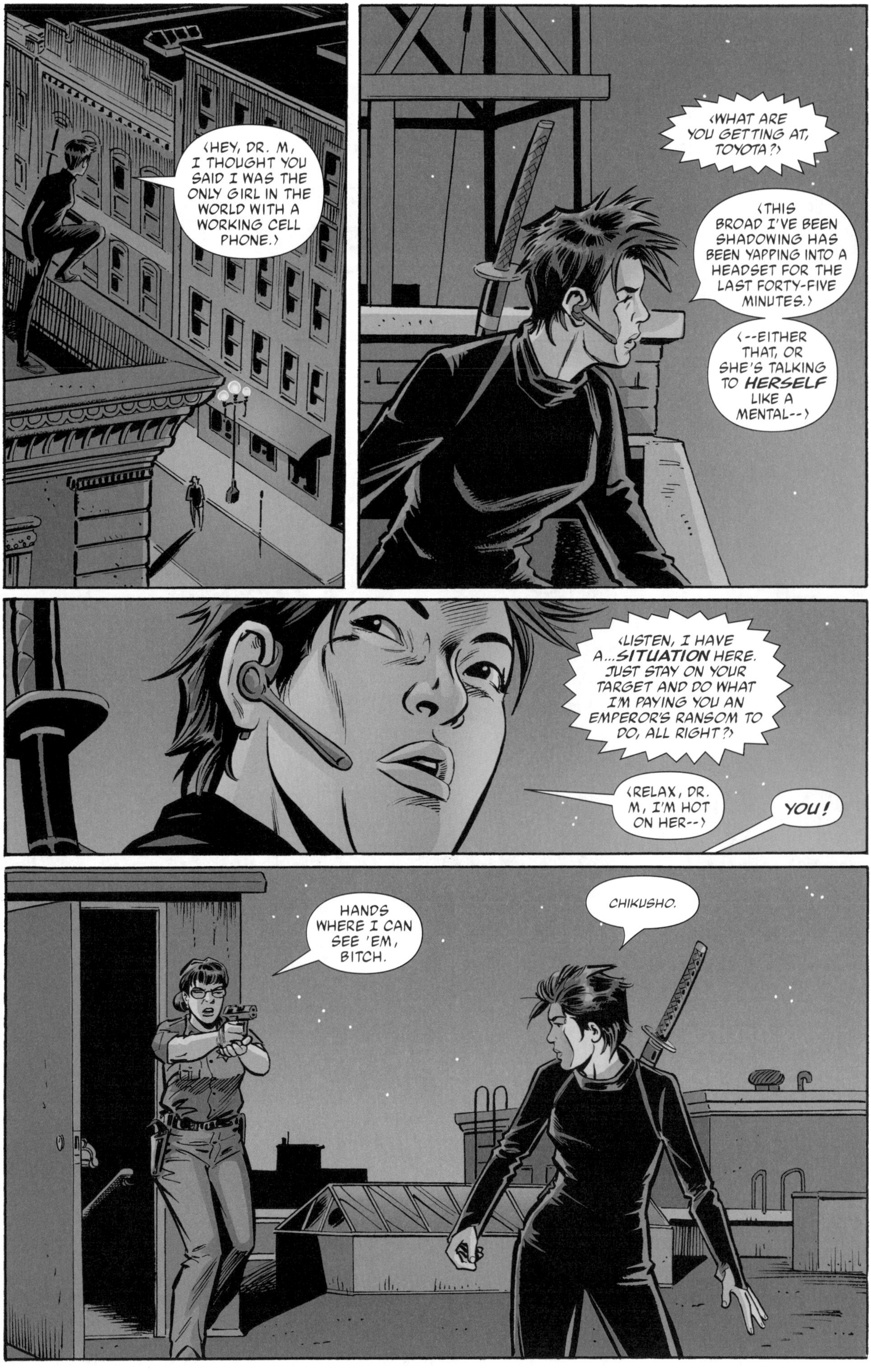
‹HEY, DR. M, I THOUGHT YOU SAID I WAS THE ONLY GIRL IN THE WORLD WITH A WORKING CELL PHONE.›
‹WHAT ARE YOU GETTING AT, TOYOTA?›
‹THIS BROAD I'VE BEEN SHADOWING HAS BEEN YAPPING INTO A HEADSET FOR THE LAST FORTY-FIVE MINUTES.›
‹--EITHER THAT, OR SHE'S TALKING TO **HERSELF** LIKE A MENTAL--›
‹LISTEN, I HAVE A...**SITUATION** HERE. JUST STAY ON YOUR TARGET AND DO WHAT I'M PAYING YOU AN EMPEROR'S RANSOM TO DO, ALL RIGHT?›
‹RELAX, DR. M, I'M HOT ON HER--›
**YOU!**
HANDS WHERE I CAN SEE 'EM, BITCH.
CHIKUSHO.

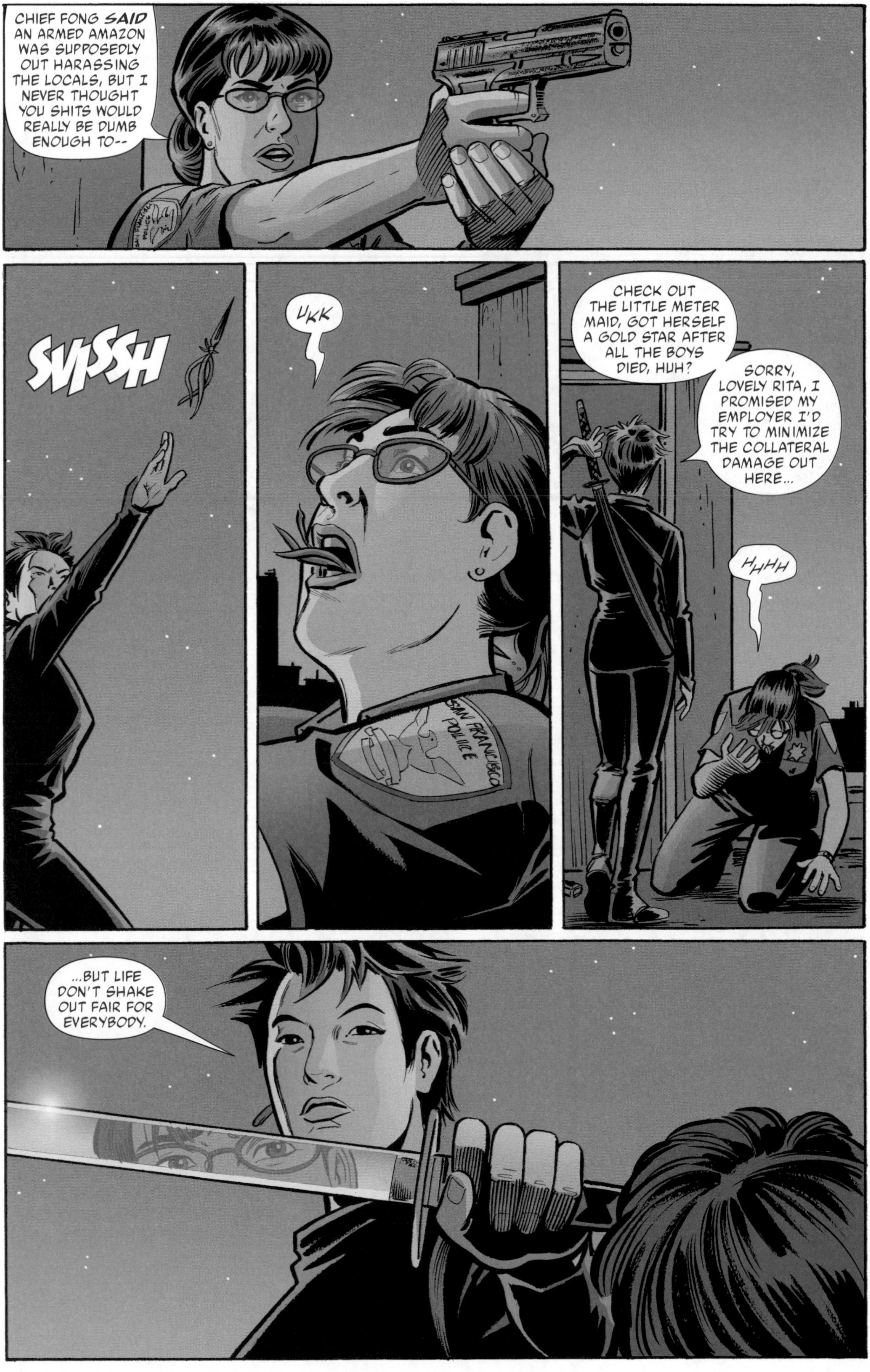
CHIEF FONG SAID AN ARMED AMAZON WAS SUPPOSEDLY OUT HARASSING THE LOCALS, BUT I NEVER THOUGHT YOU SHITS WOULD REALLY BE DUMB ENOUGH TO--
SWSSH
UKK
CHECK OUT THE LITTLE METER MAID, GOT HERSELF A GOLD STAR AFTER ALL THE BOYS DIED, HUH?
SORRY, LOVELY RITA, I PROMISED MY EMPLOYER I'D TRY TO MINIMIZE THE COLLATERAL DAMAGE OUT HERE...
HHHH
...BUT LIFE DON'T SHAKE OUT FAIR FOR EVERYBODY.

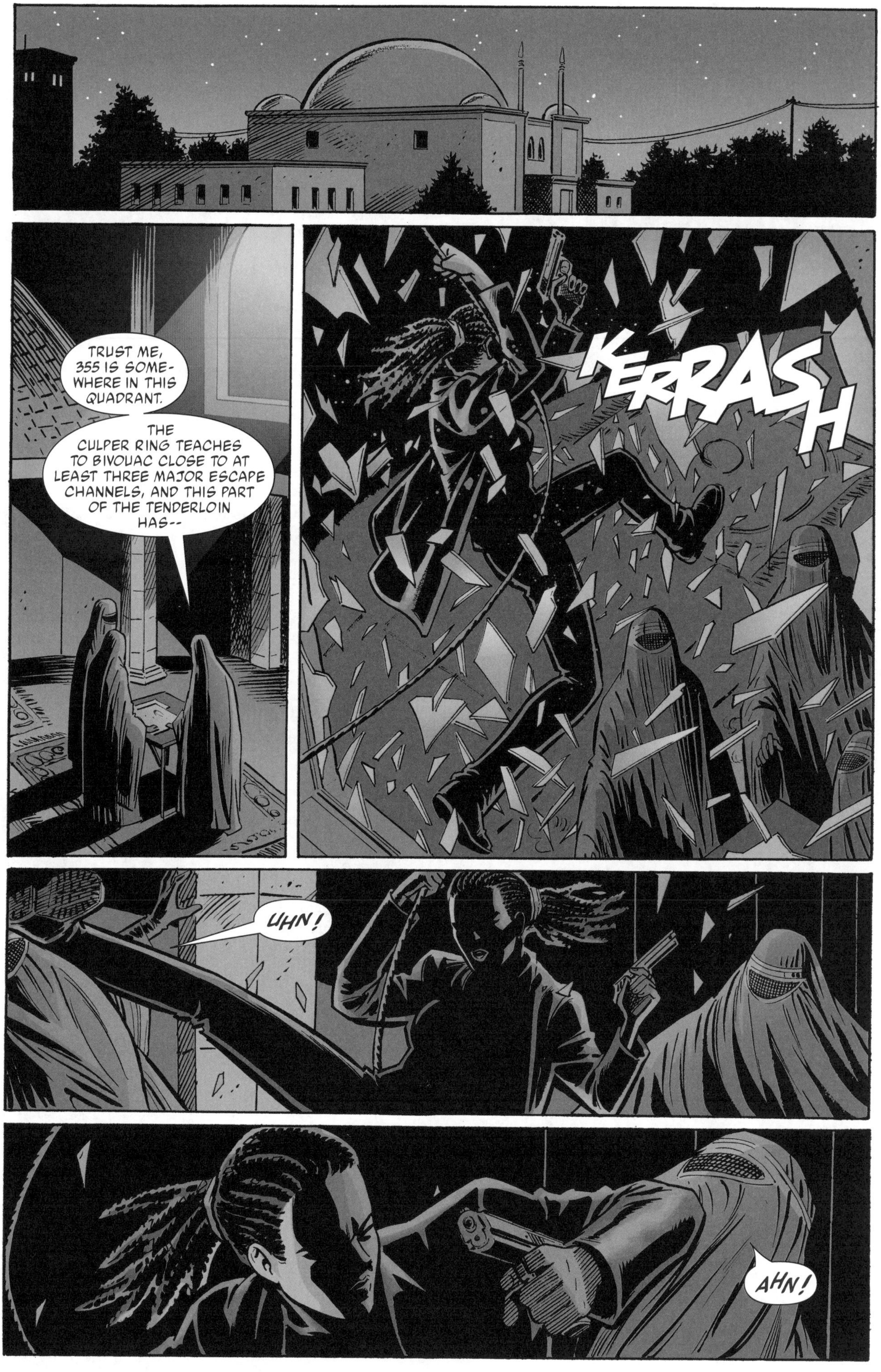
TRUST ME, 355 IS SOME-WHERE IN THIS QUADRANT.
THE CULPER RING TEACHES TO BIVOUAC CLOSE TO AT LEAST THREE MAJOR ESCAPE CHANNELS, AND THIS PART OF THE TENDERLOIN HAS--
KERRASH
UHN!
AHN!

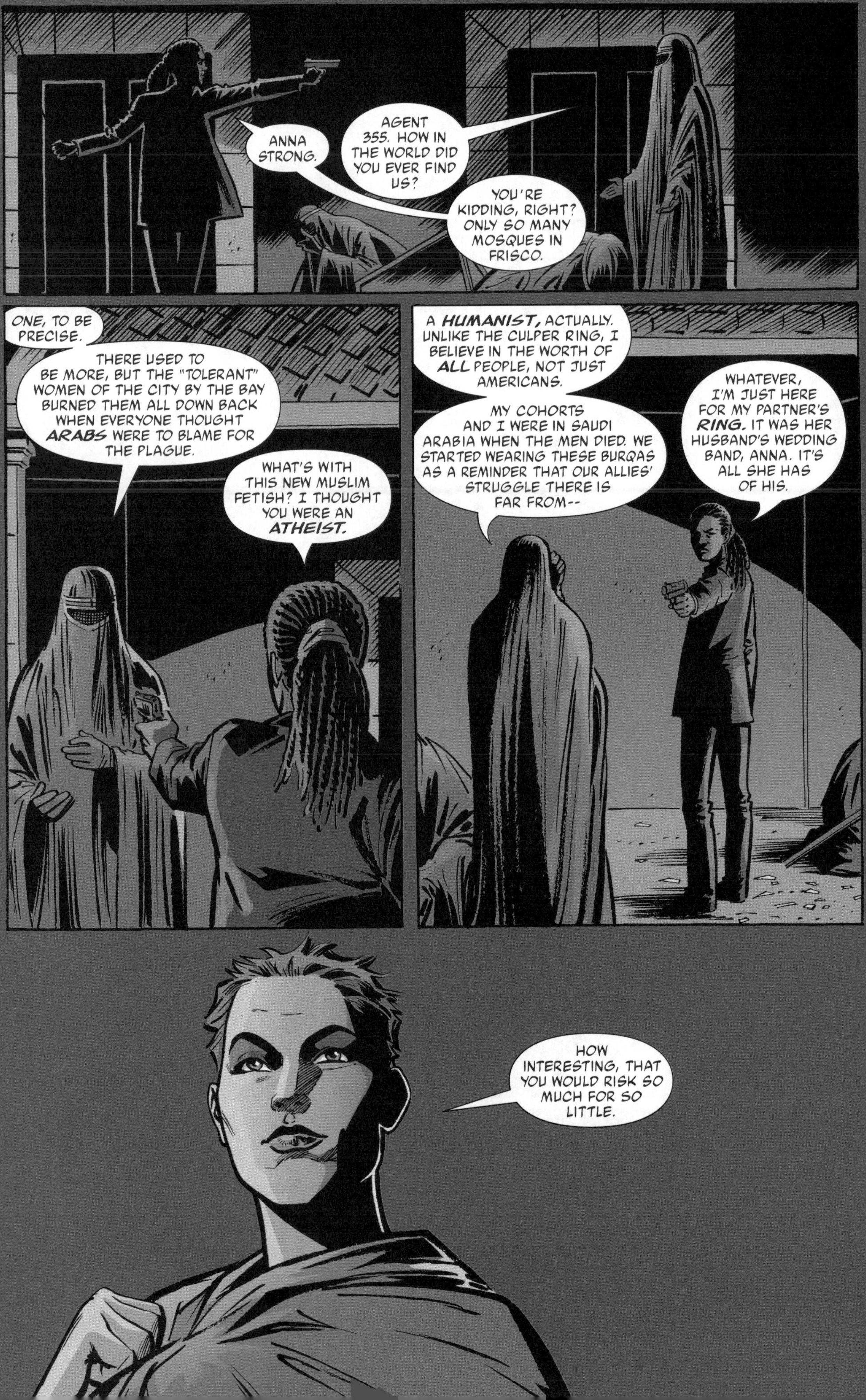
AGENT 355. HOW IN THE WORLD DID YOU EVER FIND US?
ANNA STRONG.
YOU'RE KIDDING, RIGHT? ONLY SO MANY MOSQUES IN FRISCO.
ONE, TO BE PRECISE.
THERE USED TO BE MORE, BUT THE "TOLERANT" WOMEN OF THE CITY BY THE BAY BURNED THEM ALL DOWN BACK WHEN EVERYONE THOUGHT ARABS WERE TO BLAME FOR THE PLAGUE.
WHAT'S WITH THIS NEW MUSLIM FETISH? I THOUGHT YOU WERE AN ATHEIST.
A HUMANIST, ACTUALLY. UNLIKE THE CULPER RING, I BELIEVE IN THE WORTH OF ALL PEOPLE, NOT JUST AMERICANS.
MY COHORTS AND I WERE IN SAUDI ARABIA WHEN THE MEN DIED. WE STARTED WEARING THESE BURQAS AS A REMINDER THAT OUR ALLIES' STRUGGLE THERE IS FAR FROM--
WHATEVER, I'M JUST HERE FOR MY PARTNER'S RING. IT WAS HER HUSBAND'S WEDDING BAND, ANNA. IT'S ALL SHE HAS OF HIS.
HOW INTERESTING, THAT YOU WOULD RISK SO MUCH FOR SO LITTLE.

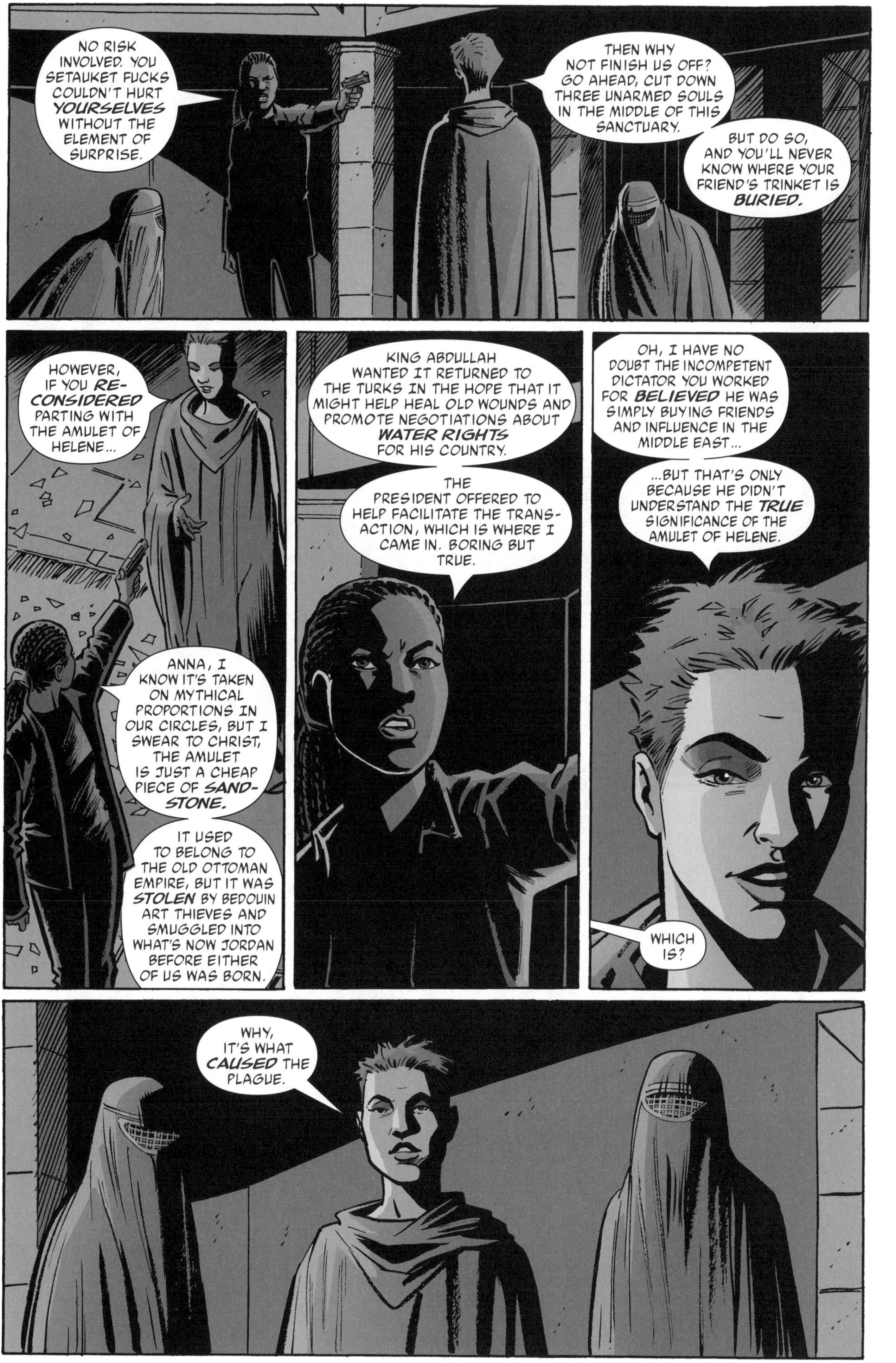
NO RISK INVOLVED. YOU SETAUKET FUCKS COULDN'T HURT YOURSELVES WITHOUT THE ELEMENT OF SURPRISE.
THEN WHY NOT FINISH US OFF? GO AHEAD, CUT DOWN THREE UNARMED SOULS IN THE MIDDLE OF THIS SANCTUARY.
BUT DO SO, AND YOU'LL NEVER KNOW WHERE YOUR FRIEND'S TRINKET IS BURIED.
HOWEVER, IF YOU RECONSIDERED PARTING WITH THE AMULET OF HELENE...
ANNA, I KNOW IT'S TAKEN ON MYTHICAL PROPORTIONS IN OUR CIRCLES, BUT I SWEAR TO CHRIST, THE AMULET IS JUST A CHEAP PIECE OF SANDSTONE.
IT USED TO BELONG TO THE OLD OTTOMAN EMPIRE, BUT IT WAS STOLEN BY BEDOUIN ART THIEVES AND SMUGGLED INTO WHAT'S NOW JORDAN BEFORE EITHER OF US WAS BORN.
KING ABDULLAH WANTED IT RETURNED TO THE TURKS IN THE HOPE THAT IT MIGHT HELP HEAL OLD WOUNDS AND PROMOTE NEGOTIATIONS ABOUT WATER RIGHTS FOR HIS COUNTRY.
THE PRESIDENT OFFERED TO HELP FACILITATE THE TRANSACTION, WHICH IS WHERE I CAME IN. BORING BUT TRUE.
OH, I HAVE NO DOUBT THE INCOMPETENT DICTATOR YOU WORKED FOR BELIEVED HE WAS SIMPLY BUYING FRIENDS AND INFLUENCE IN THE MIDDLE EAST...
...BUT THAT'S ONLY BECAUSE HE DIDN'T UNDERSTAND THE TRUE SIGNIFICANCE OF THE AMULET OF HELENE.
WHICH IS?
WHY, IT'S WHAT CAUSED THE PLAGUE.

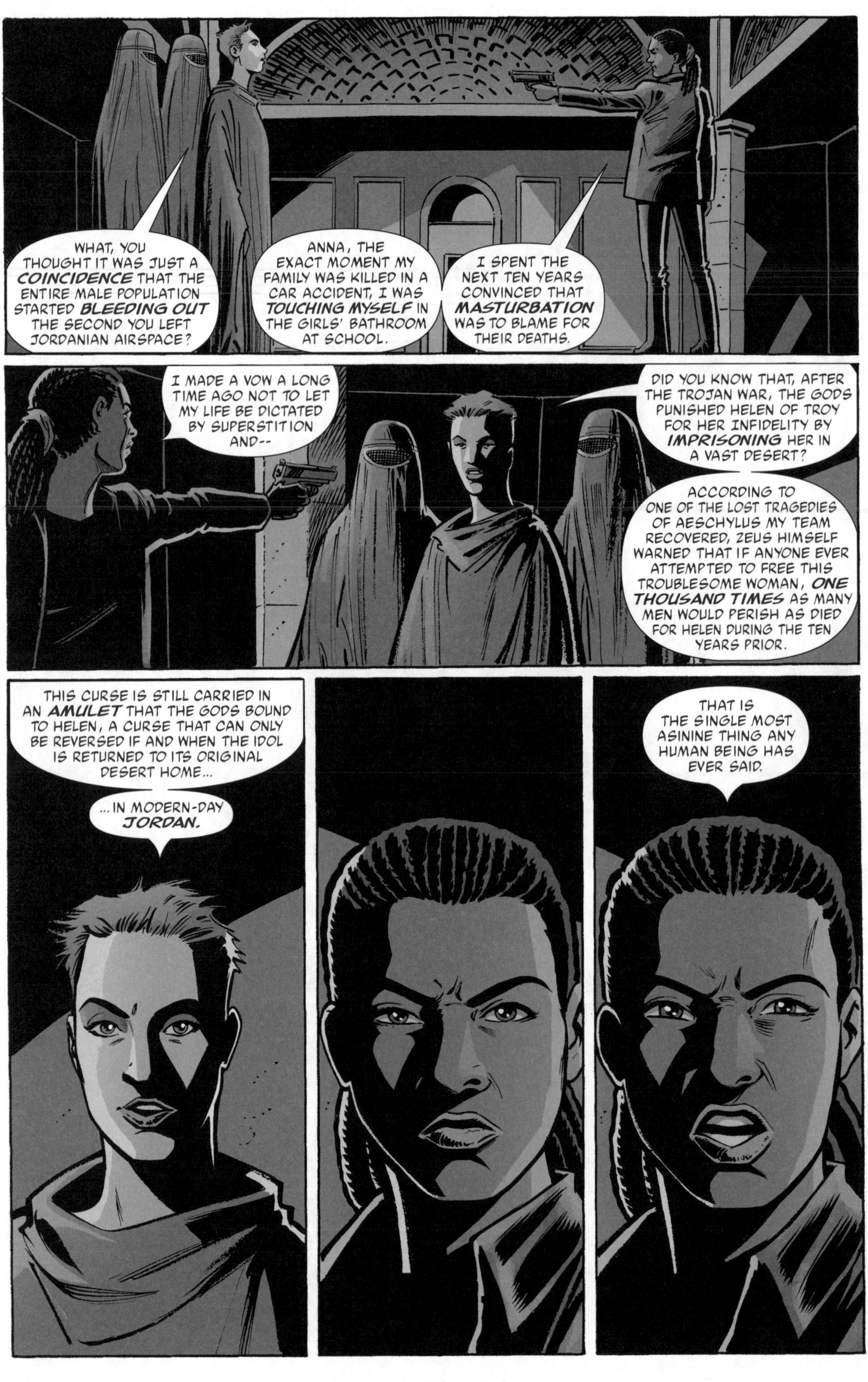
WHAT, YOU THOUGHT IT WAS JUST A COINCIDENCE THAT THE ENTIRE MALE POPULATION STARTED BLEEDING OUT THE SECOND YOU LEFT JORDANIAN AIRSPACE?
ANNA, THE EXACT MOMENT MY FAMILY WAS KILLED IN A CAR ACCIDENT, I WAS TOUCHING MYSELF IN THE GIRLS' BATHROOM AT SCHOOL.
I SPENT THE NEXT TEN YEARS CONVINCED THAT MASTURBATION WAS TO BLAME FOR THEIR DEATHS.
I MADE A VOW A LONG TIME AGO NOT TO LET MY LIFE BE DICTATED BY SUPERSTITION AND--
DID YOU KNOW THAT, AFTER THE TROJAN WAR, THE GODS PUNISHED HELEN OF TROY FOR HER INFIDELITY BY IMPRISONING HER IN A VAST DESERT?
ACCORDING TO ONE OF THE LOST TRAGEDIES OF AESCHYLUS MY TEAM RECOVERED, ZEUS HIMSELF WARNED THAT IF ANYONE EVER ATTEMPTED TO FREE THIS TROUBLESOME WOMAN, ONE THOUSAND TIMES AS MANY MEN WOULD PERISH AS DIED FOR HELEN DURING THE TEN YEARS PRIOR.
THIS CURSE IS STILL CARRIED IN AN AMULET THAT THE GODS BOUND TO HELEN, A CURSE THAT CAN ONLY BE REVERSED IF AND WHEN THE IDOL IS RETURNED TO ITS ORIGINAL DESERT HOME...
...IN MODERN-DAY JORDAN.
THAT IS THE SINGLE MOST ASININE THING ANY HUMAN BEING HAS EVER SAID.

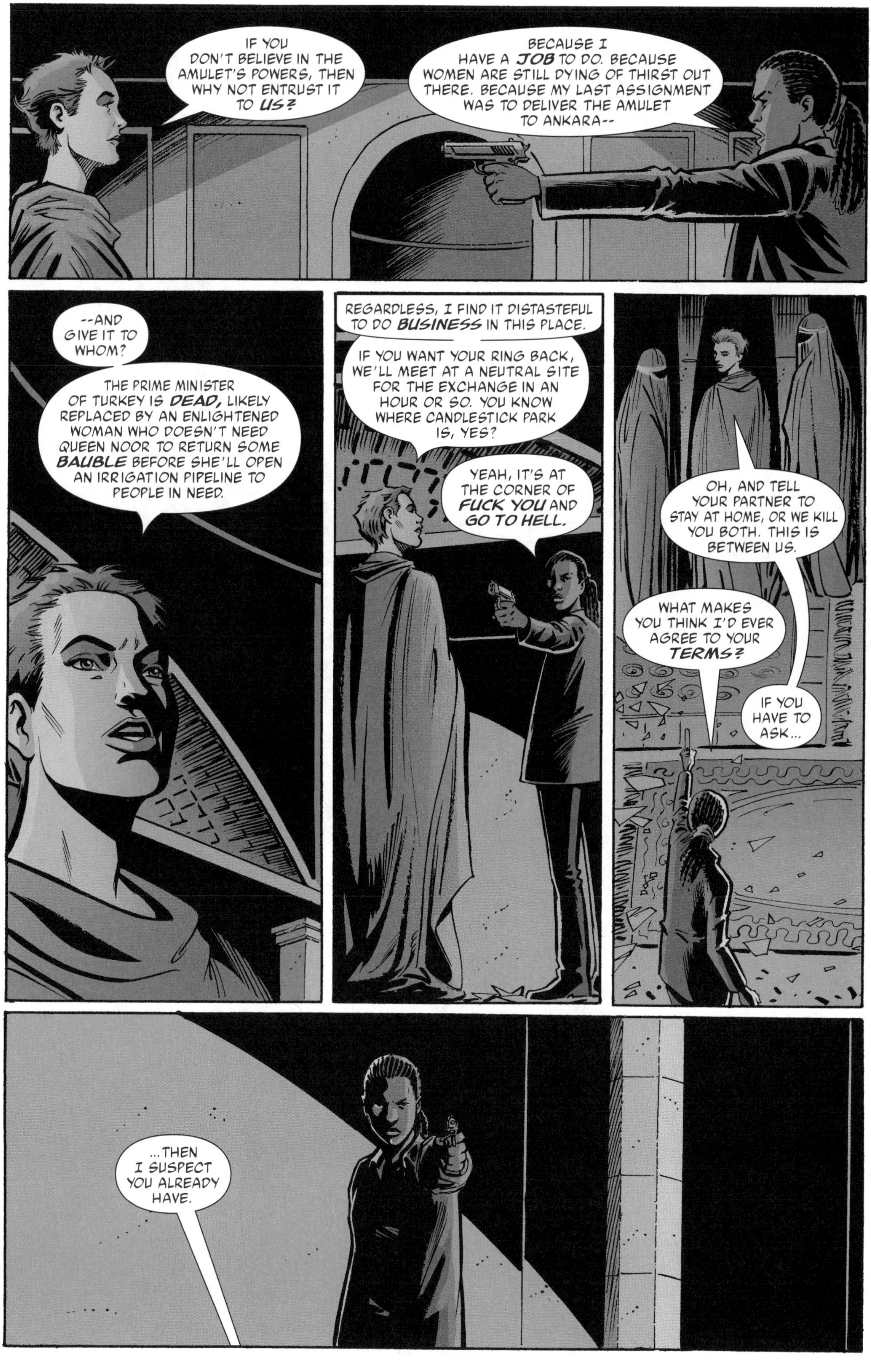
IF YOU DON'T BELIEVE IN THE AMULET'S POWERS, THEN WHY NOT ENTRUST IT TO US?
BECAUSE I HAVE A JOB TO DO. BECAUSE WOMEN ARE STILL DYING OF THIRST OUT THERE. BECAUSE MY LAST ASSIGNMENT WAS TO DELIVER THE AMULET TO ANKARA--
--AND GIVE IT TO WHOM?
THE PRIME MINISTER OF TURKEY IS DEAD, LIKELY REPLACED BY AN ENLIGHTENED WOMAN WHO DOESN'T NEED QUEEN NOOR TO RETURN SOME BAUBLE BEFORE SHE'LL OPEN AN IRRIGATION PIPELINE TO PEOPLE IN NEED.
REGARDLESS, I FIND IT DISTASTEFUL TO DO BUSINESS IN THIS PLACE.
IF YOU WANT YOUR RING BACK, WE'LL MEET AT A NEUTRAL SITE FOR THE EXCHANGE IN AN HOUR OR SO. YOU KNOW WHERE CANDLESTICK PARK IS, YES?
YEAH, IT'S AT THE CORNER OF FUCK YOU AND GO TO HELL.
OH, AND TELL YOUR PARTNER TO STAY AT HOME, OR WE KILL YOU BOTH. THIS IS BETWEEN US.
WHAT MAKES YOU THINK I'D EVER AGREE TO YOUR TERMS?
IF YOU HAVE TO ASK...
...THEN I SUSPECT YOU ALREADY HAVE.

DOC... DOCTOR... MANN...?

I'M RIGHT HERE, YORICK.

I WAS, UH, JUST PUTTING AMP IN ISOLATION. DON'T WANT YOU CATCHING *MONKEYPOX*, TOO.

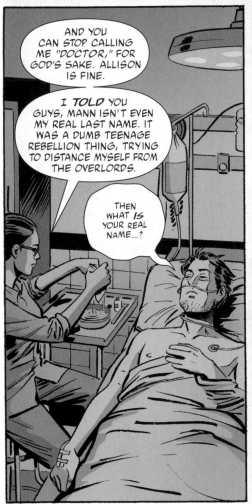

AND YOU CAN STOP CALLING ME "DOCTOR," FOR GOD'S SAKE. ALLISON IS FINE.

I *TOLD* YOU GUYS, MANN ISN'T EVEN MY REAL LAST NAME. IT WAS A DUMB TEENAGE REBELLION THING, TRYING TO DISTANCE MYSELF FROM THE OVERLORDS.

THEN WHAT *IS* YOUR REAL NAME...?

SORRY, SICKLY.

IT'S GONNA TAKE MORE THAN YOU PUKING UP YOUR SPLEEN TO GET THAT OUT OF ME.

COME ON...BACK IN 'ZONA... YOU SAID YOU'D ALWAYS TELL ME...THE *TRUTH*...

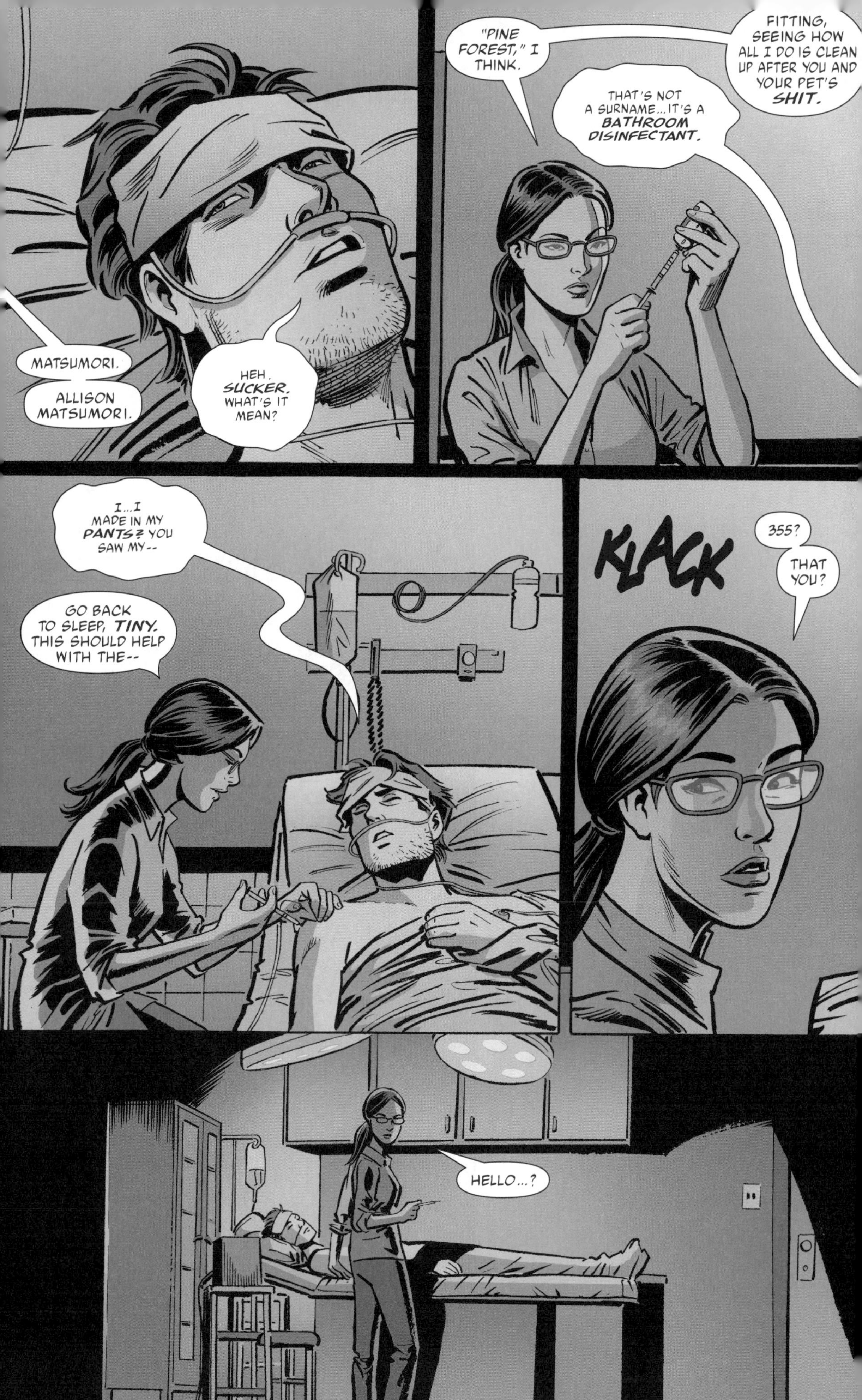
MATSUMORI.
ALLISON MATSUMORI.
HEH. SUCKER. WHAT'S IT MEAN?
"PINE FOREST," I THINK.
THAT'S NOT A SURNAME...IT'S A BATHROOM DISINFECTANT.
FITTING, SEEING HOW ALL I DO IS CLEAN UP AFTER YOU AND YOUR PET'S SHIT.
I...I MADE IN MY PANTS? YOU SAW MY--
GO BACK TO SLEEP, TINY. THIS SHOULD HELP WITH THE--
KLACK
355?
THAT YOU?
HELLO...?

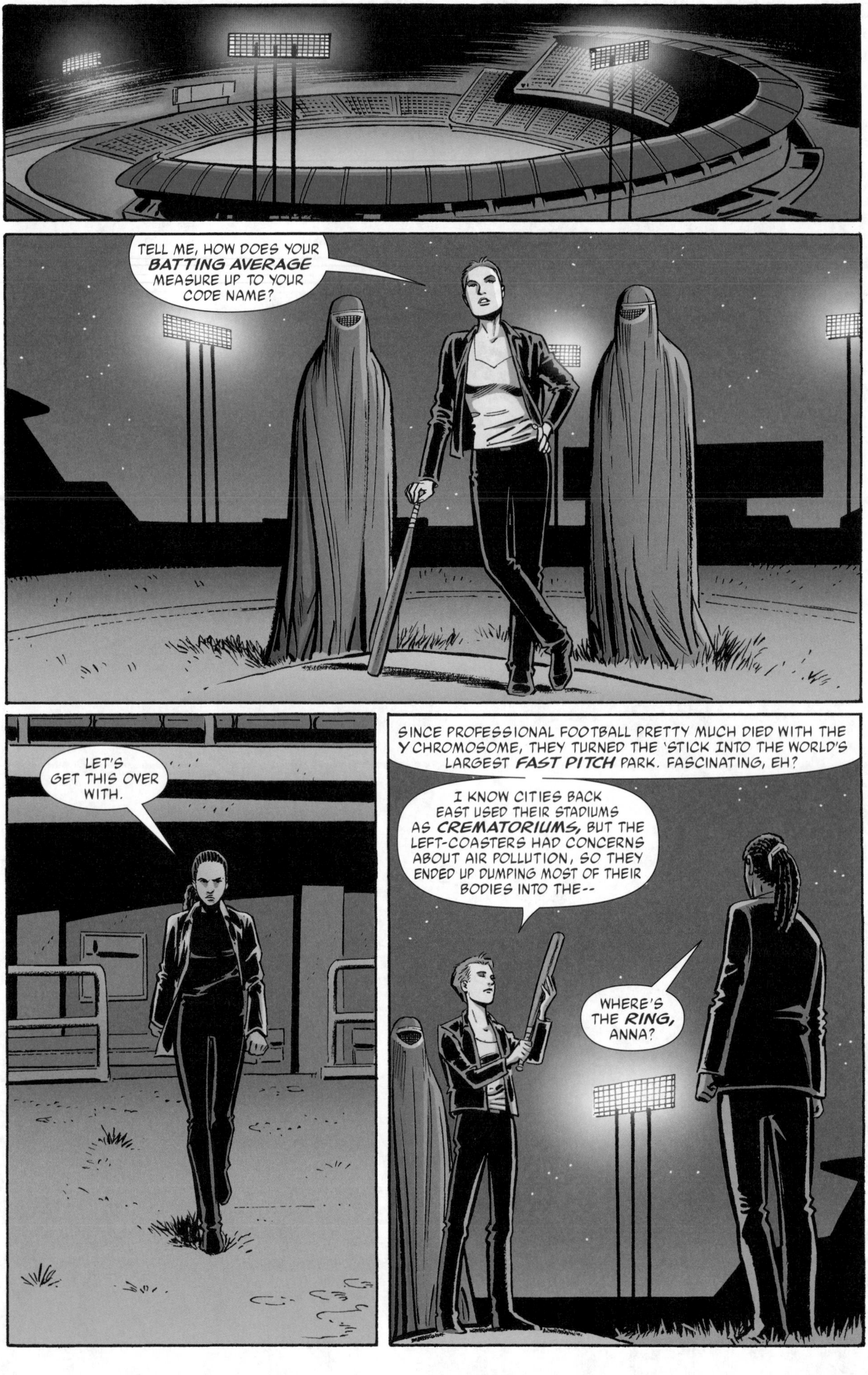

TELL ME, HOW DOES YOUR BATTING AVERAGE MEASURE UP TO YOUR CODE NAME?
LET'S GET THIS OVER WITH.
SINCE PROFESSIONAL FOOTBALL PRETTY MUCH DIED WITH THE Y CHROMOSOME, THEY TURNED THE 'STICK INTO THE WORLD'S LARGEST FAST PITCH PARK. FASCINATING, EH?
I KNOW CITIES BACK EAST USED THEIR STADIUMS AS CREMATORIUMS, BUT THE LEFT-COASTERS HAD CONCERNS ABOUT AIR POLLUTION, SO THEY ENDED UP DUMPING MOST OF THEIR BODIES INTO THE--
WHERE'S THE RING, ANNA?

DO I LOOK LIKE I *FUCK* FOR FREE?

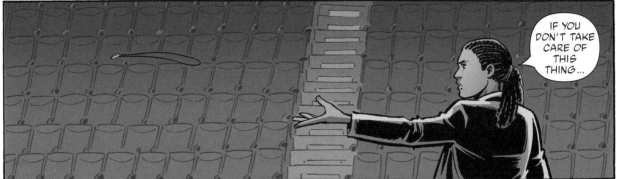

IF YOU DON'T TAKE CARE OF THIS THING...

I SWEAR BEFORE ALLAH I WILL.

AUTHENTIC?

BONA FIDE, MS. STRONG.

WELL THEN...LET'S *TAKE CARE* OF IT.

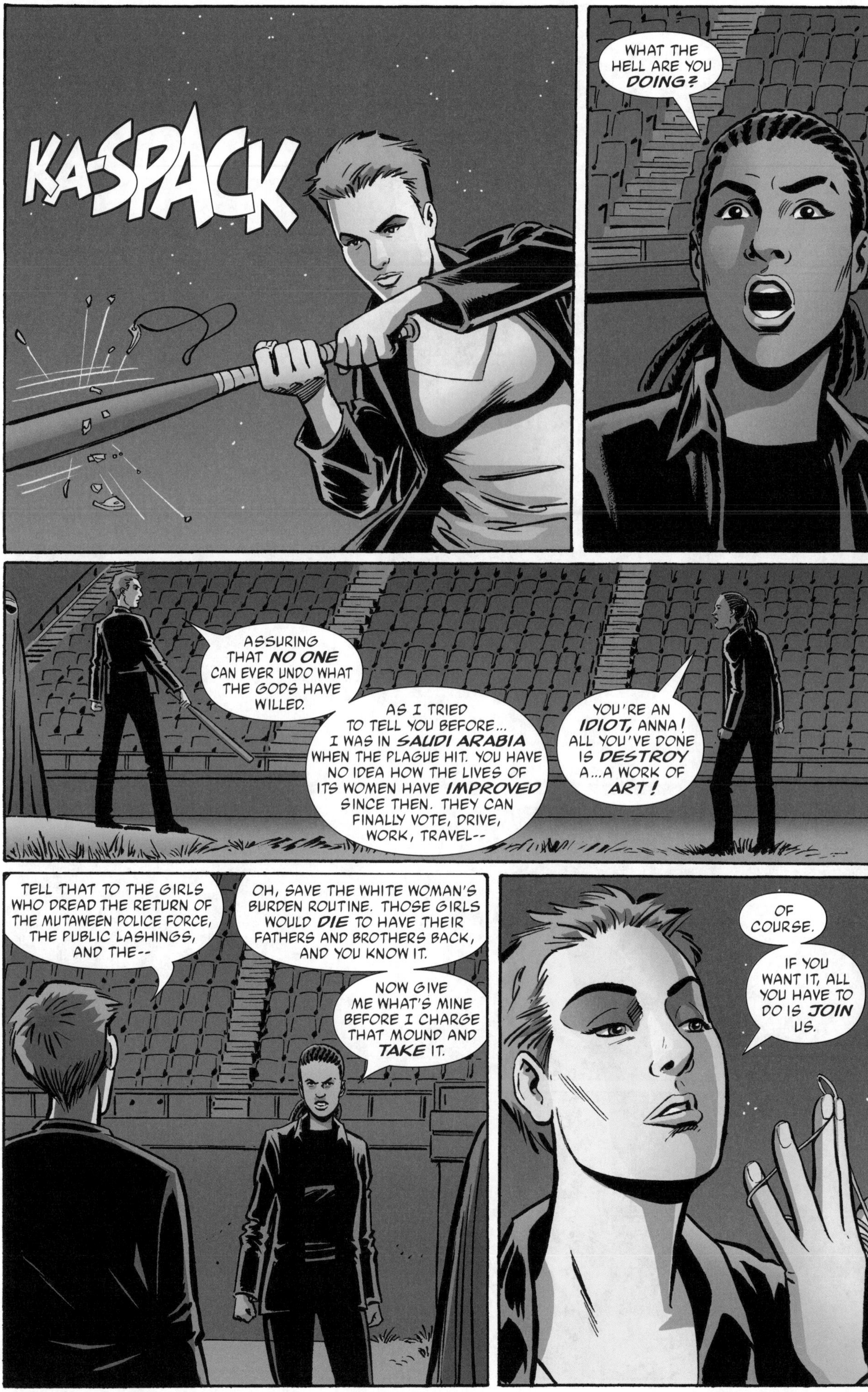
KA-SPACK
WHAT THE HELL ARE YOU DOING?
ASSURING THAT NO ONE CAN EVER UNDO WHAT THE GODS HAVE WILLED.
AS I TRIED TO TELL YOU BEFORE... I WAS IN SAUDI ARABIA WHEN THE PLAGUE HIT. YOU HAVE NO IDEA HOW THE LIVES OF ITS WOMEN HAVE IMPROVED SINCE THEN. THEY CAN FINALLY VOTE, DRIVE, WORK, TRAVEL--
YOU'RE AN IDIOT, ANNA! ALL YOU'VE DONE IS DESTROY A...A WORK OF ART!
TELL THAT TO THE GIRLS WHO DREAD THE RETURN OF THE MUTAWEEN POLICE FORCE, THE PUBLIC LASHINGS, AND THE--
OH, SAVE THE WHITE WOMAN'S BURDEN ROUTINE. THOSE GIRLS WOULD DIE TO HAVE THEIR FATHERS AND BROTHERS BACK, AND YOU KNOW IT.
NOW GIVE ME WHAT'S MINE BEFORE I CHARGE THAT MOUND AND TAKE IT.
OF COURSE.
IF YOU WANT IT, ALL YOU HAVE TO DO IS JOIN US.

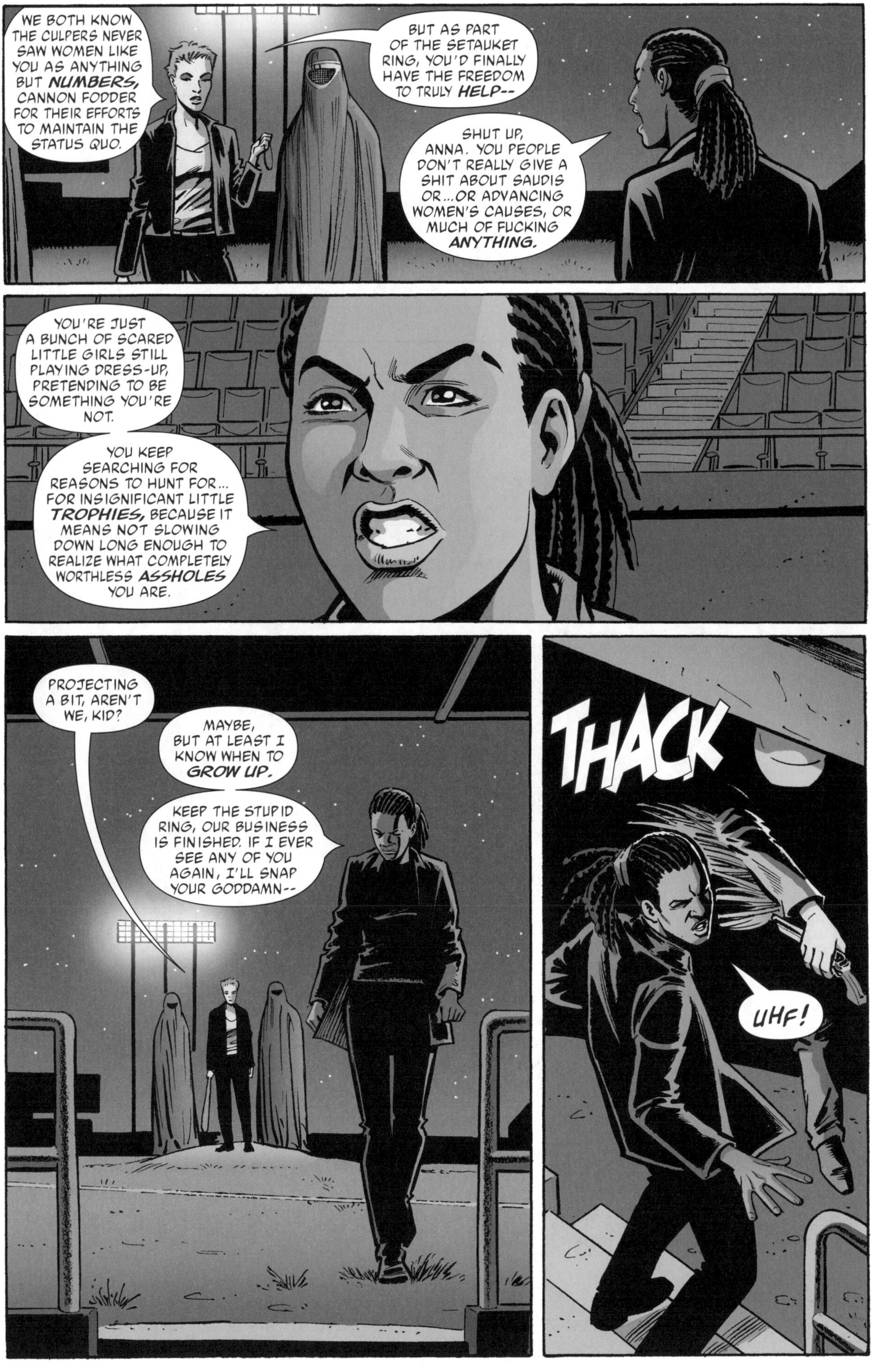
WE BOTH KNOW THE CULPERS NEVER SAW WOMEN LIKE YOU AS ANYTHING BUT **NUMBERS,** CANNON FODDER FOR THEIR EFFORTS TO MAINTAIN THE STATUS QUO.
BUT AS PART OF THE SETAUKET RING, YOU'D FINALLY HAVE THE FREEDOM TO TRULY **HELP--**
SHUT UP, ANNA. YOU PEOPLE DON'T REALLY GIVE A SHIT ABOUT SAUDIS OR...OR ADVANCING WOMEN'S CAUSES, OR MUCH OF FUCKING **ANYTHING.**
YOU'RE JUST A BUNCH OF SCARED LITTLE GIRLS STILL PLAYING DRESS-UP, PRETENDING TO BE SOMETHING YOU'RE NOT.
YOU KEEP SEARCHING FOR REASONS TO HUNT FOR... FOR INSIGNIFICANT LITTLE **TROPHIES,** BECAUSE IT MEANS NOT SLOWING DOWN LONG ENOUGH TO REALIZE WHAT COMPLETELY WORTHLESS **ASSHOLES** YOU ARE.
PROJECTING A BIT, AREN'T WE, KID?
MAYBE, BUT AT LEAST I KNOW WHEN TO **GROW UP.**
KEEP THE STUPID RING, OUR BUSINESS IS FINISHED. IF I EVER SEE ANY OF YOU AGAIN, I'LL SNAP YOUR GODDAMN--
THACK
UHF!

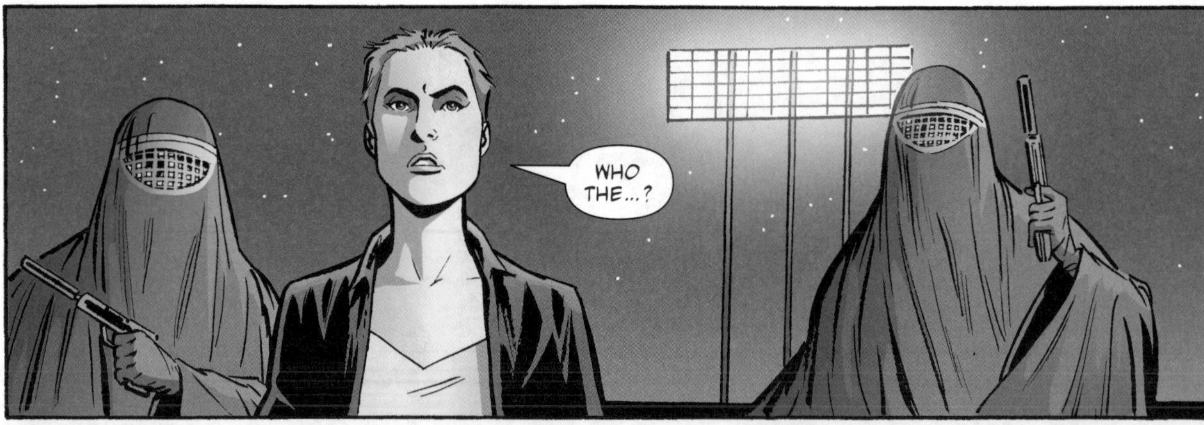
WHO THE...?

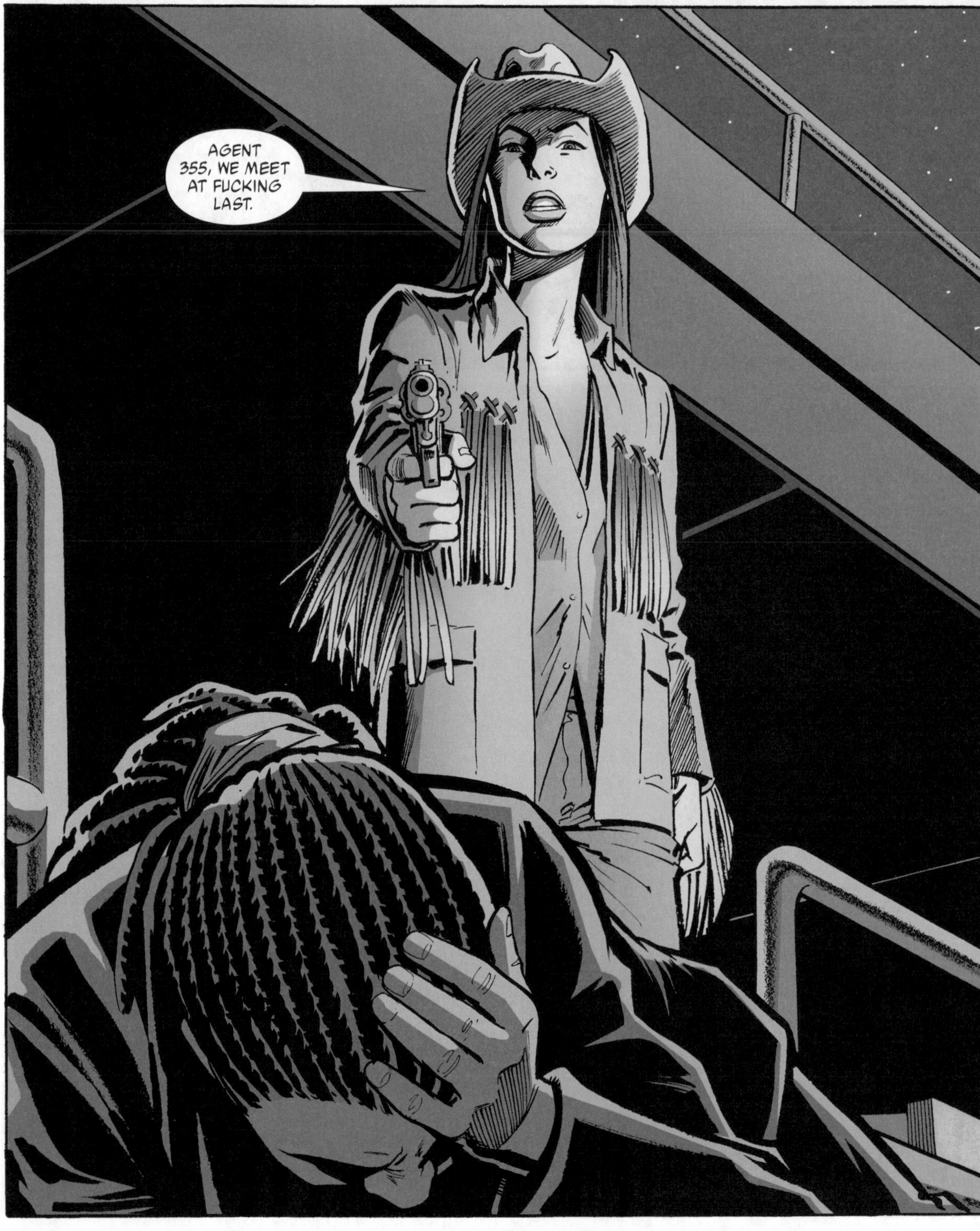
AGENT 355, WE MEET AT FUCKING LAST.

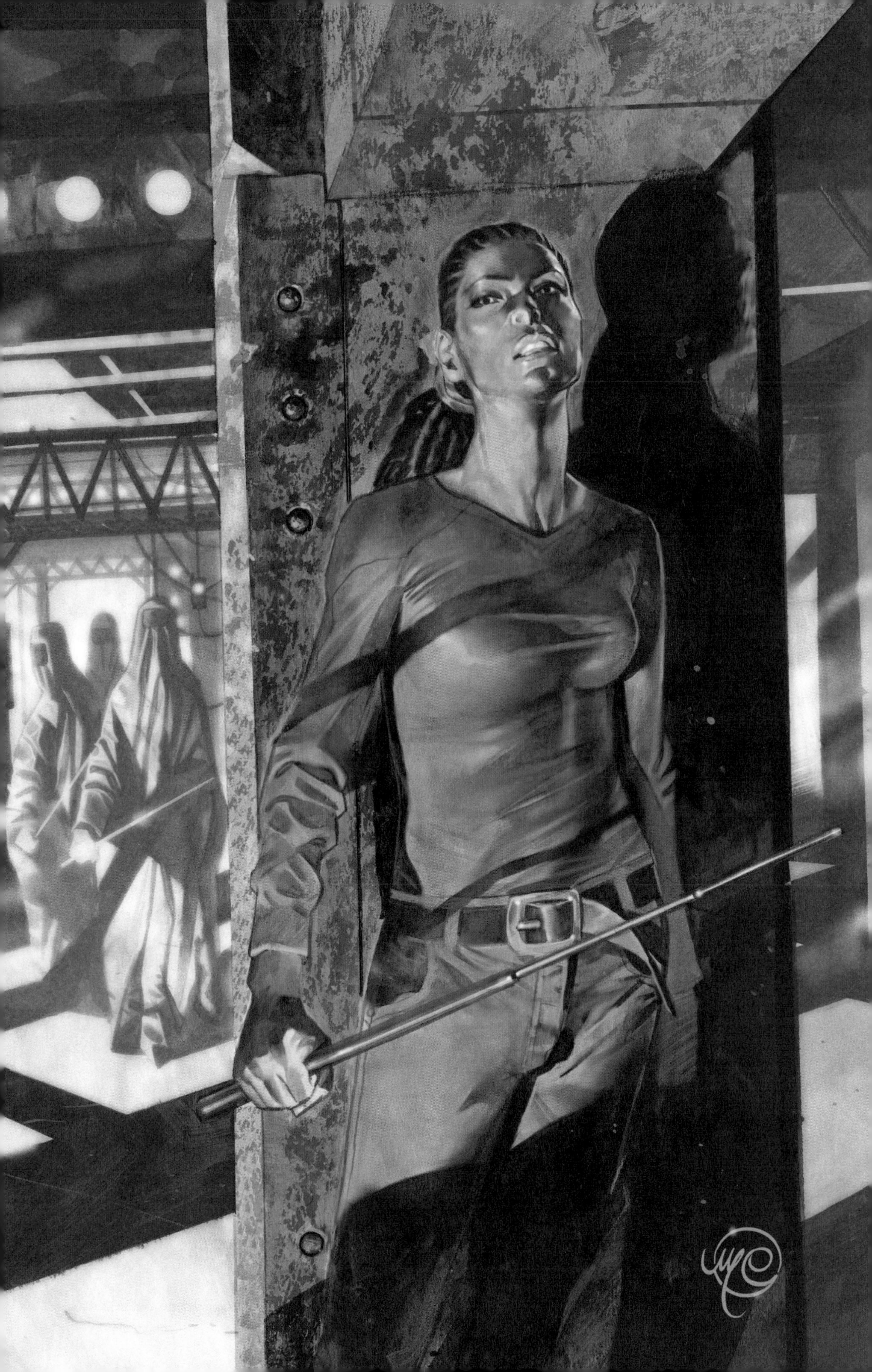

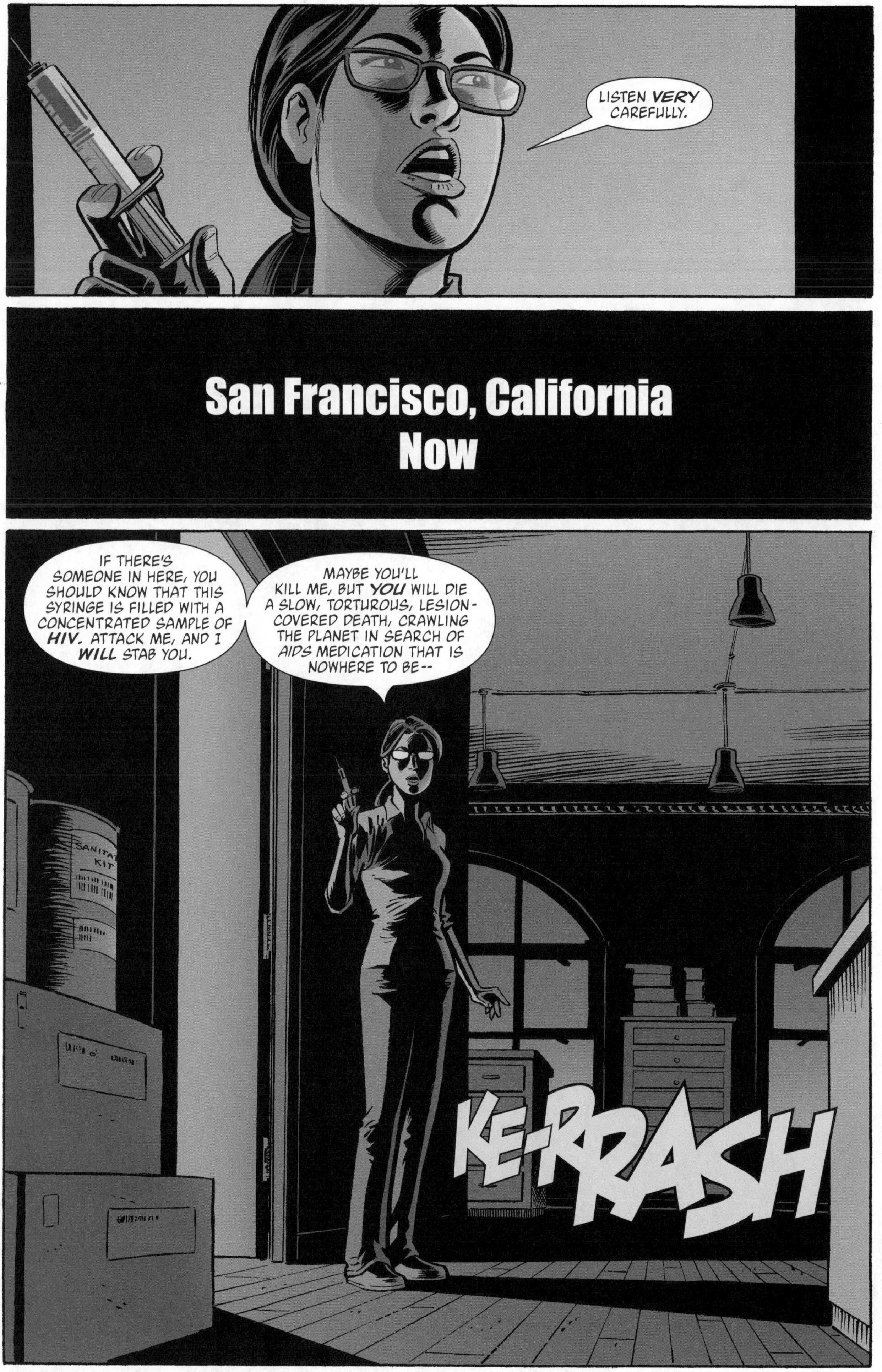
LISTEN VERY CAREFULLY.
San Francisco, California
Now
IF THERE'S SOMEONE IN HERE, YOU SHOULD KNOW THAT THIS SYRINGE IS FILLED WITH A CONCENTRATED SAMPLE OF HIV. ATTACK ME, AND I WILL STAB YOU.
MAYBE YOU'LL KILL ME, BUT YOU WILL DIE A SLOW, TORTUROUS, LESION-COVERED DEATH, CRAWLING THE PLANET IN SEARCH OF AIDS MEDICATION THAT IS NOWHERE TO BE--
KE-RRASH

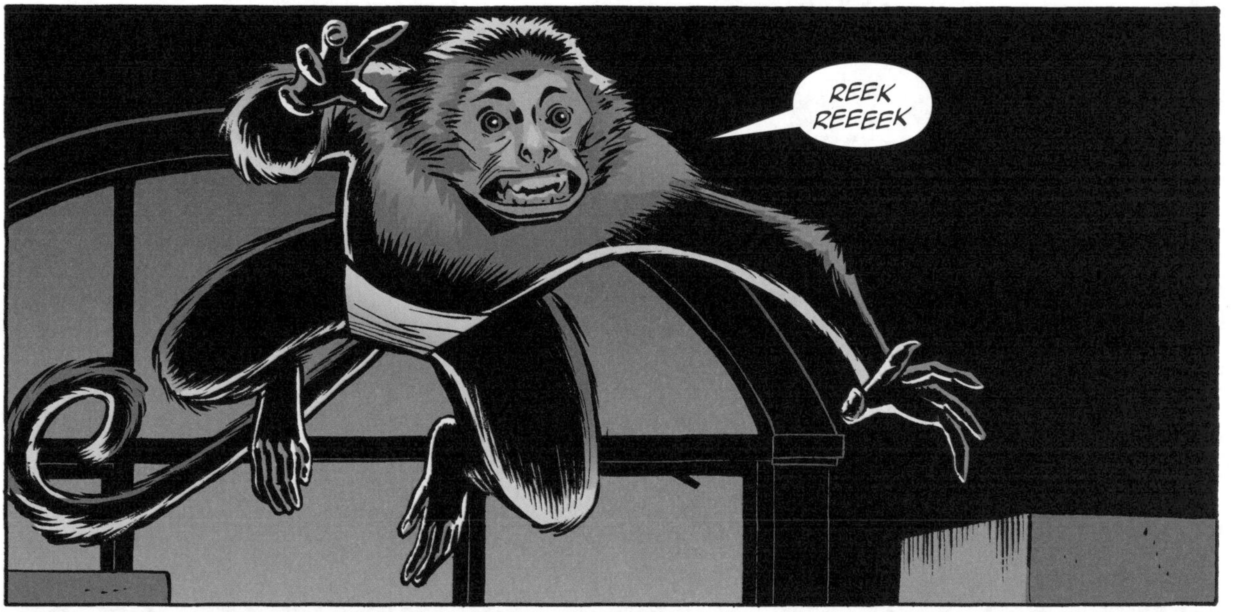
REEK REEEEEK

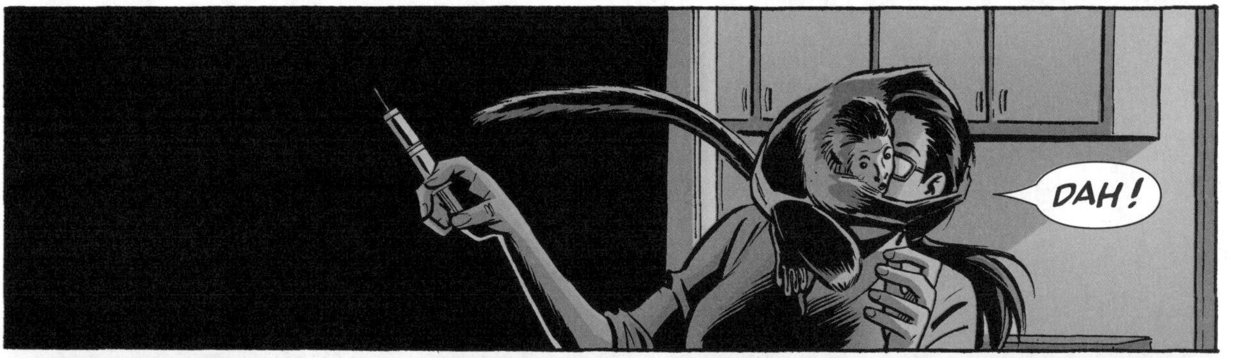
DAH!

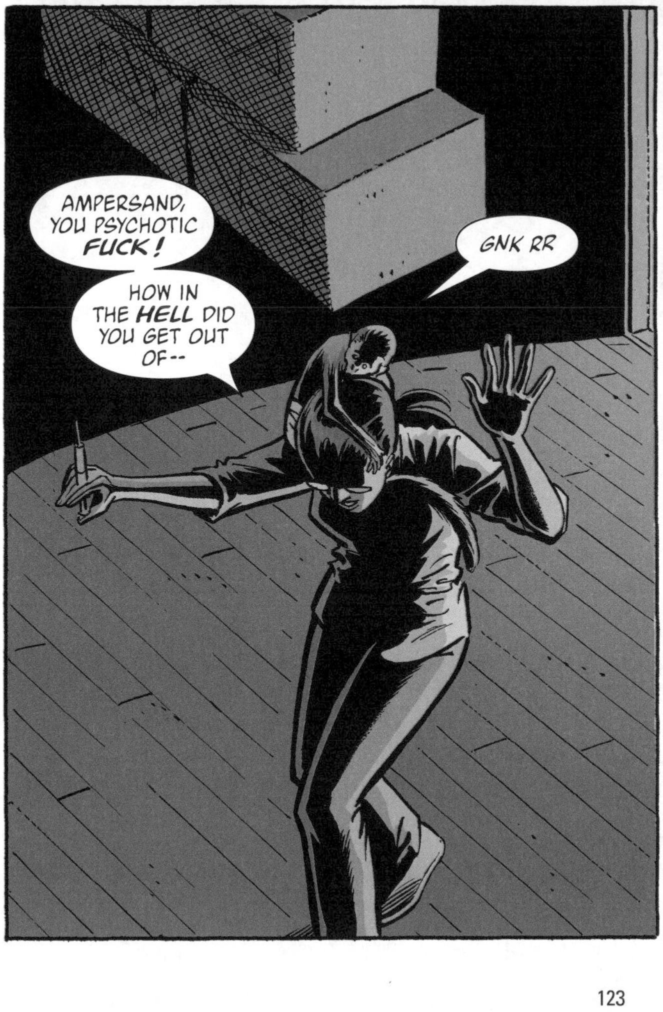
AMPERSAND, YOU PSYCHOTIC FUCK!
HOW IN THE HELL DID YOU GET OUT OF--
GNK RR

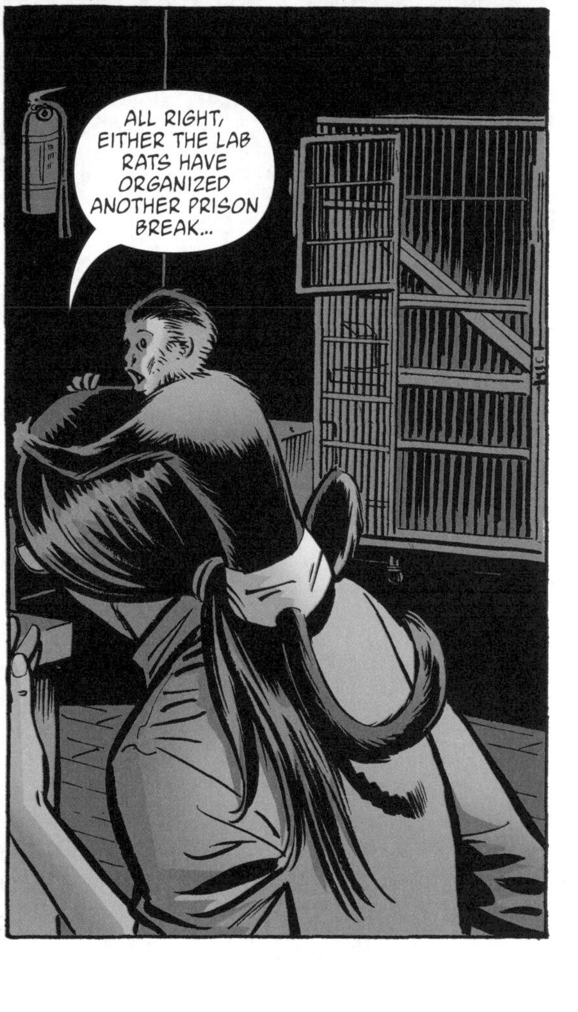
ALL RIGHT, EITHER THE LAB RATS HAVE ORGANIZED ANOTHER PRISON BREAK...

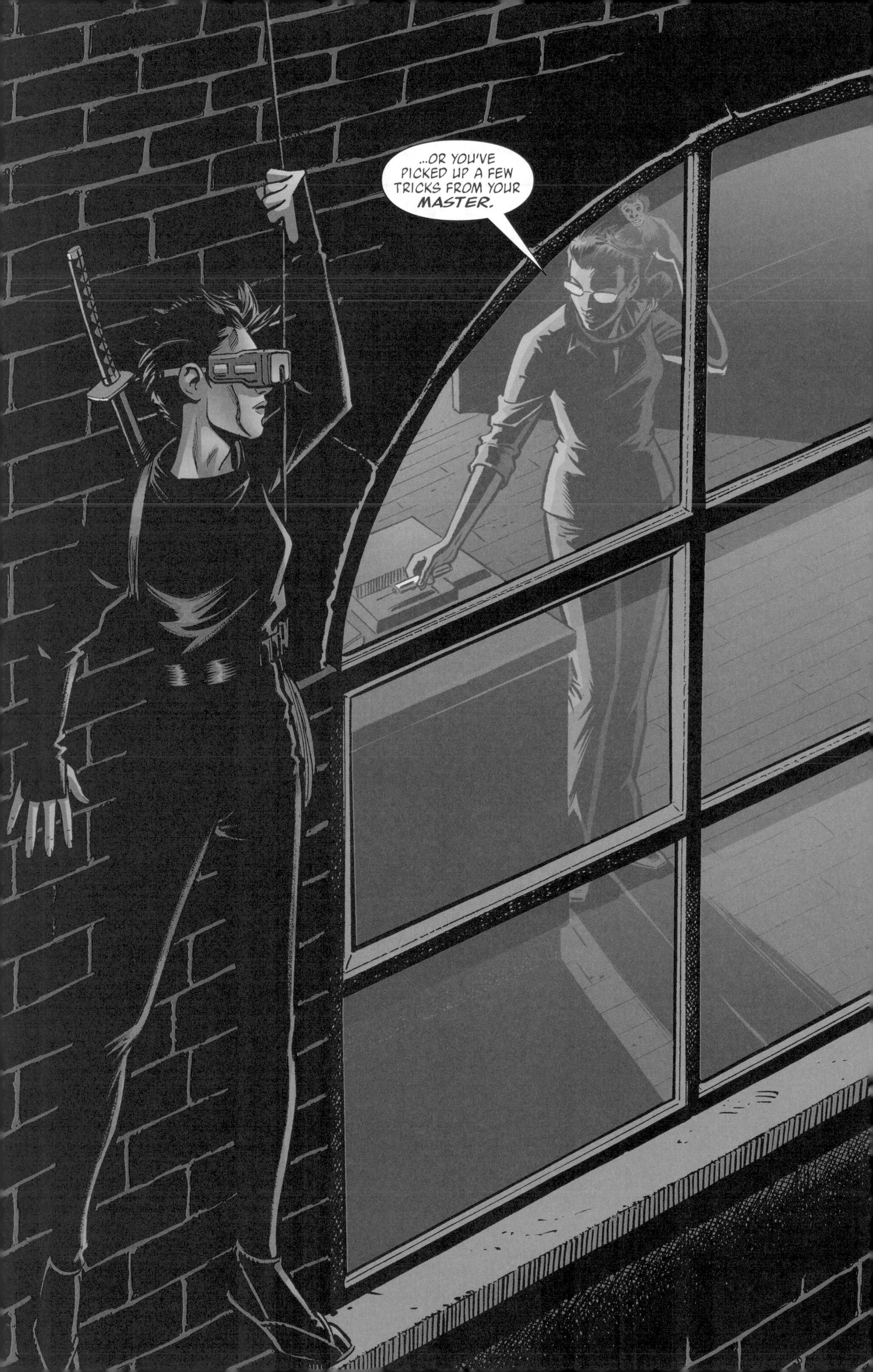
...OR YOU'VE PICKED UP A FEW TRICKS FROM YOUR MASTER.

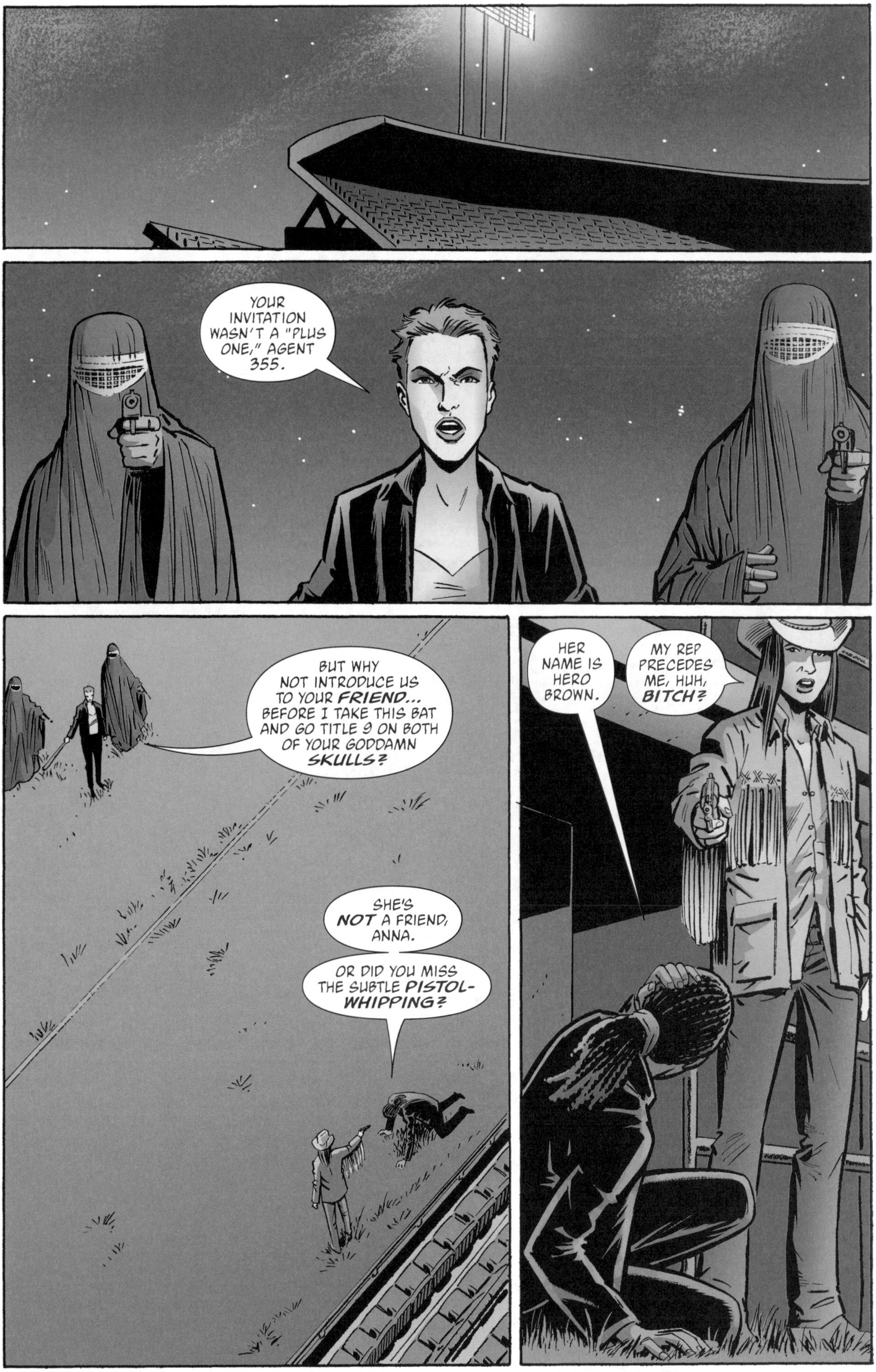
YOUR INVITATION WASN'T A "PLUS ONE," AGENT 355.
BUT WHY NOT INTRODUCE US TO YOUR FRIEND... BEFORE I TAKE THIS BAT AND GO TITLE 9 ON BOTH OF YOUR GODDAMN SKULLS?
SHE'S NOT A FRIEND, ANNA.
OR DID YOU MISS THE SUBTLE PISTOL-WHIPPING?
HER NAME IS HERO BROWN.
MY REP PRECEDES ME, HUH, BITCH?

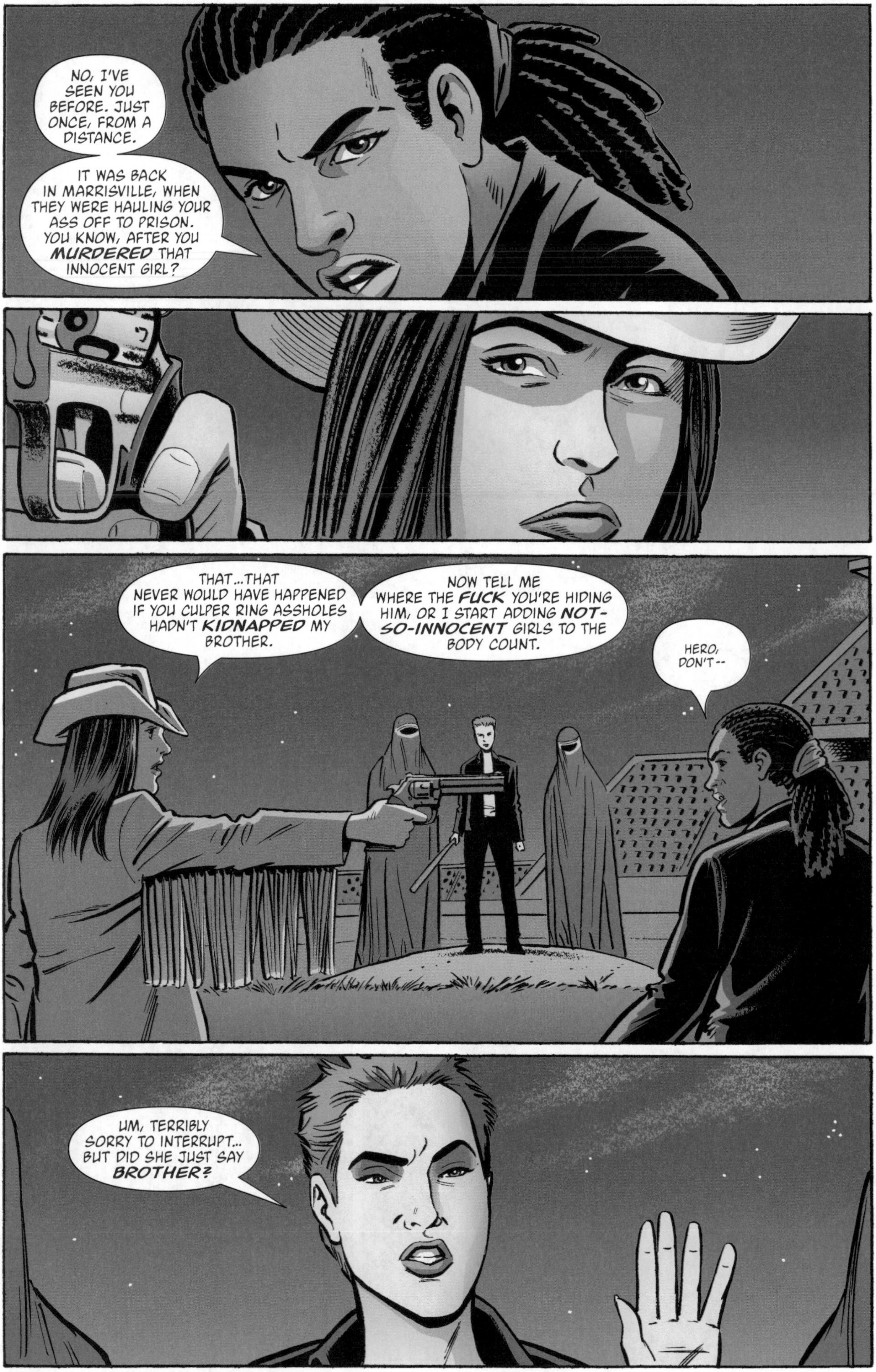
NO, I'VE SEEN YOU BEFORE. JUST ONCE, FROM A DISTANCE.
IT WAS BACK IN MARRISVILLE, WHEN THEY WERE HAULING YOUR ASS OFF TO PRISON. YOU KNOW, AFTER YOU MURDERED THAT INNOCENT GIRL?
THAT...THAT NEVER WOULD HAVE HAPPENED IF YOU CULPER RING ASSHOLES HADN'T KIDNAPPED MY BROTHER.
NOW TELL ME WHERE THE FUCK YOU'RE HIDING HIM, OR I START ADDING NOT-SO-INNOCENT GIRLS TO THE BODY COUNT.
HERO, DON'T--
UM, TERRIBLY SORRY TO INTERRUPT... BUT DID SHE JUST SAY BROTHER?

WHH...?

I'M DISAPPOINTED, YORICK.

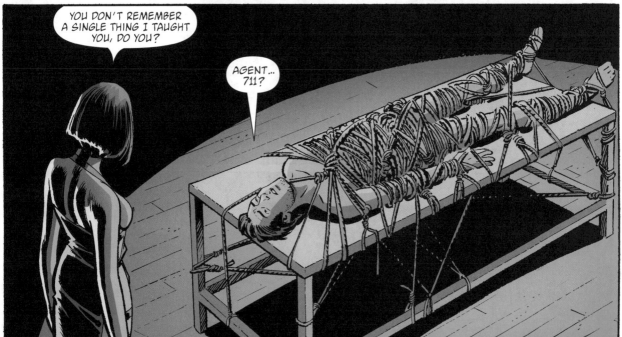

YOU DON'T REMEMBER A SINGLE THING I TAUGHT YOU, DO YOU?

AGENT... 711?

I THOUGHT YOU PROMISED TO *QUIT* YOUR FAGGY LITTLE SUICIDE ATTEMPTS?

SUICIDE? I DON'T *WANT* TO DIE, 711. I'M... I'M SICK. THE PLAGUE FINALLY CAUGHT UP WITH ME. THERE'S NOTHING I CAN DO ABOUT IT.

BULLSHIT. YOU CAN ESCAPE THIS, AS LONG AS YOU DON'T *PUSS OUT,* HARDLY HOUDINI.

I MEAN, WHAT HAPPENED TO WHATEVER THE FUCK YOU SAW WHEN YOU HAD YOUR *"EPIPHANY"?* THE THING THAT MADE YOU WANT TO *FIGHT* FOR LIFE?

WHAT WAS IT AGAIN...?

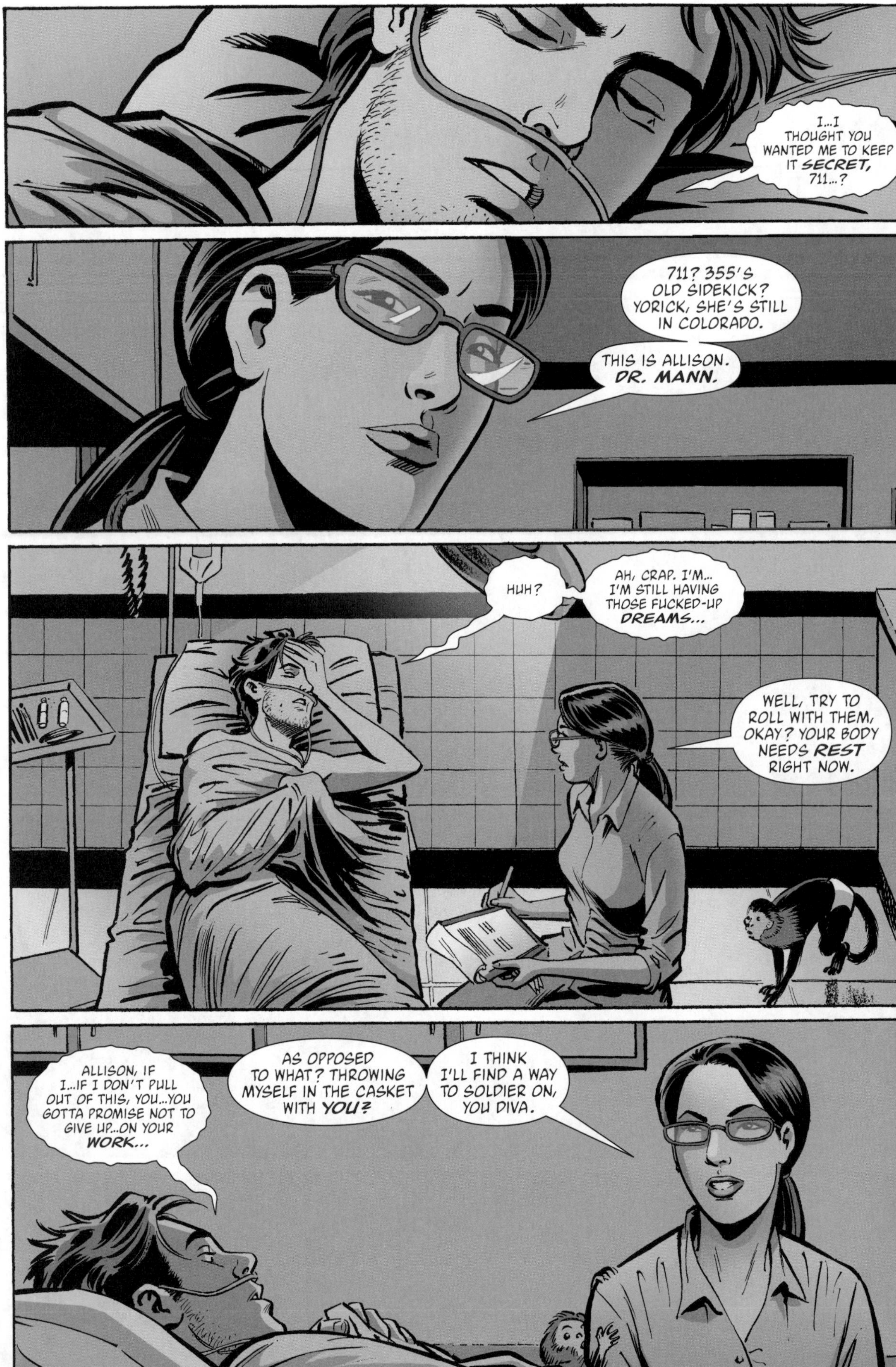
I...I THOUGHT YOU WANTED ME TO KEEP IT SECRET, 711...?
711? 355'S OLD SIDEKICK? YORICK, SHE'S STILL IN COLORADO.
THIS IS ALLISON. DR. MANN.
HUH?
AH, CRAP. I'M... I'M STILL HAVING THOSE FUCKED-UP DREAMS...
WELL, TRY TO ROLL WITH THEM, OKAY? YOUR BODY NEEDS REST RIGHT NOW.
ALLISON, IF I...IF I DON'T PULL OUT OF THIS, YOU...YOU GOTTA PROMISE NOT TO GIVE UP...ON YOUR WORK...
AS OPPOSED TO WHAT? THROWING MYSELF IN THE CASKET WITH YOU?
I THINK I'LL FIND A WAY TO SOLDIER ON, YOU DIVA.

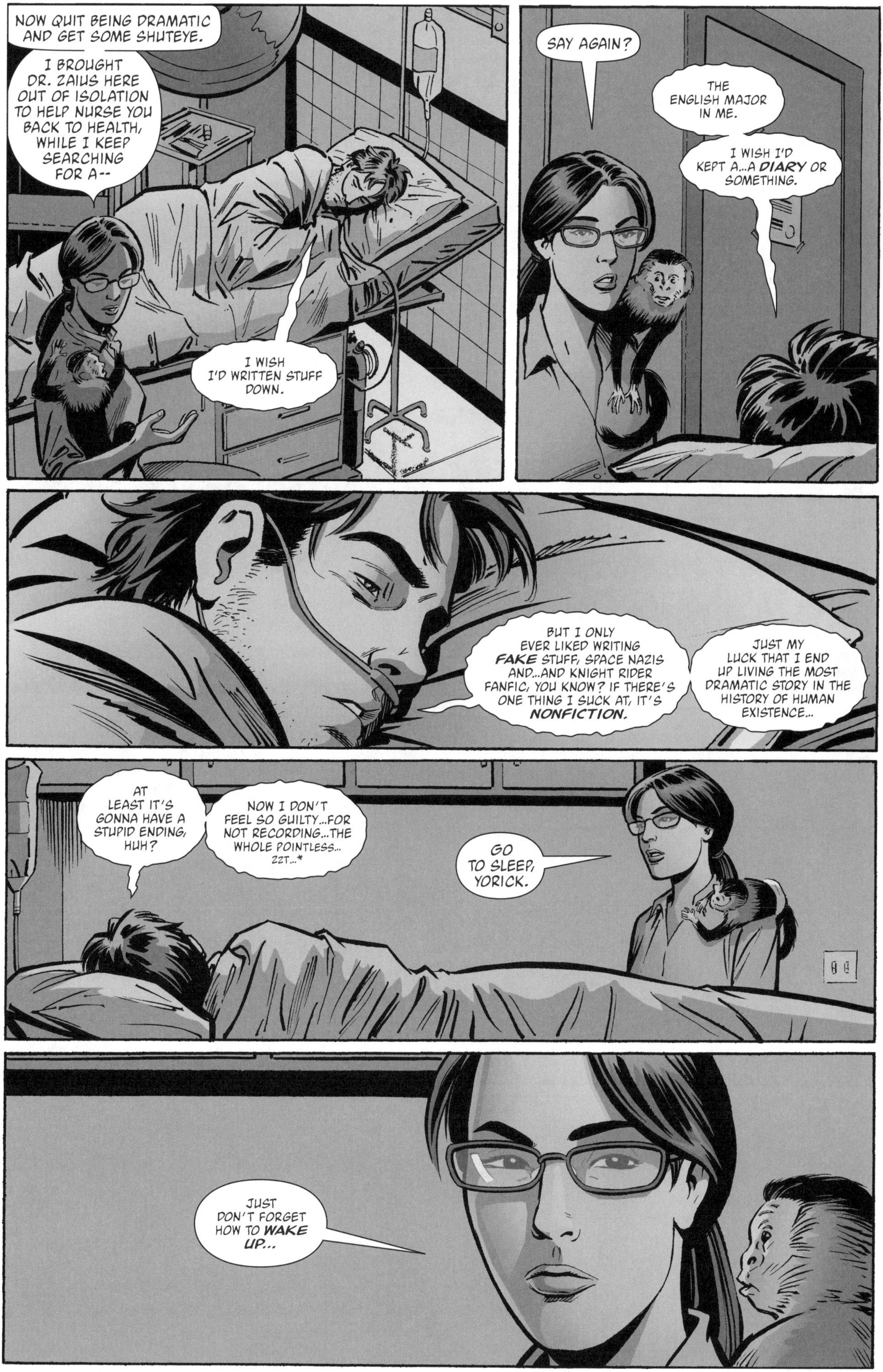
NOW QUIT BEING DRAMATIC AND GET SOME SHUTEYE.
I BROUGHT DR. ZAIUS HERE OUT OF ISOLATION TO HELP NURSE YOU BACK TO HEALTH, WHILE I KEEP SEARCHING FOR A--
I WISH I'D WRITTEN STUFF DOWN.
SAY AGAIN?
THE ENGLISH MAJOR IN ME.
I WISH I'D KEPT A...A **DIARY** OR SOMETHING.
BUT I ONLY EVER LIKED WRITING **FAKE** STUFF, SPACE NAZIS AND...AND KNIGHT RIDER FANFIC, YOU KNOW? IF THERE'S ONE THING I SUCK AT, IT'S **NONFICTION.**
JUST MY LUCK THAT I END UP LIVING THE MOST DRAMATIC STORY IN THE HISTORY OF HUMAN EXISTENCE...
AT LEAST IT'S GONNA HAVE A STUPID ENDING, HUH?
NOW I DON'T FEEL SO GUILTY...FOR NOT RECORDING...THE WHOLE POINTLESS... ZZT...*
GO TO SLEEP, YORICK.
JUST DON'T FORGET HOW TO **WAKE UP...**

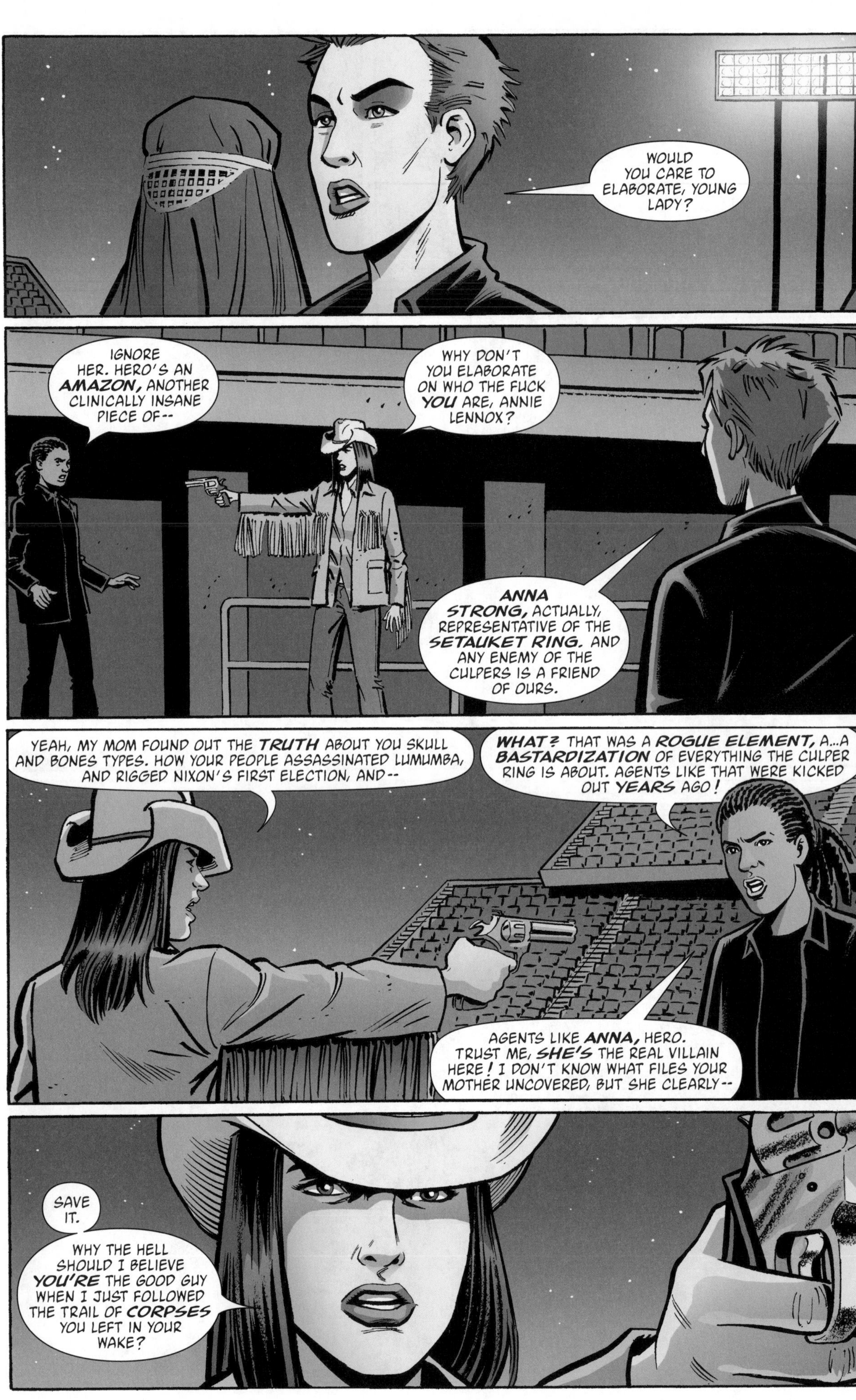

WOULD YOU CARE TO ELABORATE, YOUNG LADY?
IGNORE HER. HERO'S AN AMAZON, ANOTHER CLINICALLY INSANE PIECE OF--
WHY DON'T YOU ELABORATE ON WHO THE FUCK YOU ARE, ANNIE LENNOX?
ANNA STRONG, ACTUALLY, REPRESENTATIVE OF THE SETAUKET RING. AND ANY ENEMY OF THE CULPERS IS A FRIEND OF OURS.
YEAH, MY MOM FOUND OUT THE TRUTH ABOUT YOU SKULL AND BONES TYPES. HOW YOUR PEOPLE ASSASSINATED LUMUMBA, AND RIGGED NIXON'S FIRST ELECTION, AND--
WHAT? THAT WAS A ROGUE ELEMENT, A...A BASTARDIZATION OF EVERYTHING THE CULPER RING IS ABOUT. AGENTS LIKE THAT WERE KICKED OUT YEARS AGO!
AGENTS LIKE ANNA, HERO. TRUST ME, SHE'S THE REAL VILLAIN HERE! I DON'T KNOW WHAT FILES YOUR MOTHER UNCOVERED, BUT SHE CLEARLY--
SAVE IT.
WHY THE HELL SHOULD I BELIEVE YOU'RE THE GOOD GUY WHEN I JUST FOLLOWED THE TRAIL OF CORPSES YOU LEFT IN YOUR WAKE?

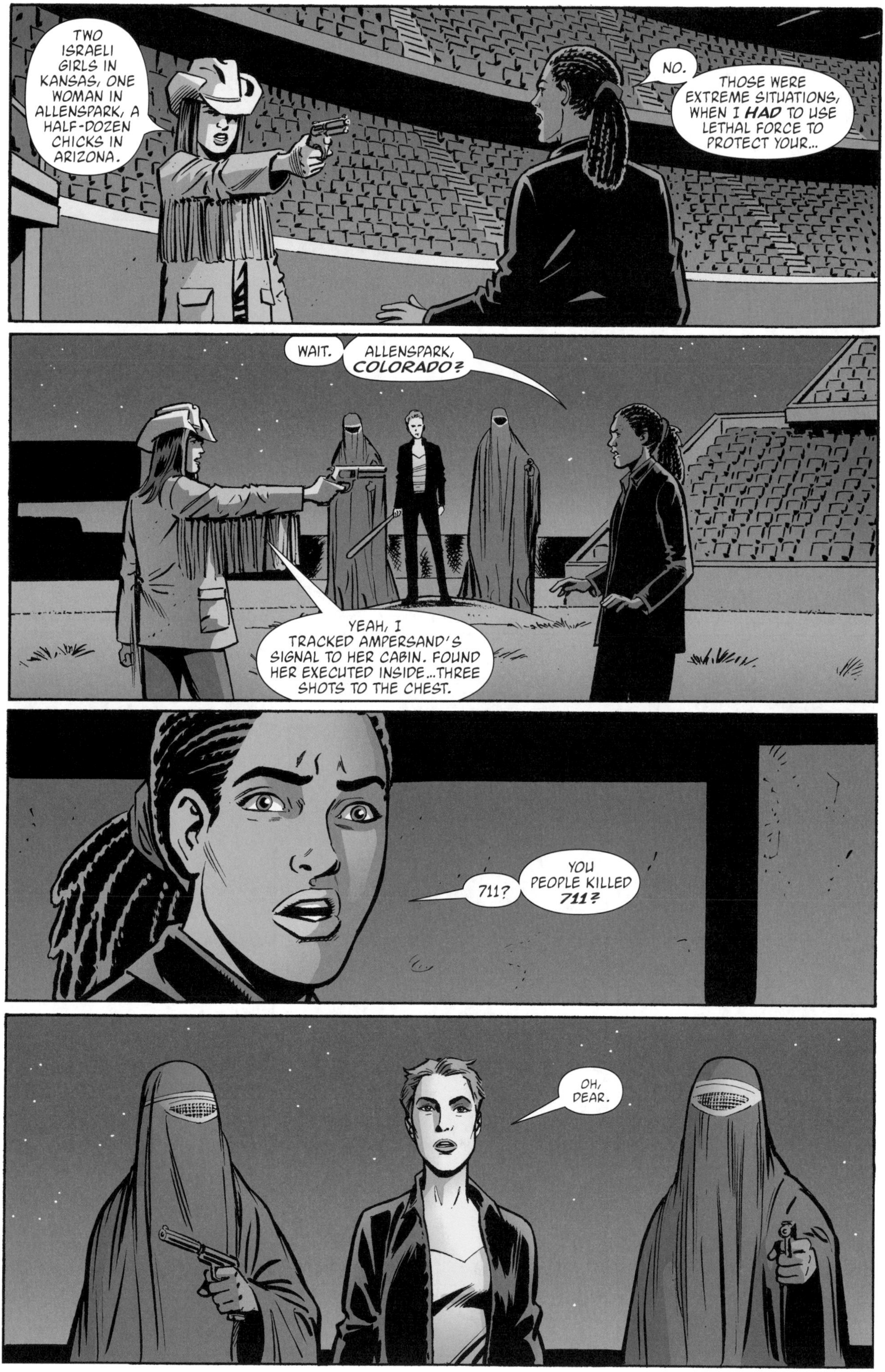
TWO ISRAELI GIRLS IN KANSAS, ONE WOMAN IN ALLENSPARK, A HALF-DOZEN CHICKS IN ARIZONA.
NO.
THOSE WERE EXTREME SITUATIONS, WHEN I **HAD** TO USE LETHAL FORCE TO PROTECT YOUR...
WAIT.
ALLENSPARK, **COLORADO?**
YEAH, I TRACKED AMPERSAND'S SIGNAL TO HER CABIN. FOUND HER EXECUTED INSIDE...THREE SHOTS TO THE CHEST.
711?
YOU PEOPLE KILLED **711?**
OH, DEAR.

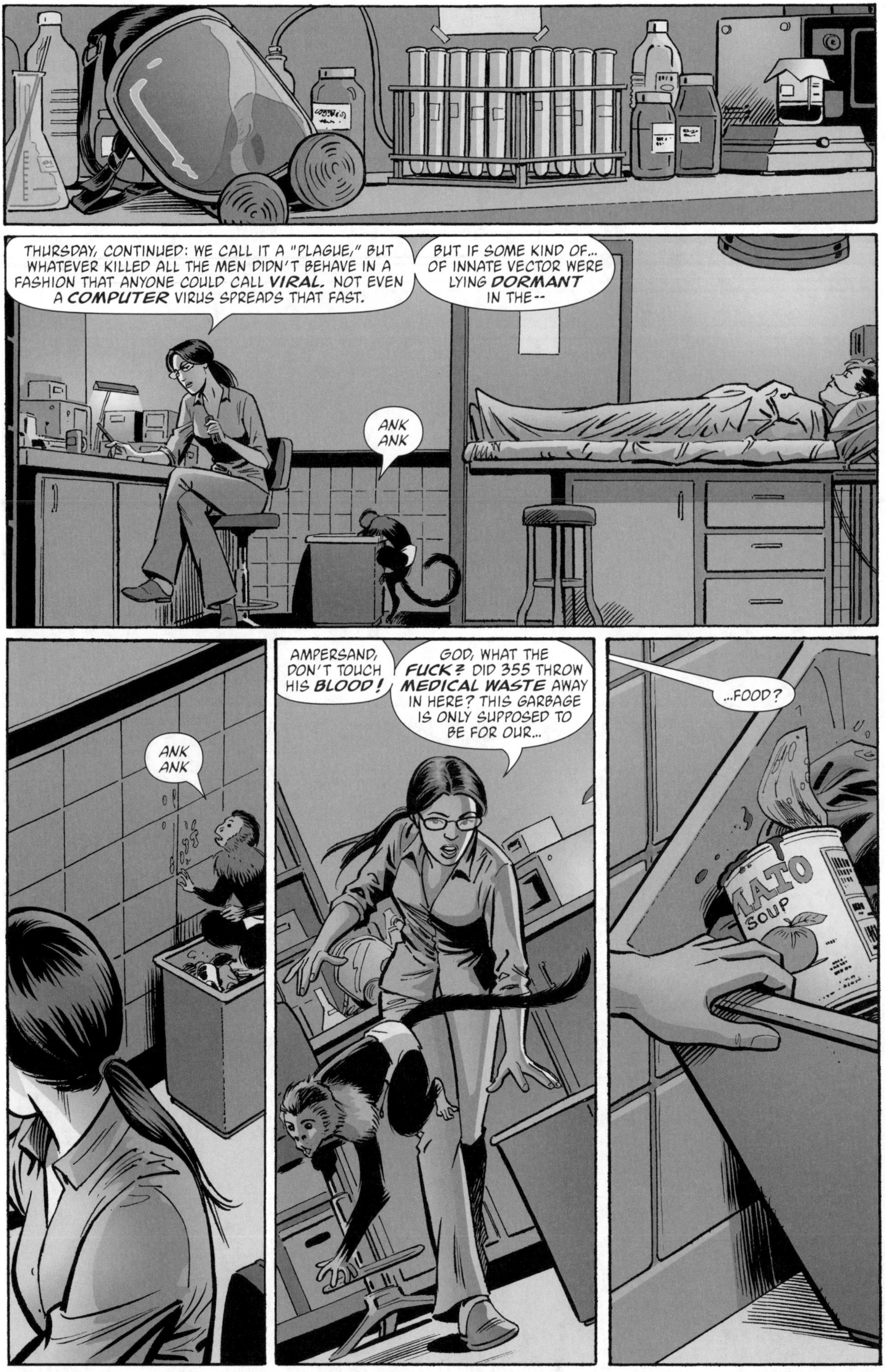
THURSDAY, CONTINUED: WE CALL IT A "PLAGUE," BUT WHATEVER KILLED ALL THE MEN DIDN'T BEHAVE IN A FASHION THAT ANYONE COULD CALL VIRAL. NOT EVEN A COMPUTER VIRUS SPREADS THAT FAST.
BUT IF SOME KIND OF... OF INNATE VECTOR WERE LYING DORMANT IN THE--
ANK ANK
ANK ANK
AMPERSAND, DON'T TOUCH HIS BLOOD!
GOD, WHAT THE FUCK? DID 355 THROW MEDICAL WASTE AWAY IN HERE? THIS GARBAGE IS ONLY SUPPOSED TO BE FOR OUR...
...FOOD?
MATO
SOUP

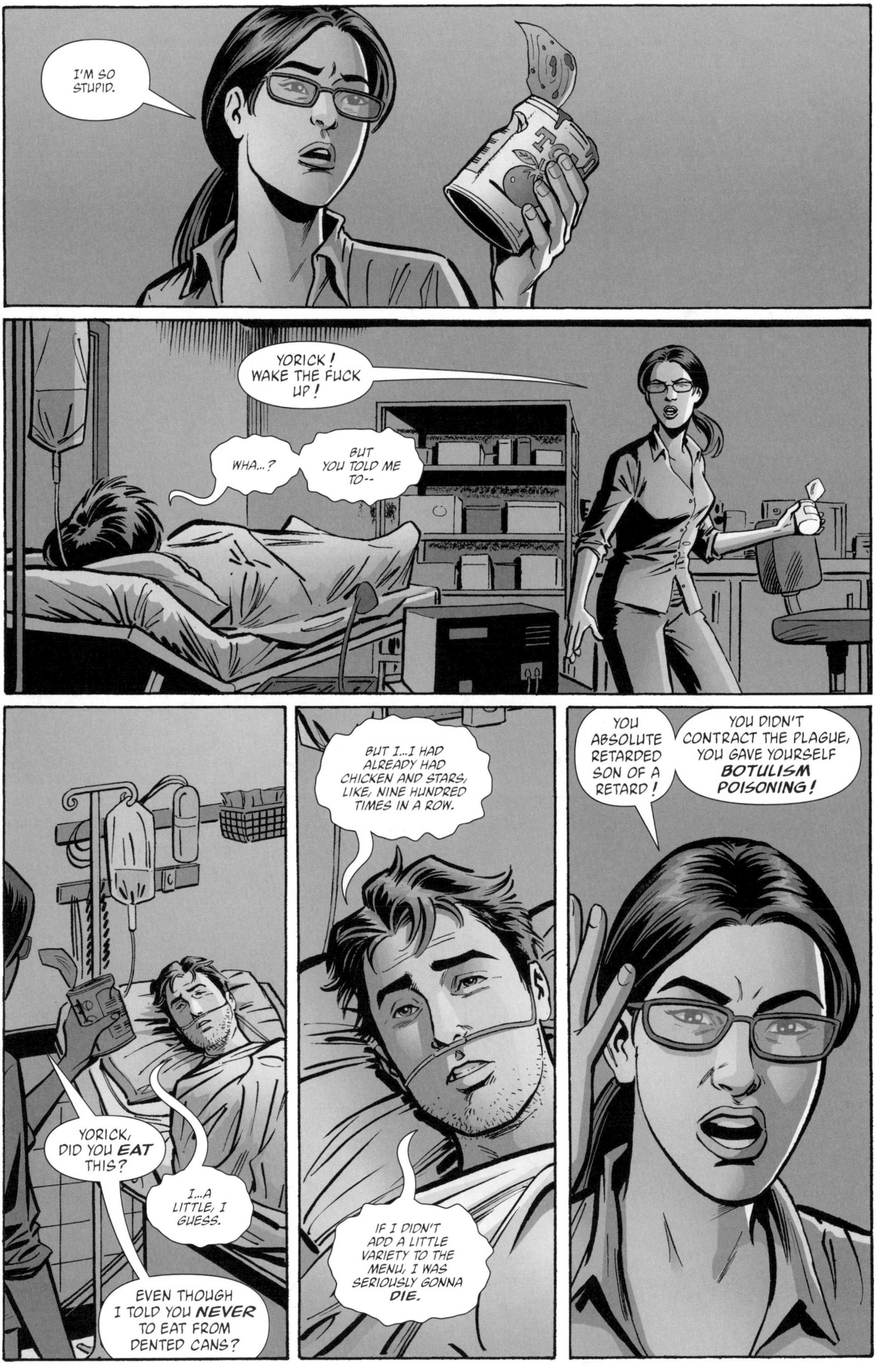
I'M SO STUPID.
YORICK! WAKE THE FUCK UP!
WHA...?
BUT YOU TOLD ME TO--
YORICK, DID YOU EAT THIS?
I...A LITTLE, I GUESS.
EVEN THOUGH I TOLD YOU NEVER TO EAT FROM DENTED CANS?
BUT I...I HAD ALREADY HAD CHICKEN AND STARS, LIKE, NINE HUNDRED TIMES IN A ROW.
IF I DIDN'T ADD A LITTLE VARIETY TO THE MENU, I WAS SERIOUSLY GONNA DIE.
YOU ABSOLUTE RETARDED SON OF A RETARD!
YOU DIDN'T CONTRACT THE PLAGUE, YOU GAVE YOURSELF BOTULISM POISONING!

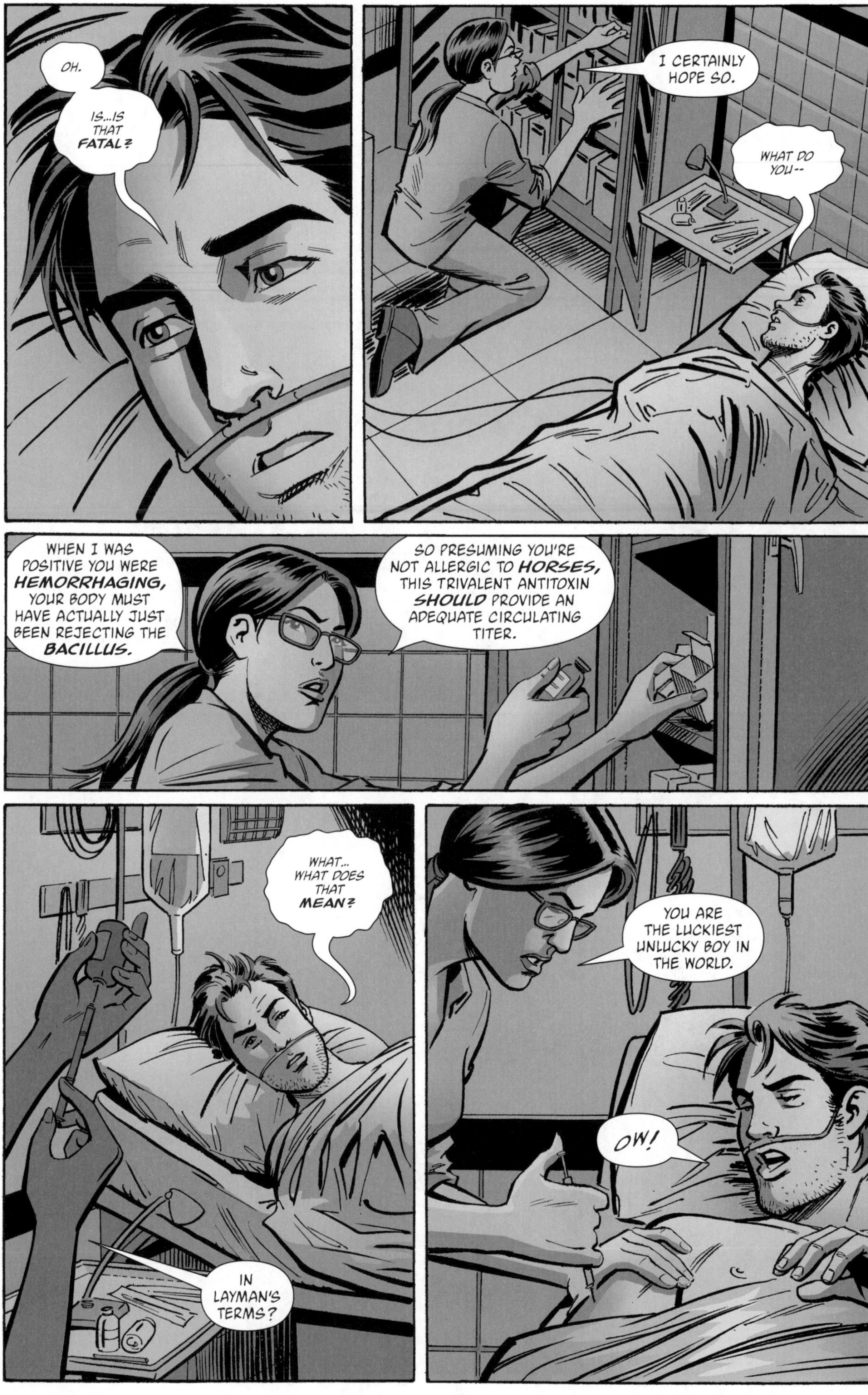
OH.
IS...IS THAT FATAL?
I CERTAINLY HOPE SO.
WHAT DO YOU--
WHEN I WAS POSITIVE YOU WERE HEMORRHAGING, YOUR BODY MUST HAVE ACTUALLY JUST BEEN REJECTING THE BACILLUS.
SO PRESUMING YOU'RE NOT ALLERGIC TO HORSES, THIS TRIVALENT ANTITOXIN SHOULD PROVIDE AN ADEQUATE CIRCULATING TITER.
WHAT... WHAT DOES THAT MEAN?
IN LAYMAN'S TERMS?
YOU ARE THE LUCKIEST UNLUCKY BOY IN THE WORLD.
OW!

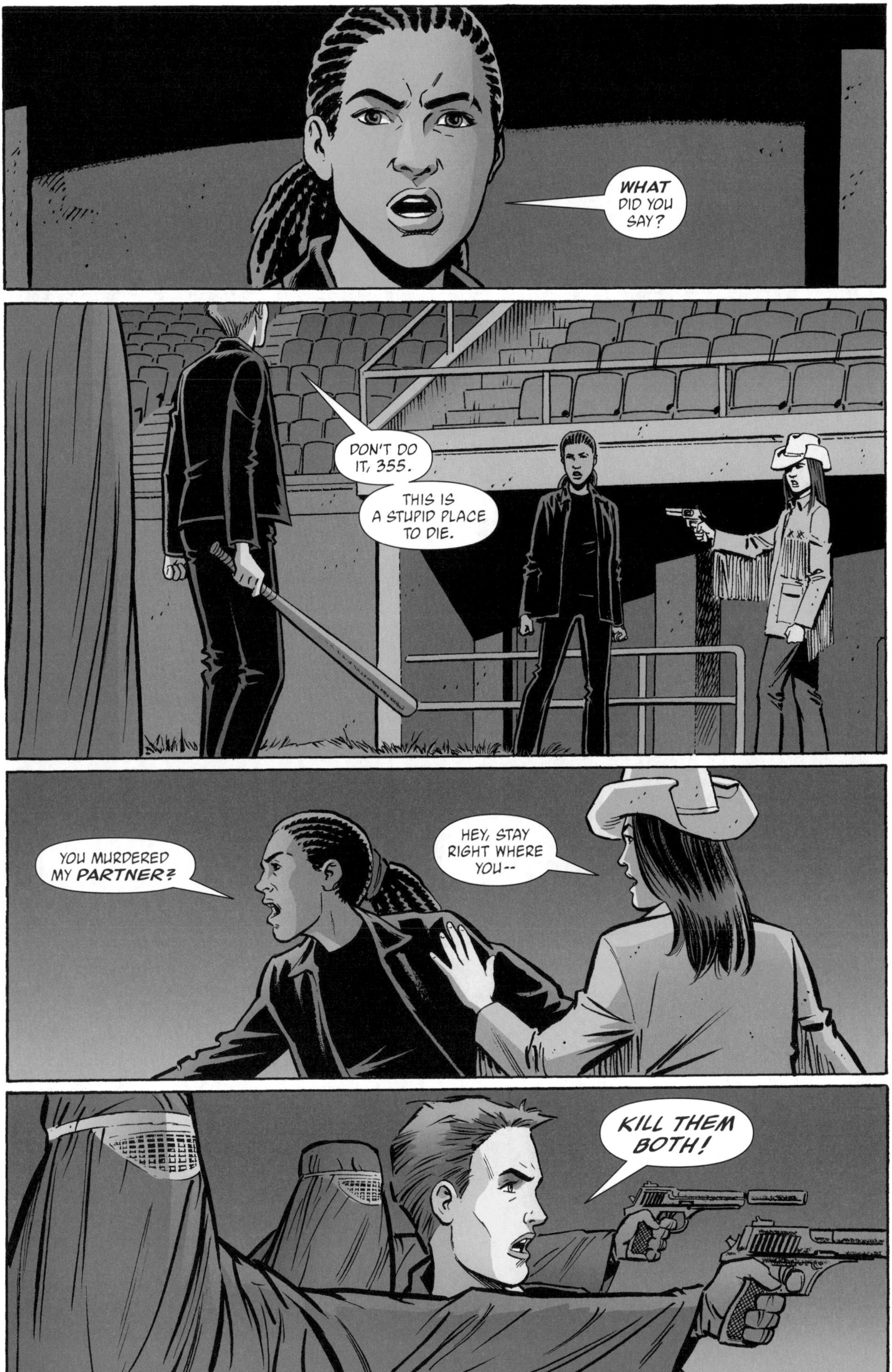
WHAT DID YOU SAY?
DON'T DO IT, 355.
THIS IS A STUPID PLACE TO DIE.
YOU MURDERED MY PARTNER?
HEY, STAY RIGHT WHERE YOU--
KILL THEM BOTH!

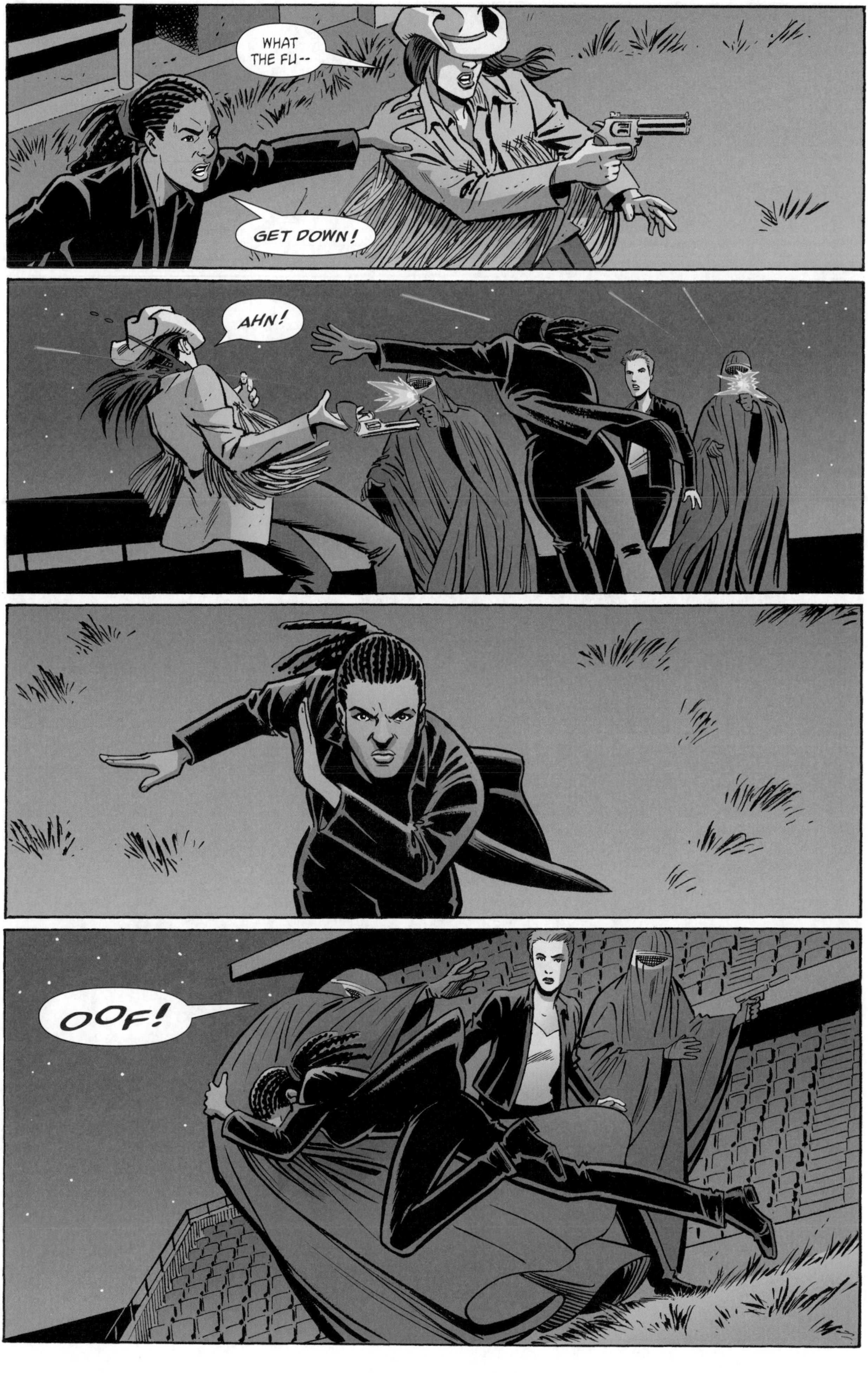
WHAT THE FU--
GET DOWN!
AHN!
OOF!

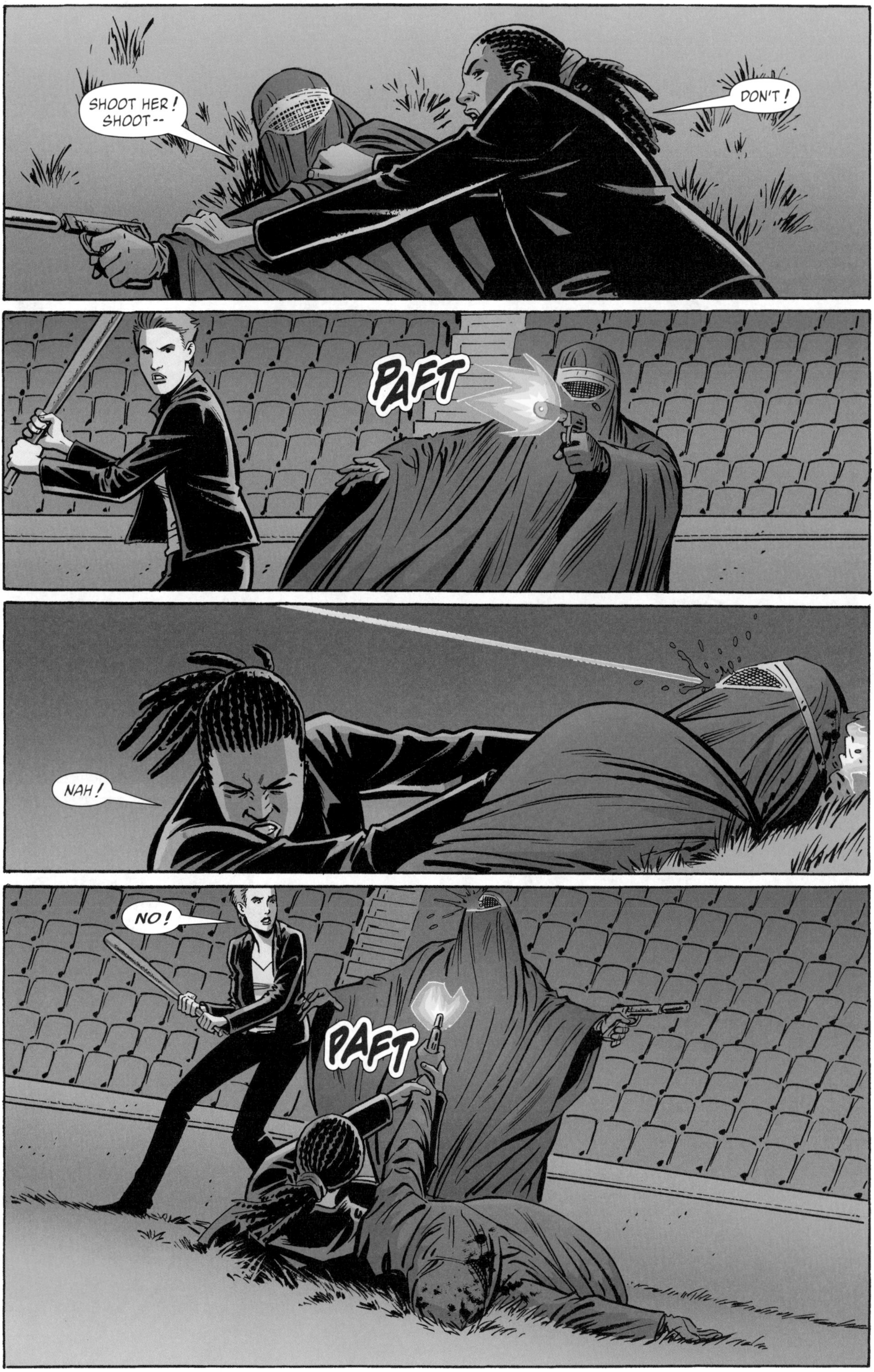

SHOOT HER! SHOOT--
DON'T!
PAFT
NAH!
NO!
PAFT

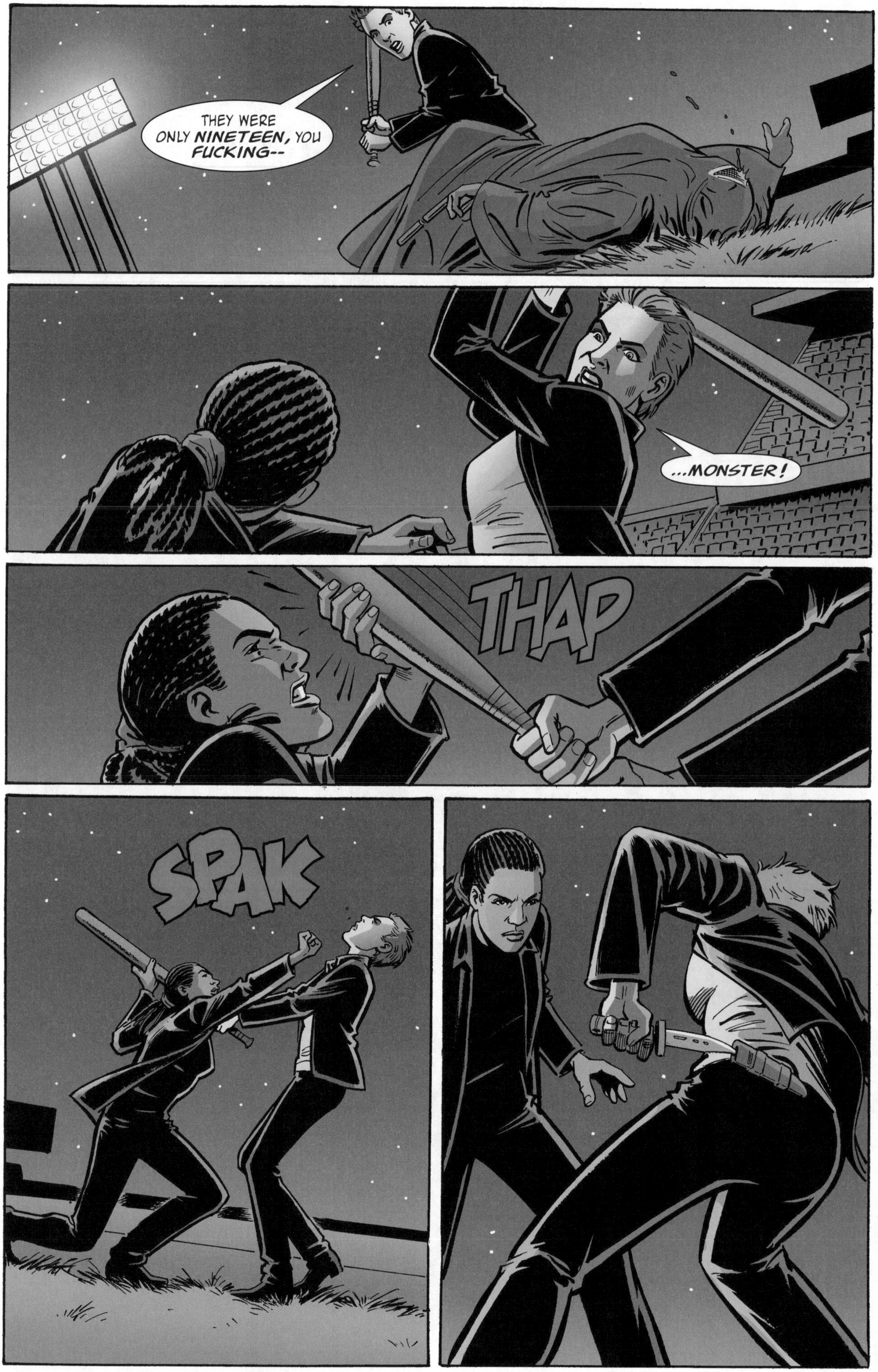
THEY WERE ONLY NINETEEN, YOU FUCKING--
...MONSTER!
THAP
SPAK

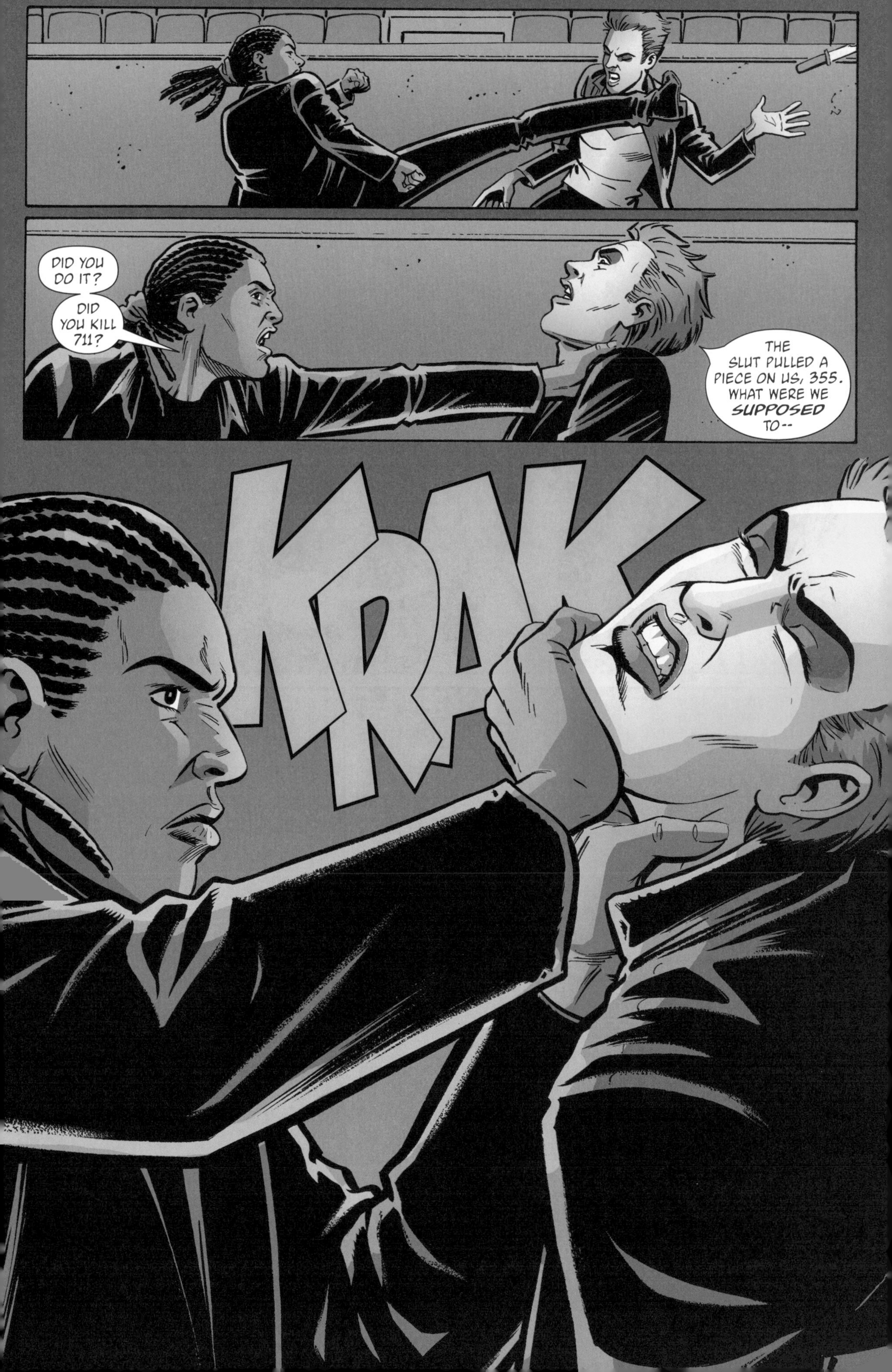
DID YOU DO IT?
DID YOU KILL 711?
THE SLUT PULLED A PIECE ON US, 355. WHAT WERE WE SUPPOSED TO--
KRAK

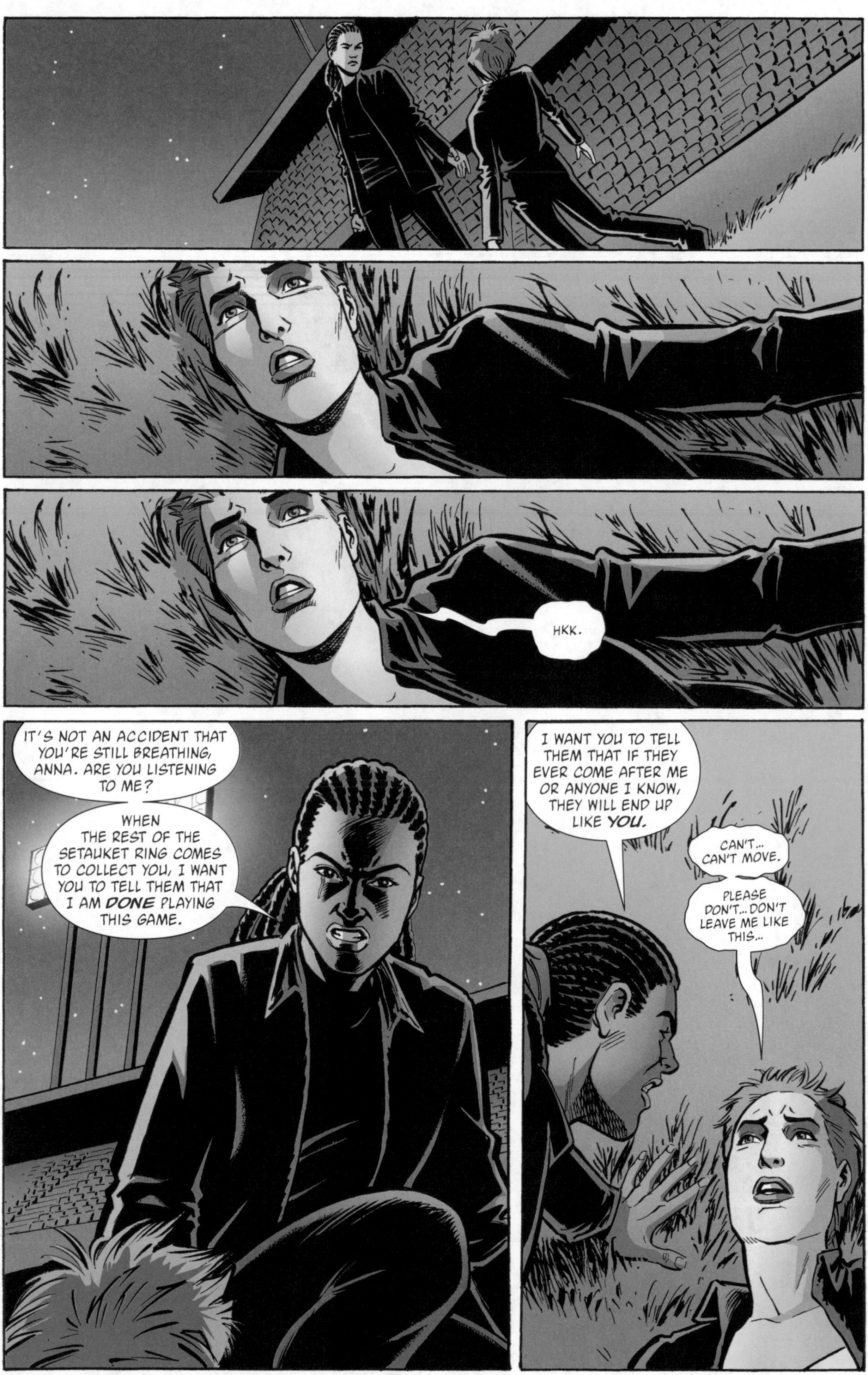
HKK.
IT'S NOT AN ACCIDENT THAT YOU'RE STILL BREATHING, ANNA. ARE YOU LISTENING TO ME?
WHEN THE REST OF THE SETAUKET RING COMES TO COLLECT YOU, I WANT YOU TO TELL THEM THAT I AM **DONE** PLAYING THIS GAME.
I WANT YOU TO TELL THEM THAT IF THEY EVER COME AFTER ME OR ANYONE I KNOW, THEY WILL END UP LIKE ***YOU.***
CAN'T... CAN'T MOVE.
PLEASE DON'T... DON'T LEAVE ME LIKE THIS...

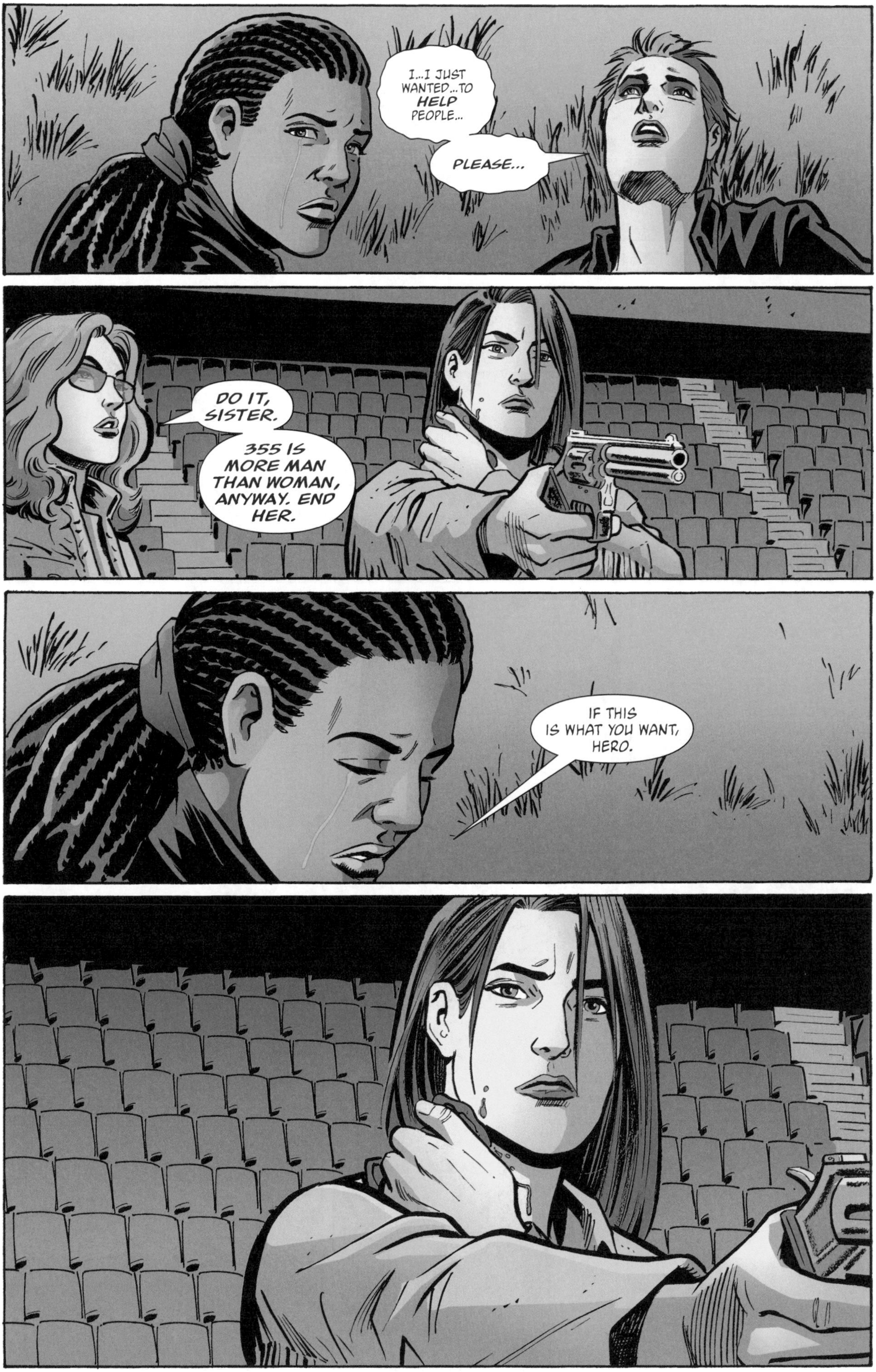
I...I JUST WANTED...TO HELP PEOPLE...
PLEASE...
DO IT, SISTER.
355 IS MORE MAN THAN WOMAN, ANYWAY. END HER.
IF THIS IS WHAT YOU WANT, HERO.

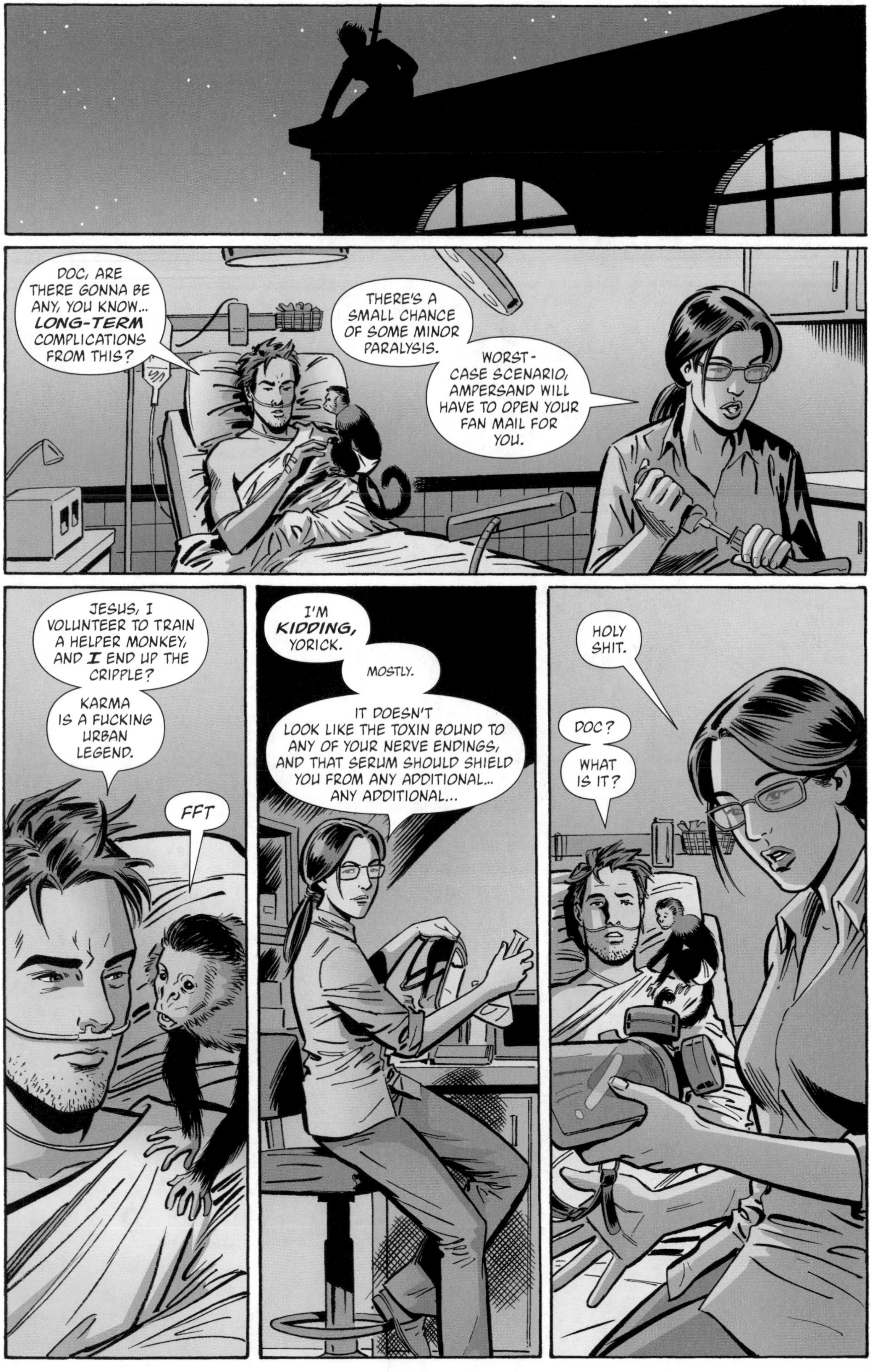
DOC, ARE THERE GONNA BE ANY, YOU KNOW... LONG-TERM COMPLICATIONS FROM THIS?
THERE'S A SMALL CHANCE OF SOME MINOR PARALYSIS.
WORST-CASE SCENARIO, AMPERSAND WILL HAVE TO OPEN YOUR FAN MAIL FOR YOU.
JESUS, I VOLUNTEER TO TRAIN A HELPER MONKEY, AND I END UP THE CRIPPLE?
KARMA IS A FUCKING URBAN LEGEND.
FFT
I'M KIDDING, YORICK.
MOSTLY.
IT DOESN'T LOOK LIKE THE TOXIN BOUND TO ANY OF YOUR NERVE ENDINGS, AND THAT SERUM SHOULD SHIELD YOU FROM ANY ADDITIONAL... ANY ADDITIONAL...
HOLY SHIT.
DOC?
WHAT IS IT?

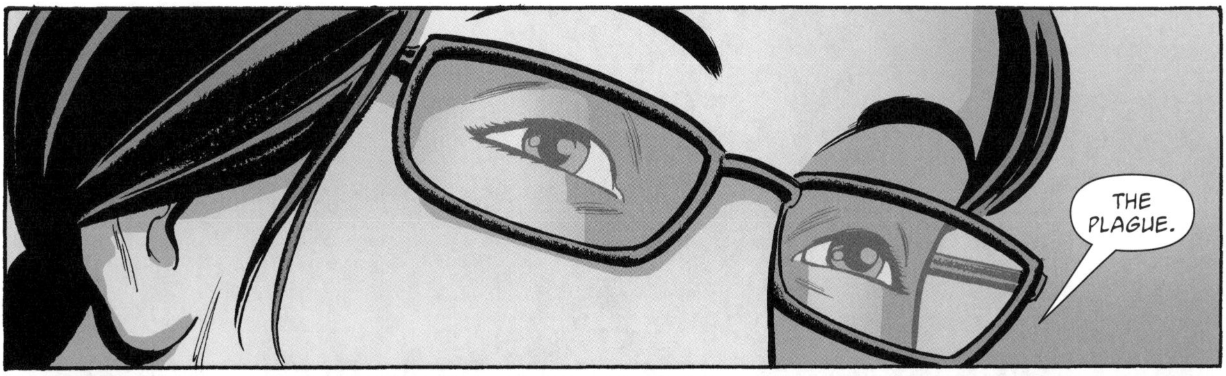
THE PLAGUE.

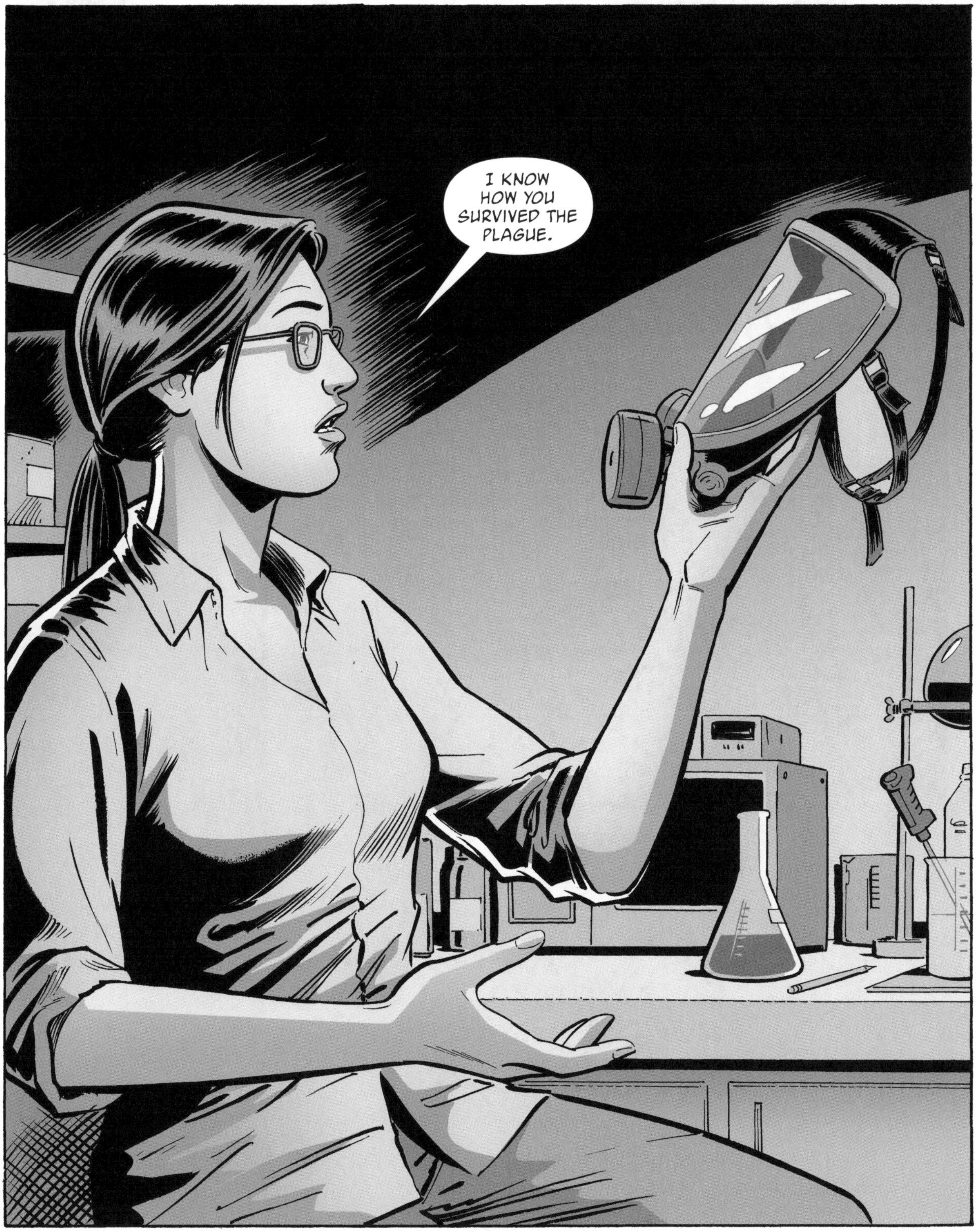
I KNOW HOW YOU SURVIVED THE PLAGUE.

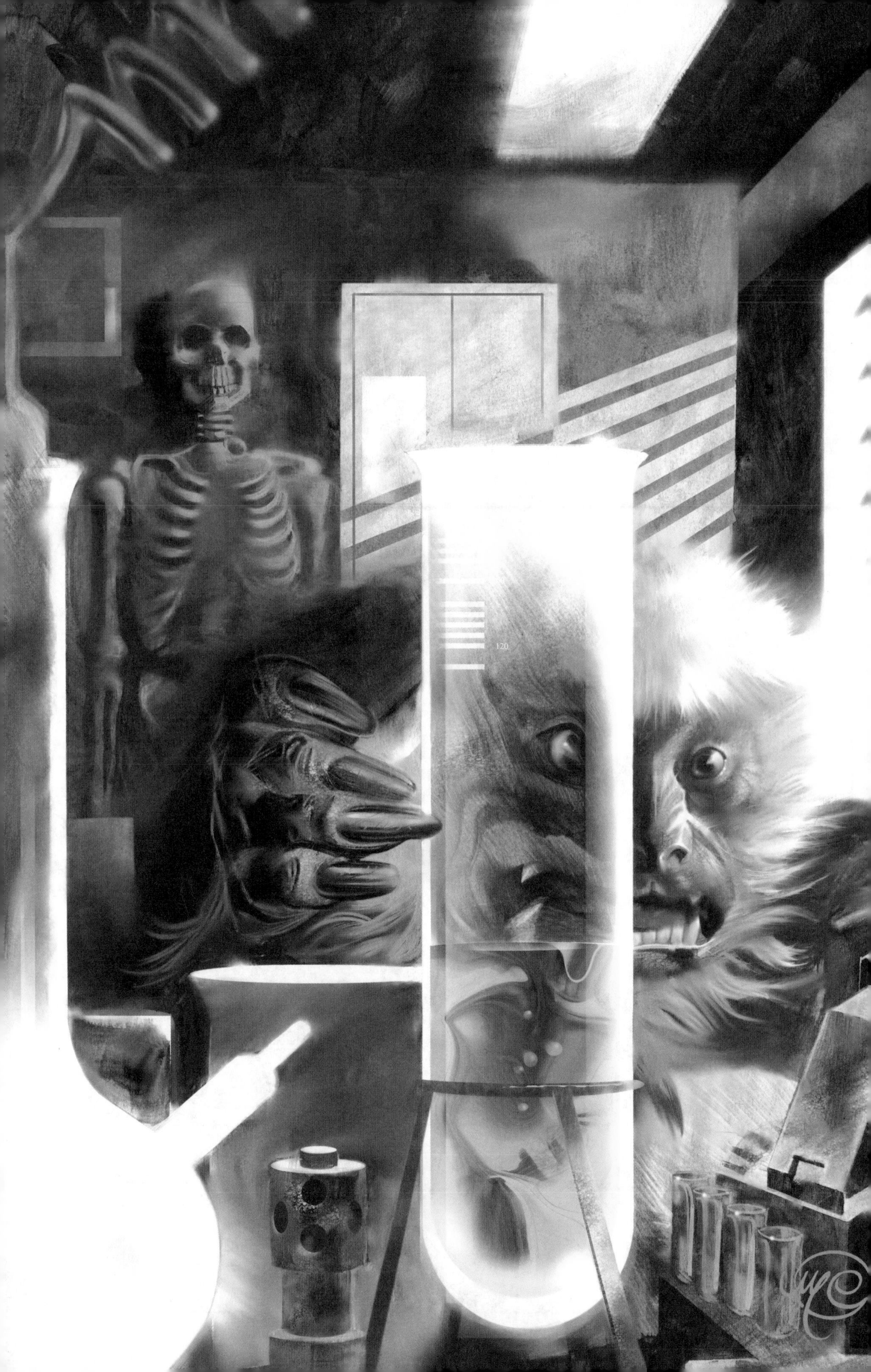

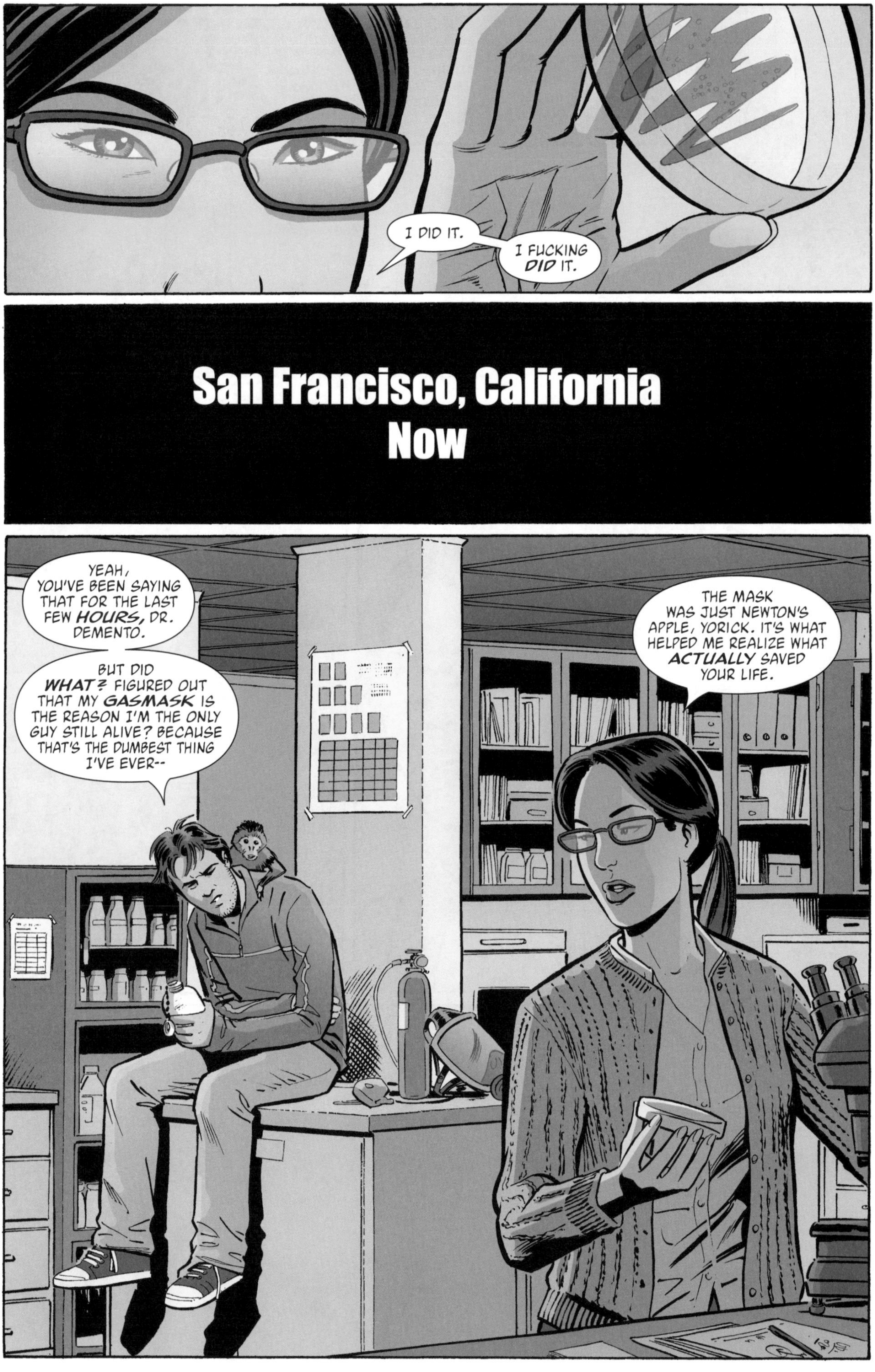
I DID IT.
I FUCKING DID IT.
San Francisco, California
Now
YEAH, YOU'VE BEEN SAYING THAT FOR THE LAST FEW HOURS, DR. DEMENTO.
BUT DID WHAT? FIGURED OUT THAT MY GASMASK IS THE REASON I'M THE ONLY GUY STILL ALIVE? BECAUSE THAT'S THE DUMBEST THING I'VE EVER--
THE MASK WAS JUST NEWTON'S APPLE, YORICK. IT'S WHAT HELPED ME REALIZE WHAT ACTUALLY SAVED YOUR LIFE.

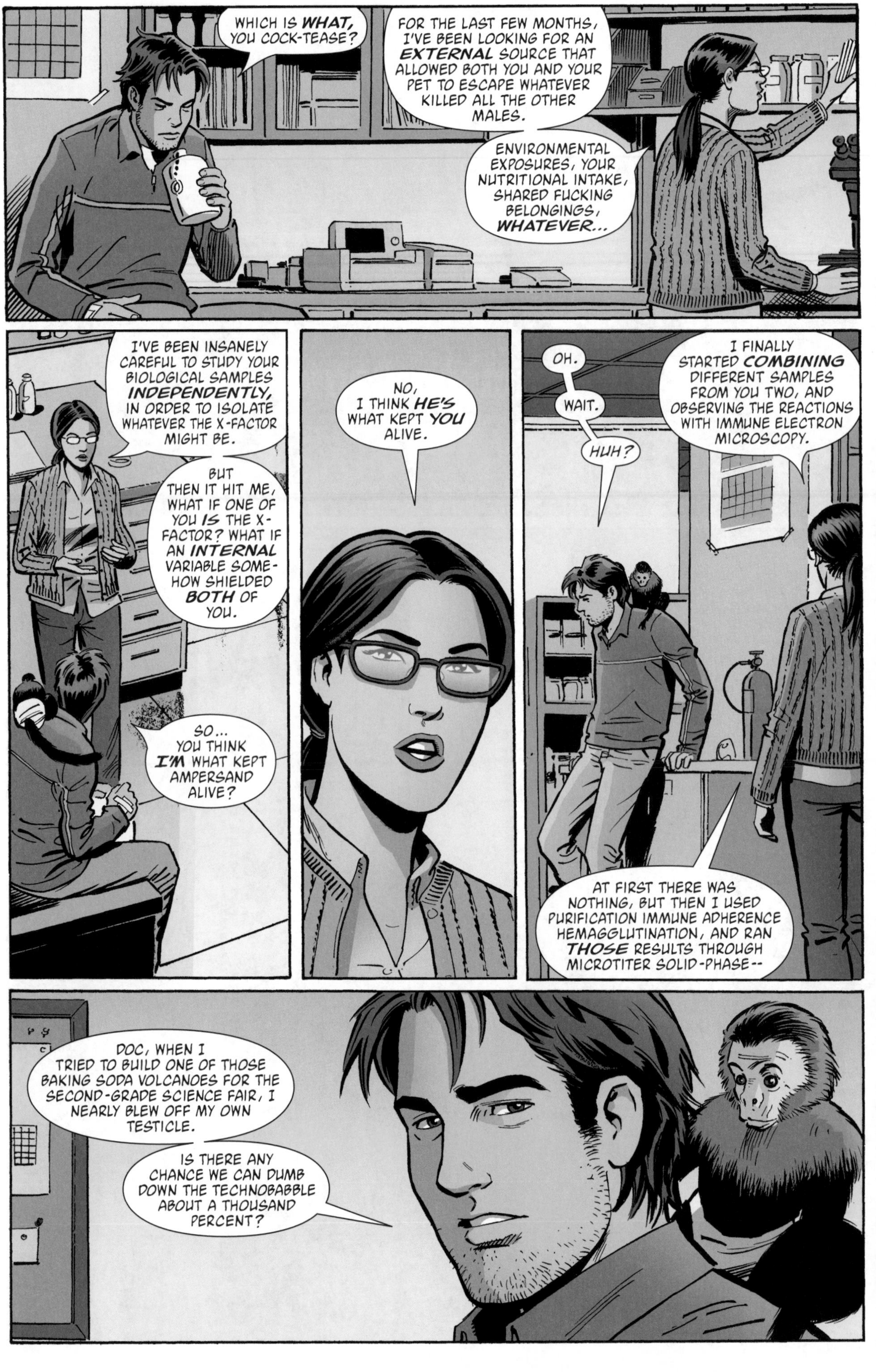
WHICH IS WHAT, YOU COCK-TEASE?
FOR THE LAST FEW MONTHS, I'VE BEEN LOOKING FOR AN EXTERNAL SOURCE THAT ALLOWED BOTH YOU AND YOUR PET TO ESCAPE WHATEVER KILLED ALL THE OTHER MALES.
ENVIRONMENTAL EXPOSURES, YOUR NUTRITIONAL INTAKE, SHARED FUCKING BELONGINGS, WHATEVER...
I'VE BEEN INSANELY CAREFUL TO STUDY YOUR BIOLOGICAL SAMPLES INDEPENDENTLY, IN ORDER TO ISOLATE WHATEVER THE X-FACTOR MIGHT BE.
BUT THEN IT HIT ME, WHAT IF ONE OF YOU IS THE X-FACTOR? WHAT IF AN INTERNAL VARIABLE SOME-HOW SHIELDED BOTH OF YOU.
SO... YOU THINK I'M WHAT KEPT AMPERSAND ALIVE?
NO, I THINK HE'S WHAT KEPT YOU ALIVE.
OH.
WAIT.
HUH?
I FINALLY STARTED COMBINING DIFFERENT SAMPLES FROM YOU TWO, AND OBSERVING THE REACTIONS WITH IMMUNE ELECTRON MICROSCOPY.
AT FIRST THERE WAS NOTHING, BUT THEN I USED PURIFICATION IMMUNE ADHERENCE HEMAGGLUTINATION, AND RAN THOSE RESULTS THROUGH MICROTITER SOLID-PHASE--
DOC, WHEN I TRIED TO BUILD ONE OF THOSE BAKING SODA VOLCANOES FOR THE SECOND-GRADE SCIENCE FAIR, I NEARLY BLEW OFF MY OWN TESTICLE.
IS THERE ANY CHANCE WE CAN DUMB DOWN THE TECHNOBABBLE ABOUT A THOUSAND PERCENT?

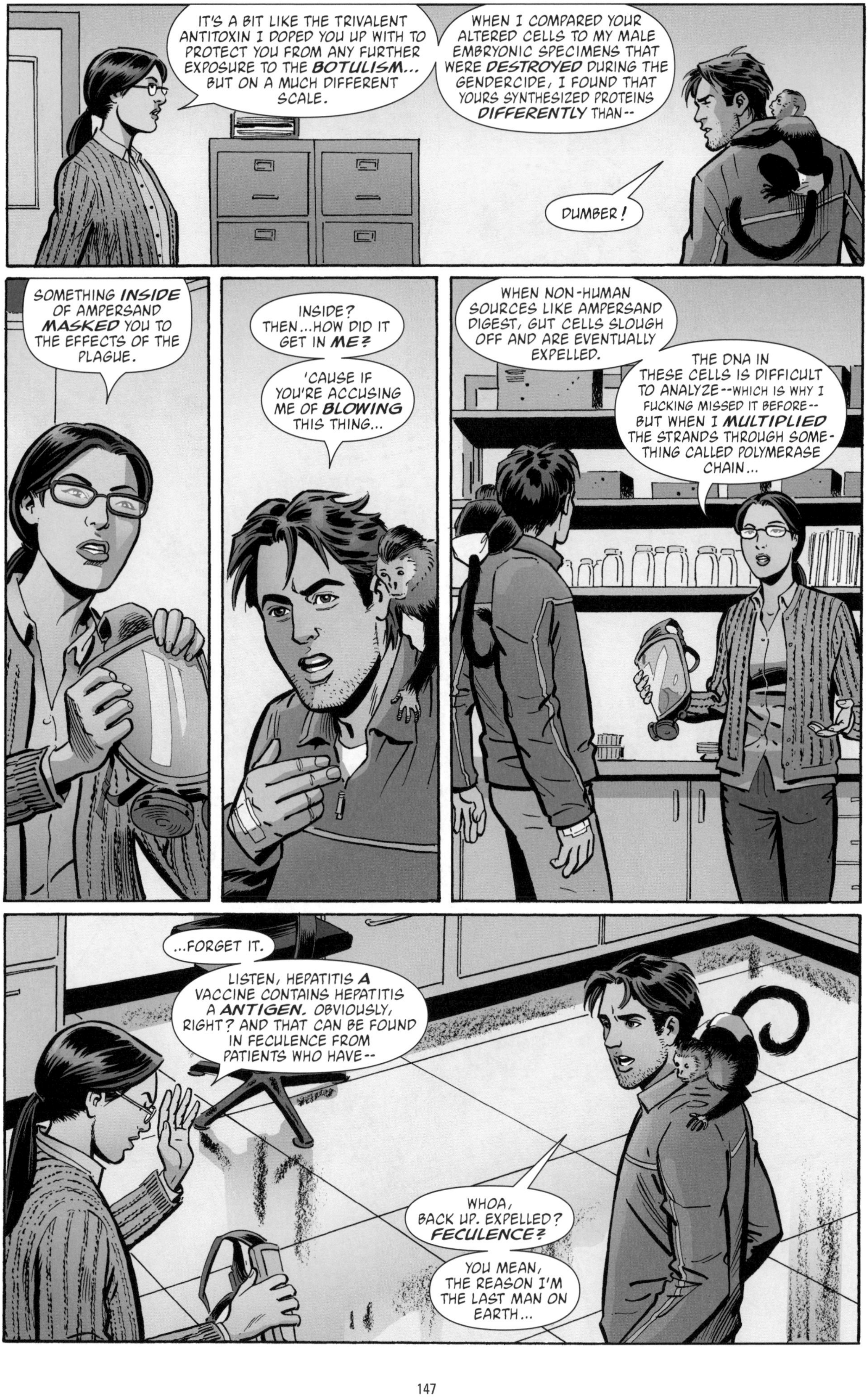
IT'S A BIT LIKE THE TRIVALENT ANTITOXIN I DOPED YOU UP WITH TO PROTECT YOU FROM ANY FURTHER EXPOSURE TO THE **BOTULISM...** BUT ON A MUCH DIFFERENT SCALE.
WHEN I COMPARED YOUR ALTERED CELLS TO MY MALE EMBRYONIC SPECIMENS THAT WERE **DESTROYED** DURING THE GENDERCIDE, I FOUND THAT YOURS SYNTHESIZED PROTEINS **DIFFERENTLY** THAN--
DUMBER!
SOMETHING **INSIDE** OF AMPERSAND **MASKED** YOU TO THE EFFECTS OF THE PLAGUE.
INSIDE? THEN...HOW DID IT GET IN **ME?**
'CAUSE IF YOU'RE ACCUSING ME OF **BLOWING** THIS THING...
WHEN NON-HUMAN SOURCES LIKE AMPERSAND DIGEST, GUT CELLS SLOUGH OFF AND ARE EVENTUALLY EXPELLED.
THE DNA IN THESE CELLS IS DIFFICULT TO ANALYZE--WHICH IS WHY I FUCKING MISSED IT BEFORE--BUT WHEN I **MULTIPLIED** THE STRANDS THROUGH SOMETHING CALLED POLYMERASE CHAIN...
...FORGET IT.
LISTEN, HEPATITIS **A** VACCINE CONTAINS HEPATITIS A **ANTIGEN.** OBVIOUSLY, RIGHT? AND THAT CAN BE FOUND IN FECULENCE FROM PATIENTS WHO HAVE--
WHOA, BACK UP. EXPELLED? **FECULENCE?**
YOU MEAN, THE REASON I'M THE LAST MAN ON EARTH...

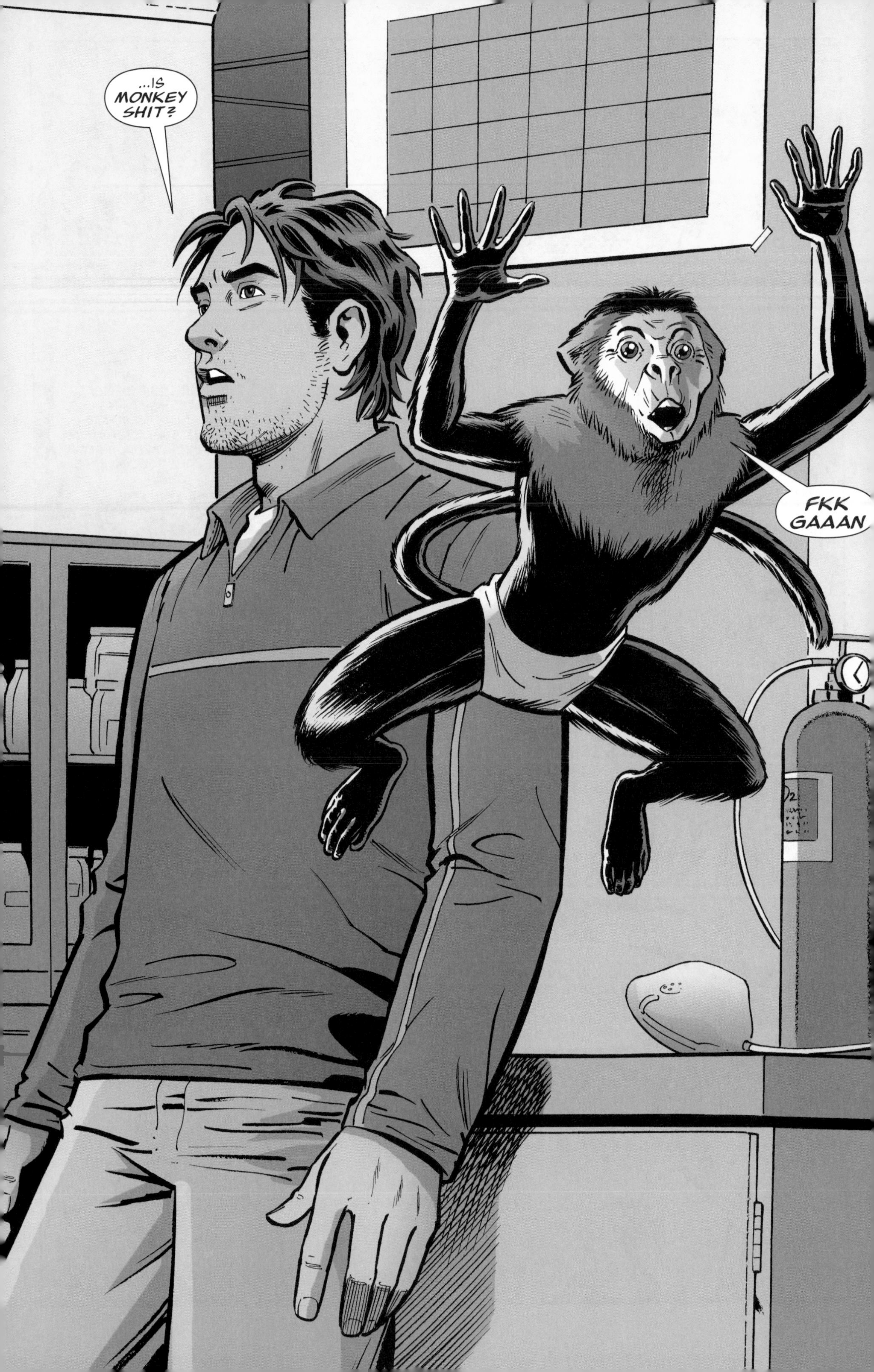
...IS MONKEY SHIT?
FKK GAAAN

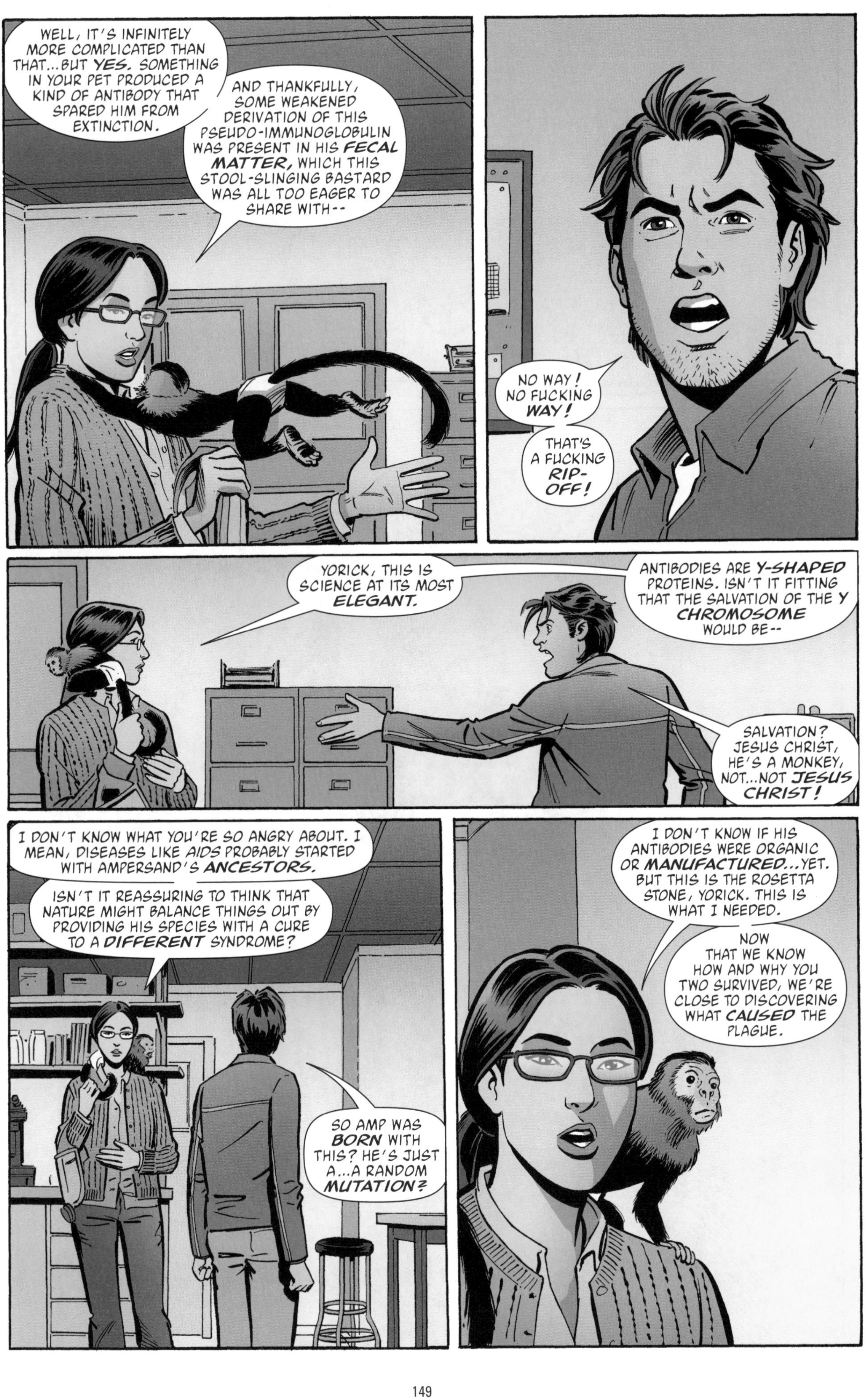
WELL, IT'S INFINITELY MORE COMPLICATED THAN THAT...BUT YES. SOMETHING IN YOUR PET PRODUCED A KIND OF ANTIBODY THAT SPARED HIM FROM EXTINCTION.
AND THANKFULLY, SOME WEAKENED DERIVATION OF THIS PSEUDO-IMMUNOGLOBULIN WAS PRESENT IN HIS FECAL MATTER, WHICH THIS STOOL-SLINGING BASTARD WAS ALL TOO EAGER TO SHARE WITH--
NO WAY! NO FUCKING WAY!
THAT'S A FUCKING RIP-OFF!
YORICK, THIS IS SCIENCE AT ITS MOST ELEGANT.
ANTIBODIES ARE Y-SHAPED PROTEINS. ISN'T IT FITTING THAT THE SALVATION OF THE Y CHROMOSOME WOULD BE--
SALVATION? JESUS CHRIST, HE'S A MONKEY, NOT...NOT JESUS CHRIST!
I DON'T KNOW WHAT YOU'RE SO ANGRY ABOUT. I MEAN, DISEASES LIKE AIDS PROBABLY STARTED WITH AMPERSAND'S ANCESTORS.
ISN'T IT REASSURING TO THINK THAT NATURE MIGHT BALANCE THINGS OUT BY PROVIDING HIS SPECIES WITH A CURE TO A DIFFERENT SYNDROME?
SO AMP WAS BORN WITH THIS? HE'S JUST A...A RANDOM MUTATION?
I DON'T KNOW IF HIS ANTIBODIES WERE ORGANIC OR MANUFACTURED...YET. BUT THIS IS THE ROSETTA STONE, YORICK. THIS IS WHAT I NEEDED.
NOW THAT WE KNOW HOW AND WHY YOU TWO SURVIVED, WE'RE CLOSE TO DISCOVERING WHAT CAUSED THE PLAGUE.

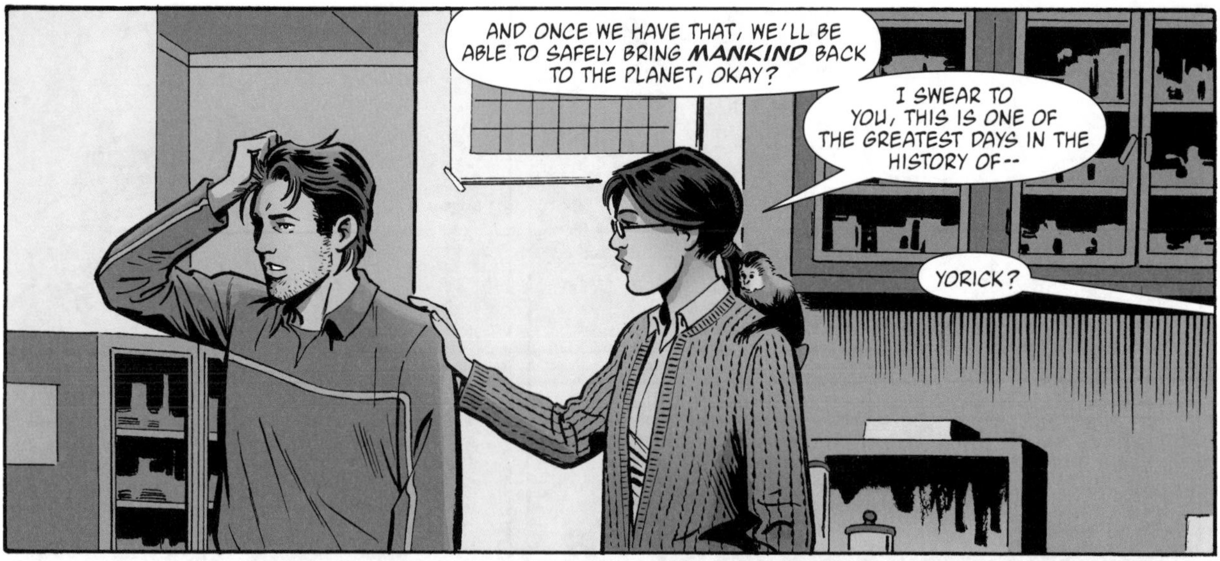
AND ONCE WE HAVE THAT, WE'LL BE ABLE TO SAFELY BRING MANKIND BACK TO THE PLANET, OKAY?
I SWEAR TO YOU, THIS IS ONE OF THE GREATEST DAYS IN THE HISTORY OF--
YORICK?

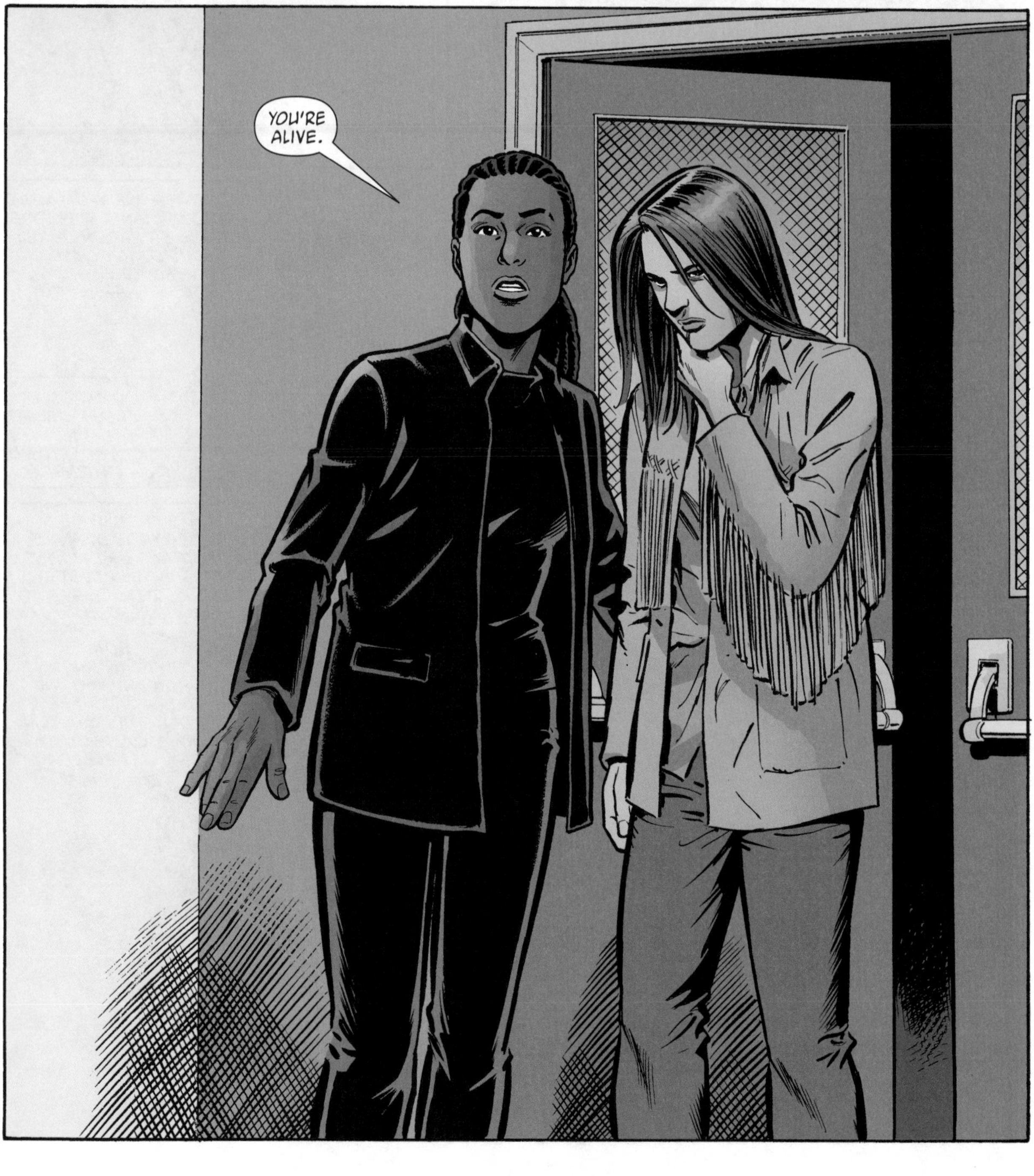
YOU'RE ALIVE.

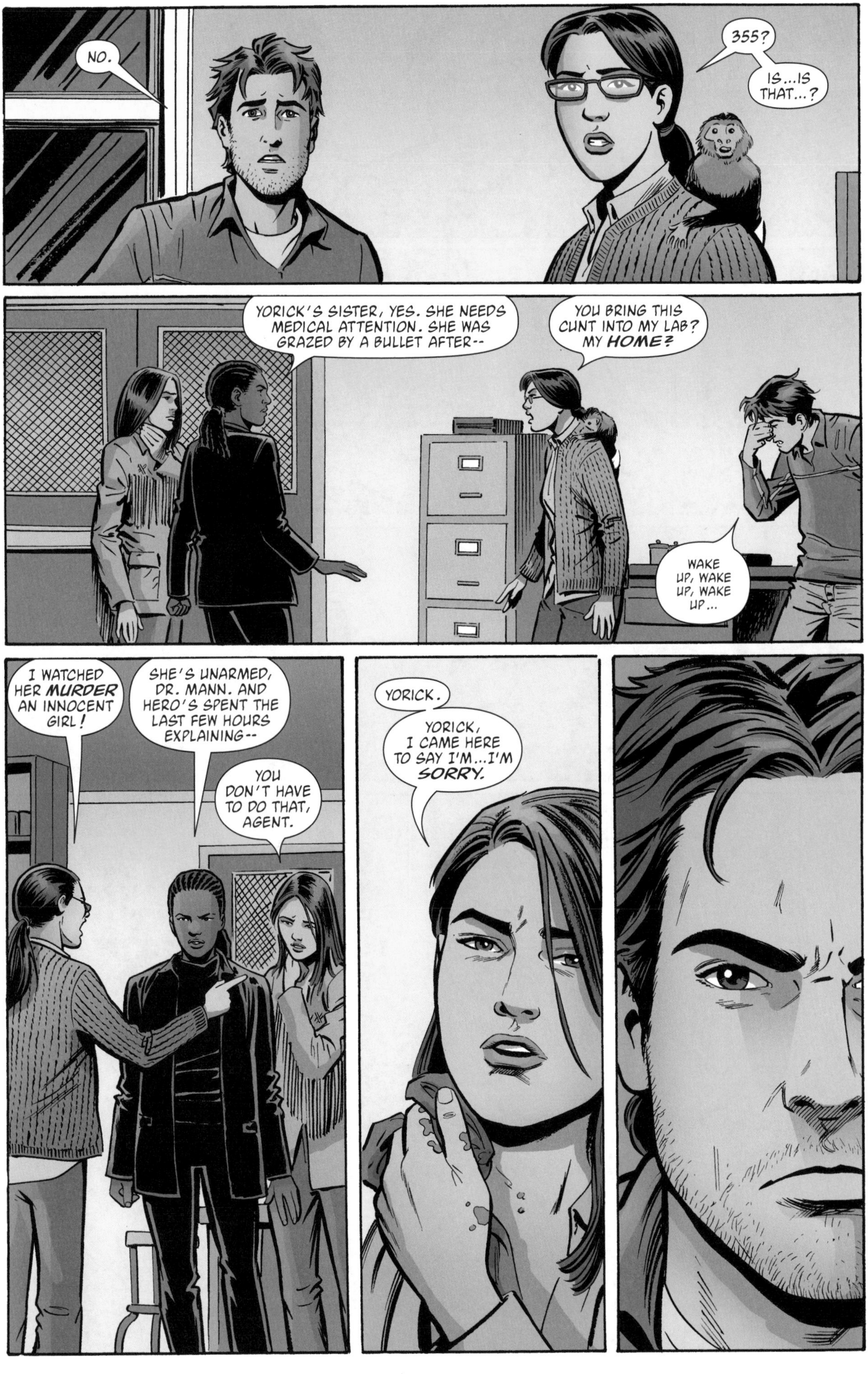
NO.
355?
IS...IS THAT...?
YORICK'S SISTER, YES. SHE NEEDS MEDICAL ATTENTION. SHE WAS GRAZED BY A BULLET AFTER--
YOU BRING THIS CUNT INTO MY LAB? MY *HOME?*
WAKE UP, WAKE UP, WAKE UP...
I WATCHED HER *MURDER* AN INNOCENT GIRL!
SHE'S UNARMED, DR. MANN. AND HERO'S SPENT THE LAST FEW HOURS EXPLAINING--
YOU DON'T HAVE TO DO THAT, AGENT.
YORICK.
YORICK, I CAME HERE TO SAY I'M...I'M *SORRY.*

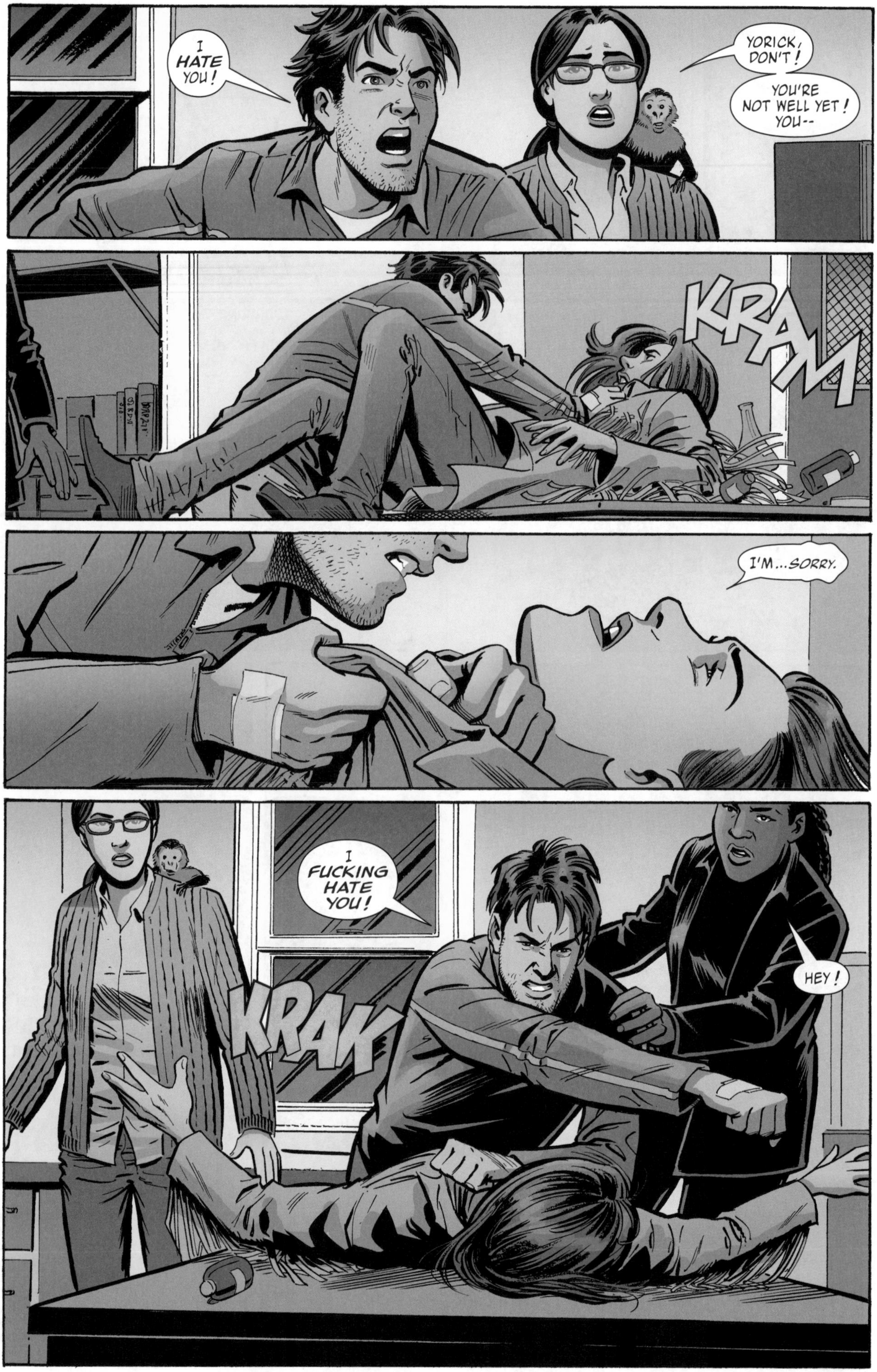
I HATE YOU!
YORICK, DON'T!
YOU'RE NOT WELL YET! YOU--
KRAM
I'M...SORRY.
I FUCKING HATE YOU!
KRAK
HEY!

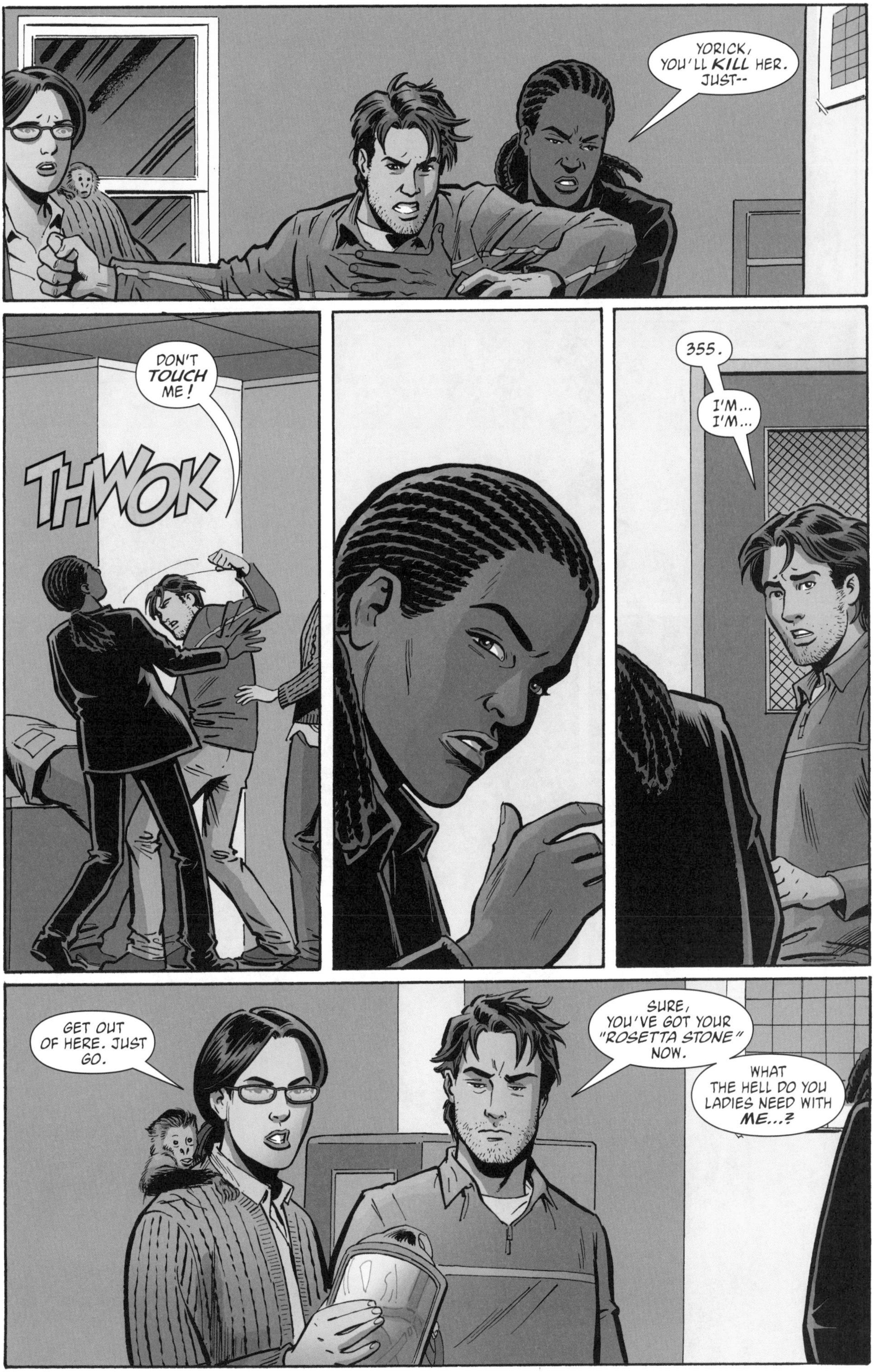
YORICK, YOU'LL KILL HER. JUST--
DON'T TOUCH ME!
THWOK
355.
I'M... I'M...
GET OUT OF HERE. JUST GO.
SURE, YOU'VE GOT YOUR "ROSETTA STONE" NOW.
WHAT THE HELL DO YOU LADIES NEED WITH ME...?

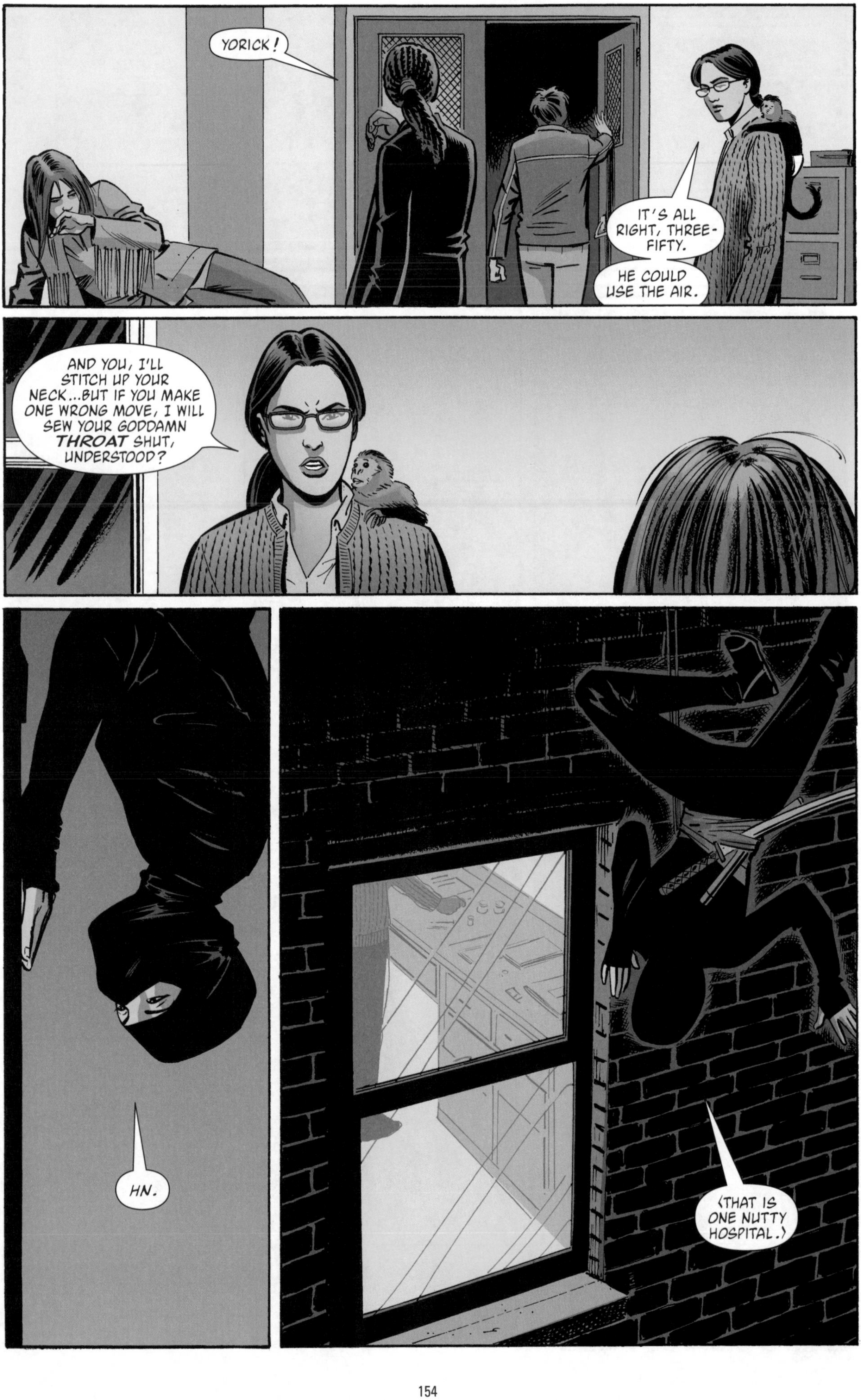
YORICK!
IT'S ALL RIGHT, THREE-FIFTY.
HE COULD USE THE AIR.
AND YOU, I'LL STITCH UP YOUR NECK...BUT IF YOU MAKE ONE WRONG MOVE, I WILL SEW YOUR GODDAMN THROAT SHUT, UNDERSTOOD?
HN.
‹THAT IS ONE NUTTY HOSPITAL.›

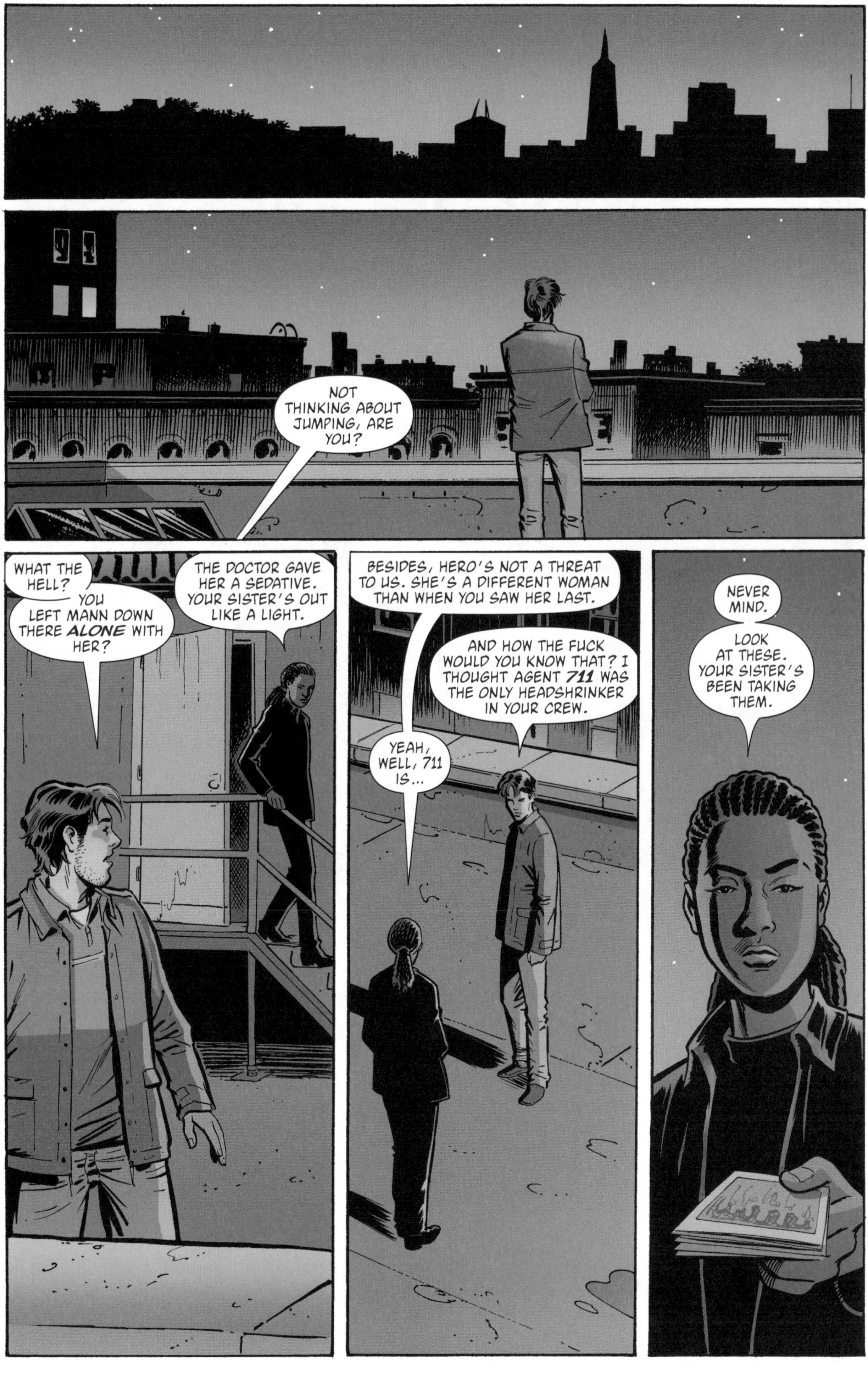
NOT THINKING ABOUT JUMPING, ARE YOU?
WHAT THE HELL?
YOU LEFT MANN DOWN THERE ALONE WITH HER?
THE DOCTOR GAVE HER A SEDATIVE. YOUR SISTER'S OUT LIKE A LIGHT.
BESIDES, HERO'S NOT A THREAT TO US. SHE'S A DIFFERENT WOMAN THAN WHEN YOU SAW HER LAST.
AND HOW THE FUCK WOULD YOU KNOW THAT? I THOUGHT AGENT 711 WAS THE ONLY HEADSHRINKER IN YOUR CREW.
YEAH, WELL, 711 IS...
NEVER MIND.
LOOK AT THESE. YOUR SISTER'S BEEN TAKING THEM.

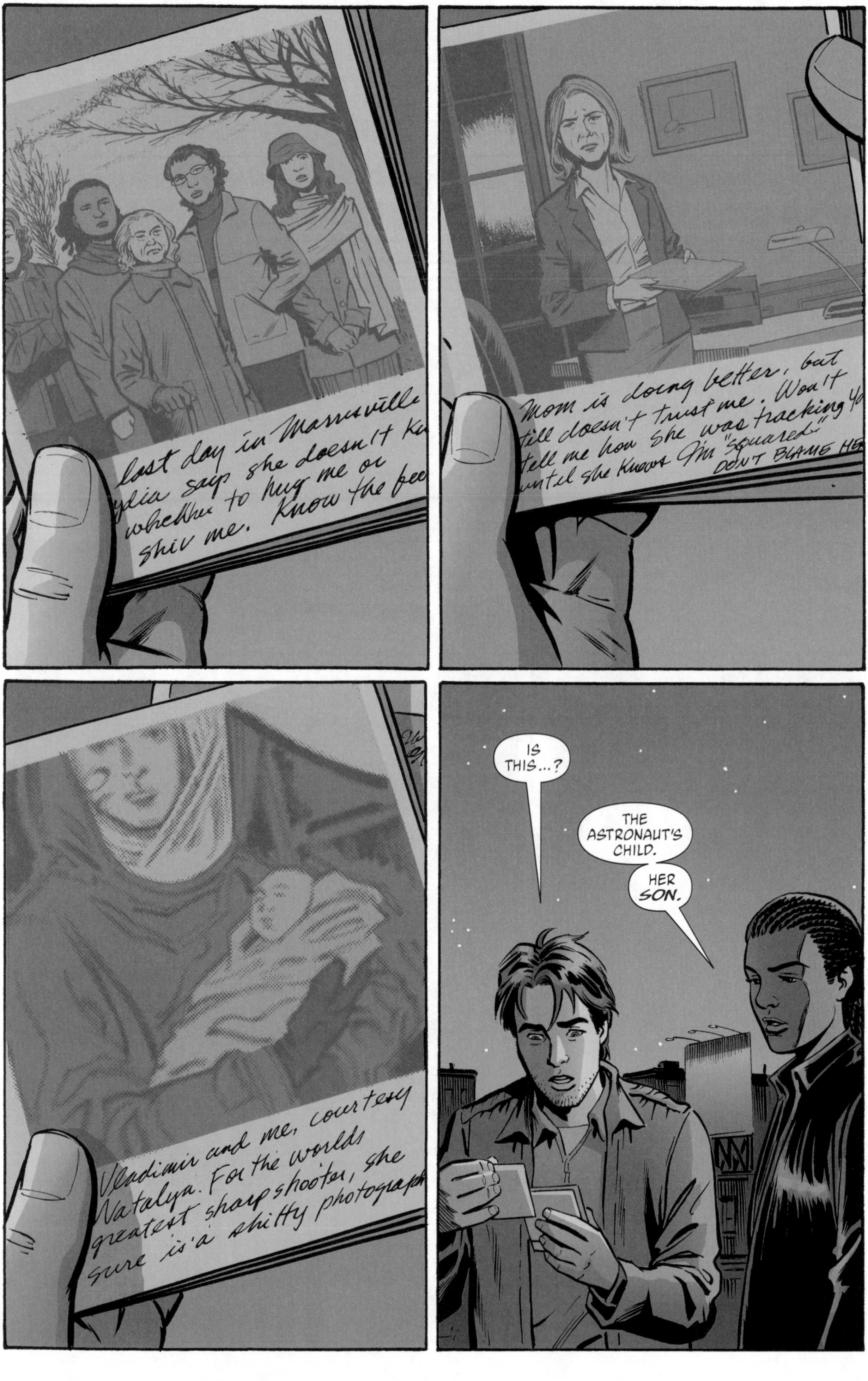
last day in Marysville
ydia says she doesn't kn
whether to hug me or
shiv me. Know the fee
Mom is doing better, but
till doesn't trust me. Won't
tell me how she was tracking yo
until she knows I'm "squared"
DON'T BLAME HE
Vladimir and me, courtesy
Natalya. For the worlds
greatest sharpshooter, she
sure is a shitty photograph
IS THIS...?
THE ASTRONAUT'S CHILD.
HER SON.

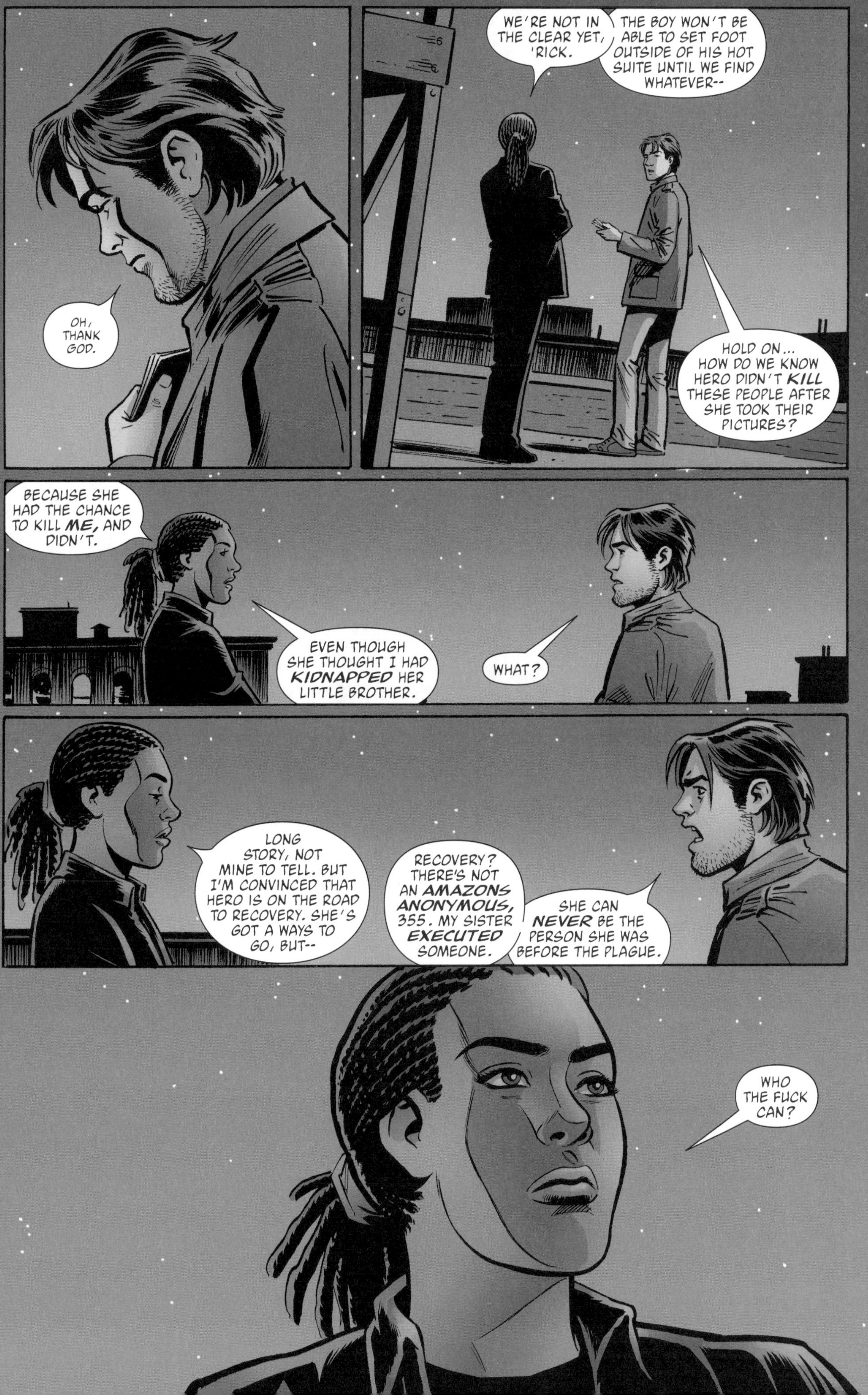
OH, THANK GOD.
WE'RE NOT IN THE CLEAR YET, 'RICK.
THE BOY WON'T BE ABLE TO SET FOOT OUTSIDE OF HIS HOT SUITE UNTIL WE FIND WHATEVER--
HOLD ON... HOW DO WE KNOW HERO DIDN'T KILL THESE PEOPLE AFTER SHE TOOK THEIR PICTURES?
BECAUSE SHE HAD THE CHANCE TO KILL ME, AND DIDN'T.
EVEN THOUGH SHE THOUGHT I HAD KIDNAPPED HER LITTLE BROTHER.
WHAT?
LONG STORY, NOT MINE TO TELL. BUT I'M CONVINCED THAT HERO IS ON THE ROAD TO RECOVERY. SHE'S GOT A WAYS TO GO, BUT--
RECOVERY? THERE'S NOT AN AMAZONS ANONYMOUS, 355. MY SISTER EXECUTED SOMEONE.
SHE CAN NEVER BE THE PERSON SHE WAS BEFORE THE PLAGUE.
WHO THE FUCK CAN?

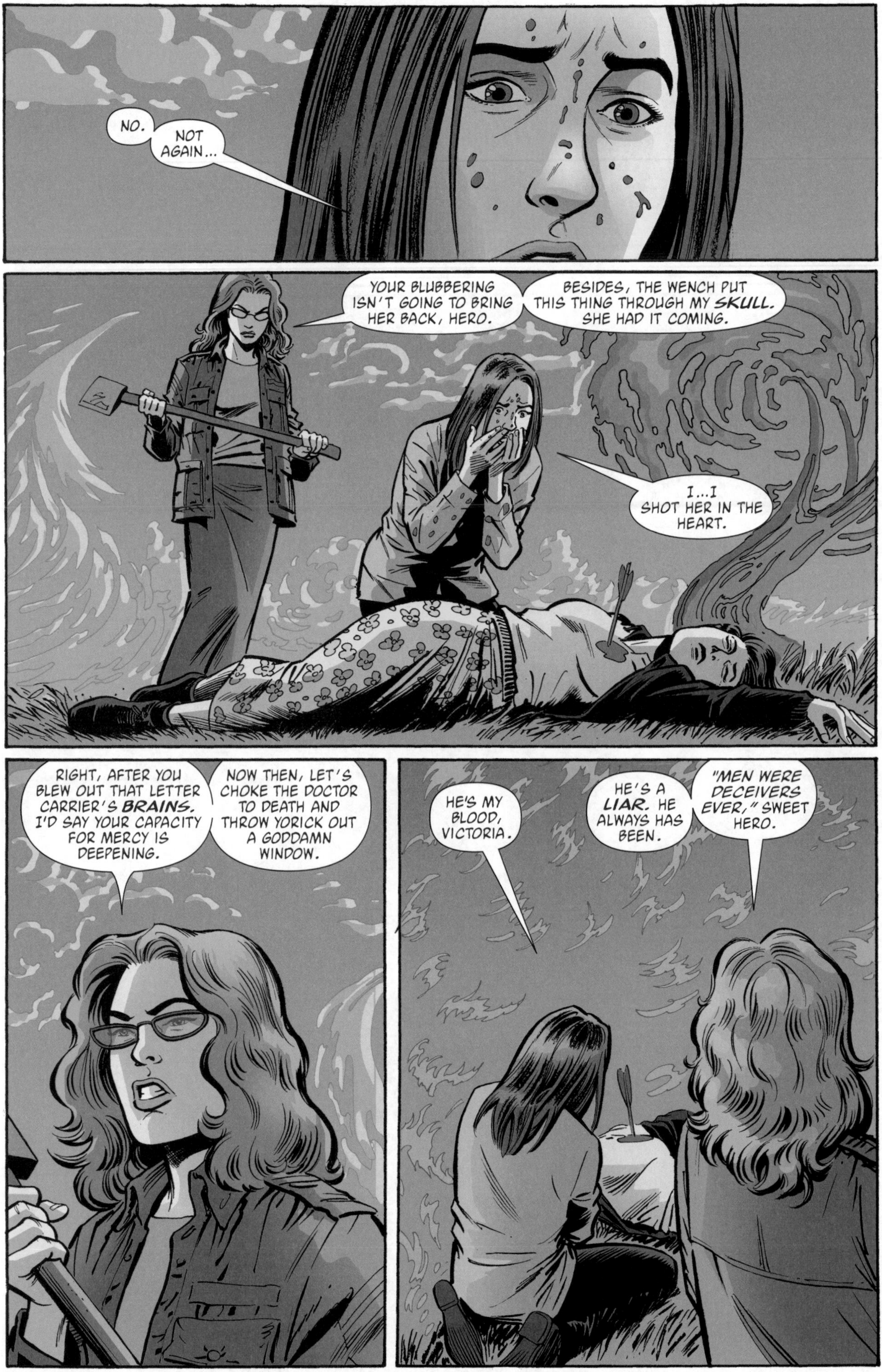
NO.
NOT AGAIN...
YOUR BLUBBERING ISN'T GOING TO BRING HER BACK, HERO.
BESIDES, THE WENCH PUT THIS THING THROUGH MY SKULL. SHE HAD IT COMING.
I...I SHOT HER IN THE HEART.
RIGHT, AFTER YOU BLEW OUT THAT LETTER CARRIER'S BRAINS. I'D SAY YOUR CAPACITY FOR MERCY IS DEEPENING.
NOW THEN, LET'S CHOKE THE DOCTOR TO DEATH AND THROW YORICK OUT A GODDAMN WINDOW.
HE'S MY BLOOD, VICTORIA.
HE'S A LIAR. HE ALWAYS HAS BEEN.
"MEN WERE DECEIVERS EVER," SWEET HERO.

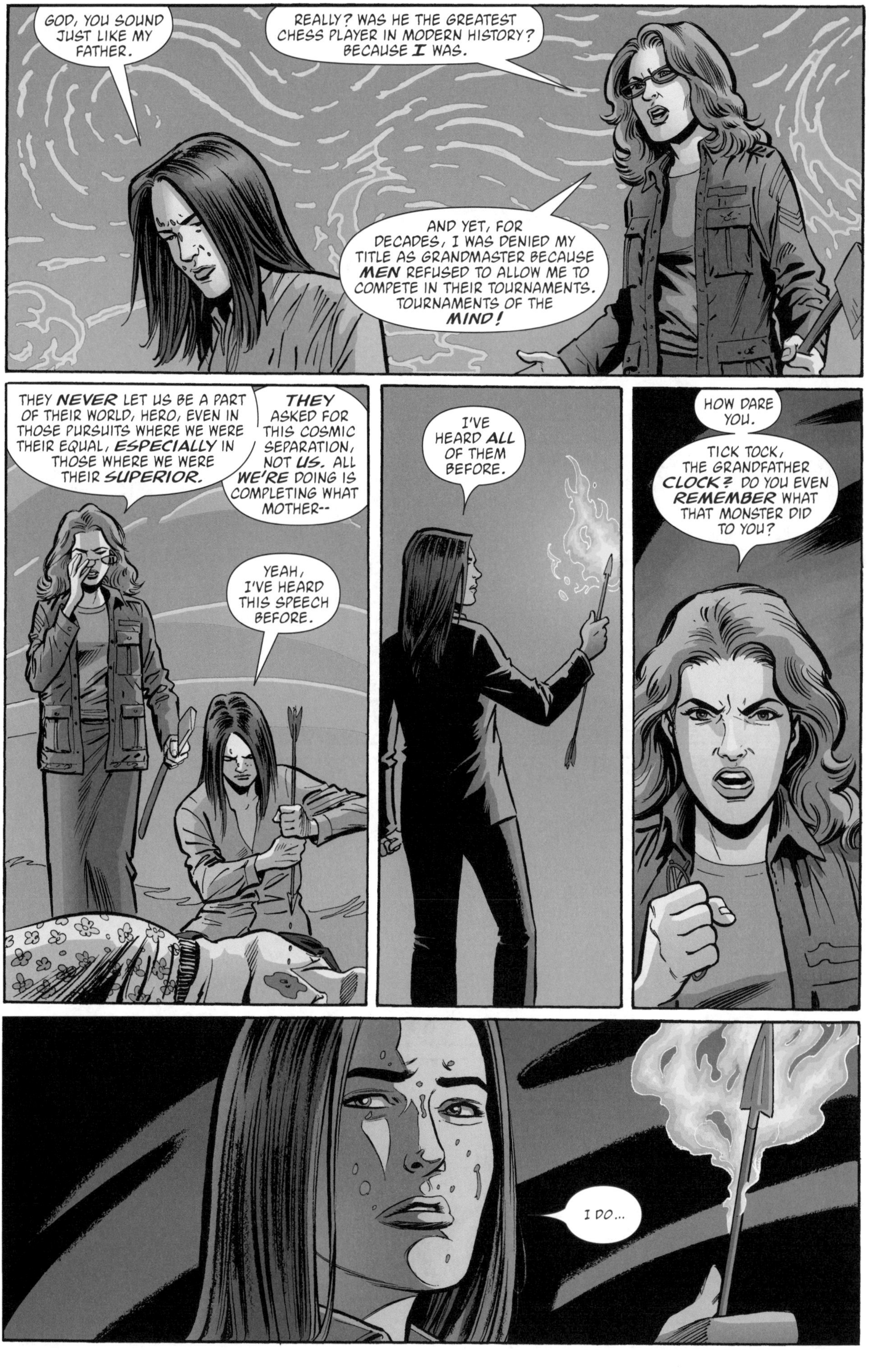
GOD, YOU SOUND JUST LIKE MY FATHER.
REALLY? WAS HE THE GREATEST CHESS PLAYER IN MODERN HISTORY? BECAUSE I WAS.
AND YET, FOR DECADES, I WAS DENIED MY TITLE AS GRANDMASTER BECAUSE MEN REFUSED TO ALLOW ME TO COMPETE IN THEIR TOURNAMENTS. TOURNAMENTS OF THE MIND!
THEY NEVER LET US BE A PART OF THEIR WORLD, HERO, EVEN IN THOSE PURSUITS WHERE WE WERE THEIR EQUAL, ESPECIALLY IN THOSE WHERE WE WERE THEIR SUPERIOR.
THEY ASKED FOR THIS COSMIC SEPARATION, NOT US. ALL WE'RE DOING IS COMPLETING WHAT MOTHER--
YEAH, I'VE HEARD THIS SPEECH BEFORE.
I'VE HEARD ALL OF THEM BEFORE.
HOW DARE YOU.
TICK TOCK, THE GRANDFATHER CLOCK? DO YOU EVEN REMEMBER WHAT THAT MONSTER DID TO YOU?
I DO...

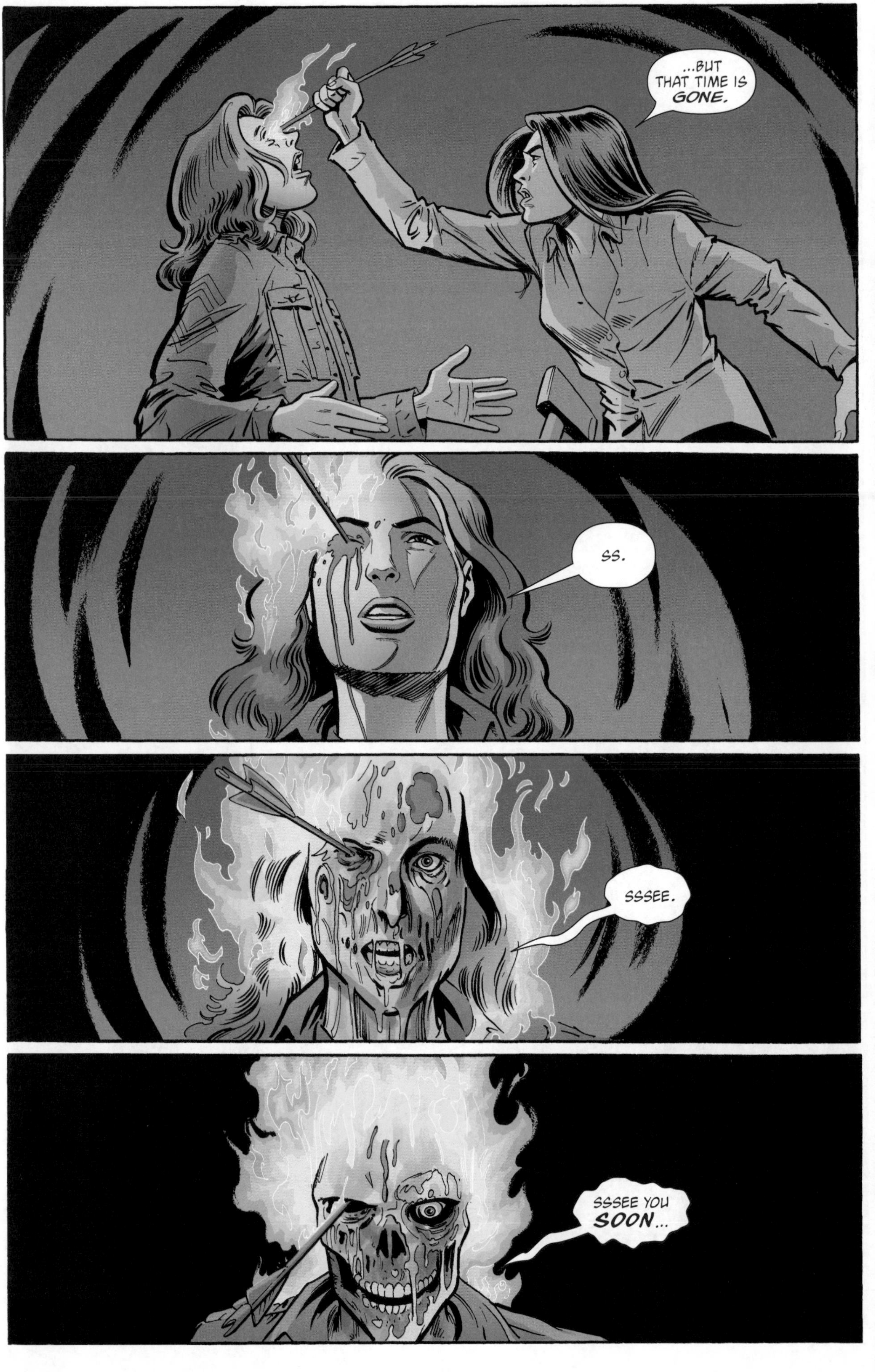
...BUT THAT TIME IS GONE.
SS.
SSSEE.
SSSEE YOU SOON...

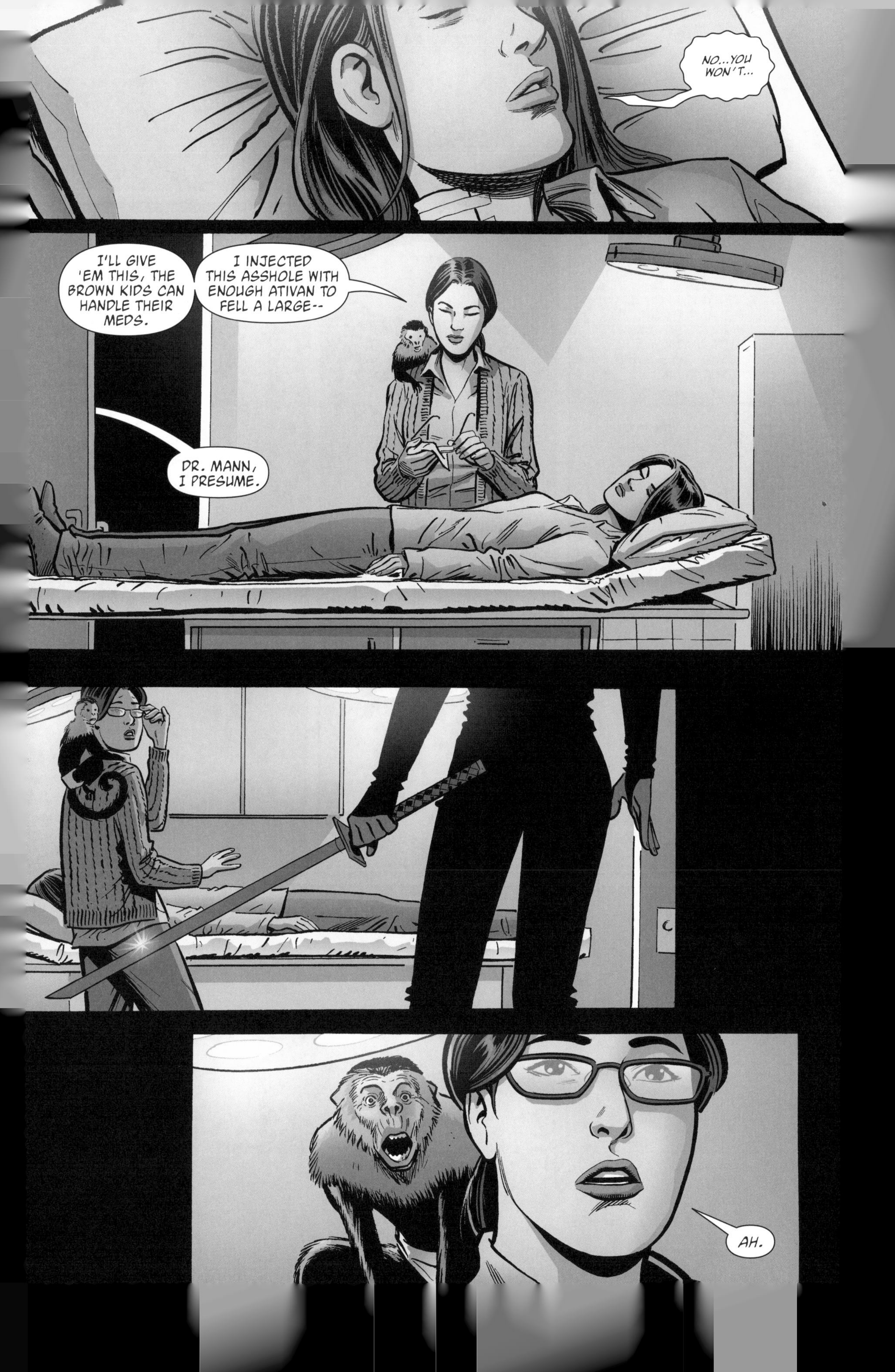
NO...YOU WON'T...
I'LL GIVE 'EM THIS, THE BROWN KIDS CAN HANDLE THEIR MEDS.
I INJECTED THIS ASSHOLE WITH ENOUGH ATIVAN TO FELL A LARGE--
DR. MANN, I PRESUME.
AH.

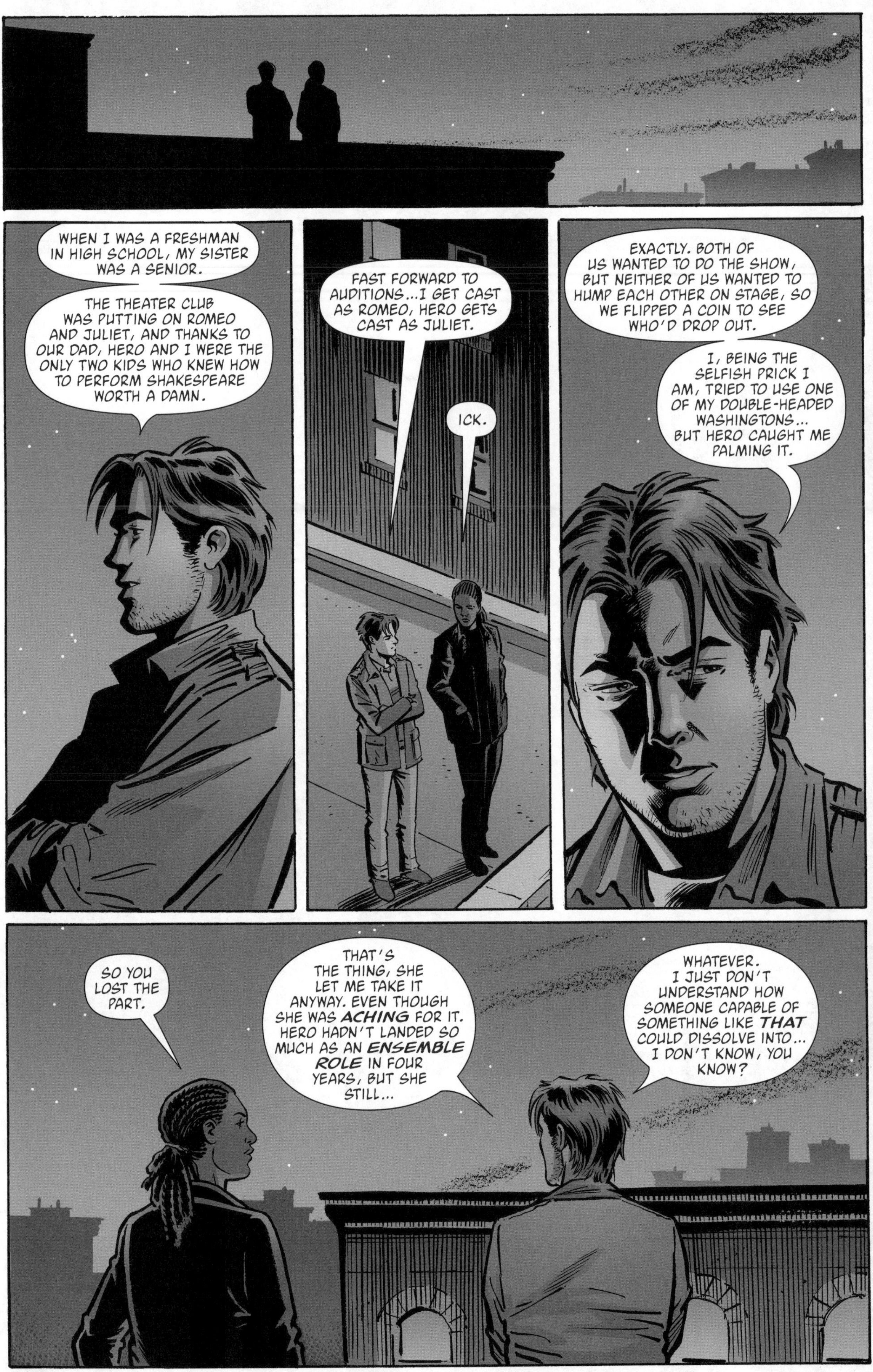
WHEN I WAS A FRESHMAN IN HIGH SCHOOL, MY SISTER WAS A SENIOR.
THE THEATER CLUB WAS PUTTING ON ROMEO AND JULIET, AND THANKS TO OUR DAD, HERO AND I WERE THE ONLY TWO KIDS WHO KNEW HOW TO PERFORM SHAKESPEARE WORTH A DAMN.
FAST FORWARD TO AUDITIONS...I GET CAST AS ROMEO, HERO GETS CAST AS JULIET.
ICK.
EXACTLY. BOTH OF US WANTED TO DO THE SHOW, BUT NEITHER OF US WANTED TO HUMP EACH OTHER ON STAGE, SO WE FLIPPED A COIN TO SEE WHO'D DROP OUT.
I, BEING THE SELFISH PRICK I AM, TRIED TO USE ONE OF MY DOUBLE-HEADED WASHINGTONS... BUT HERO CAUGHT ME PALMING IT.
SO YOU LOST THE PART.
THAT'S THE THING, SHE LET ME TAKE IT ANYWAY. EVEN THOUGH SHE WAS ACHING FOR IT. HERO HADN'T LANDED SO MUCH AS AN ENSEMBLE ROLE IN FOUR YEARS, BUT SHE STILL...
WHATEVER. I JUST DON'T UNDERSTAND HOW SOMEONE CAPABLE OF SOMETHING LIKE THAT COULD DISSOLVE INTO... I DON'T KNOW, YOU KNOW?

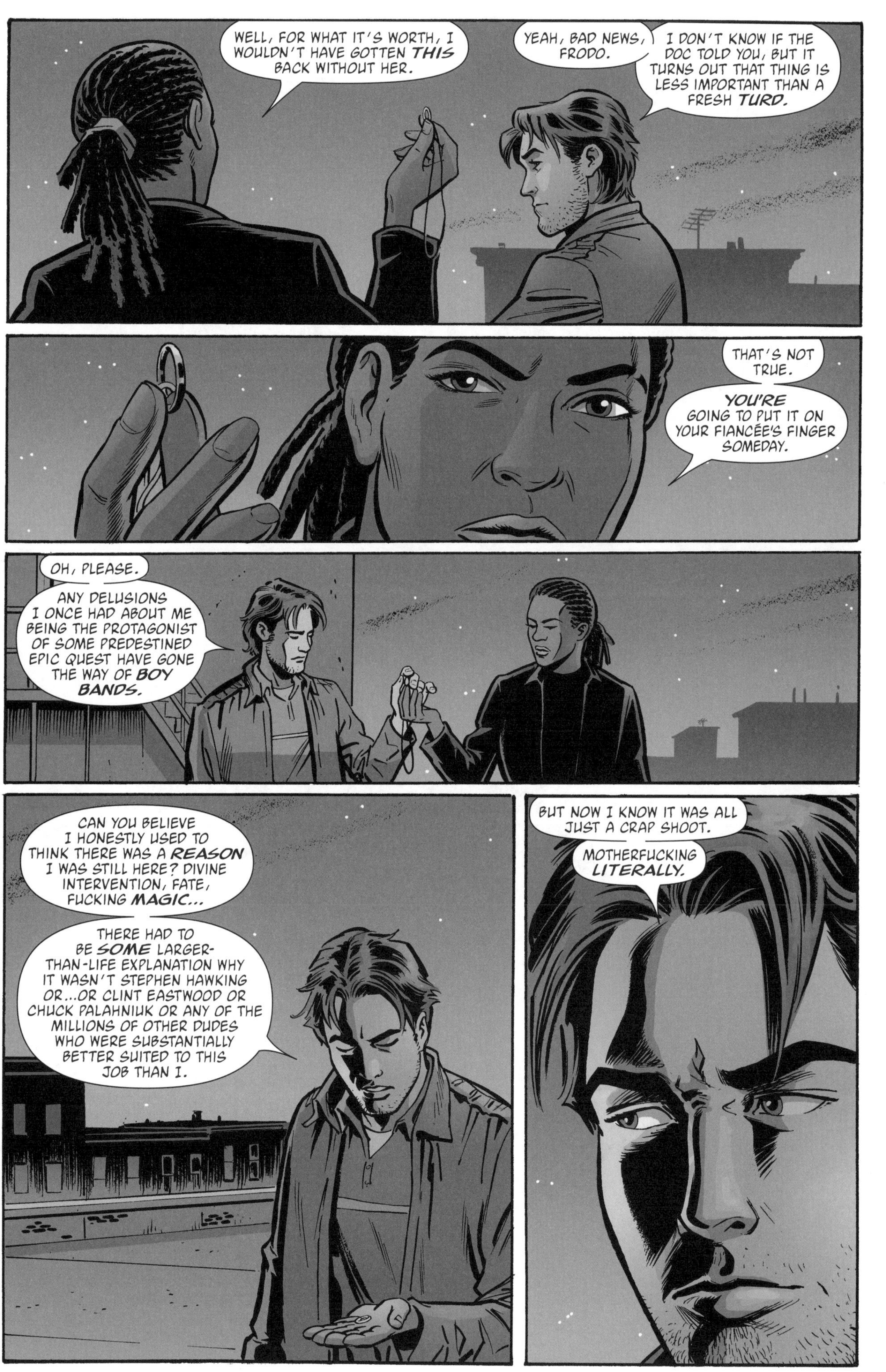
WELL, FOR WHAT IT'S WORTH, I WOULDN'T HAVE GOTTEN THIS BACK WITHOUT HER.
YEAH, BAD NEWS, FRODO.
I DON'T KNOW IF THE DOC TOLD YOU, BUT IT TURNS OUT THAT THING IS LESS IMPORTANT THAN A FRESH TURD.
THAT'S NOT TRUE.
YOU'RE GOING TO PUT IT ON YOUR FIANCÉE'S FINGER SOMEDAY.
OH, PLEASE.
ANY DELUSIONS I ONCE HAD ABOUT ME BEING THE PROTAGONIST OF SOME PREDESTINED EPIC QUEST HAVE GONE THE WAY OF BOY BANDS.
CAN YOU BELIEVE I HONESTLY USED TO THINK THERE WAS A REASON I WAS STILL HERE? DIVINE INTERVENTION, FATE, FUCKING MAGIC...
THERE HAD TO BE SOME LARGER-THAN-LIFE EXPLANATION WHY IT WASN'T STEPHEN HAWKING OR...OR CLINT EASTWOOD OR CHUCK PALAHNIUK OR ANY OF THE MILLIONS OF OTHER DUDES WHO WERE SUBSTANTIALLY BETTER SUITED TO THIS JOB THAN I.
BUT NOW I KNOW IT WAS ALL JUST A CRAP SHOOT.
MOTHERFUCKING LITERALLY.

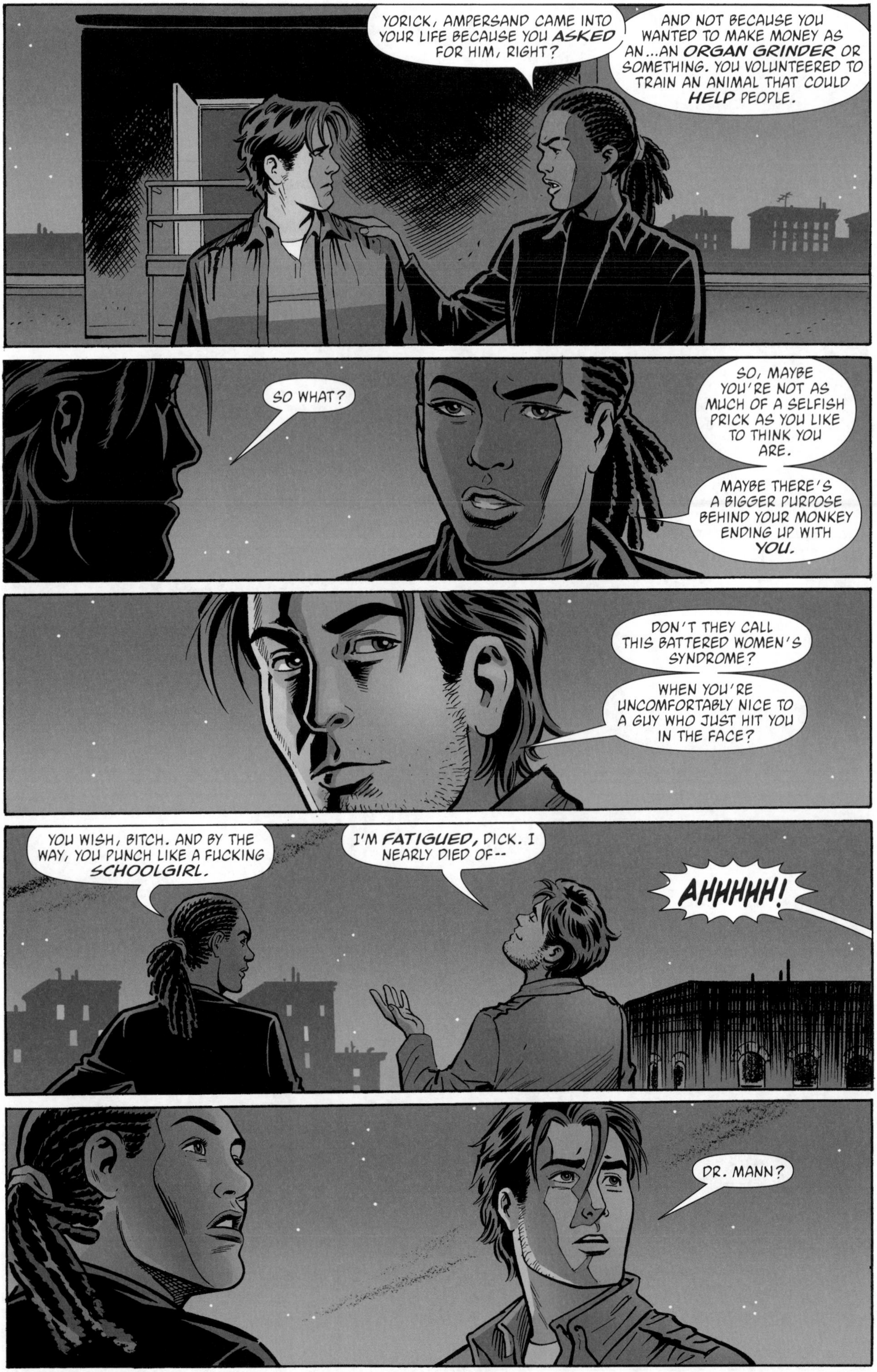
YORICK, AMPERSAND CAME INTO YOUR LIFE BECAUSE YOU ASKED FOR HIM, RIGHT?
AND NOT BECAUSE YOU WANTED TO MAKE MONEY AS AN...AN ORGAN GRINDER OR SOMETHING. YOU VOLUNTEERED TO TRAIN AN ANIMAL THAT COULD HELP PEOPLE.
SO WHAT?
SO, MAYBE YOU'RE NOT AS MUCH OF A SELFISH PRICK AS YOU LIKE TO THINK YOU ARE.
MAYBE THERE'S A BIGGER PURPOSE BEHIND YOUR MONKEY ENDING UP WITH YOU.
DON'T THEY CALL THIS BATTERED WOMEN'S SYNDROME?
WHEN YOU'RE UNCOMFORTABLY NICE TO A GUY WHO JUST HIT YOU IN THE FACE?
YOU WISH, BITCH. AND BY THE WAY, YOU PUNCH LIKE A FUCKING SCHOOLGIRL.
I'M FATIGUED, DICK. I NEARLY DIED OF--
AHHHHH!
DR. MANN?

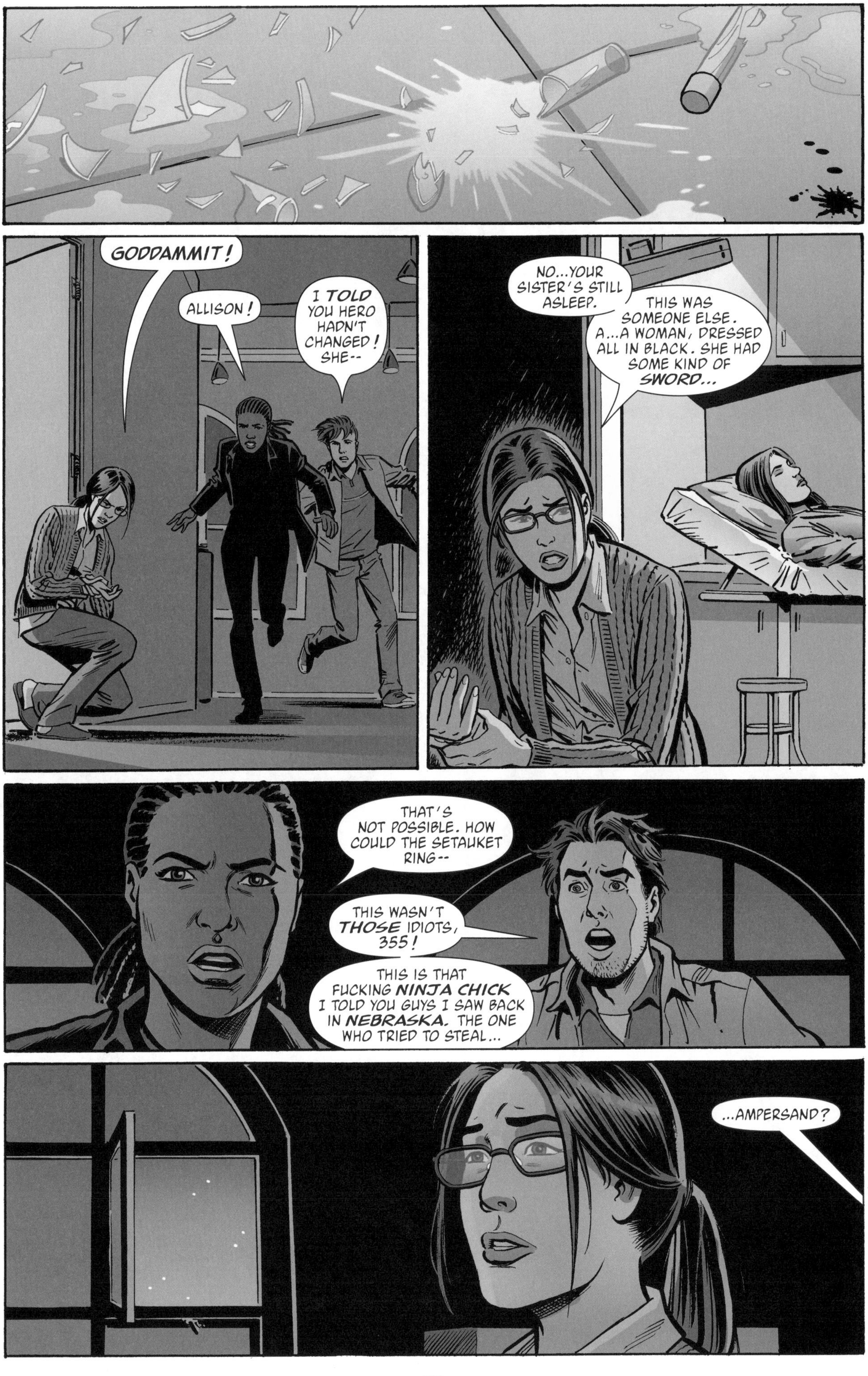
GODDAMMIT!
ALLISON!
I TOLD YOU HERO HADN'T CHANGED! SHE--
NO...YOUR SISTER'S STILL ASLEEP.
THIS WAS SOMEONE ELSE. A...A WOMAN, DRESSED ALL IN BLACK. SHE HAD SOME KIND OF SWORD...
THAT'S NOT POSSIBLE. HOW COULD THE SETAUKET RING--
THIS WASN'T THOSE IDIOTS, 355!
THIS IS THAT FUCKING NINJA CHICK I TOLD YOU GUYS I SAW BACK IN NEBRASKA. THE ONE WHO TRIED TO STEAL...
...AMPERSAND?

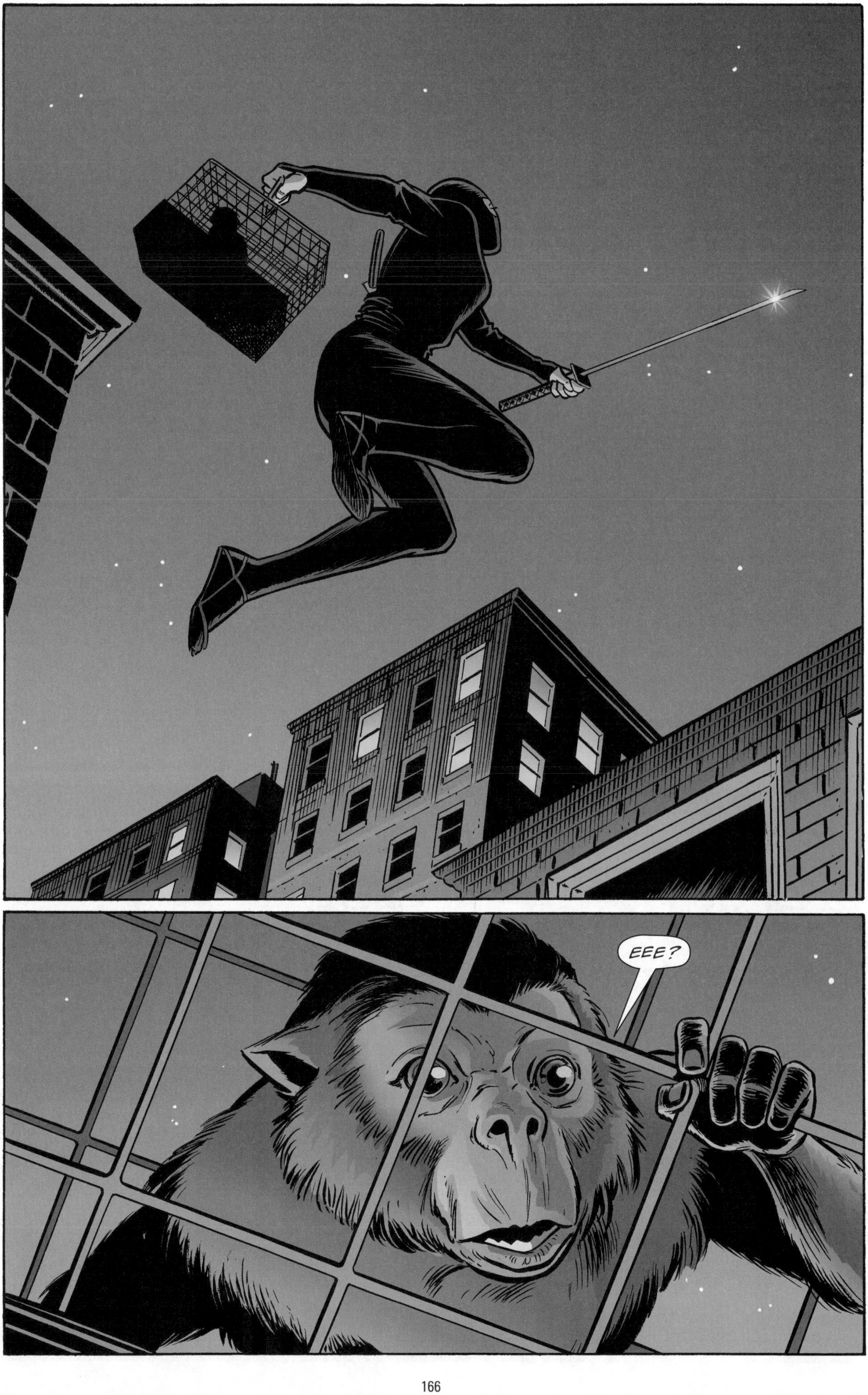
EEE?

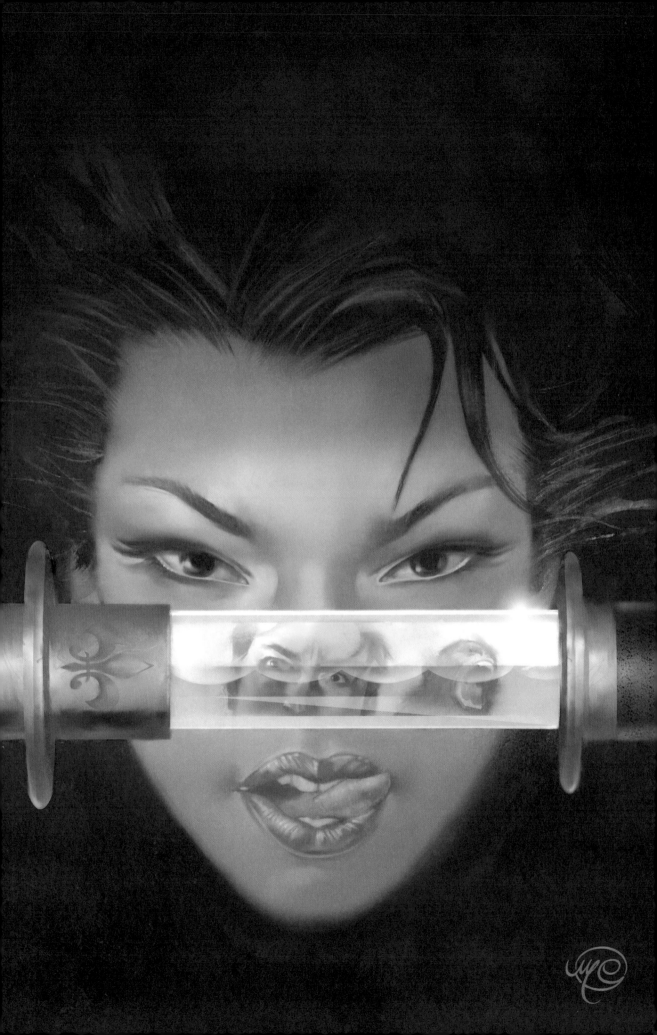

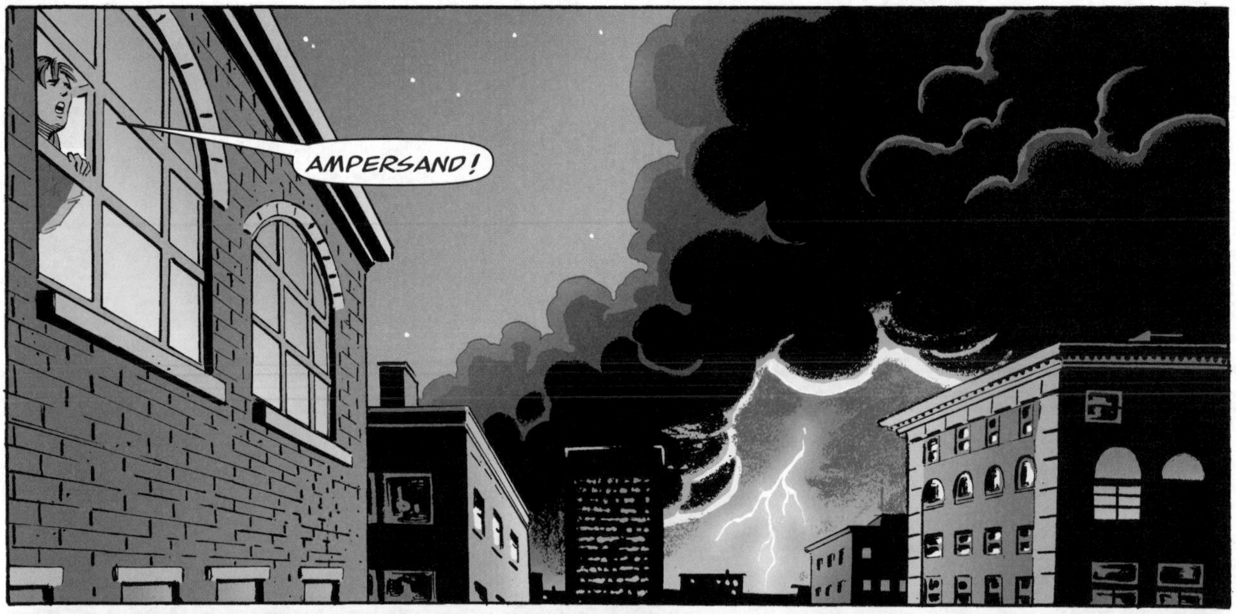
AMPERSAND!

San Francisco, California
Now

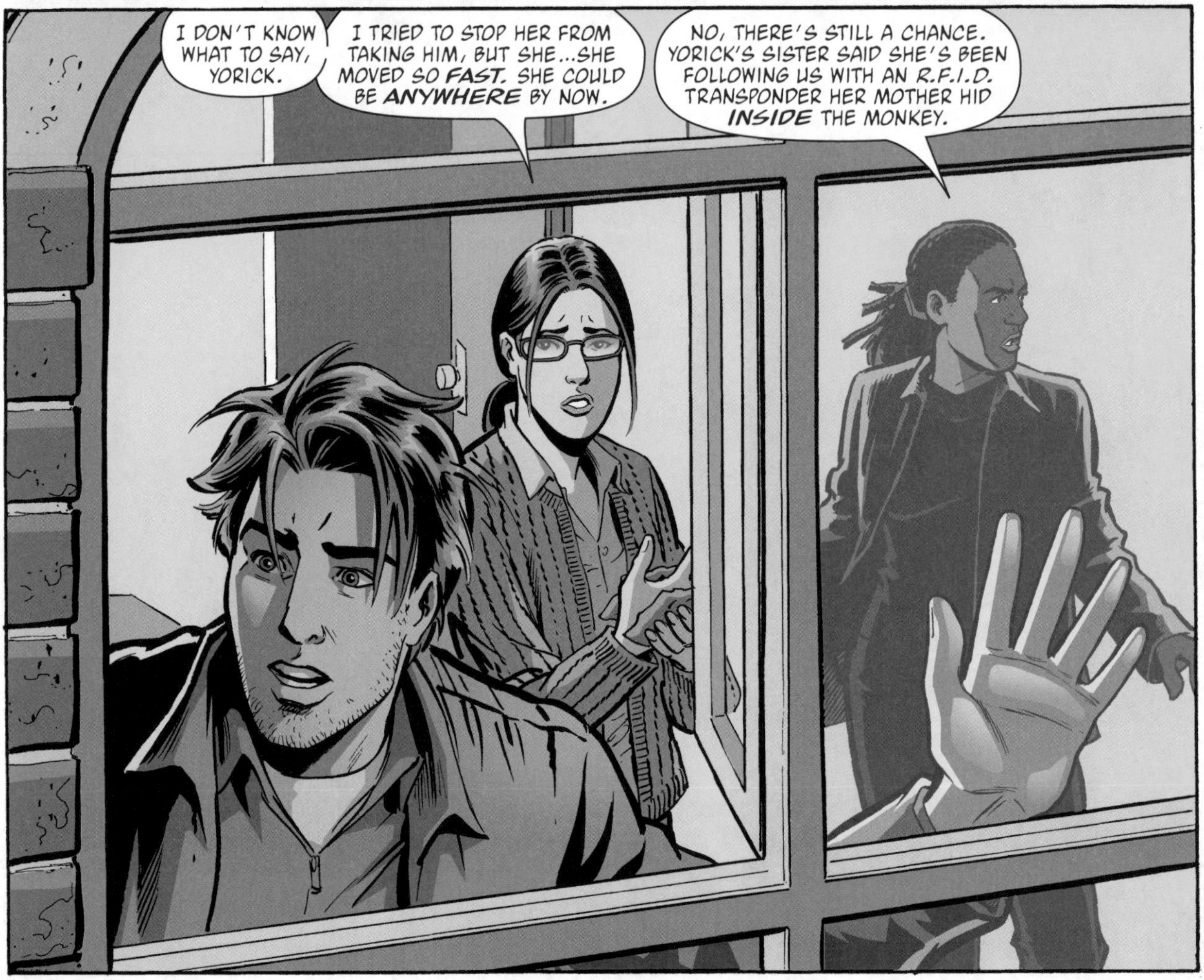
I DON'T KNOW WHAT TO SAY, YORICK.
I TRIED TO STOP HER FROM TAKING HIM, BUT SHE...SHE MOVED SO *FAST.* SHE COULD BE *ANYWHERE* BY NOW.
NO, THERE'S STILL A CHANCE. YORICK'S SISTER SAID SHE'S BEEN FOLLOWING US WITH AN R.F.I.D. TRANSPONDER HER MOTHER HID *INSIDE* THE MONKEY.

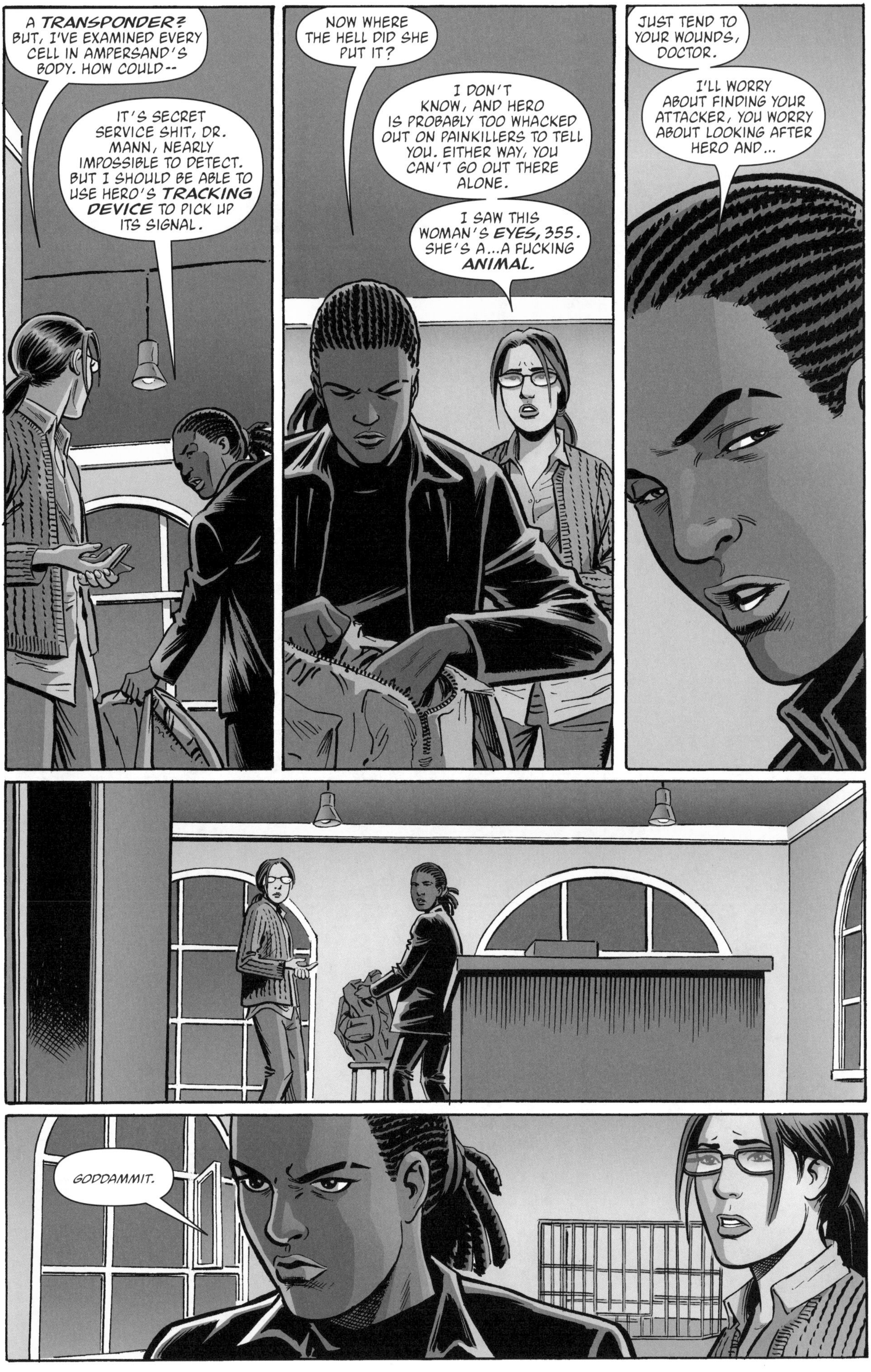
A TRANSPONDER? BUT, I'VE EXAMINED EVERY CELL IN AMPERSAND'S BODY. HOW COULD--
IT'S SECRET SERVICE SHIT, DR. MANN, NEARLY IMPOSSIBLE TO DETECT. BUT I SHOULD BE ABLE TO USE HERO'S TRACKING DEVICE TO PICK UP ITS SIGNAL.
NOW WHERE THE HELL DID SHE PUT IT?
I DON'T KNOW, AND HERO IS PROBABLY TOO WHACKED OUT ON PAINKILLERS TO TELL YOU. EITHER WAY, YOU CAN'T GO OUT THERE ALONE.
I SAW THIS WOMAN'S EYES, 355. SHE'S A...A FUCKING ANIMAL.
JUST TEND TO YOUR WOUNDS, DOCTOR.
I'LL WORRY ABOUT FINDING YOUR ATTACKER, YOU WORRY ABOUT LOOKING AFTER HERO AND...
GODDAMMIT.

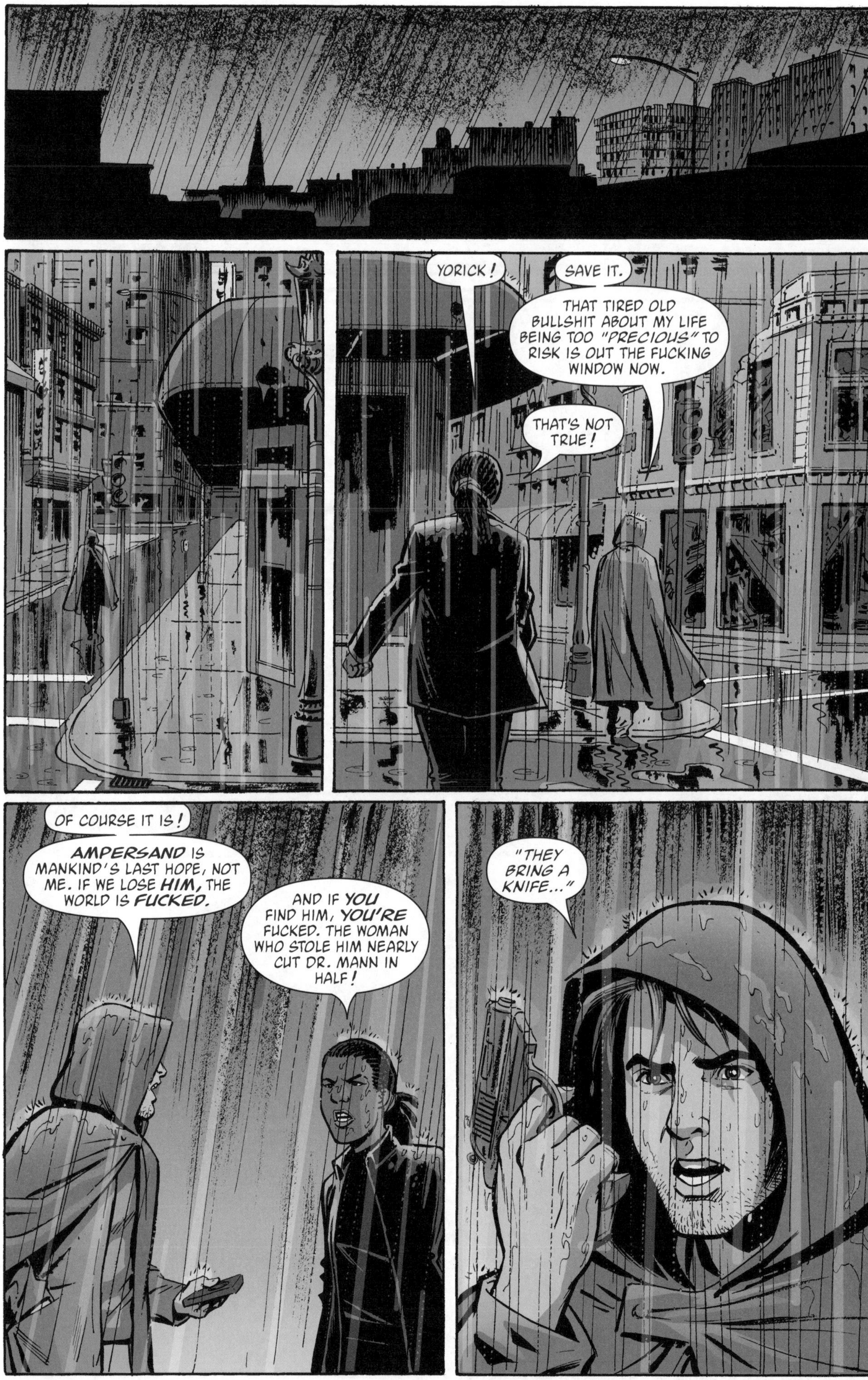
YORICK!
SAVE IT.
THAT TIRED OLD BULLSHIT ABOUT MY LIFE BEING TOO "PRECIOUS" TO RISK IS OUT THE FUCKING WINDOW NOW.
THAT'S NOT TRUE!
OF COURSE IT IS!
AMPERSAND IS MANKIND'S LAST HOPE, NOT ME. IF WE LOSE HIM, THE WORLD IS FUCKED.
AND IF YOU FIND HIM, YOU'RE FUCKED. THE WOMAN WHO STOLE HIM NEARLY CUT DR. MANN IN HALF!
"THEY BRING A KNIFE..."

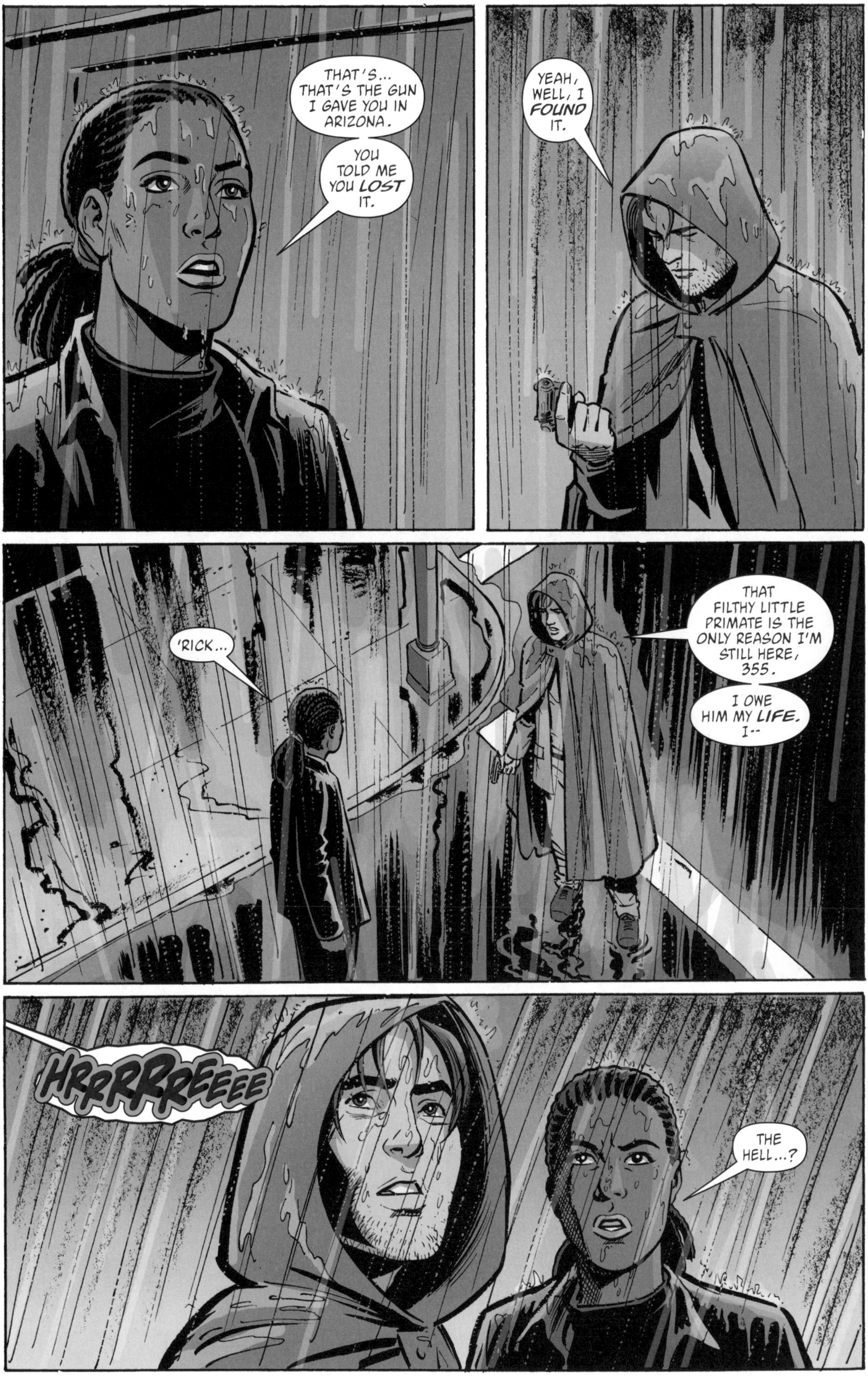
THAT'S... THAT'S THE GUN I GAVE YOU IN ARIZONA.
YOU TOLD ME YOU LOST IT.
YEAH, WELL, I FOUND IT.
'RICK...
THAT FILTHY LITTLE PRIMATE IS THE ONLY REASON I'M STILL HERE, 355.
I OWE HIM MY LIFE. I--
HRRRRREEEEE
THE HELL...?

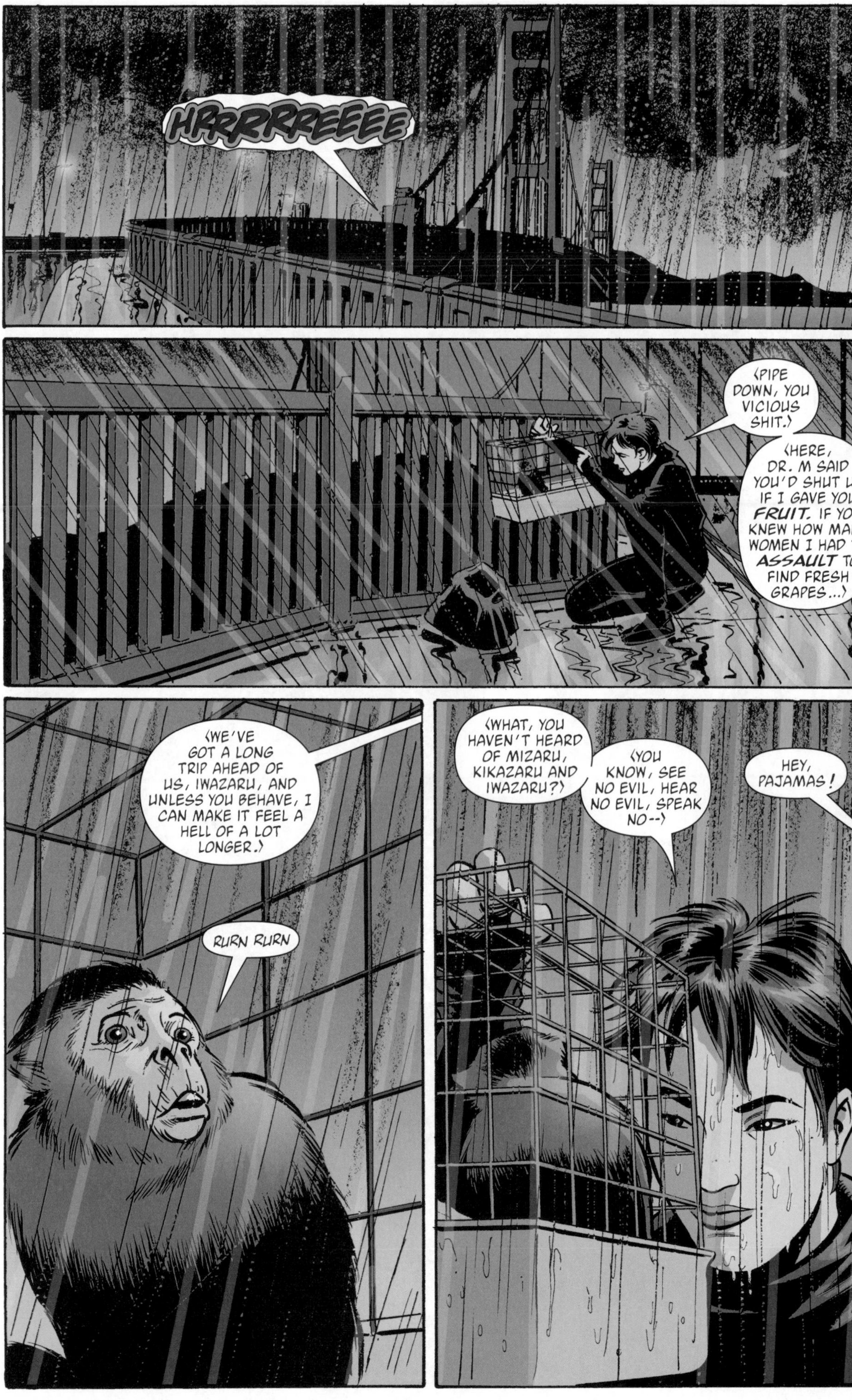
HRRRRREEEE
‹PIPE DOWN, YOU VICIOUS SHIT.›
‹HERE, DR. M SAID YOU'D SHUT UP IF I GAVE YOU FRUIT. IF YOU KNEW HOW MANY WOMEN I HAD TO ASSAULT TO FIND FRESH GRAPES...›
‹WE'VE GOT A LONG TRIP AHEAD OF US, IWAZARU, AND UNLESS YOU BEHAVE, I CAN MAKE IT FEEL A HELL OF A LOT LONGER.›
RURN RURN
‹WHAT, YOU HAVEN'T HEARD OF MIZARU, KIKAZARU AND IWAZARU?›
‹YOU KNOW, SEE NO EVIL, HEAR NO EVIL, SPEAK NO--›
HEY, PAJAMAS!

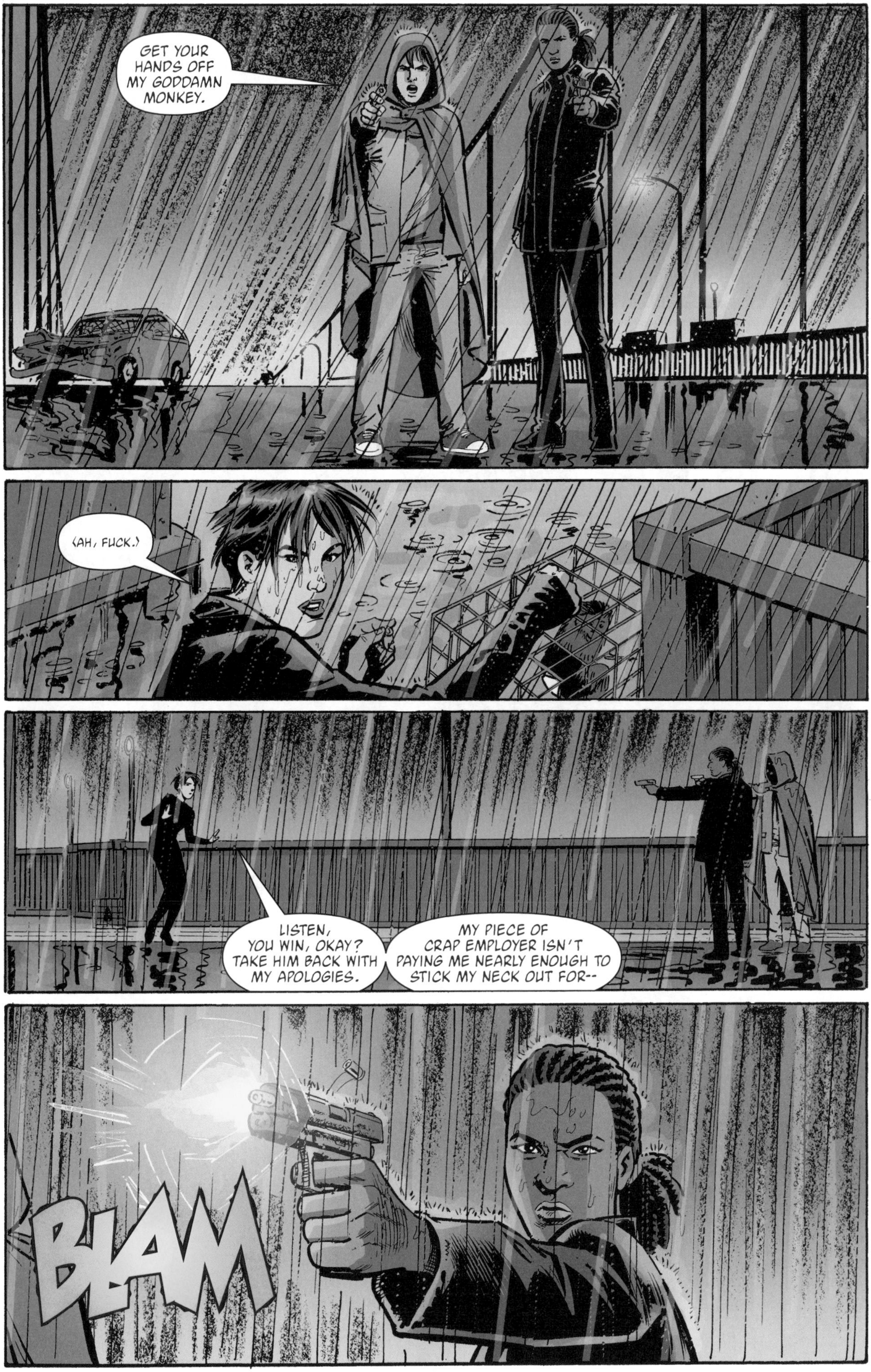
GET YOUR HANDS OFF MY GODDAMN MONKEY.
‹AH, FUCK.›
LISTEN, YOU WIN, OKAY? TAKE HIM BACK WITH MY APOLOGIES.
MY PIECE OF CRAP EMPLOYER ISN'T PAYING ME NEARLY ENOUGH TO STICK MY NECK OUT FOR--
BLAM

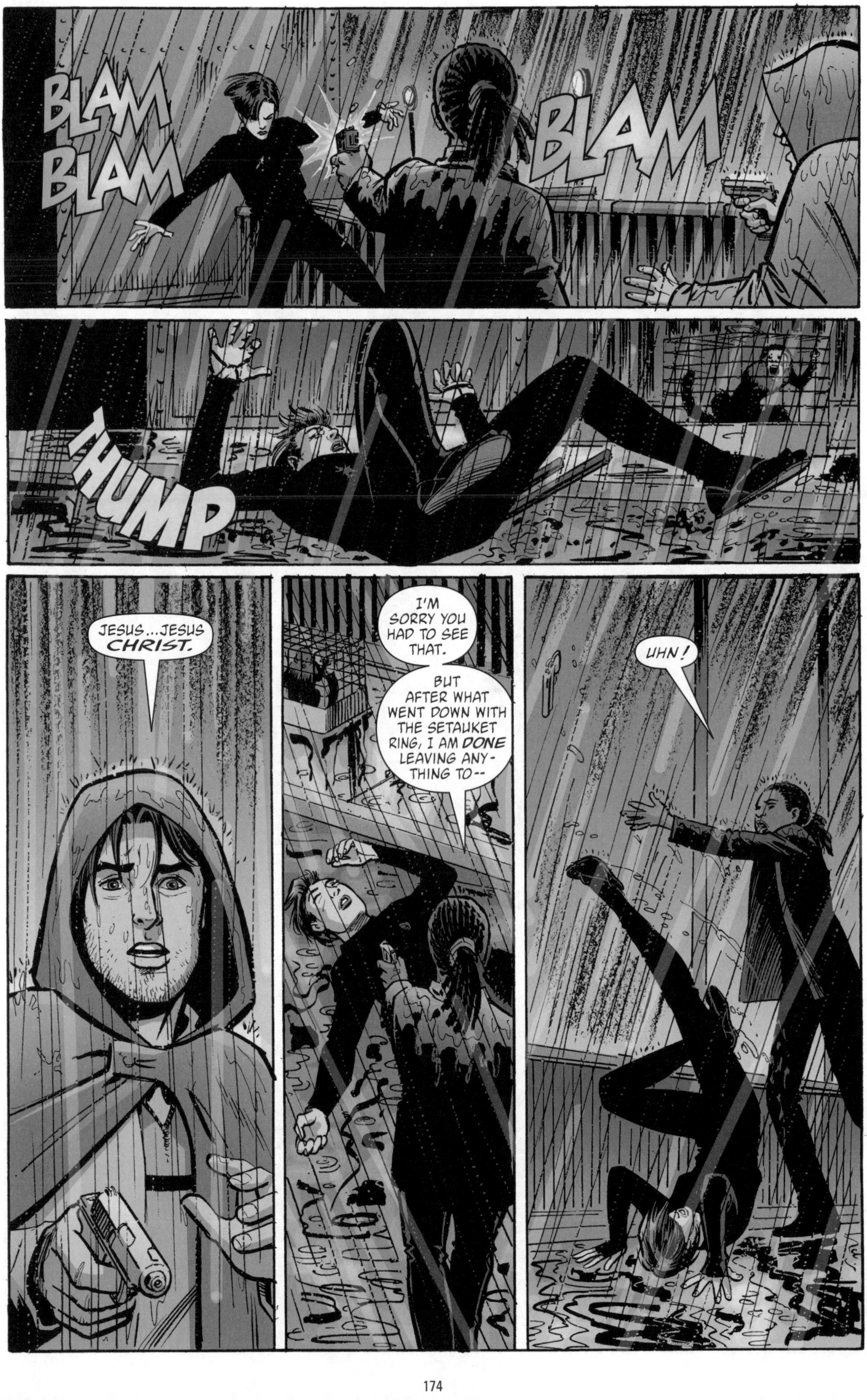
BLAM
BLAM
BLAM
THUMP
JESUS...JESUS CHRIST.
I'M SORRY YOU HAD TO SEE THAT.
BUT AFTER WHAT WENT DOWN WITH THE SETAUKET RING, I AM DONE LEAVING ANY-THING TO--
UHN!

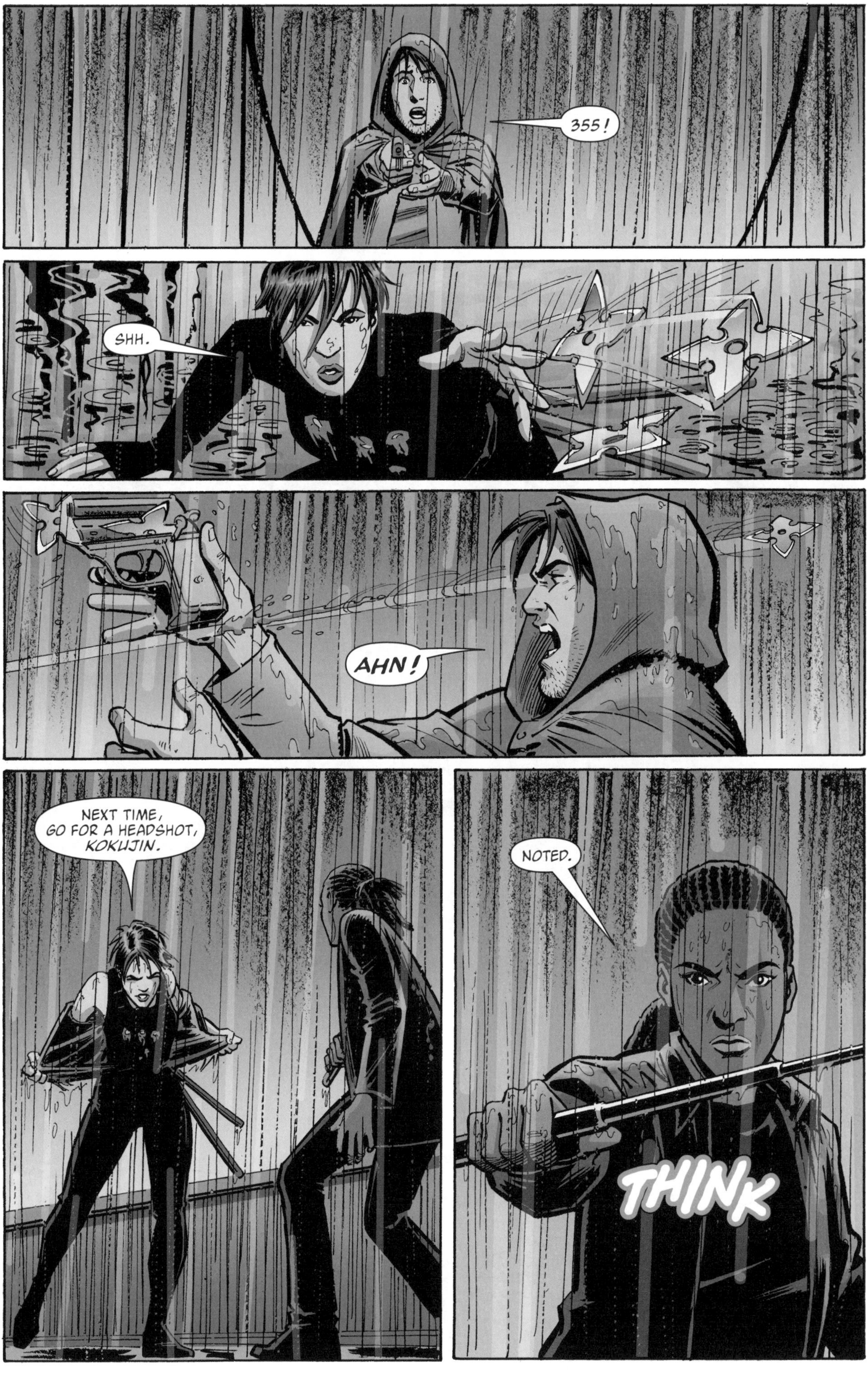
355!
SHH.
AHN!
NEXT TIME, GO FOR A HEADSHOT, KOKUJIN.
NOTED.
THINK

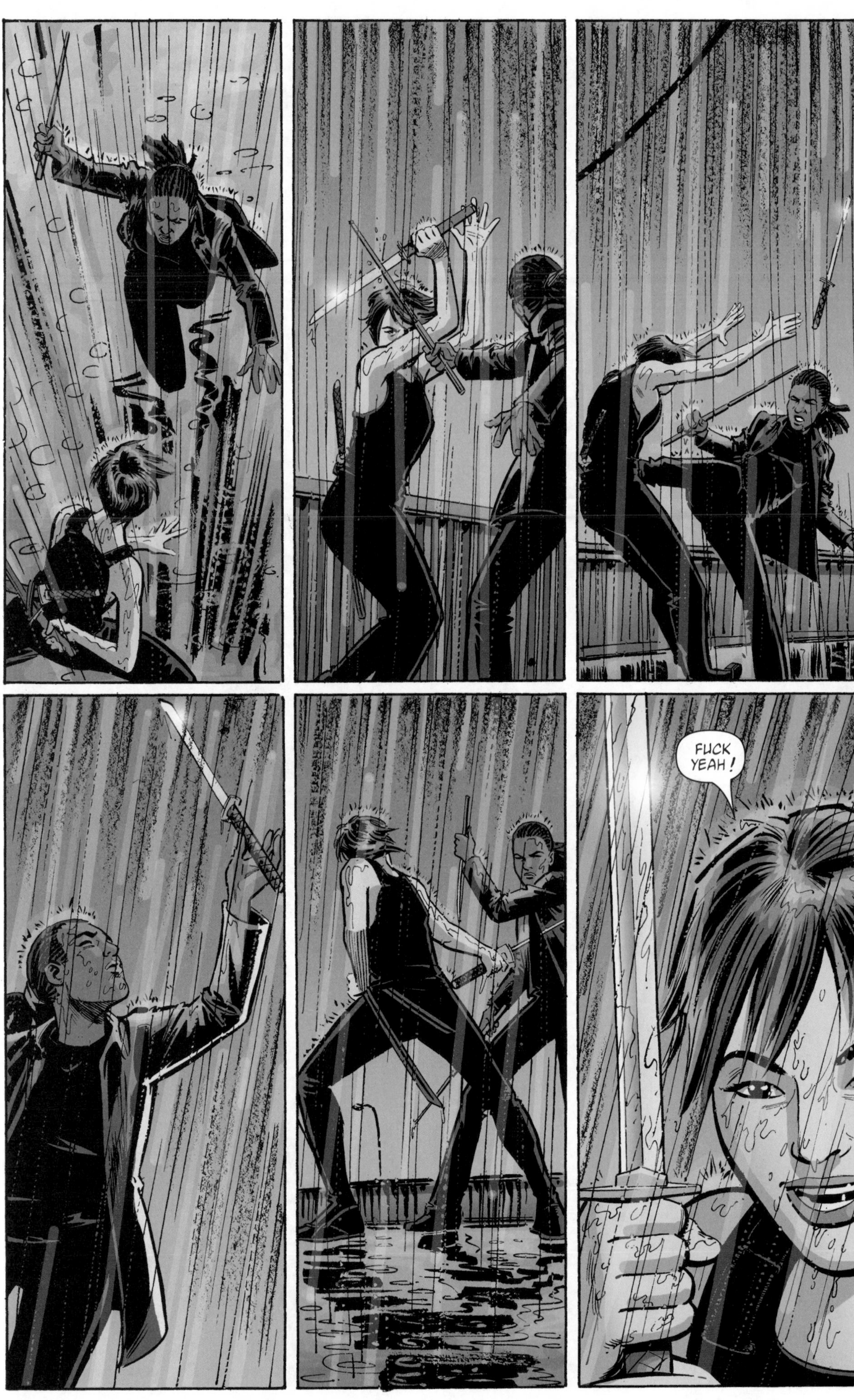
FUCK YEAH!

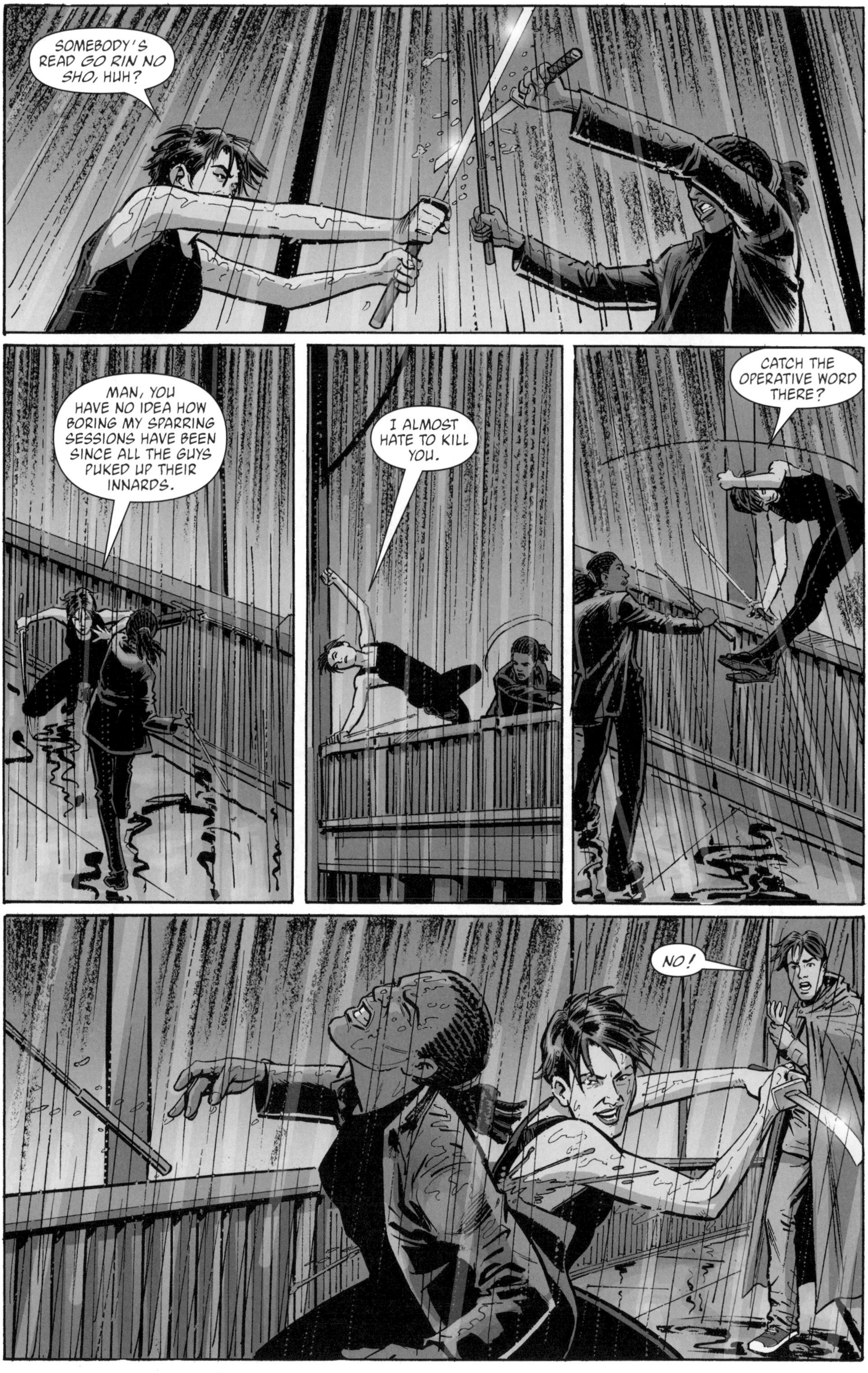

SOMEBODY'S READ GO RIN NO SHO, HUH?
MAN, YOU HAVE NO IDEA HOW BORING MY SPARRING SESSIONS HAVE BEEN SINCE ALL THE GUYS PUKED UP THEIR INNARDS.
I ALMOST HATE TO KILL YOU.
CATCH THE OPERATIVE WORD THERE?
NO!

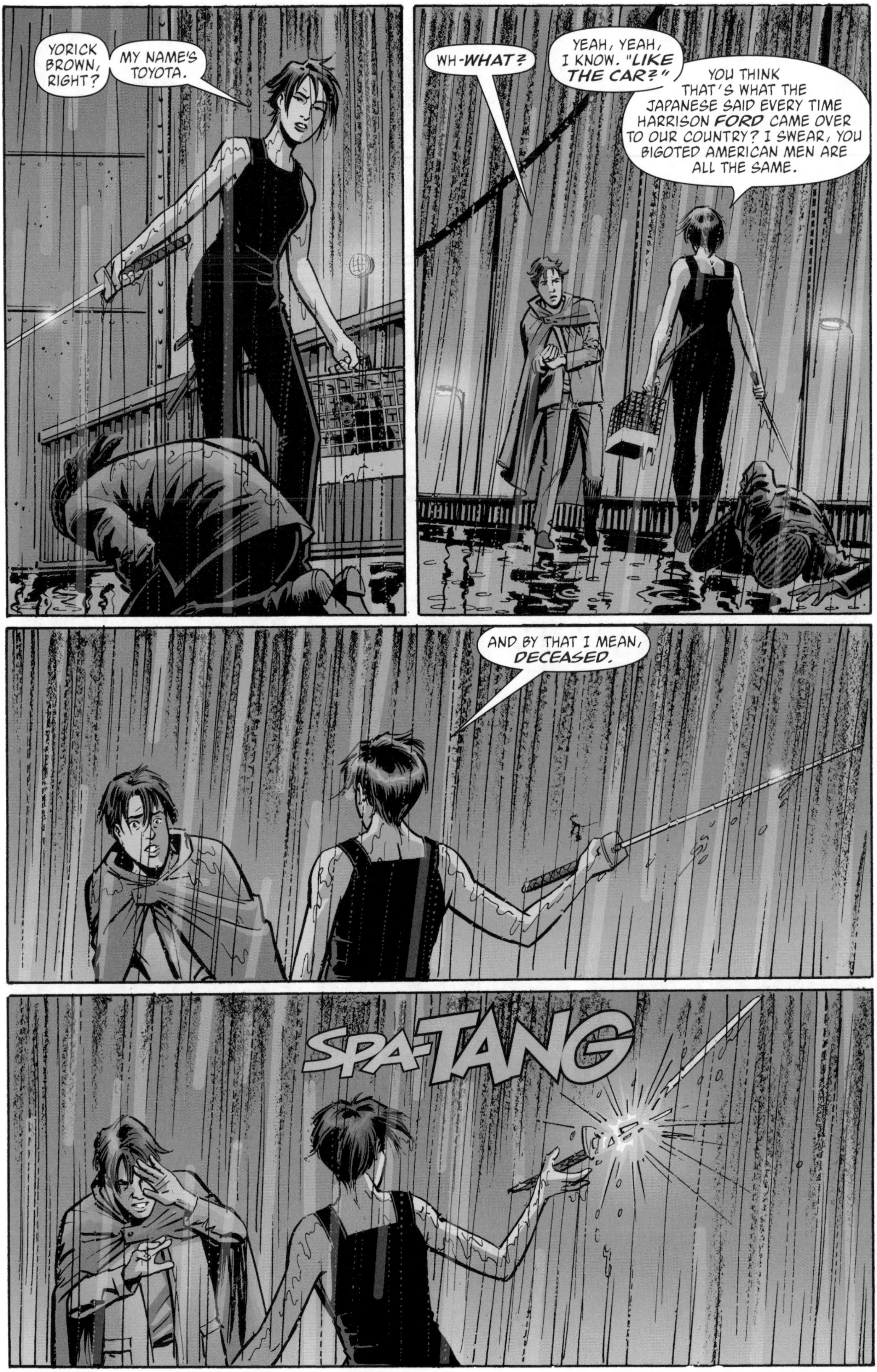
YORICK BROWN, RIGHT?
MY NAME'S TOYOTA.
WH-WHAT?
YEAH, YEAH, I KNOW. "LIKE THE CAR?"
YOU THINK THAT'S WHAT THE JAPANESE SAID EVERY TIME HARRISON FORD CAME OVER TO OUR COUNTRY? I SWEAR, YOU BIGOTED AMERICAN MEN ARE ALL THE SAME.
AND BY THAT I MEAN, DECEASED.
SPA-TANG

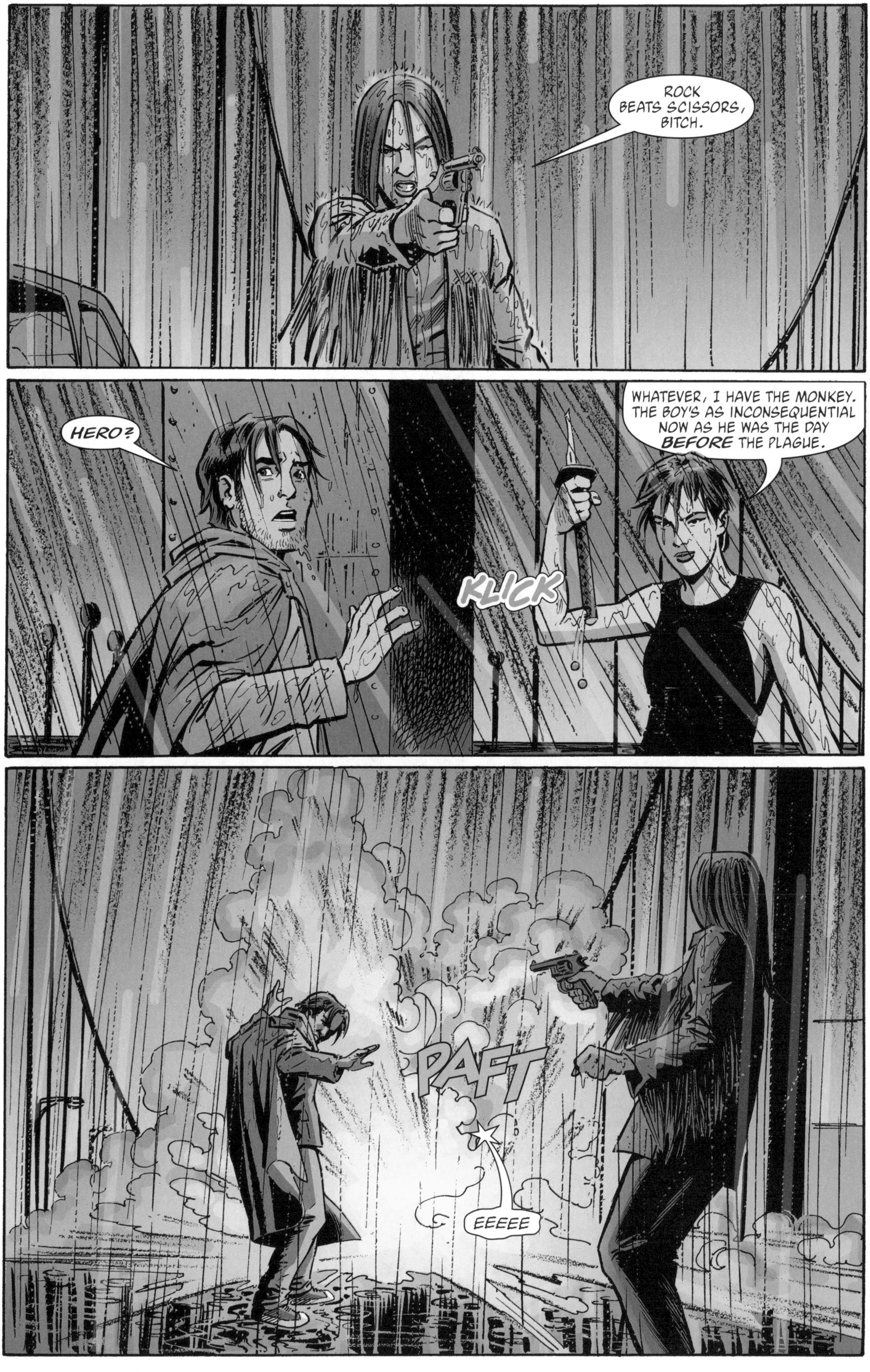
ROCK BEATS SCISSORS, BITCH.
HERO?
WHATEVER, I HAVE THE MONKEY. THE BOY'S AS INCONSEQUENTIAL NOW AS HE WAS THE DAY BEFORE THE PLAGUE.
KLICK
PAFT
EEEEE

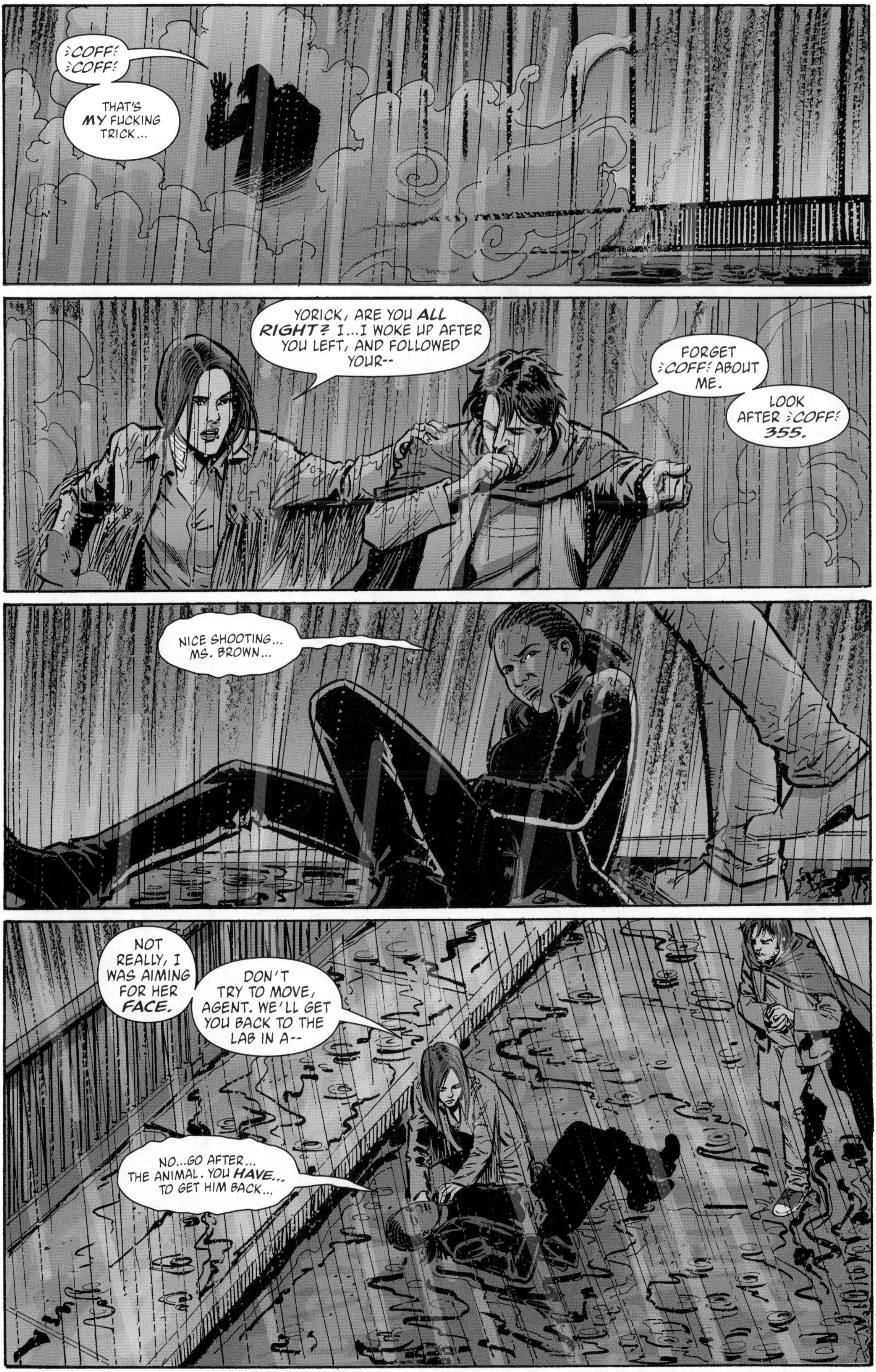
COFF COFF
THAT'S MY FUCKING TRICK...
YORICK, ARE YOU ALL RIGHT? I...I WOKE UP AFTER YOU LEFT, AND FOLLOWED YOUR--
FORGET COFF ABOUT ME.
LOOK AFTER COFF 355.
NICE SHOOTING... MS. BROWN...
NOT REALLY, I WAS AIMING FOR HER FACE.
DON'T TRY TO MOVE, AGENT. WE'LL GET YOU BACK TO THE LAB IN A--
NO...GO AFTER... THE ANIMAL. YOU HAVE... TO GET HIM BACK...

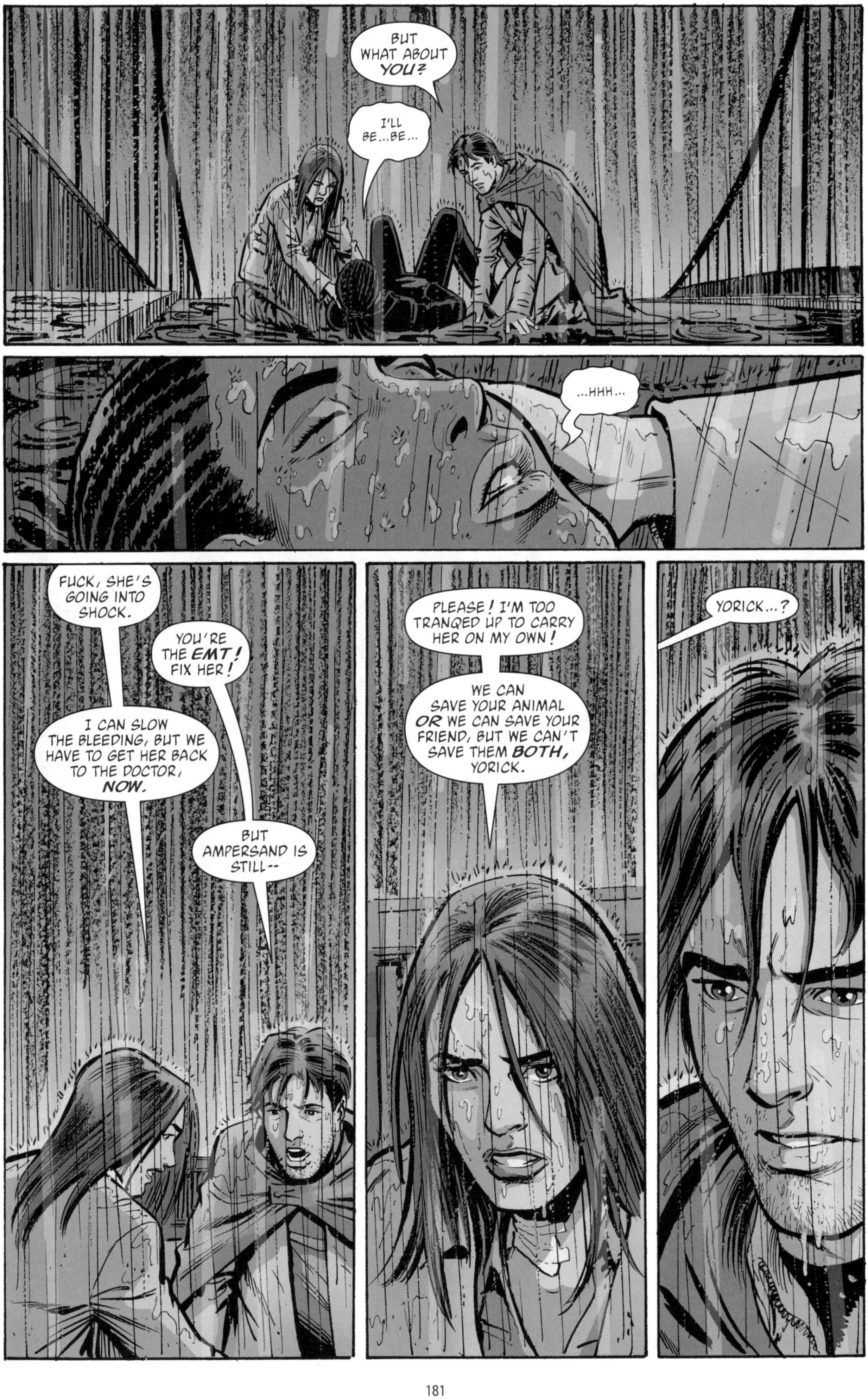
BUT WHAT ABOUT YOU?
I'LL BE...BE...
...HHH...
FUCK, SHE'S GOING INTO SHOCK.
YOU'RE THE EMT! FIX HER!
I CAN SLOW THE BLEEDING, BUT WE HAVE TO GET HER BACK TO THE DOCTOR, NOW.
BUT AMPERSAND IS STILL--
PLEASE! I'M TOO TRANQED UP TO CARRY HER ON MY OWN!
WE CAN SAVE YOUR ANIMAL OR WE CAN SAVE YOUR FRIEND, BUT WE CAN'T SAVE THEM BOTH, YORICK.
YORICK...?

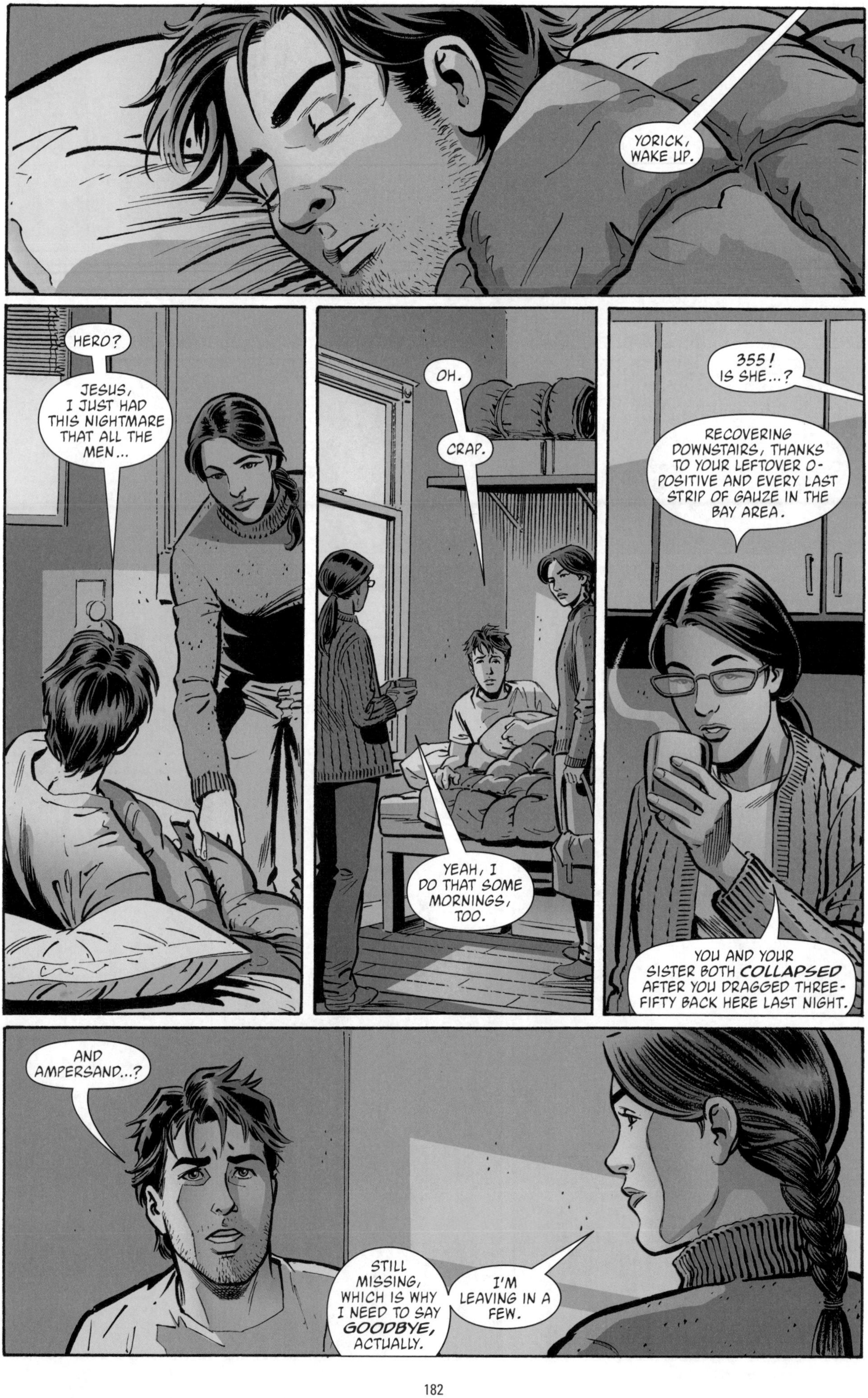
YORICK, WAKE UP.
HERO?
JESUS, I JUST HAD THIS NIGHTMARE THAT ALL THE MEN...
OH.
CRAP.
YEAH, I DO THAT SOME MORNINGS, TOO.
355! IS SHE...?
RECOVERING DOWNSTAIRS, THANKS TO YOUR LEFTOVER O-POSITIVE AND EVERY LAST STRIP OF GAUZE IN THE BAY AREA.
YOU AND YOUR SISTER BOTH COLLAPSED AFTER YOU DRAGGED THREE-FIFTY BACK HERE LAST NIGHT.
AND AMPERSAND...?
STILL MISSING, WHICH IS WHY I NEED TO SAY GOODBYE, ACTUALLY.
I'M LEAVING IN A FEW.

TO LOOK FOR AMP? I'M COMING WITH YOU.

YORICK, YOU WERE IN NO SHAPE FOR MONKEY HUNTING WHEN YOU WERE IN PEAK PHYSICAL CONDITION--AN EXPRESSION I USE LIGHTLY--MUCH LESS WHEN YOU'RE STILL RECOVERING FROM A DEBILITATING ILLNESS.

BESIDES, HERO *ISN'T* GOING AFTER YOUR PET.

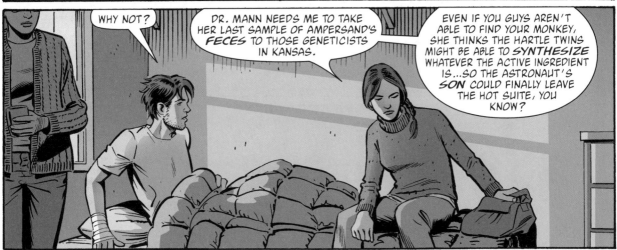

WHY NOT?

DR. MANN NEEDS ME TO TAKE HER LAST SAMPLE OF AMPERSAND'S *FECES* TO THOSE GENETICISTS IN KANSAS.

EVEN IF YOU GUYS AREN'T ABLE TO FIND YOUR MONKEY, SHE THINKS THE HARTLE TWINS MIGHT BE ABLE TO *SYNTHESIZE* WHATEVER THE ACTIVE INGREDIENT IS...SO THE ASTRONAUT'S *SON* COULD FINALLY LEAVE THE HOT SUITE, YOU KNOW?

AND YOU TRUST *HERO* TO PULL THIS OFF?

BETTER HER THAN ME.

BY ALL ACCOUNTS, YOUR SISTER SAVED AT LEAST *TWO* LIVES LAST NIGHT. ALL *I* DID WAS LOSE THE KEY TO HUMANITY'S CONTINUED EXISTENCE.

I'D SAY IT'S MY TURN TO BE THE VILLAIN.

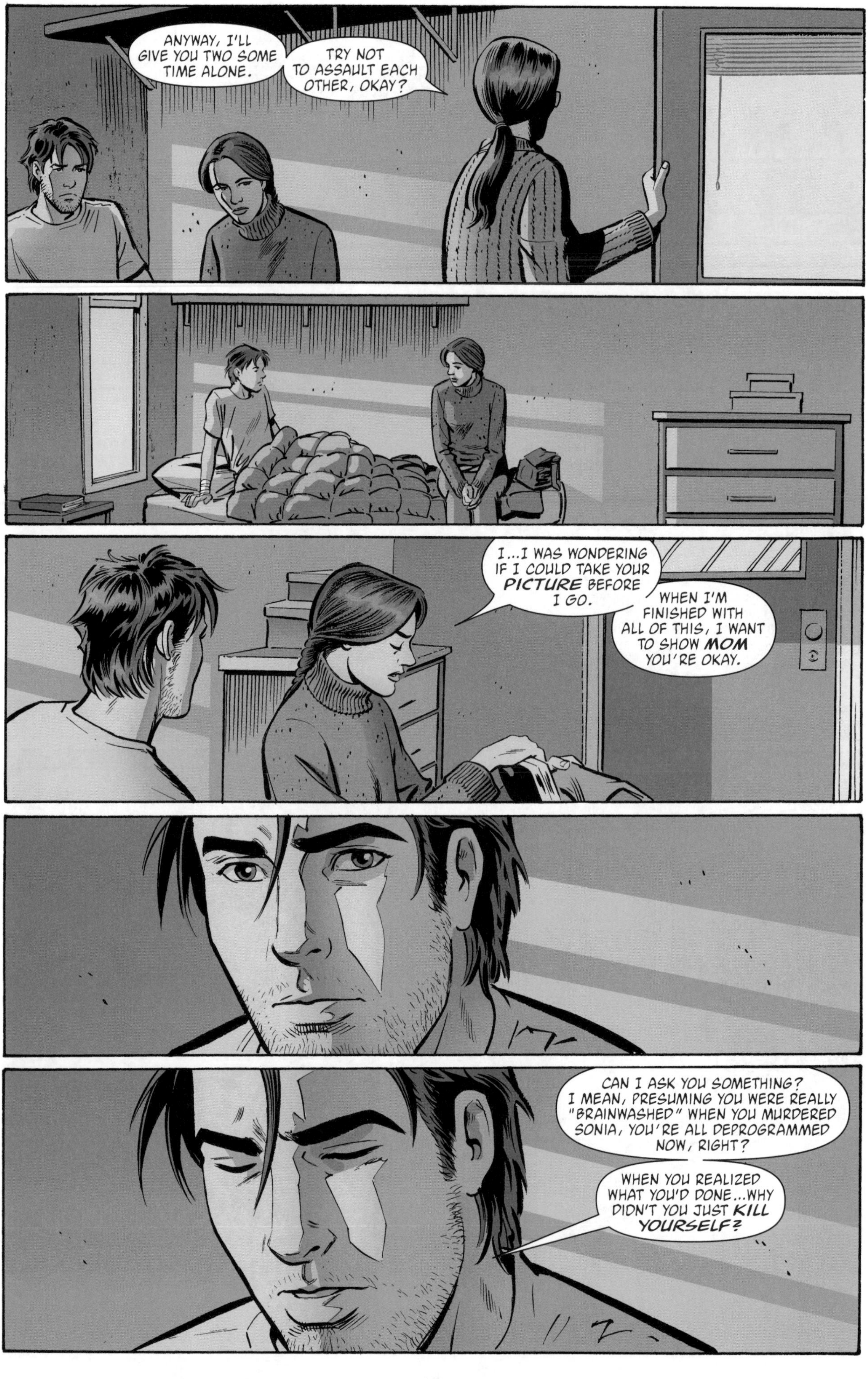
ANYWAY, I'LL GIVE YOU TWO SOME TIME ALONE.
TRY NOT TO ASSAULT EACH OTHER, OKAY?
I...I WAS WONDERING IF I COULD TAKE YOUR **PICTURE** BEFORE I GO.
WHEN I'M FINISHED WITH ALL OF THIS, I WANT TO SHOW **MOM** YOU'RE OKAY.
CAN I ASK YOU SOMETHING? I MEAN, PRESUMING YOU WERE REALLY "BRAINWASHED" WHEN YOU MURDERED SONIA, YOU'RE ALL DEPROGRAMMED NOW, RIGHT?
WHEN YOU REALIZED WHAT YOU'D DONE...WHY DIDN'T YOU JUST **KILL YOURSELF?**

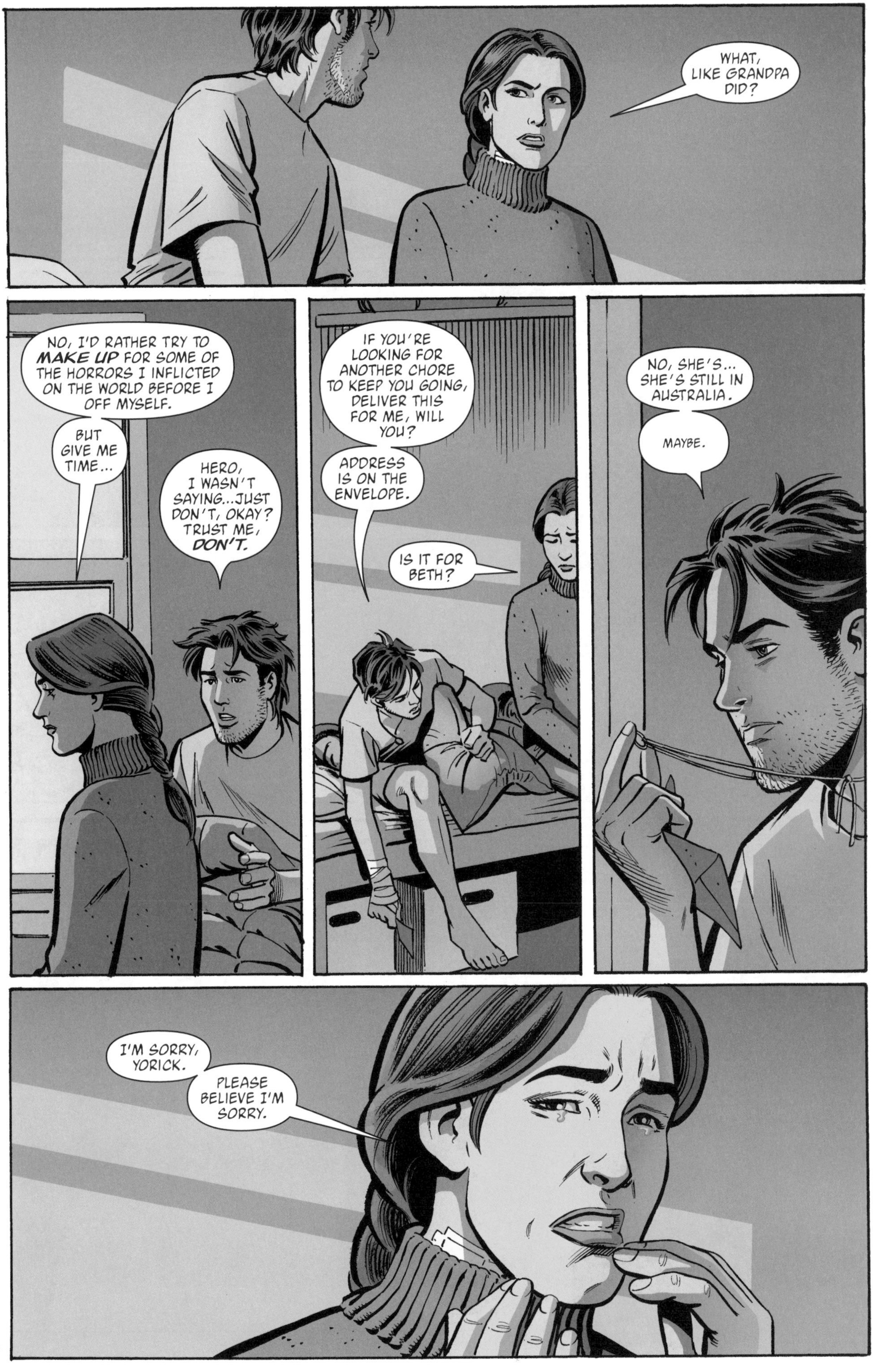
WHAT, LIKE GRANDPA DID?
NO, I'D RATHER TRY TO **MAKE UP** FOR SOME OF THE HORRORS I INFLICTED ON THE WORLD BEFORE I OFF MYSELF.
BUT GIVE ME TIME...
HERO, I WASN'T SAYING...JUST DON'T, OKAY? TRUST ME, **DON'T.**
IF YOU'RE LOOKING FOR ANOTHER CHORE TO KEEP YOU GOING, DELIVER THIS FOR ME, WILL YOU?
ADDRESS IS ON THE ENVELOPE.
IS IT FOR BETH?
NO, SHE'S... SHE'S STILL IN AUSTRALIA.
MAYBE.
I'M SORRY, YORICK.
PLEASE BELIEVE I'M SORRY.

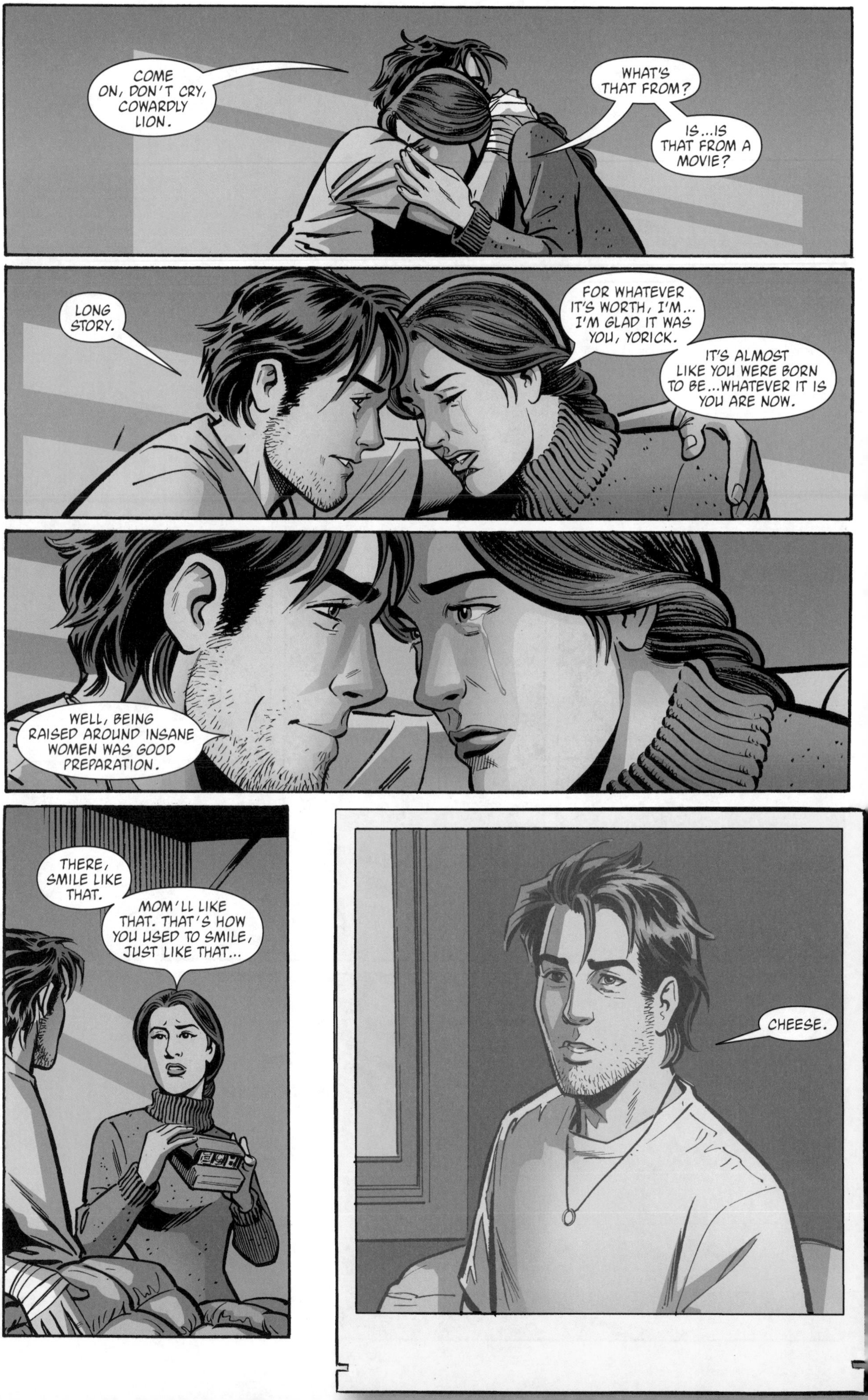
COME ON, DON'T CRY, COWARDLY LION.
WHAT'S THAT FROM?
IS...IS THAT FROM A MOVIE?
LONG STORY.
FOR WHATEVER IT'S WORTH, I'M... I'M GLAD IT WAS YOU, YORICK.
IT'S ALMOST LIKE YOU WERE BORN TO BE...WHATEVER IT IS YOU ARE NOW.
WELL, BEING RAISED AROUND INSANE WOMEN WAS GOOD PREPARATION.
THERE, SMILE LIKE THAT.
MOM'LL LIKE THAT. THAT'S HOW YOU USED TO SMILE, JUST LIKE THAT...
CHEESE.

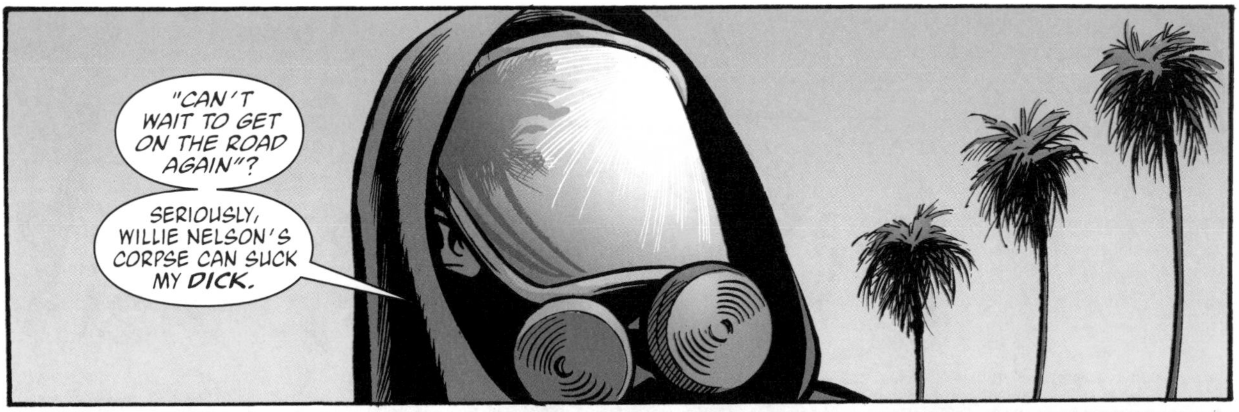
"CAN'T WAIT TO GET ON THE ROAD AGAIN"?
SERIOUSLY, WILLIE NELSON'S CORPSE CAN SUCK MY DICK.

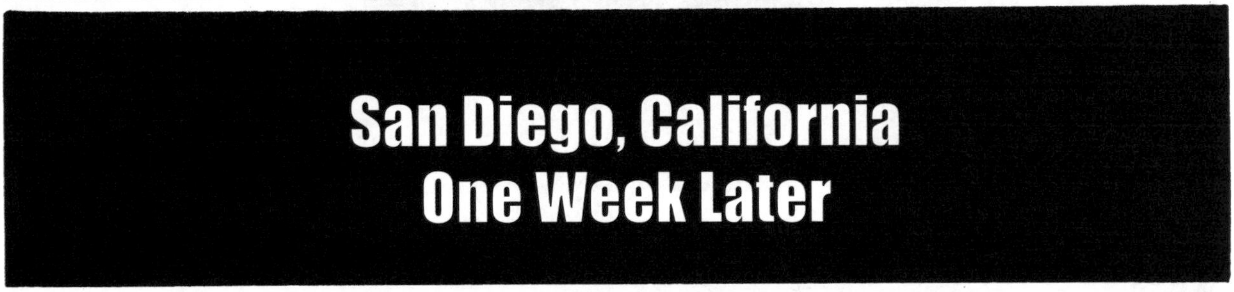
San Diego, California
One Week Later

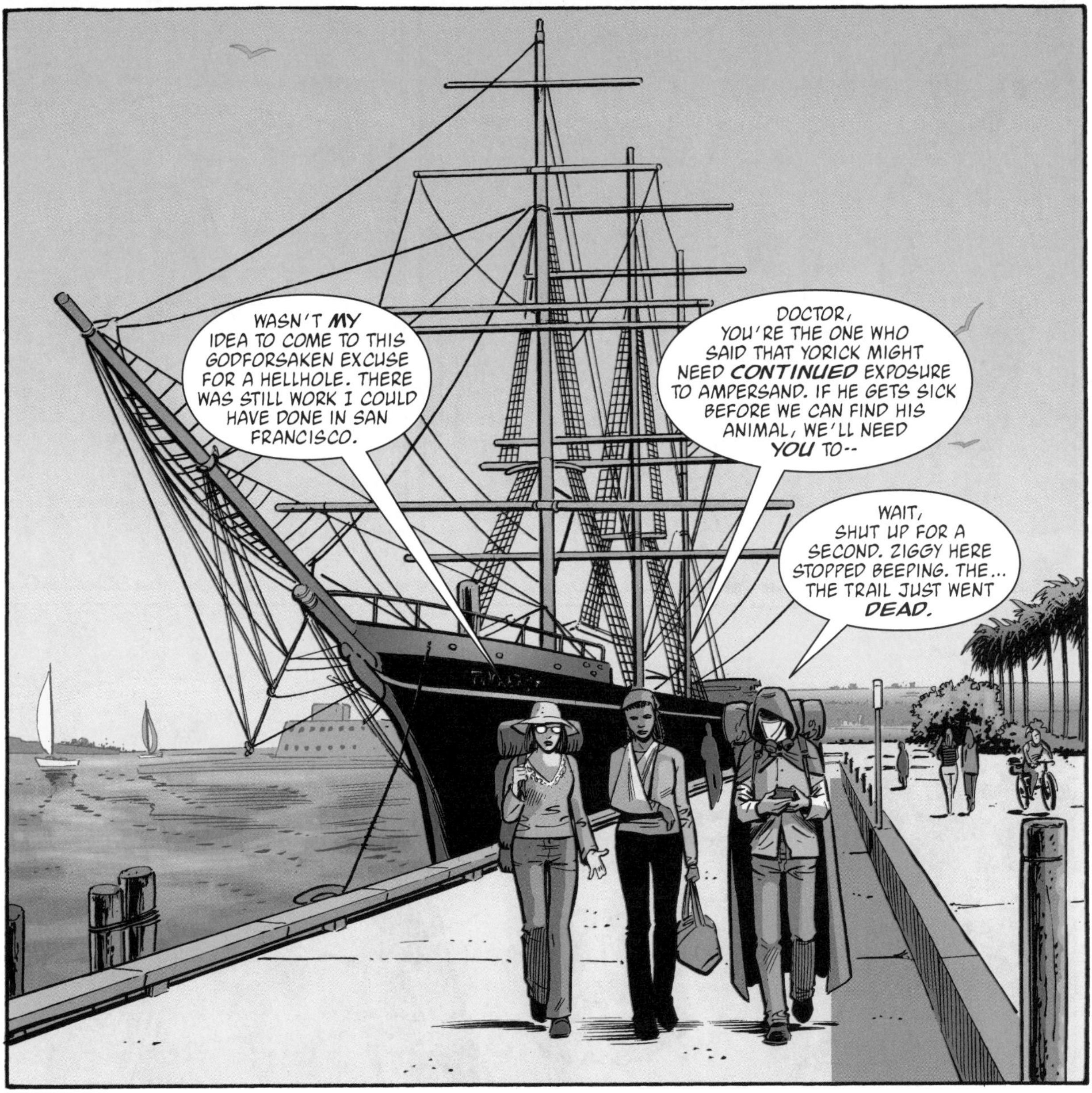
WASN'T MY IDEA TO COME TO THIS GODFORSAKEN EXCUSE FOR A HELLHOLE. THERE WAS STILL WORK I COULD HAVE DONE IN SAN FRANCISCO.
DOCTOR, YOU'RE THE ONE WHO SAID THAT YORICK MIGHT NEED CONTINUED EXPOSURE TO AMPERSAND. IF HE GETS SICK BEFORE WE CAN FIND HIS ANIMAL, WE'LL NEED YOU TO--
WAIT, SHUT UP FOR A SECOND. ZIGGY HERE STOPPED BEEPING. THE... THE TRAIL JUST WENT DEAD.

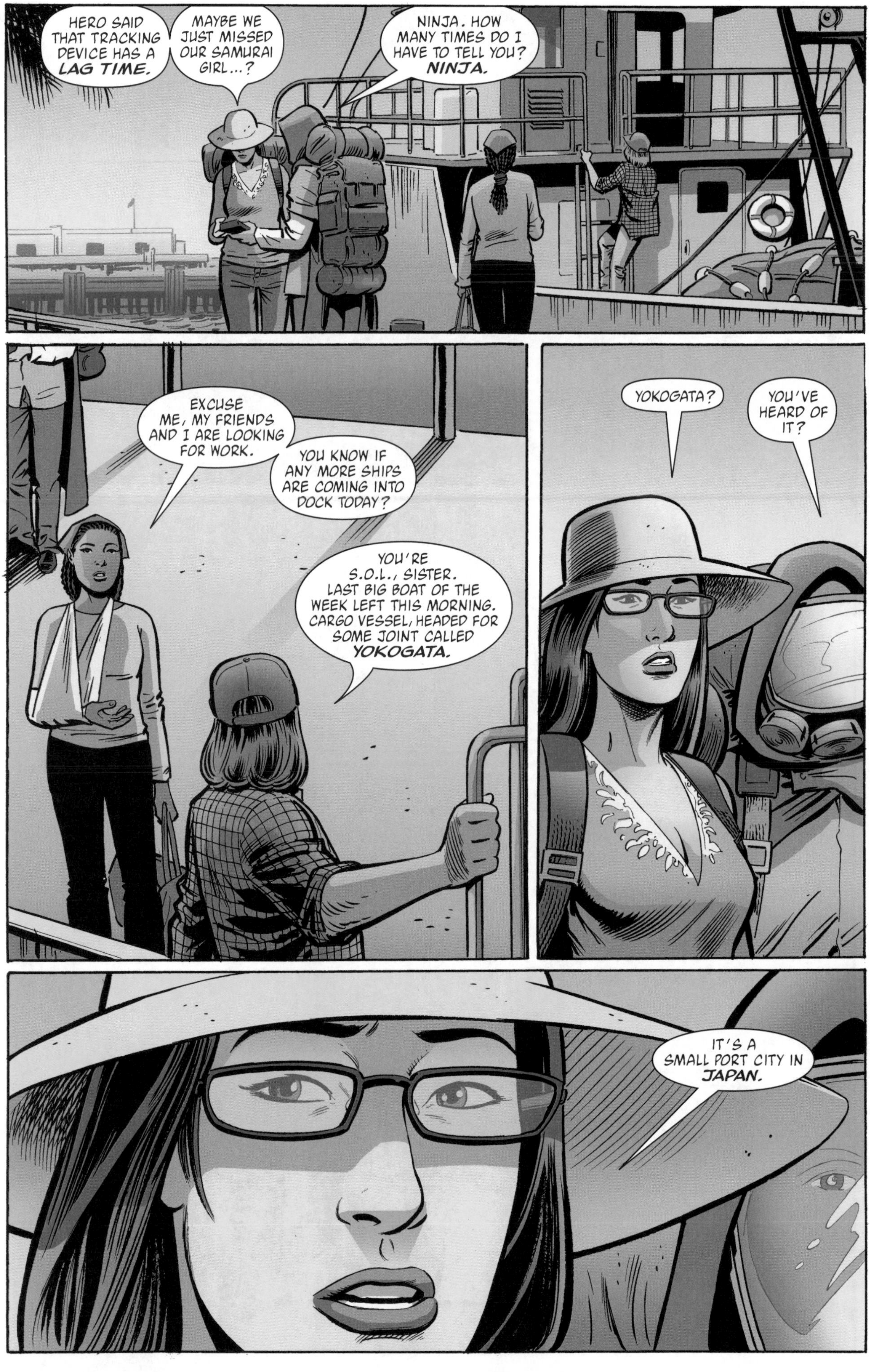
HERO SAID THAT TRACKING DEVICE HAS A **LAG TIME.**
MAYBE WE JUST MISSED OUR SAMURAI GIRL...?
NINJA. HOW MANY TIMES DO I HAVE TO TELL YOU? **NINJA.**
EXCUSE ME, MY FRIENDS AND I ARE LOOKING FOR WORK.
YOU KNOW IF ANY MORE SHIPS ARE COMING INTO DOCK TODAY?
YOU'RE S.O.L., SISTER. LAST BIG BOAT OF THE WEEK LEFT THIS MORNING. CARGO VESSEL, HEADED FOR SOME JOINT CALLED **YOKOGATA.**
YOKOGATA?
YOU'VE HEARD OF IT?
IT'S A SMALL PORT CITY IN **JAPAN.**

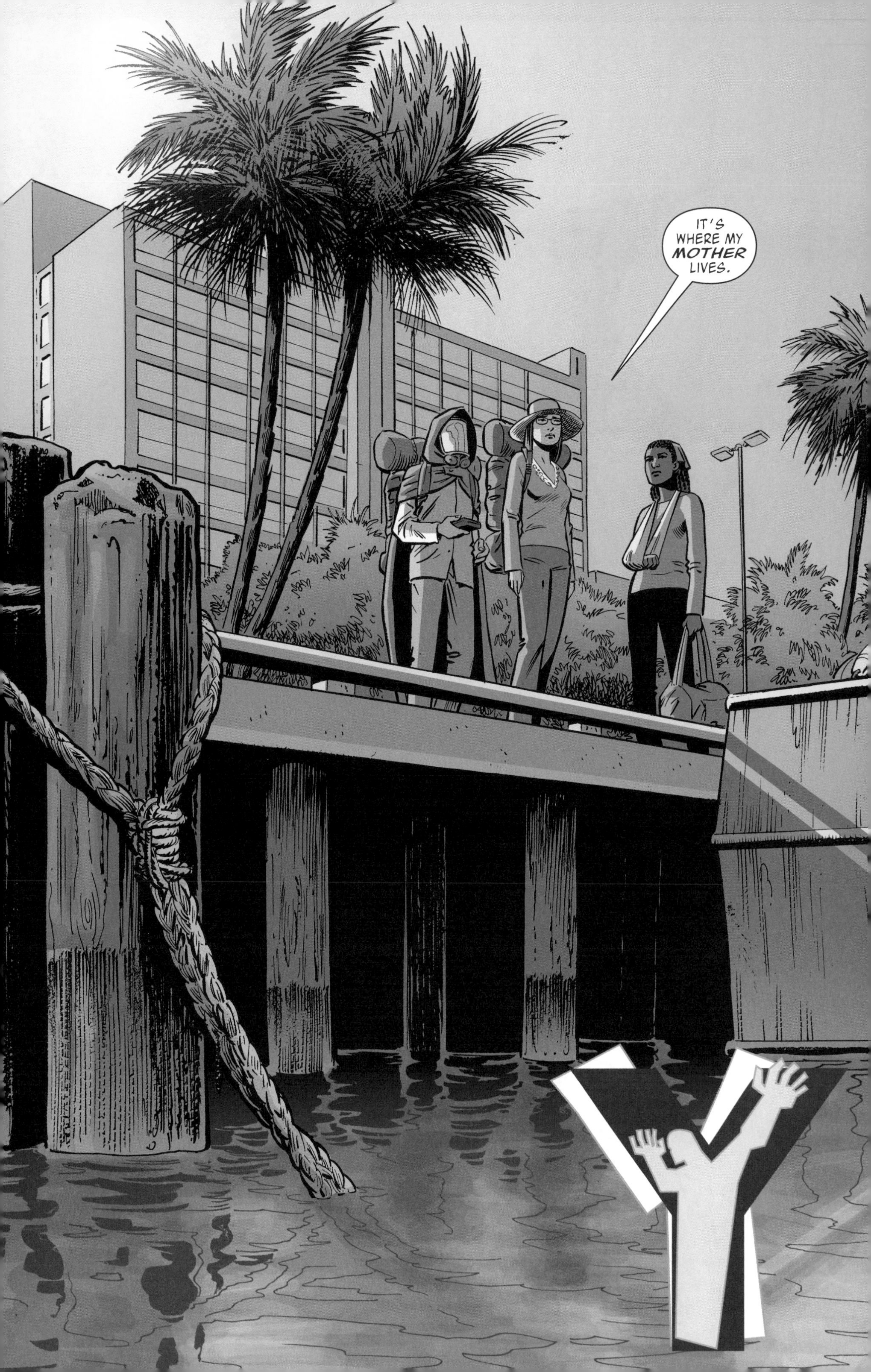
IT'S WHERE MY *MOTHER* LIVES.

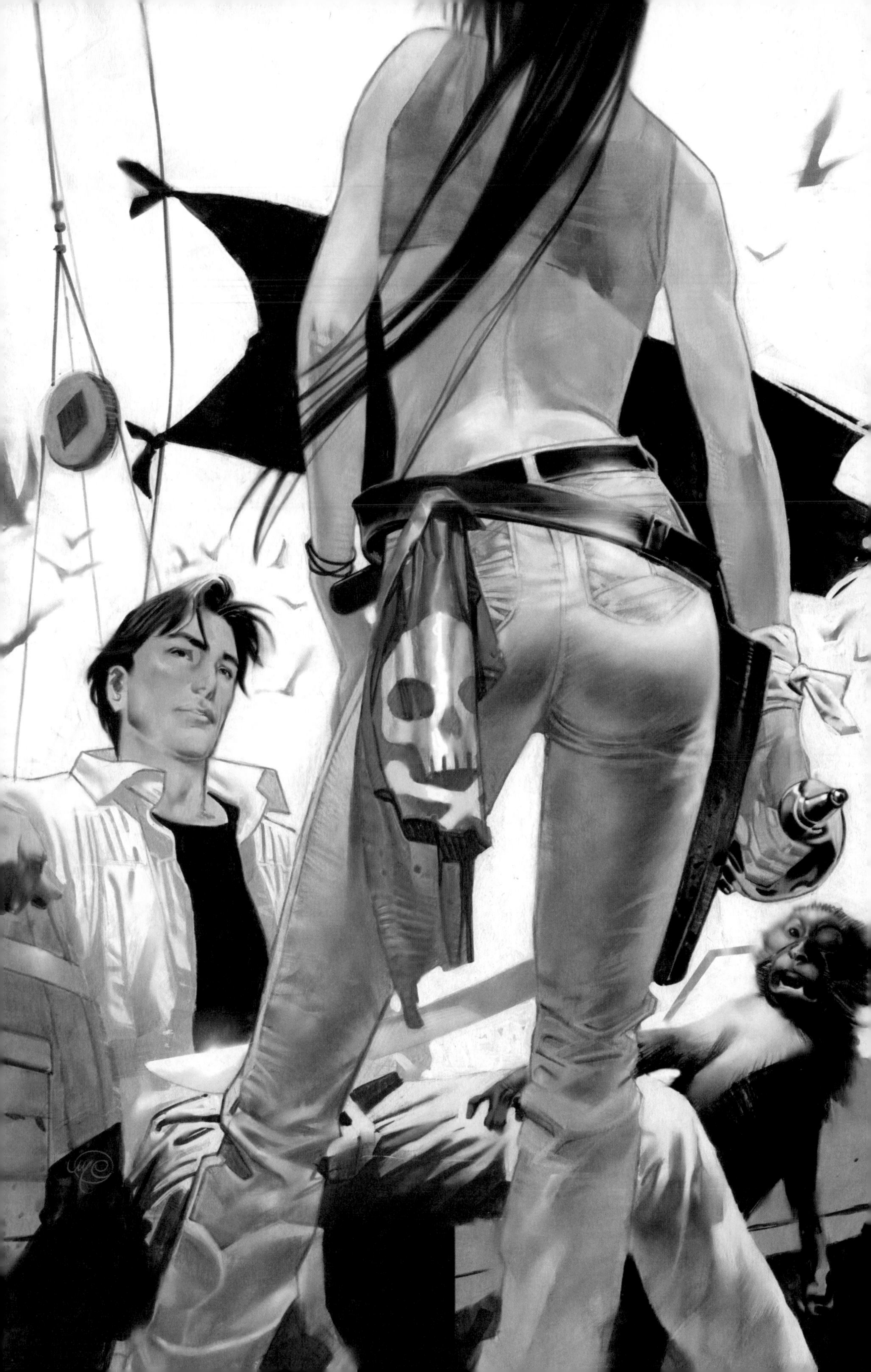

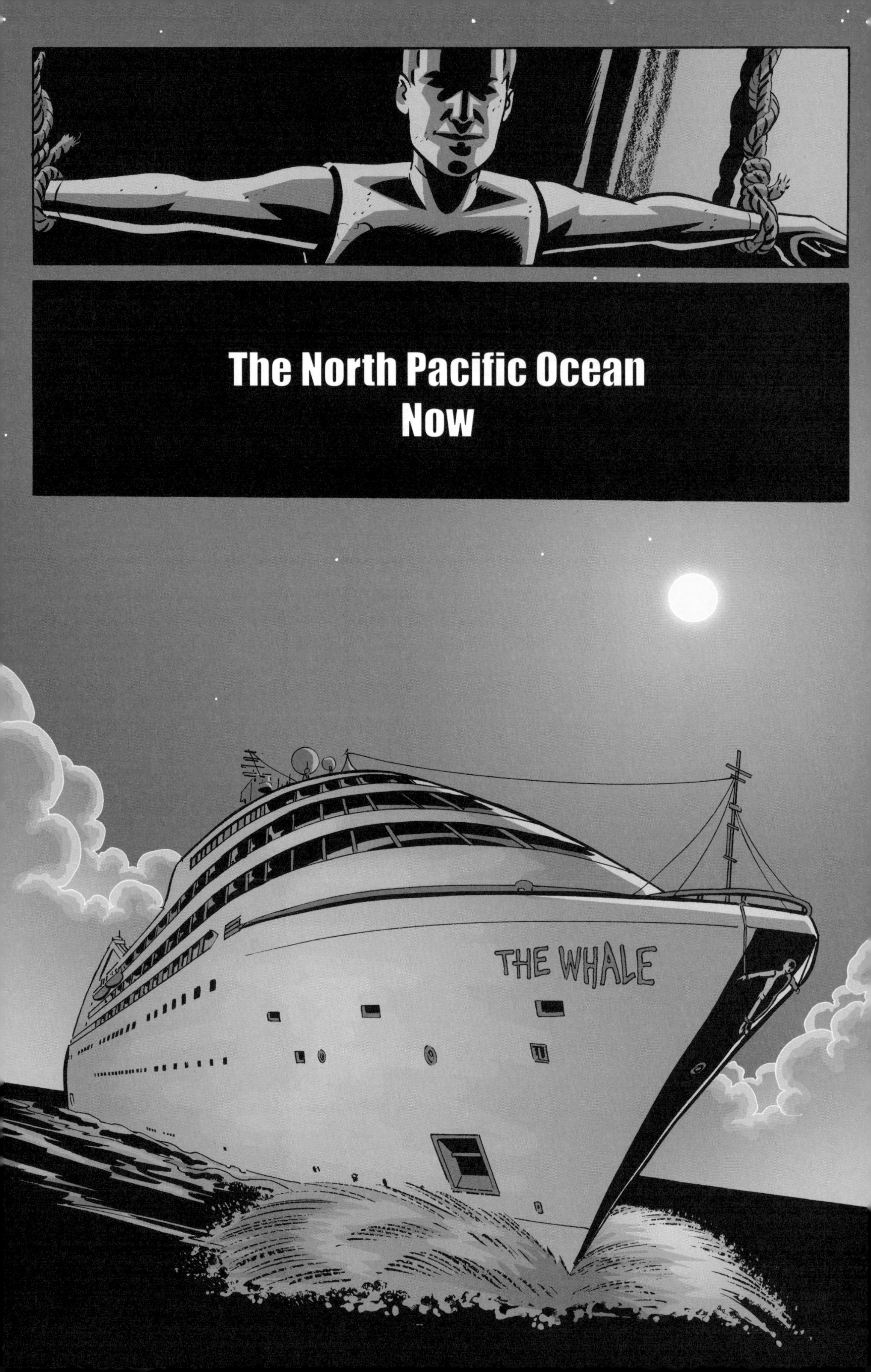
The North Pacific Ocean
Now
THE WHALE

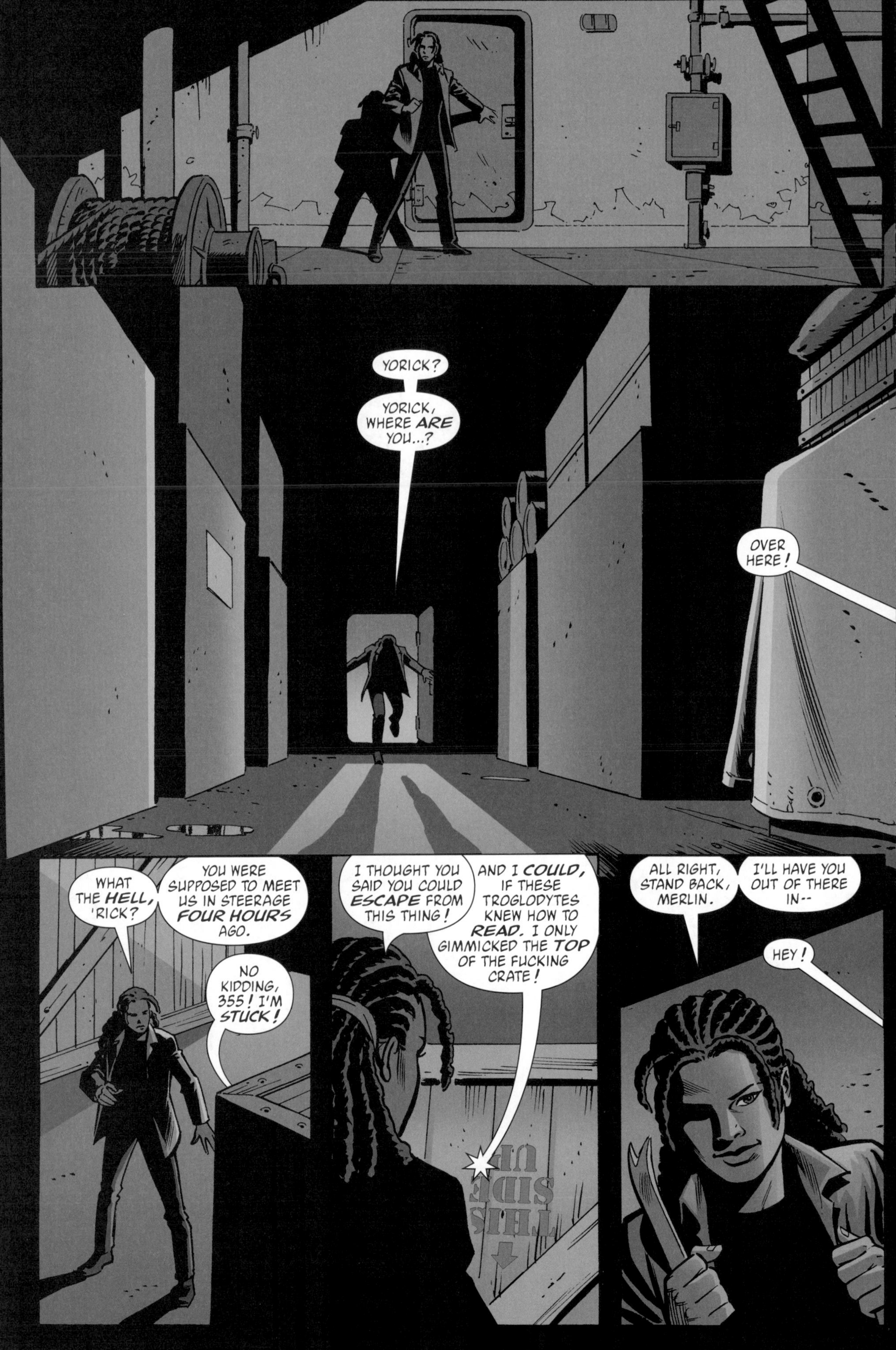
YORICK?
YORICK, WHERE ARE YOU...?
OVER HERE!
WHAT THE HELL, 'RICK?
YOU WERE SUPPOSED TO MEET US IN STEERAGE FOUR HOURS AGO.
NO KIDDING, 355! I'M STUCK!
I THOUGHT YOU SAID YOU COULD ESCAPE FROM THIS THING!
AND I COULD, IF THESE TROGLODYTES KNEW HOW TO READ. I ONLY GIMMICKED THE TOP OF THE FUCKING CRATE!
THIS SIDE UP
ALL RIGHT, STAND BACK, MERLIN.
I'LL HAVE YOU OUT OF THERE IN--
HEY!

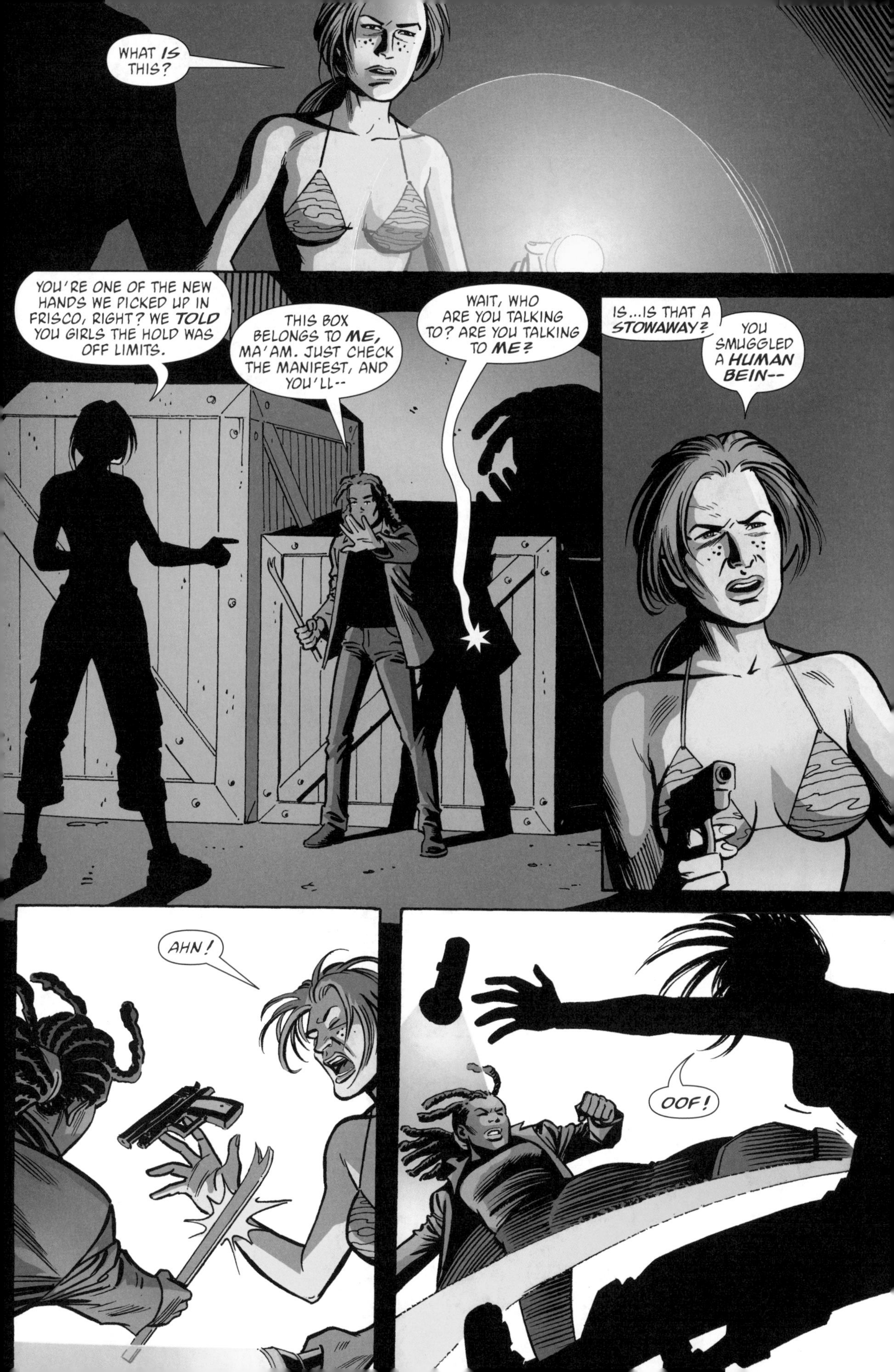
WHAT IS THIS?
YOU'RE ONE OF THE NEW HANDS WE PICKED UP IN FRISCO, RIGHT? WE TOLD YOU GIRLS THE HOLD WAS OFF LIMITS.
THIS BOX BELONGS TO ME, MA'AM. JUST CHECK THE MANIFEST, AND YOU'LL--
WAIT, WHO ARE YOU TALKING TO? ARE YOU TALKING TO ME?
IS...IS THAT A STOWAWAY?
YOU SMUGGLED A HUMAN BEIN--
AHN!
OOF!

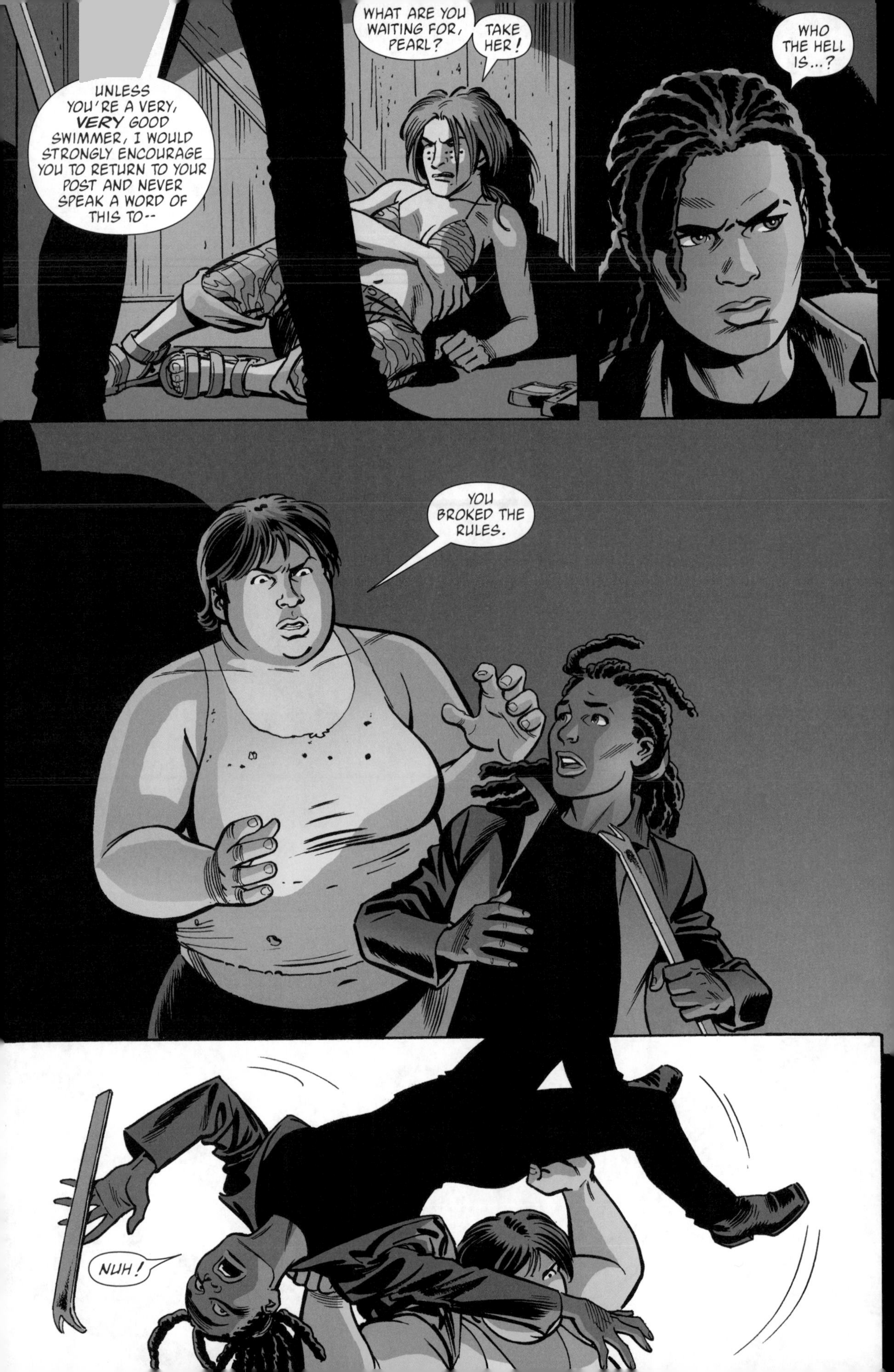
UNLESS YOU'RE A VERY, VERY GOOD SWIMMER, I WOULD STRONGLY ENCOURAGE YOU TO RETURN TO YOUR POST AND NEVER SPEAK A WORD OF THIS TO--
WHAT ARE YOU WAITING FOR, PEARL?
TAKE HER!
WHO THE HELL IS...?
YOU BROKED THE RULES.
NUH!

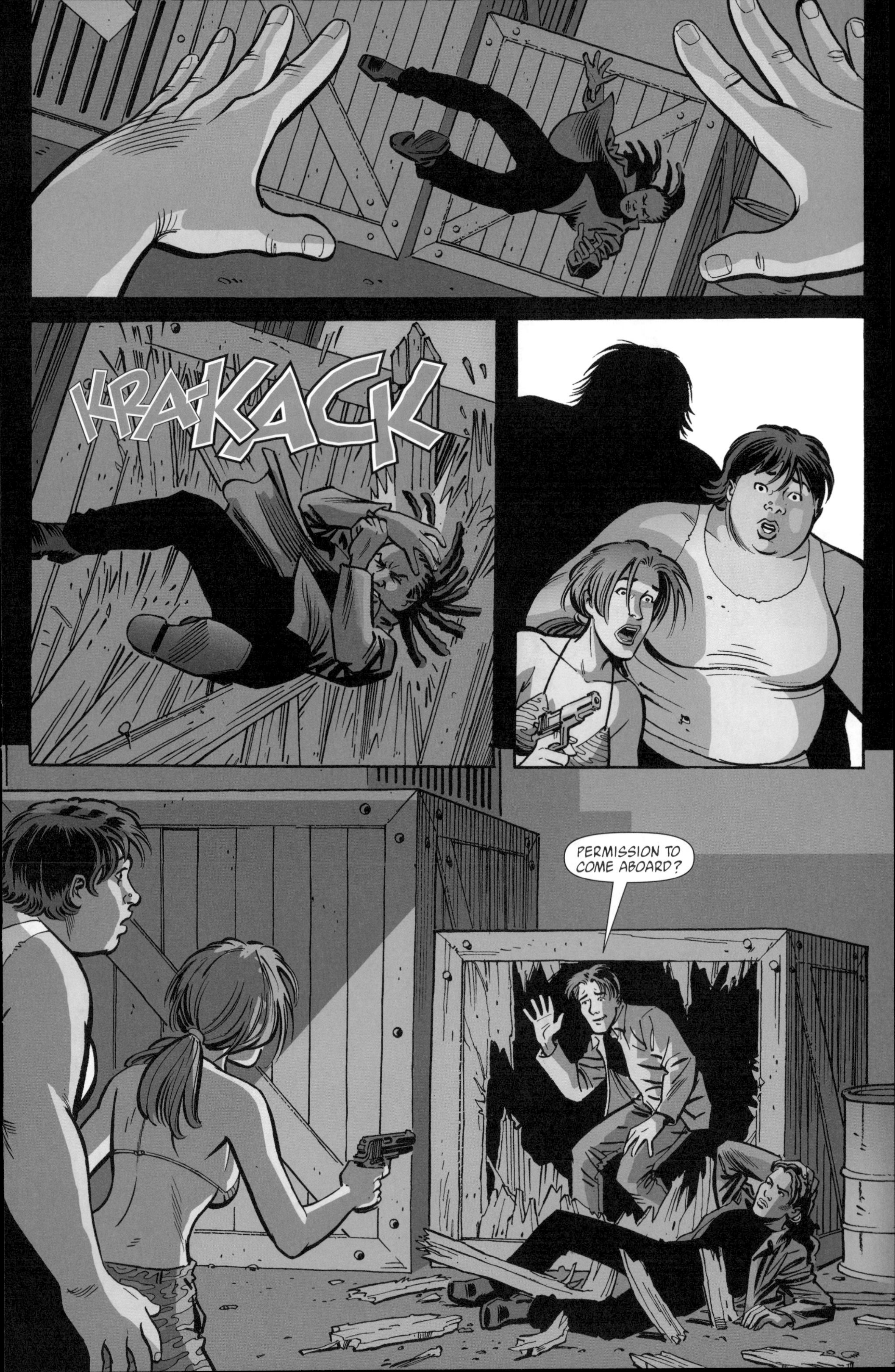
KRA-KACK
PERMISSION TO COME ABOARD?

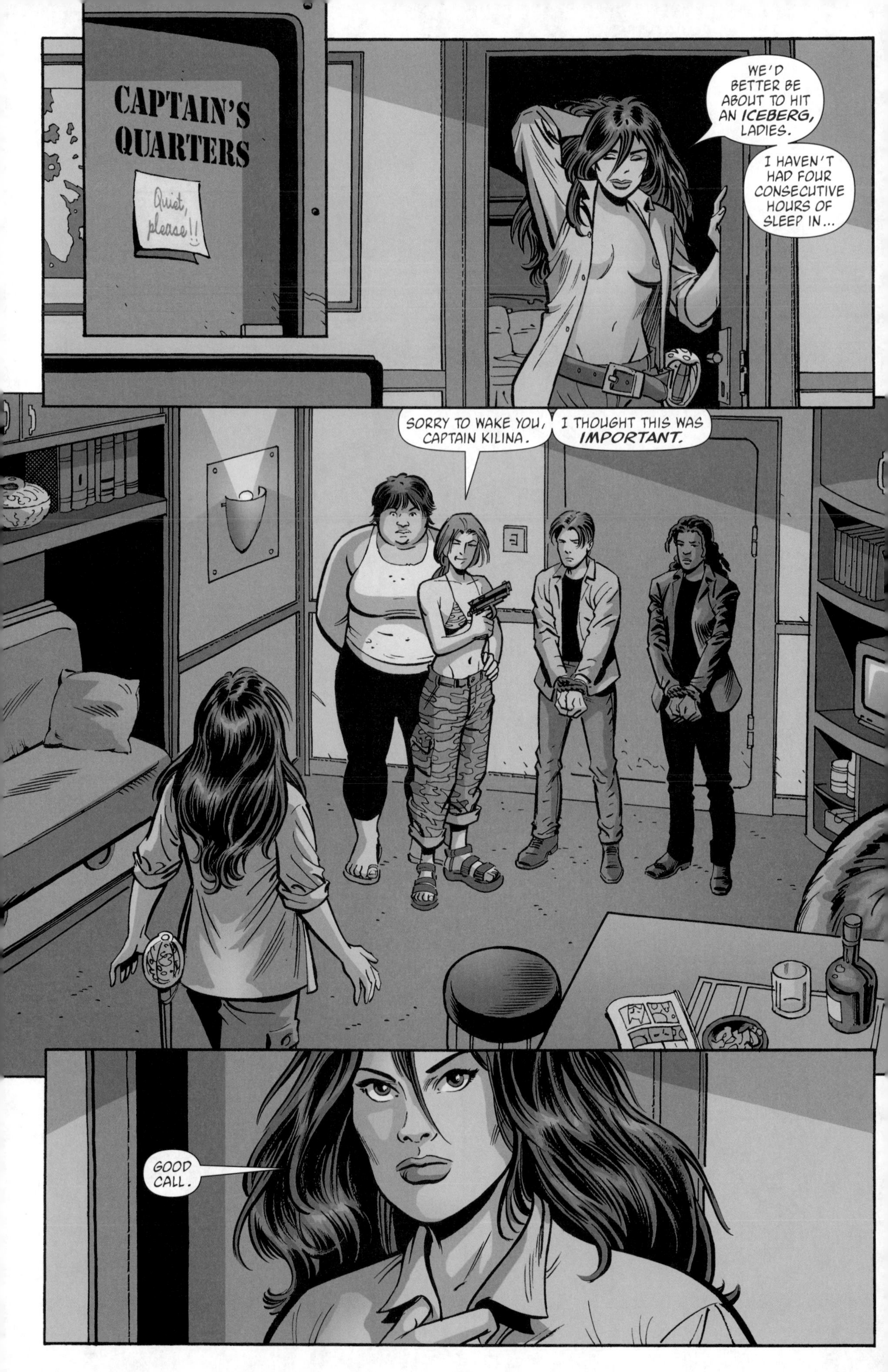
CAPTAIN'S QUARTERS
Quiet, please!!
WE'D BETTER BE ABOUT TO HIT AN ICEBERG, LADIES.
I HAVEN'T HAD FOUR CONSECUTIVE HOURS OF SLEEP IN...
SORRY TO WAKE YOU, CAPTAIN KILINA.
I THOUGHT THIS WAS IMPORTANT.
GOOD CALL.

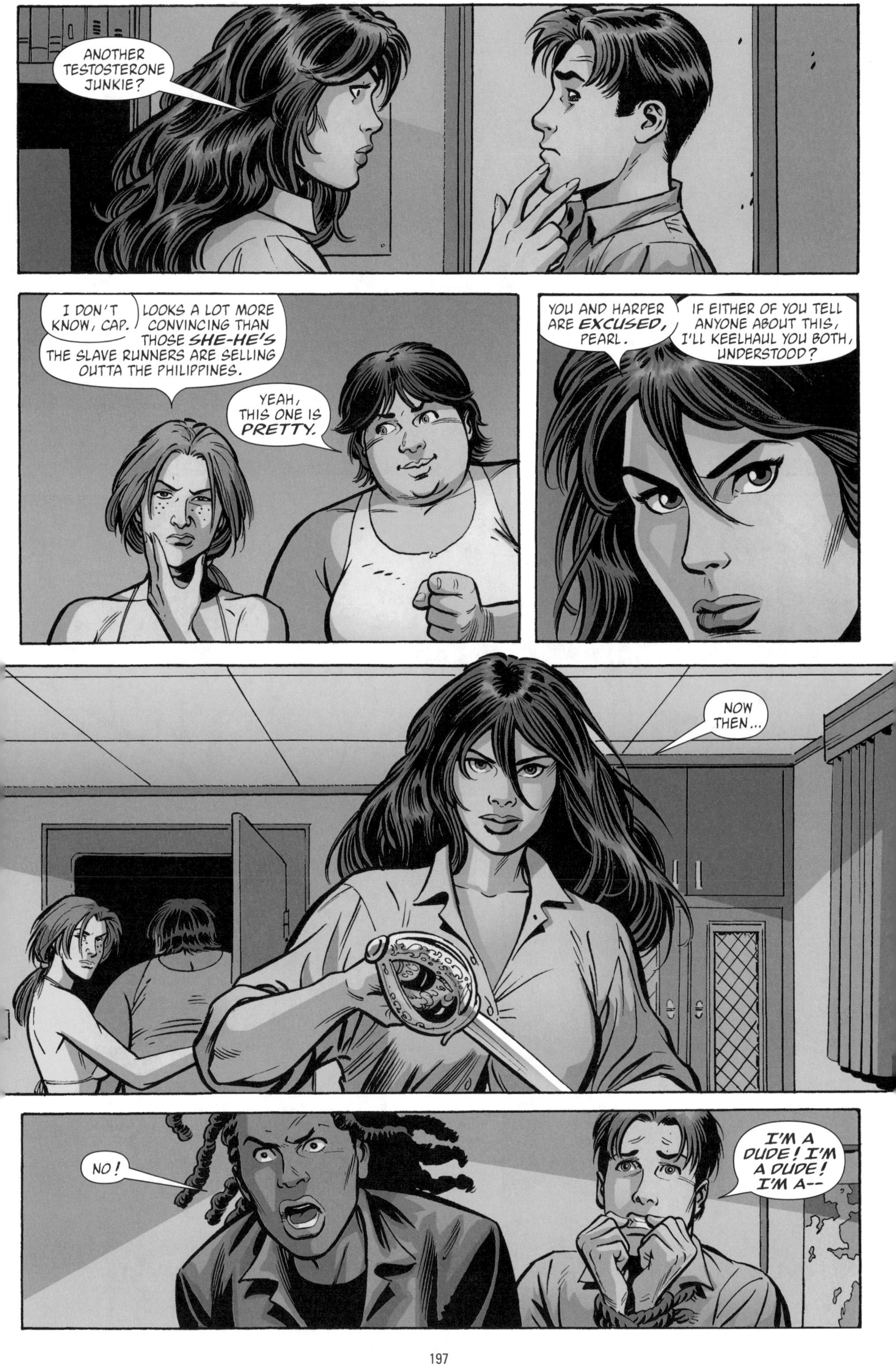
ANOTHER TESTOSTERONE JUNKIE?
I DON'T KNOW, CAP.
LOOKS A LOT MORE CONVINCING THAN THOSE SHE-HE'S THE SLAVE RUNNERS ARE SELLING OUTTA THE PHILIPPINES.
YEAH, THIS ONE IS PRETTY.
YOU AND HARPER ARE EXCUSED, PEARL.
IF EITHER OF YOU TELL ANYONE ABOUT THIS, I'LL KEELHAUL YOU BOTH, UNDERSTOOD?
NOW THEN...
NO!
I'M A DUDE! I'M A DUDE! I'M A--

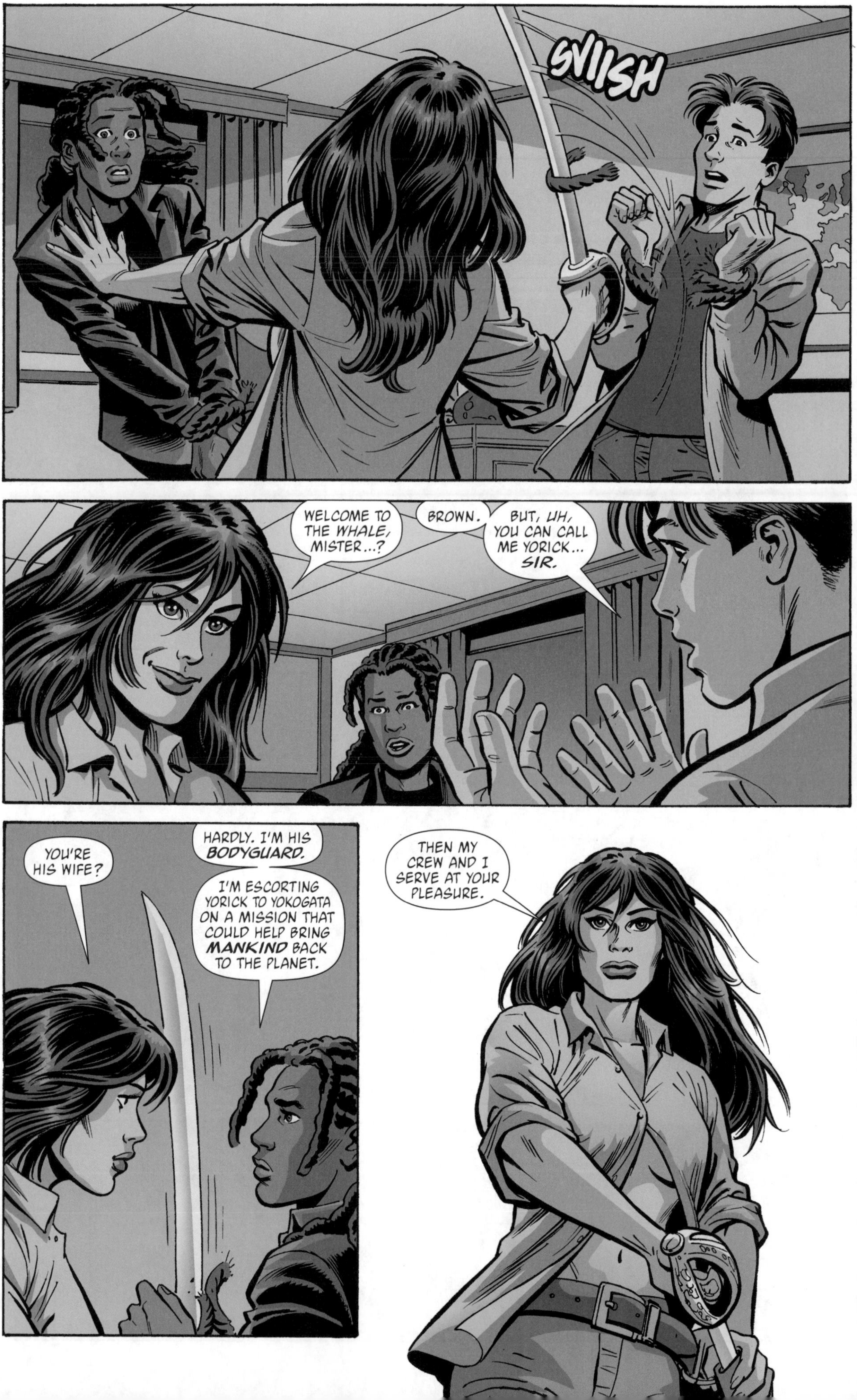
SVIISH
WELCOME TO THE WHALE, MISTER...?
BROWN.
BUT, UH, YOU CAN CALL ME YORICK... SIR.
YOU'RE HIS WIFE?
HARDLY. I'M HIS BODYGUARD.
I'M ESCORTING YORICK TO YOKOGATA ON A MISSION THAT COULD HELP BRING MANKIND BACK TO THE PLANET.
THEN MY CREW AND I SERVE AT YOUR PLEASURE.

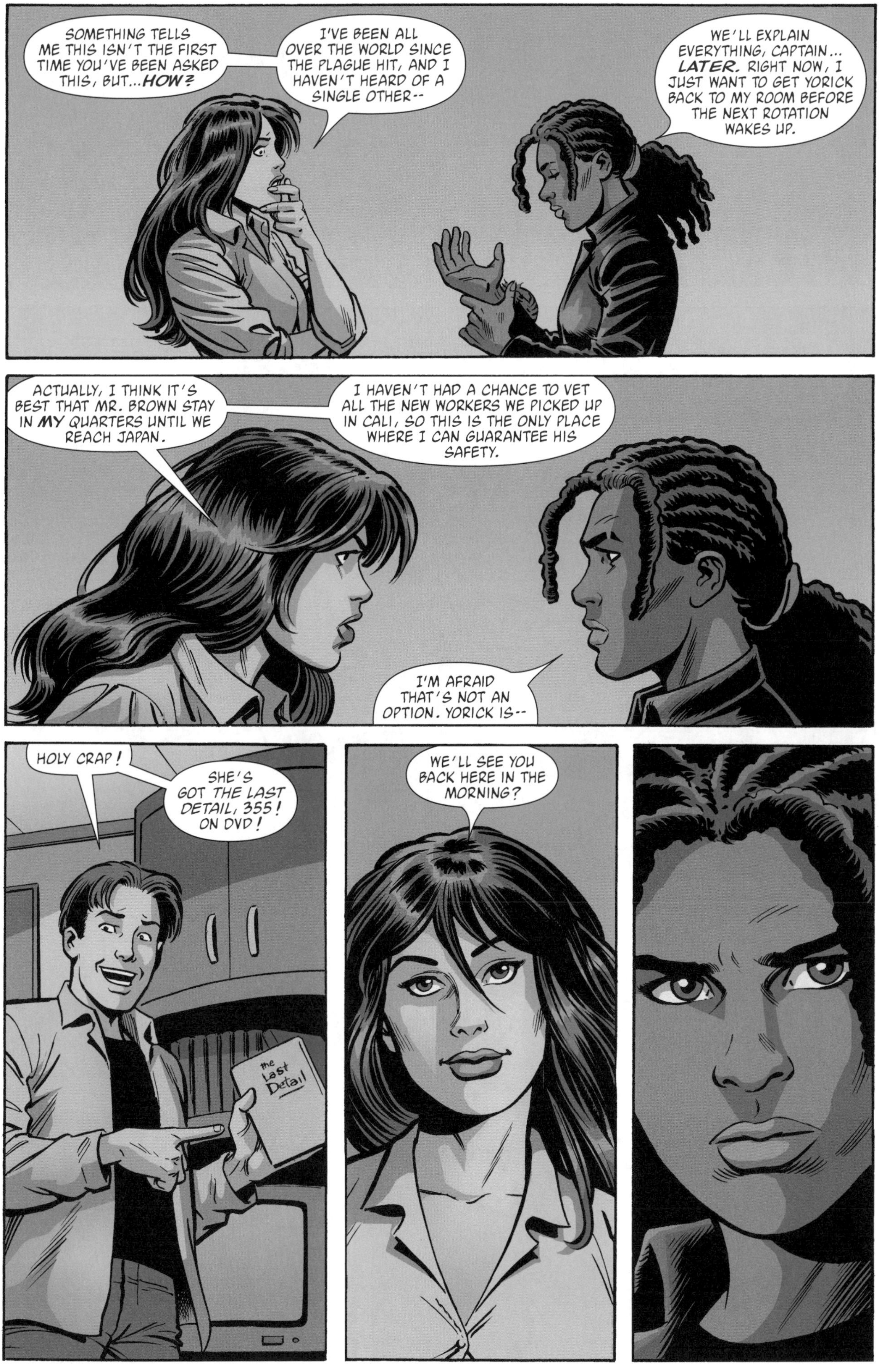
SOMETHING TELLS ME THIS ISN'T THE FIRST TIME YOU'VE BEEN ASKED THIS, BUT...HOW?
I'VE BEEN ALL OVER THE WORLD SINCE THE PLAGUE HIT, AND I HAVEN'T HEARD OF A SINGLE OTHER--
WE'LL EXPLAIN EVERYTHING, CAPTAIN... LATER. RIGHT NOW, I JUST WANT TO GET YORICK BACK TO MY ROOM BEFORE THE NEXT ROTATION WAKES UP.
ACTUALLY, I THINK IT'S BEST THAT MR. BROWN STAY IN MY QUARTERS UNTIL WE REACH JAPAN.
I HAVEN'T HAD A CHANCE TO VET ALL THE NEW WORKERS WE PICKED UP IN CALI, SO THIS IS THE ONLY PLACE WHERE I CAN GUARANTEE HIS SAFETY.
I'M AFRAID THAT'S NOT AN OPTION. YORICK IS--
HOLY CRAP!
SHE'S GOT THE LAST DETAIL, 355! ON DVD!
the Last Detail
WE'LL SEE YOU BACK HERE IN THE MORNING?

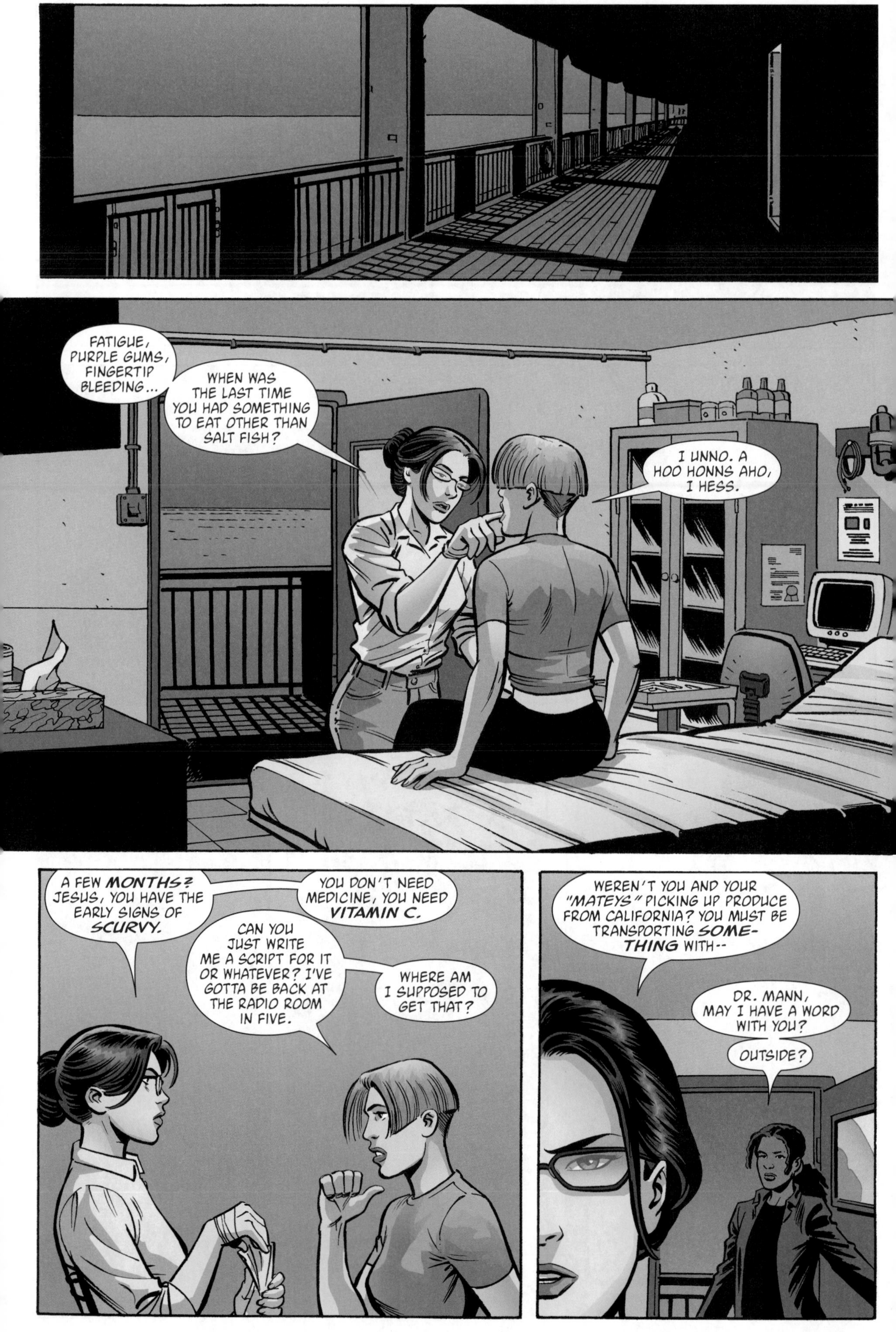
FATIGUE, PURPLE GUMS, FINGERTIP BLEEDING...
WHEN WAS THE LAST TIME YOU HAD SOMETHING TO EAT OTHER THAN SALT FISH?
I UNNO. A HOO HONNS AHO, I HESS.
A FEW MONTHS? JESUS, YOU HAVE THE EARLY SIGNS OF SCURVY.
YOU DON'T NEED MEDICINE, YOU NEED VITAMIN C.
CAN YOU JUST WRITE ME A SCRIPT FOR IT OR WHATEVER? I'VE GOTTA BE BACK AT THE RADIO ROOM IN FIVE.
WHERE AM I SUPPOSED TO GET THAT?
WEREN'T YOU AND YOUR "MATEYS" PICKING UP PRODUCE FROM CALIFORNIA? YOU MUST BE TRANSPORTING SOMETHING WITH--
DR. MANN, MAY I HAVE A WORD WITH YOU?
OUTSIDE?

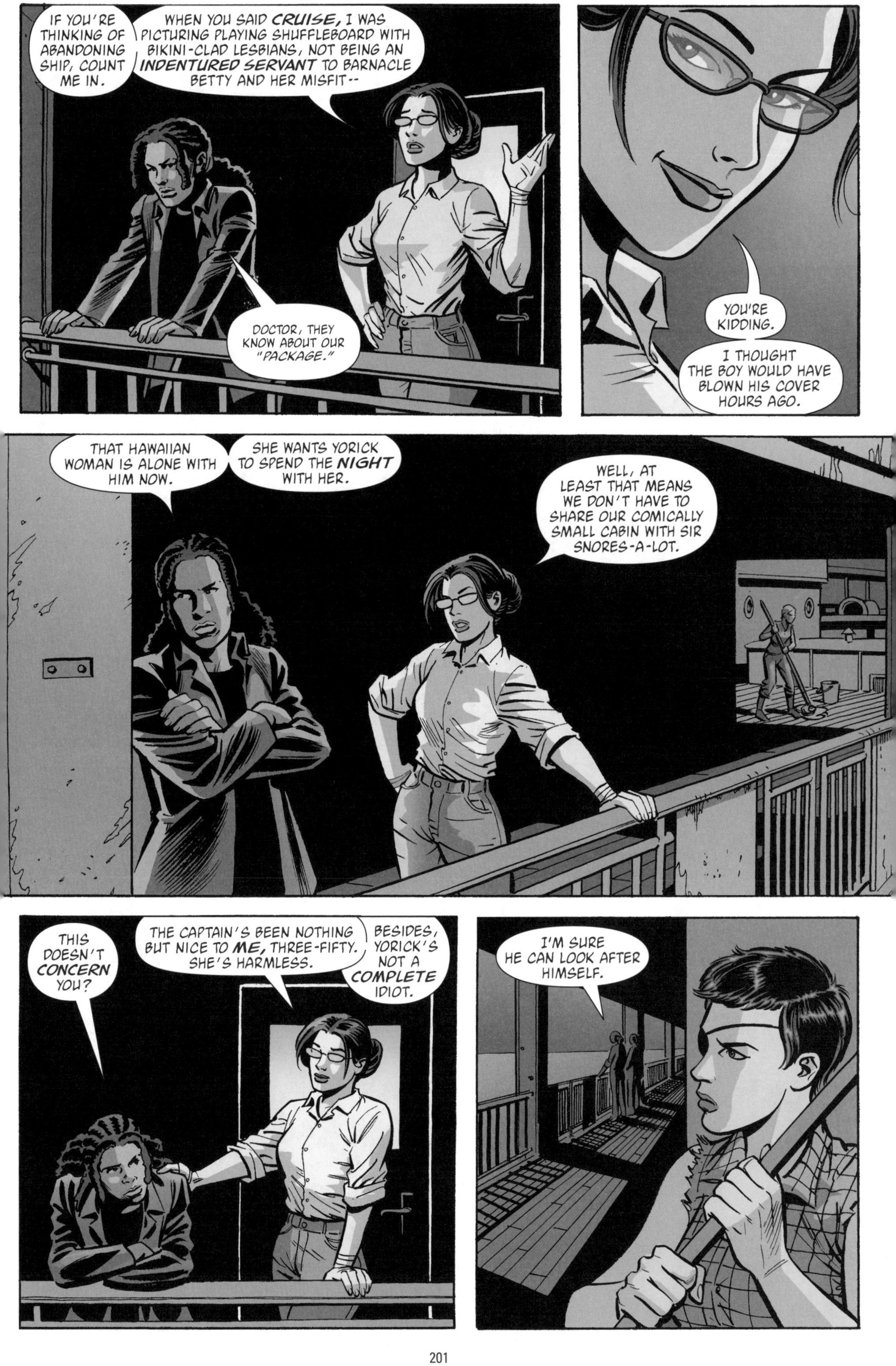
IF YOU'RE THINKING OF ABANDONING SHIP, COUNT ME IN.
WHEN YOU SAID CRUISE, I WAS PICTURING PLAYING SHUFFLEBOARD WITH BIKINI-CLAD LESBIANS, NOT BEING AN INDENTURED SERVANT TO BARNACLE BETTY AND HER MISFIT--
DOCTOR, THEY KNOW ABOUT OUR "PACKAGE."
YOU'RE KIDDING.
I THOUGHT THE BOY WOULD HAVE BLOWN HIS COVER HOURS AGO.
THAT HAWAIIAN WOMAN IS ALONE WITH HIM NOW.
SHE WANTS YORICK TO SPEND THE NIGHT WITH HER.
WELL, AT LEAST THAT MEANS WE DON'T HAVE TO SHARE OUR COMICALLY SMALL CABIN WITH SIR SNORES-A-LOT.
THIS DOESN'T CONCERN YOU?
THE CAPTAIN'S BEEN NOTHING BUT NICE TO ME, THREE-FIFTY. SHE'S HARMLESS.
BESIDES, YORICK'S NOT A COMPLETE IDIOT.
I'M SURE HE CAN LOOK AFTER HIMSELF.

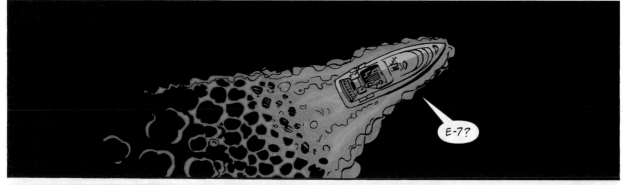

E-7?

CRAP, YOU SUNK MY DESTROYER.

I WOULD TELL YOUR CARRIER TO START MANNING ITS LIFEBOATS, TOO.

ANYWAY, YOU WERE SAYING ABOUT THE ASTRONAUT'S BABY...?

OH, RIGHT. I MIGHT BE THE LAST MAN ON EARTH, BUT CIBA'S SON IS THE FIRST BOY.

AND IF THERE'S EVER GOING TO BE ANY MORE OF US, MY FRIENDS AND I HAVE TO FIND AMPERSAND.

SORRY?

HE'S WHAT SAVED MY LIFE, BELIEVE IT OR NOT.

AMP'S MY PET--

GLEEE!

BA-FUCK!

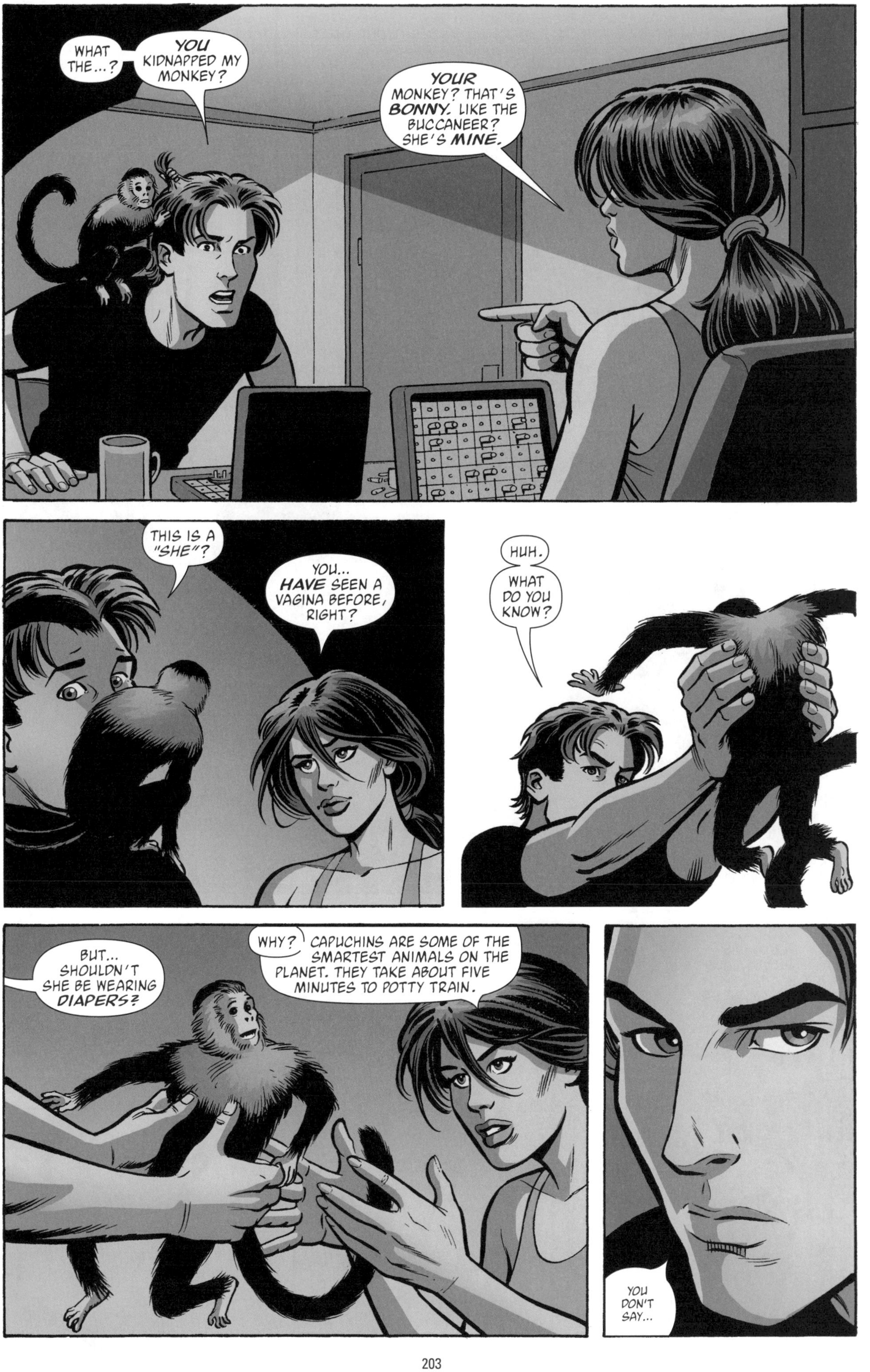
WHAT THE...?
YOU KIDNAPPED MY MONKEY?
YOUR MONKEY? THAT'S BONNY. LIKE THE BUCCANEER? SHE'S MINE.
THIS IS A "SHE"?
YOU... HAVE SEEN A VAGINA BEFORE, RIGHT?
HUH.
WHAT DO YOU KNOW?
BUT... SHOULDN'T SHE BE WEARING DIAPERS?
WHY?
CAPUCHINS ARE SOME OF THE SMARTEST ANIMALS ON THE PLANET. THEY TAKE ABOUT FIVE MINUTES TO POTTY TRAIN.
YOU DON'T SAY...

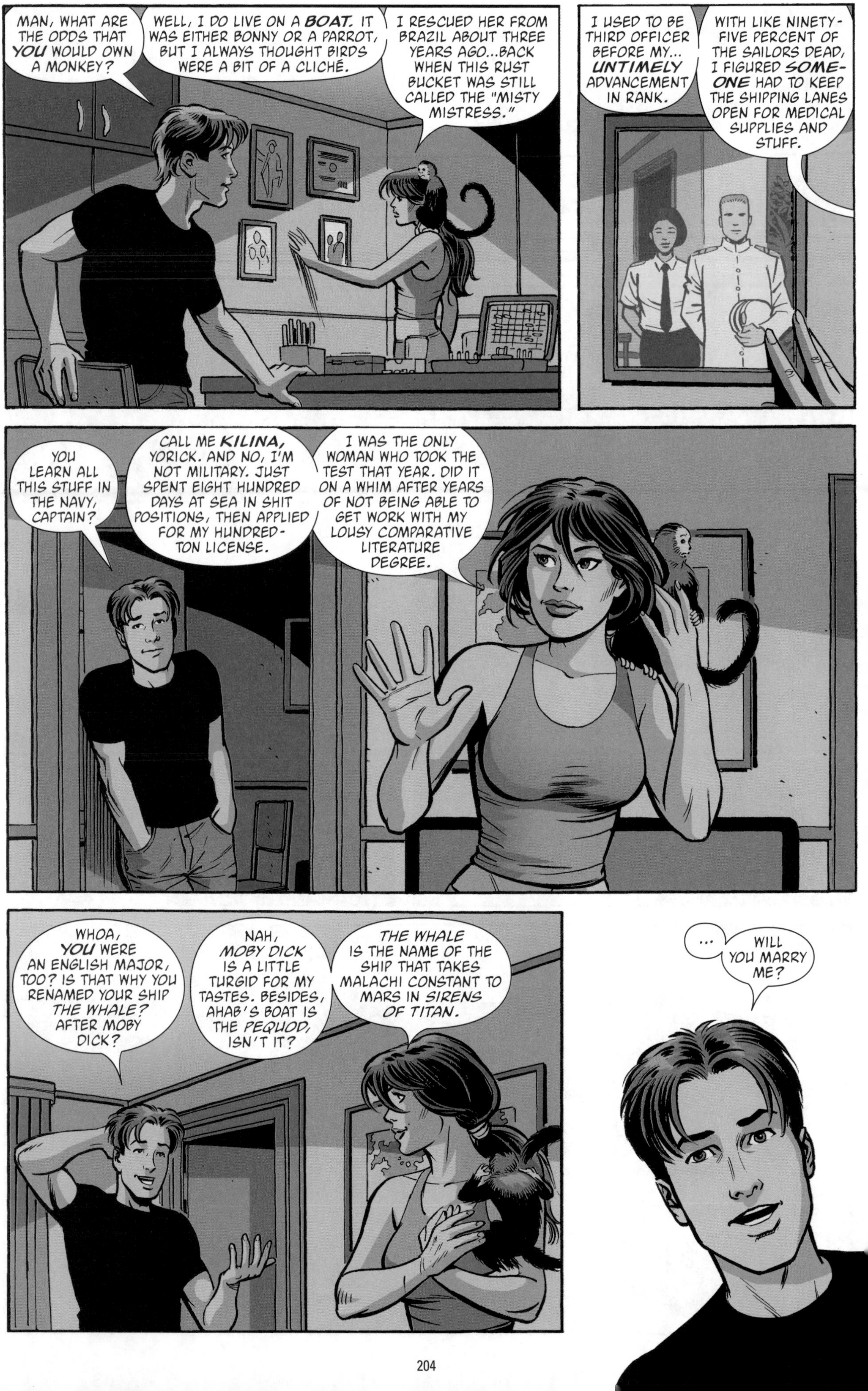
MAN, WHAT ARE THE ODDS THAT YOU WOULD OWN A MONKEY?
WELL, I DO LIVE ON A BOAT. IT WAS EITHER BONNY OR A PARROT, BUT I ALWAYS THOUGHT BIRDS WERE A BIT OF A CLICHÉ.
I RESCUED HER FROM BRAZIL ABOUT THREE YEARS AGO...BACK WHEN THIS RUST BUCKET WAS STILL CALLED THE "MISTY MISTRESS."
I USED TO BE THIRD OFFICER BEFORE MY... UNTIMELY ADVANCEMENT IN RANK.
WITH LIKE NINETY-FIVE PERCENT OF THE SAILORS DEAD, I FIGURED SOME-ONE HAD TO KEEP THE SHIPPING LANES OPEN FOR MEDICAL SUPPLIES AND STUFF.
YOU LEARN ALL THIS STUFF IN THE NAVY, CAPTAIN?
CALL ME KILINA, YORICK. AND NO, I'M NOT MILITARY. JUST SPENT EIGHT HUNDRED DAYS AT SEA IN SHIT POSITIONS, THEN APPLIED FOR MY HUNDRED-TON LICENSE.
I WAS THE ONLY WOMAN WHO TOOK THE TEST THAT YEAR. DID IT ON A WHIM AFTER YEARS OF NOT BEING ABLE TO GET WORK WITH MY LOUSY COMPARATIVE LITERATURE DEGREE.
WHOA, YOU WERE AN ENGLISH MAJOR, TOO? IS THAT WHY YOU RENAMED YOUR SHIP THE WHALE? AFTER MOBY DICK?
NAH, MOBY DICK IS A LITTLE TURGID FOR MY TASTES. BESIDES, AHAB'S BOAT IS THE PEQUOD, ISN'T IT?
THE WHALE IS THE NAME OF THE SHIP THAT TAKES MALACHI CONSTANT TO MARS IN SIRENS OF TITAN.
...
WILL YOU MARRY ME?

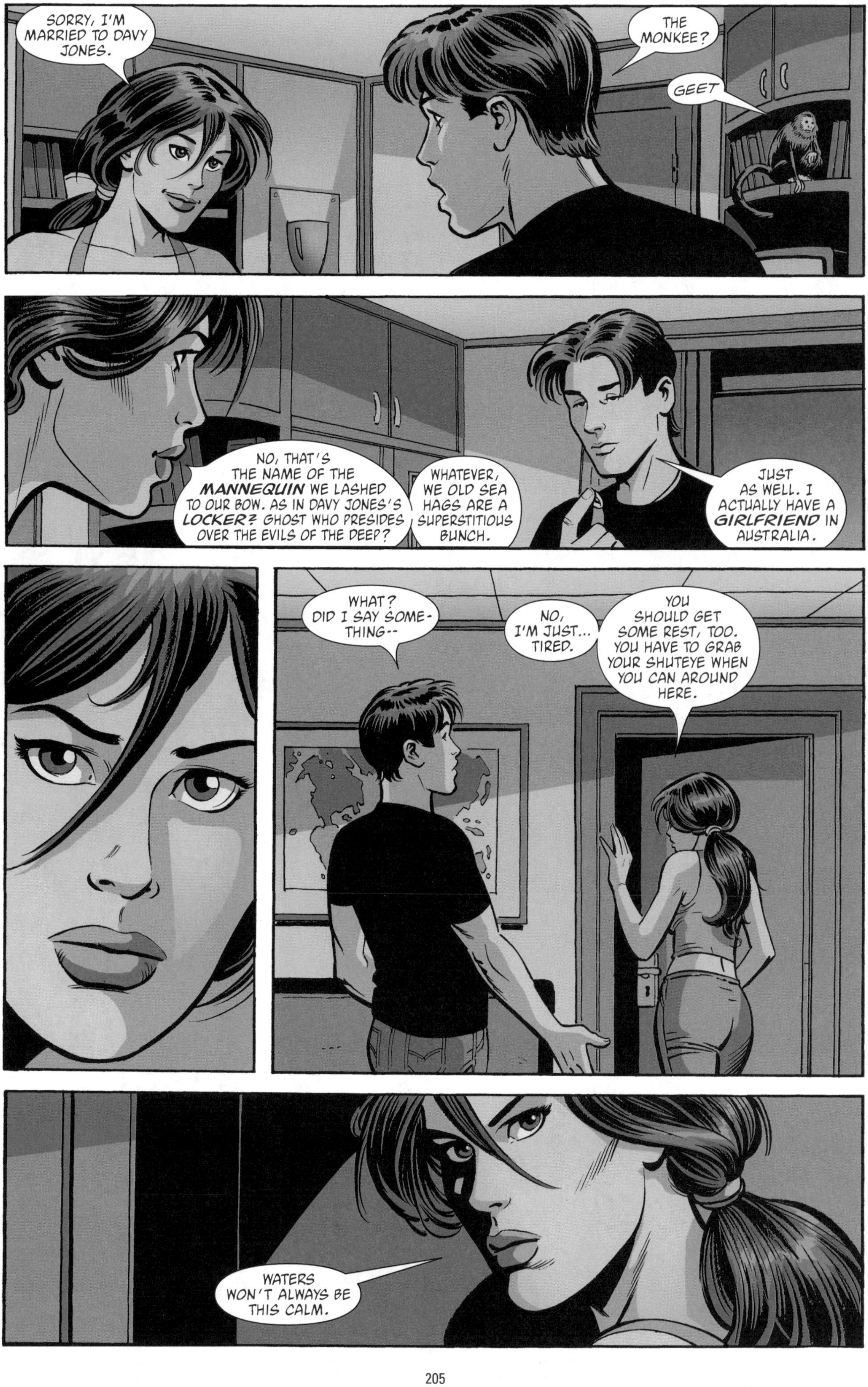
SORRY, I'M MARRIED TO DAVY JONES.
THE MONKEE?
GEET
NO, THAT'S THE NAME OF THE MANNEQUIN WE LASHED TO OUR BOW. AS IN DAVY JONES'S LOCKER? GHOST WHO PRESIDES OVER THE EVILS OF THE DEEP?
WHATEVER, WE OLD SEA HAGS ARE A SUPERSTITIOUS BUNCH.
JUST AS WELL. I ACTUALLY HAVE A GIRLFRIEND IN AUSTRALIA.
WHAT? DID I SAY SOME-THING--
NO, I'M JUST... TIRED.
YOU SHOULD GET SOME REST, TOO. YOU HAVE TO GRAB YOUR SHUTEYE WHEN YOU CAN AROUND HERE.
WATERS WON'T ALWAYS BE THIS CALM.

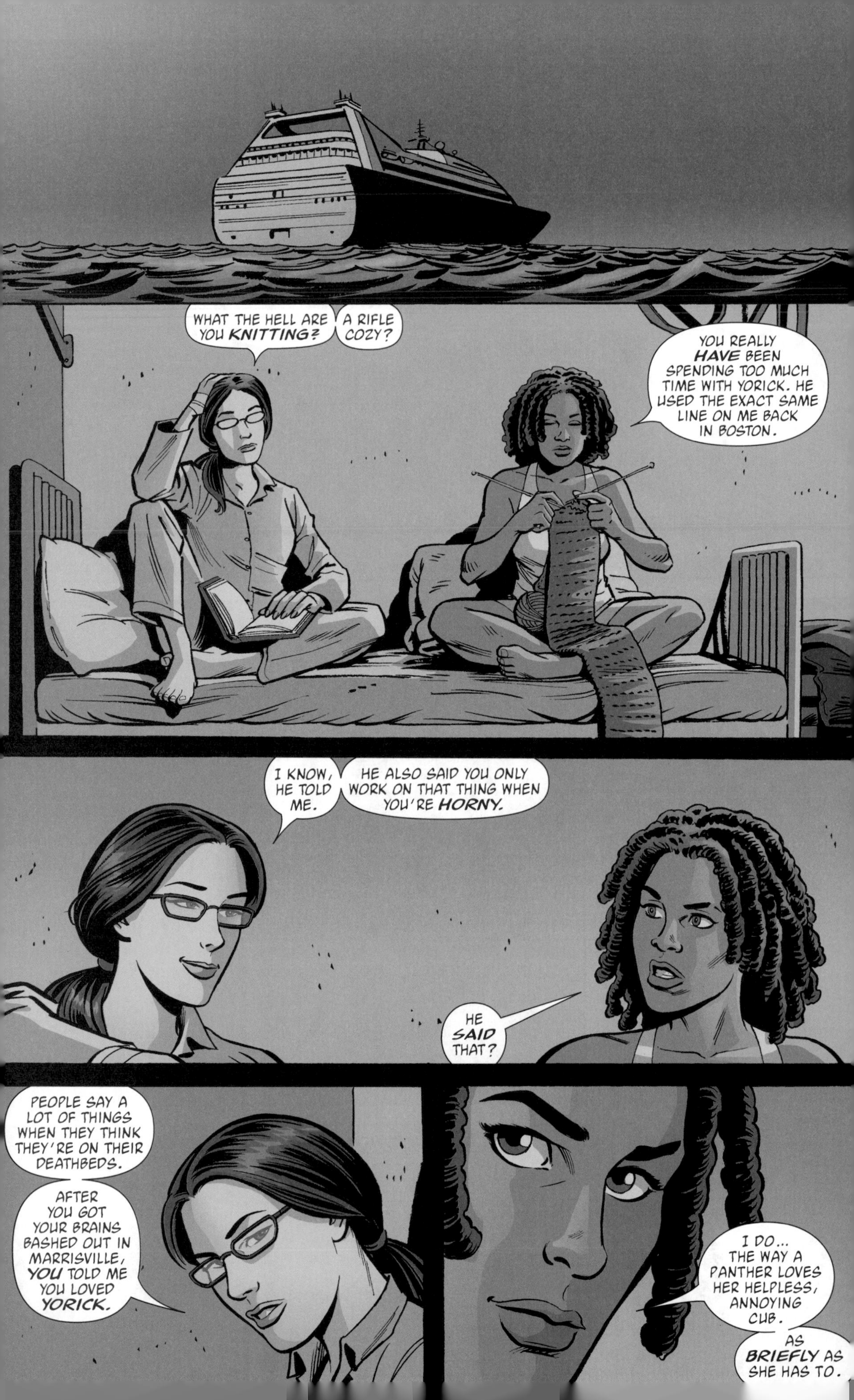
WHAT THE HELL ARE YOU KNITTING?
A RIFLE COZY?
YOU REALLY HAVE BEEN SPENDING TOO MUCH TIME WITH YORICK. HE USED THE EXACT SAME LINE ON ME BACK IN BOSTON.
I KNOW, HE TOLD ME.
HE ALSO SAID YOU ONLY WORK ON THAT THING WHEN YOU'RE HORNY.
HE SAID THAT?
PEOPLE SAY A LOT OF THINGS WHEN THEY THINK THEY'RE ON THEIR DEATHBEDS.
AFTER YOU GOT YOUR BRAINS BASHED OUT IN MARRISVILLE, YOU TOLD ME YOU LOVED YORICK.
I DO... THE WAY A PANTHER LOVES HER HELPLESS, ANNOYING CUB.
AS BRIEFLY AS SHE HAS TO.

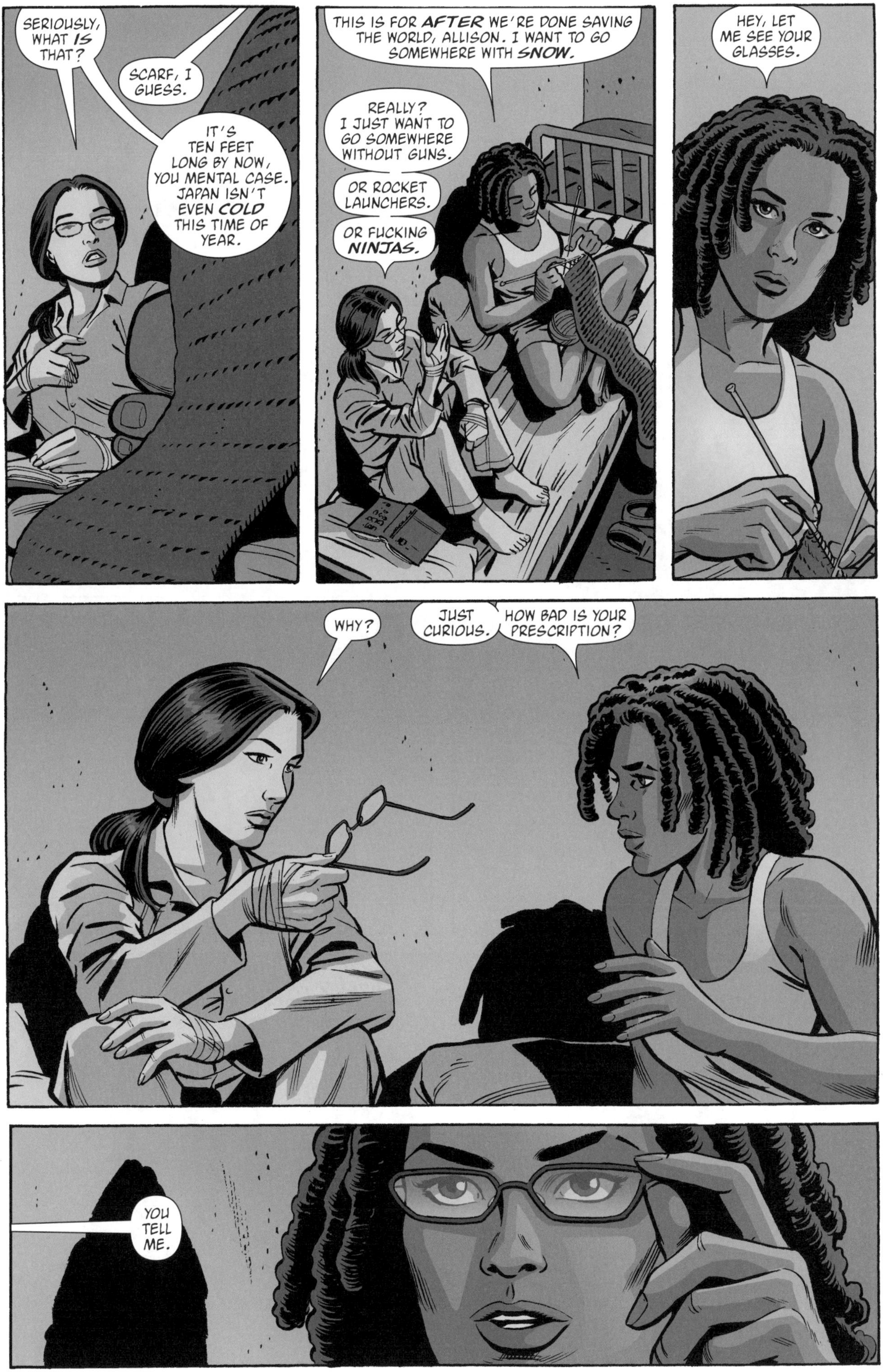
SERIOUSLY, WHAT *IS* THAT?
SCARF, I GUESS.
IT'S TEN FEET LONG BY NOW, YOU MENTAL CASE. JAPAN ISN'T EVEN *COLD* THIS TIME OF YEAR.
THIS IS FOR *AFTER* WE'RE DONE SAVING THE WORLD, ALLISON. I WANT TO GO SOMEWHERE WITH *SNOW.*
REALLY? I JUST WANT TO GO SOMEWHERE WITHOUT GUNS.
OR ROCKET LAUNCHERS.
OR FUCKING *NINJAS.*
HEY, LET ME SEE YOUR GLASSES.
WHY?
JUST CURIOUS.
HOW BAD IS YOUR PRESCRIPTION?
YOU TELL ME.

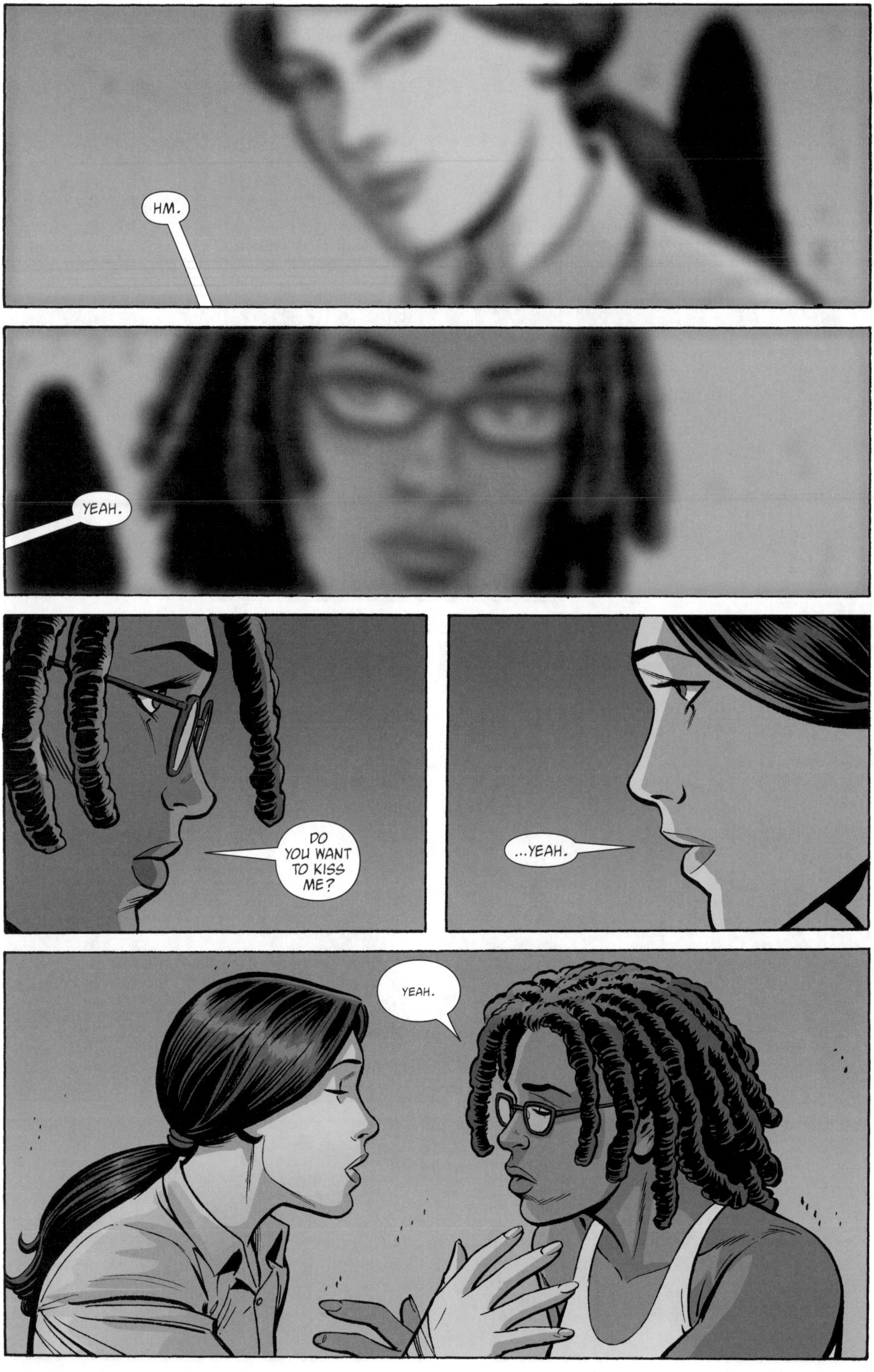
HM.
YEAH.
DO YOU WANT TO KISS ME?
...YEAH.
YEAH.

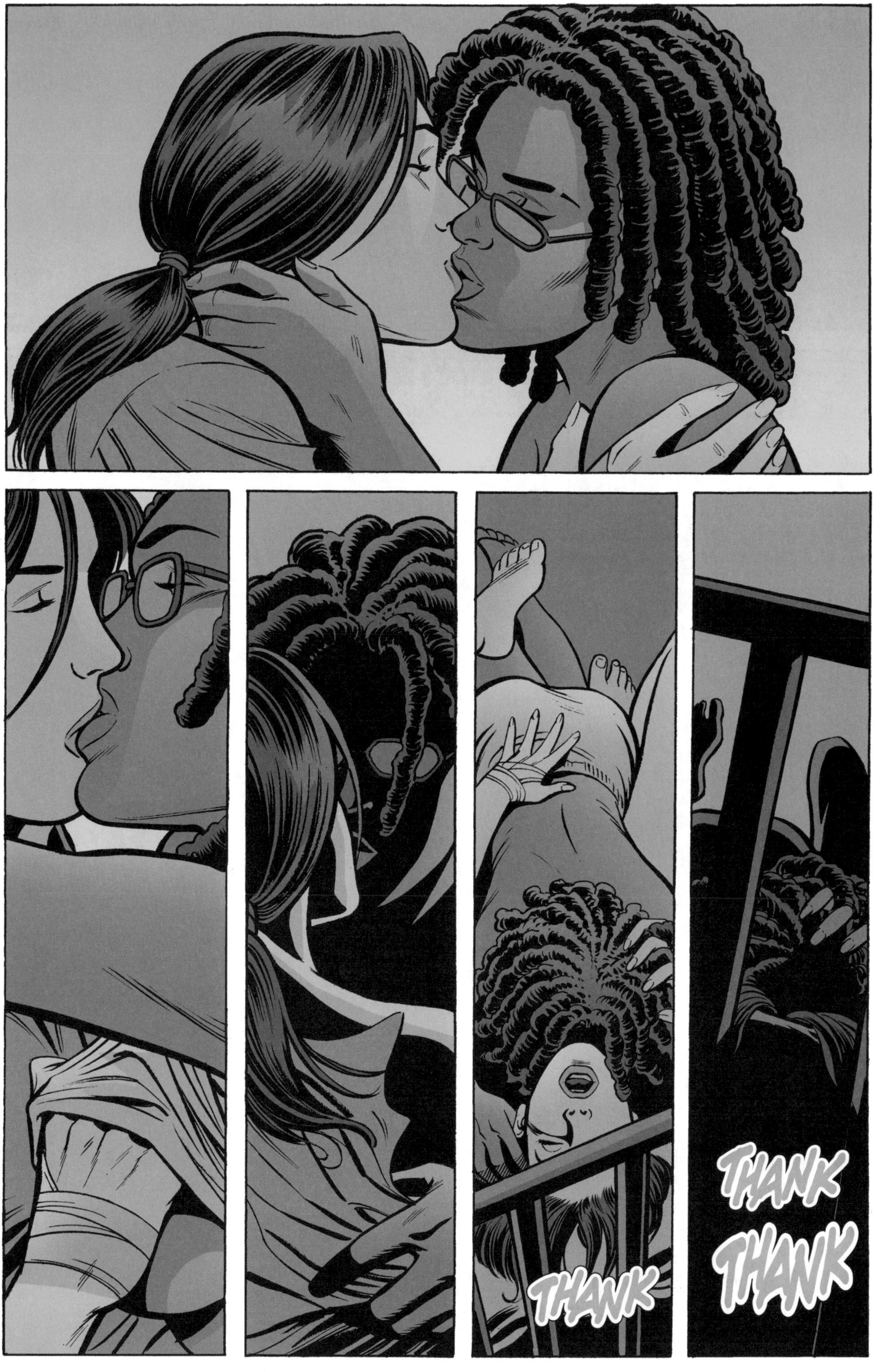
THANK
THANK
THANK

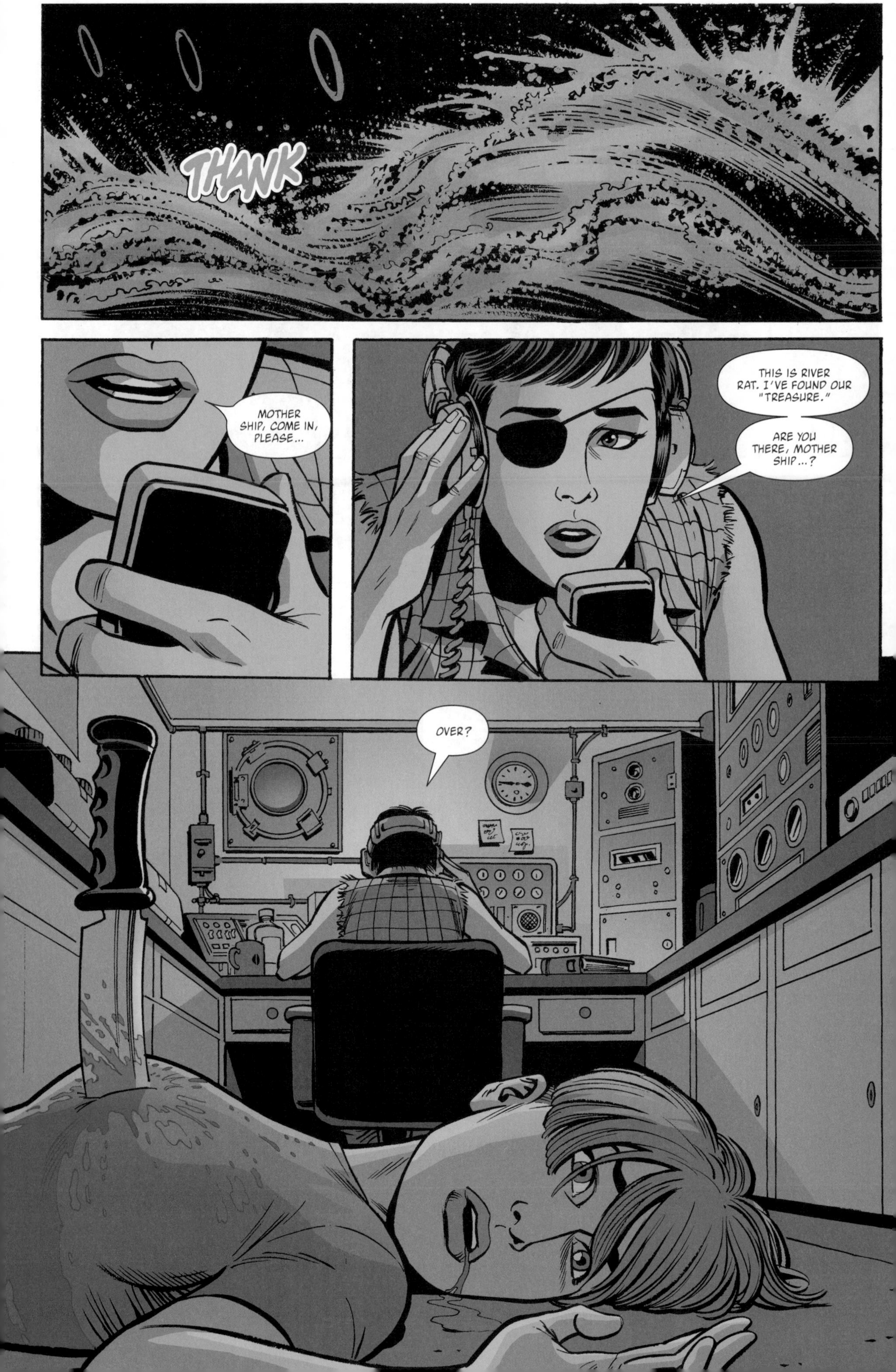
THANK
MOTHER SHIP, COME IN, PLEASE...
THIS IS RIVER RAT. I'VE FOUND OUR "TREASURE."
ARE YOU THERE, MOTHER SHIP...?
OVER?

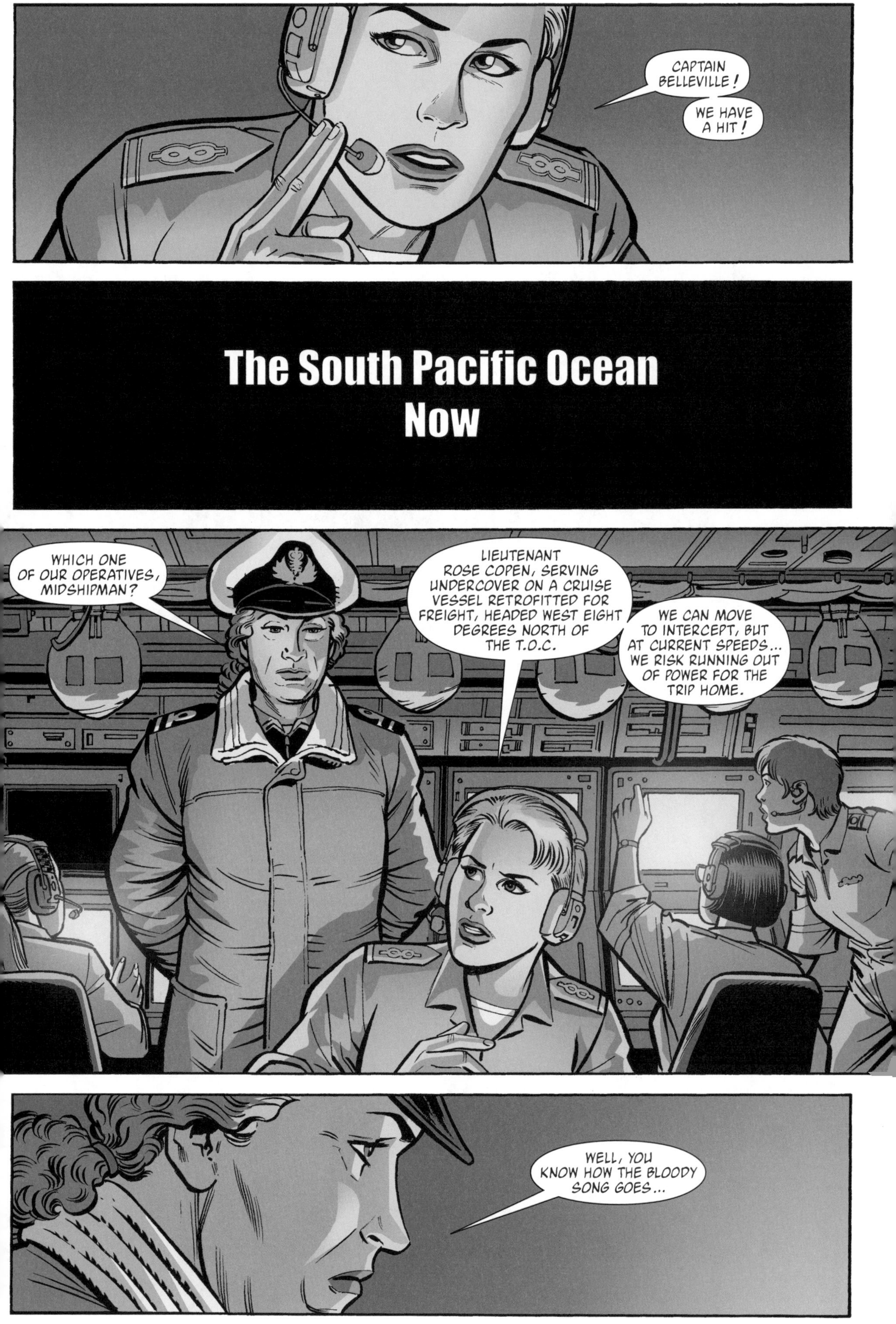
CAPTAIN BELLEVILLE!
WE HAVE A HIT!
The South Pacific Ocean
Now
WHICH ONE OF OUR OPERATIVES, MIDSHIPMAN?
LIEUTENANT ROSE COPEN, SERVING UNDERCOVER ON A CRUISE VESSEL RETROFITTED FOR FREIGHT, HEADED WEST EIGHT DEGREES NORTH OF THE T.O.C.
WE CAN MOVE TO INTERCEPT, BUT AT CURRENT SPEEDS... WE RISK RUNNING OUT OF POWER FOR THE TRIP HOME.
WELL, YOU KNOW HOW THE BLOODY SONG GOES...

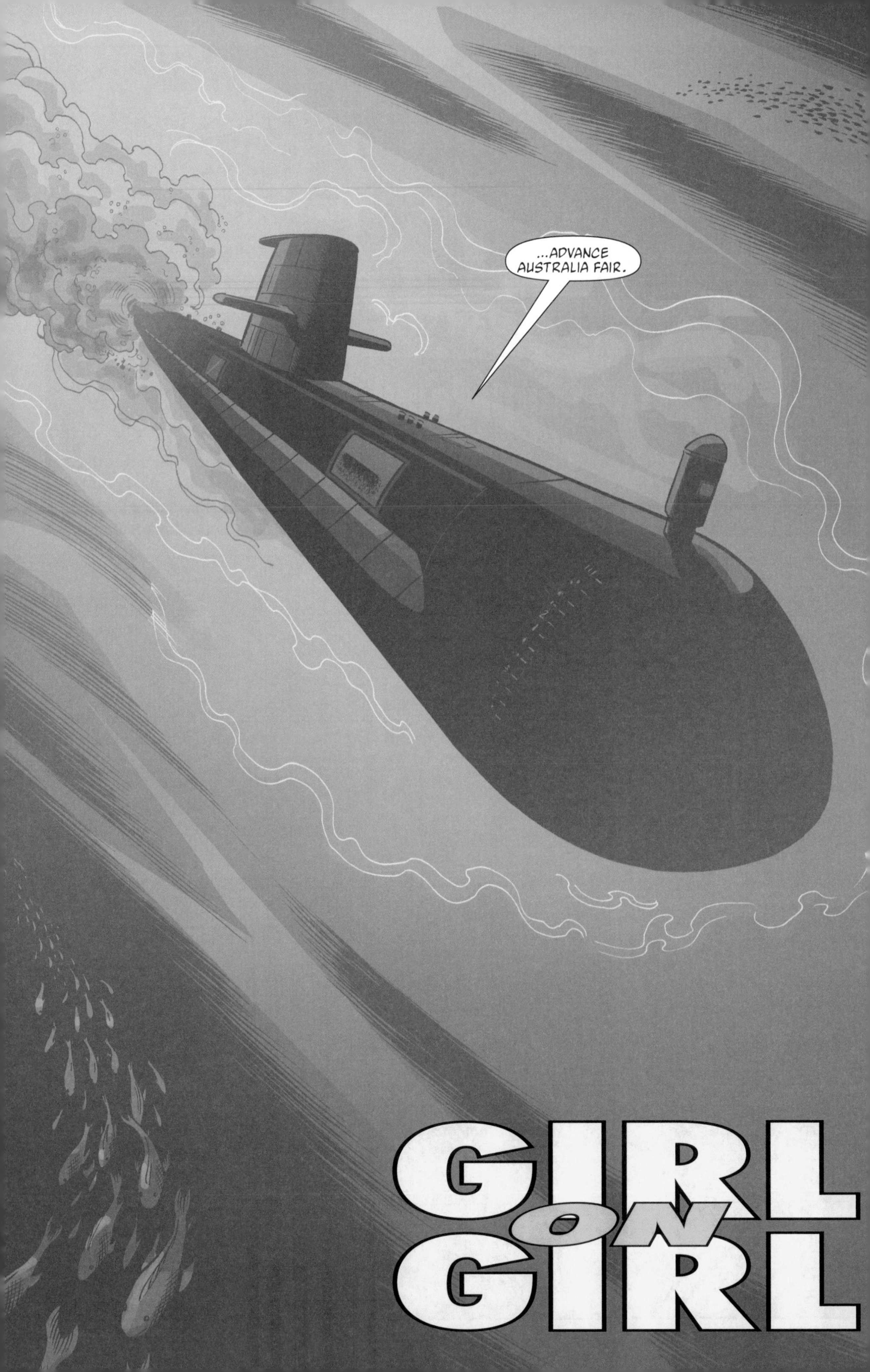
...ADVANCE AUSTRALIA FAIR.
GIRL ON GIRL

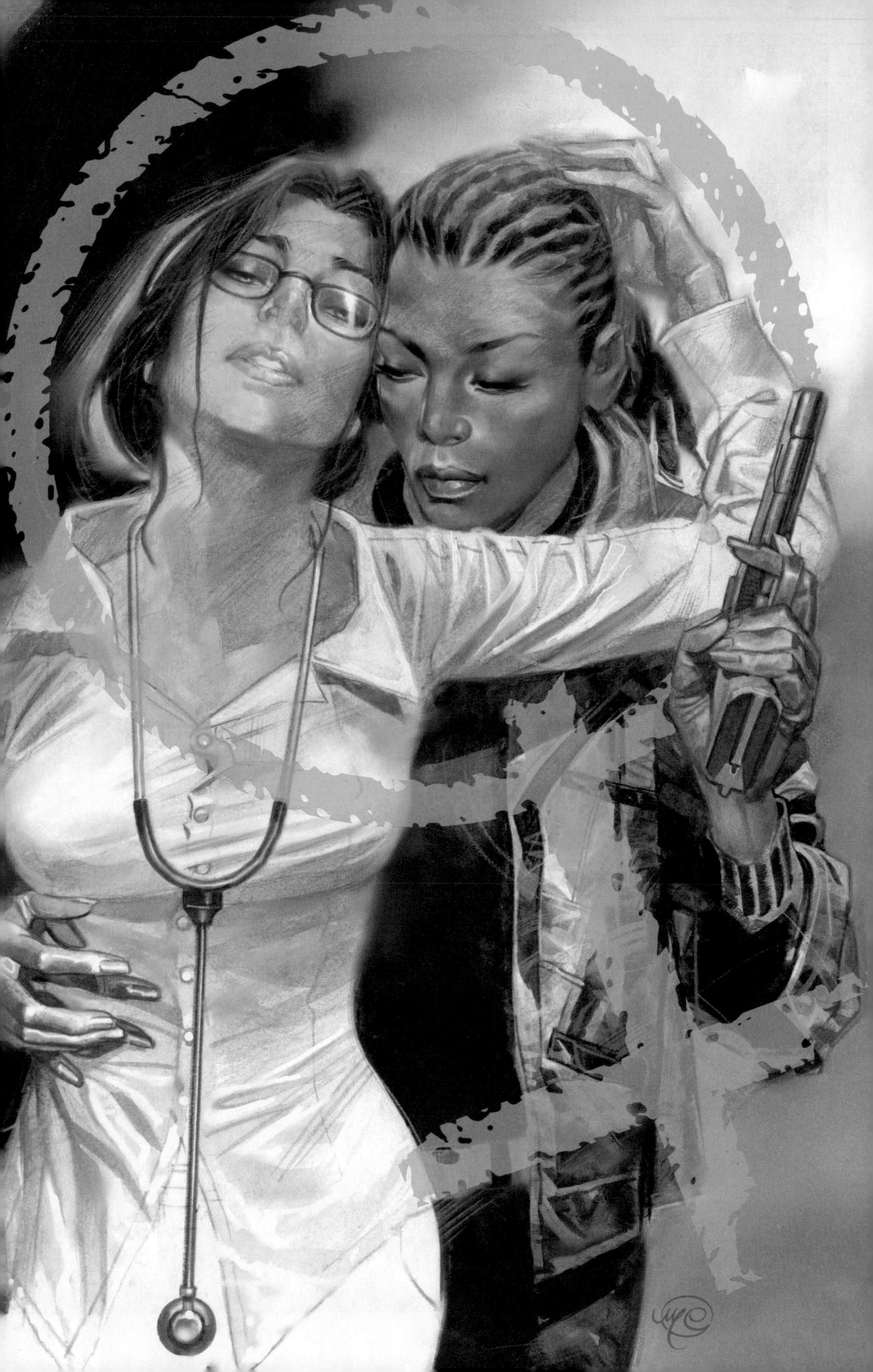

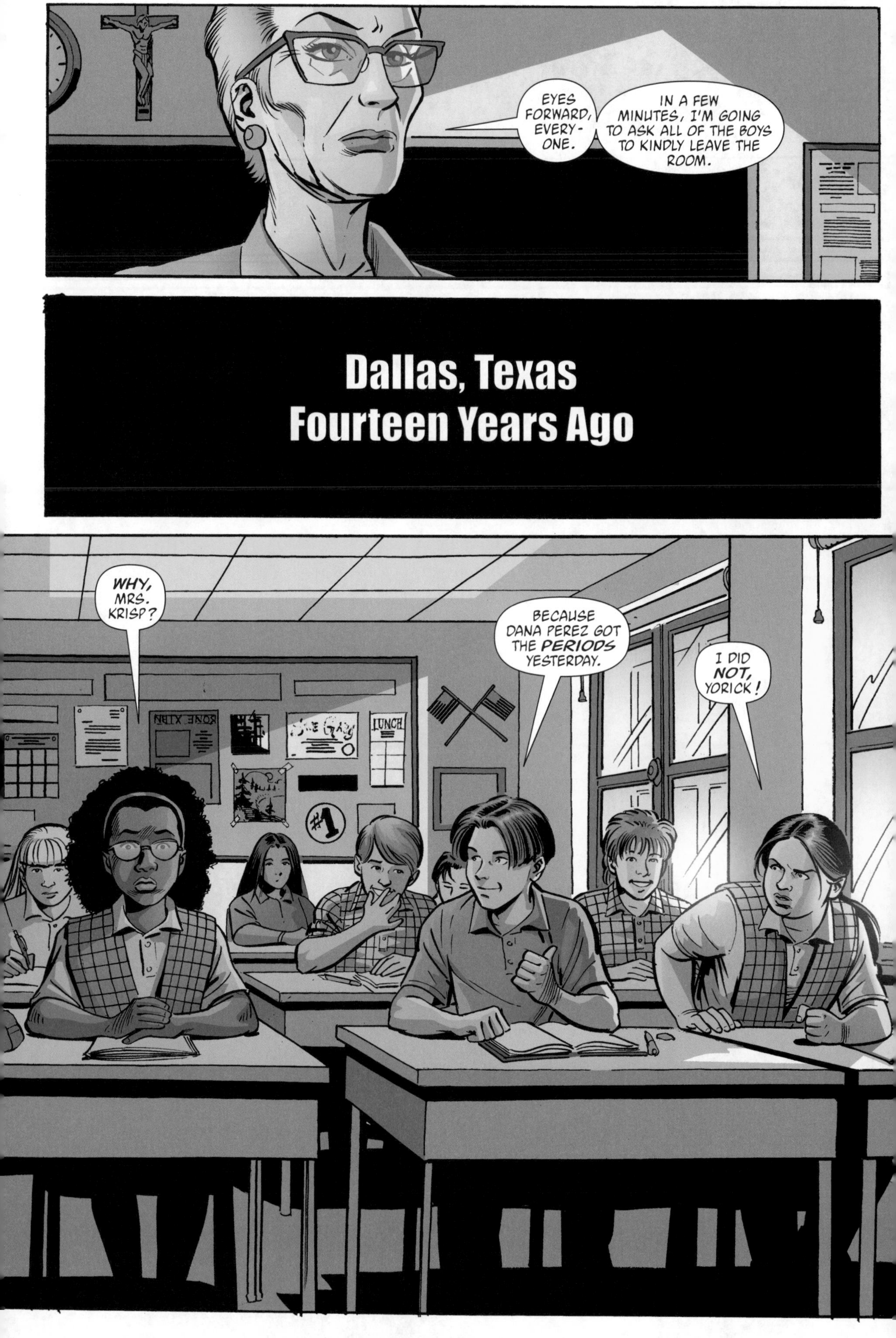
EYES FORWARD, EVERY-ONE.
IN A FEW MINUTES, I'M GOING TO ASK ALL OF THE BOYS TO KINDLY LEAVE THE ROOM.
Dallas, Texas
Fourteen Years Ago
WHY, MRS. KRISP?
BECAUSE DANA PEREZ GOT THE PERIODS YESTERDAY.
I DID NOT, YORICK!

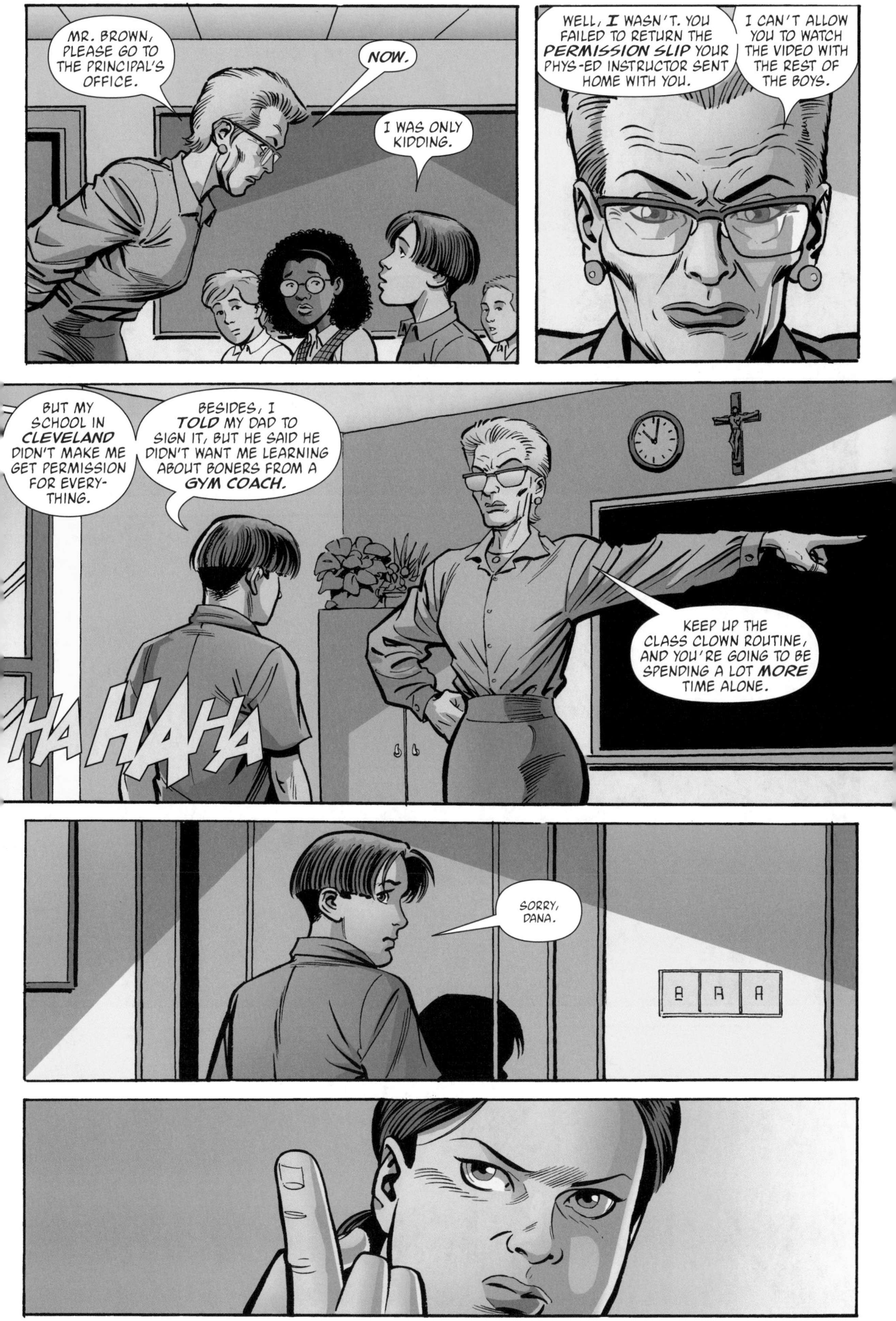

MR. BROWN, PLEASE GO TO THE PRINCIPAL'S OFFICE.
NOW.
I WAS ONLY KIDDING.
WELL, I WASN'T. YOU FAILED TO RETURN THE PERMISSION SLIP YOUR PHYS-ED INSTRUCTOR SENT HOME WITH YOU.
I CAN'T ALLOW YOU TO WATCH THE VIDEO WITH THE REST OF THE BOYS.
BUT MY SCHOOL IN CLEVELAND DIDN'T MAKE ME GET PERMISSION FOR EVERY-THING.
BESIDES, I TOLD MY DAD TO SIGN IT, BUT HE SAID HE DIDN'T WANT ME LEARNING ABOUT BONERS FROM A GYM COACH.
HAHAHA
KEEP UP THE CLASS CLOWN ROUTINE, AND YOU'RE GOING TO BE SPENDING A LOT MORE TIME ALONE.
SORRY, DANA.

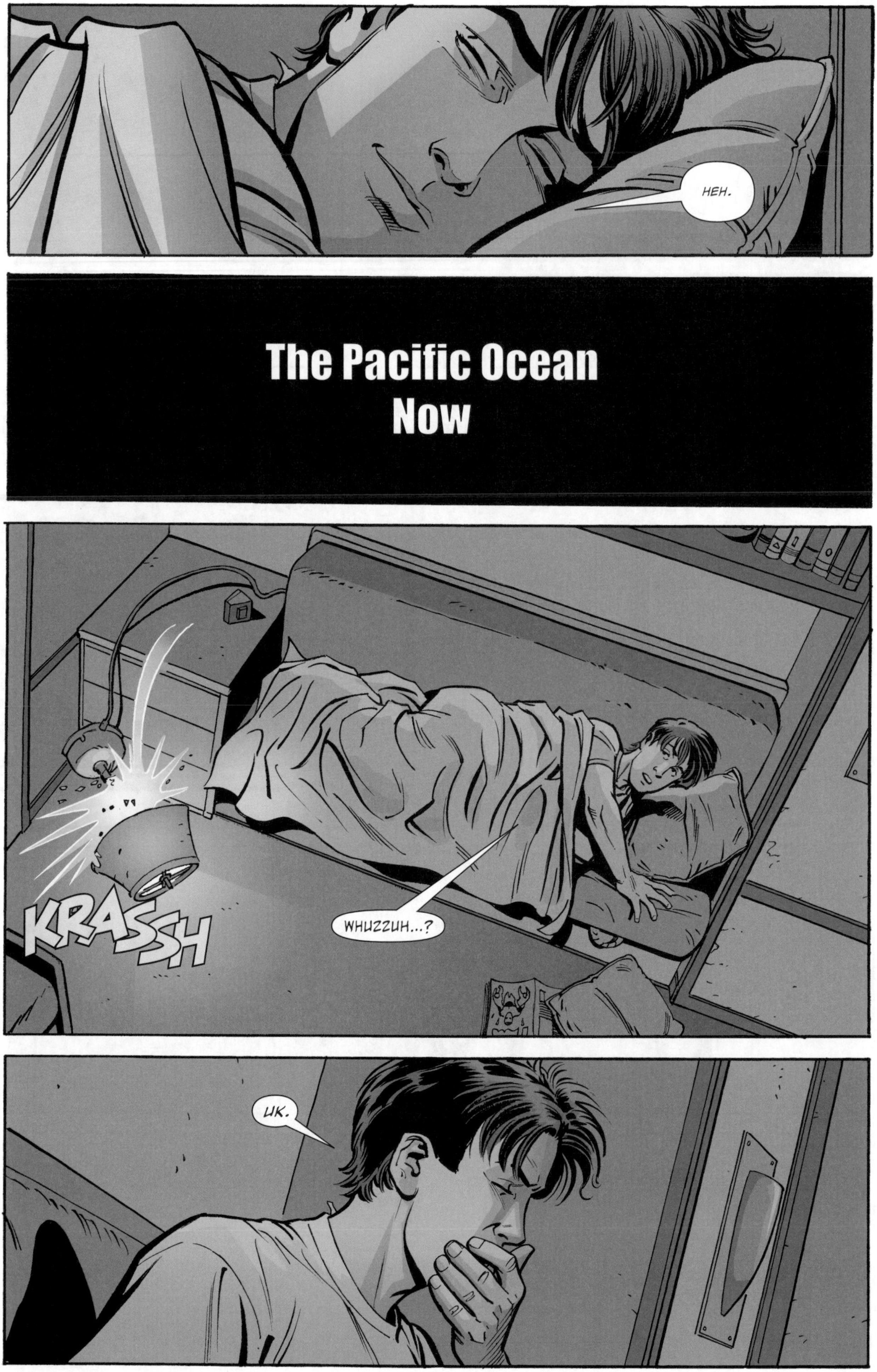
HEH.
The Pacific Ocean
Now
KRASSH
WHUZZUH...?
UK.

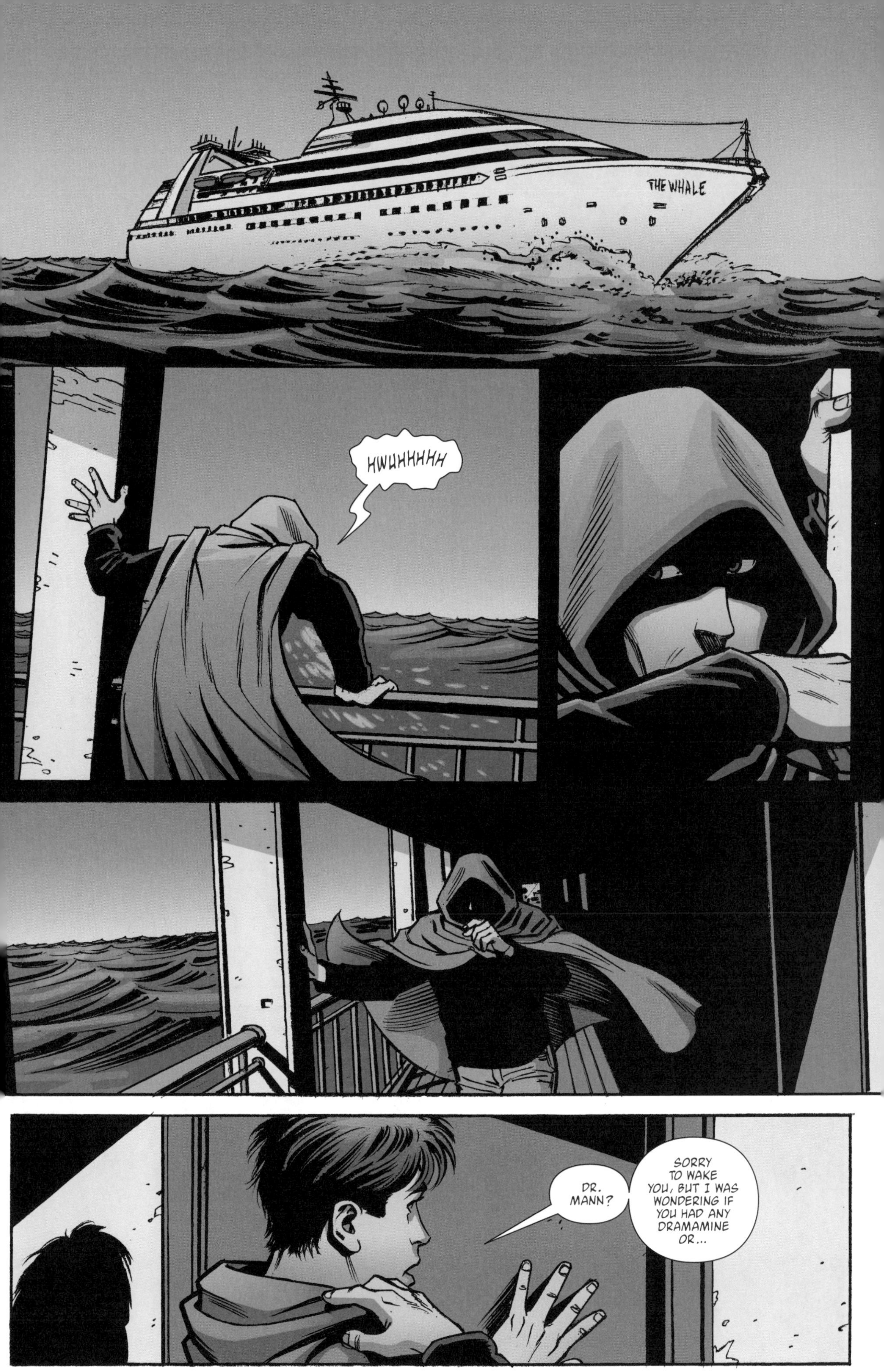
THE WHALE
HWUHHHHH
DR. MANN?
SORRY TO WAKE YOU, BUT I WAS WONDERING IF YOU HAD ANY DRAMAMINE OR...

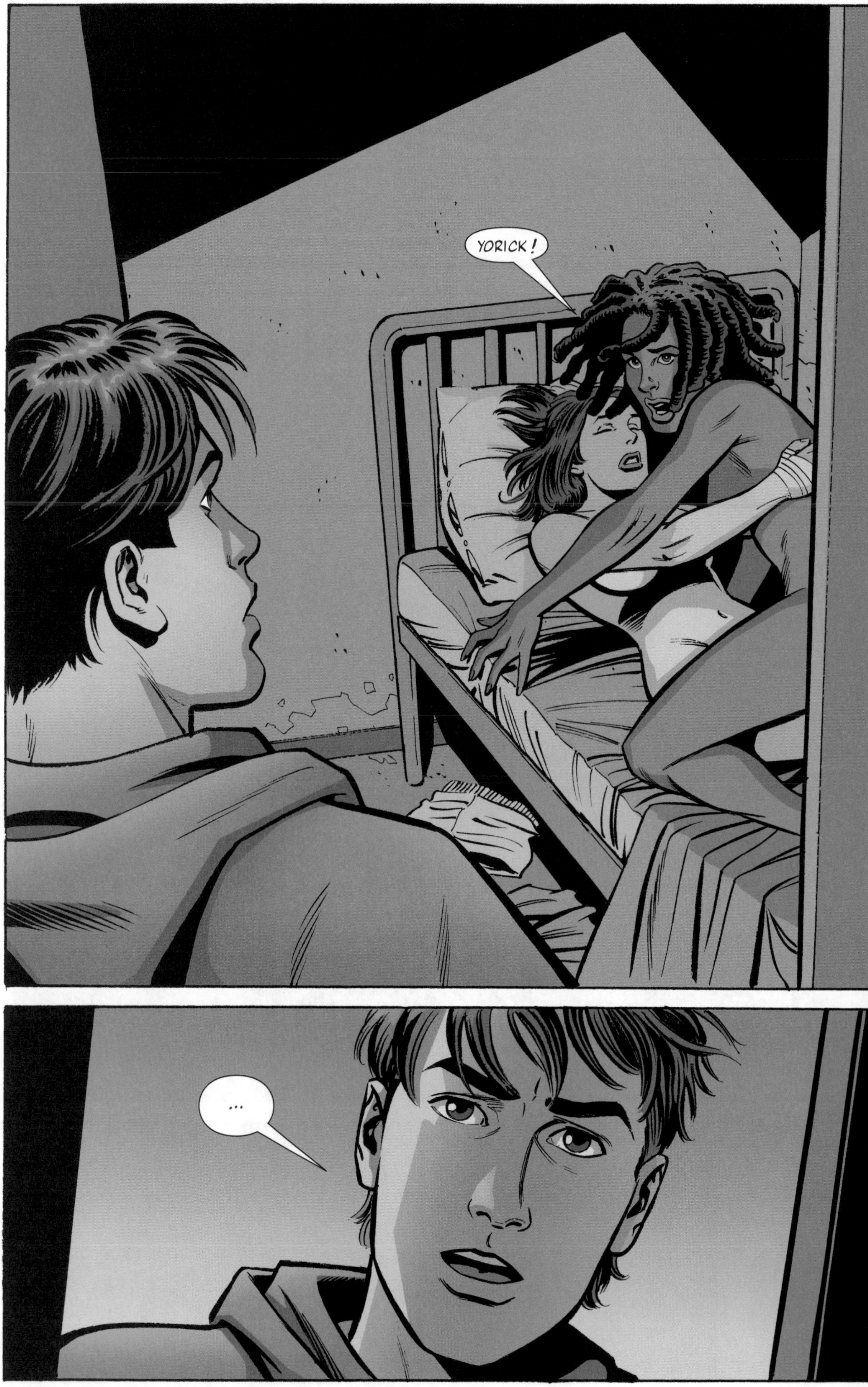
YORICK!
...

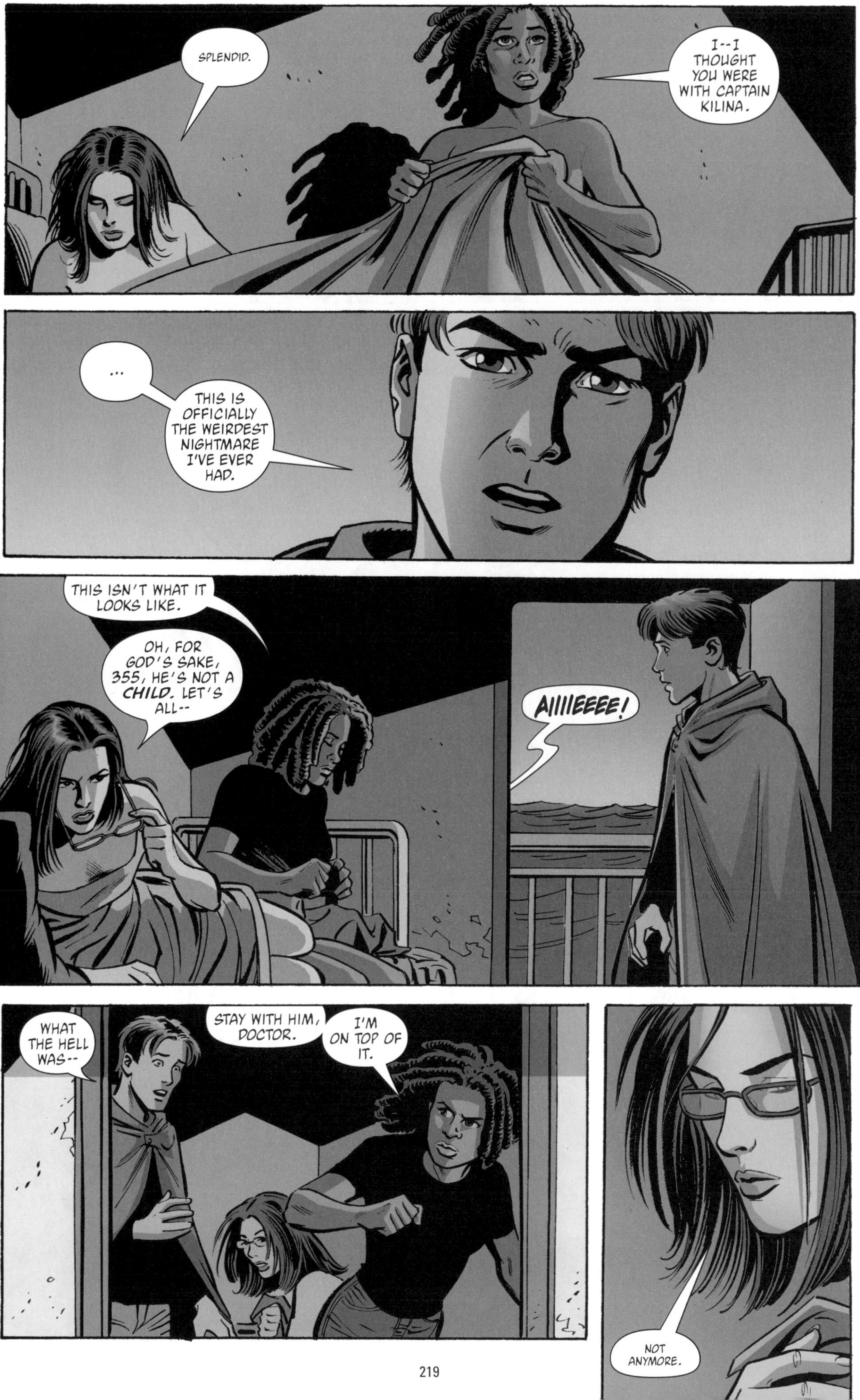
SPLENDID.
I--I THOUGHT YOU WERE WITH CAPTAIN KILINA.
...
THIS IS OFFICIALLY THE WEIRDEST NIGHTMARE I'VE EVER HAD.
THIS ISN'T WHAT IT LOOKS LIKE.
OH, FOR GOD'S SAKE, 355, HE'S NOT A CHILD. LET'S ALL--
AIIIEEEE!
WHAT THE HELL WAS--
STAY WITH HIM, DOCTOR.
I'M ON TOP OF IT.
NOT ANYMORE.

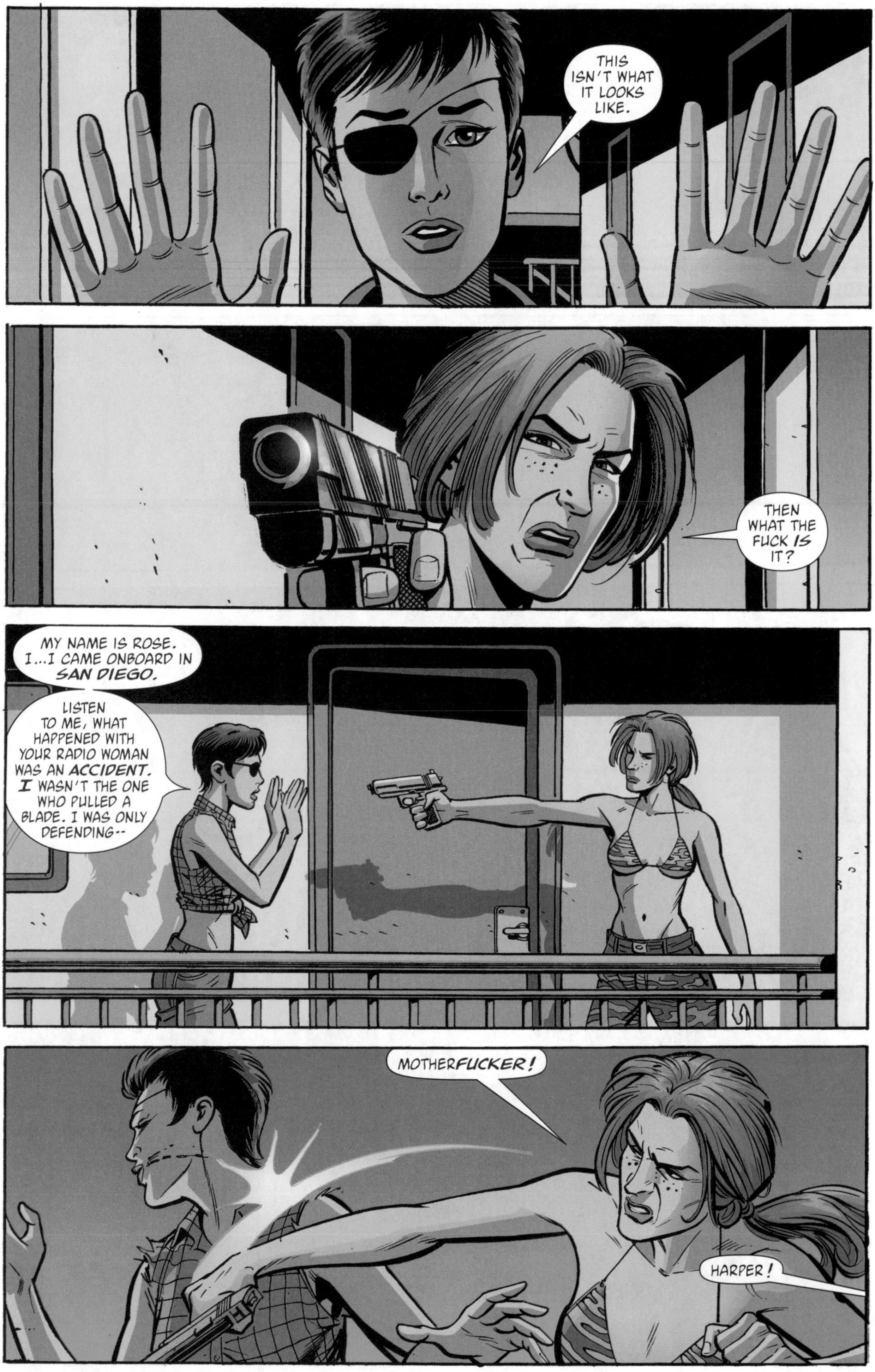
THIS ISN'T WHAT IT LOOKS LIKE.
THEN WHAT THE FUCK *IS* IT?
MY NAME IS ROSE. I...I CAME ONBOARD IN **SAN DIEGO.**
LISTEN TO ME, WHAT HAPPENED WITH YOUR RADIO WOMAN WAS AN **ACCIDENT.** ***I*** WASN'T THE ONE WHO PULLED A BLADE. I WAS ONLY DEFENDING--
MOTHER***FUCKER!***
HARPER!

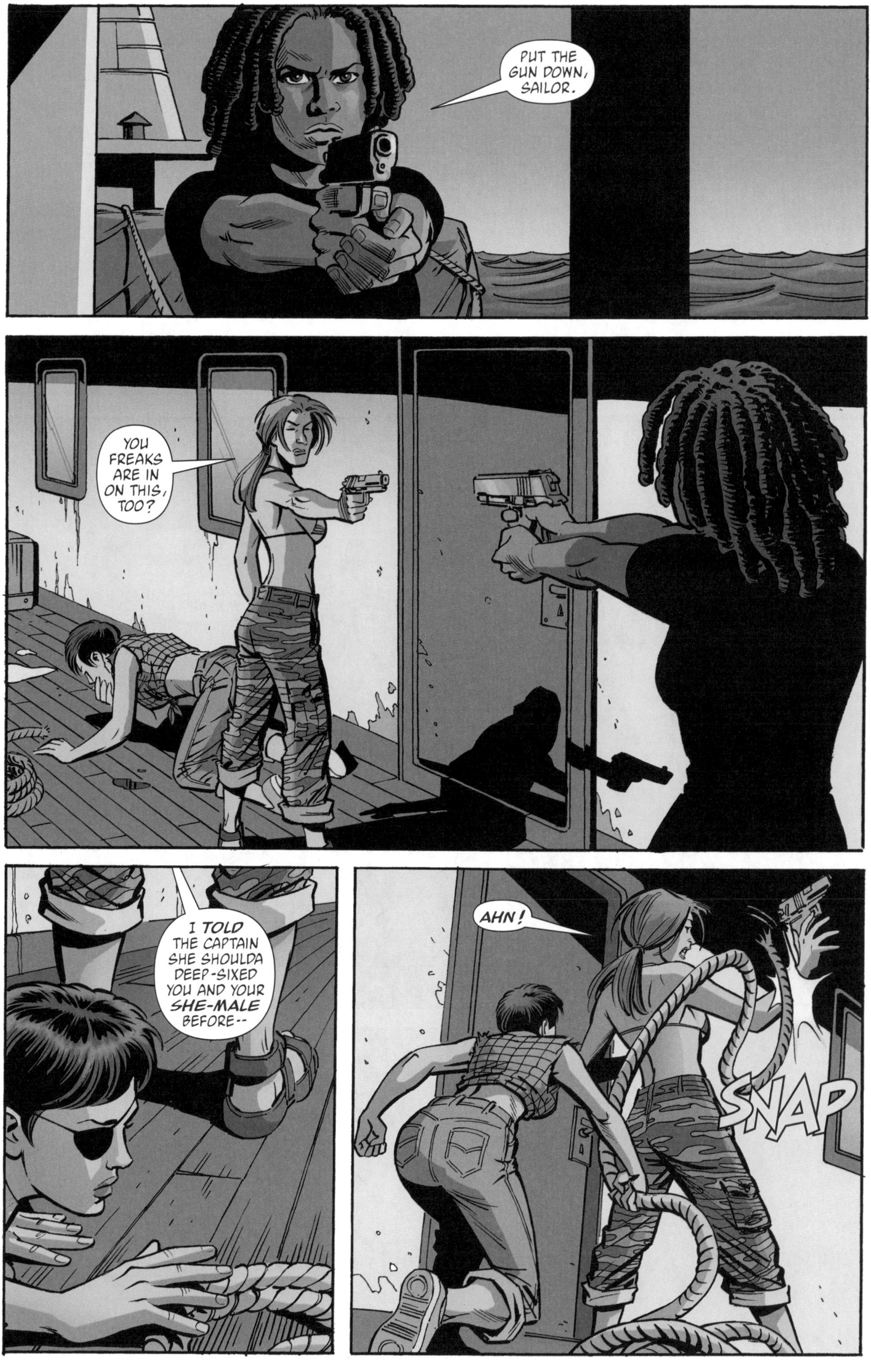
PUT THE GUN DOWN, SAILOR.
YOU FREAKS ARE IN ON THIS, TOO?
I TOLD THE CAPTAIN SHE SHOULDA DEEP-SIXED YOU AND YOUR SHE-MALE BEFORE--
AHN!
SNAP

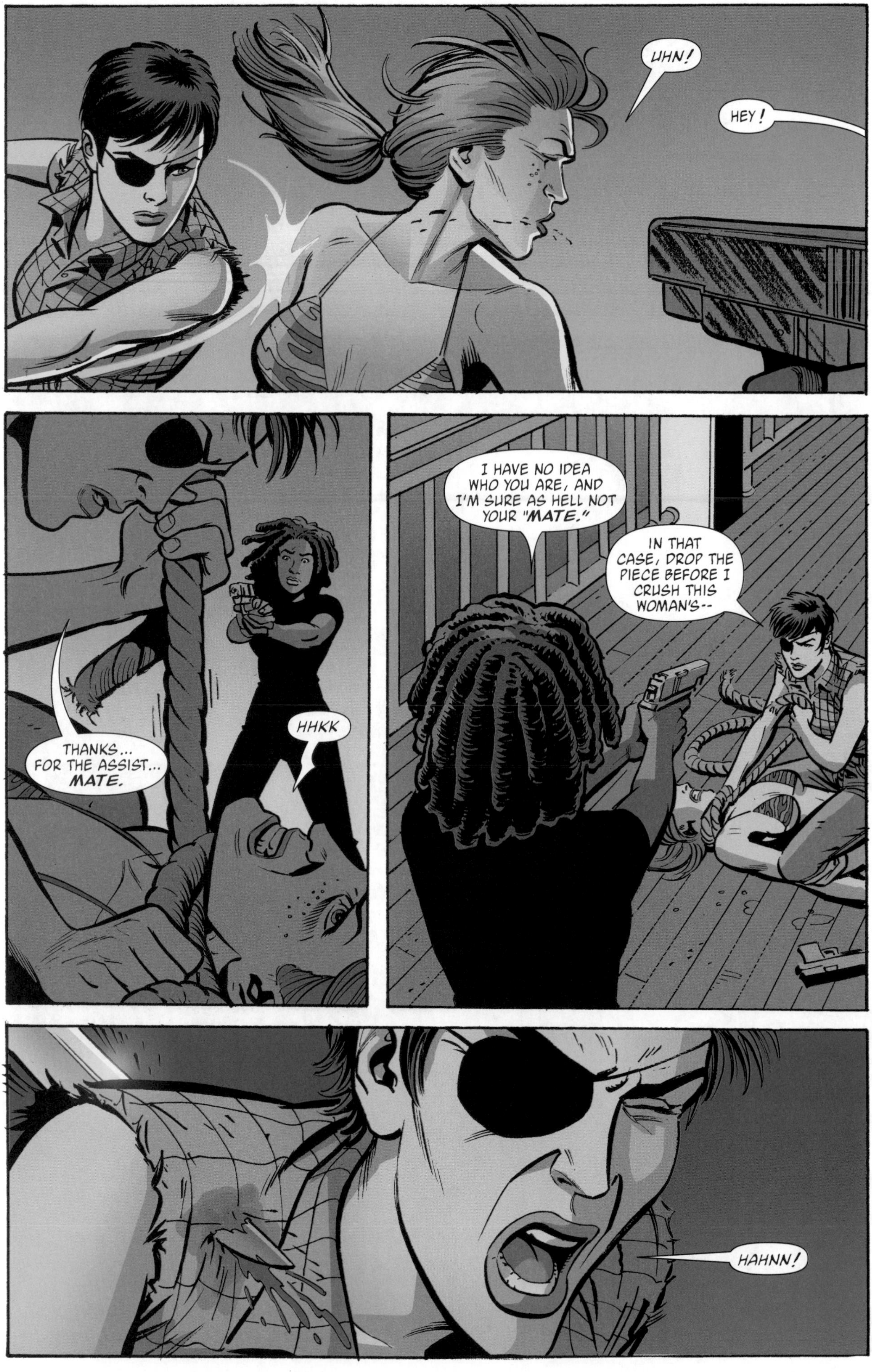
UHN!
HEY!
THANKS...
FOR THE ASSIST...
MATE.
HHKK
I HAVE NO IDEA WHO YOU ARE, AND I'M SURE AS HELL NOT YOUR "MATE."
IN THAT CASE, DROP THE PIECE BEFORE I CRUSH THIS WOMAN'S--
HAHNN!

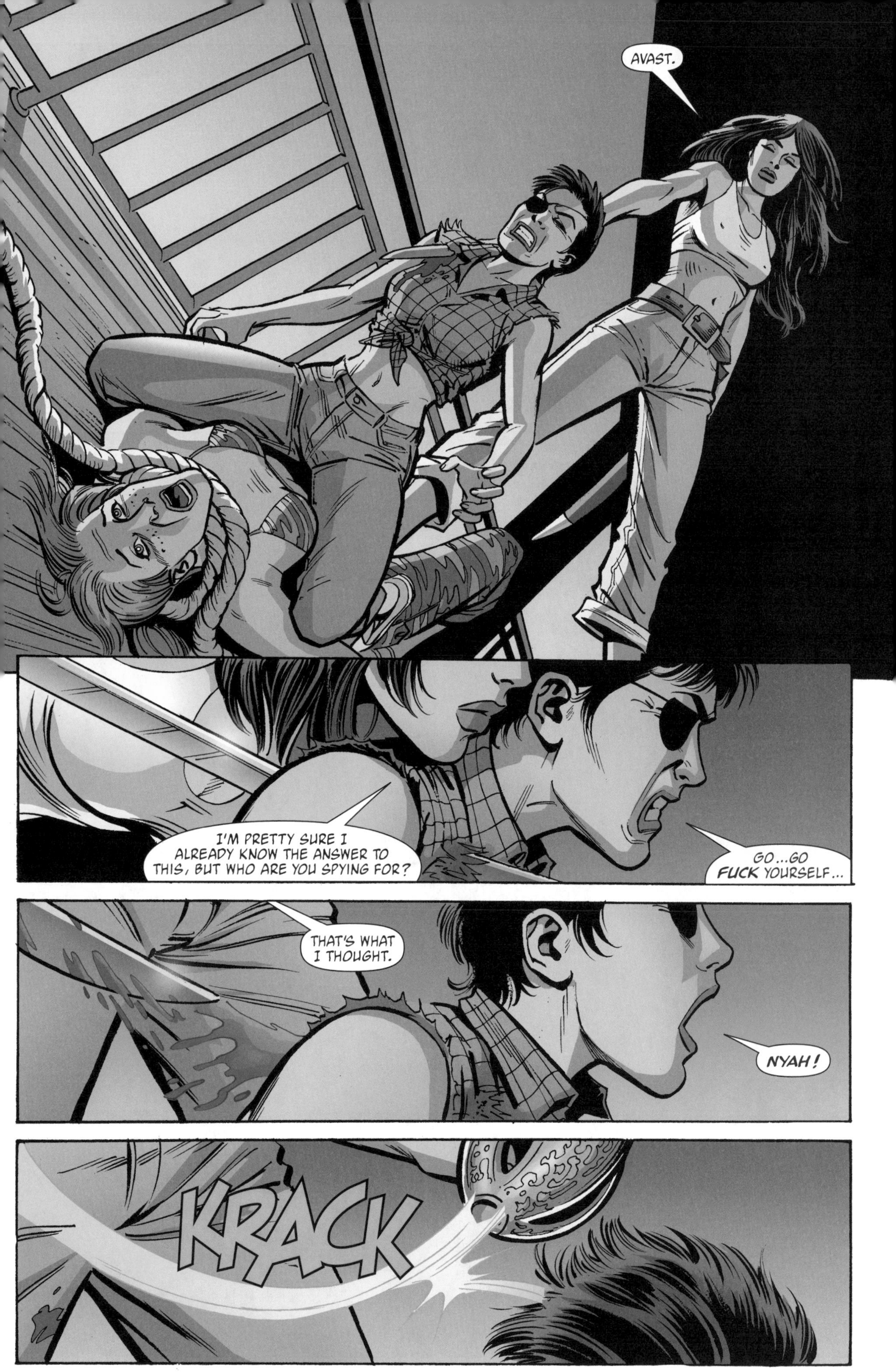
AVAST.
I'M PRETTY SURE I ALREADY KNOW THE ANSWER TO THIS, BUT WHO ARE YOU SPYING FOR?
GO...GO **FUCK** YOURSELF...
THAT'S WHAT I THOUGHT.
NYAH!
KRACK

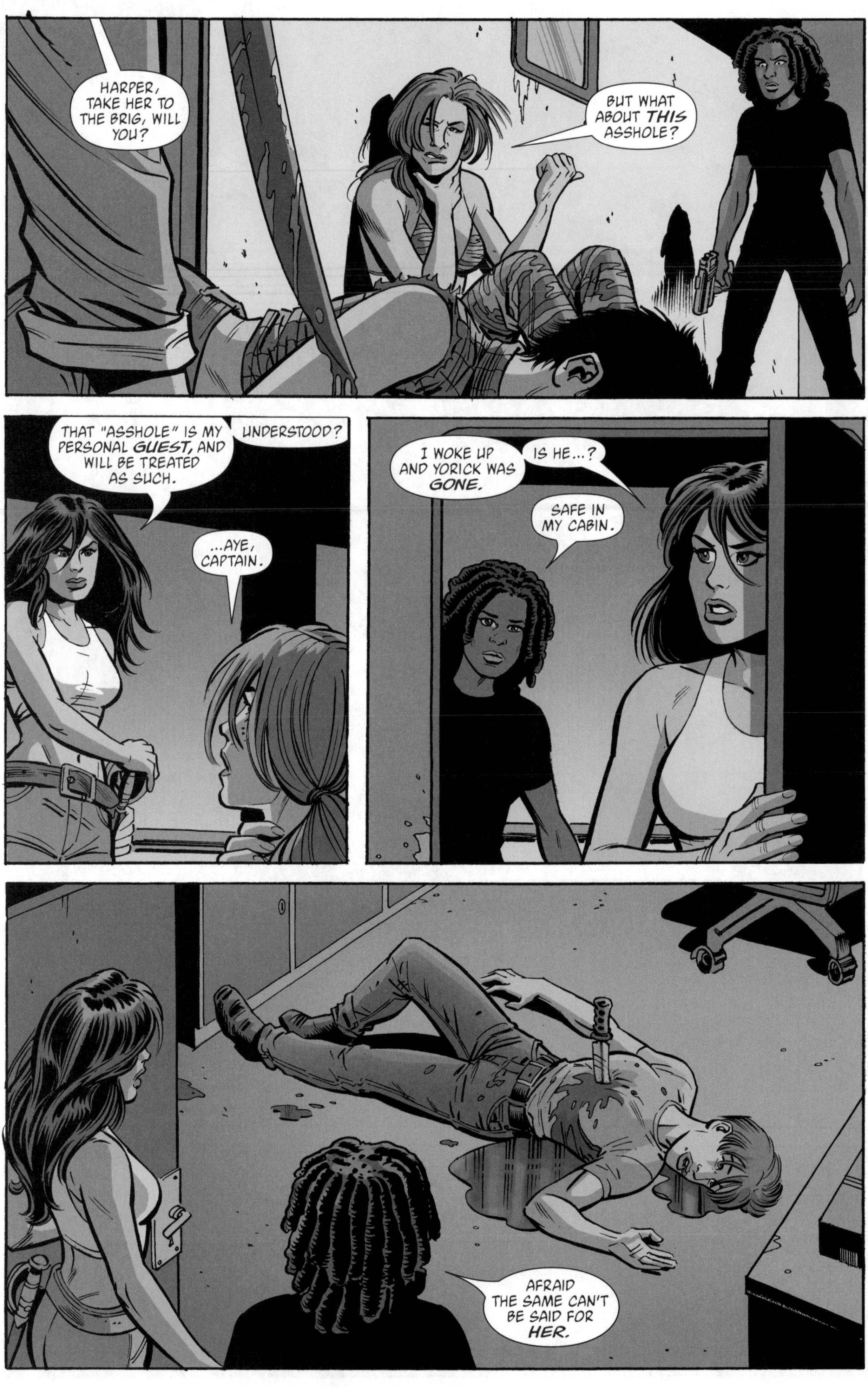
HARPER, TAKE HER TO THE BRIG, WILL YOU?
BUT WHAT ABOUT THIS ASSHOLE?
THAT "ASSHOLE" IS MY PERSONAL GUEST, AND WILL BE TREATED AS SUCH.
UNDERSTOOD?
...AYE, CAPTAIN.
I WOKE UP AND YORICK WAS GONE.
IS HE...?
SAFE IN MY CABIN.
AFRAID THE SAME CAN'T BE SAID FOR HER.

GODDAMMIT.

YOU SAID HER KILLER IS A **SPY**?

NO OFFENSE TO **YOUR** PROFESSION, AGENT. THE WHORE WHO DID THIS IS NOTHING BUT A SCUM-SUCKING **PIRATE**.

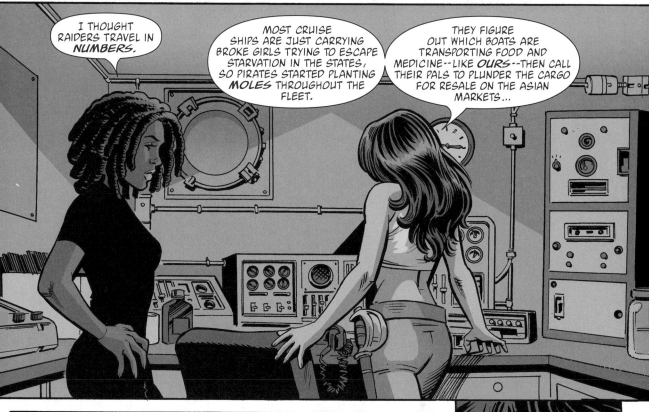

I THOUGHT RAIDERS TRAVEL IN **NUMBERS**.

MOST CRUISE SHIPS ARE JUST CARRYING BROKE GIRLS TRYING TO ESCAPE STARVATION IN THE STATES, SO PIRATES STARTED PLANTING **MOLES** THROUGHOUT THE FLEET.

THEY FIGURE OUT WHICH BOATS ARE TRANSPORTING FOOD AND MEDICINE--LIKE **OURS**--THEN CALL THEIR PALS TO PLUNDER THE CARGO FOR RESALE ON THE ASIAN MARKETS...

**SHIT.** IF SHE WAS BROADCASTING AT FREQUENCIES THIS LOW, SHE WAS PROBABLY TRYING TO SIGNAL A COLLINS CLASS.

SORRY?

YOU KNOW THE OLD LINE...

WHAT'S LONG AND HARD AND FILLED WITH SEMEN?

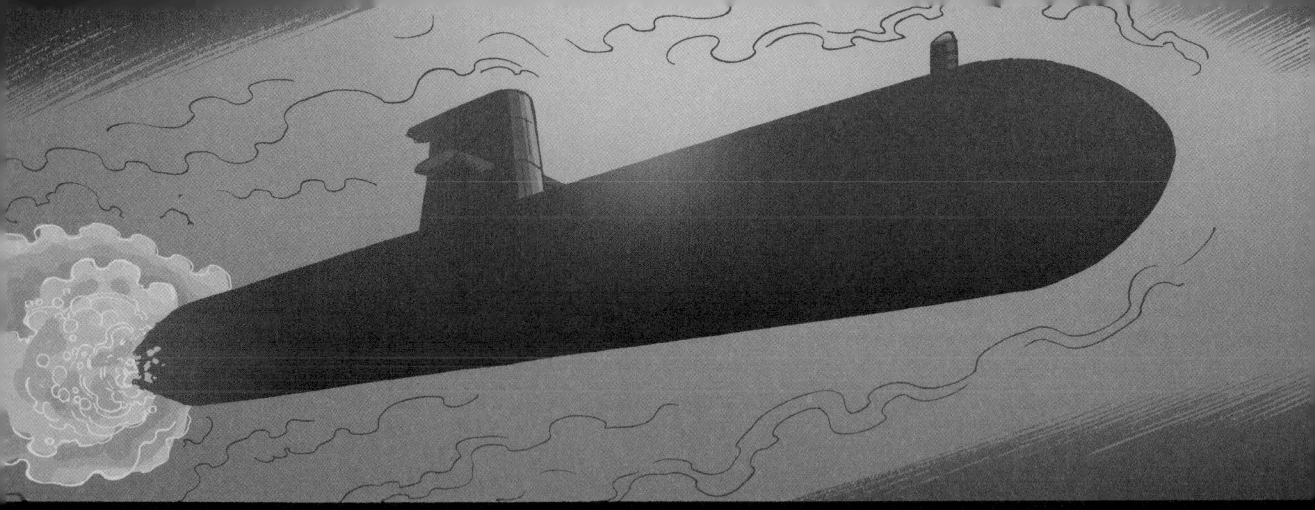

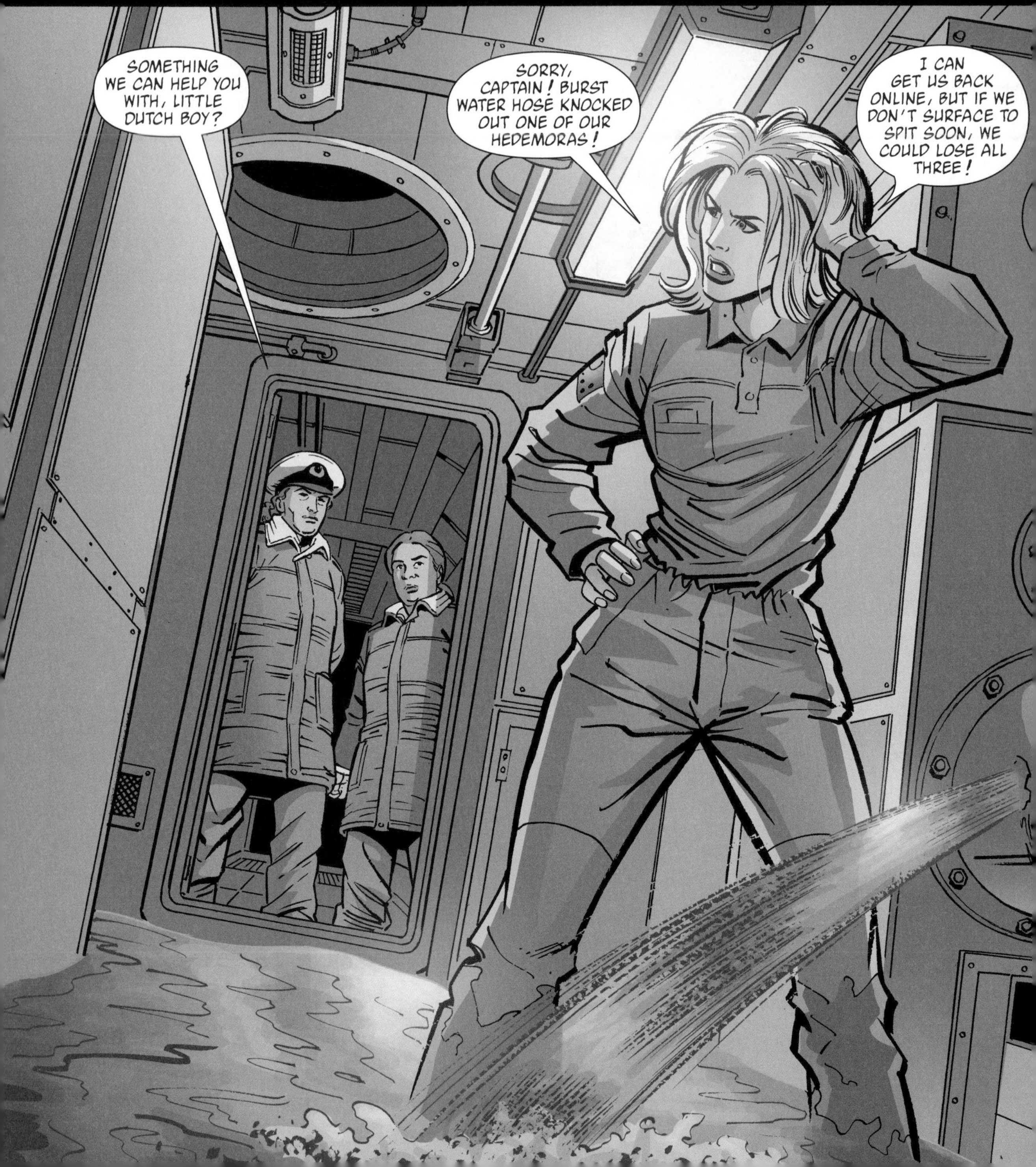
SOMETHING WE CAN HELP YOU WITH, LITTLE DUTCH BOY?
SORRY, CAPTAIN! BURST WATER HOSE KNOCKED OUT ONE OF OUR HEDEMORAS!
I CAN GET US BACK ONLINE, BUT IF WE DON'T SURFACE TO SPIT SOON, WE COULD LOSE ALL THREE!

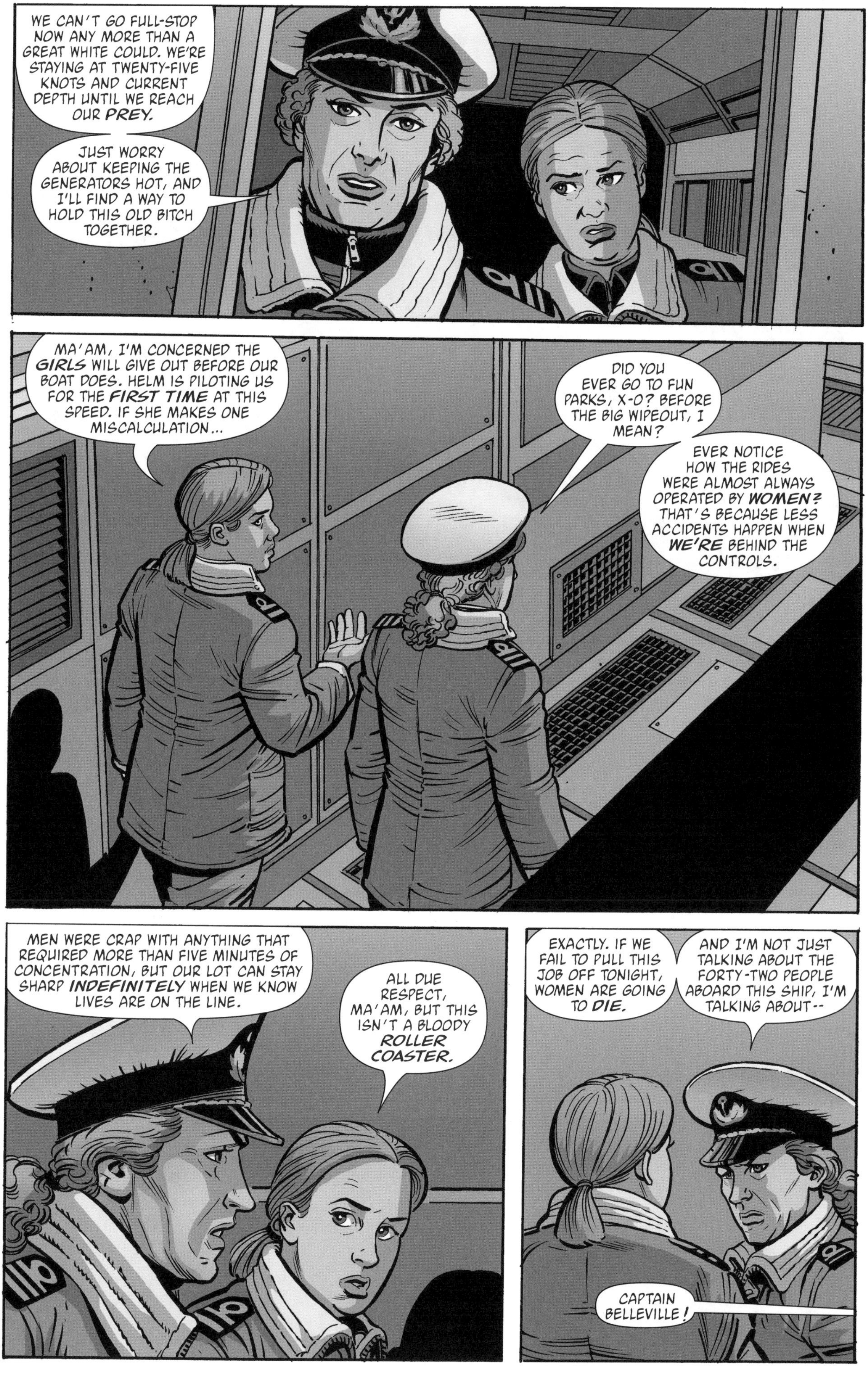
WE CAN'T GO FULL-STOP NOW ANY MORE THAN A GREAT WHITE COULD. WE'RE STAYING AT TWENTY-FIVE KNOTS AND CURRENT DEPTH UNTIL WE REACH OUR PREY.
JUST WORRY ABOUT KEEPING THE GENERATORS HOT, AND I'LL FIND A WAY TO HOLD THIS OLD BITCH TOGETHER.
MA'AM, I'M CONCERNED THE GIRLS WILL GIVE OUT BEFORE OUR BOAT DOES. HELM IS PILOTING US FOR THE FIRST TIME AT THIS SPEED. IF SHE MAKES ONE MISCALCULATION...
DID YOU EVER GO TO FUN PARKS, X-O? BEFORE THE BIG WIPEOUT, I MEAN?
EVER NOTICE HOW THE RIDES WERE ALMOST ALWAYS OPERATED BY WOMEN? THAT'S BECAUSE LESS ACCIDENTS HAPPEN WHEN WE'RE BEHIND THE CONTROLS.
MEN WERE CRAP WITH ANYTHING THAT REQUIRED MORE THAN FIVE MINUTES OF CONCENTRATION, BUT OUR LOT CAN STAY SHARP INDEFINITELY WHEN WE KNOW LIVES ARE ON THE LINE.
ALL DUE RESPECT, MA'AM, BUT THIS ISN'T A BLOODY ROLLER COASTER.
EXACTLY. IF WE FAIL TO PULL THIS JOB OFF TONIGHT, WOMEN ARE GOING TO DIE.
AND I'M NOT JUST TALKING ABOUT THE FORTY-TWO PEOPLE ABOARD THIS SHIP, I'M TALKING ABOUT--
CAPTAIN BELLEVILLE!

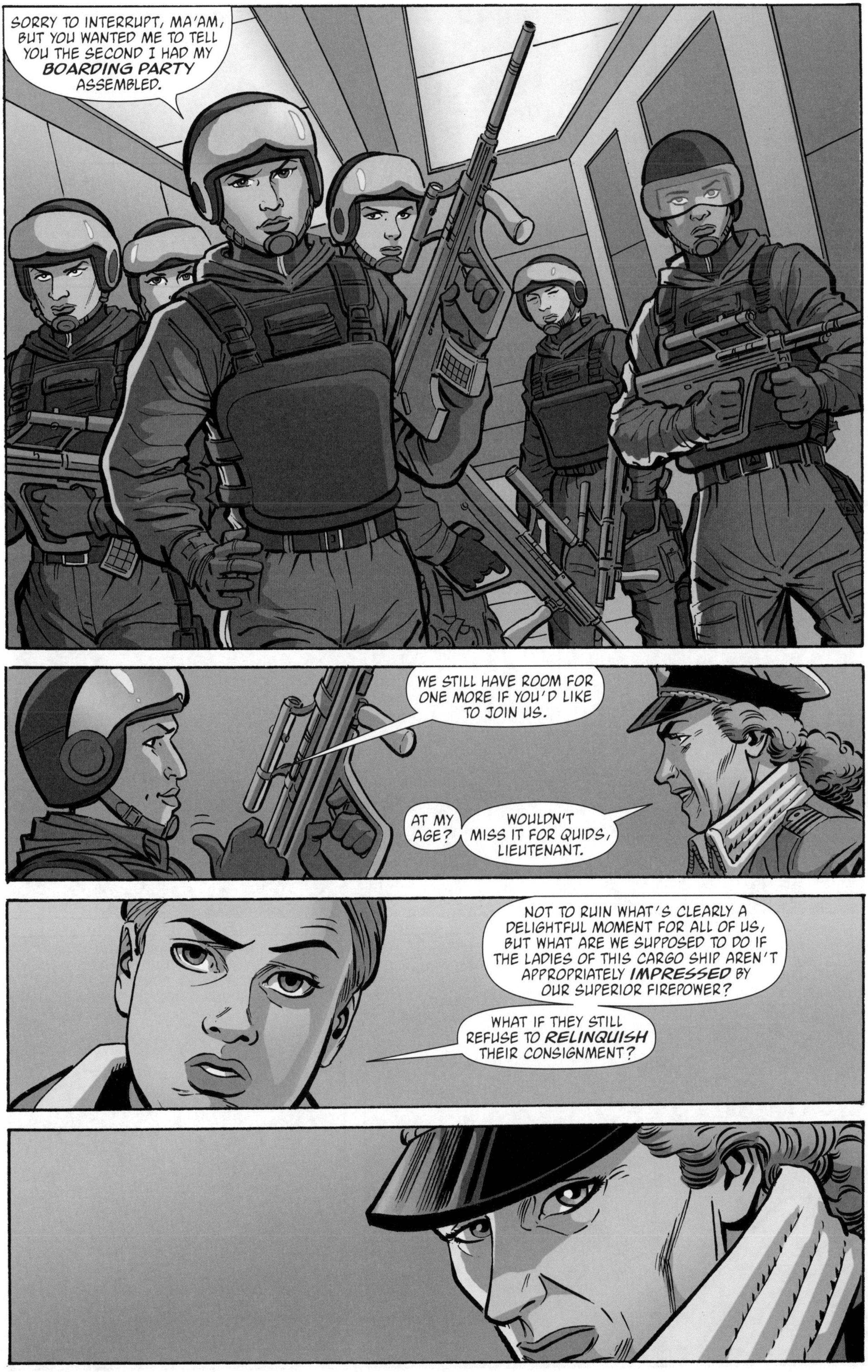
SORRY TO INTERRUPT, MA'AM, BUT YOU WANTED ME TO TELL YOU THE SECOND I HAD MY BOARDING PARTY ASSEMBLED.
WE STILL HAVE ROOM FOR ONE MORE IF YOU'D LIKE TO JOIN US.
AT MY AGE?
WOULDN'T MISS IT FOR QUIDS, LIEUTENANT.
NOT TO RUIN WHAT'S CLEARLY A DELIGHTFUL MOMENT FOR ALL OF US, BUT WHAT ARE WE SUPPOSED TO DO IF THE LADIES OF THIS CARGO SHIP AREN'T APPROPRIATELY IMPRESSED BY OUR SUPERIOR FIREPOWER?
WHAT IF THEY STILL REFUSE TO RELINQUISH THEIR CONSIGNMENT?

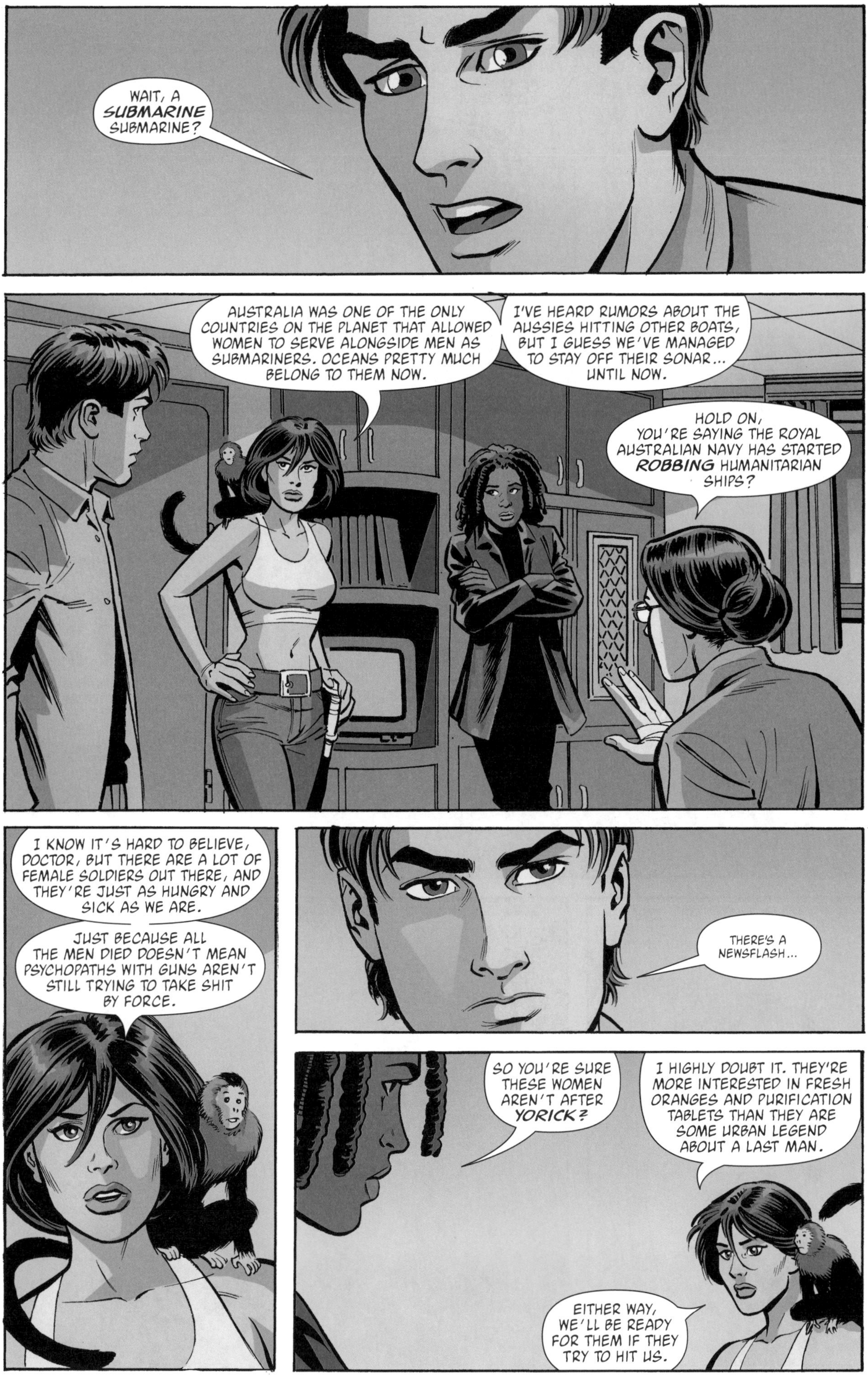
WAIT, A SUBMARINE SUBMARINE?
AUSTRALIA WAS ONE OF THE ONLY COUNTRIES ON THE PLANET THAT ALLOWED WOMEN TO SERVE ALONGSIDE MEN AS SUBMARINERS. OCEANS PRETTY MUCH BELONG TO THEM NOW.
I'VE HEARD RUMORS ABOUT THE AUSSIES HITTING OTHER BOATS, BUT I GUESS WE'VE MANAGED TO STAY OFF THEIR SONAR... UNTIL NOW.
HOLD ON, YOU'RE SAYING THE ROYAL AUSTRALIAN NAVY HAS STARTED ROBBING HUMANITARIAN SHIPS?
I KNOW IT'S HARD TO BELIEVE, DOCTOR, BUT THERE ARE A LOT OF FEMALE SOLDIERS OUT THERE, AND THEY'RE JUST AS HUNGRY AND SICK AS WE ARE.
JUST BECAUSE ALL THE MEN DIED DOESN'T MEAN PSYCHOPATHS WITH GUNS AREN'T STILL TRYING TO TAKE SHIT BY FORCE.
THERE'S A NEWSFLASH...
SO YOU'RE SURE THESE WOMEN AREN'T AFTER YORICK?
I HIGHLY DOUBT IT. THEY'RE MORE INTERESTED IN FRESH ORANGES AND PURIFICATION TABLETS THAN THEY ARE SOME URBAN LEGEND ABOUT A LAST MAN.
EITHER WAY, WE'LL BE READY FOR THEM IF THEY TRY TO HIT US.

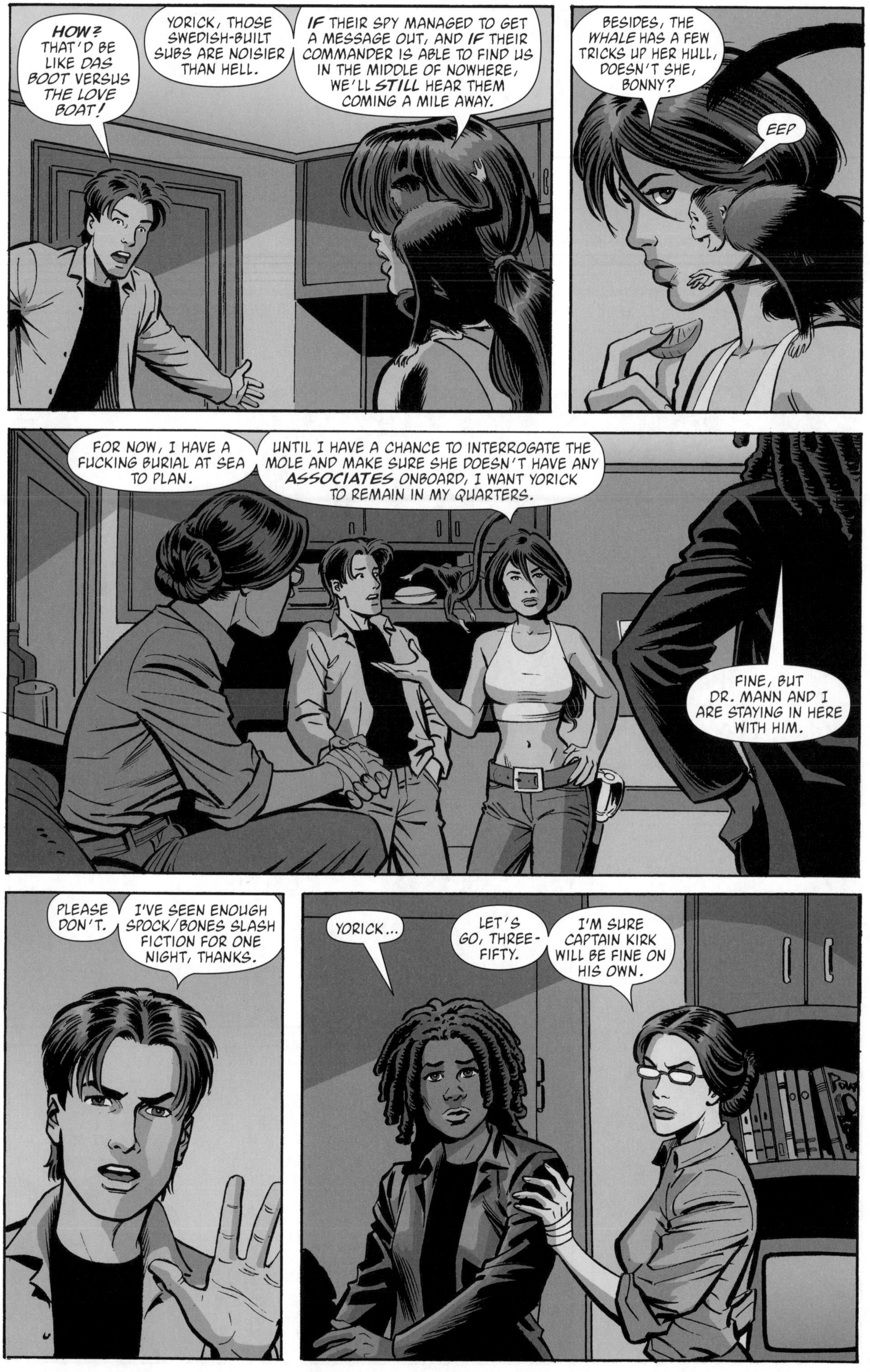
HOW? THAT'D BE LIKE DAS BOOT VERSUS THE LOVE BOAT!
YORICK, THOSE SWEDISH-BUILT SUBS ARE NOISIER THAN HELL.
IF THEIR SPY MANAGED TO GET A MESSAGE OUT, AND IF THEIR COMMANDER IS ABLE TO FIND US IN THE MIDDLE OF NOWHERE, WE'LL STILL HEAR THEM COMING A MILE AWAY.
BESIDES, THE WHALE HAS A FEW TRICKS UP HER HULL, DOESN'T SHE, BONNY?
EEP
FOR NOW, I HAVE A FUCKING BURIAL AT SEA TO PLAN.
UNTIL I HAVE A CHANCE TO INTERROGATE THE MOLE AND MAKE SURE SHE DOESN'T HAVE ANY ASSOCIATES ONBOARD, I WANT YORICK TO REMAIN IN MY QUARTERS.
FINE, BUT DR. MANN AND I ARE STAYING IN HERE WITH HIM.
PLEASE DON'T.
I'VE SEEN ENOUGH SPOCK/BONES SLASH FICTION FOR ONE NIGHT, THANKS.
YORICK...
LET'S GO, THREE-FIFTY.
I'M SURE CAPTAIN KIRK WILL BE FINE ON HIS OWN.

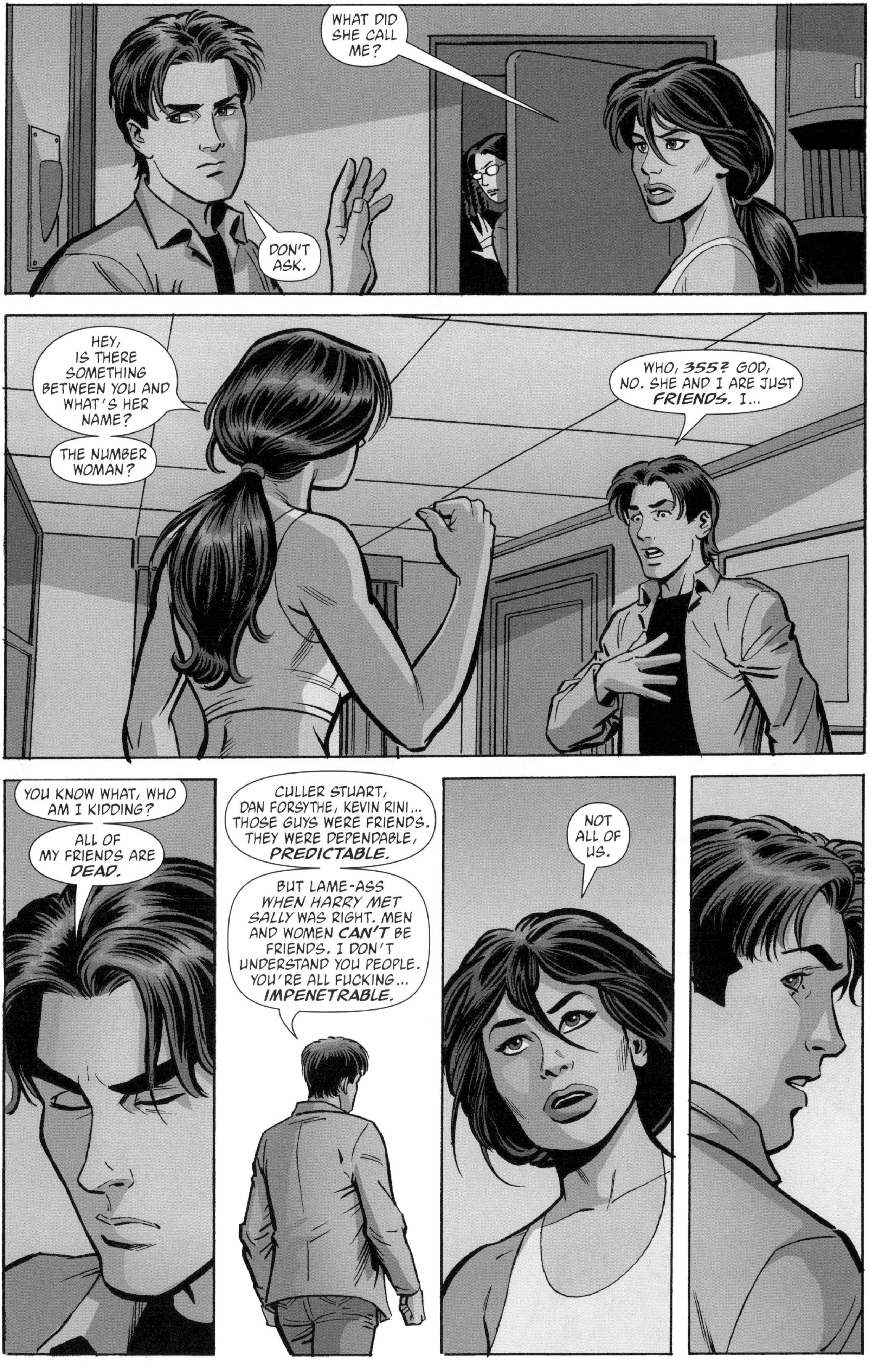
WHAT DID SHE CALL ME?
DON'T ASK.
HEY, IS THERE SOMETHING BETWEEN YOU AND WHAT'S HER NAME?
THE NUMBER WOMAN?
WHO, 355? GOD, NO. SHE AND I ARE JUST FRIENDS. I...
YOU KNOW WHAT, WHO AM I KIDDING?
ALL OF MY FRIENDS ARE DEAD.
CULLER STUART, DAN FORSYTHE, KEVIN RINI... THOSE GUYS WERE FRIENDS. THEY WERE DEPENDABLE, PREDICTABLE.
BUT LAME-ASS WHEN HARRY MET SALLY WAS RIGHT. MEN AND WOMEN CAN'T BE FRIENDS. I DON'T UNDERSTAND YOU PEOPLE. YOU'RE ALL FUCKING... IMPENETRABLE.
NOT ALL OF US.

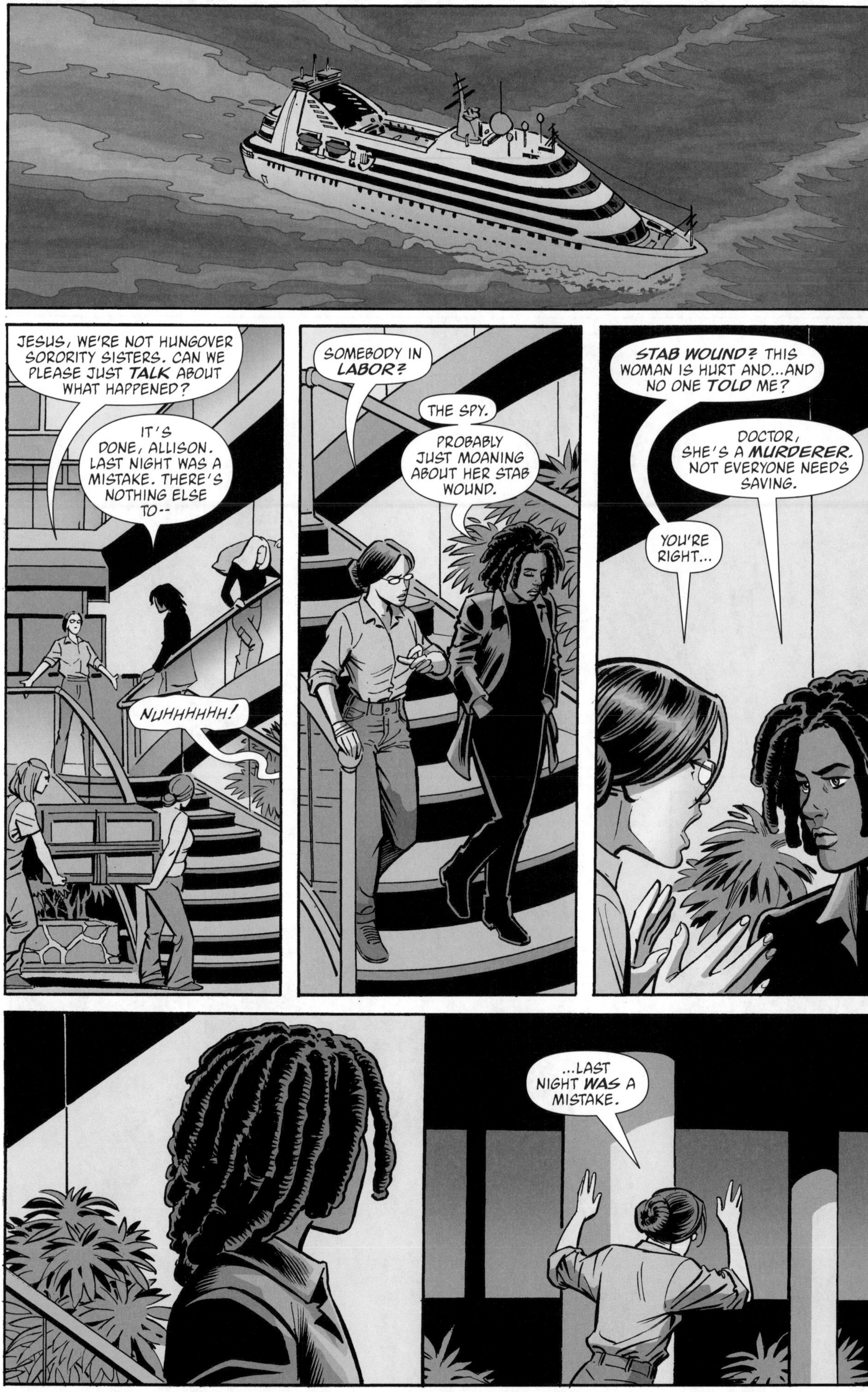
JESUS, WE'RE NOT HUNGOVER SORORITY SISTERS. CAN WE PLEASE JUST TALK ABOUT WHAT HAPPENED?
IT'S DONE, ALLISON. LAST NIGHT WAS A MISTAKE. THERE'S NOTHING ELSE TO--
NUHHHHHH!
SOMEBODY IN LABOR?
THE SPY.
PROBABLY JUST MOANING ABOUT HER STAB WOUND.
STAB WOUND? THIS WOMAN IS HURT AND...AND NO ONE TOLD ME?
DOCTOR, SHE'S A MURDERER. NOT EVERYONE NEEDS SAVING.
YOU'RE RIGHT...
...LAST NIGHT WAS A MISTAKE.

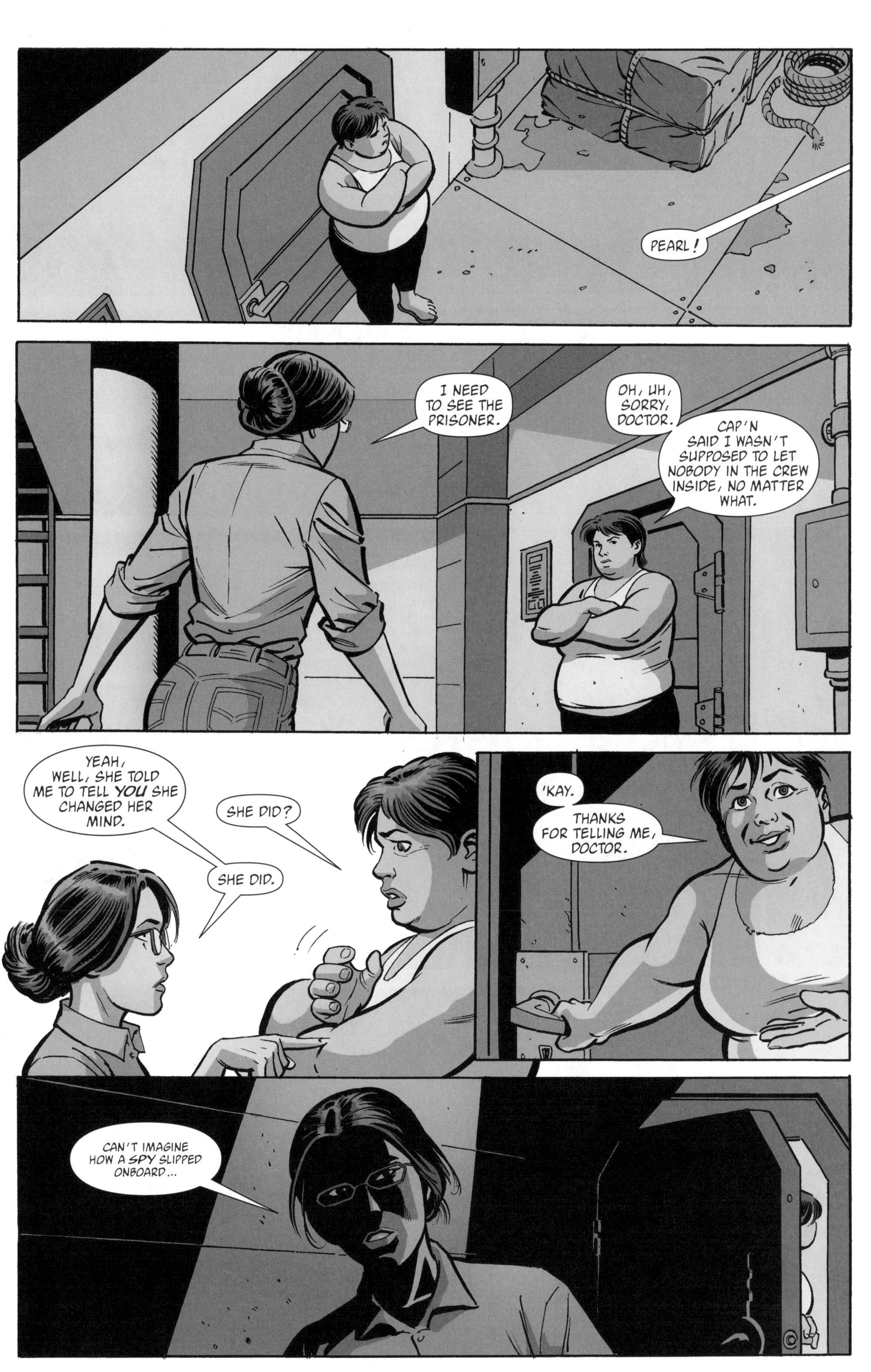
PEARL!
I NEED TO SEE THE PRISONER.
OH, UH, SORRY, DOCTOR.
CAP'N SAID I WASN'T SUPPOSED TO LET NOBODY IN THE CREW INSIDE, NO MATTER WHAT.
YEAH, WELL, SHE TOLD ME TO TELL YOU SHE CHANGED HER MIND.
SHE DID?
SHE DID.
'KAY.
THANKS FOR TELLING ME, DOCTOR.
CAN'T IMAGINE HOW A SPY SLIPPED ONBOARD...

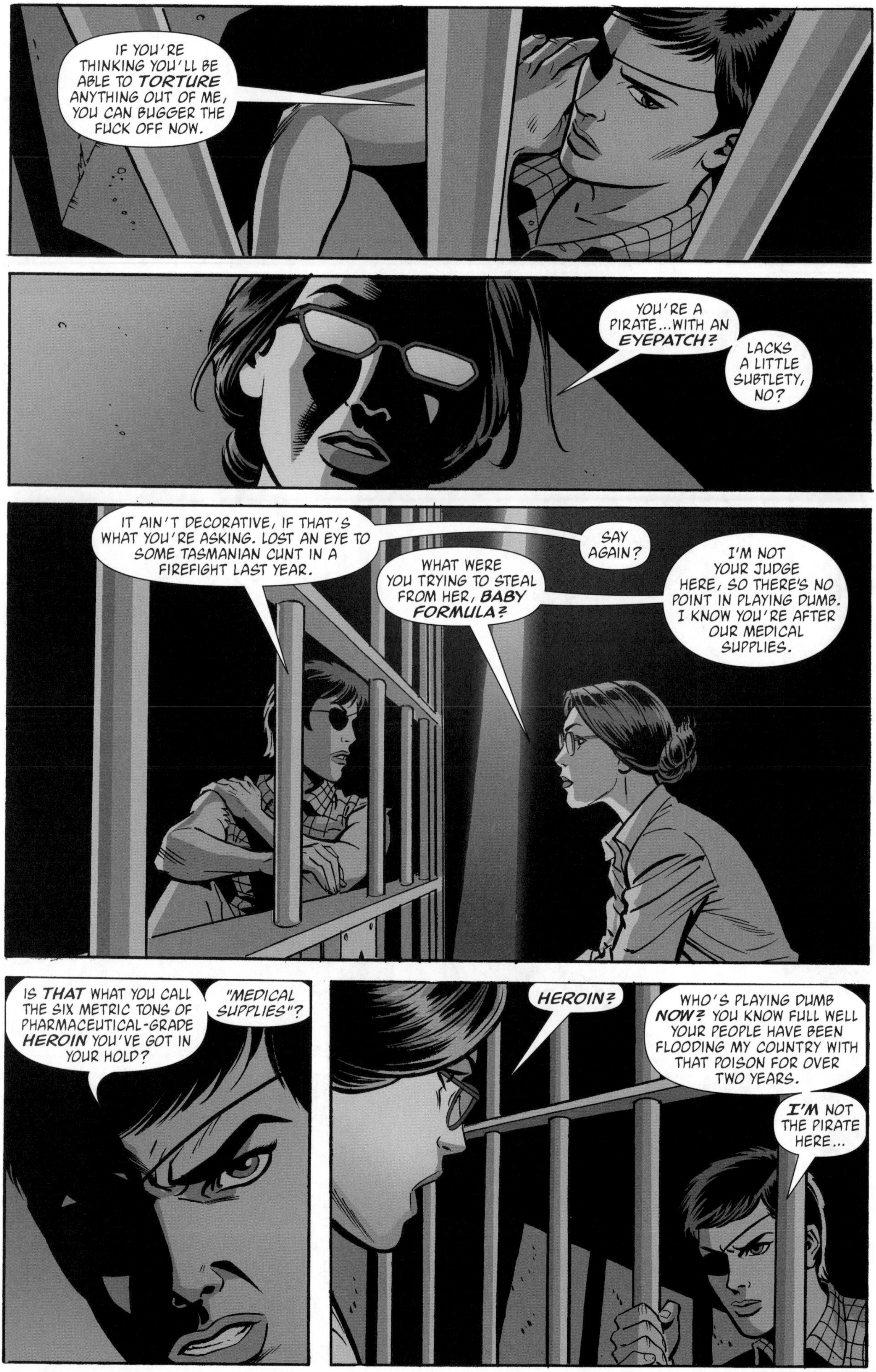

IF YOU'RE THINKING YOU'LL BE ABLE TO TORTURE ANYTHING OUT OF ME, YOU CAN BUGGER THE FUCK OFF NOW.
YOU'RE A PIRATE...WITH AN EYEPATCH?
LACKS A LITTLE SUBTLETY, NO?
IT AIN'T DECORATIVE, IF THAT'S WHAT YOU'RE ASKING. LOST AN EYE TO SOME TASMANIAN CUNT IN A FIREFIGHT LAST YEAR.
SAY AGAIN?
WHAT WERE YOU TRYING TO STEAL FROM HER, BABY FORMULA?
I'M NOT YOUR JUDGE HERE, SO THERE'S NO POINT IN PLAYING DUMB. I KNOW YOU'RE AFTER OUR MEDICAL SUPPLIES.
IS THAT WHAT YOU CALL THE SIX METRIC TONS OF PHARMACEUTICAL-GRADE HEROIN YOU'VE GOT IN YOUR HOLD?
"MEDICAL SUPPLIES"?
HEROIN?
WHO'S PLAYING DUMB NOW? YOU KNOW FULL WELL YOUR PEOPLE HAVE BEEN FLOODING MY COUNTRY WITH THAT POISON FOR OVER TWO YEARS.
I'M NOT THE PIRATE HERE...

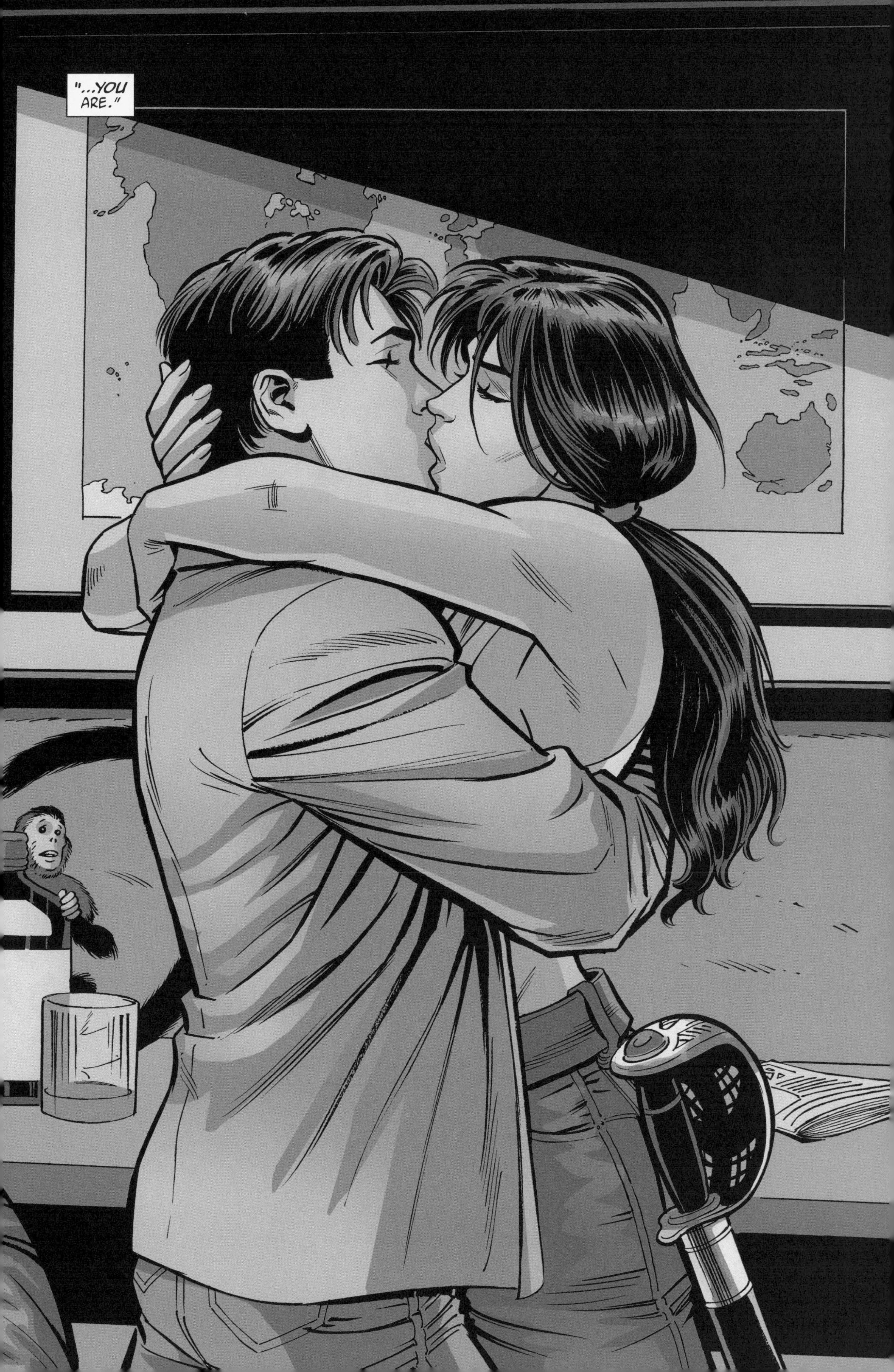
"...YOU ARE."

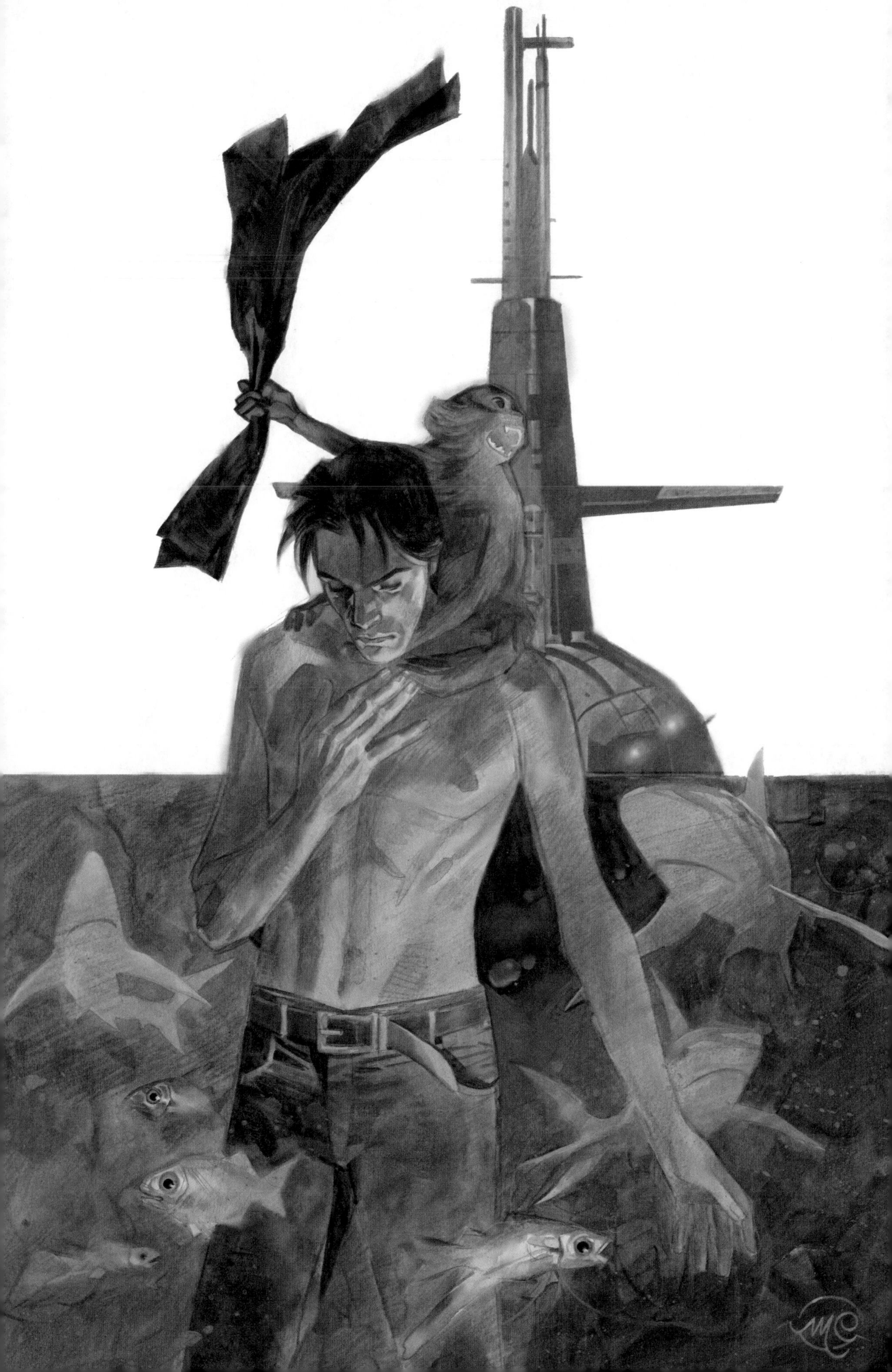

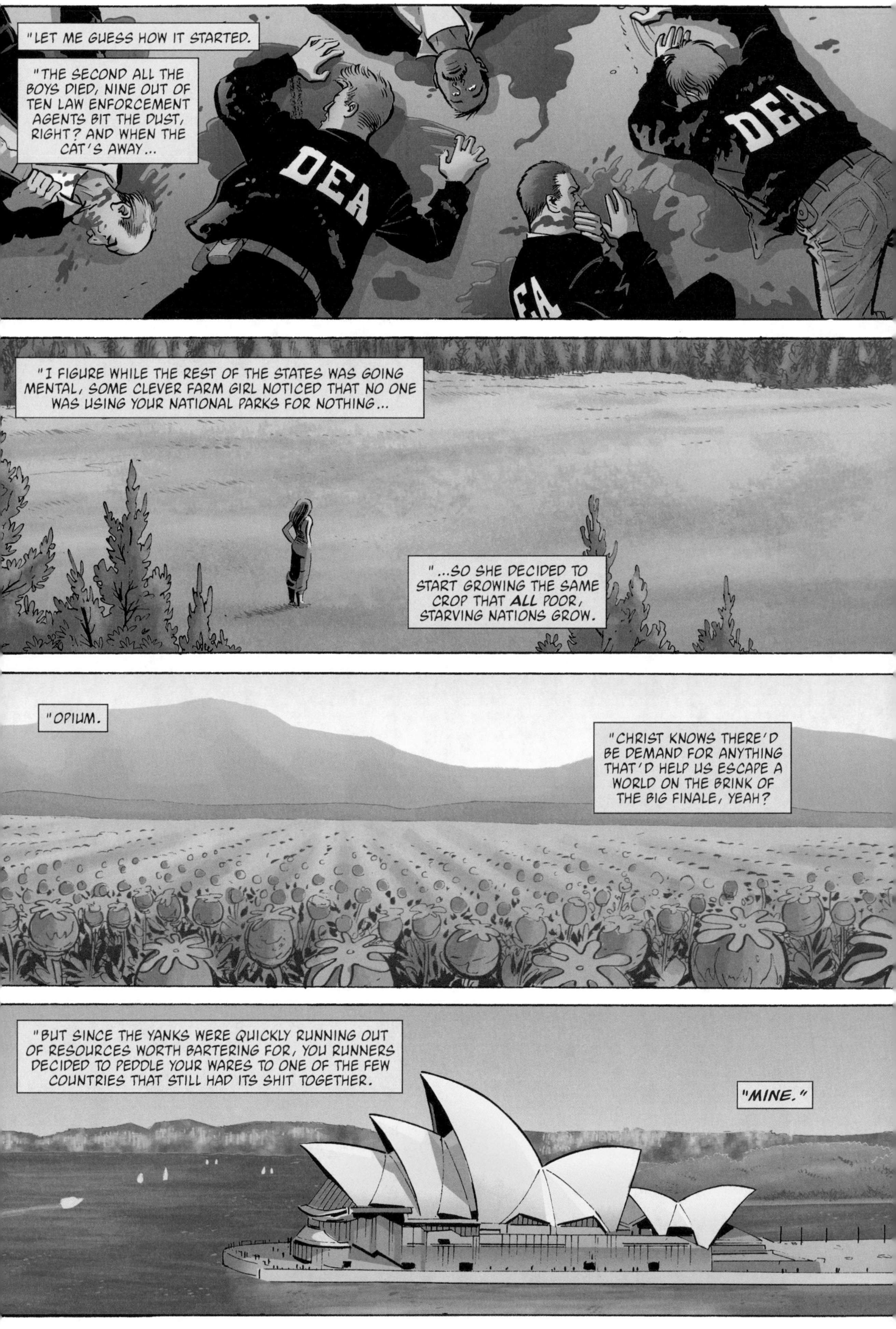
"LET ME GUESS HOW IT STARTED.
"THE SECOND ALL THE BOYS DIED, NINE OUT OF TEN LAW ENFORCEMENT AGENTS BIT THE DUST, RIGHT? AND WHEN THE CAT'S AWAY...
DEA
DEA
DEA
"I FIGURE WHILE THE REST OF THE STATES WAS GOING MENTAL, SOME CLEVER FARM GIRL NOTICED THAT NO ONE WAS USING YOUR NATIONAL PARKS FOR NOTHING...
"...SO SHE DECIDED TO START GROWING THE SAME CROP THAT ALL POOR, STARVING NATIONS GROW.
"OPIUM.
"CHRIST KNOWS THERE'D BE DEMAND FOR ANYTHING THAT'D HELP US ESCAPE A WORLD ON THE BRINK OF THE BIG FINALE, YEAH?
"BUT SINCE THE YANKS WERE QUICKLY RUNNING OUT OF RESOURCES WORTH BARTERING FOR, YOU RUNNERS DECIDED TO PEDDLE YOUR WARES TO ONE OF THE FEW COUNTRIES THAT STILL HAD ITS SHIT TOGETHER.
"MINE."

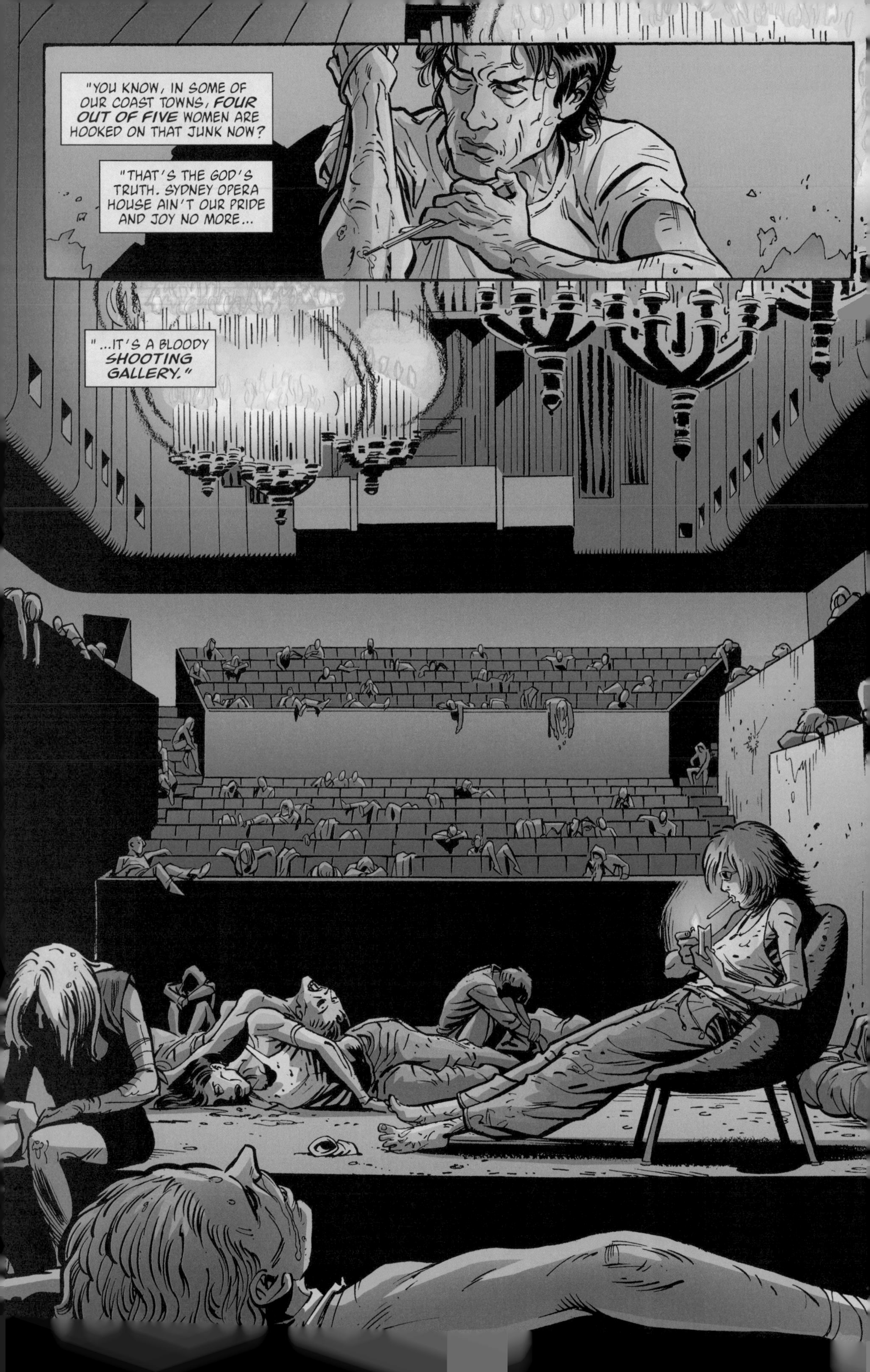
"YOU KNOW, IN SOME OF OUR COAST TOWNS, FOUR OUT OF FIVE WOMEN ARE HOOKED ON THAT JUNK NOW?
"THAT'S THE GOD'S TRUTH. SYDNEY OPERA HOUSE AIN'T OUR PRIDE AND JOY NO MORE...
"...IT'S A BLOODY SHOOTING GALLERY."

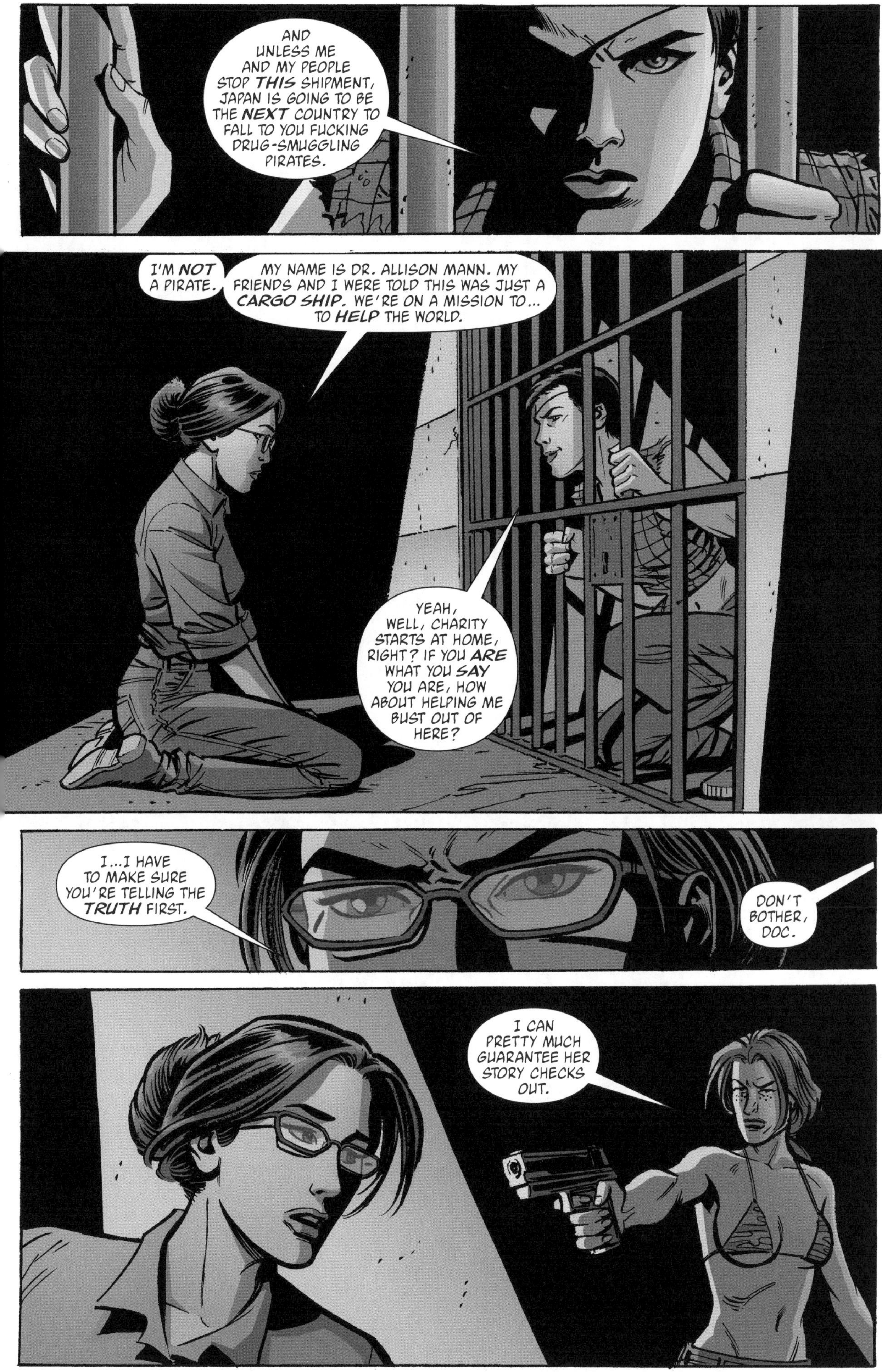
AND UNLESS ME AND MY PEOPLE STOP THIS SHIPMENT, JAPAN IS GOING TO BE THE NEXT COUNTRY TO FALL TO YOU FUCKING DRUG-SMUGGLING PIRATES.
I'M NOT A PIRATE.
MY NAME IS DR. ALLISON MANN. MY FRIENDS AND I WERE TOLD THIS WAS JUST A CARGO SHIP. WE'RE ON A MISSION TO... TO HELP THE WORLD.
YEAH, WELL, CHARITY STARTS AT HOME, RIGHT? IF YOU ARE WHAT YOU SAY YOU ARE, HOW ABOUT HELPING ME BUST OUT OF HERE?
I...I HAVE TO MAKE SURE YOU'RE TELLING THE TRUTH FIRST.
DON'T BOTHER, DOC.
I CAN PRETTY MUCH GUARANTEE HER STORY CHECKS OUT.

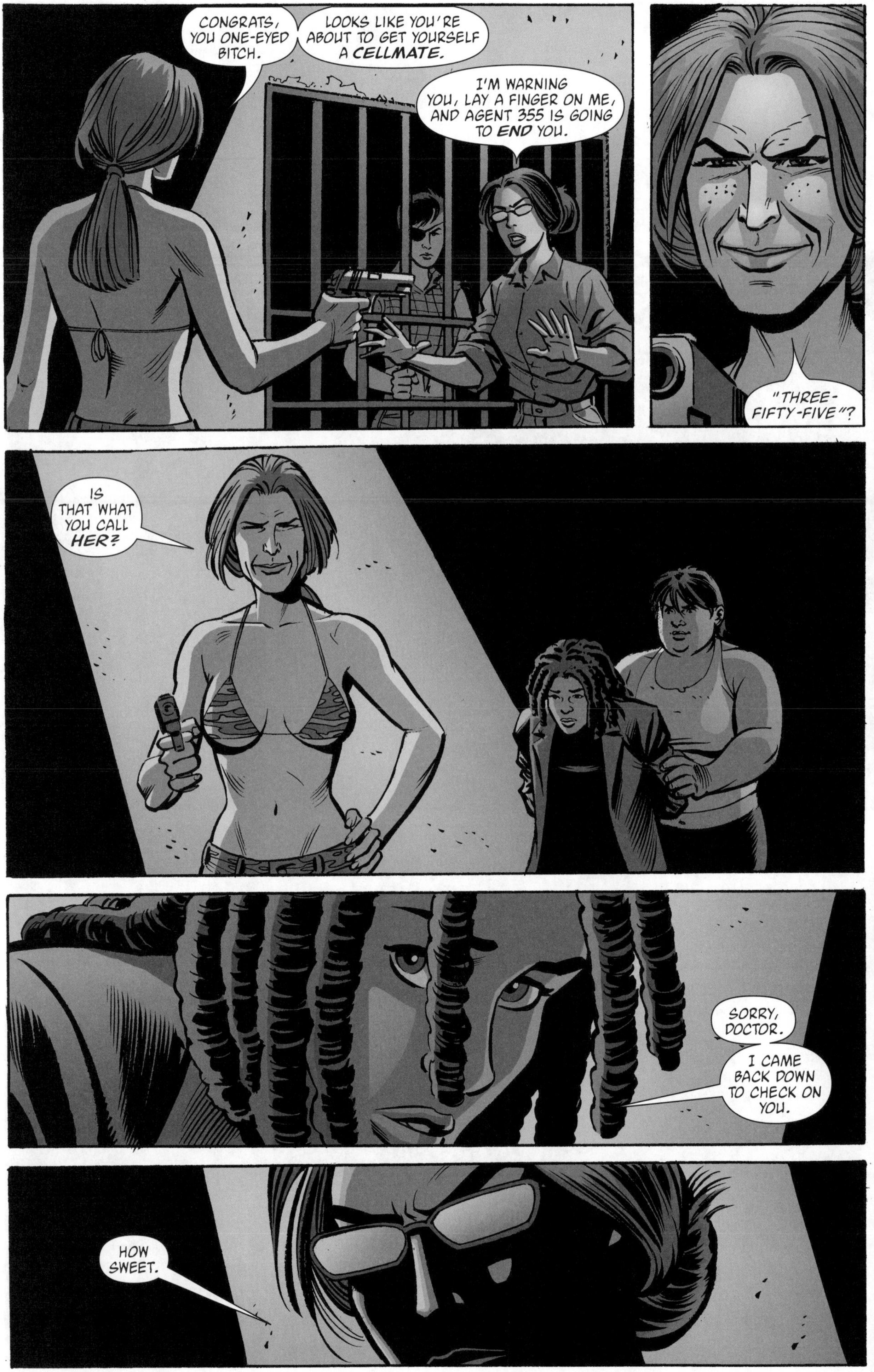
CONGRATS, YOU ONE-EYED BITCH.
LOOKS LIKE YOU'RE ABOUT TO GET YOURSELF A CELLMATE.
I'M WARNING YOU, LAY A FINGER ON ME, AND AGENT 355 IS GOING TO END YOU.
"THREE-FIFTY-FIVE"?
IS THAT WHAT YOU CALL HER?
SORRY, DOCTOR.
I CAME BACK DOWN TO CHECK ON YOU.
HOW SWEET.

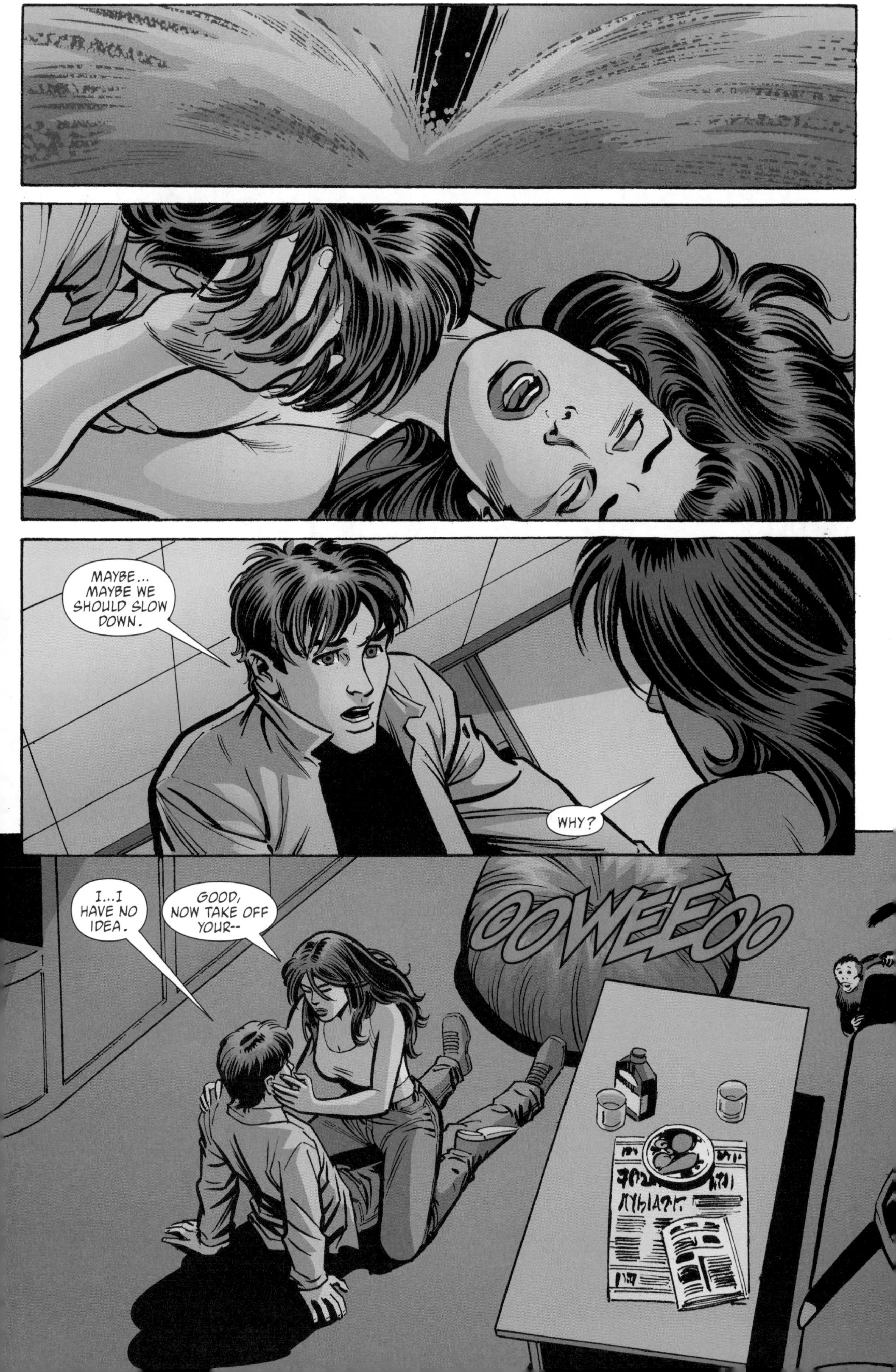
MAYBE... MAYBE WE SHOULD SLOW DOWN.
WHY?
I...I HAVE NO IDEA.
GOOD, NOW TAKE OFF YOUR--
OOWEEOO

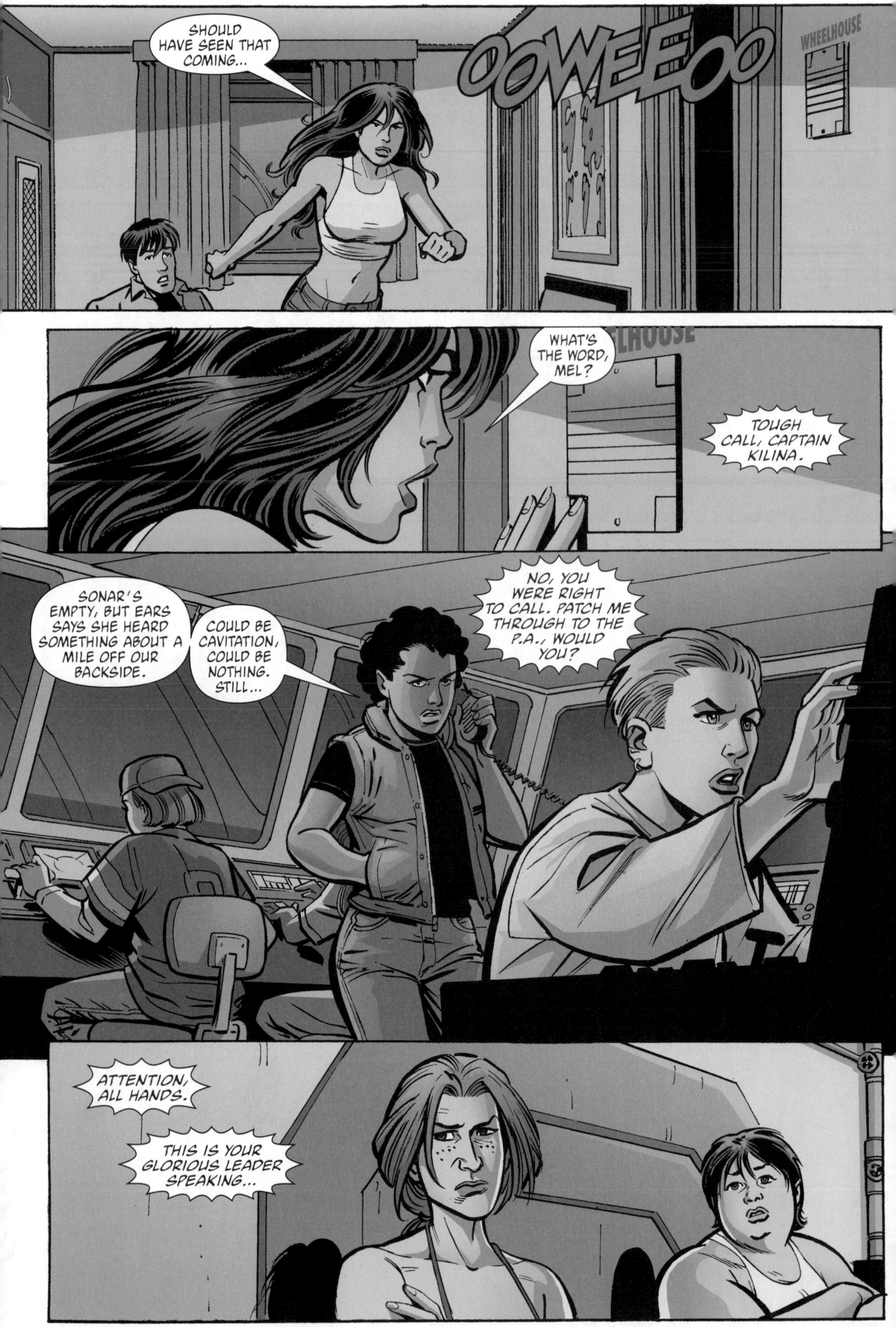
SHOULD HAVE SEEN THAT COMING...
OOWEEOO
WHEELHOUSE
WHAT'S THE WORD, MEL?
TOUGH CALL, CAPTAIN KILINA.
SONAR'S EMPTY, BUT EARS SAYS SHE HEARD SOMETHING ABOUT A MILE OFF OUR BACKSIDE.
COULD BE CAVITATION, COULD BE NOTHING. STILL...
NO, YOU WERE RIGHT TO CALL. PATCH ME THROUGH TO THE P.A., WOULD YOU?
ATTENTION, ALL HANDS.
THIS IS YOUR GLORIOUS LEADER SPEAKING...

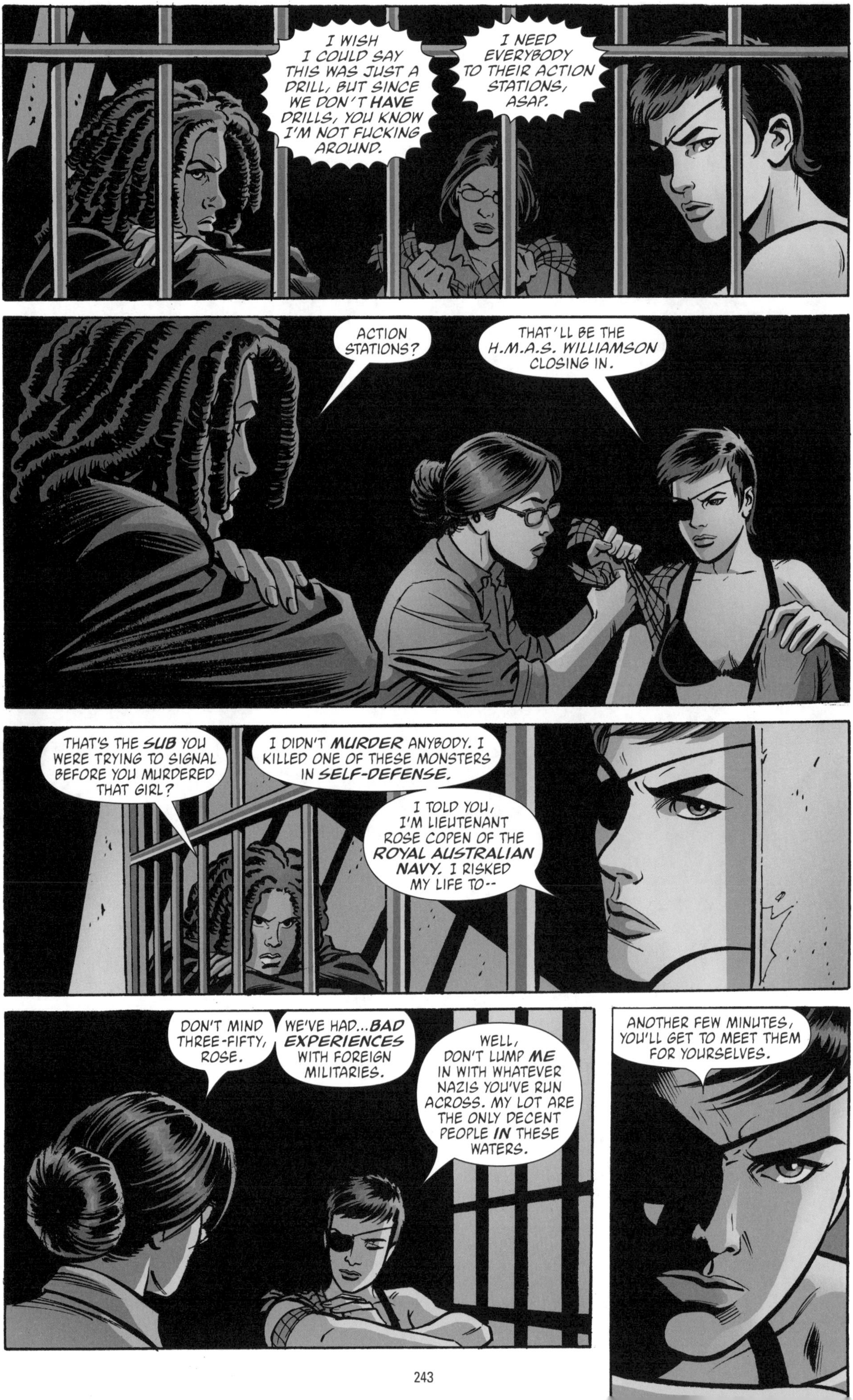
I WISH I COULD SAY THIS WAS JUST A DRILL, BUT SINCE WE DON'T HAVE DRILLS, YOU KNOW I'M NOT FUCKING AROUND.
I NEED EVERYBODY TO THEIR ACTION STATIONS, ASAP.
ACTION STATIONS?
THAT'LL BE THE H.M.A.S. WILLIAMSON CLOSING IN.
THAT'S THE SUB YOU WERE TRYING TO SIGNAL BEFORE YOU MURDERED THAT GIRL?
I DIDN'T MURDER ANYBODY. I KILLED ONE OF THESE MONSTERS IN SELF-DEFENSE.
I TOLD YOU, I'M LIEUTENANT ROSE COPEN OF THE ROYAL AUSTRALIAN NAVY. I RISKED MY LIFE TO--
DON'T MIND THREE-FIFTY, ROSE.
WE'VE HAD...BAD EXPERIENCES WITH FOREIGN MILITARIES.
WELL, DON'T LUMP ME IN WITH WHATEVER NAZIS YOU'VE RUN ACROSS. MY LOT ARE THE ONLY DECENT PEOPLE IN THESE WATERS.
ANOTHER FEW MINUTES, YOU'LL GET TO MEET THEM FOR YOURSELVES.

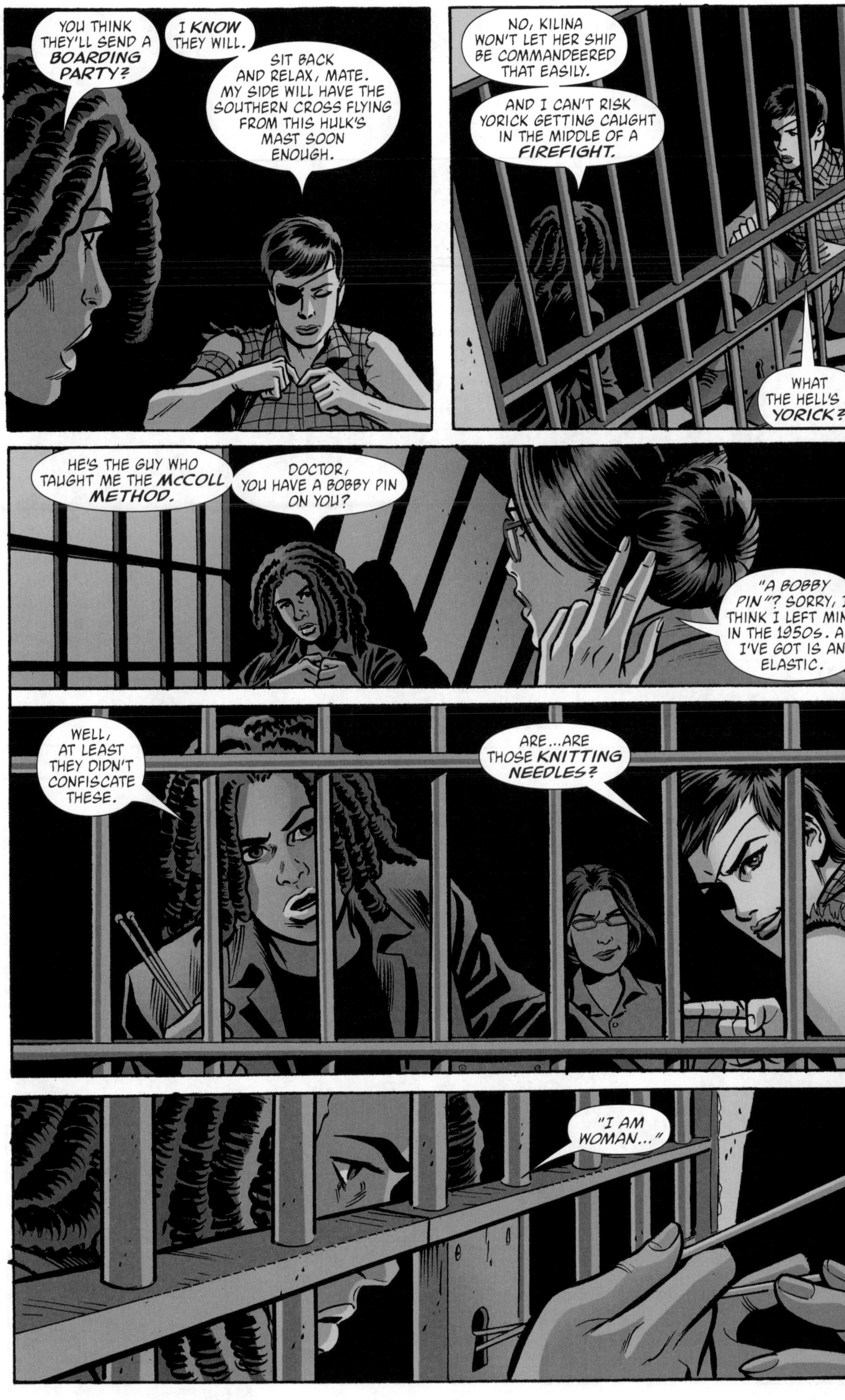
YOU THINK THEY'LL SEND A BOARDING PARTY?
I KNOW THEY WILL.
SIT BACK AND RELAX, MATE. MY SIDE WILL HAVE THE SOUTHERN CROSS FLYING FROM THIS HULK'S MAST SOON ENOUGH.
NO, KILINA WON'T LET HER SHIP BE COMMANDEERED THAT EASILY.
AND I CAN'T RISK YORICK GETTING CAUGHT IN THE MIDDLE OF A FIREFIGHT.
WHAT THE HELL'S A YORICK?
HE'S THE GUY WHO TAUGHT ME THE McCOLL METHOD.
DOCTOR, YOU HAVE A BOBBY PIN ON YOU?
"A BOBBY PIN"? SORRY, I THINK I LEFT MINE IN THE 1950s. ALL I'VE GOT IS AN ELASTIC.
WELL, AT LEAST THEY DIDN'T CONFISCATE THESE.
ARE...ARE THOSE KNITTING NEEDLES?
"I AM WOMAN..."

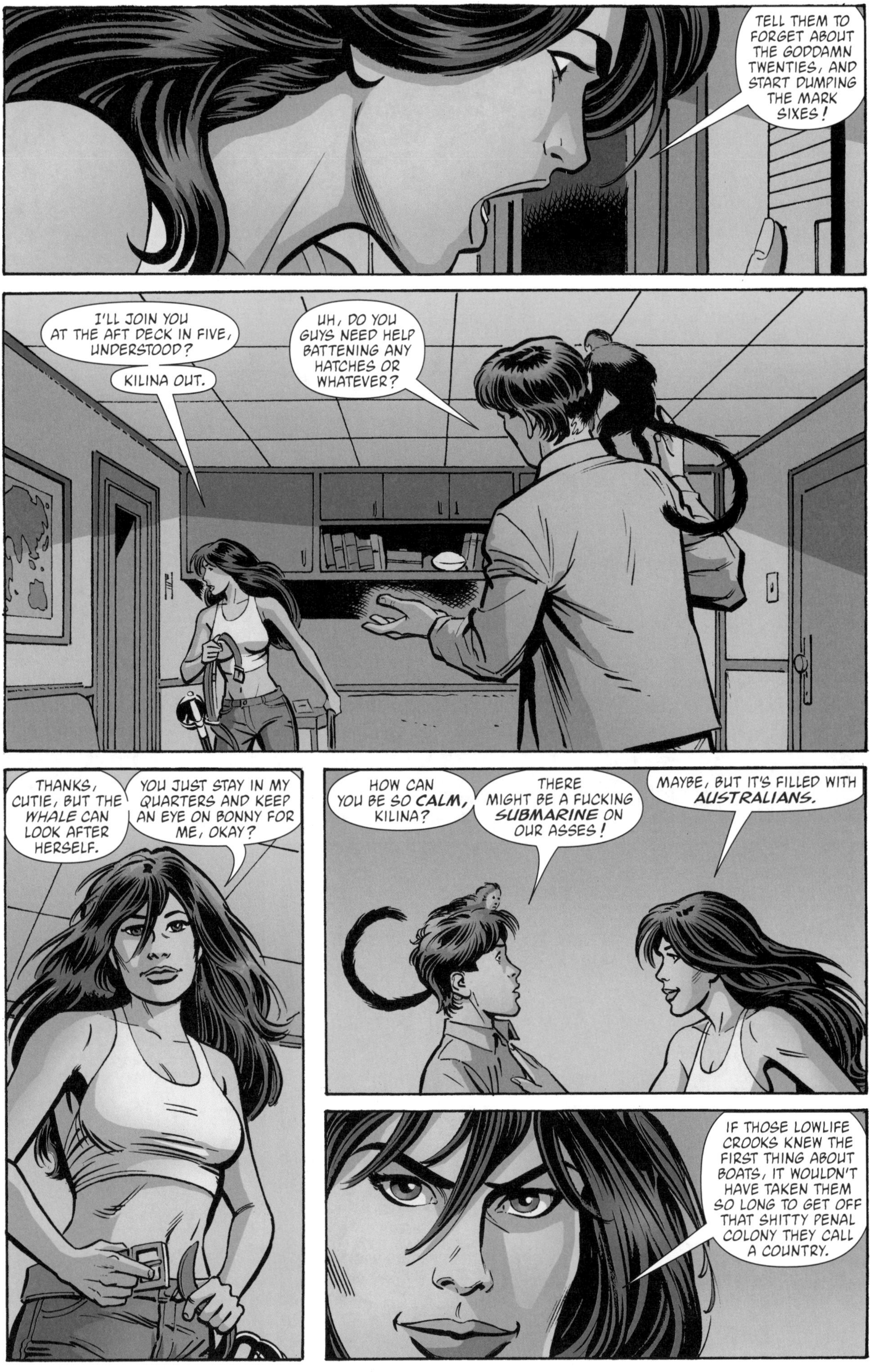
TELL THEM TO FORGET ABOUT THE GODDAMN TWENTIES, AND START DUMPING THE MARK SIXES!
I'LL JOIN YOU AT THE AFT DECK IN FIVE, UNDERSTOOD?
KILINA OUT.
UH, DO YOU GUYS NEED HELP BATTENING ANY HATCHES OR WHATEVER?
THANKS, CUTIE, BUT THE WHALE CAN LOOK AFTER HERSELF.
YOU JUST STAY IN MY QUARTERS AND KEEP AN EYE ON BONNY FOR ME, OKAY?
HOW CAN YOU BE SO CALM, KILINA?
THERE MIGHT BE A FUCKING SUBMARINE ON OUR ASSES!
MAYBE, BUT IT'S FILLED WITH AUSTRALIANS.
IF THOSE LOWLIFE CROOKS KNEW THE FIRST THING ABOUT BOATS, IT WOULDN'T HAVE TAKEN THEM SO LONG TO GET OFF THAT SHITTY PENAL COLONY THEY CALL A COUNTRY.

GO-TEAM IS PREPPED FOR STORMY WEATHER, CAPTAIN BELLEVILLE.

FINE, WE'LL RISE JUST SHY OF SURFACE, AND LET YOU GIRLS OUT INTO THE DRINK.

IF THE COAST IS CLEAR, YOU CAN INFLATE YOUR RAFT, DOCK WITH THE CRUISE SHIP, AND SCALE ITS HULL. REMEMBER, FIRST PRIORITY IS TAKING CONTROL OF THEIR BRIDGE, AND--

MA'AM!

THERE'S...THERE'S SOMETHING IN THE WATER. LOOKS LIKE A COUPLE OF CONTAINERS, THROWN OFF OUR TARGET'S STERN.

MAYBE THEY'RE DUMPING THEIR HEROIN SUPPLY BEFORE WE CAN BOARD...?

NO, THOSE ARE SINKING TOO FAST TO BE ORDINARY FREIGHT. THEY LOOK MORE LIKE...

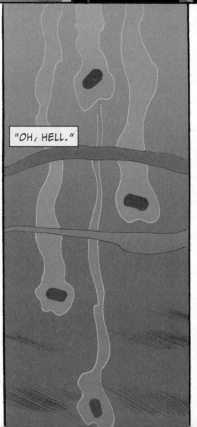

"OH, HELL."

SPLASHES! SPLA--

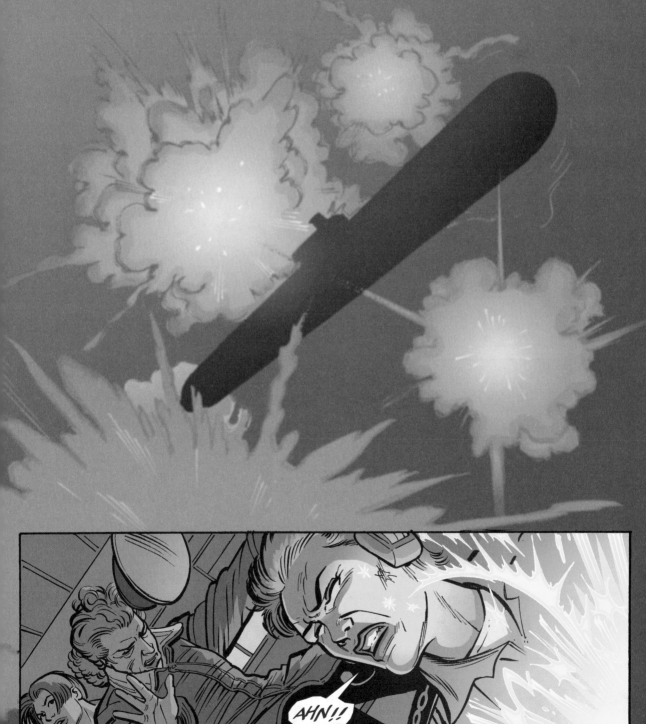

AHN!!

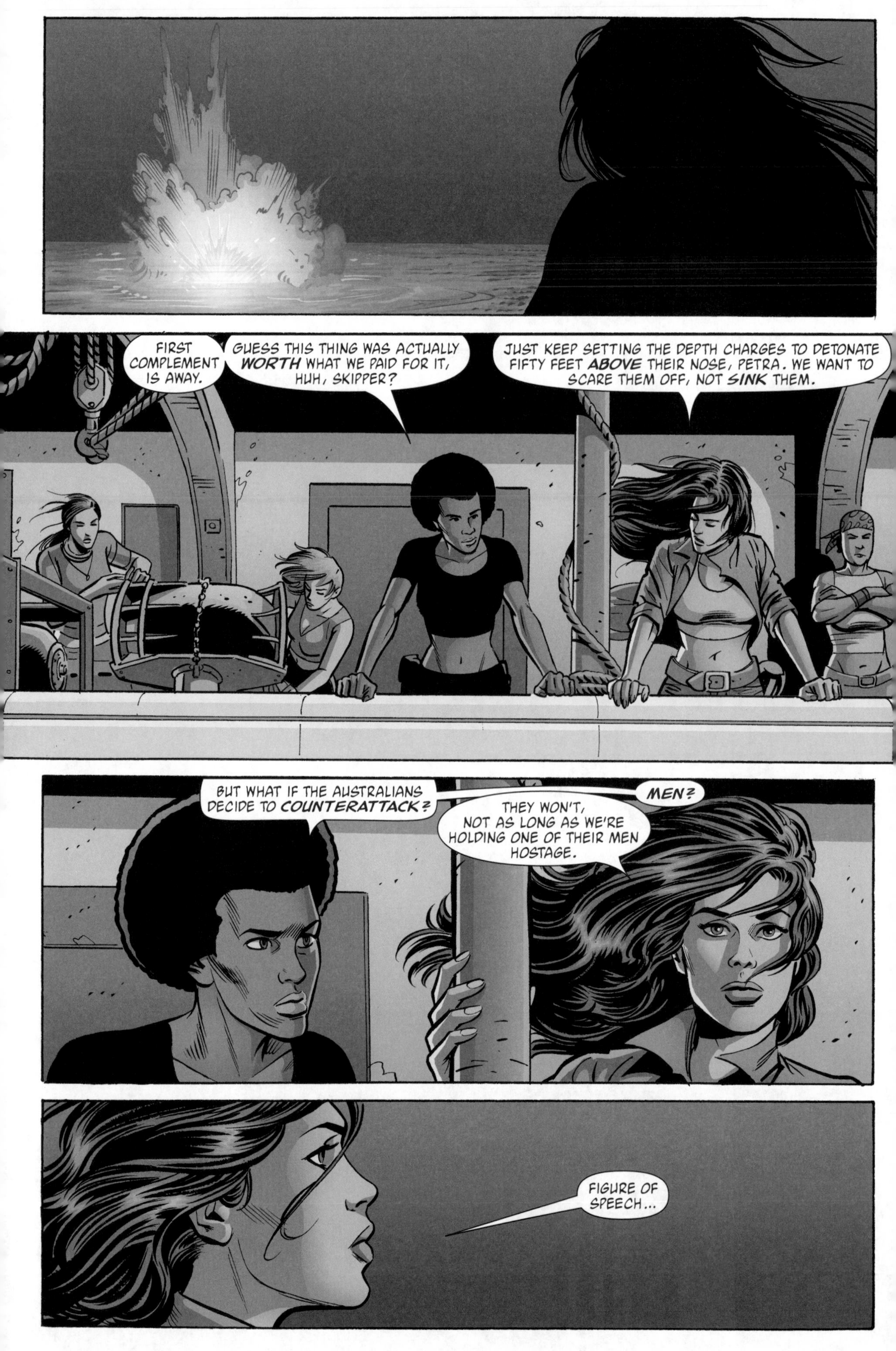
FIRST COMPLEMENT IS AWAY.
GUESS THIS THING WAS ACTUALLY WORTH WHAT WE PAID FOR IT, HUH, SKIPPER?
JUST KEEP SETTING THE DEPTH CHARGES TO DETONATE FIFTY FEET ABOVE THEIR NOSE, PETRA. WE WANT TO SCARE THEM OFF, NOT SINK THEM.
BUT WHAT IF THE AUSTRALIANS DECIDE TO COUNTERATTACK?
THEY WON'T, NOT AS LONG AS WE'RE HOLDING ONE OF THEIR MEN HOSTAGE.
MEN?
FIGURE OF SPEECH...

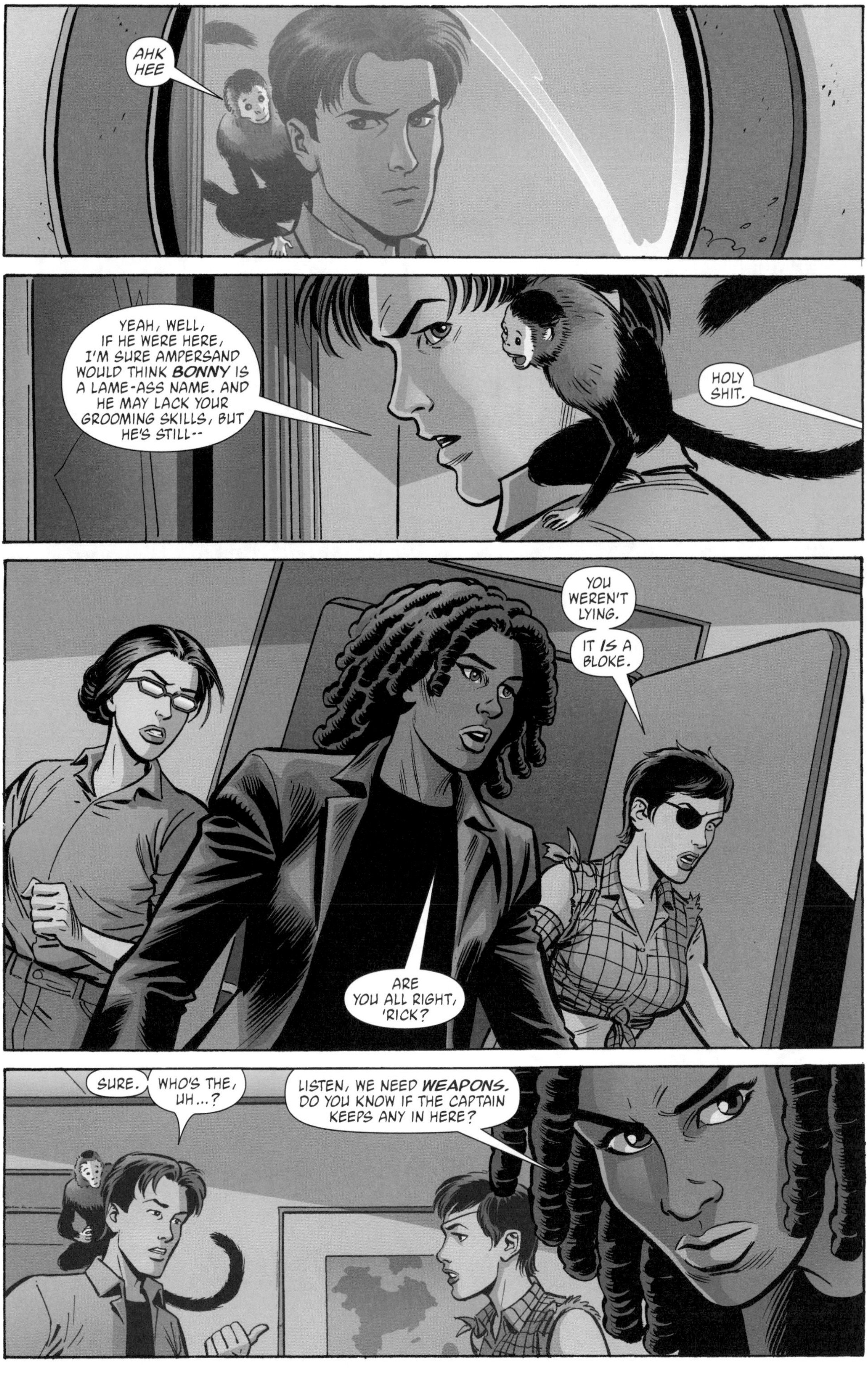
AHK HEE
YEAH, WELL, IF HE WERE HERE, I'M SURE AMPERSAND WOULD THINK BONNY IS A LAME-ASS NAME. AND HE MAY LACK YOUR GROOMING SKILLS, BUT HE'S STILL--
HOLY SHIT.
YOU WEREN'T LYING.
IT IS A BLOKE.
ARE YOU ALL RIGHT, 'RICK?
SURE.
WHO'S THE, UH...?
LISTEN, WE NEED WEAPONS. DO YOU KNOW IF THE CAPTAIN KEEPS ANY IN HERE?

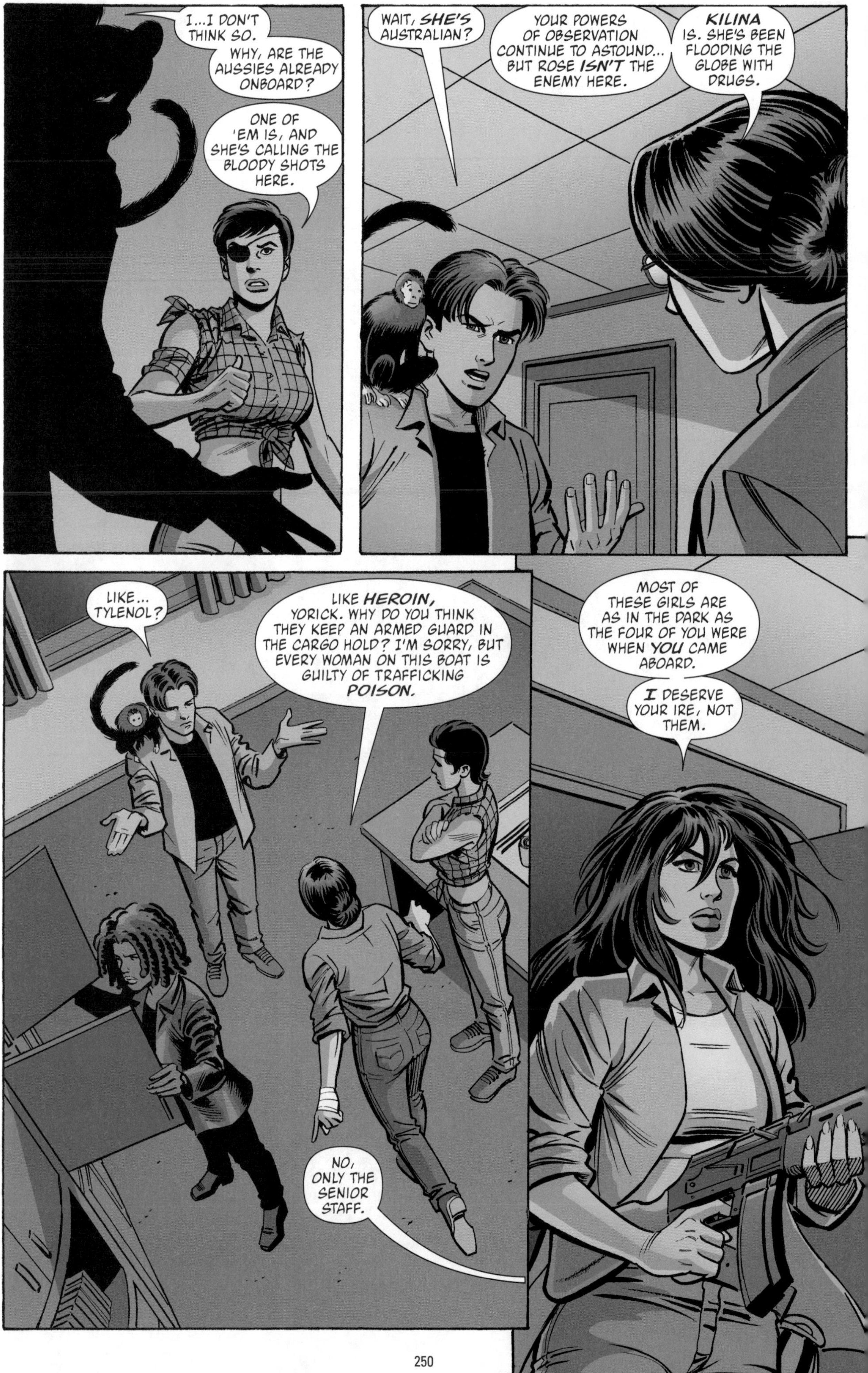
I...I DON'T THINK SO.
WHY, ARE THE AUSSIES ALREADY ONBOARD?
ONE OF 'EM IS, AND SHE'S CALLING THE BLOODY SHOTS HERE.
WAIT, SHE'S AUSTRALIAN?
YOUR POWERS OF OBSERVATION CONTINUE TO ASTOUND... BUT ROSE ISN'T THE ENEMY HERE.
KILINA IS. SHE'S BEEN FLOODING THE GLOBE WITH DRUGS.
LIKE... TYLENOL?
LIKE HEROIN, YORICK. WHY DO YOU THINK THEY KEEP AN ARMED GUARD IN THE CARGO HOLD? I'M SORRY, BUT EVERY WOMAN ON THIS BOAT IS GUILTY OF TRAFFICKING POISON.
NO, ONLY THE SENIOR STAFF.
MOST OF THESE GIRLS ARE AS IN THE DARK AS THE FOUR OF YOU WERE WHEN YOU CAME ABOARD.
I DESERVE YOUR IRE, NOT THEM.

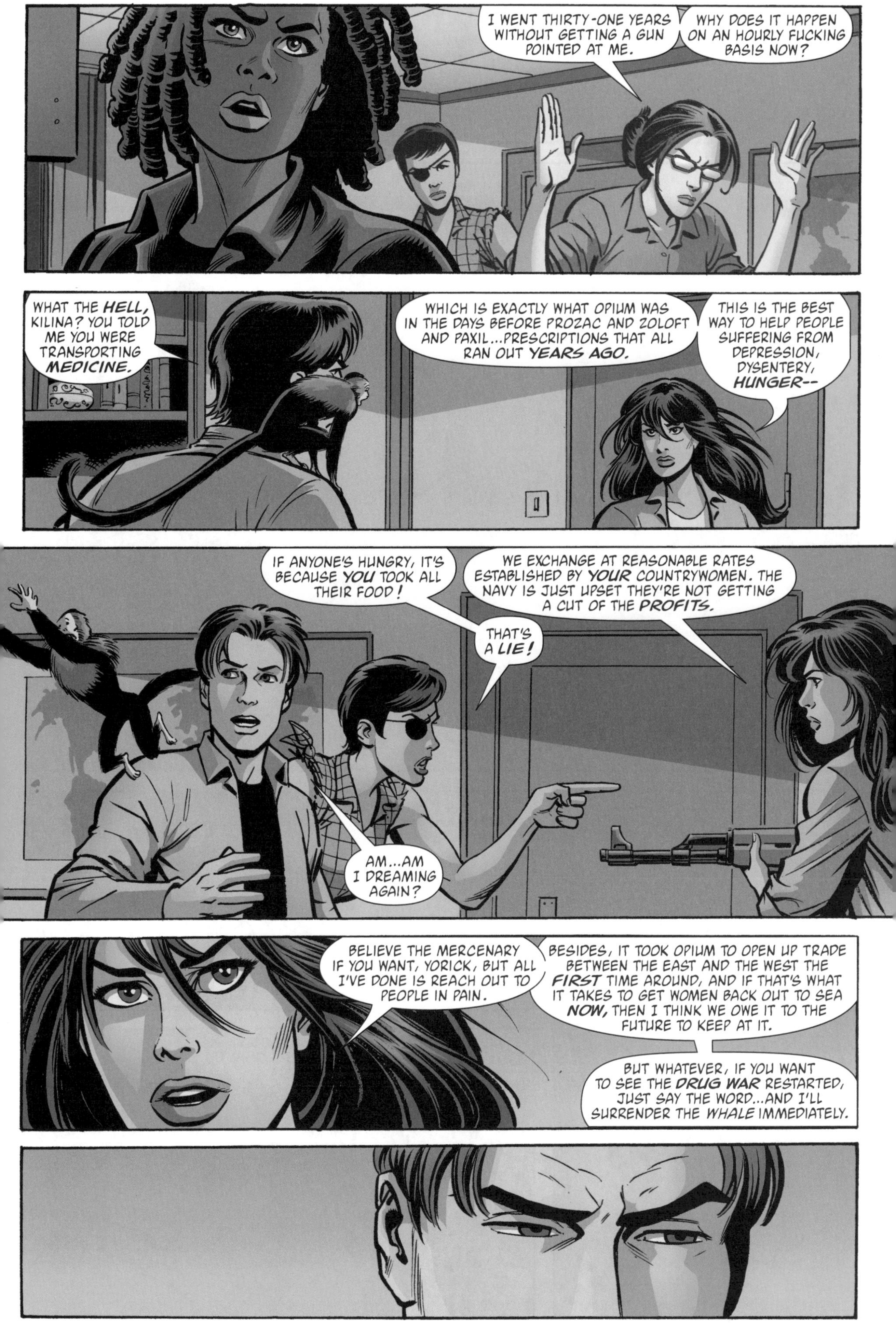
I WENT THIRTY-ONE YEARS WITHOUT GETTING A GUN POINTED AT ME.
WHY DOES IT HAPPEN ON AN HOURLY FUCKING BASIS NOW?
WHAT THE HELL, KILINA? YOU TOLD ME YOU WERE TRANSPORTING MEDICINE.
WHICH IS EXACTLY WHAT OPIUM WAS IN THE DAYS BEFORE PROZAC AND ZOLOFT AND PAXIL...PRESCRIPTIONS THAT ALL RAN OUT YEARS AGO.
THIS IS THE BEST WAY TO HELP PEOPLE SUFFERING FROM DEPRESSION, DYSENTERY, HUNGER--
IF ANYONE'S HUNGRY, IT'S BECAUSE YOU TOOK ALL THEIR FOOD!
WE EXCHANGE AT REASONABLE RATES ESTABLISHED BY YOUR COUNTRYWOMEN. THE NAVY IS JUST UPSET THEY'RE NOT GETTING A CUT OF THE PROFITS.
THAT'S A LIE!
AM...AM I DREAMING AGAIN?
BELIEVE THE MERCENARY IF YOU WANT, YORICK, BUT ALL I'VE DONE IS REACH OUT TO PEOPLE IN PAIN.
BESIDES, IT TOOK OPIUM TO OPEN UP TRADE BETWEEN THE EAST AND THE WEST THE FIRST TIME AROUND, AND IF THAT'S WHAT IT TAKES TO GET WOMEN BACK OUT TO SEA NOW, THEN I THINK WE OWE IT TO THE FUTURE TO KEEP AT IT.
BUT WHATEVER, IF YOU WANT TO SEE THE DRUG WAR RESTARTED, JUST SAY THE WORD...AND I'LL SURRENDER THE WHALE IMMEDIATELY.

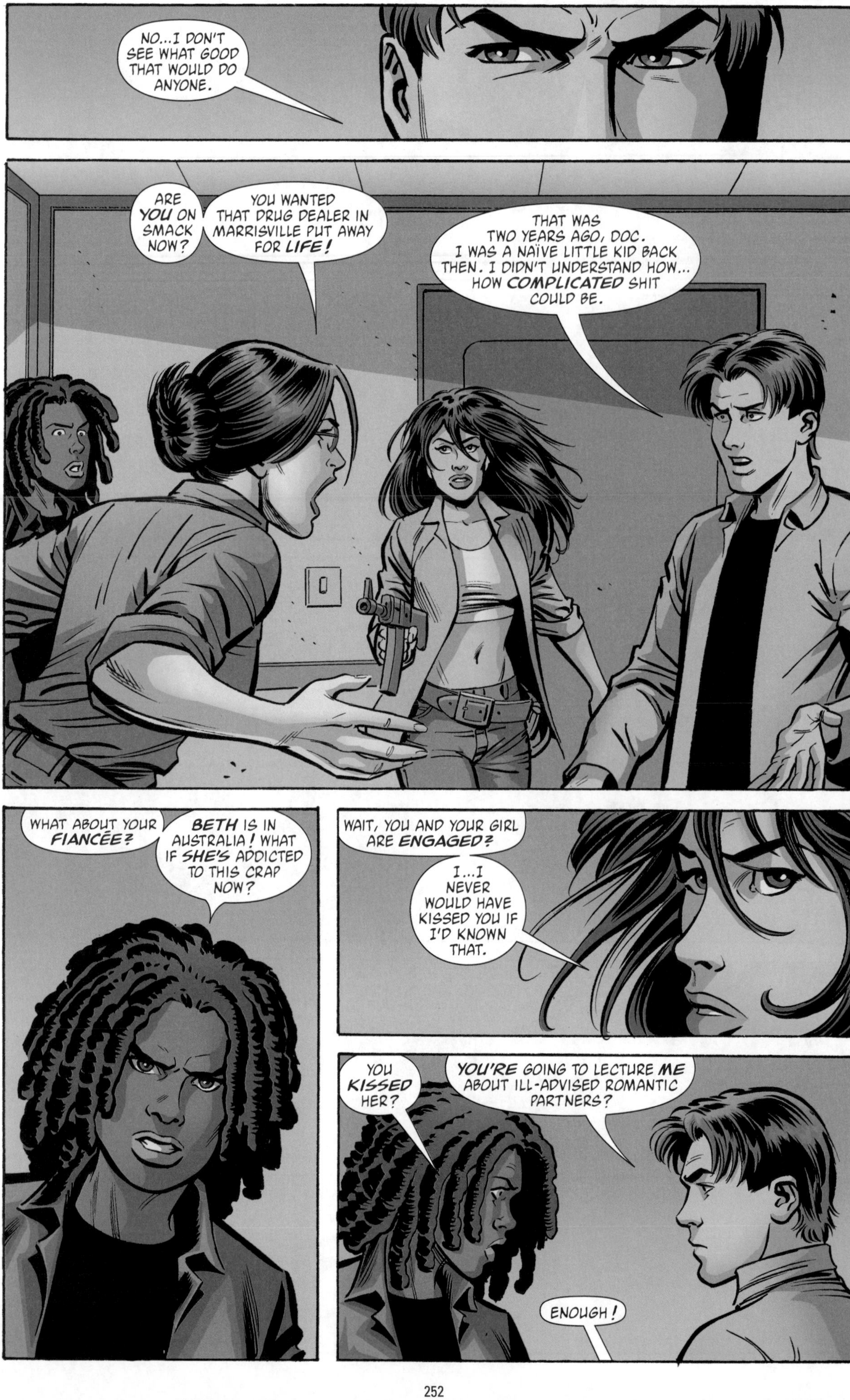
NO...I DON'T SEE WHAT GOOD THAT WOULD DO ANYONE.
ARE YOU ON SMACK NOW?
YOU WANTED THAT DRUG DEALER IN MARRISVILLE PUT AWAY FOR LIFE!
THAT WAS TWO YEARS AGO, DOC. I WAS A NAÏVE LITTLE KID BACK THEN. I DIDN'T UNDERSTAND HOW... HOW COMPLICATED SHIT COULD BE.
WHAT ABOUT YOUR FIANCÉE?
BETH IS IN AUSTRALIA! WHAT IF SHE'S ADDICTED TO THIS CRAP NOW?
WAIT, YOU AND YOUR GIRL ARE ENGAGED?
I...I NEVER WOULD HAVE KISSED YOU IF I'D KNOWN THAT.
YOU KISSED HER?
YOU'RE GOING TO LECTURE ME ABOUT ILL-ADVISED ROMANTIC PARTNERS?
ENOUGH!

YOU CAN SETTLE YOUR DOMESTIC DISPUTE AFTER WE DROP OFF OUR SHIPMENT IN *YOKOGATA*.

RIGHT NOW, I NEED THE LADIES BACK IN THE BRIG...FOR THEIR OWN SAFETY, OF COURSE.

ABSOLUTELY NOT.

YORICK, THE CYCLOPS OVER THERE *OFFED* A MEMBER OF MY CREW.

YOU'RE LUCKY I DON'T MAKE HER WALK THE *GANGPLANK* FOR--

KROOM

UHN!

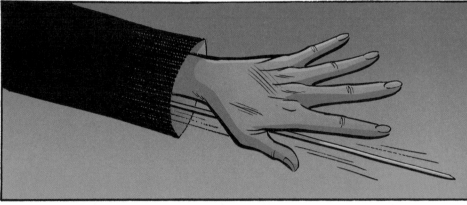

253

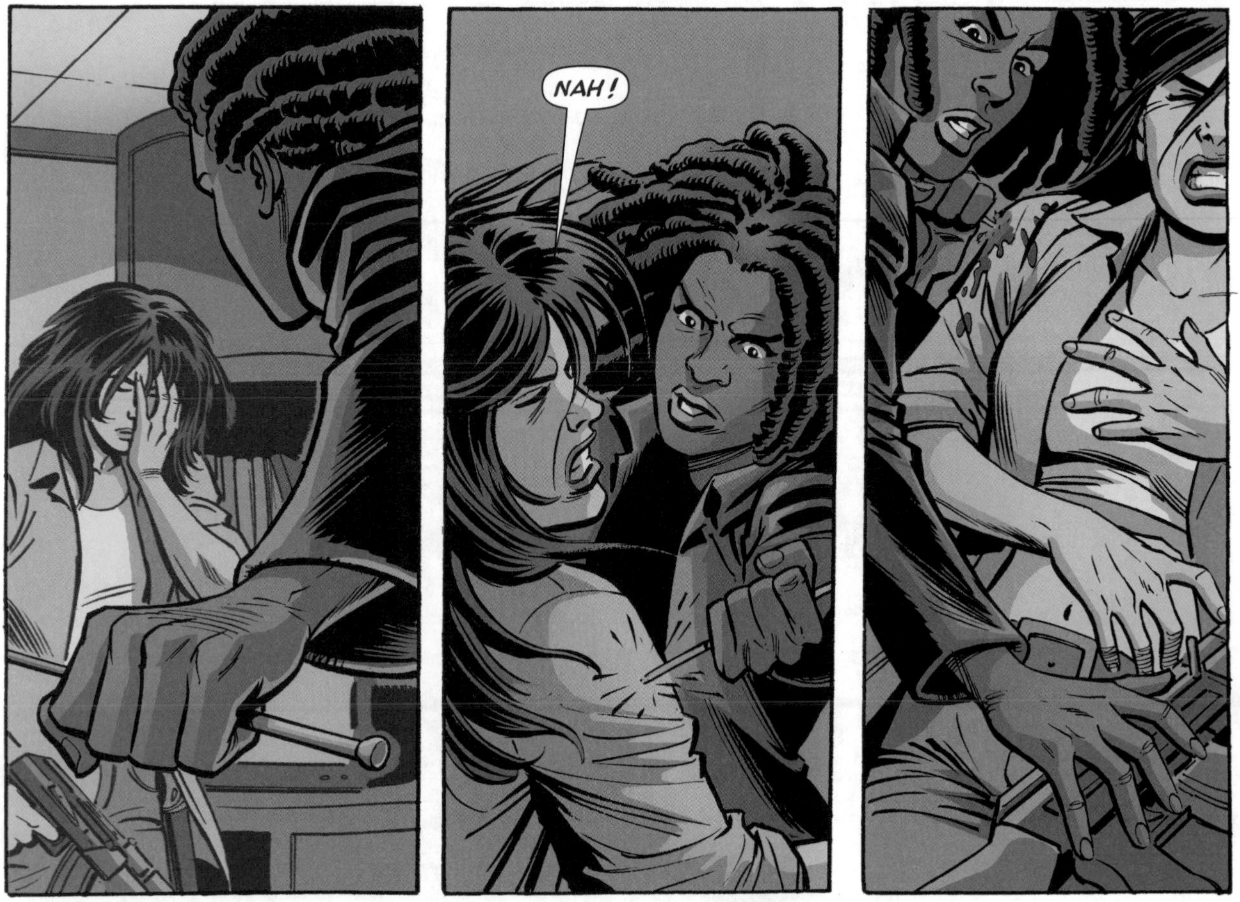
NAH!

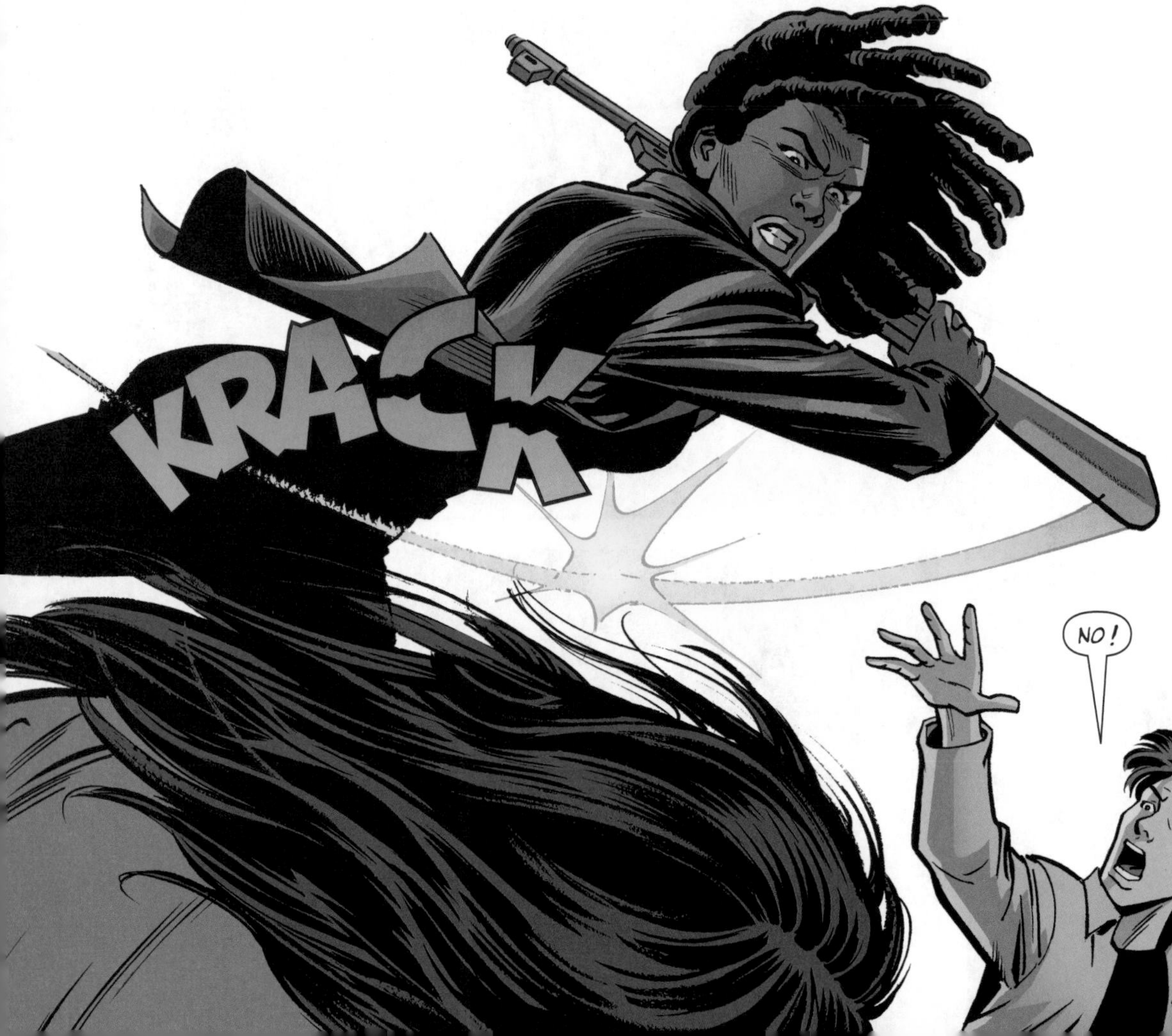
KRACK
NO!

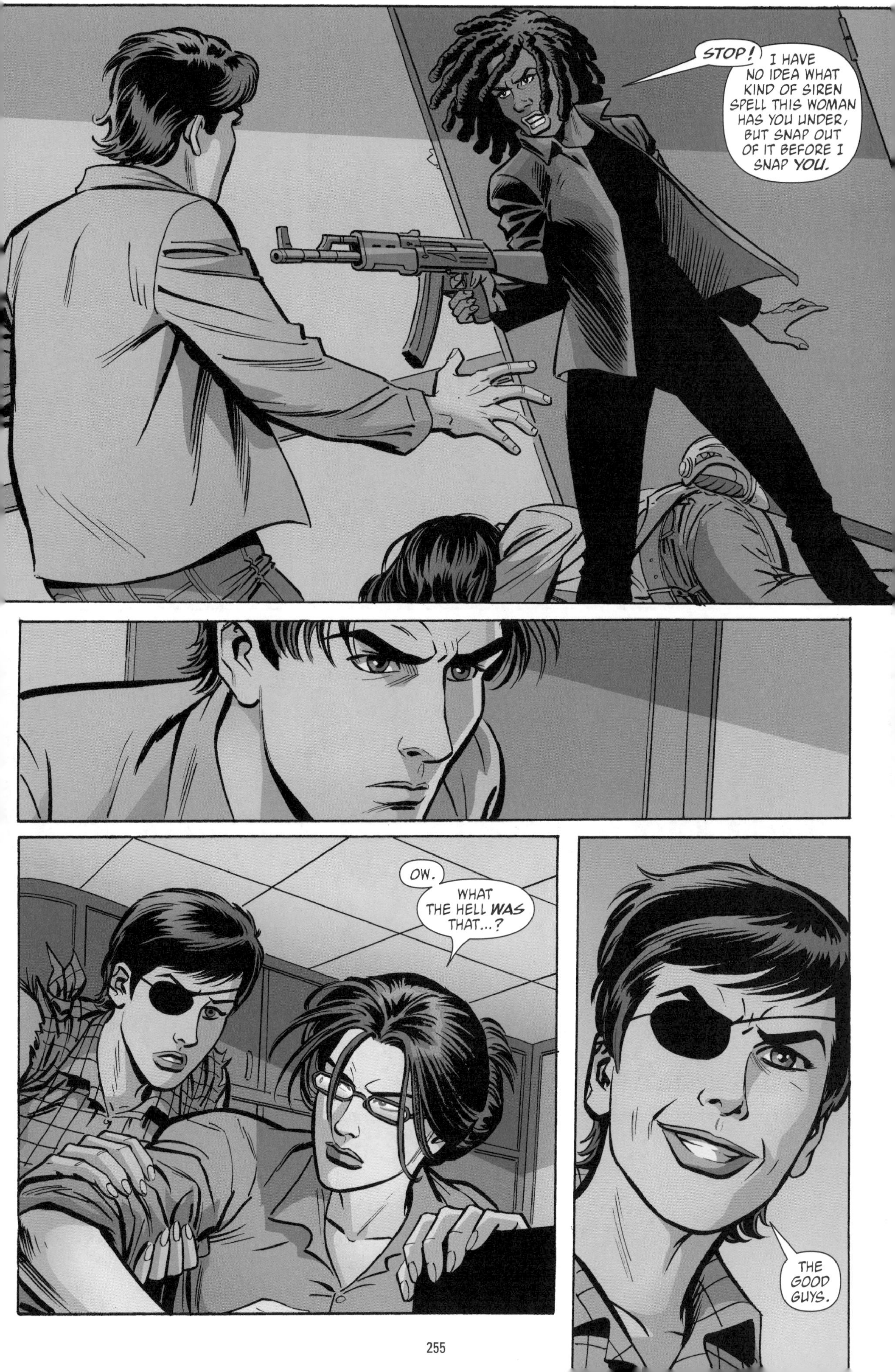
STOP! I HAVE NO IDEA WHAT KIND OF SIREN SPELL THIS WOMAN HAS YOU UNDER, BUT SNAP OUT OF IT BEFORE I SNAP YOU.
OW.
WHAT THE HELL WAS THAT...?
THE GOOD GUYS.

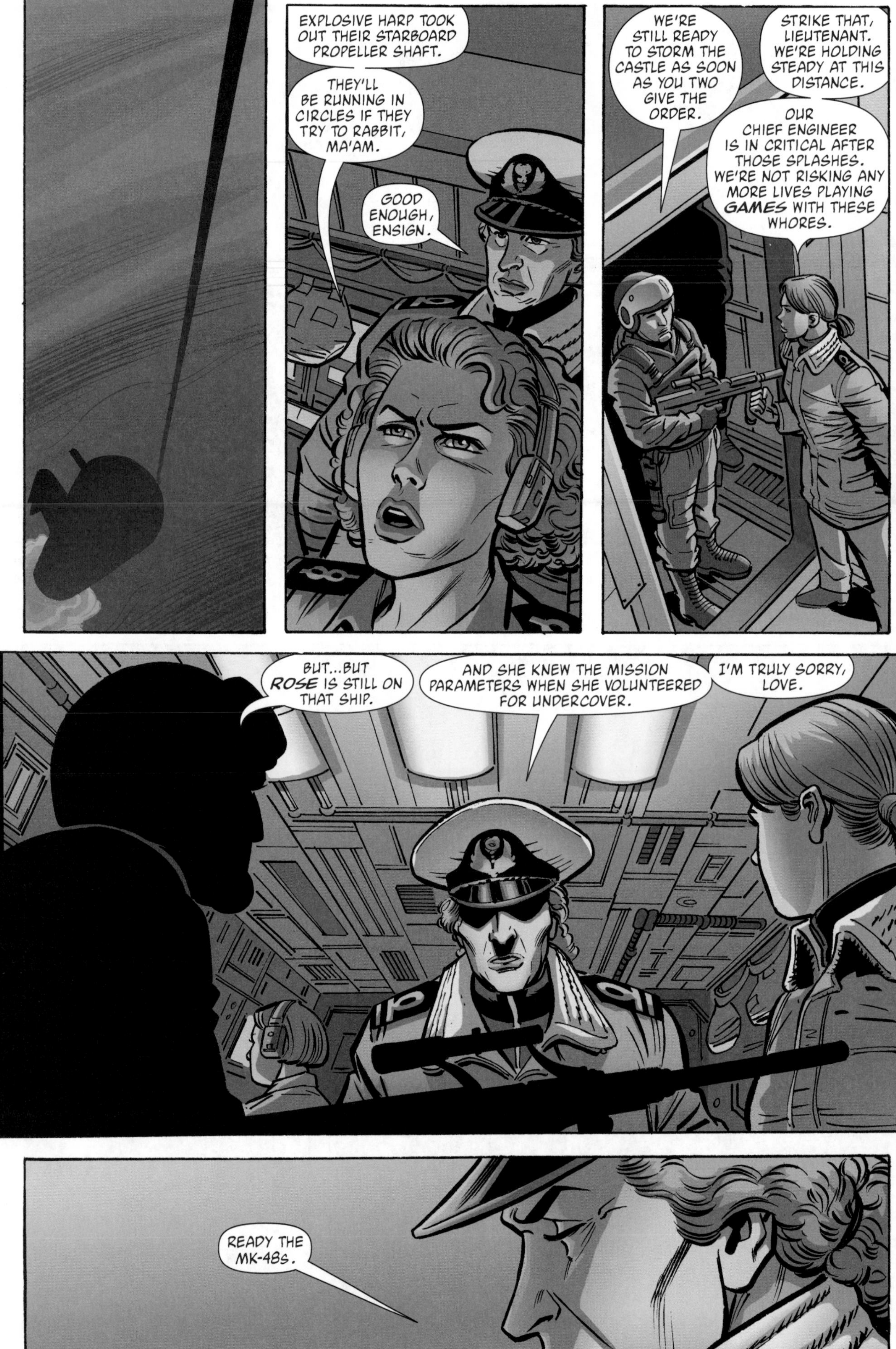
EXPLOSIVE HARP TOOK OUT THEIR STARBOARD PROPELLER SHAFT.
THEY'LL BE RUNNING IN CIRCLES IF THEY TRY TO RABBIT, MA'AM.
GOOD ENOUGH, ENSIGN.
WE'RE STILL READY TO STORM THE CASTLE AS SOON AS YOU TWO GIVE THE ORDER.
STRIKE THAT, LIEUTENANT. WE'RE HOLDING STEADY AT THIS DISTANCE.
OUR CHIEF ENGINEER IS IN CRITICAL AFTER THOSE SPLASHES. WE'RE NOT RISKING ANY MORE LIVES PLAYING GAMES WITH THESE WHORES.
BUT...BUT ROSE IS STILL ON THAT SHIP.
AND SHE KNEW THE MISSION PARAMETERS WHEN SHE VOLUNTEERED FOR UNDERCOVER.
I'M TRULY SORRY, LOVE.
READY THE MK-48s.

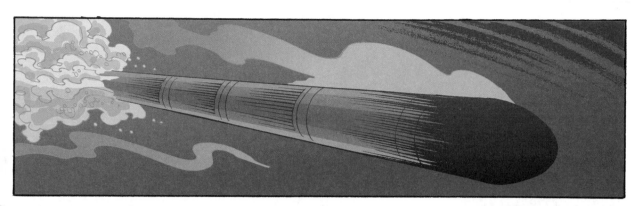

CAPTAIN, THIS IS NAVS!

TORPEDO SIGHTED OFF OUR PORT!

CAPTAIN, SHOULD WE ABANDON SHIP?

355, I--

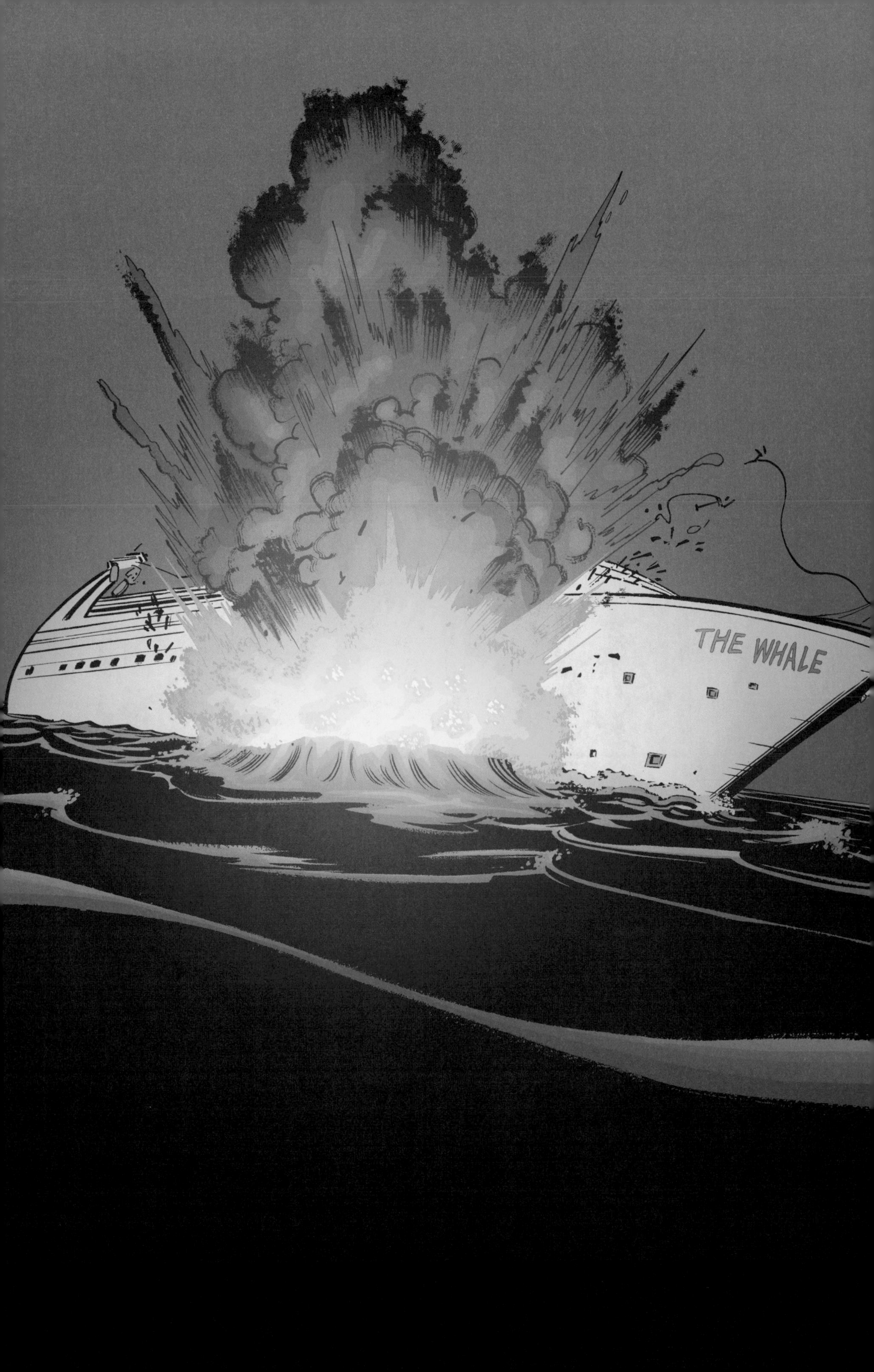
THE WHALE

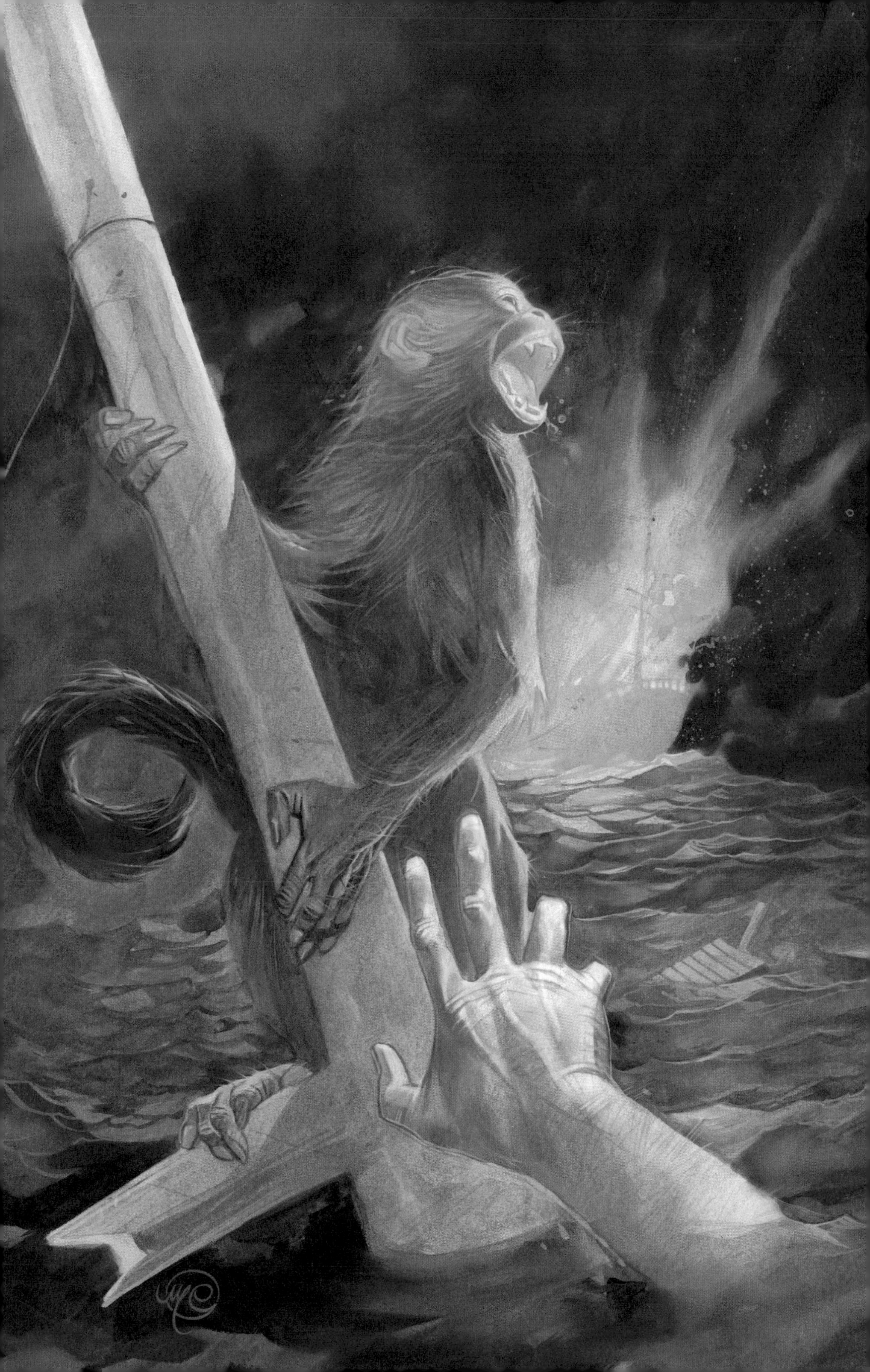

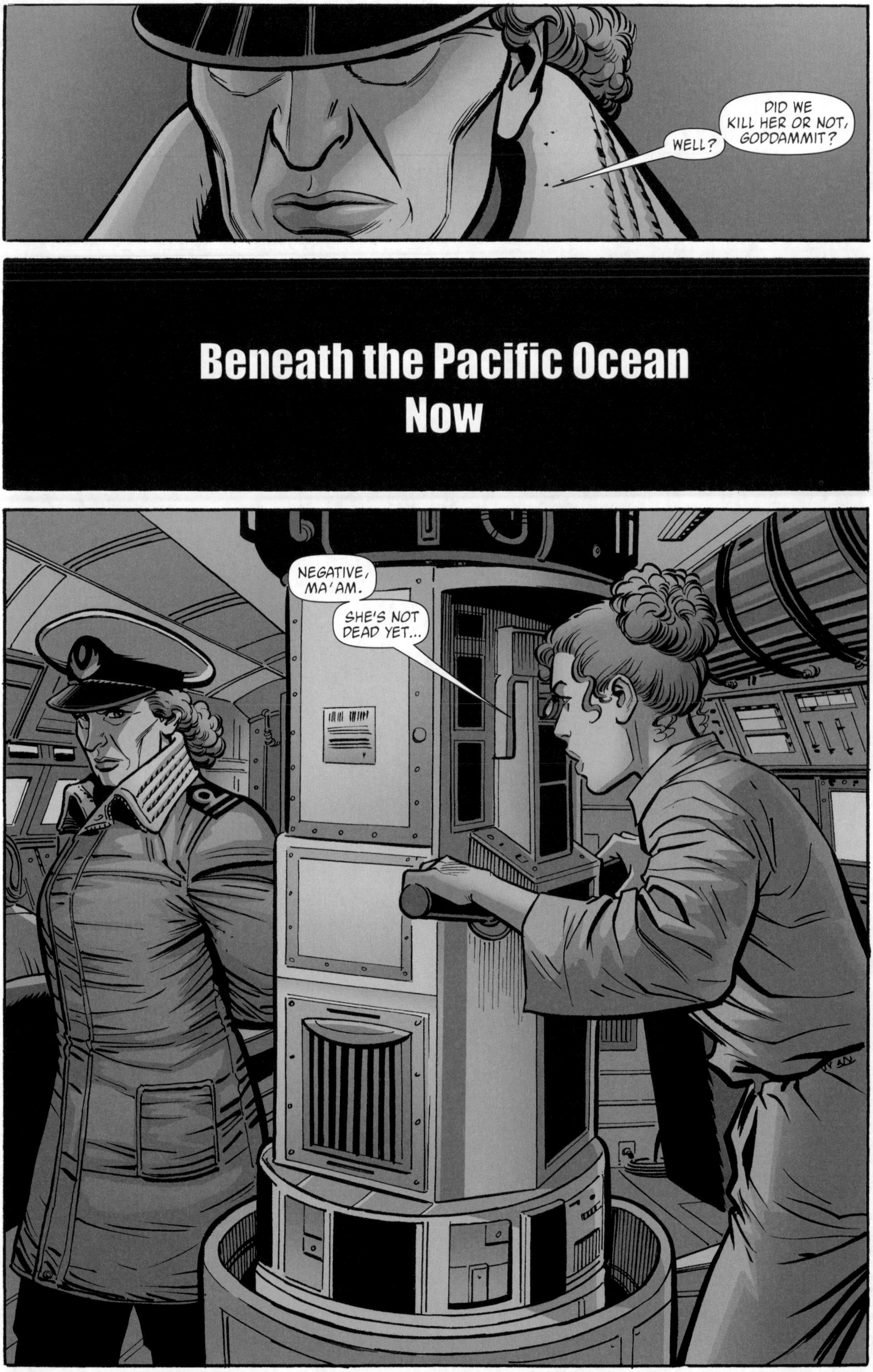
WELL?
DID WE KILL HER OR NOT, GODDAMMIT?
Beneath the Pacific Ocean
Now
NEGATIVE, MA'AM.
SHE'S NOT DEAD YET...

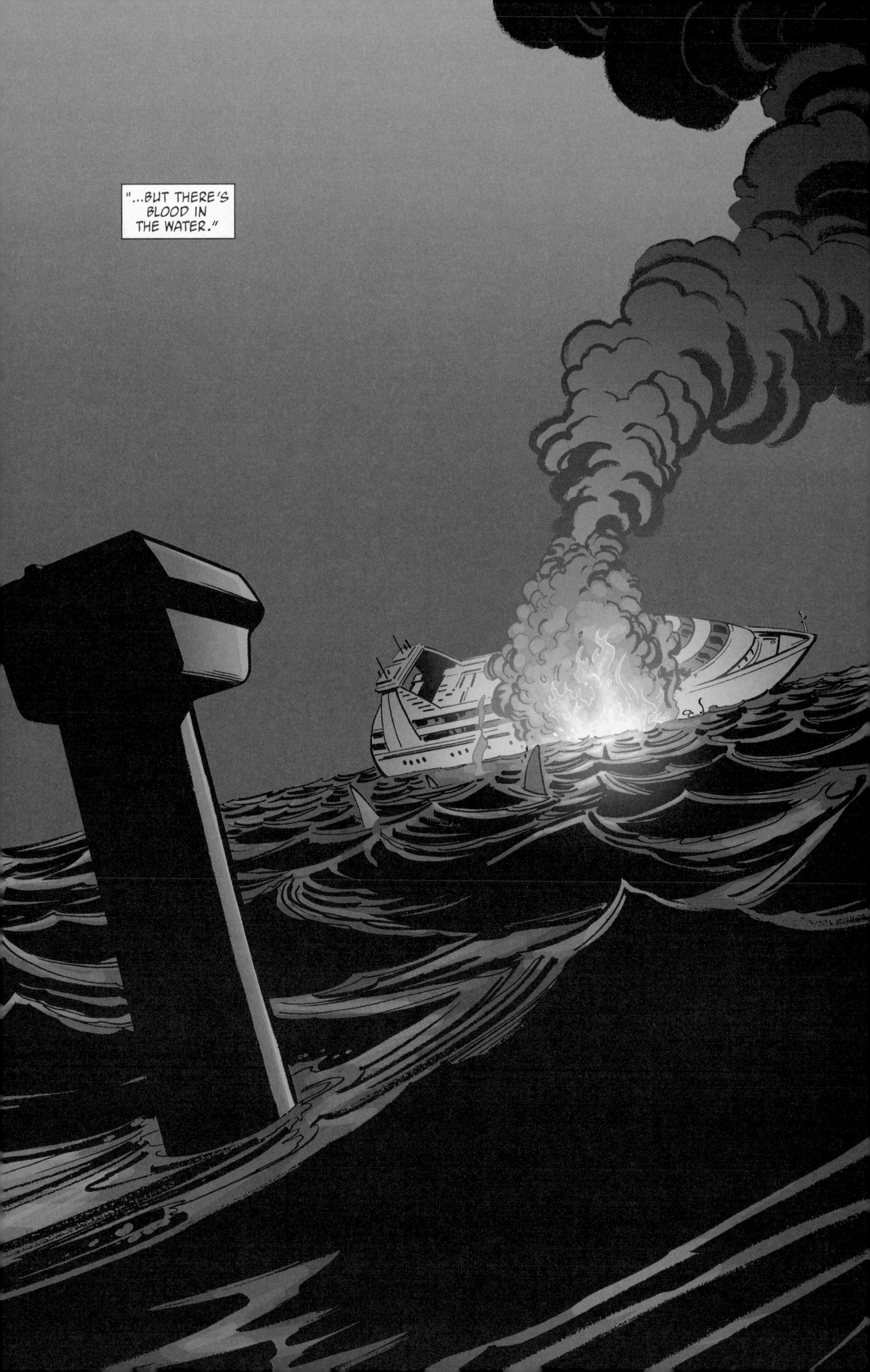
"...BUT THERE'S BLOOD IN THE WATER."

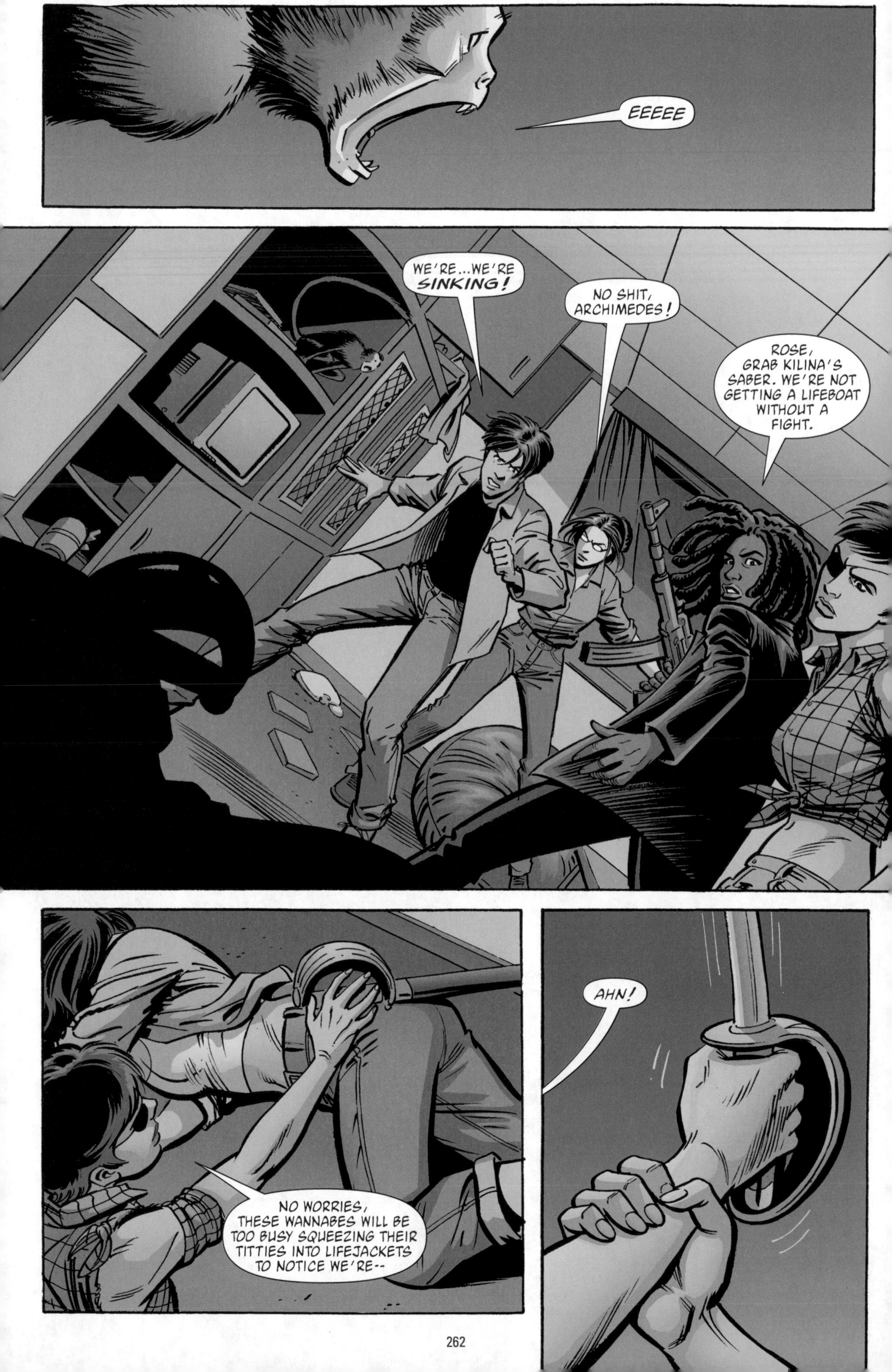
EEEEE
WE'RE...WE'RE SINKING!
NO SHIT, ARCHIMEDES!
ROSE, GRAB KILINA'S SABER. WE'RE NOT GETTING A LIFEBOAT WITHOUT A FIGHT.
NO WORRIES, THESE WANNABES WILL BE TOO BUSY SQUEEZING THEIR TITTIES INTO LIFEJACKETS TO NOTICE WE'RE--
AHN!

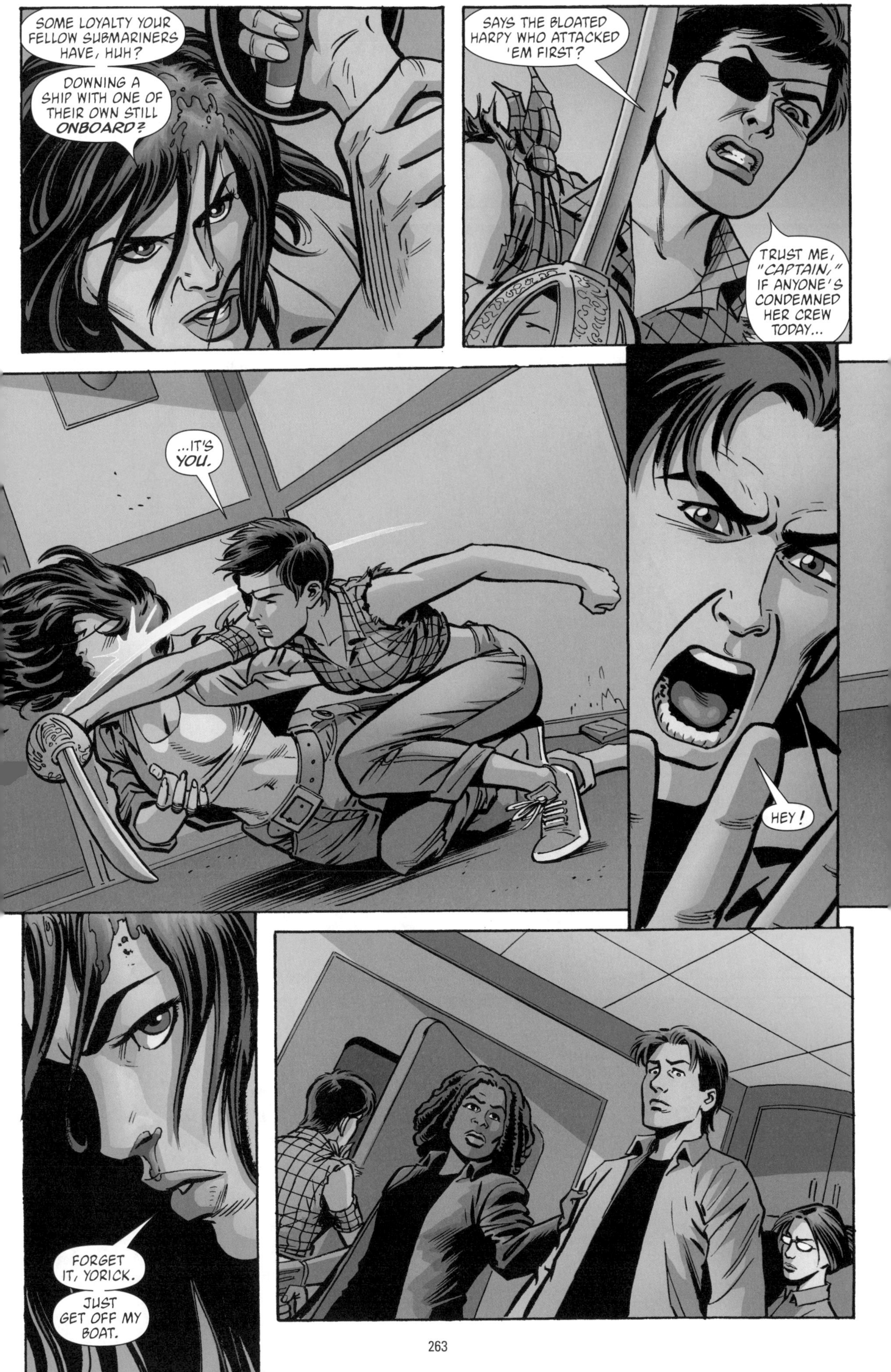

SOME LOYALTY YOUR FELLOW SUBMARINERS HAVE, HUH?
DOWNING A SHIP WITH ONE OF THEIR OWN STILL ONBOARD?
SAYS THE BLOATED HARPY WHO ATTACKED 'EM FIRST?
TRUST ME, "CAPTAIN," IF ANYONE'S CONDEMNED HER CREW TODAY...
...IT'S YOU.
HEY!
FORGET IT, YORICK.
JUST GET OFF MY BOAT.

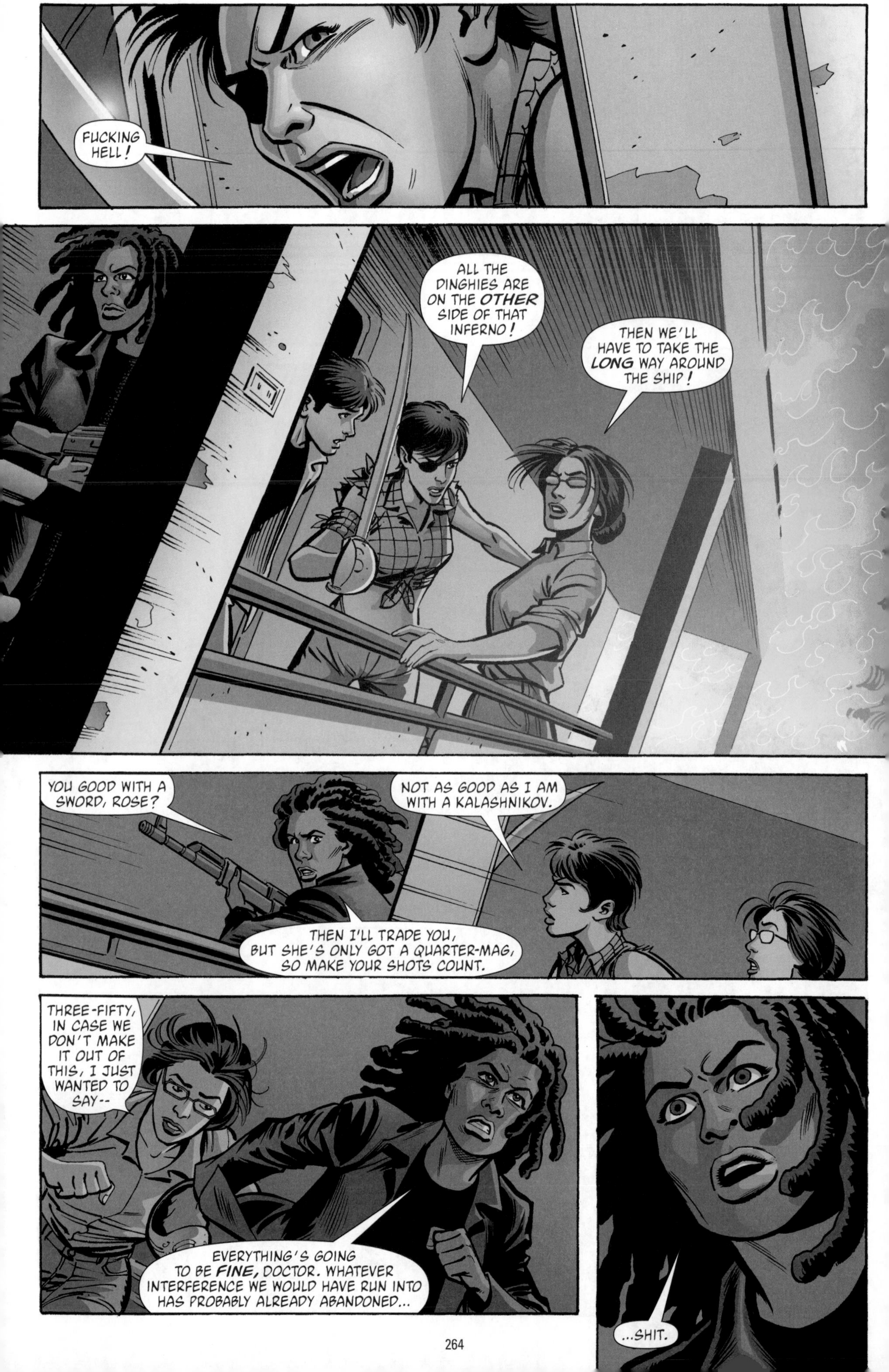
FUCKING HELL!
ALL THE DINGHIES ARE ON THE OTHER SIDE OF THAT INFERNO!
THEN WE'LL HAVE TO TAKE THE LONG WAY AROUND THE SHIP!
YOU GOOD WITH A SWORD, ROSE?
NOT AS GOOD AS I AM WITH A KALASHNIKOV.
THEN I'LL TRADE YOU, BUT SHE'S ONLY GOT A QUARTER-MAG, SO MAKE YOUR SHOTS COUNT.
THREE-FIFTY, IN CASE WE DON'T MAKE IT OUT OF THIS, I JUST WANTED TO SAY--
EVERYTHING'S GOING TO BE FINE, DOCTOR. WHATEVER INTERFERENCE WE WOULD HAVE RUN INTO HAS PROBABLY ALREADY ABANDONED...
...SHIT.

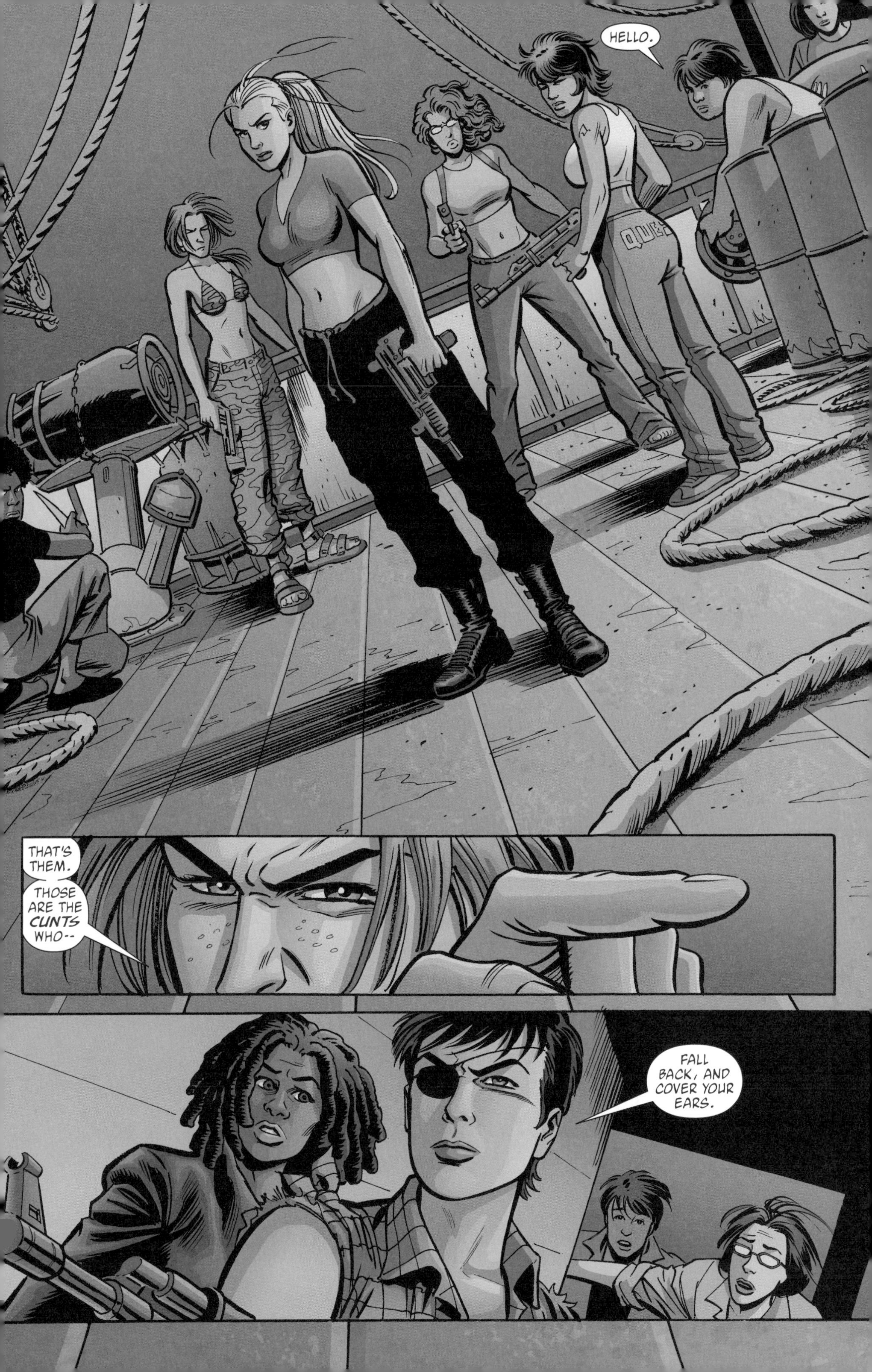

HELLO.
THAT'S THEM.
THOSE ARE THE *CUNTS* WHO--
FALL BACK, AND COVER YOUR EARS.

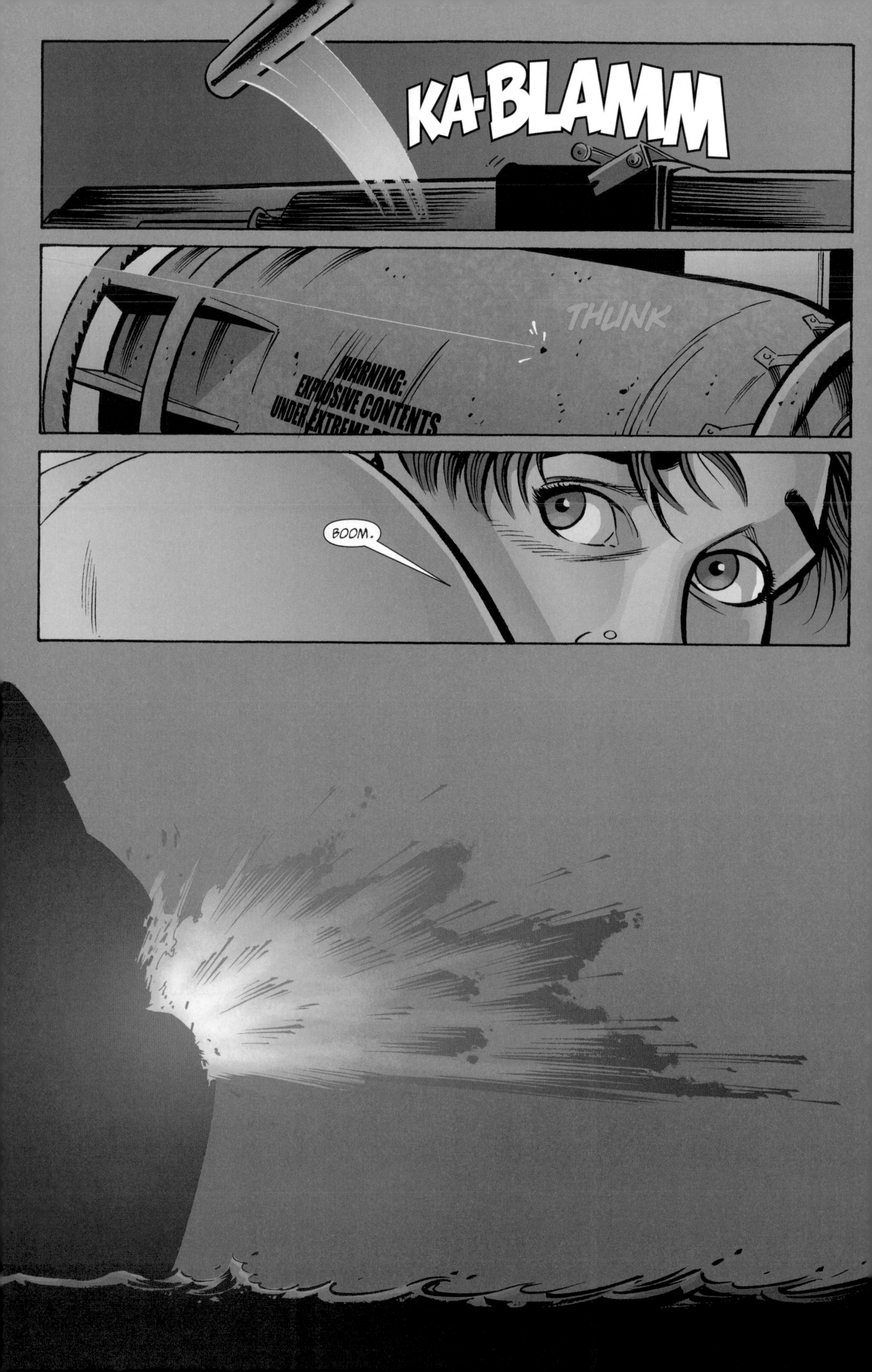
KA-BLAMM
THUNK
WARNING:
EXPLOSIVE CONTENTS
BOOM.

UNF!

ROSE!
ARE YOU **ALL RIGHT**?

WHAT?

HOW THE HELL DID YOU HIT A PRIMER CHARGE THE SIZE OF A **WALNUT**? YOU DON'T EVEN HAVE DEPTH PERCEPTION!

SAY AGAIN?

WHAT THE **FUCK** ARE YOU SO IMPRESSED WITH, 355? SHE JUST OBLITERATED OUR ONLY OTHER ACCESS TO THE **LIFEBOATS**!

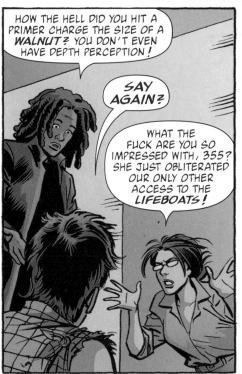

WE'LL HAVE TO CUT ACROSS THROUGH THE **CARGO HOLD**, DOC.

HOW, YORICK?

THEIR HEROIN SUPPLY IS LOCKED LIKE FORT KNOX, AND DEADEYE DICKLESS JUST **BLEW UP** EVERY WOMAN WHO MIGHT HAVE HAD A **KEY**.

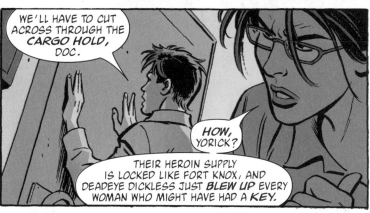

ANYONE GOT A BOBBY PIN?

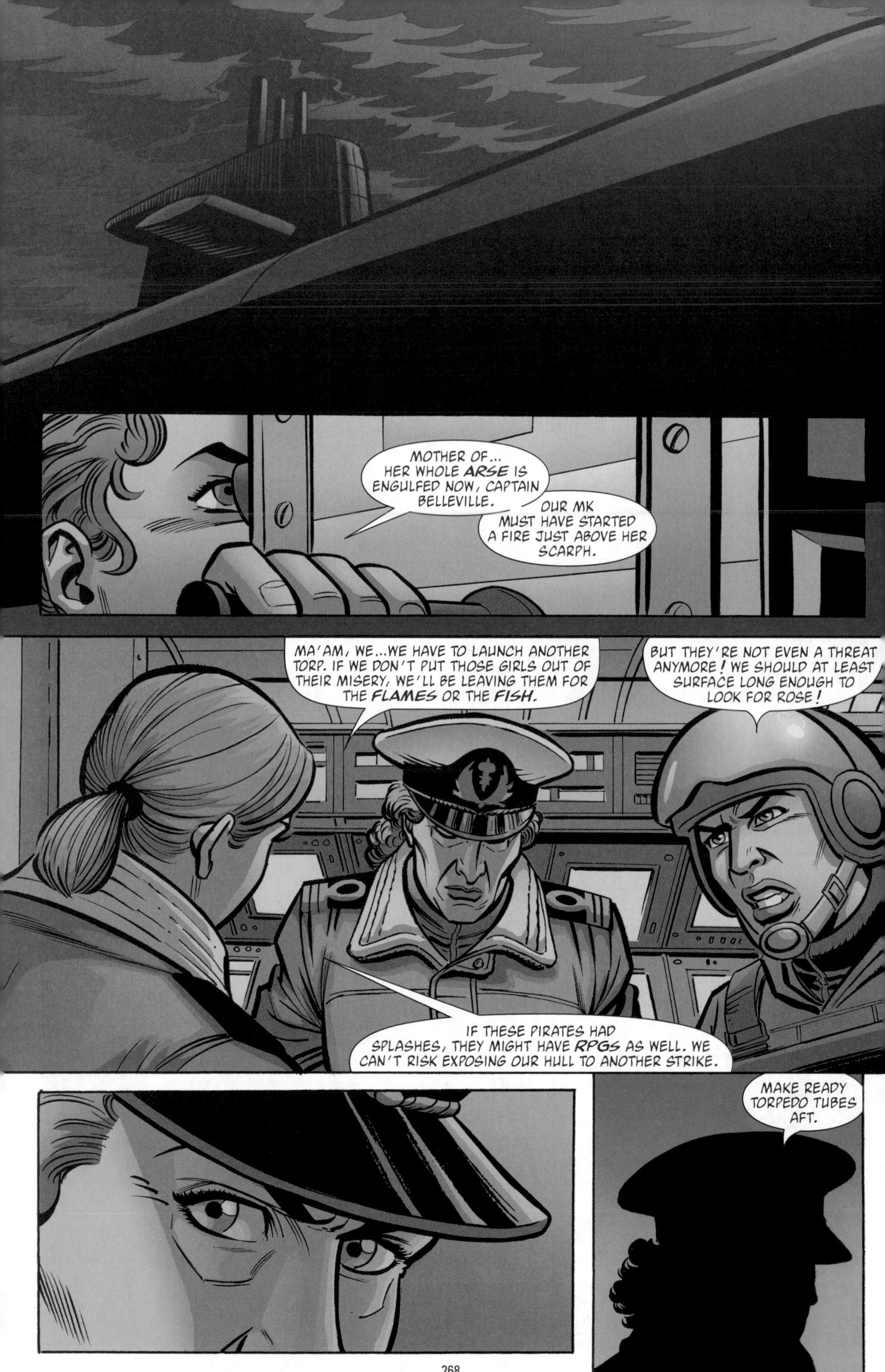
MOTHER OF... HER WHOLE ARSE IS ENGULFED NOW, CAPTAIN BELLEVILLE.
OUR MK MUST HAVE STARTED A FIRE JUST ABOVE HER SCARPH.
MA'AM, WE...WE HAVE TO LAUNCH ANOTHER TORP. IF WE DON'T PUT THOSE GIRLS OUT OF THEIR MISERY, WE'LL BE LEAVING THEM FOR THE FLAMES OR THE FISH.
BUT THEY'RE NOT EVEN A THREAT ANYMORE! WE SHOULD AT LEAST SURFACE LONG ENOUGH TO LOOK FOR ROSE!
IF THESE PIRATES HAD SPLASHES, THEY MIGHT HAVE RPGS AS WELL. WE CAN'T RISK EXPOSING OUR HULL TO ANOTHER STRIKE.
MAKE READY TORPEDO TUBES AFT.

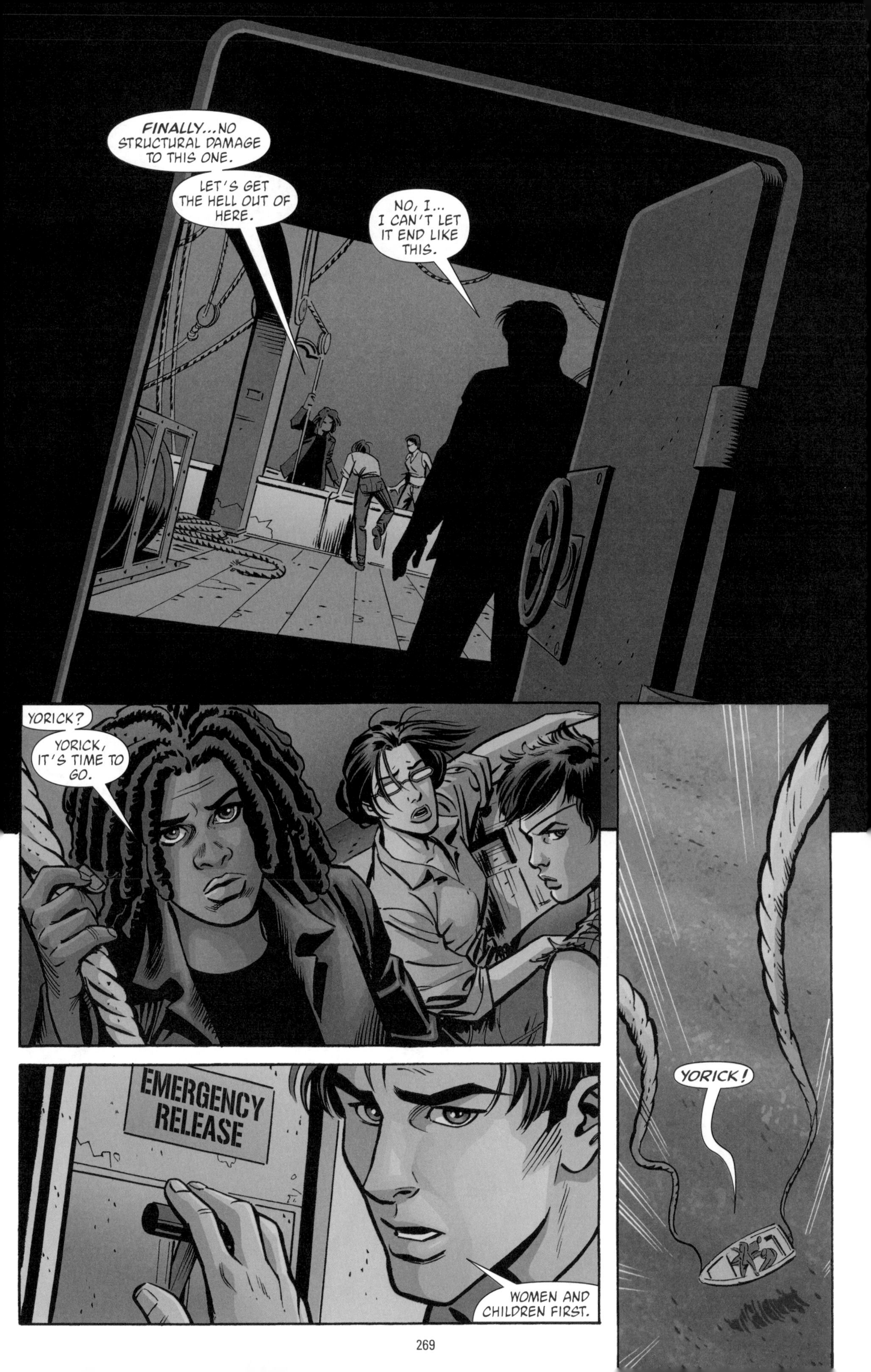
FINALLY...NO STRUCTURAL DAMAGE TO THIS ONE.
LET'S GET THE HELL OUT OF HERE.
NO, I... I CAN'T LET IT END LIKE THIS.
YORICK?
YORICK, IT'S TIME TO GO.
YORICK!
EMERGENCY RELEASE
WOMEN AND CHILDREN FIRST.

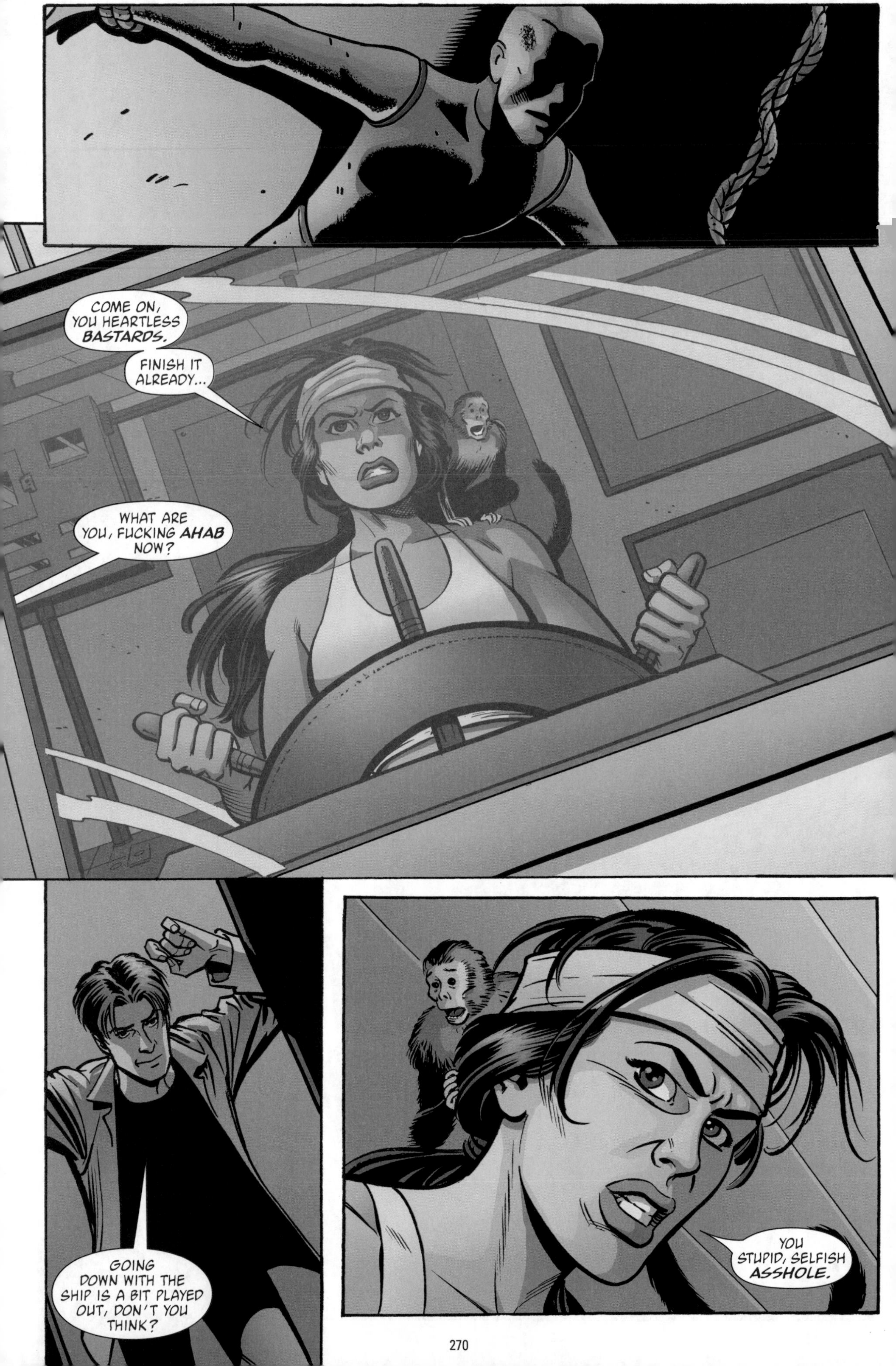
COME ON, YOU HEARTLESS BASTARDS.
FINISH IT ALREADY...
WHAT ARE YOU, FUCKING AHAB NOW?
GOING DOWN WITH THE SHIP IS A BIT PLAYED OUT, DON'T YOU THINK?
YOU STUPID, SELFISH ASSHOLE.

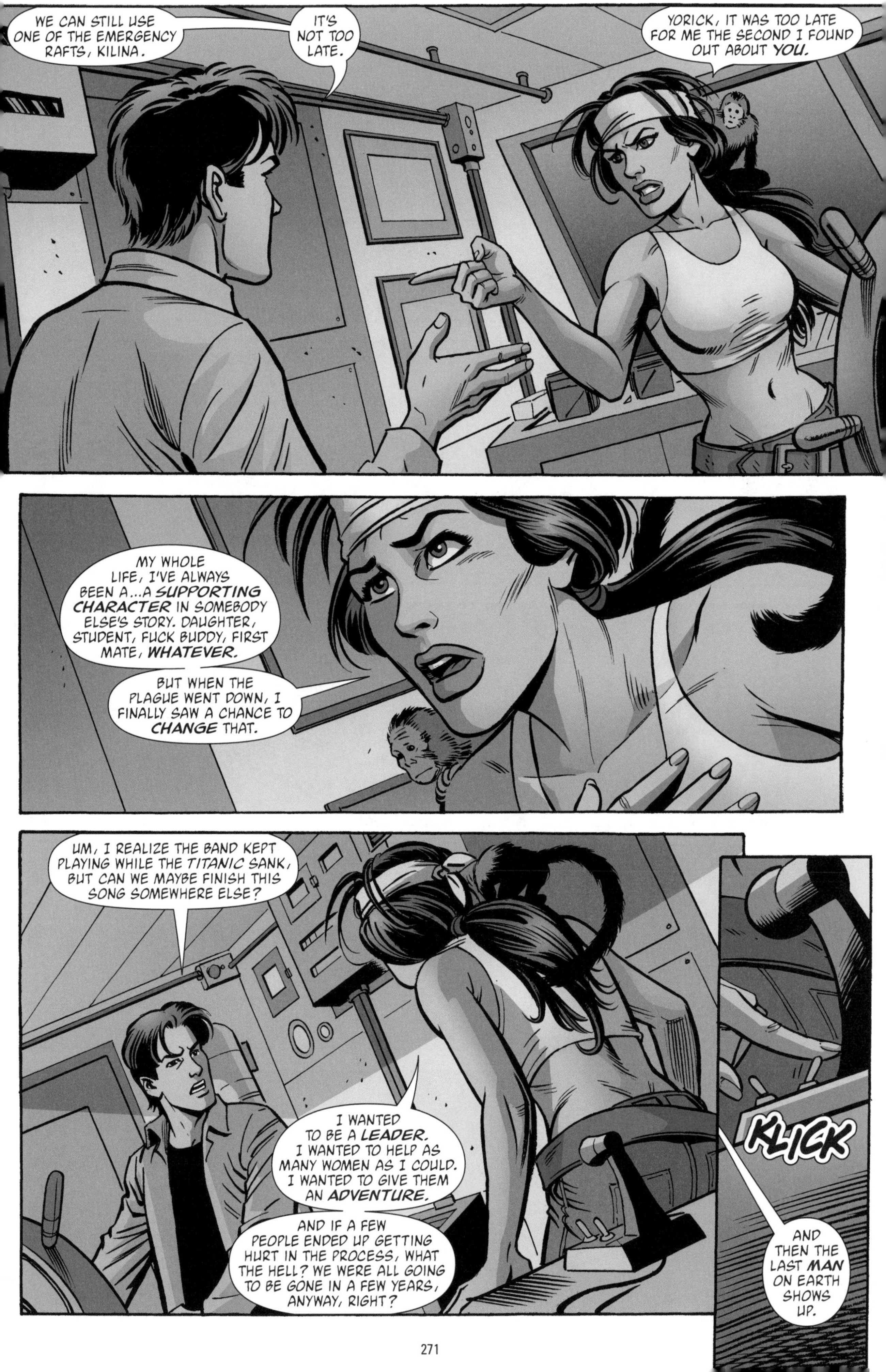
WE CAN STILL USE ONE OF THE EMERGENCY RAFTS, KILINA.
IT'S NOT TOO LATE.
YORICK, IT WAS TOO LATE FOR ME THE SECOND I FOUND OUT ABOUT YOU.
MY WHOLE LIFE, I'VE ALWAYS BEEN A...A SUPPORTING CHARACTER IN SOMEBODY ELSE'S STORY. DAUGHTER, STUDENT, FUCK BUDDY, FIRST MATE, WHATEVER.
BUT WHEN THE PLAGUE WENT DOWN, I FINALLY SAW A CHANCE TO CHANGE THAT.
UM, I REALIZE THE BAND KEPT PLAYING WHILE THE TITANIC SANK, BUT CAN WE MAYBE FINISH THIS SONG SOMEWHERE ELSE?
I WANTED TO BE A LEADER. I WANTED TO HELP AS MANY WOMEN AS I COULD. I WANTED TO GIVE THEM AN ADVENTURE.
AND IF A FEW PEOPLE ENDED UP GETTING HURT IN THE PROCESS, WHAT THE HELL? WE WERE ALL GOING TO BE GONE IN A FEW YEARS, ANYWAY, RIGHT?
KLICK
AND THEN THE LAST MAN ON EARTH SHOWS UP.

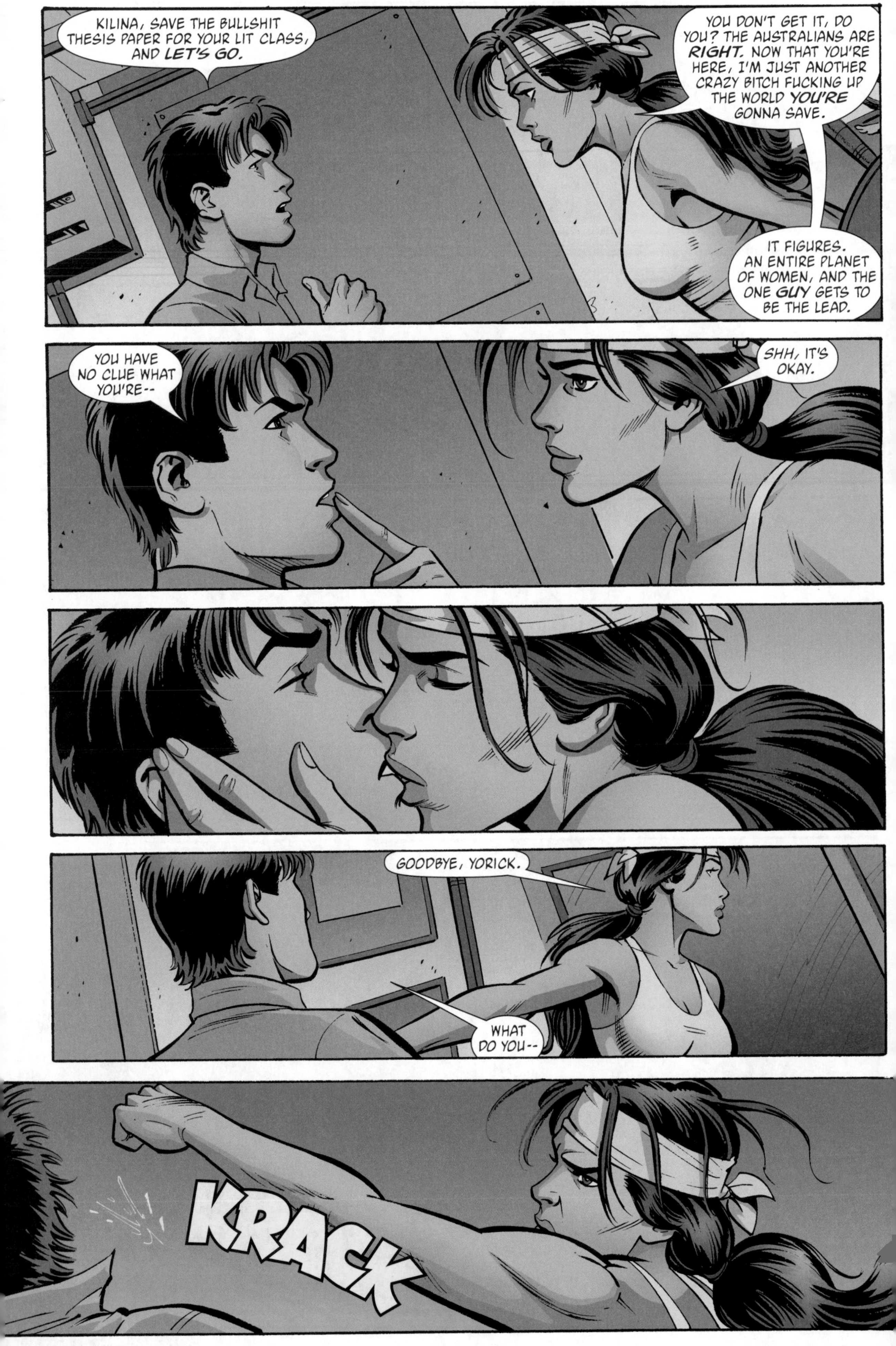
KILINA, SAVE THE BULLSHIT THESIS PAPER FOR YOUR LIT CLASS, AND LET'S GO.
YOU DON'T GET IT, DO YOU? THE AUSTRALIANS ARE RIGHT. NOW THAT YOU'RE HERE, I'M JUST ANOTHER CRAZY BITCH FUCKING UP THE WORLD YOU'RE GONNA SAVE.
IT FIGURES. AN ENTIRE PLANET OF WOMEN, AND THE ONE GUY GETS TO BE THE LEAD.
YOU HAVE NO CLUE WHAT YOU'RE--
SHH, IT'S OKAY.
GOODBYE, YORICK.
WHAT DO YOU--
KRACK

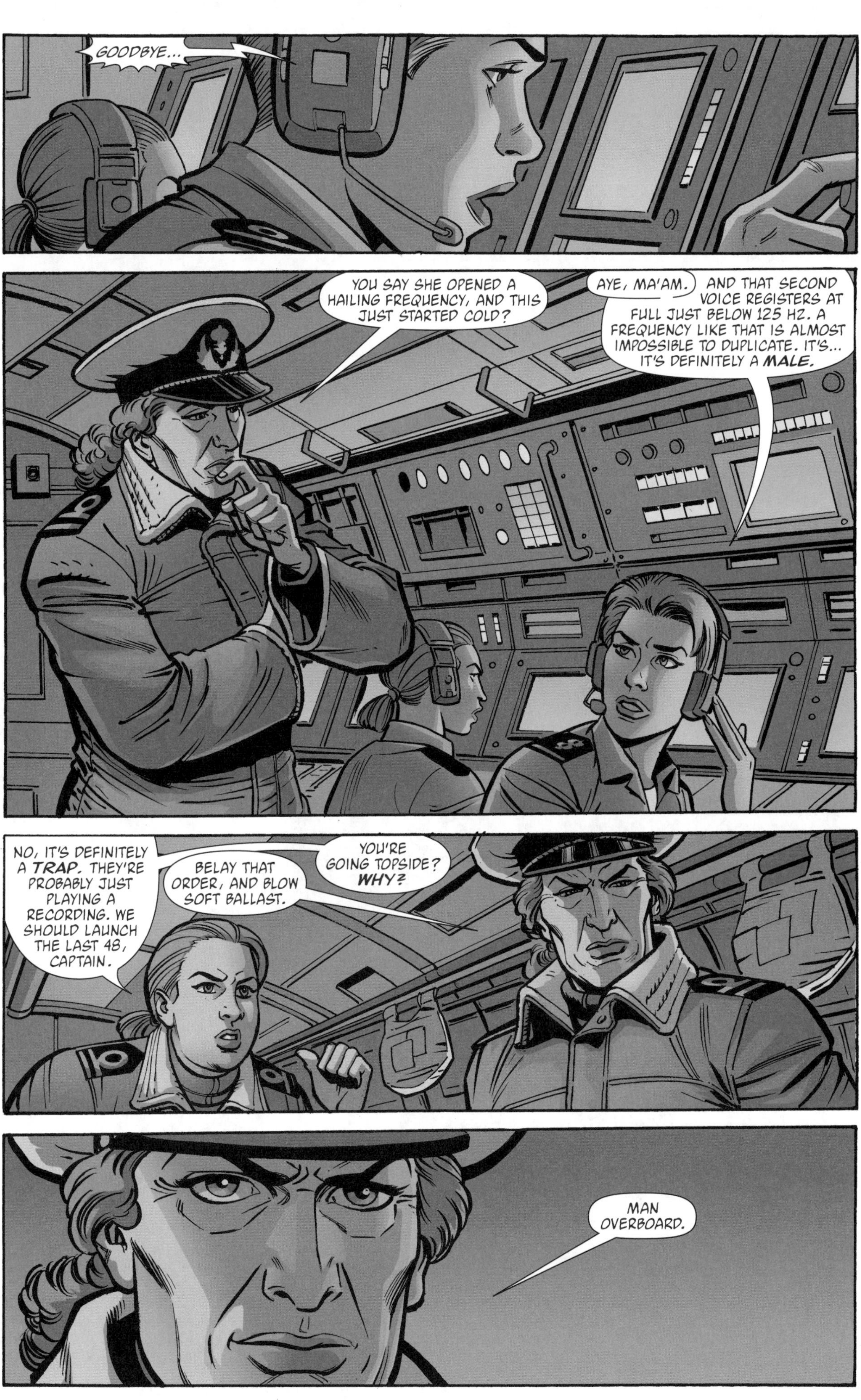
GOODBYE...
YOU SAY SHE OPENED A HAILING FREQUENCY, AND THIS JUST STARTED COLD?
AYE, MA'AM.
AND THAT SECOND VOICE REGISTERS AT FULL JUST BELOW 125 HZ. A FREQUENCY LIKE THAT IS ALMOST IMPOSSIBLE TO DUPLICATE. IT'S... IT'S DEFINITELY A **MALE.**
NO, IT'S DEFINITELY A **TRAP.** THEY'RE PROBABLY JUST PLAYING A RECORDING. WE SHOULD LAUNCH THE LAST 48, CAPTAIN.
BELAY THAT ORDER, AND BLOW SOFT BALLAST.
YOU'RE GOING TOPSIDE? **WHY?**
MAN OVERBOARD.

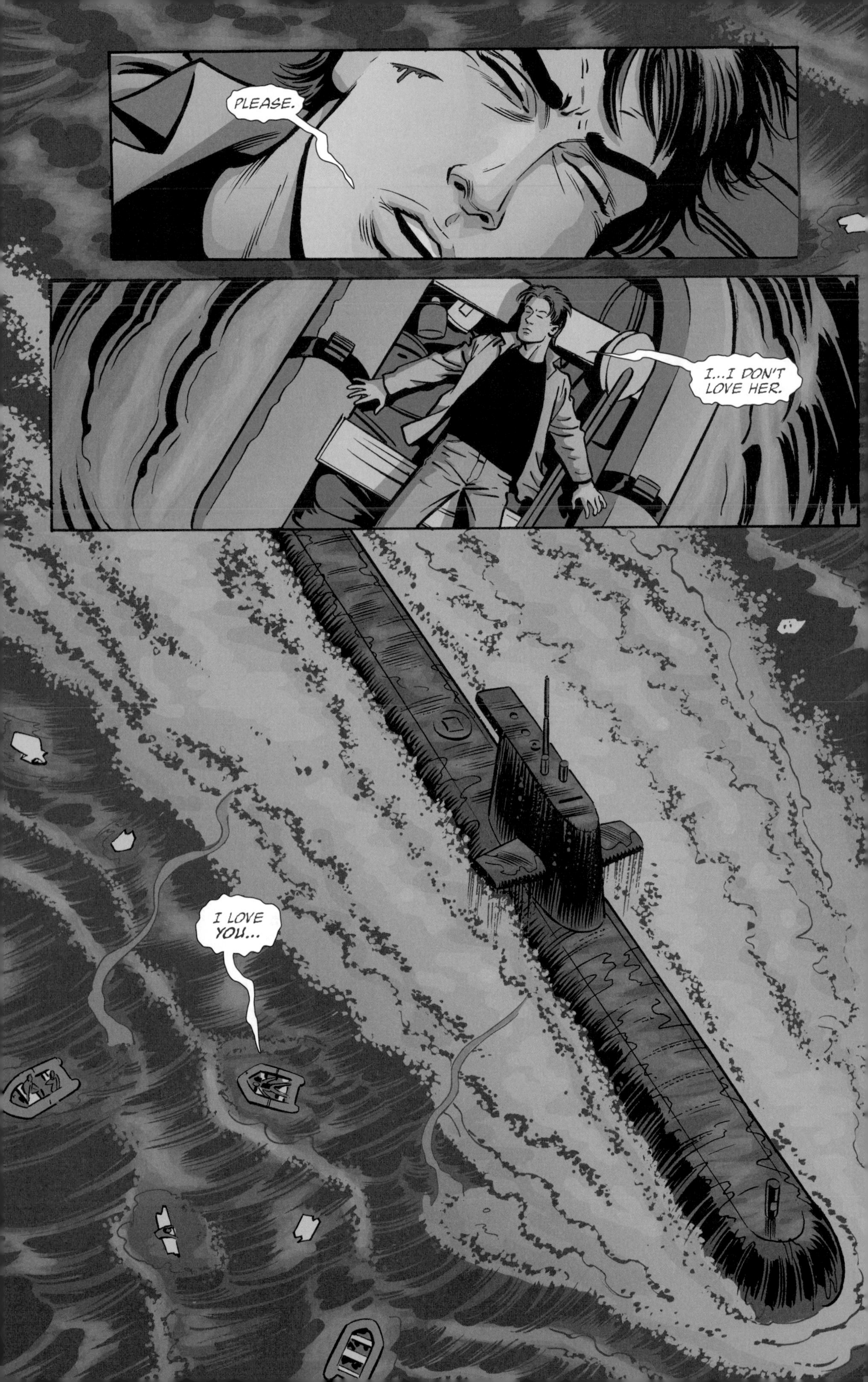
PLEASE.
I...I DON'T LOVE HER.
I LOVE YOU...

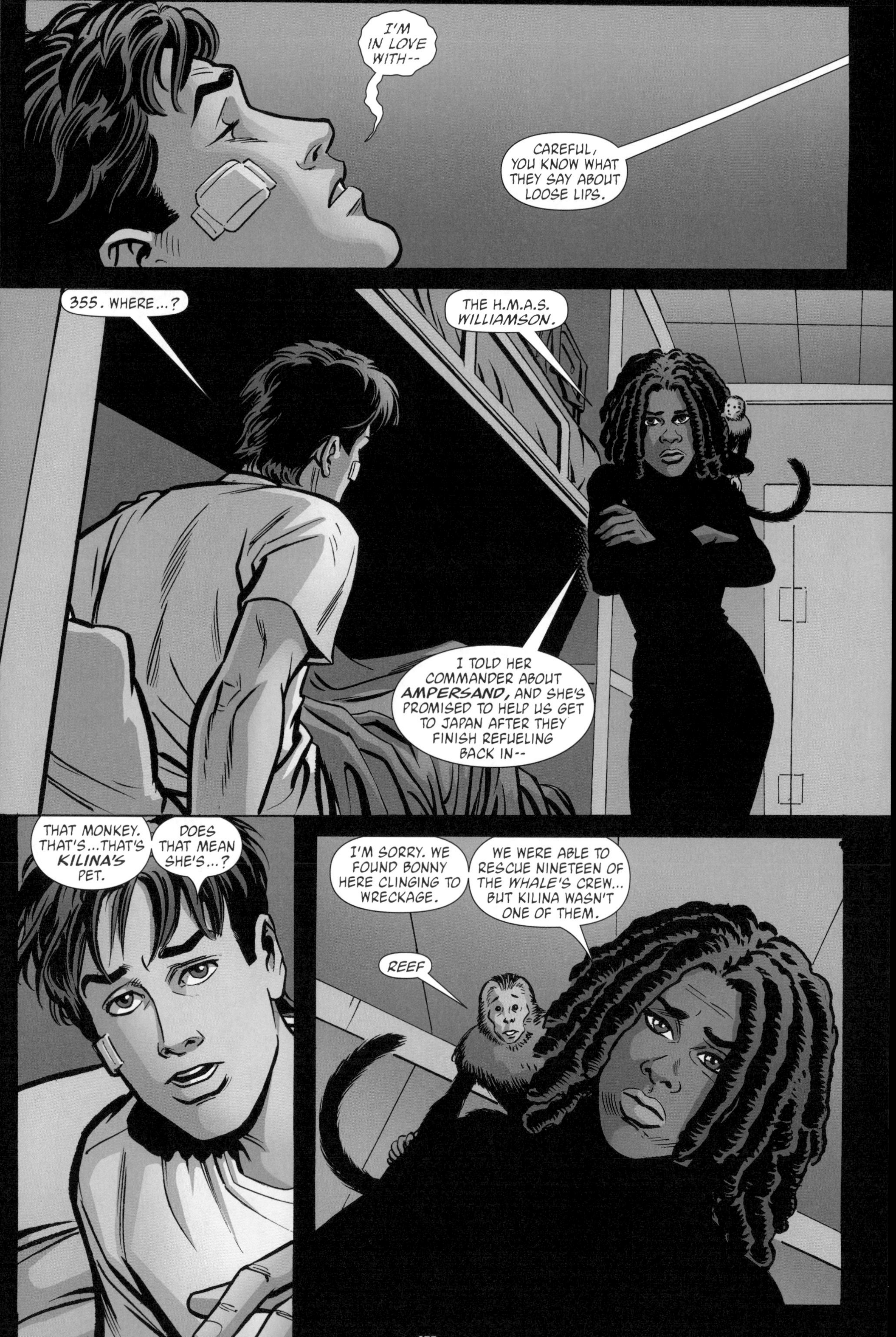
I'M IN LOVE WITH--
CAREFUL, YOU KNOW WHAT THEY SAY ABOUT LOOSE LIPS.
355. WHERE...?
THE H.M.A.S. *WILLIAMSON.*
I TOLD HER COMMANDER ABOUT **AMPERSAND,** AND SHE'S PROMISED TO HELP US GET TO JAPAN AFTER THEY FINISH REFUELING BACK IN--
THAT MONKEY. THAT'S...THAT'S ***KILINA'S*** PET.
DOES THAT MEAN SHE'S...?
I'M SORRY. WE FOUND BONNY HERE CLINGING TO WRECKAGE.
WE WERE ABLE TO RESCUE NINETEEN OF THE *WHALE'S* CREW... BUT KILINA WASN'T ONE OF THEM.
*REEF*

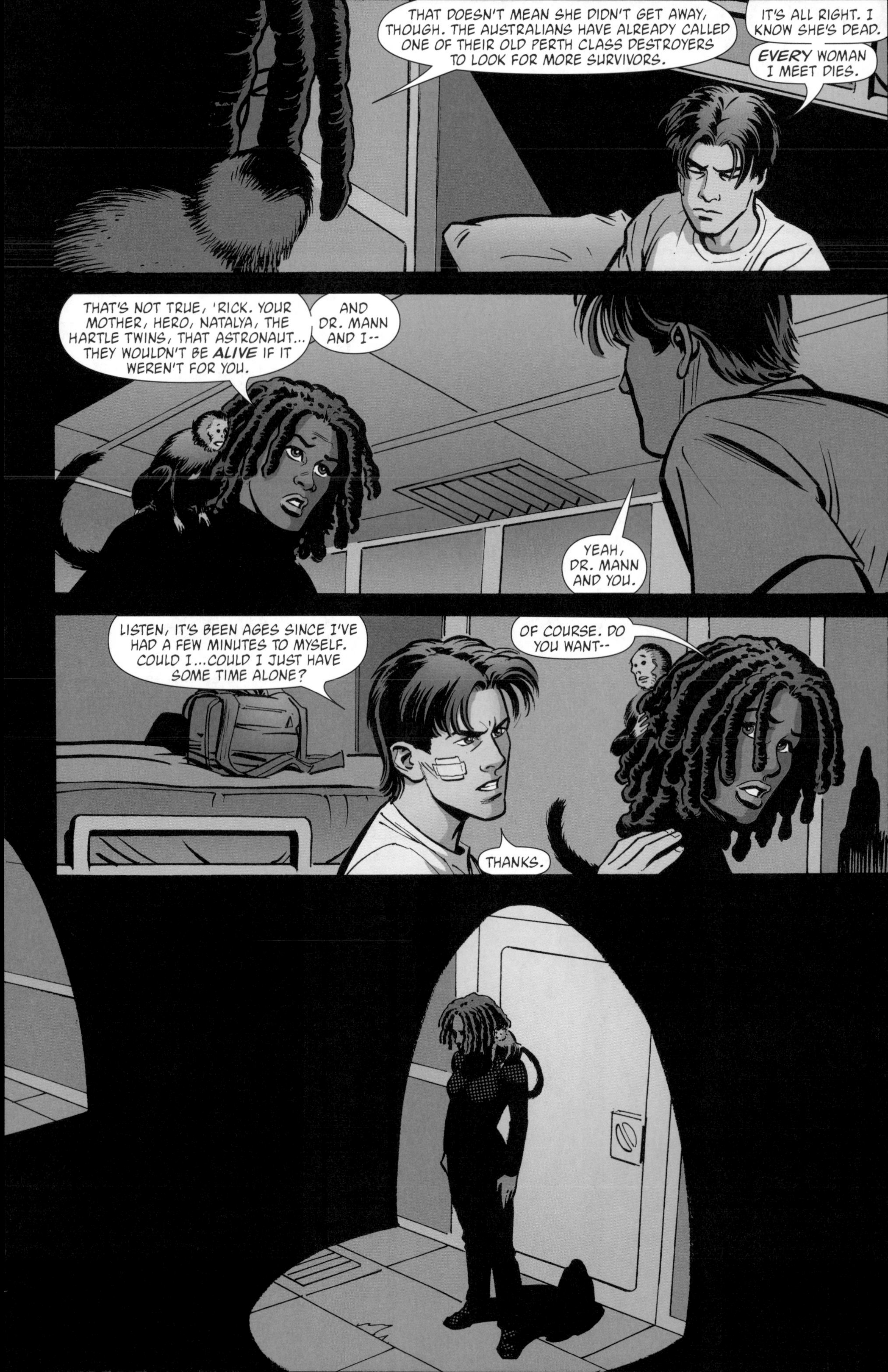
THAT DOESN'T MEAN SHE DIDN'T GET AWAY, THOUGH. THE AUSTRALIANS HAVE ALREADY CALLED ONE OF THEIR OLD PERTH CLASS DESTROYERS TO LOOK FOR MORE SURVIVORS.
IT'S ALL RIGHT. I KNOW SHE'S DEAD.
EVERY WOMAN I MEET DIES.
THAT'S NOT TRUE, 'RICK. YOUR MOTHER, HERO, NATALYA, THE HARTLE TWINS, THAT ASTRONAUT... THEY WOULDN'T BE ALIVE IF IT WEREN'T FOR YOU.
AND DR. MANN AND I--
YEAH, DR. MANN AND YOU.
LISTEN, IT'S BEEN AGES SINCE I'VE HAD A FEW MINUTES TO MYSELF. COULD I...COULD I JUST HAVE SOME TIME ALONE?
OF COURSE. DO YOU WANT--
THANKS.

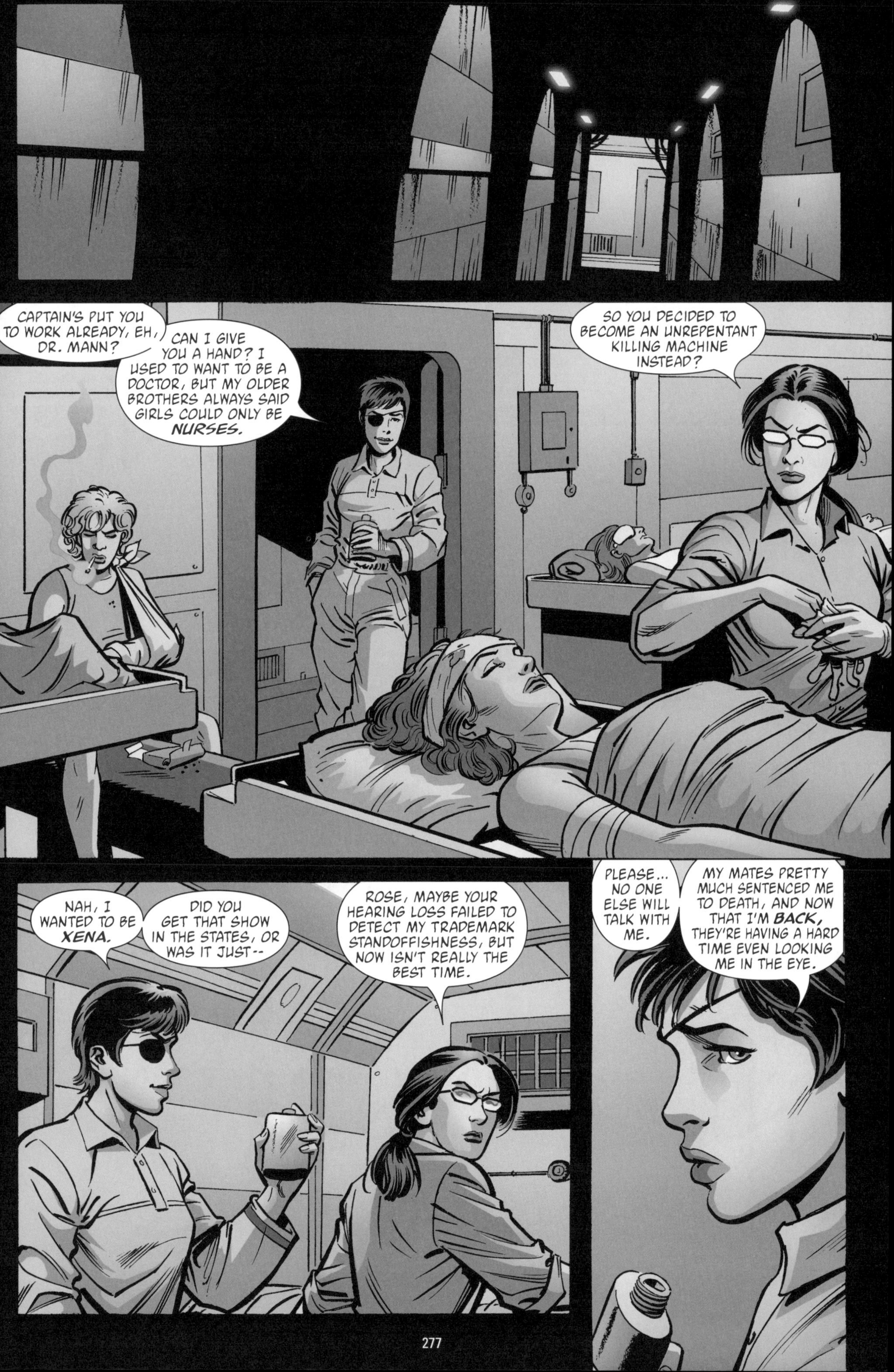

CAPTAIN'S PUT YOU TO WORK ALREADY, EH, DR. MANN?
CAN I GIVE YOU A HAND? I USED TO WANT TO BE A DOCTOR, BUT MY OLDER BROTHERS ALWAYS SAID GIRLS COULD ONLY BE NURSES.
SO YOU DECIDED TO BECOME AN UNREPENTANT KILLING MACHINE INSTEAD?
NAH, I WANTED TO BE XENA.
DID YOU GET THAT SHOW IN THE STATES, OR WAS IT JUST--
ROSE, MAYBE YOUR HEARING LOSS FAILED TO DETECT MY TRADEMARK STANDOFFISHNESS, BUT NOW ISN'T REALLY THE BEST TIME.
PLEASE... NO ONE ELSE WILL TALK WITH ME.
MY MATES PRETTY MUCH SENTENCED ME TO DEATH, AND NOW THAT I'M BACK, THEY'RE HAVING A HARD TIME EVEN LOOKING ME IN THE EYE.

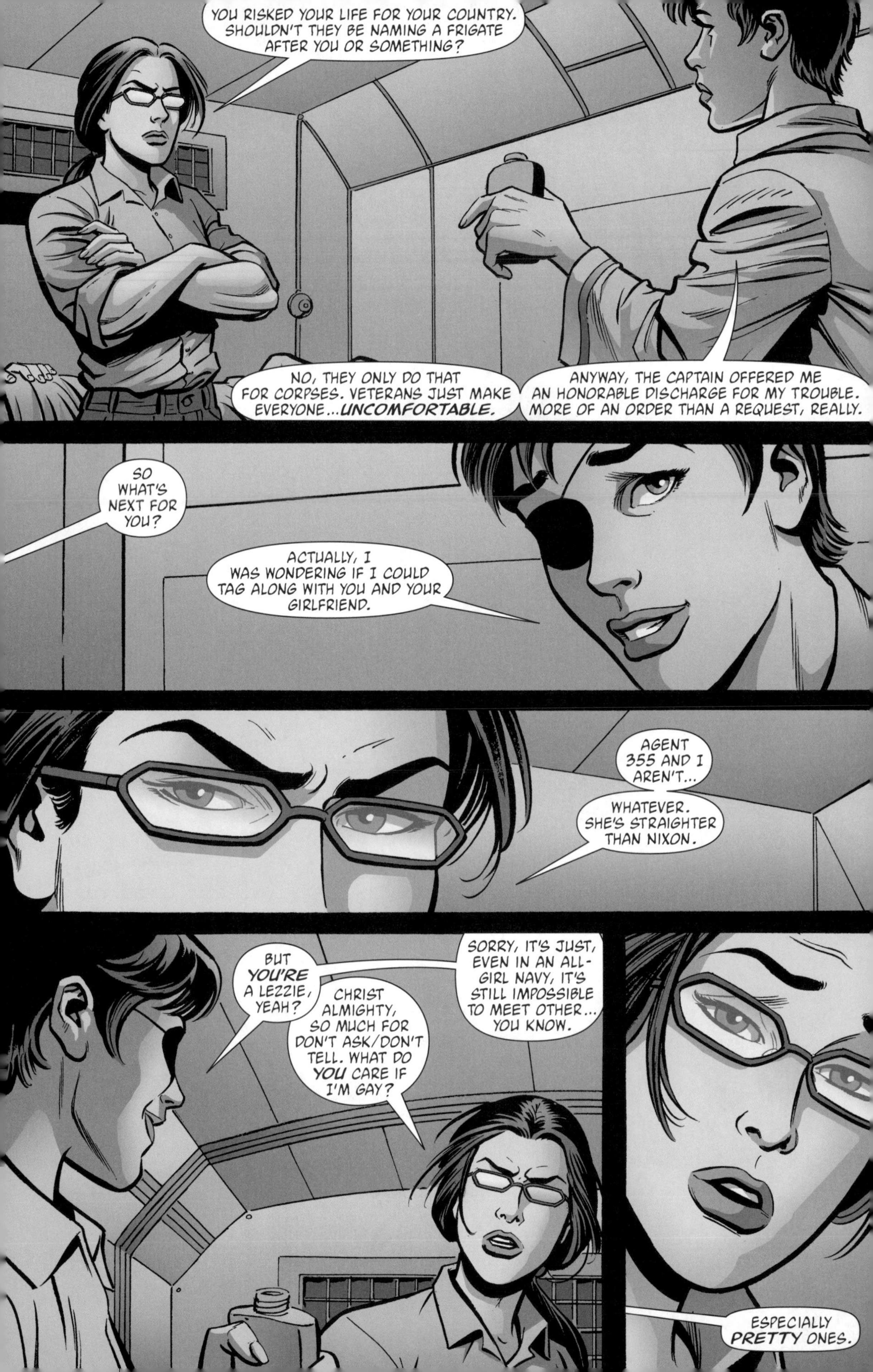
YOU RISKED YOUR LIFE FOR YOUR COUNTRY. SHOULDN'T THEY BE NAMING A FRIGATE AFTER YOU OR SOMETHING?
NO, THEY ONLY DO THAT FOR CORPSES. VETERANS JUST MAKE EVERYONE... UNCOMFORTABLE.
ANYWAY, THE CAPTAIN OFFERED ME AN HONORABLE DISCHARGE FOR MY TROUBLE. MORE OF AN ORDER THAN A REQUEST, REALLY.
SO WHAT'S NEXT FOR YOU?
ACTUALLY, I WAS WONDERING IF I COULD TAG ALONG WITH YOU AND YOUR GIRLFRIEND.
AGENT 355 AND I AREN'T...
WHATEVER. SHE'S STRAIGHTER THAN NIXON.
BUT YOU'RE A LEZZIE, YEAH?
CHRIST ALMIGHTY, SO MUCH FOR DON'T ASK/DON'T TELL. WHAT DO YOU CARE IF I'M GAY?
SORRY, IT'S JUST, EVEN IN AN ALL-GIRL NAVY, IT'S STILL IMPOSSIBLE TO MEET OTHER... YOU KNOW.
ESPECIALLY PRETTY ONES.

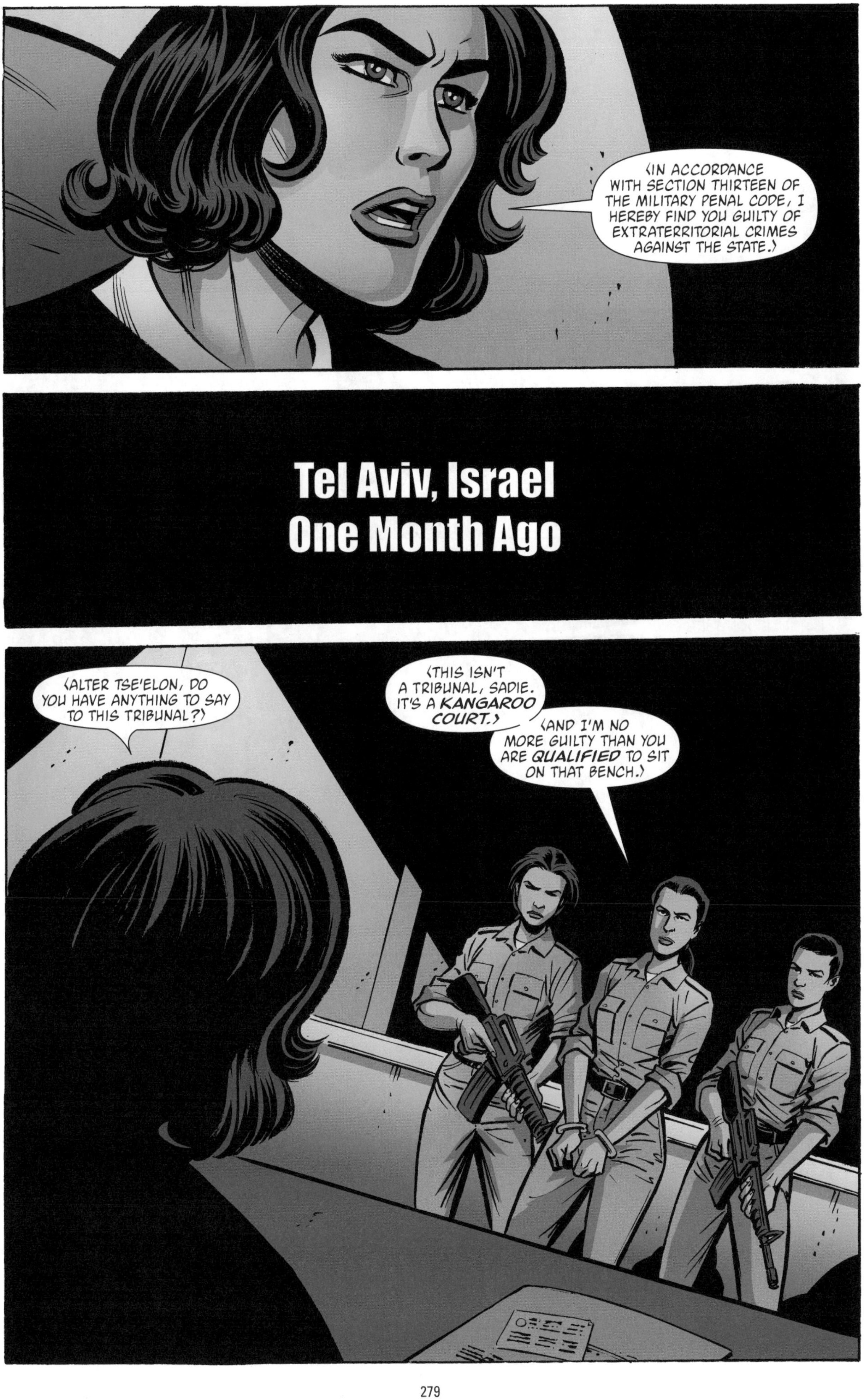
‹IN ACCORDANCE WITH SECTION THIRTEEN OF THE MILITARY PENAL CODE, I HEREBY FIND YOU GUILTY OF EXTRATERRITORIAL CRIMES AGAINST THE STATE.›
Tel Aviv, Israel
One Month Ago
‹ALTER TSE'ELON, DO YOU HAVE ANYTHING TO SAY TO THIS TRIBUNAL?›
‹THIS ISN'T A TRIBUNAL, SADIE. IT'S A KANGAROO COURT.›
‹AND I'M NO MORE GUILTY THAN YOU ARE QUALIFIED TO SIT ON THAT BENCH.›

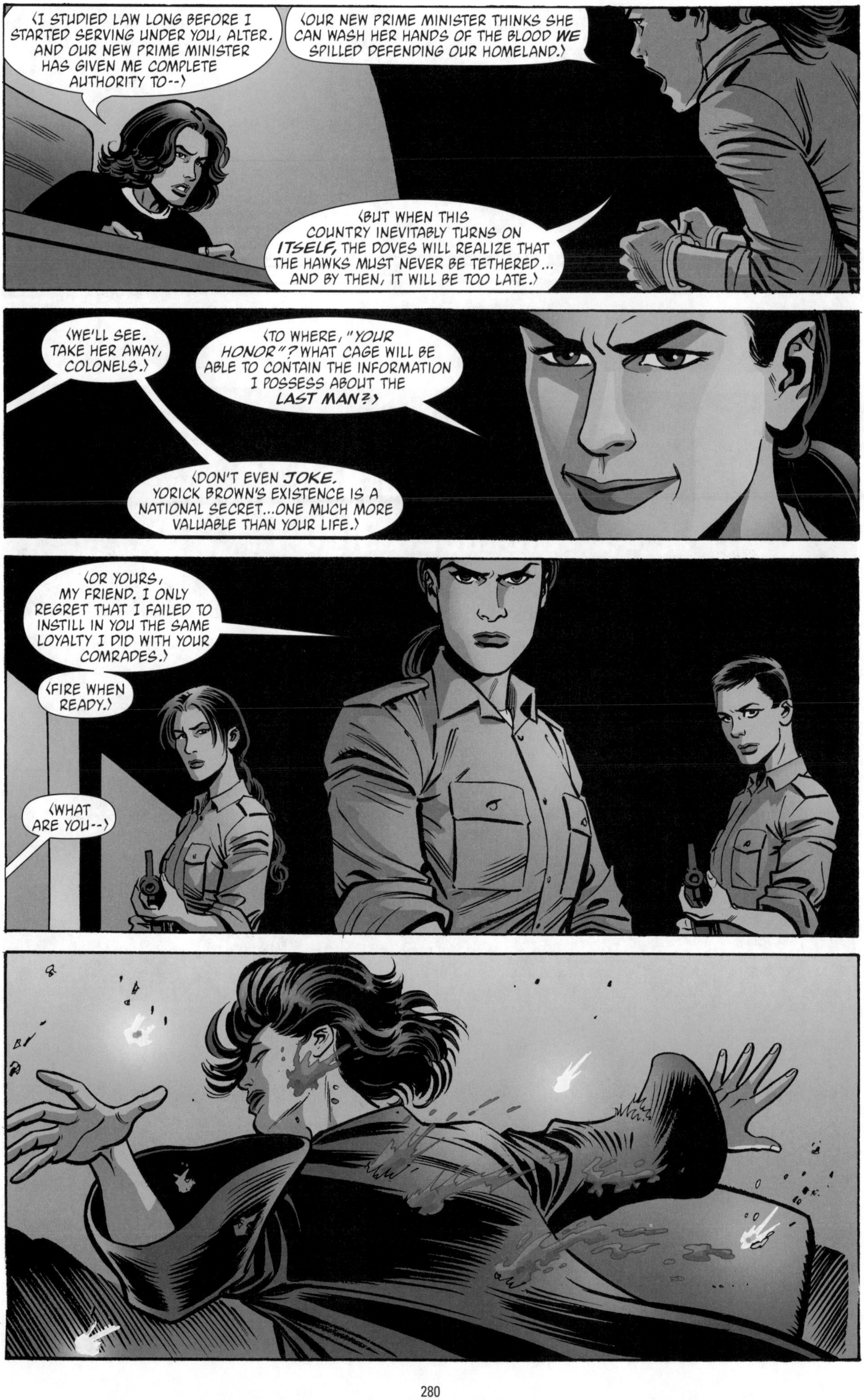

⟨I STUDIED LAW LONG BEFORE I STARTED SERVING UNDER YOU, ALTER. AND OUR NEW PRIME MINISTER HAS GIVEN ME COMPLETE AUTHORITY TO--⟩
⟨OUR NEW PRIME MINISTER THINKS SHE CAN WASH HER HANDS OF THE BLOOD WE SPILLED DEFENDING OUR HOMELAND.⟩
⟨BUT WHEN THIS COUNTRY INEVITABLY TURNS ON ITSELF, THE DOVES WILL REALIZE THAT THE HAWKS MUST NEVER BE TETHERED... AND BY THEN, IT WILL BE TOO LATE.⟩
⟨WE'LL SEE. TAKE HER AWAY, COLONELS.⟩
⟨TO WHERE, "YOUR HONOR"? WHAT CAGE WILL BE ABLE TO CONTAIN THE INFORMATION I POSSESS ABOUT THE LAST MAN?⟩
⟨DON'T EVEN JOKE. YORICK BROWN'S EXISTENCE IS A NATIONAL SECRET...ONE MUCH MORE VALUABLE THAN YOUR LIFE.⟩
⟨OR YOURS, MY FRIEND. I ONLY REGRET THAT I FAILED TO INSTILL IN YOU THE SAME LOYALTY I DID WITH YOUR COMRADES.⟩
⟨FIRE WHEN READY.⟩
⟨WHAT ARE YOU--⟩

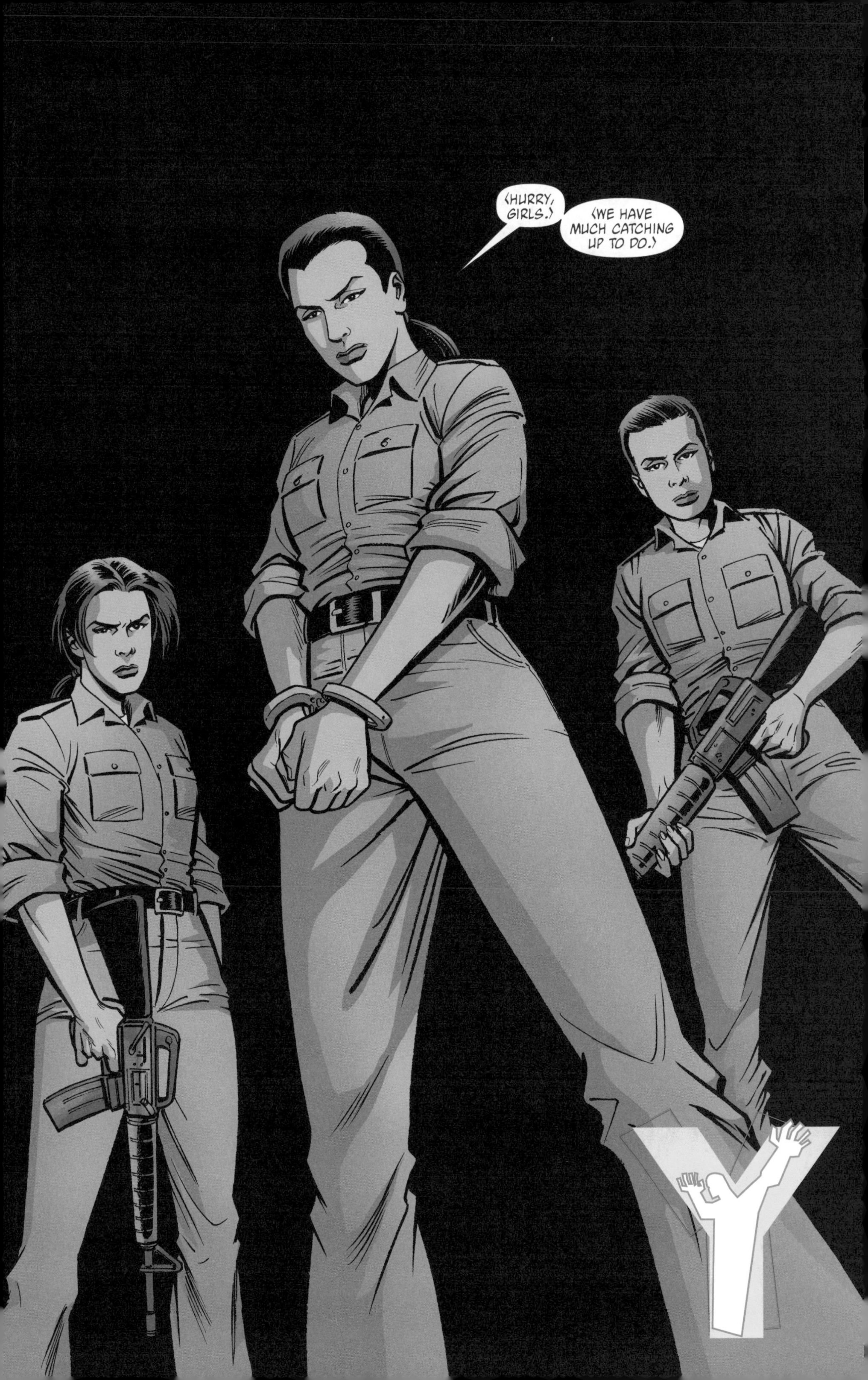
‹HURRY, GIRLS.›
‹WE HAVE MUCH CATCHING UP TO DO.›

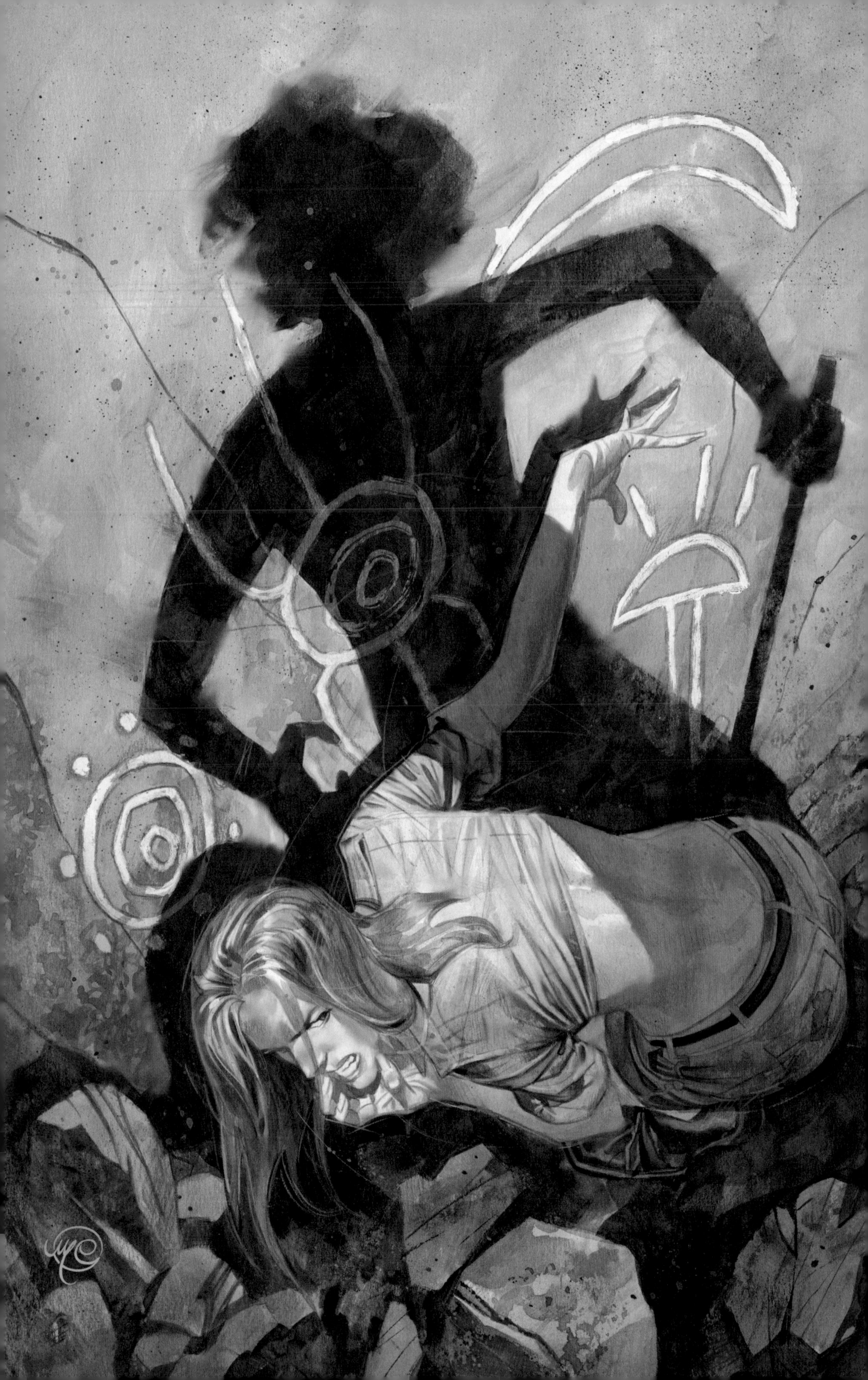

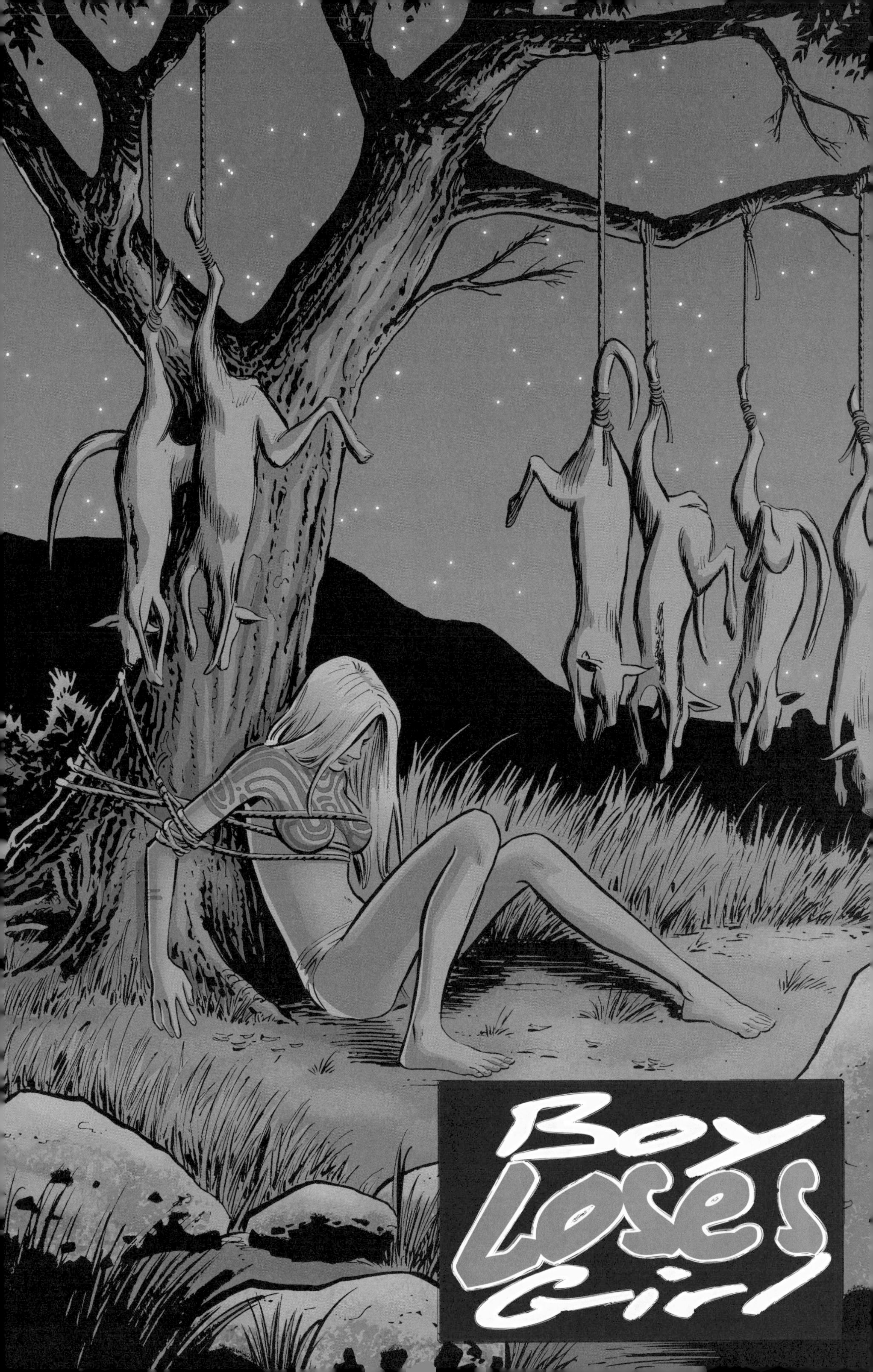
Boy
Loses
Girl

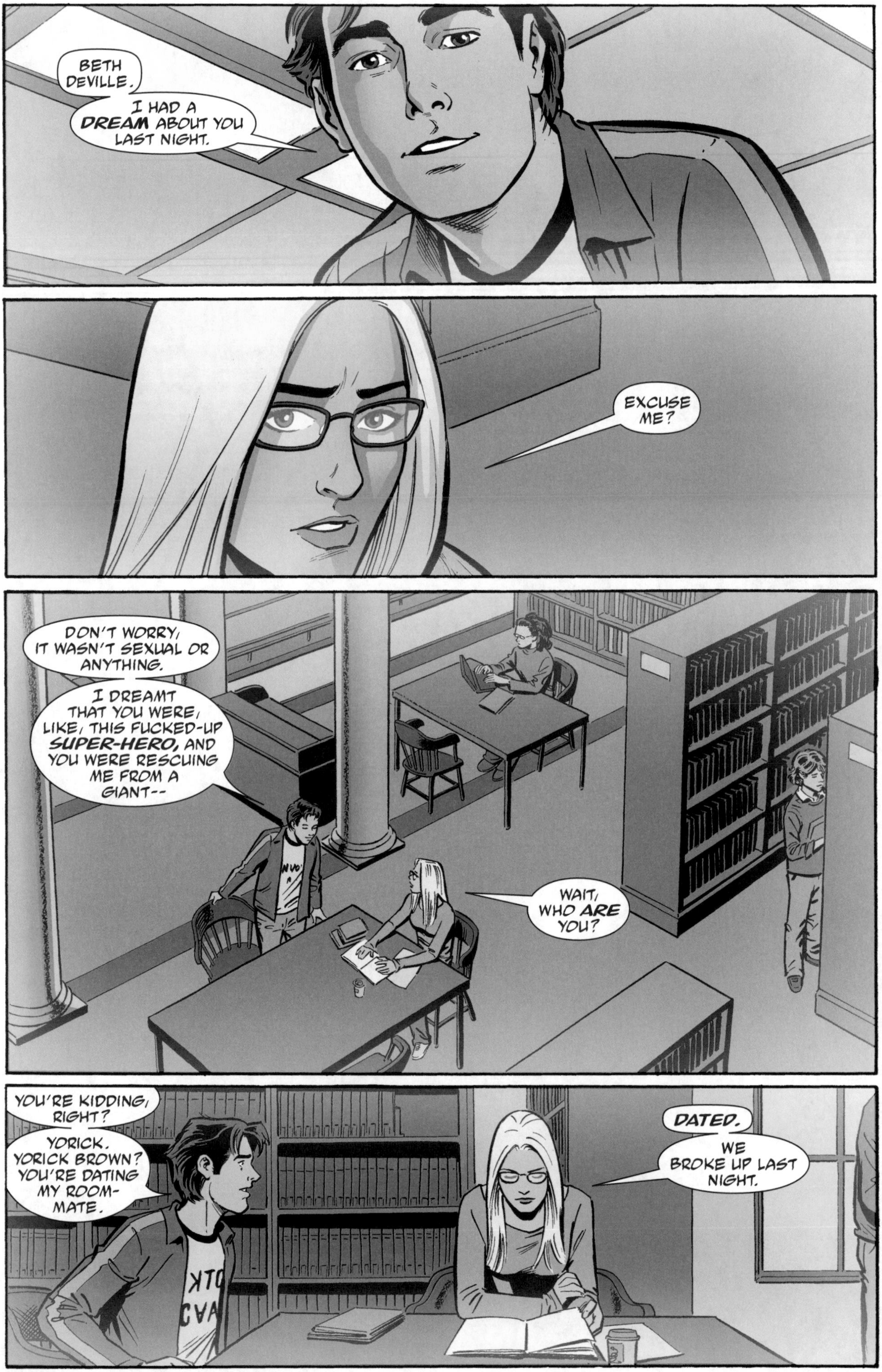
BETH DEVILLE.
I HAD A DREAM ABOUT YOU LAST NIGHT.
EXCUSE ME?
DON'T WORRY, IT WASN'T SEXUAL OR ANYTHING.
I DREAMT THAT YOU WERE, LIKE, THIS FUCKED-UP SUPER-HERO, AND YOU WERE RESCUING ME FROM A GIANT--
WAIT, WHO ARE YOU?
YOU'RE KIDDING, RIGHT?
YORICK. YORICK BROWN? YOU'RE DATING MY ROOM-MATE.
DATED.
WE BROKE UP LAST NIGHT.

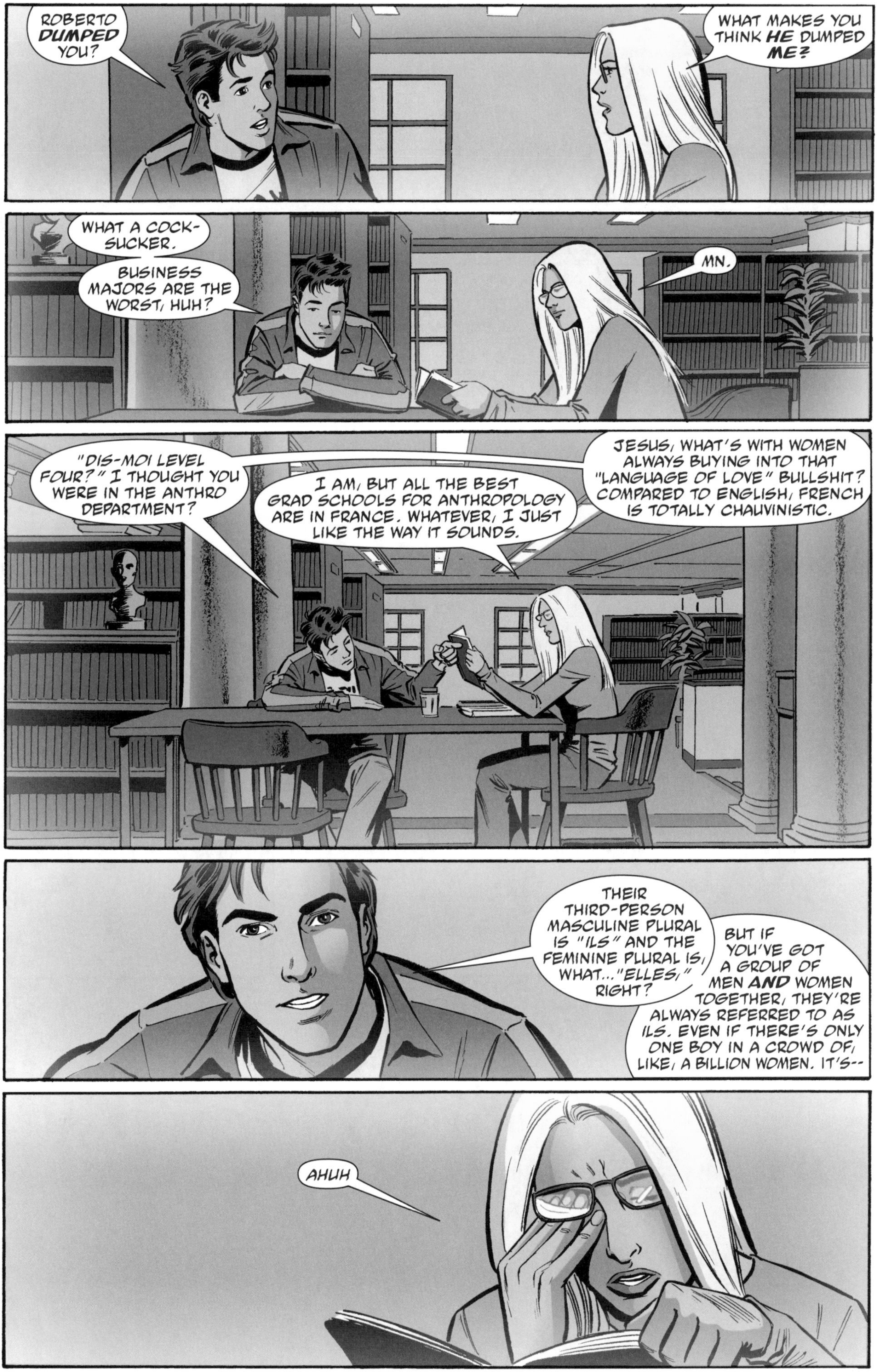
ROBERTO DUMPED YOU?
WHAT MAKES YOU THINK HE DUMPED ME?
WHAT A COCK-SUCKER.
BUSINESS MAJORS ARE THE WORST, HUH?
MN.
"DIS-MOI LEVEL FOUR?" I THOUGHT YOU WERE IN THE ANTHRO DEPARTMENT?
I AM, BUT ALL THE BEST GRAD SCHOOLS FOR ANTHROPOLOGY ARE IN FRANCE. WHATEVER, I JUST LIKE THE WAY IT SOUNDS.
JESUS, WHAT'S WITH WOMEN ALWAYS BUYING INTO THAT "LANGUAGE OF LOVE" BULLSHIT? COMPARED TO ENGLISH, FRENCH IS TOTALLY CHAUVINISTIC.
THEIR THIRD-PERSON MASCULINE PLURAL IS "ILS" AND THE FEMININE PLURAL IS, WHAT..."ELLES," RIGHT?
BUT IF YOU'VE GOT A GROUP OF MEN AND WOMEN TOGETHER, THEY'RE ALWAYS REFERRED TO AS ILS. EVEN IF THERE'S ONLY ONE BOY IN A CROWD OF, LIKE, A BILLION WOMEN. IT'S--
AHUH

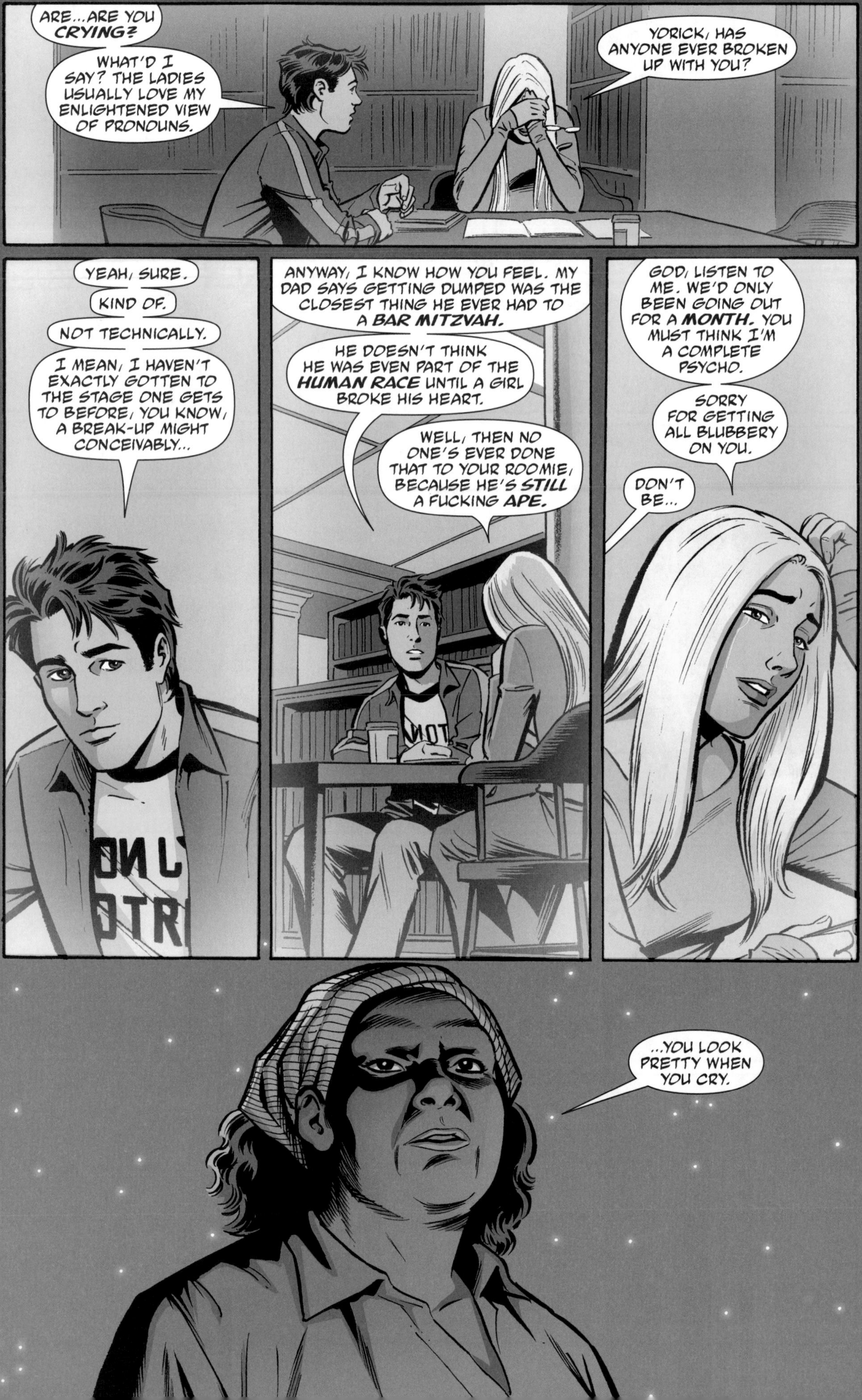
ARE...ARE YOU CRYING?
WHAT'D I SAY? THE LADIES USUALLY LOVE MY ENLIGHTENED VIEW OF PRONOUNS.
YORICK, HAS ANYONE EVER BROKEN UP WITH YOU?
YEAH, SURE.
KIND OF.
NOT TECHNICALLY.
I MEAN, I HAVEN'T EXACTLY GOTTEN TO THE STAGE ONE GETS TO BEFORE, YOU KNOW, A BREAK-UP MIGHT CONCEIVABLY...
ANYWAY, I KNOW HOW YOU FEEL. MY DAD SAYS GETTING DUMPED WAS THE CLOSEST THING HE EVER HAD TO A BAR MITZVAH.
HE DOESN'T THINK HE WAS EVEN PART OF THE HUMAN RACE UNTIL A GIRL BROKE HIS HEART.
WELL, THEN NO ONE'S EVER DONE THAT TO YOUR ROOMIE, BECAUSE HE'S STILL A FUCKING APE.
GOD, LISTEN TO ME. WE'D ONLY BEEN GOING OUT FOR A MONTH. YOU MUST THINK I'M A COMPLETE PSYCHO.
SORRY FOR GETTING ALL BLUBBERY ON YOU.
DON'T BE...
...YOU LOOK PRETTY WHEN YOU CRY.

WHAT?

I **SAID**, HOW THE HELL ARE WE SUPPOSED TO GET OUT OF HERE?

THE GUIDES ARE GONE, HALF OUR CLASS IS **DEAD**, THE SAT-PHONE SUDDENLY DOESN'T WORK FOR SHIT, AND OUR RATIONS ARE FUCKING **TOXIC!**

SETTLE, MARGO. WE DON'T **KNOW** THAT THE FOOD KILLED THEM.

WELL, THAT'S BLOODY REASSURING, BOSS. MAYBE IT'S JUST **EBOLA.**

NO, IT WAS THE **ABOS.**

WATCH YOUR MOUTH.

THINK ABOUT IT.

WHY'D THE PROF SAY THE LOCALS DIDN'T WANT WHITES KILLING OFF ANY MORE KANGAROOS, EVEN THOUGH THE GODDAMN SKIPPERS HAVE BEEN CHOKING THE LAND TO DEATH?

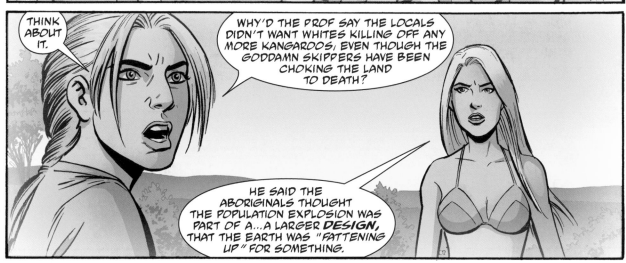

HE SAID THE ABORIGINALS THOUGHT THE POPULATION EXPLOSION WAS PART OF A...A LARGER **DESIGN,** THAT THE EARTH WAS "FATTENING UP" FOR SOMETHING.

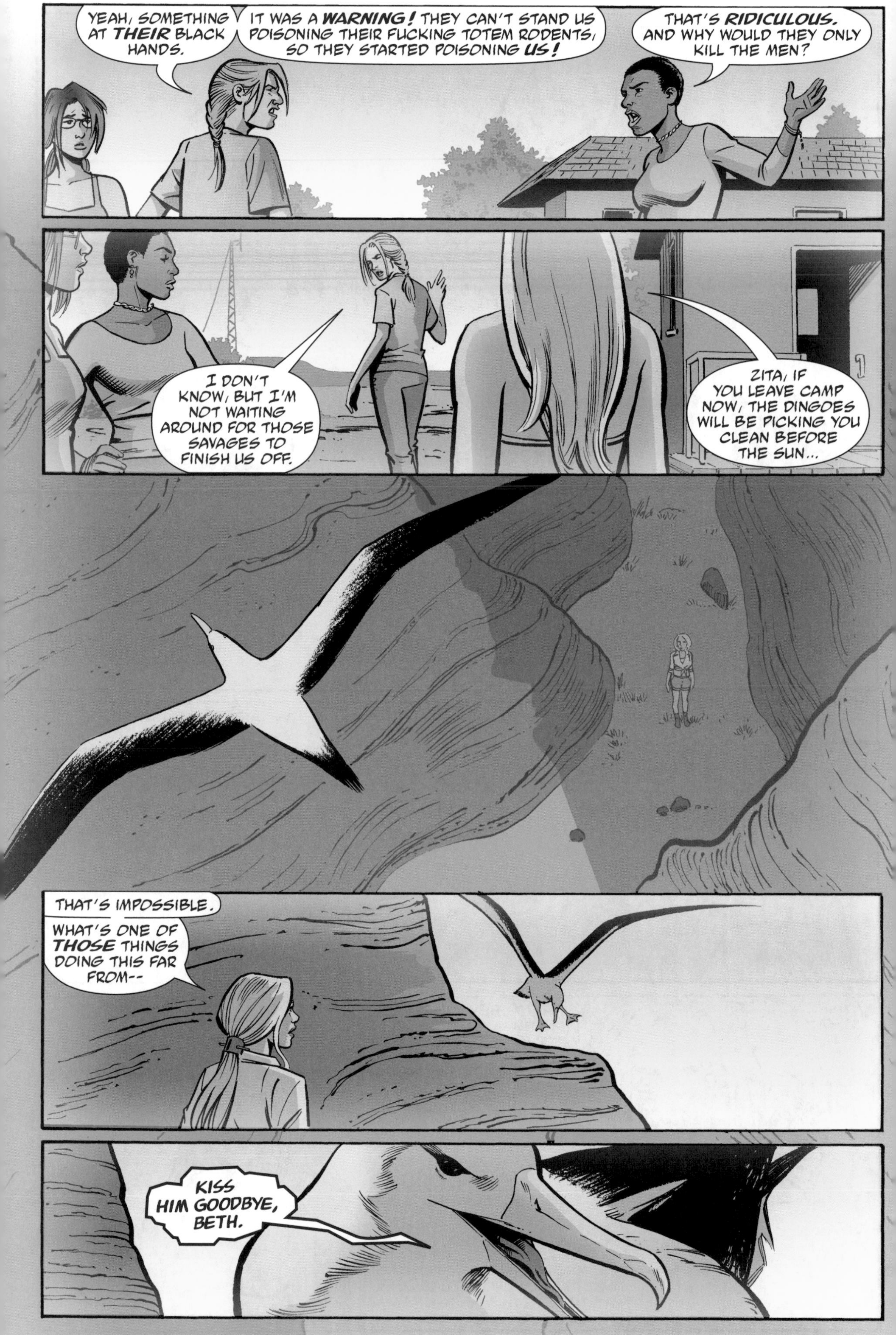
YEAH, SOMETHING AT THEIR BLACK HANDS.
IT WAS A WARNING! THEY CAN'T STAND US POISONING THEIR FUCKING TOTEM RODENTS, SO THEY STARTED POISONING US!
THAT'S RIDICULOUS. AND WHY WOULD THEY ONLY KILL THE MEN?
I DON'T KNOW, BUT I'M NOT WAITING AROUND FOR THOSE SAVAGES TO FINISH US OFF.
ZITA, IF YOU LEAVE CAMP NOW, THE DINGOES WILL BE PICKING YOU CLEAN BEFORE THE SUN...
THAT'S IMPOSSIBLE.
WHAT'S ONE OF THOSE THINGS DOING THIS FAR FROM--
KISS HIM GOODBYE, BETH.

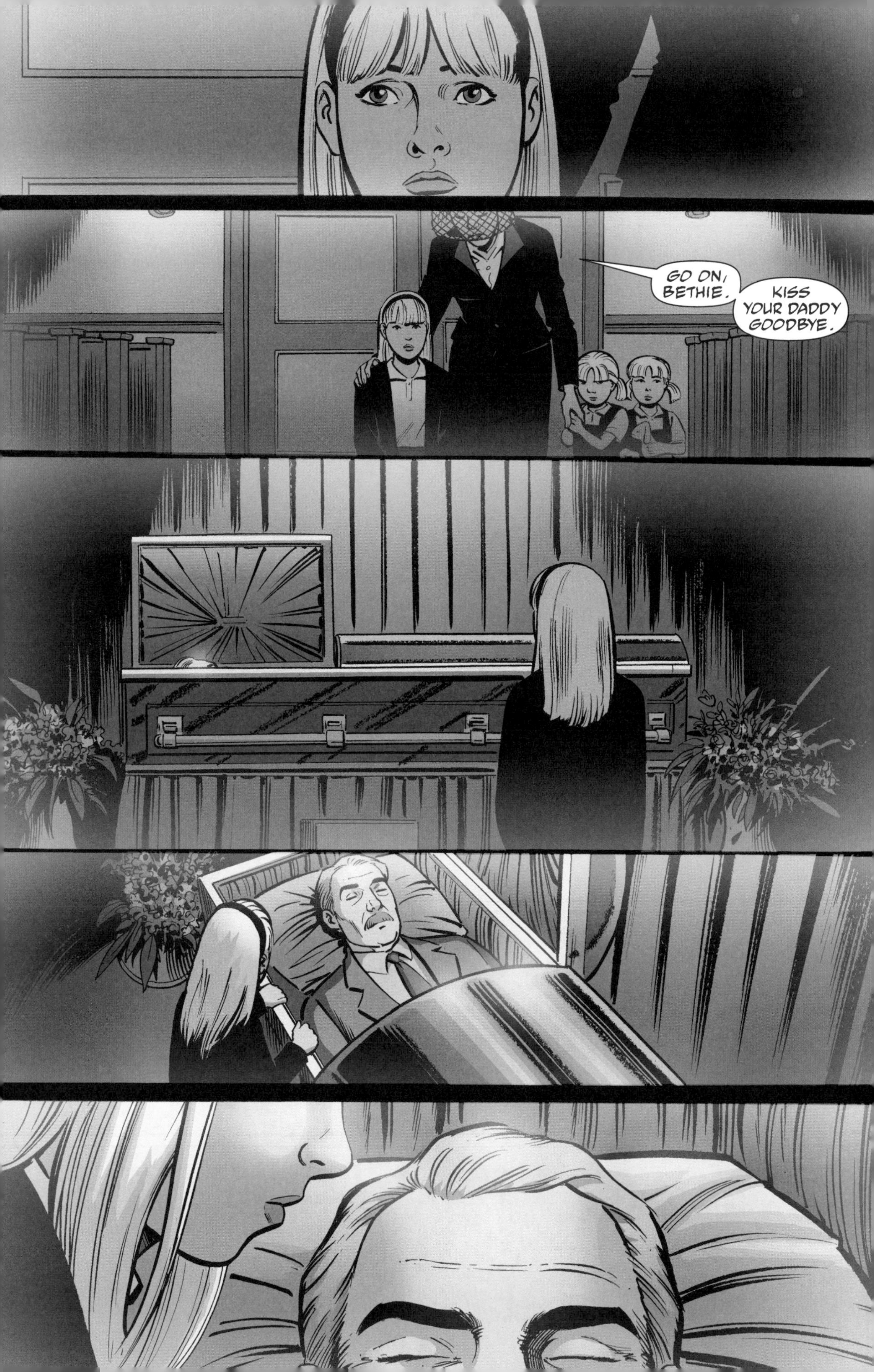
GO ON, BETHIE.
KISS YOUR DADDY GOODBYE.

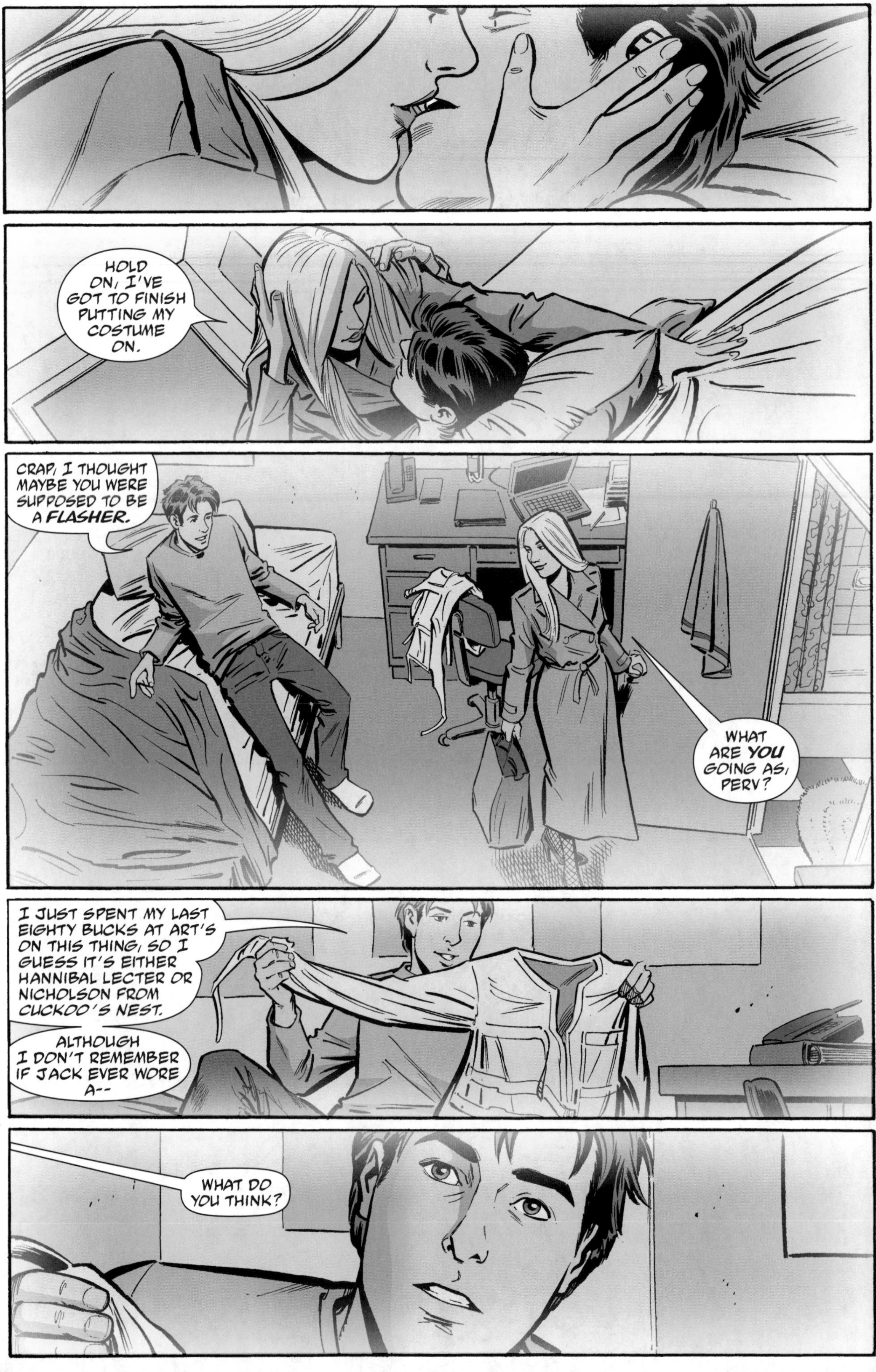
HOLD ON, I'VE GOT TO FINISH PUTTING MY COSTUME ON.
CRAP, I THOUGHT MAYBE YOU WERE SUPPOSED TO BE A FLASHER.
WHAT ARE YOU GOING AS, PERV?
I JUST SPENT MY LAST EIGHTY BUCKS AT ART'S ON THIS THING, SO I GUESS IT'S EITHER HANNIBAL LECTER OR NICHOLSON FROM CUCKOO'S NEST.
ALTHOUGH I DON'T REMEMBER IF JACK EVER WORE A--
WHAT DO YOU THINK?

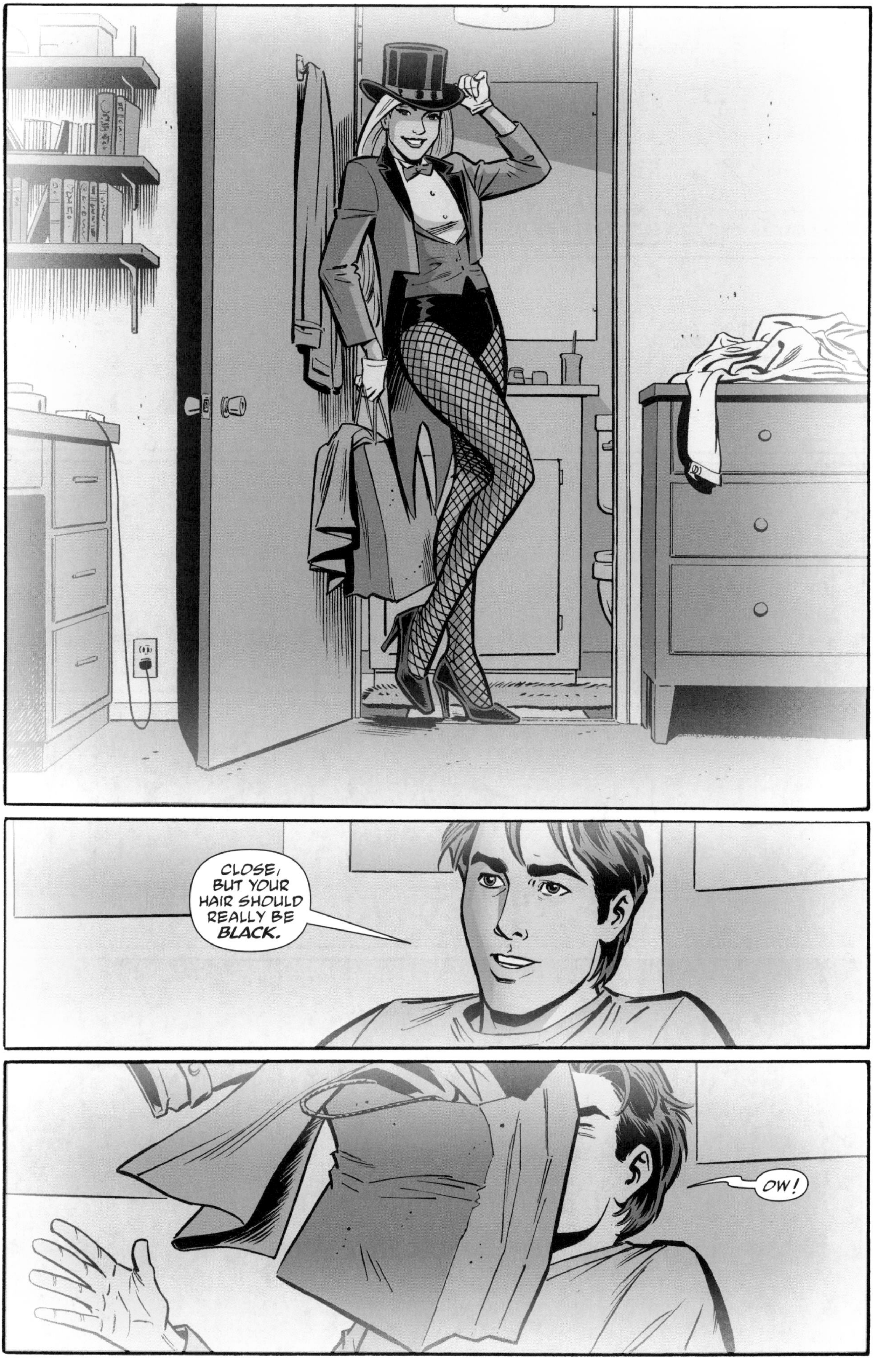
CLOSE, BUT YOUR HAIR SHOULD REALLY BE BLACK.
OW!

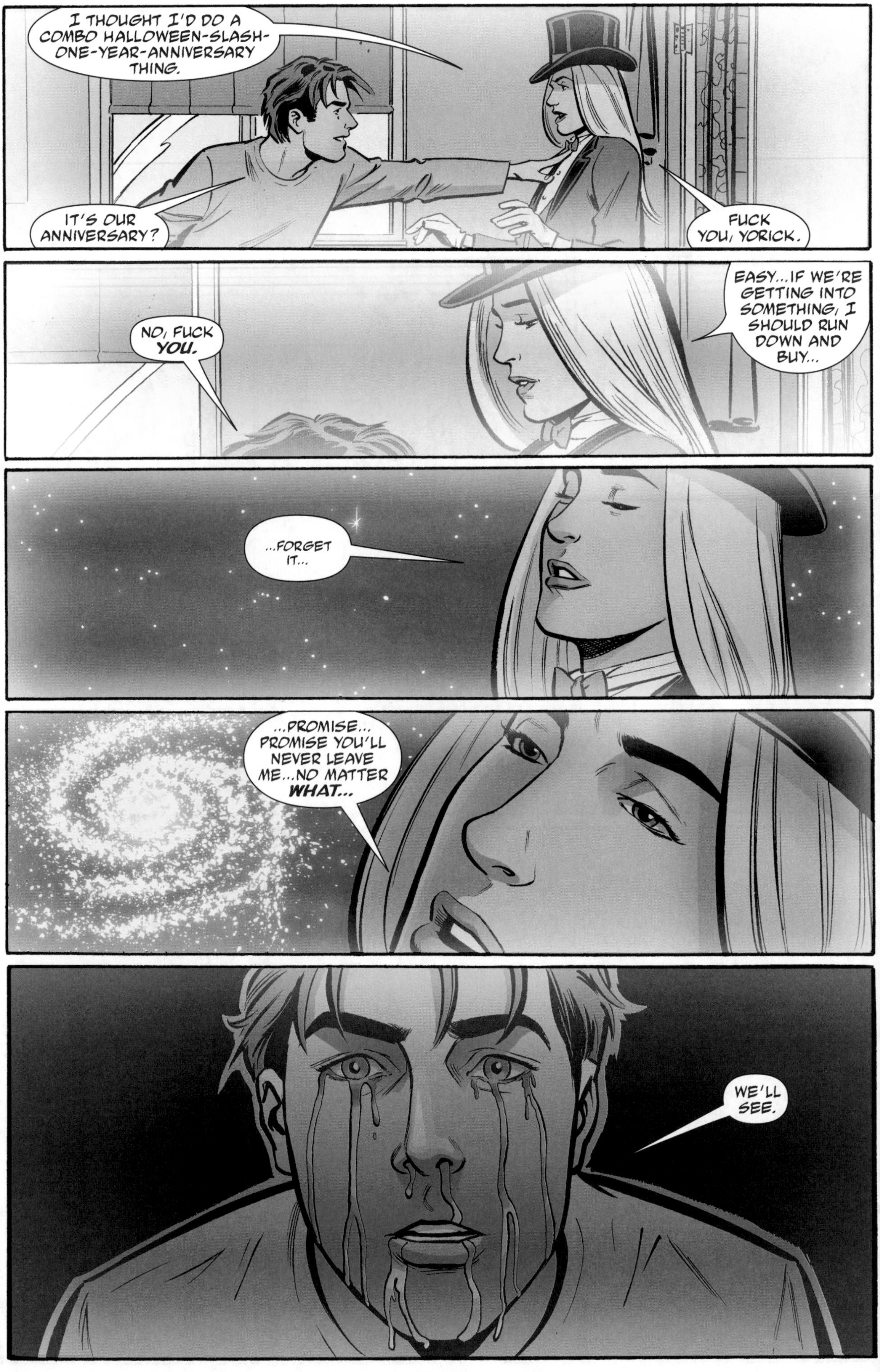
I THOUGHT I'D DO A COMBO HALLOWEEN-SLASH-ONE-YEAR-ANNIVERSARY THING.
IT'S OUR ANNIVERSARY?
FUCK YOU, YORICK.
NO, FUCK YOU.
EASY...IF WE'RE GETTING INTO SOMETHING, I SHOULD RUN DOWN AND BUY...
...FORGET IT...
...PROMISE... PROMISE YOU'LL NEVER LEAVE ME...NO MATTER WHAT...
WE'LL SEE.

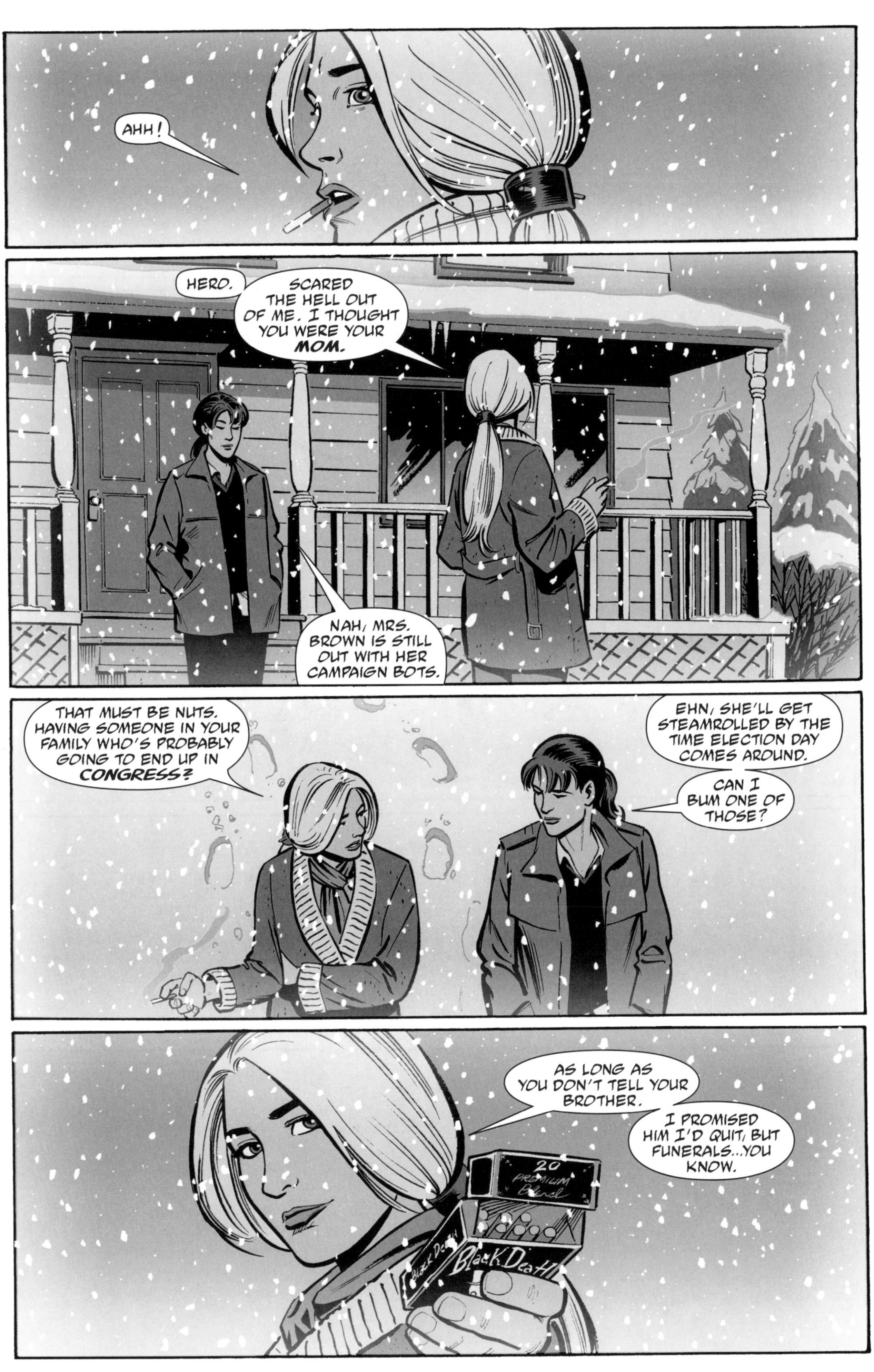
AHH!
HERO.
SCARED THE HELL OUT OF ME. I THOUGHT YOU WERE YOUR **MOM.**
NAH, MRS. BROWN IS STILL OUT WITH HER CAMPAIGN BOTS.
THAT MUST BE NUTS. HAVING SOMEONE IN YOUR FAMILY WHO'S PROBABLY GOING TO END UP IN **CONGRESS?**
EHN, SHE'LL GET STEAMROLLED BY THE TIME ELECTION DAY COMES AROUND.
CAN I BUM ONE OF THOSE?
AS LONG AS YOU DON'T TELL YOUR BROTHER.
I PROMISED HIM I'D QUIT, BUT FUNERALS...YOU KNOW.
20 PREMIUM Blend
Black Death

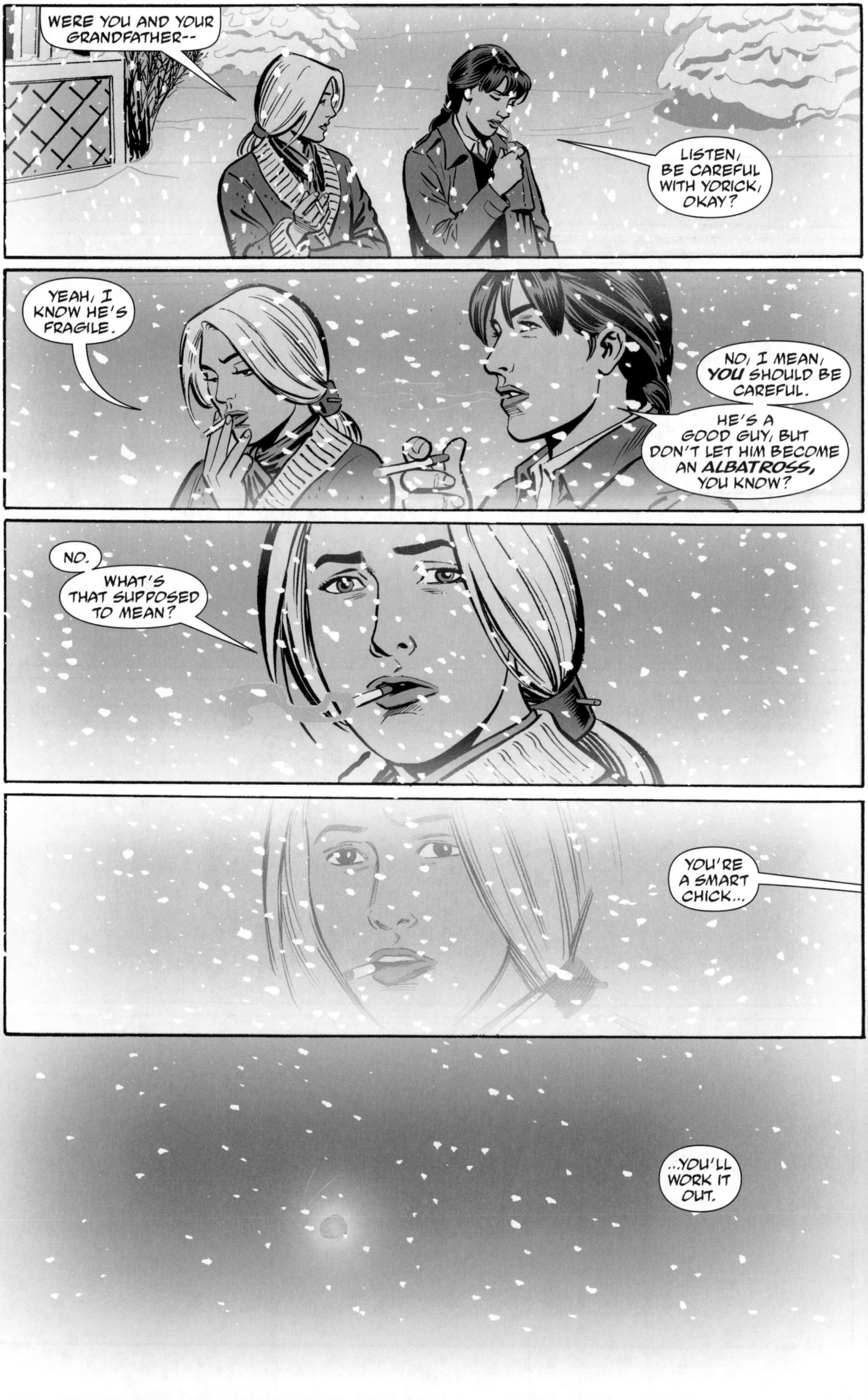
WERE YOU AND YOUR GRANDFATHER--
LISTEN, BE CAREFUL WITH YORICK, OKAY?
YEAH, I KNOW HE'S FRAGILE.
NO, I MEAN, YOU SHOULD BE CAREFUL.
HE'S A GOOD GUY, BUT DON'T LET HIM BECOME AN ALBATROSS, YOU KNOW?
NO.
WHAT'S THAT SUPPOSED TO MEAN?
YOU'RE A SMART CHICK...
...YOU'LL WORK IT OUT.

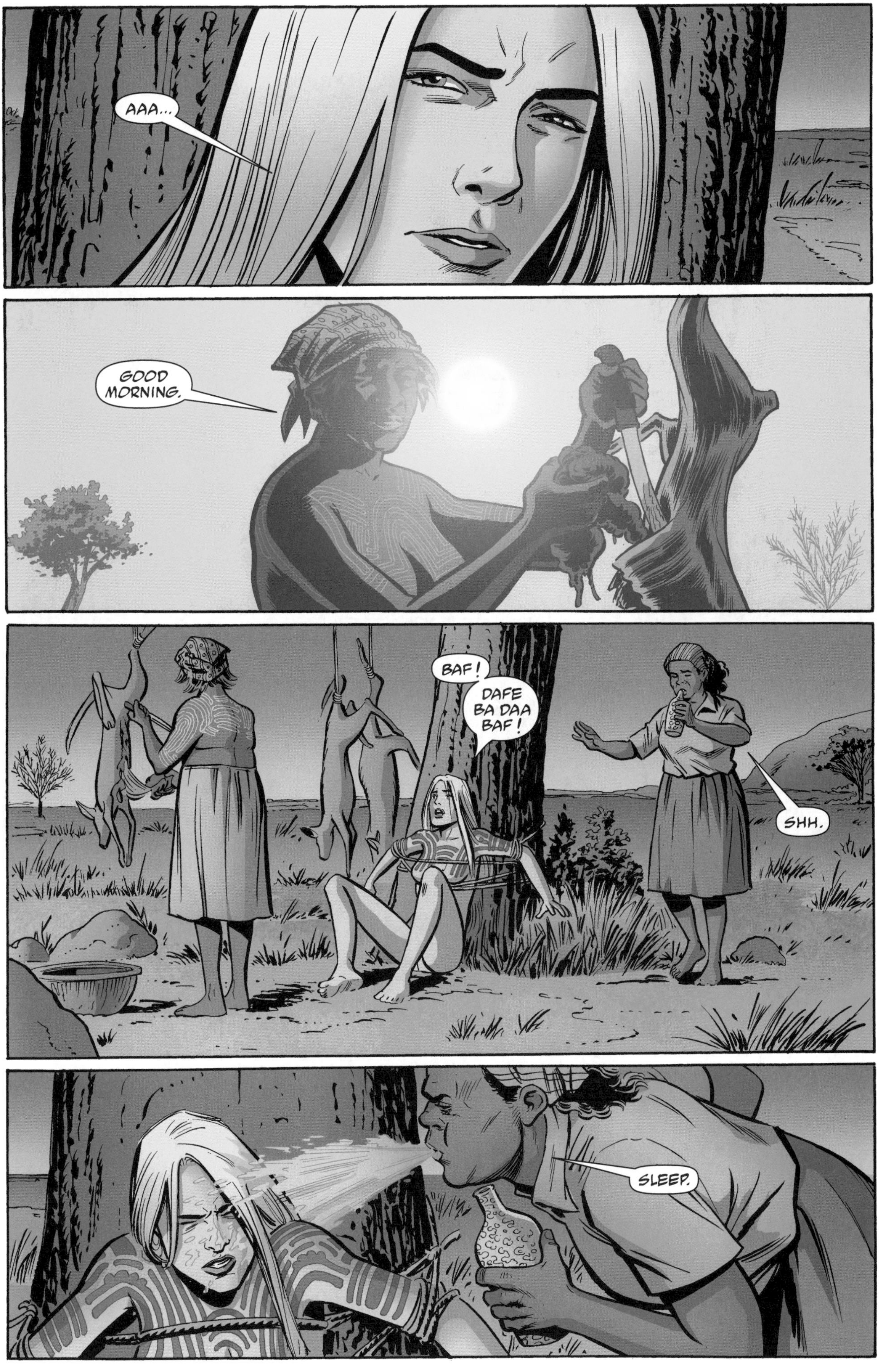
AAA...
GOOD MORNING.
BAF! DAFE BA DAA BAF!
SHH.
SLEEP.

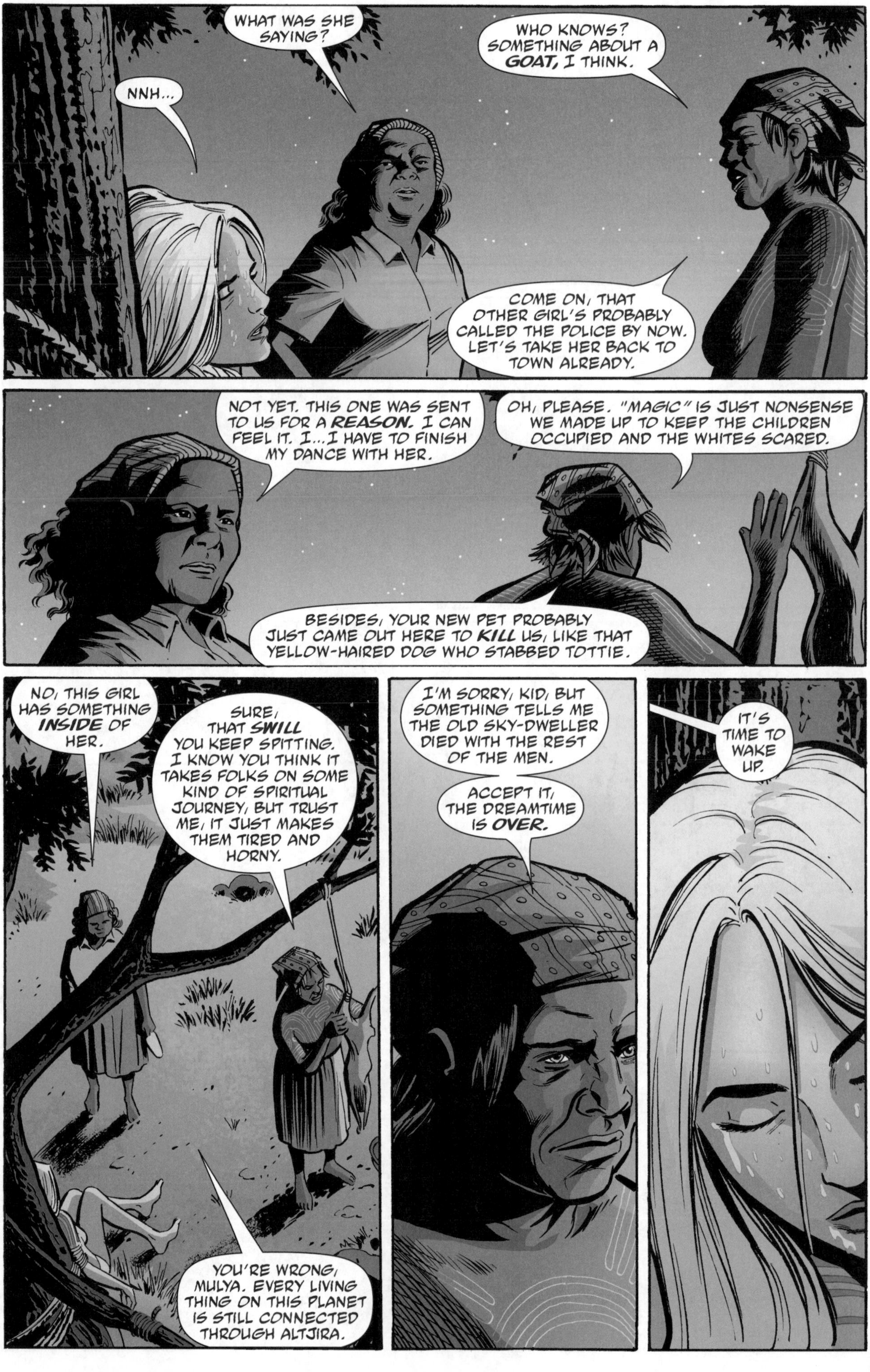
WHAT WAS SHE SAYING?
NNH...
WHO KNOWS? SOMETHING ABOUT A GOAT, I THINK.
COME ON, THAT OTHER GIRL'S PROBABLY CALLED THE POLICE BY NOW. LET'S TAKE HER BACK TO TOWN ALREADY.
NOT YET. THIS ONE WAS SENT TO US FOR A REASON. I CAN FEEL IT. I...I HAVE TO FINISH MY DANCE WITH HER.
OH, PLEASE. "MAGIC" IS JUST NONSENSE WE MADE UP TO KEEP THE CHILDREN OCCUPIED AND THE WHITES SCARED.
BESIDES, YOUR NEW PET PROBABLY JUST CAME OUT HERE TO KILL US, LIKE THAT YELLOW-HAIRED DOG WHO STABBED TOTTIE.
NO, THIS GIRL HAS SOMETHING INSIDE OF HER.
SURE, THAT SWILL YOU KEEP SPITTING. I KNOW YOU THINK IT TAKES FOLKS ON SOME KIND OF SPIRITUAL JOURNEY, BUT TRUST ME, IT JUST MAKES THEM TIRED AND HORNY.
YOU'RE WRONG, MULYA. EVERY LIVING THING ON THIS PLANET IS STILL CONNECTED THROUGH ALTJIRA.
I'M SORRY, KID, BUT SOMETHING TELLS ME THE OLD SKY-DWELLER DIED WITH THE REST OF THE MEN.
ACCEPT IT, THE DREAMTIME IS OVER.
IT'S TIME TO WAKE UP.

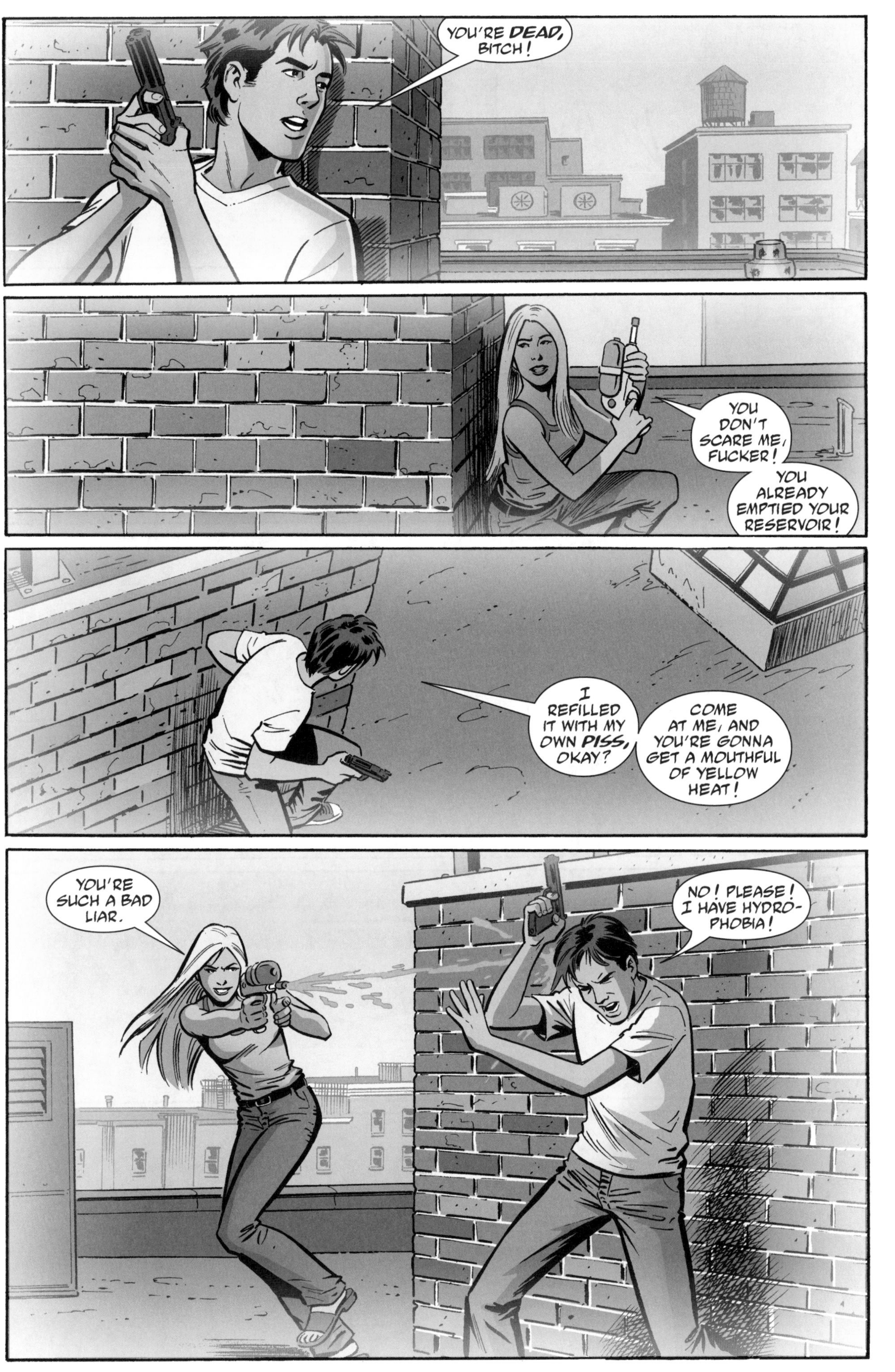
YOU'RE DEAD, BITCH!
YOU DON'T SCARE ME, FUCKER!
YOU ALREADY EMPTIED YOUR RESERVOIR!
I REFILLED IT WITH MY OWN PISS, OKAY?
COME AT ME, AND YOU'RE GONNA GET A MOUTHFUL OF YELLOW HEAT!
YOU'RE SUCH A BAD LIAR.
NO! PLEASE! I HAVE HYDRO-PHOBIA!

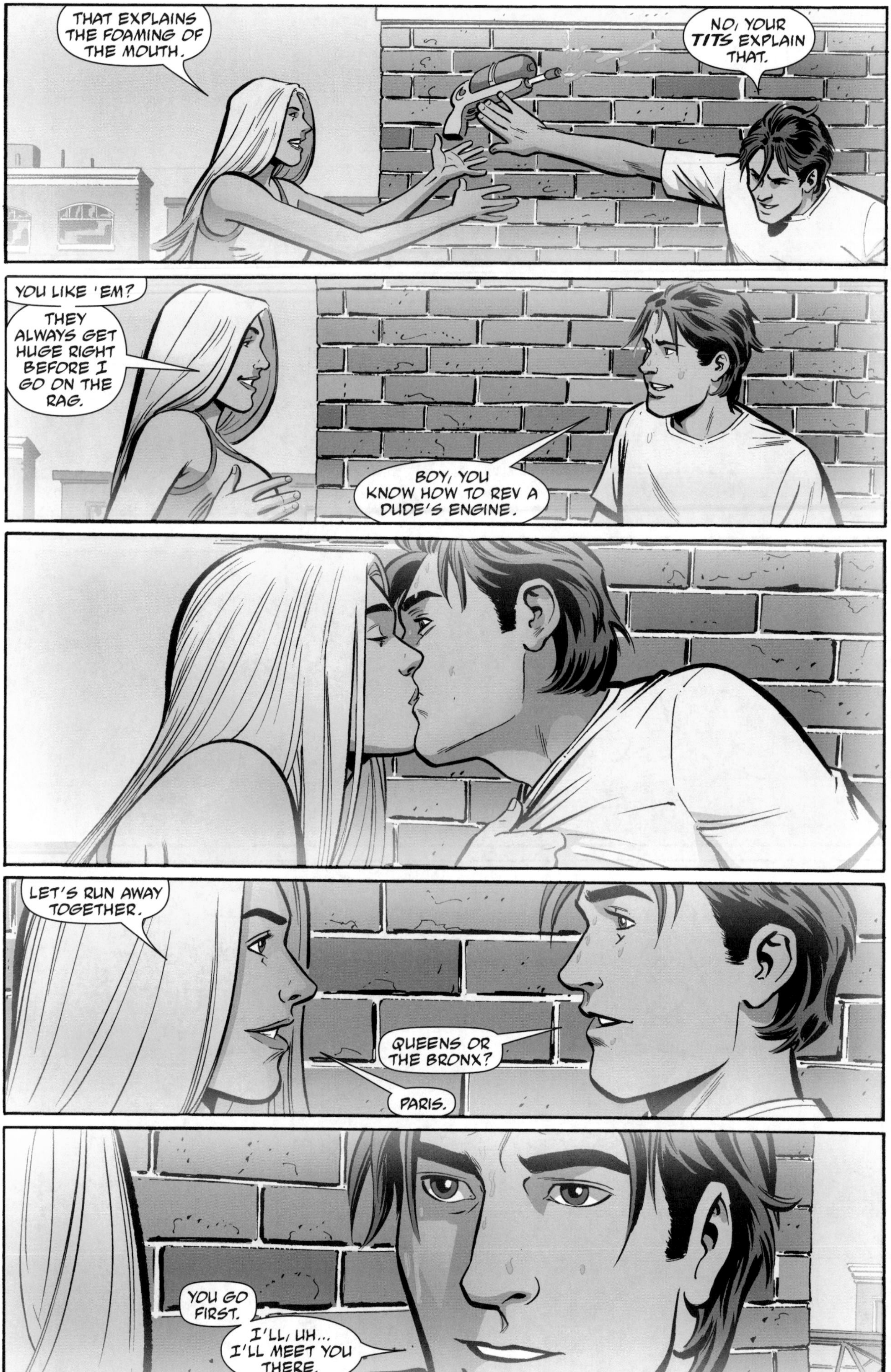
THAT EXPLAINS THE FOAMING OF THE MOUTH.
NO, YOUR TITS EXPLAIN THAT.
YOU LIKE 'EM?
THEY ALWAYS GET HUGE RIGHT BEFORE I GO ON THE RAG.
BOY, YOU KNOW HOW TO REV A DUDE'S ENGINE.
LET'S RUN AWAY TOGETHER.
QUEENS OR THE BRONX?
PARIS.
YOU GO FIRST.
I'LL, UH... I'LL MEET YOU THERE.

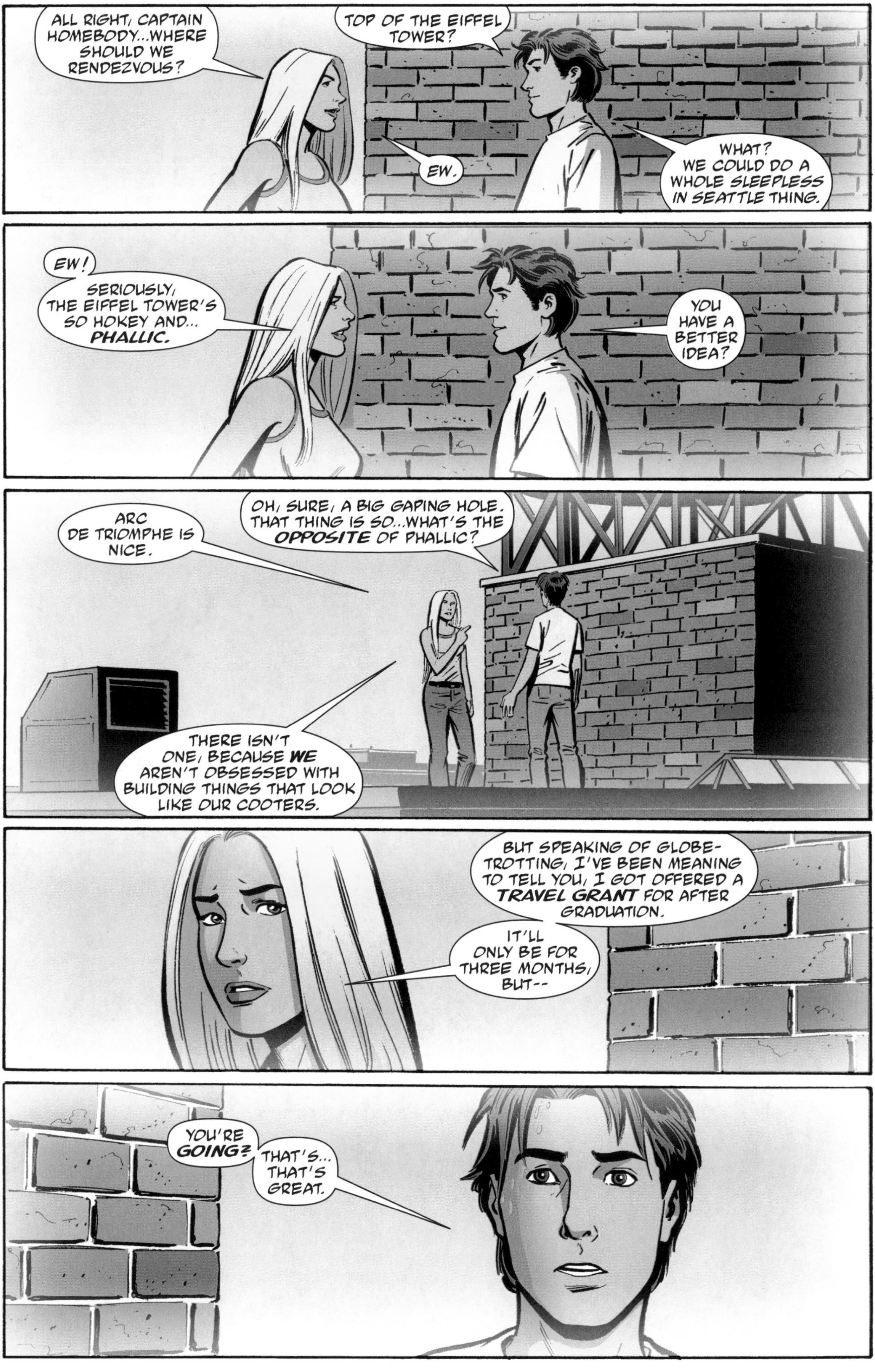
ALL RIGHT, CAPTAIN HOMEBODY...WHERE SHOULD WE RENDEZVOUS?
TOP OF THE EIFFEL TOWER?
EW.
WHAT? WE COULD DO A WHOLE SLEEPLESS IN SEATTLE THING.
EW!
SERIOUSLY, THE EIFFEL TOWER'S SO HOKEY AND... PHALLIC.
YOU HAVE A BETTER IDEA?
ARC DE TRIOMPHE IS NICE.
OH, SURE, A BIG GAPING HOLE. THAT THING IS SO...WHAT'S THE OPPOSITE OF PHALLIC?
THERE ISN'T ONE, BECAUSE WE AREN'T OBSESSED WITH BUILDING THINGS THAT LOOK LIKE OUR COOTERS.
BUT SPEAKING OF GLOBE-TROTTING, I'VE BEEN MEANING TO TELL YOU, I GOT OFFERED A TRAVEL GRANT FOR AFTER GRADUATION.
IT'LL ONLY BE FOR THREE MONTHS, BUT--
YOU'RE GOING?
THAT'S... THAT'S GREAT.

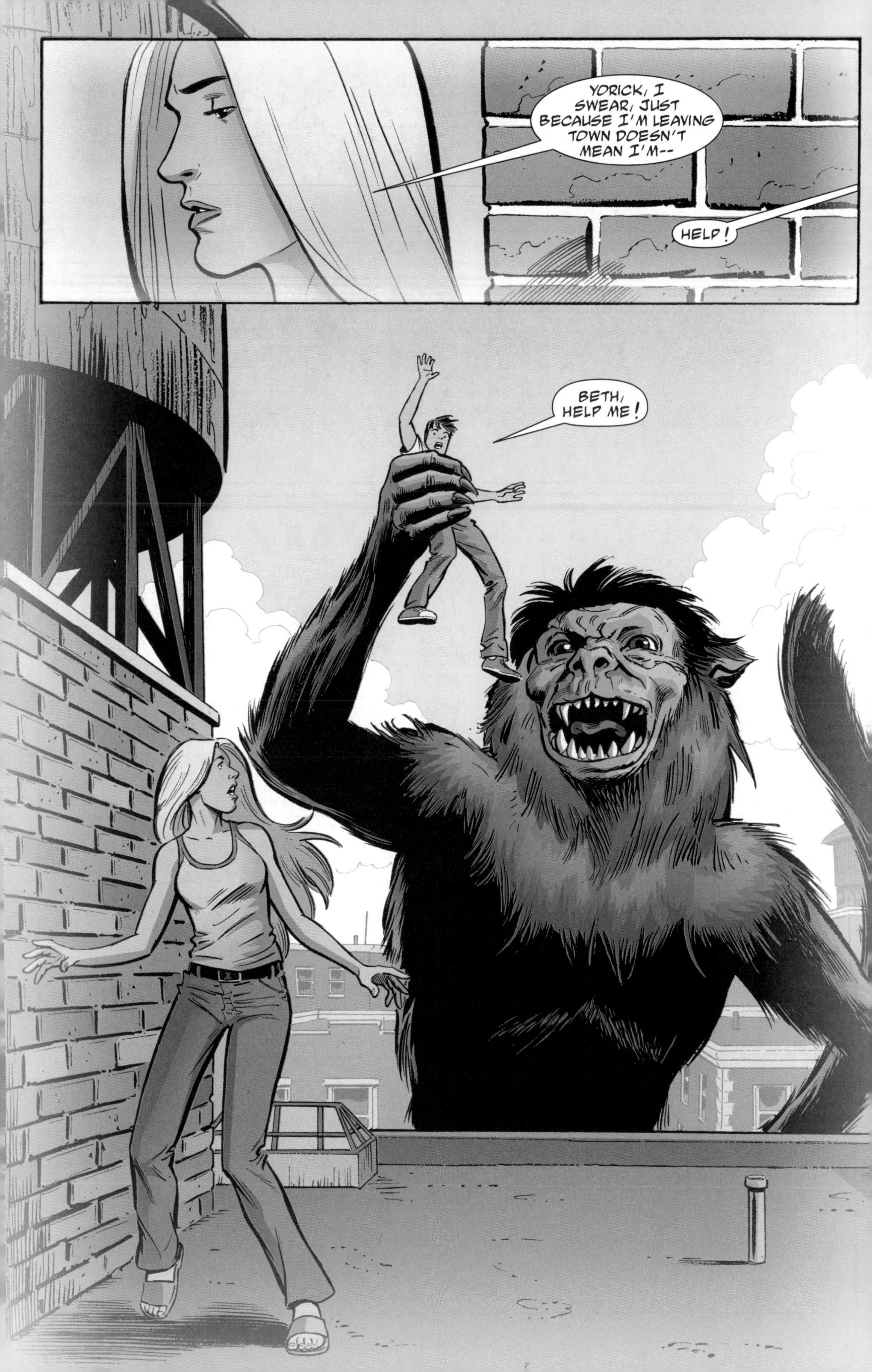
YORICK, I SWEAR, JUST BECAUSE I'M LEAVING TOWN DOESN'T MEAN I'M--
HELP!
BETH, HELP ME!

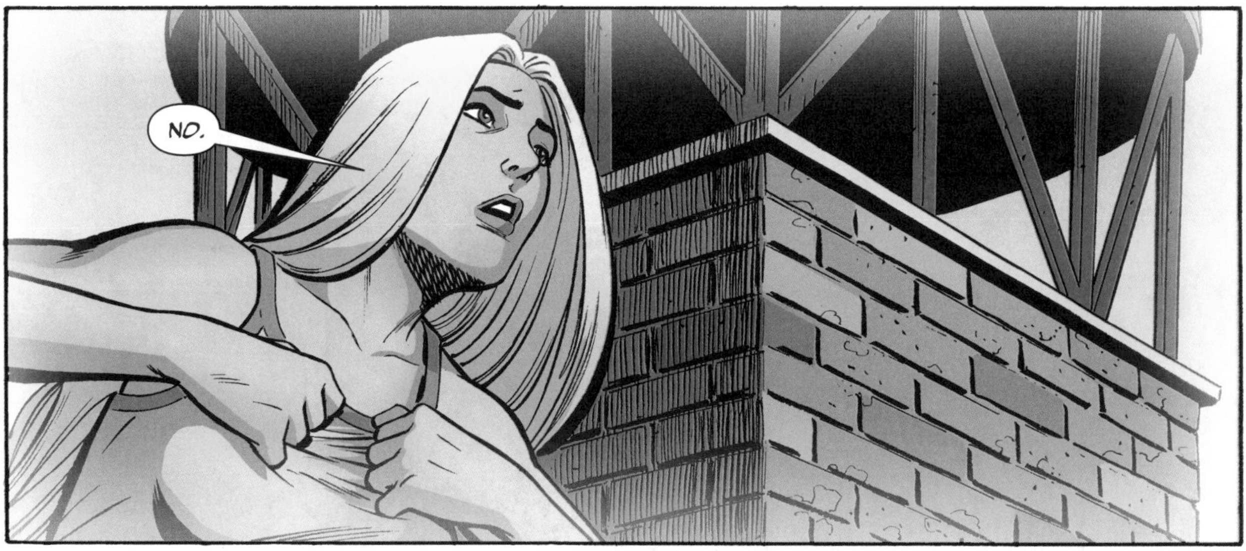
NO.

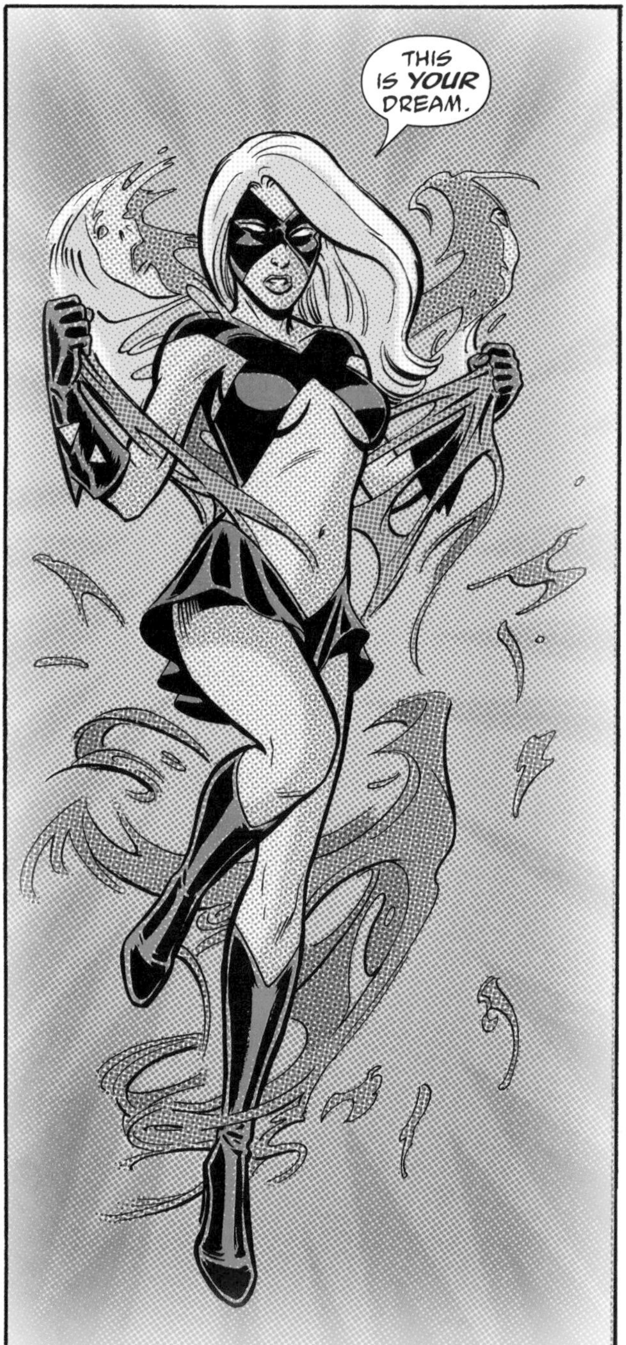
THIS IS **YOUR** DREAM.

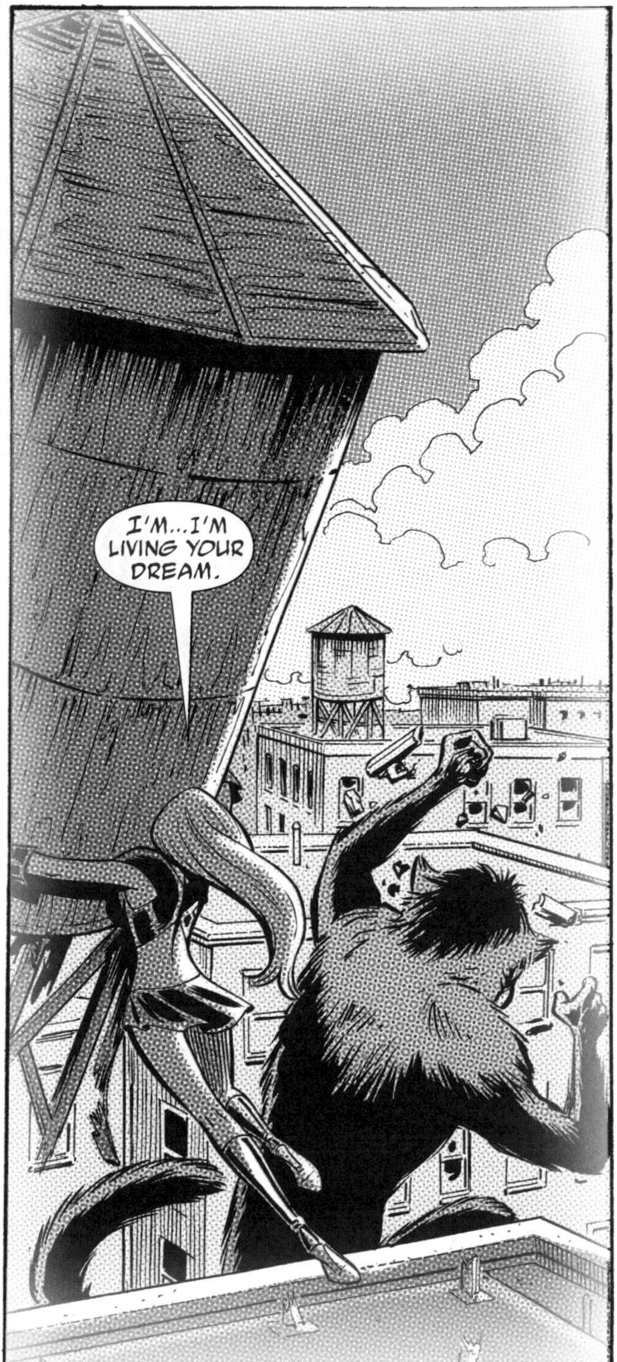
I'M...I'M LIVING YOUR DREAM.

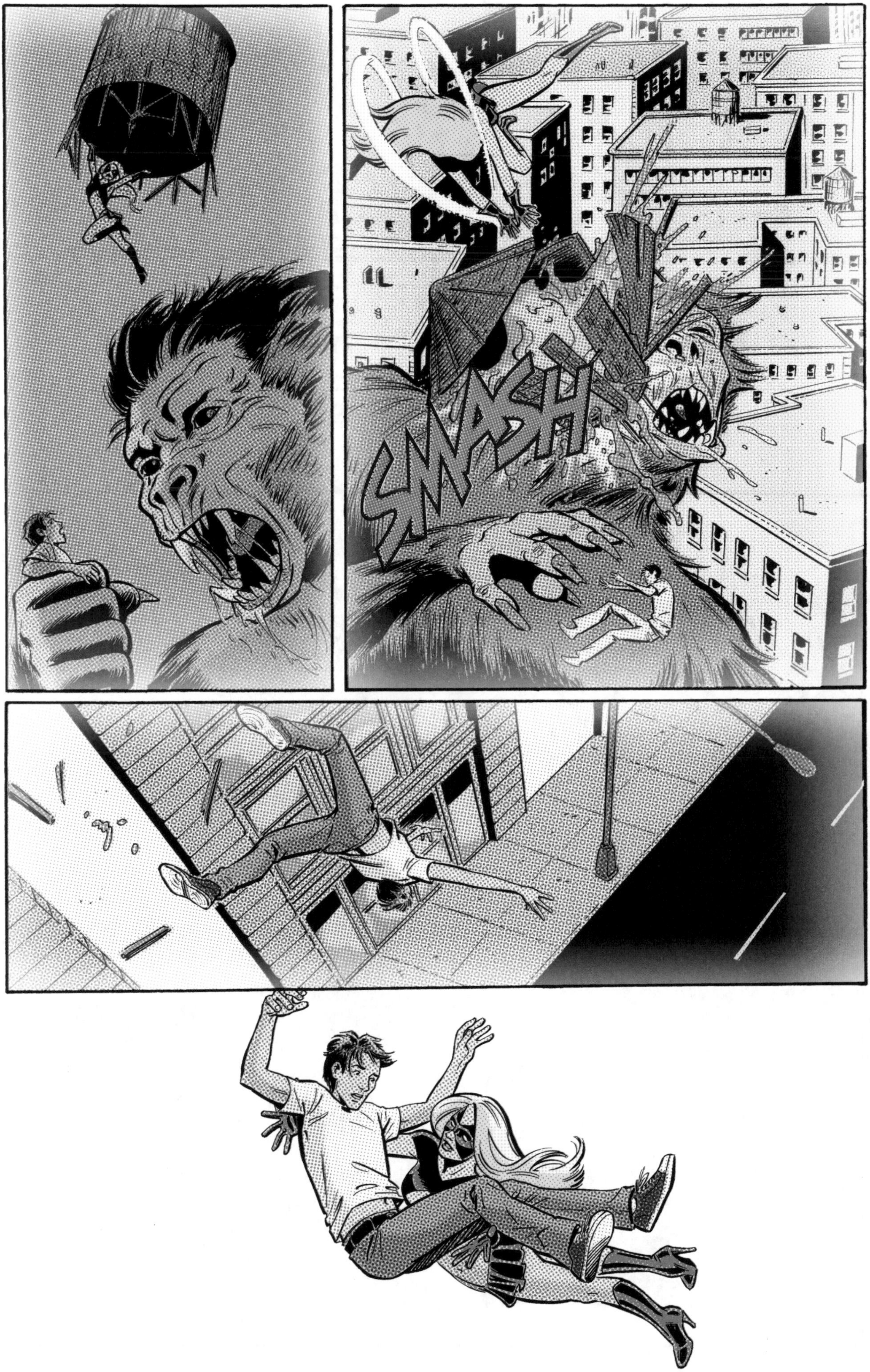
SMASH

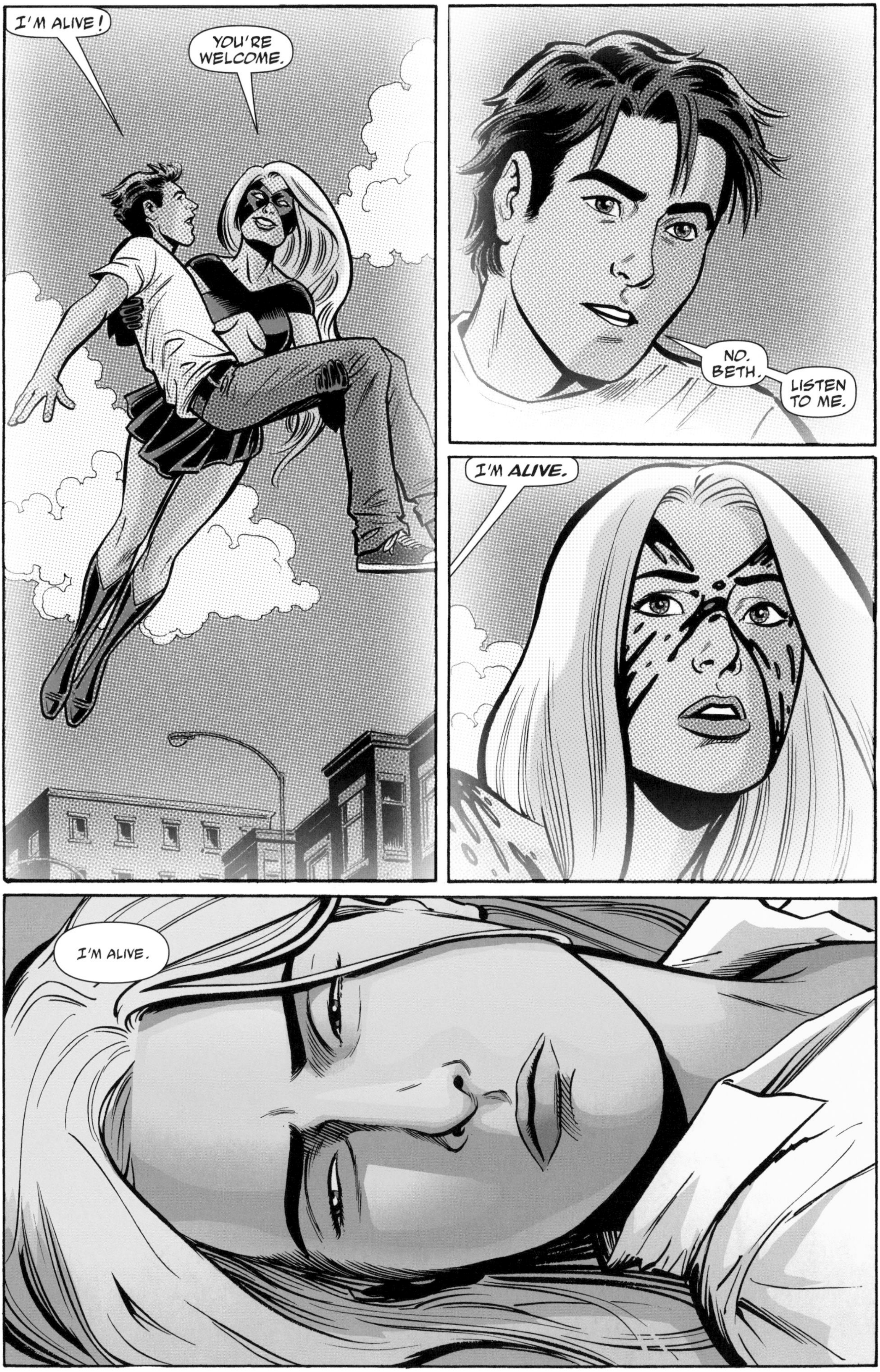
I'M ALIVE!
YOU'RE WELCOME.
NO. BETH.
LISTEN TO ME.
I'M ALIVE.
I'M ALIVE.

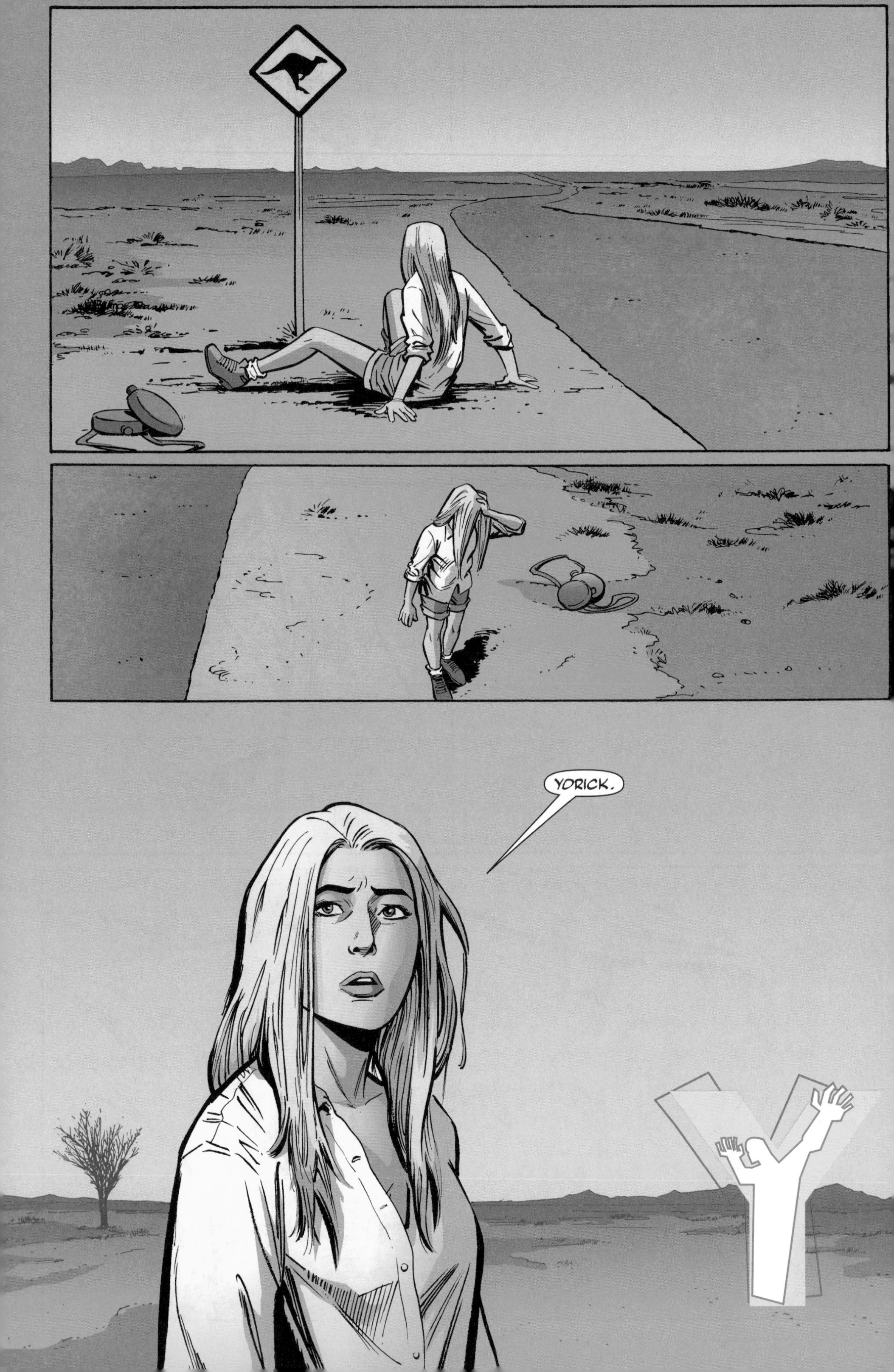
YORICK.

# Y: THE SCRIPT

The complete script to Y: THE LAST MAN #36
by co-creator and writer Brian K. Vaughan.

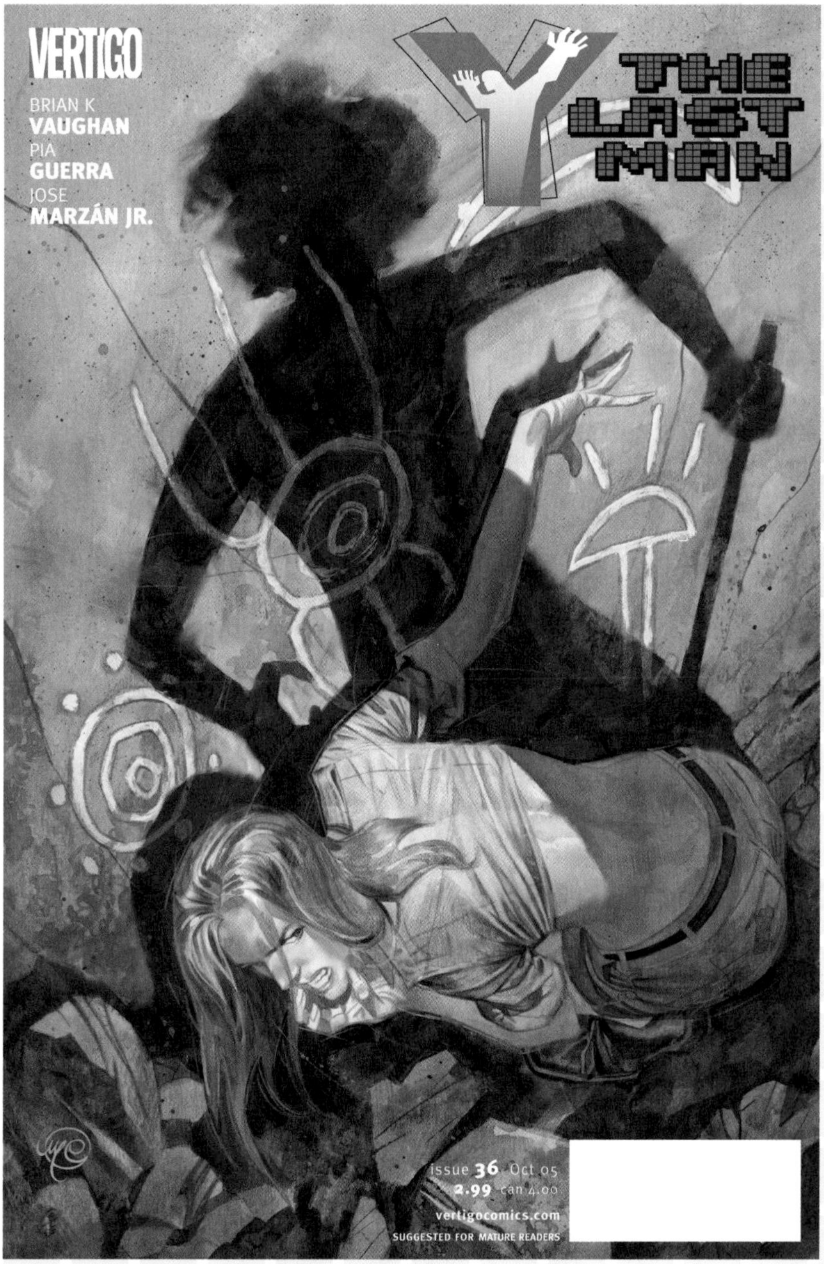
VERTIGO
BRIAN K VAUGHAN
PIA GUERRA
JOSE MARZÁN JR.
Y THE LAST MAN
issue 36 Oct 05
2.99 can 4.00
vertigocomics.com
SUGGESTED FOR MATURE READERS

**"Boy Loses Girl"**

The Full Script for Y #36

Prepared for Vertigo Comics

April 4, 2004

Brian K. Vaughan

## Page One

**Page One, SPLASH**

To welcome you back in style, Pia, we're going to open with this SPLASH of Yorick's old girlfriend BETH DEVILLE, who is unconscious, mostly naked (only wearing panties), and tightly bound by handmade ropes to the trunk of a medium-sized tree in the middle of the Australian Outback. It's night, but moonlight reveals that Beth is flanked by SIX DEAD KANGA-ROOS, tied upside-down by their tails to branches on either side of her. Our twenty-something heroine has Warlpiri tribal markings painted on her bare breasts in what appears to be BLOOD.

Please leave room for our title and credits at the very *bottom* fourth of this page!

1) <u>Title:</u>

# BOY LOSES GIRL

2) <u>Credits:</u>
Brian K. Vaughan
Writer

Pia Guerra
Penciller

José Marzán, Jr.
Inker

Clem Robins
Letterer

Zylonol
Colorist

Massimo Carnevale
Cover Artist

Casey Seijas
Assistant Editor

Will Dennis
Editor

Y: The Last Man Created by Vaughan and Guerra

## Page Two

### Page Two, Panel One

Smash cut to a few years in the past for the page-wide establishing shot of YORICK BROWN, circa his sophomore year of college.

1) <u>Yorick</u>: Beth Deville.
2) <u>Yorick</u>: I had a *dream* about you last night.

### Page Two, Panel Two

Cut over to a similarly framed shot of Beth, same age. She's wearing her glasses, and she looks up at us with confusion.

3) <u>Beth</u>: Excuse me?

### Page Two, Panel Three

Pull out to the largest panel of the page, as we reveal that Yorick has just taken a seat at a desk across from Beth inside of a large COLLEGE LIBRARY. Other STUDENTS can be milling around in the background. Beth puts down her book to stare at this weird kid. (And Pia, even when these next few scenes are in a naturalistic setting, they're all part of Beth's dream, so feel free to add subtle surreal touches throughout.)

4) <u>Yorick</u>: Don't worry, it wasn't sexual or anything.
5) <u>Yorick</u>: I dreamt that you were, like, this fucked-up *super-hero*, and you were rescuing me from a giant—

6) <u>Beth</u>: Wait, who *are* you?

### Page Two, Panel Four

Push in closer on the two. Yorick looks a little offended, as Beth returns to her book.

7) <u>Yorick</u>: You're kidding, right?
8) <u>Yorick</u>: Yorick. Yorick Brown? You're dating my *roommate*.

9) <u>Beth</u>: *Dated*.
10) <u>Beth</u>: We broke up last night.

## Page Three

### Page Three, Panel One

Change angles on the two. Now it's Beth's turn to look offended.

1) <u>Yorick</u>: Roberto *dumped* you?

2) <u>Beth</u>: What makes you think *he* dumped *me*?

**Page Three, Panel Two**

Similar framing, but as Yorick leans in, Beth returns to her book, which we can now see is a French textbook.

3) <u>Yorick</u>: What a cocksucker.
4) <u>Yorick</u>: Business majors are the worst, huh?

5) <u>Beth</u>: Mn.

**Page Three, Panel Three**

Pull out to the largest panel of the page, as Yorick tips up Beth's book to get a better look at its cover. Beth has given up trying to get rid of this dude.

6) <u>Yorick</u>: "Dis-Moi Level Four?" I thought you were in the anthro department?

7) <u>Beth</u>: I am, but all the best grad schools for anthropology are in France. Whatever, I just like the way it sounds.

8) <u>Yorick</u>: Jesus, what's with women always buying into that "language of love" bull-shit? Compared to English, French is totally chauvinistic.

**Page Three, Panel Four**

This is just a shot of brash English major Yorick, spouting off one of his patented Useless Factoids™.

9) <u>Yorick</u>: Their third-person masculine plural is "ils" and the feminine plural is, what... "elles," right?
10) <u>Yorick</u>: But if you've got a group of men *and* women together, they're always referred to as *ils*. Even if there's only one boy in a crowd of, like, a billion women. It's—

**Page Three, Panel Five**

Cut back to Beth, as she suddenly begins CRYING.

11) <u>Beth</u>: *ahuh*

## Page Four

**Page Four, Panel One**

Pull out to a shot of both characters for this largest panel of the page, as Beth takes off her glasses to rub her eyes. Yorick doesn't know what the fuck is going on.

1) <u>Yorick</u>: Are... are you *crying*?
2) <u>Yorick</u>: What'd I say? The ladies usually love my enlightened view of pronouns.

3) <u>Beth</u>: Yorick, has anyone ever broken up with you?

**Page Four, Panel Two**

This is just a shot of Yorick, at the prime of his reign as King of All Dorks.

4) <u>Yorick</u>: Yeah, sure.
5) <u>Yorick</u>: Kind of.
6) <u>Yorick</u>: Not technically.
7) <u>Yorick</u>: I mean, I haven't exactly gotten to the stage one gets to before, you know, a break-up might conceivably...

**Page Four, Panel Three**

Pull out to a shot of both characters, as Yorick genuinely tries to console Beth.

8) <u>Yorick</u>: Anyway, I know how you feel. My dad says getting dumped was the closest thing he ever had to a *bar mitzvah*.
9) <u>Yorick</u>: He doesn't think he was even part of the *human race* until a girl broke his heart.

10) <u>Beth</u>: Well, then no one's ever done that to your roomie, because he's still a fucking *ape*.

**Page Four, Panel Four**
This is just a shot of Beth, looking at us. Mascara is running down her spectacles-free face, but she still looks nice.

11) <u>Beth</u>: God, listen to me. We'd only been going out for a *month*. You must think I'm a complete psycho.
12) <u>Beth</u>: Sorry for getting all blubbery on you.

13) <u>Yorick (from off)</u>: Don't be…

**Page Four, Panel Five**
Cut over to where Yorick was just sitting, but now he's suddenly and mysteriously been replaced by an ABORIGINAL WOMAN (Warlpiri again) in her early thirties. She's looking at us impassively as she finishes Yorick's thought:

14) <u>Aboriginal Woman</u>: …you look pretty when you cry.

## Page Five

**Page Five, Panel One**
Smash cut to the day of the Plague for this close-up of Beth, wearing what she had on way back in Issue #1.

1) <u>Beth</u>: What?

**Page Five, Panel Two**
Pull out to the largest panel of the page for this shot of Beth's campsite, which looks like a horrific crime scene. There's a DEAD MALE PROFESSOR and THREE DEAD MALE STUDENTS lying about, one or two partially covered with sleeping bags as makeshift shrouds. Standing around Beth are her three surviving classmates: MARGO (the blue-haired girl we first saw in Issue #25), CAMILLA (a Black teenager), and ZITA (an unattractive blonde Australian girl with a big nose and a braided ponytail; she'll eventually become the corpse we saw back in #25). Camilla is crying and Margo is freaking out, but Beth is calm and collected, clearly the leader. It's late afternoon.

2) <u>Margo</u>: I *said*, how the hell are we supposed to get out of here?
3) <u>Margo</u>: The guides are gone, half our class is *dead*, the sat-phone suddenly doesn't work for shit, and our rations are fucking *toxic*!

4) <u>Beth</u>: Settle, Margo. We don't *know* that the food killed them.

**Page Five, Panel Three**
Change angles for this shot of Margo, Zita and Camilla. Margo looks hopeless. Zita makes a startling accusation, and Camilla shoots her a dirty look for her choice of words.

5) <u>Margo</u>: Well, that's bloody reassuring, boss. Maybe it's just *Ebola*.

6) <u>Zita</u>: No, it was the *Abos*.

7) <u>Camilla</u>: Watch your mouth.

**Page Five, Panel Four**
Change angles for an angry Zita and a rational Beth.

8) <u>Zita</u>: Think about it.
9) <u>Zita</u>: Why'd the Prof say the locals didn't want whites killing off any more kangaroos,

even though the goddamn skippers have been choking the land to death?

      10) <u>Beth</u>: He said the Aboriginals thought the population explosion was part of a... a larger *design*, that the earth was "fattening up" for something.

## Page Six

### Page Six, Panel One
      Change angles for this shot of Zita and Camilla.

      1) <u>Zita</u>: Yeah, something at *their* black hands.
      2) <u>Zita</u>: It was a *warning*! They can't stand us poisoning their fucking totem rodents, so they started poisoning *us*!

      3) <u>Camilla</u>: That's ridiculous. And why would they only kill the men?

### Page Six, Panel Two
      Change angles for this shot of Beth and Zita, as Beth tries to stop her classmate from departing.

      4) <u>Zita</u>: I don't know, but I'm not waiting around for those savages to finish us off.

      5) <u>Beth</u>: Zita, if you leave camp now, the dingoes will be picking you clean before the sun...

### Page Six, Panel Three
      Change angles for this largest panel of the page. We're high in the air with a STARTLINGLY WHITE ALBATROSS, as it suddenly swoops into frame. We can see a transfixed Beth looking up at us on the ground below.

      No Copy

### Page Six, Panel Four
      Push in on a stunned Beth, who watches the albatross LAND at her eye-level on a nearby boulder (or whatever). This moment never actually happened, Pia, so feel free to play up the surreal nature of it all.

      6) <u>Beth</u>: That's impossible.
      7) <u>Beth</u>: What's one of *those* things doing this far from—

### Page Six, Panel Five
      Push in close on the Albatross, as it suddenly begins to TALK.

      8) <u>Albatross</u>*: Kiss him goodbye, Beth.

      *(Clem—As a bit of a dream sequence shout-out to Sandman, can this bird's font/ balloon please be in the style of the Dreaming's resident raven, Matthew? Sorry I don't have reference, but I suspect Vertigo might have an example or two...)*

## Page Seven

### Page Seven, Panel One
      Smash cut into the past for this page-wide shot of SIX-YEAR-OLD BETH, complete with adorable bangs. She's wearing a dark funeral dress, and she looks *frightened*.

      No Copy

### Page Seven, Panel Two
      Pull out to this shot of Beth, who is being gently pushed towards us by her GRIEVING MOTHER. Beth's two YOUNGER SISTERS are hiding behind their mom.

1) <u>Mrs. Deville</u>: Go on, Bethie.
2) <u>Mrs. Deville</u>: Kiss your daddy goodbye.

**Page Seven, Panel Three**
We're behind Beth for this largest panel of the page, as she approaches an OPEN CASKET, eerily lit from above in this otherwise pitch-black room.

No Copy

**Page Seven, Panel Four**
This is an *overhead* shot of Little Beth nervously approaching her DEAD FATHER, a mustachioed man in his late fifties, who's lying in the open coffin.

No Copy

**Page Seven, Panel Five**
Push in eerily close on Beth, as she closes her eyes and leans in to kiss her dad's cold cheek. Her lips are less than an inch away from his lips here.

No Copy

# Page Eight

**Page Eight, Panel One**
Smash cut to Yorick's junior year of college for this page-wide shot of he and Beth KISSING passionately.

No Copy

**Page Eight, Panel Two**
Similar framing, but now Beth pulls away to smile at her boyfriend.

1) <u>Beth</u>: Hold on, I've got to finish putting my costume on.

**Page Eight, Panel Three**
Pull out to the largest panel of the page, as we reveal that we're inside of Yorick's small, messy college dorm room, decorated appropriately. Yorick takes a seat on his bed, as Beth (who we can now see is wearing a LONG TRENCHCOAT, and carrying a SHOPPING BAG) walks into the nearby bathroom.

2) <u>Yorick</u>: Crap, I thought maybe you were supposed to be a *flasher*.

3) <u>Beth</u>: What are *you* going as, perv?

**Page Eight, Panel Four**
Push in on Yorick, as he holds up his familiar STRAITJACKET from Issue #1.

4) <u>Yorick</u>: I just spent my last eighty bucks at Art's on this thing, so I guess it's either Hannibal Lecter or Nicholson from Cuckoo's Nest.
5) <u>Yorick</u>: Although I don't remember if Jack ever wore a—

**Page Eight, Panel Five**
Push in close on a comically dumbfounded Yorick, as he looks up at his off-panel love.

6) <u>Beth (from off)</u>: What do you think?

# Page Nine

**Page Nine, Panel One**
Cut over to Beth for this largest panel of the page, at least a half-SPLASH, as she sexily